Economics of the Environment

Selected Readings

FOURTH EDITION

Economics
of the
Environment

Selected Readings

FOURTH EDITION

Edited by

Robert N. Stavins

HARVARD UNIVERSITY

W. W. Norton & Company

New York   London

For Daniel and Julia

The text of this book is composed in New Aster
with the display set in Frutiger and Europa Arabesque
Composition by Matrix Publishing Services
Manufacturing by Maple-Vail, Binghamton, NY
Book design by Joan Greenfield

Library of Congress Cataloging-in-Publication Data

Economics of the environment : selected readings / edited by
Robert N. Stavins—4th ed.
       p.   cm.
    Includes bibliographical references.
    ISBN 0-393-97523-1 (pbk.)
    1. Pollution—Economic aspects.   2. Environmental policy—Costs.
I. Stavins, R. N. (Robert N.), 1948–
    HC79.P55 D65   1999
    363.7—dc21   99-43410
                                                                      CIP

ISBN 0-393-97523-1 (pbk.)

W. W. Norton & Company, Inc., 500 Fifth Avenue
New York, N.Y. 10110
www.wwnorton.com

W. W. Norton & Company Ltd., 10 Coptic Street
London WC1A 1PU

1 2 3 4 5 6 7 8 9 0

Contents

Introduction

It was nearly three decades ago that the first edition of this volume appeared, edited by my Harvard colleagues, Robert and Nancy Dorfman. In the intervening years, the area of environmental economics has evolved from a relatively obscure application of welfare economics to a legitimate field in its own right, combining elements from public finance, industrial organization, microeconomic theory, and many other areas of economics. The number of scholarly articles on the environment appearing in mainstream economics periodicals has increased significantly, as has the number of economics journals dedicated exclusively to environmental and resource topics.

During this same thirty years, there has been a proliferation of environmental economics textbooks. Even the best of these texts, however, cannot (and are not intended to) provide direct access to timely and original contributions by the field's leading scholars. As nearly all teachers (and many students) of environmental economics recognize, it is necessary to supplement the structural rigor of a text with original readings from the literature. This volume assembles a set of important readings that instructors will find to be a particularly valuable complement to their lectures. Any single volume, of course, can contain no more than a small sample of the best articles in such a diverse field. Nevertheless, the scope of the volume is comprehensive, the list of authors is a "who's who" of environmental economics, and the articles are timely, with more than three-fourths published since 1990, and one-third since 1998.

In order to make these readings accessible to diverse practitioners, as well as students at all levels, a central criterion used in the selection process was that articles should not only be sound, original, and well written, but also relatively nontechnical. That is, there is little use of formal mathematics in the articles that comprise this volume. This should not be confused with a lack of rigor, however, for these articles meet the highest standards of economic scholarship.

Part I of the volume provides an overview of the field and a review of its foundations. New articles are combined with some of the classics of the field. Don Fullerton and I start things off with a brief essay about how economists actually think about the environment. This is followed by Garrett Hardin's frequently cited article on the tragedy of the commons, and Ronald Coase's classic treatment of social costs and bargaining. Maureen Cropper and Wallace Oates' more recent survey of the field is also included, as is Robert Solow's insightful treatment of an economic perspective of sustainability.

Part II examines the costs of environmental protection. This might seem to be an area without controversy or current analytical interest, but that is certainly not the case. We begin with a survey article by Adam Jaffe and his colleagues that reviews and synthesizes much of the empirical evidence on the relationship between environmental regulation and so-called "competitiveness." A revisionist view is provided by Michael Porter and Claas van der Linde, who suggest that the conventional approach to thinking about the costs of environmental protection is fundamentally flawed. Karen Palmer, Wallace Oates, and Paul Portney provide a careful response.

In Part III, the focus turns to the other side of the analytic ledger—the benefits of environmental protection. This is an area that has been even more contentious—both in the policy world and among scholars—than have methods for analyzing the costs of environmental protection. Here the challenging question is how environmental amenities can be valued in economic terms for analytic purposes. Kerry Smith provides an introduction and overview, which is followed by a debate on the stated-preference method known as "contingent valuation." Paul Portney outlines the structure and importance of the debate, Michael Hanemann makes the affirmative case, and Peter Diamond and Jerry Hausman provide the critique.

There are two principal policy questions that need to be addressed in the environmental realm: how much environmental protection is desirable; and how should that degree of environmental protection be achieved. The first of these questions is addressed in Part IV and the second in Part V. In Part IV, the criterion of economic efficiency and the analytical tool of benefit-cost analysis are considered as ways of judging the goals of environmental policy. In an introductory essay, Kenneth Arrow and his coauthors ask whether there is a role for benefit-cost analysis to play in environmental, health, and safety regulation. Then, Kip Viscusi makes the case for greater reliance on benefit-cost analysis in policy formulation, and Steven Kelman provides an ethically based critique. This is followed by a set of responses.

Part V examines the policy instruments—the means—that can be employed to achieve given environmental targets or goals. This is an area where economists have made their greatest inroads of influence in the policy world, with tremendous changes having taken place over the past decade in the reception given by politicians and policy makers to so-called market-based or economic-incentive instruments for environmental protection. Tom Tietenberg provides an introduction to these innovative approaches, including both taxes and tradeable permit systems. Lawrence Goulder focuses his attention on a particularly new development in this literature—the performance and cost of alternative policy instruments in the presence of existing, distortionary taxes. Robert Hahn turns our attention to tradeable permit systems, and examines their use in actual public policies. Finally, Michael Sandel provides a timely critique of these systems, with responses offered by Eric Maskin, Steven Shavell, and others.

The next three parts of the book treat particularly important environmental-policy problem areas. In Part VI, the topic is acid rain, caused in the United States principally by emissions of sulfur dioxide (SO_2) from coal-burning electric generating plants. Richard Schmalensee, Paul Joskow, Denny Ellerman, and their colleagues examine the performance of the innovative SO_2 allowance trading system, set up by the Clean Air Act Amendments of 1990. Following that, I examine the lessons that can be learned from this grand experiment with market-based environmental policy.

Part VII is dedicated to investigations of economic dimensions of global climate change, which may in the long term prove to be the most significant environmental problem that has arisen, both in terms of its potential damages and in terms of the costs of addressing it. William Nordhaus provides an outline of economic dimensions of the problem. Thomas Schelling investigates the costs and distributional implications of addressing global warming; and Henry Jacoby, Ronald Prinn, and Richard Schmalensee examine fundamental issues associated with the Kyoto Protocol, the international policy established in 1997 to deal with this global environmental threat.

Part VIII examines another new area of exploration in environmental economics: ecological values. Much of U.S. environmental regulation has targeted—often with considerable success—the human-health consequences of environmental degradation, but much less attention has been given to effects on ecological systems. David Simpson provides a structured overview of an economic perspective.

Andrew Metrick and Martin Weitzman describe their statistical analysis of why Federal policy efforts have been aimed at preserving and protecting some species, but not others.

The final section of the book, Part IX, departs from the normative concerns of much of the volume to examine instead interesting and important questions of political economy. It turns out that an economic perspective can provide useful insights on questions that might at first seem to be fundamentally political. Nathaniel Keohane, Richard Revesz, and I utilize an economic framework to ask why our political system has produced the particular set of environmental policy instruments it has. Then, Paul Joskow and Richard Schmalensee address similar questions in a detailed, empirical analysis of the Congressional allocation of SO_2 allowances in 1990. Finally, Jason Shogren builds on his experience in 1997 as a senior staff economist at the White House Council of Economic Advisers to develop insights about the relationship between environmental economics, policy, and politics.

A final note: I want to acknowledge the great debt that is owed to Robert and Nancy Dorfman, who originated this volume three decades ago, and who have nurtured it through three editions. It was in response to their invitation that I agreed to carry on this effort. On their behalf, I want to thank readers of previous editions who have sent their comments and suggestions for revisions. Thanks are also due to Ruben Lubowski for excellent research assistance. I invite all readers of this edition, whether practitioners, teachers, or students, to send me or the publisher any thoughts or suggestions for future editions.

Rob Stavins
Cambridge, Massachusetts
July, 1999

I

Overview and Principles

1   *How Economists See the Environment**

*How Economists See the Environment**

Don Fullerton

Robert N. Stavins

Don Fullerton is Addison Baker Duncan Centennial Professor of Economics, Department of Economics, University of Texas at Austin, and Research Associate at the National Bureau of Economic Research; and Robert N. Stavins is Albert Pratt Professor of Business and Government, John F. Kennedy School of Government, Harvard University, and University Fellow at Resources for the Future.

On a topic such as the environment, communication among those from different disciplines in the natural and social sciences is both important and difficult. Economists themselves may have contributed to some misunderstandings about how they think about the environment, perhaps through enthusiasm for market solutions, perhaps by neglecting to make explicit all the necessary qualifications, and perhaps simply by the use of jargon.

There are several prevalent myths about how economists think about the environment. By examining them here, we hope to explain how economists really do think about the natural environment.

Myth of the Universal Market

The first myth is that economists believe that the market solves all problems. The "first theorem of welfare economics," as taught to generations of economics students, is that private markets are perfectly efficient on their own, with no interference from government, provided certain conditions are met.

This theorem, easily proved, is exceptionally powerful, because it means that no one needs to tell producers of goods and services what to sell to which consumers. Instead, self-interested producers and consumers meet in the market-place, engage in trade, and thereby achieve the greatest good for the

"How Economists See the Environment," by Don Fullerton and Robert Stavins, from *Nature* 395: 6701. Reprinted from *Nature* copyright © 1998 by Macmillan Magazines Ltd.

*The authors are grateful for suggestions from Robert Frosch, Robert Hahn, Gilbert Metcalf, Richard Revesz and Thomas Schelling.

greatest number, as if "guided by an invisible hand."[1] This maximum general welfare is what economists mean by the "efficiency" of competitive markets. Economists in business schools are particularly fond of identifying markets where the necessary conditions are met, such as the stock market, where many buyers and sellers operate with good information and low transaction costs to trade well-defined commodities with enforced rights of ownership.

Other economists, especially those in public policy schools, have a different approach to this theorem. By clarifying the conditions under which markets are efficient, the theorem also identifies the conditions under which they are not. Private markets are perfectly efficient only if there are no public goods, no externalities, no monopoly buyers or sellers, no increasing returns to scale, no information problems, no transaction costs, no taxes, no common property and no other "distortions" between the costs paid by buyers and the benefits received by sellers. Those conditions are obviously very restrictive, and they are usually not all satisfied simultaneously in the real world.

When a market thus fails, this same theorem offers guidance. For any particular market, it asks whether the number of sellers is sufficiently small to warrant antitrust action, whether the returns to scale are great enough to justify tolerating a single producer in a regulated market, or whether the benefits from the good are public in a way that might justify outright gov-

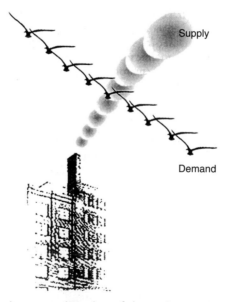

An economist's view of the environment.

[1]Smith, A. *An Inquiry into the Nature and Causes of the Wealth of Nations* (Whitestone, Dublin, 1776).

ernment provision of it. A public good, like the light from a lighthouse, benefits additional users at no cost to society.

Environmental economists are interested in pollution and other externalities, where some consequences of producing or consuming a good or service are external to the market (not considered by producers or consumers). With a negative externality, such as environmental pollution, the total social cost of production may exceed the value to consumers. If the market is left to itself, too many pollution-generating products are made.

Similarly, natural-resource economists are interested in common property, or open-access resources, where anyone can extract or harvest the resource freely and no one recognizes the full cost of using the resource. Extractors consider only their own direct and immediate costs, not the costs to others of increased scarcity ("user cost" or "scarcity rent"). The result is that the resource is depleted too quickly.

So, the market by itself demonstrably does not solve all problems. Indeed, in the environmental domain, perfectly functioning markets are the exception rather than the rule. Governments can try to correct these market failures, for example by restricting pollutant emissions or limiting access to open-access resources, which can improve welfare and lead to greater efficiency.

Myth of Market Solutions

A second common myth is that economists always recommend a market solution to a market problem. Economists tend to search for instruments of public policy that can fix one market essentially by introducing another, allowing each to operate efficiently on its own. If pollution imposes large external costs, for example, the government can establish a market for rights to emit a limited amount of that pollutant. Such a market for tradable emission permits will work if there are many buyers and sellers, all are well informed, and the other conditions of the "first theorem" are met. In this case, the government's role is to enforce the rights and responsibilities of permit ownership, so that each unit of emissions is matched by the ownership of one emission permit. Then the market for the output will also work, as the producer has to pay a price for each permit that reflects the social cost of the associated pollution. Equivalently, producers can be required to pay a tax on their emissions that reflects the external social cost. Either way, the result in theory will be the efficient amount of pollution abatement, undertaken at minimum aggregate abatement cost.

This tradable-permit approach has much to recommend it, and can be just the right solution in some cases, but it is still a "market." Therefore the outcome will be efficient only if certain conditions are met. But these conditions are not always met.[2] Could the sale of permits be mo-

---

[2]Hahn, R. W. & Hester, G. L. *Ecol. Law Q.* 16, 361–406 (1989).

nopolized by a small number of buyers or sellers? Do problems arise
from inadequate information or significant transaction costs? Will the
government find it too costly to measure emissions? If the answer to any
such question is yes, the permit market may work less than optimally.
The environmental goal may still be met, but at more than minimum
cost.

As an example, to reduce acid rain in the United States, amendments
to the Clean Air Act of 1990 require electricity generators to hold a permit for each tonne of SO_2 they emit. A robust market for the permits has
emerged, in which well-defined prices are broadly known to many potential buyers and sellers. Through continuous emissions monitoring, the
government can track SO_2 emissions from each plant. Equally important,
penalties are significantly greater than incremental abatement costs and
hence are sufficient to ensure compliance. Overall, this market works;
acid rain deposition is being reduced by 50 per cent in a cost-effective
manner.[3]

A permit market achieves this efficiency through trades because any
company that has high abatement costs can buy permits from another that
has low costs, so reducing the total cost of abating pollution. These trades
also switch the source of the pollution from one company to another, which
is unimportant when any emissions equally affect the whole trading area.
This "perfect mixing" assumption is certainly valid for global problems such
as greenhouse gases or the effect of chlorofluorocarbons on the stratospheric ozone layer. It may also work reasonably well for a regional problem such as acid rain, because acid deposition in downwind states of New
England is about equally affected by SO_2 emissions that were traded among
upwind sources in Ohio, Indiana or Illinois. But it does not work perfectly,
as acid rain in New England may increase if a plant there sells permits to
a plant in the mid-west.

At the other extreme, many environmental problems might not be addressed appropriately by tradable-permit systems or other market-based
policy instruments.[4] One example is a hazardous air pollutant such as benzene that does not mix in the airshed and so can cause localized "hotspots."
Because a company can buy permits and increase local emissions, permit
trading does not ensure that each location will meet a specific standard.
Moreover, the damages caused by local concentrations may increase nonlinearly. If so, then even a permit system that reduces total emissions might
allow trades that move those emissions to a high-impact location and thus
increase total damages.

The bottom line is that no specific policy instrument, or even set
of policy instruments, is a panacea. Market instruments do not always provide the best solutions, and sometimes not even satisfactory
solutions.

---

[3]Schmalensee, R. *et al. J. Econ. Perspect.* 12 No. 3 (Summer 1998).
[4]Hahn, R. W. & Stavins, R. N. *Am. Econ. Rev.* 82, 464–468 (1992).

Myth of Market Prices

The next myth is that, when non-market solutions are considered, economists still use only market prices to evaluate them. No matter what policy instrument is chosen, the environmental goal of that policy must be identified. For example, should vehicle emissions be reduced by 10, 20 or 50 per cent? Economists frequently try to identify the most efficient degree of control that provides the greatest net benefit. This means, of course, that both benefits and costs need to be evaluated. True enough, economists typically favour using market prices, whenever possible, to carry out such evaluations, because these prices reveal how members of society actually value the scarce amenities and resources under consideration.

Economists are wary of asking people how much they value something, as respondents may not provide honest assessments of their own valuations. Instead, actions may reveal their preferences, as when individuals pay more for a house in a neighbourhood with cleaner air, all else being equal.[5]

This is not to suggest that economists are concerned only with the financial value of things. Far from it. The financial flows that make up the gross national product represent only a fraction of all economic flows. The scope of economics encompasses the allocation and use of all scarce resources. For example, the economic value of the human-health damages of environmental pollution is greater than the sum of health-care costs and lost wages (or lost productivity), as it includes what lawyers would call "pain and suffering." Economists might use a market price indirectly to measure revealed rather than stated preferences, but the goal is to measure the total value of the loss that individuals incur.

To take another example, the economic value of part of the Amazon rainforest is not limited to its financial value as a repository of future pharmaceutical products or as a location for ecotourism. That "use" value may only be a small part of the properly defined economic valuation. For decades, economists have recognized the importance of "non-use" value of environmental amenities such as wilderness areas or endangered species. The public nature of these goods make it particularly difficult to quantify these values empirically, as we cannot use market prices! The important fact is that benefit–cost analysis of environmental policies, virtually by definition, cannot rely exclusively on market prices.[6]

Economists insist on trying to convert all these disparate values into monetary terms because a common unit of measure is needed to be able to add them up. How else can we combine the benefits of ten extra miles of visibility plus some amount of reduced morbidity, and then compare these total benefits with the total cost of installing scrubbers to clean stack gases at coal-fired power plants? Money, after all, is simply a medium of exchange, a convenient way to add together or compare disparate goods and services.

---

[5]Smith, V. K. & Huang, J.-C. *J. Polit. Econ.* 103, 209–227 (1995).
[6]Arrow, K. *et al. Science* 272, 221–222 (1996).

Myth of Efficiency

The last myth we address here is that these economic analyses are concerned only with efficiency rather than distribution. Many economists do give more attention to measures of aggregate social welfare than to measures of the distribution of the benefits and costs of policies among members of society. The reason is that an improvement in economic efficiency can be determined by a simple and unambiguous criterion—an increase in total net benefits. What constitutes an improvement in distributional equity, on the other hand, is inevitably the subject of considerable dispute. Nevertheless, many economists do analyse distributional issues thoroughly. The more difficult problem, not yet solved in a satisfactory manner, is how to combine efficiency and distributional issues in a unified analysis.

Available data often permit reliable estimates of the impacts of environmental policies on important subgroups of the population.[7] On the other hand, environmental regulations are neither effective nor efficient tools for achieving redistributional goals. The best economic analyses recognize the contributions and limitations of efficiency and distributional measures.

Where Does This Leave Us?

To summarize, economists do not necessarily believe that the market solves all problems. Indeed, many economists, ourselves included, make a living out of analysing market failures such as environmental pollution in which laissez-faire policy leads not to social efficiency, but to inefficiency. When economists identify market problems, their tendency is first to consider the feasibility of market solutions because of their potential cost-effectiveness, but market-based approaches to environmental protection are no panacea. When market or non-market solutions to environmental problems are being assessed, economists do not limit their analysis to financial considerations but use money as a unit of measurement in the absence of a more convenient unit. And although the efficiency criterion is by definition aggregate in nature, economic analysis can reveal much about the distribution of the benefits and costs of environmental policy.

Having identified and sought to dispel four prevalent myths about how economists think about the natural environment, we acknowledge that our profession bears some responsibility for the existence of such misunderstandings. Like their colleagues in other social and natural sciences, academic economists focus their greatest energies on communicating to their peers within their own discipline. Greater effort can certainly be made to improve communication across disciplinary boundaries.

---

[7]Christiansen, G. B. & Tietenberg, T. H. in *Handbook of Natural Resource and Energy Economics* Vol. 1 (eds Kneese, A. V. & Sweeney, J. L.) 345–393 (North-Holland, Amsterdam, 1985).

2   *The Tragedy of the Commons*

Garrett Hardin

Garrett Hardin is Professor Emeritus of Biology at the University of California at Santa Barbara.

At the end of a thoughtful article on the future of nuclear war, J. B. Wiesner and H. F. York concluded that "Both sides in the arms race are . . . confronted by the dilemma of steadily increasing military power and steadily decreasing national security. *It is our considered professional judgment that this dilemma has no technical solution.* If the great powers continue to look for solutions in the area of science and technology only, the result will be to worsen the situation."[1]

I would like to focus your attention not on the subject of the article (national security in a nuclear world) but on the kind of conclusion they reached, namely, that there is no technical solution to the problem. An implicit and almost universal assumption of discussions published in professional and semipopular scientific journals is that the problem under discussion has a technical solution. A technical solution may be defined as one that requires a change only in the techniques of the natural sciences, demanding little or nothing in the way of change in human values or ideas of morality.

In our day (though not in earlier times) technical solutions are always welcome. Because of previous failures in prophecy, it takes courage to assert that a desired technical solution is not possible. Wiesner and York exhibited this courage; publishing in a science journal, they insisted that the solution to the problem was not to be found in the natural sciences. They cautiously qualified their statement with the phrase, "It is our considered professional judgment. . . ." Whether they were right or not is not the concern of the present article. Rather, the concern here is with the important concept of a class of human problems which can be called "no technical solution problems," and more specifically, with the identification and discussion of one of these.

It is easy to show that the class is not a null class. Recall the game of tick-tack-toe. Consider the problem, "How can I win the game of tick-tack-toe?" It is well known that I cannot, if I assume (in keeping with the conventions of game theory) that my opponent understands the game perfectly. Put another way, there is no "technical solution" to the problem. I can win

---

[1]J. B. Wiesner and H. F. York, *Scientific American* 211 (No. 4), 27 (1964).

only by giving a radical meaning to the word "win." I can hit my opponent over the head; or I can falsify the records. Every way in which I "win" involves, in some sense, an abandonment of the game, as we intuitively understand it. (I can also, of course, openly abandon the game—refuse to play it. This is what most adults do.)

The class of "no technical solution problems" has members. My thesis is that the "population problem," as conventionally conceived, is a member of this class. How it is conventionally conceived needs some comment. It is fair to say that most people who anguish over the population problem are trying to find a way to avoid the evils of overpopulation without relinquishing any of the privileges they now enjoy. They think that farming the seas or developing new strains of wheat will solve the problem—technologically. I try to show here that the solution they seek cannot be found. The population problem cannot be solved in a technical way, any more than can the problem of winning the game of tick-tack-toe.

What Shall We Maximize?

Population, as Malthus said, naturally tends to grow "geometrically," or, as we would now say, exponentially. In a finite world this means that the per-capita share of the world's goods must decrease. Is ours a finite world?

A fair defense can be put forward for the view that the world is infinite; or that we do not know that it is not. But, in terms of the practical problems that we must face in the next few generations with the foreseeable technology, it is clear that we will greatly increase human misery if we do not, during the immediate future, assume that the world available to the terrestrial human population is finite. "Space" is no escape.[2]

A finite world can support only a finite population; therefore, population growth must eventually equal zero. (The case of perpetual wide fluctuations above and below zero is a trivial variant that need not be discussed.) When this condition is met, what will be the situation of mankind? Specifically, can Bentham's goal of "the greatest good for the greatest number" be realized?

No—for two reasons, each sufficient by itself. The first is a theoretical one. It is not mathematically possible to maximize for two (or more) variables at the same time. This was clearly stated by von Neumann and Morgenstern,[3] but the principle is implicit in the theory of partial differential equations, dating back at least to D'Alembert (1717–1783).

[2] G. Hardin, *Journal of Heredity* 50, 68 (1959), S. von Hoernor, *Science* 137, 18 (1962).
[3] J. von Neumann and O. Morgenstern, *Theory of Games and Economic Behavior* (Princeton University Press, Princeton, N.J., 1947), p. 11.

The second reason springs directly from biological facts. To live, any organism must have a source of energy (for example, food). This energy is utilized for two purposes: mere maintenance and work. For man, maintenance of life requires about 1600 kilocalories a day ("maintenance calories"). Anything that he does over and above merely staying alive will be defined as work, and is supported by "work calories" which he takes in. Work calories are used not only for what we call work in common speech; they are also required for all forms of enjoyment, from swimming and automobile racing to playing music and writing poetry. If our goal is to maximize population it is obvious what we must do: We must make the work calories per person approach as close to zero as possible. No gourmet meals, no vacations, no sports, no music, no literature, no art. . . . I think that everyone will grant, without argument or proof, that maximizing population does not maximize goods. Bentham's goal is impossible.

In reaching this conclusion I have made the usual assumption that it is the acquisition of energy that is the problem. The appearance of atomic energy has led some to question this assumption. However, given an infinite source of energy, population growth still produces an inescapable problem. The problem of the acquisition of energy is replaced by the problem of its dissipation, as J. H. Fremlin has so wittily shown.[4] The arithmetic signs in the analysis are, as it were, reversed; but Bentham's goal is unobtainable.

The optimum population is, then, less than the maximum. The difficulty of defining the optimum is enormous; so far as I know, no one has seriously tackled this problem. Reaching an acceptable and stable solution will surely require more than one generation of hard analytical work—and much persuasion.

We want the maximum good per person; but what is good? To one person it is wilderness, to another it is ski lodges for thousands. To one it is estuaries to nourish ducks for hunters to shoot; to another it is factory land. Comparing one good with another is, we usually say, impossible because goods are incommensurable. Incommensurables cannot be compared.

Theoretically this may be true; but in real life incommensurables *are* commensurable. Only a criterion of judgment and a system of weighting are needed. In nature the criterion is survival. Is it better for a species to be small and hideable, or large and powerful? Natural selection commensurates the incommensurables. The compromise achieved depends on a natural weighting of the values of the variables.

Man must imitate this process. There is no doubt that in fact he already does, but unconsciously. It is when the hidden decisions are made explicit that the arguments begin. The problem for the years ahead is to work out an acceptable theory of weighting. Synergistic effects, nonlinear variation, and difficulties in discounting the future make the intellectual problem difficult, but not (in principle) insoluble.

---

[4]J. H. Fremlin, *New Scientist*, No. 415 (1964), p. 285.

Has any cultural group solved this practical problem at the present time, even on an intuitive level? One simple fact proves that none has: there is no prosperous population in the world today that has, and has had for some time, a growth rate of zero. Any people that has intuitively identified its optimum point will soon reach it, after which its growth rate becomes and remains zero.

Of course, a positive growth rate might be taken as evidence that a population is below its optimum. However, by any reasonable standards, the most rapidly growing populations on earth today are (in general) the most miserable. This association (which need not be invariable) casts doubt on the optimistic assumption that the positive growth rate of a population is evidence that it has yet to reach its optimum.

We can make little progress in working toward optimum population size until we explicitly exorcise the spirit of Adam Smith in the field of practical demography. In economic affairs, *The Wealth of Nations* (1776) popularized the "invisible hand," the idea that an individual who "intends only his own gain," is, as it were, "led by an invisible hand to promote . . . the public interest."[5] Adam Smith did not assert that this was invariably true, and perhaps neither did any of his followers. But he contributed to a dominant tendency of thought that has ever since interfered with positive action based on rational analysis, namely, the tendency to assume that decisions reached individually will, in fact, be the best decisions for an entire society. If this assumption is correct it justifies the continuance of our present policy of *laissez faire* in reproduction. If it is correct we can assume that men will control their individual fecundity so as to produce the optimum population. If the assumption is not correct, we need to reexamine our individual freedoms to see which ones are defensible.

Tragedy of Freedom in a Commons

The rebuttal to the invisible hand in population control is to be found in a scenario first sketched in a little-known pamphlet in 1833 by a mathematical amateur named William Forster Lloyd (1794–1852).[6] We may well call it "the tragedy of the commons," using the word "tragedy" as the philosopher Whitehead used it: "The essence of dramatic tragedy is not unhappiness. It resides in the solemnity of the remorseless working of things." He then goes on to say, "This inevitableness of destiny can only be illustrated in terms of human life by incidents which in fact involve unhappiness. For it is only by them that the futility of escape can be made evident in the drama."[7]

---

[5]A. Smith, *The Wealth of Nations* (Modern Library, New York, 1937), p. 423.

[6]W. F. Lloyd, *Two Lectures on the Checks to Population* (Oxford University Press, Oxford, England, 1833).

[7]A. N. Whitehead, *Science and the Modern World* (Mentor, New York, 1948), p. 17.

The tragedy of the commons develops in this way. Picture a pasture open to all. It is to be expected that each herdsman will try to keep as many cattle as possible on the commons. Such an arrangement may work reasonably satisfactorily for centuries because tribal wars, poaching, and disease keep the numbers of both man and beast well below the carrying capacity of the land. Finally, however, comes the day of reckoning, that is, the day when the long-desired goal of social stability becomes a reality. At this point, the inherent logic of the commons remorselessly generates tragedy.

As a rational being, each herdsman seeks to maximize his gain. Explicitly or implicitly, more or less consciously, he asks, "What is the utility *to me* of adding one more animal to my herd?" This utility has one negative and one positive component.

1. The positive component is a function of the increment of one animal. Since the herdsman receives all the proceeds from the sale of the additional animal, the positive utility is nearly +1.

2. The negative component is a function of the additional overgrazing created by one more animal. Since, however, the effects of overgrazing are shared by all the herdsmen, the negative utility for any particular decision-making herdsman is only a fraction of −1.

Adding together the component partial utilities, the rational herdsman concludes that the only sensible course for him to pursue is to add another animal to his herd. And another. . . . But this is the conclusion reached by each and every rational herdsman sharing a commons. Therein is the tragedy. Each man is locked into a system that compels him to increase his herd without limit—in a world that is limited. Ruin is the destination toward which all men rush, each pursuing his own best interest in a society that believes in the freedom of the commons. Freedom in a commons brings ruin to all.

Some would say that this is a platitude. Would that it were! In a sense, it was learned thousands of years ago, but natural selection favors the forces of psychological denial.[8] The individual benefits as an individual from his ability to deny the truth even though society as a whole, of which he is a part, suffers. Education can counteract the natural tendency to do the wrong thing, but the inexorable succession of generations requires that the basis for this knowledge be constantly refreshed.

A simple incident that occurred a few years ago in Leominster, Massachusetts, shows how perishable the knowledge is. During the Christmas shopping season the parking meters downtown were covered with plastic bags that bore tags reading: "Do not open until after Christmas. Free parking courtesy of the mayor and city council." In other words, facing the prospect of an increased demand for already scarce space, the city fathers reinstituted the system of the commons. (Cynically, we suspect that they gained more votes than they lost by this retrogressive act.)

---

[8]G. Hardin, Ed., *Population, Evolution, and Birth Control* (Freeman, San Francisco, 1964), p. 56.

In an approximate way, the logic of the commons has been understood for a long time, perhaps since the discovery of agriculture or the invention of private property in real estate. But it is understood mostly only in special cases which are not sufficiently generalized. Even at this late date, cattlemen leasing national land on the Western ranges demonstrate no more than an ambivalent understanding, in constantly pressuring federal authorities to increase the head count to the point where overgrazing produces erosion and weed-dominance. Likewise, the oceans of the world continue to suffer from the survival of the philosophy of the commons. Maritime nations still respond automatically to the shibboleth of the "freedom of the seas." Professing to believe in the "inexhaustible resources of the oceans," they bring species after species of fish and whales closer to extinction.[9]

The National Parks present another instance of the working out of the tragedy of the commons. At present, they are open to all, without limit. The parks themselves are limited in extent—there is only one Yosemite Valley—whereas population seems to grow without limit. The values that visitors seek in the parks are steadily eroded. Plainly, we must soon cease to treat the parks as commons or they will be of no value to anyone.

What shall we do? We have several options. We might sell them off as private property. We might keep them as public property, but allocate the right to enter them. The allocation might be on the basis of wealth, by the use of an auction system. It might be on the basis of merit, as defined by some agreed-upon standards. It might be by lottery. Or it might be on a first-come, first-served basis, administered to long queues. These, I think, are all objectionable. But we must choose—or acquiesce in the destruction of the commons that we call our National Parks.

Pollution

In a reverse way, the tragedy of the commons reappears in problems of pollution. Here it is not a question of taking something out of the commons, but of putting something in—sewage, or chemical, radioactive, and heat wastes into water; noxious and dangerous fumes into the air; and distracting and unpleasant advertising signs into the line of slight. The calculations of utility are much the same as before. The rational man finds that his share of the cost of the wastes he discharges into the commons is less than the cost of purifying his wastes before releasing them. Since this is true for everyone, we are locked into a system of "fouling our own nest," so long as we behave only as independent, rational, free-enterprisers.

The tragedy of the commons as a food basket is averted by private property, or something formally like it. But the air and waters surrounding us

---

[9]S. McVay, *Scientific American* 216 (No. 8), 13 (1966).

cannot readily be fenced, and so the tragedy of the commons as a cesspool must be prevented by different means, by coercive laws or taxing devices that make it cheaper for the polluter to treat his pollutants than to discharge them untreated. We have not progressed as far with the solution of this problem as we have with the first. Indeed, our particular concept of private property, which deters us from exhausting the positive resources of the earth, favors pollution. The owner of a factory on the bank of a stream—whose property extends to the middle of the stream—often has difficulty seeing why it is not his natural right to muddy the waters flowing past his door. The law, always behind the times, requires elaborate stitching and fitting to adapt it to this newly perceived aspect of the commons.

The pollution problem is a consequence of population. It did not much matter how a lonely American frontiersman disposed of his waste. "Flowing water purifies itself every ten miles," my grandfather used to say, and the myth was near enough to the truth when he was a boy, for there were not too many people. But as population became denser, the natural chemical and biological recycling processes became overloaded, calling for a redefinition of property rights.

How to Legislate Temperance?

Analysis of the pollution problem as a function of population density uncovers a not generally recognized principle of morality, namely: *the morality of an act is a function of the state of the system at the time it is performed.*[10] Using the commons as a cesspool does not harm the general public under frontier conditions, because there is no public; the same behavior in a metropolis is unbearable. A hundred and fifty years ago a plainsman could kill an American bison, cut out only the tongue for his dinner, and discard the rest of the animal. He was not in any important sense being wasteful. Today, with only a few thousand bison left, we would be appalled at such behavior.

In passing, it is worth noting that the morality of an act cannot be determined from a photograph. One does not know whether a man killing an elephant or setting fire to the grassland is harming others until one knows the total system in which his act appears. "One picture is worth a thousand words," said an ancient Chinese; but it may take ten thousand words to validate it. It is as tempting to ecologists as it is to reformers in general to try to persuade others by way of the photographic shortcut. But the essence of an argument cannot be photographed: it must be presented rationally—in words.

---

[10]J. Fletcher, *Situation Ethics* (Westminster, Philadelphia, 1966).

That morality is system-sensitive escaped the attention of most codifiers of ethics in the past. "Thou shalt not . . ." is the form of traditional ethical directives which make no allowance for particular circumstances. The laws of our society follow the pattern of ancient ethics, and therefore are poorly suited to governing a complex, crowded, changeable world. Our epicyclic solution is to augment statutory law with administrative law. Since it is practically impossible to spell out all the conditions under which it is safe to burn trash in the backyard or to run an automobile without smog control, by law we delegate the details to bureaus. The result is administrative law, which is rightly feared for an ancient reason—*Quis custodiet ipsos custodes?*—Who shall watch the watchers themselves? John Adams said that we must have a "government of laws and not men." Bureau administrators, trying to evaluate the morality of acts in the total system, are singularly liable to corruption, producing a government by men, not laws.

Prohibition is easy to legislate (though not necessarily to enforce); but how do we legislate temperance? Experience indicates that it can be accomplished best through the mediation of administrative law. We limit possibilities unnecessarily if we suppose that the sentiment of *Quis custodiet* denies us the use of administrative law. We should rather retain the phrase as a perpetual reminder of fearful dangers we cannot avoid. The great challenge facing us now is to invent the corrective feedbacks that are needed to keep custodians honest. We must find ways to legitimate the needed authority of both the custodians and the corrective feedbacks.

Freedom to Breed Is Intolerable

The tragedy of the commons is involved in population problems in another way. In a world governed solely by the principle of "dog eat dog"— if indeed there ever was such a world—how many children a family had would not be a matter of public concern. Parents who bred too exuberantly would leave fewer descendants, not more, because they would be unable to care adequately for their children. David Lack and others have found that such a negative feedback demonstrably controls the fecundity of birds.[11] But men are not birds, and have not acted like them for millenniums, at least.

If each human family were dependent only on its own resources; *if* the children of improvident parents starved to death; *if*, thus, overbreeding brought its own "punishment" to the germ line—*then* there would be no public interest in controlling the breeding of families. But our society is deeply committed to the welfare state,[12] and hence is confronted with another aspect of the tragedy of the commons.

In a welfare state, how shall we deal with the family, the religion, the race, or the class (or indeed any distinguishable and cohesive group) that

---

[11]D. Lack, *The Natural Regulation of Animal Numbers* (Clarendon Press, Oxford, England, 1954).
[12]H. Girvetz, *From Wealth to Welfare* (Stanford University Press, Stanford, Calif., 1950).

adopts overbreeding as a policy to secure its own aggrandizement?[13] To couple the concept of freedom to breed with the belief that everyone born has an equal right to the commons is to lock the world into a tragic course of action.

Unfortunately this is just the course of action that is being pursued by the United States. In late 1967, some thirty nations agreed to the following: "The Universal Declaration of Human Rights describes the family as the natural and fundamental unit of society. It follows that any choice and decision with regard to the size of the family must irrevocably rest with the family itself, and cannot be made by anyone else."[14]

It is painful to have to deny categorically the validity of this right; denying it, one feels as uncomfortable as a resident of Salem, Massachusetts, who denied the reality of witches in the seventeenth century. At the present time, in liberal quarters, something like a taboo acts to inhibit criticism of the United Nations. There is a feeling that the United Nations is "our last and best hope," that we shouldn't find fault with it; we shouldn't play into the hands of the archconservatives. However, let us not forget what Robert Louis Stevenson said: "The truth that is suppressed by friends is the readiest weapon of the enemy." If we love the truth we must openly deny the validity of the Universal Declaration of Human Rights, even though it is promoted by the United Nations. We should also join with Kingsley Davis[15] in attempting to get Planned Parenthood–World Population to see the error of its ways in embracing the same tragic ideal.

Conscience Is Self-Eliminating

It is a mistake to think that we can control the breeding of mankind in the long run by an appeal to conscience. Charles Galton Darwin made this point when he spoke on the centennial of the publication of his grandfather's great book. The argument is straightforward and Darwinian.

People vary. Confronted with appeals to limit breeding, some people will undoubtedly respond to the plea more than others. Those who have more children will produce a larger fraction of the next generation than those with more susceptible consciences. The differences will be accentuated, generation by generation.

In C. G. Darwin's words: "It may well be that it would take hundreds of generations for the progenitive instinct to develop in this way, but if it should do so, nature would have taken her revenge, and the variety *Homo contracipiens* would become extinct and would be replaced by the variety *Homo progenitivus*."[16]

---

[13]G. Hardin, *Perspectives in Biology and Medicine* 6, 366 (1963).

[14]U Thant, *International Planned Parenthood News*, No. 168 (February 1968), p. 3.

[15]K. Davis, *Science* 158, 730 (1967).

[16]S. Tax, Ed., *Evolution After Darwin* (University of Chicago Press, Chicago, 1960), vol. 2, p. 469.

The argument assumes that conscience or the desire for children (no matter which) is hereditary—but hereditary only in the most general formal sense. The result will be the same whether the attitude is transmitted through germ cells, or exosomatically, to use A. J. Lotka's term. (If one denies the latter possibility as well as the former, then what's the point of education?) The argument has here been stated in the context of the population problem, but it applies equally well to any instance in which society appeals to an individual exploiting a commons to restrains himself for the general good—by means of his conscience. To make such an appeal is to set up a selective system that works toward the elimination of conscience from the race.

Pathogenic Effects of Conscience

The long-term disadvantage of an appeal to conscience should be enough to condemn it; but it has serious short-term disadvantages as well. If we ask a man who is exploiting a commons to desist "in the name of conscience," what are we saying to him? What does he hear?—not only at the moment but also in the wee small hours of the night when, half asleep, he remembers not merely the words we used but also the nonverbal communication cues we gave him unawares? Sooner or later, consciously or subconsciously, he senses that he has received two communications, and that they are contradictory: 1. (intended communication) "If you don't do as we ask, we will openly condemn you for not acting like a responsible citizen"; 2. (the unintended communication) "If you *do* behave as we ask, we will secretly condemn you for a simpleton who can be shamed into standing aside while the rest of us exploit the commons."

Everyman then is caught in what Bateson has called a "double bind." Bateson and his co-workers have made a plausible case for viewing the double bind as an important causative factor in the genesis of schizophrenia.[17] The double bind may not always be so damaging, but it always endangers the mental health of anyone to whom it is applied. "A bad conscience," said Nietzsche, "is a kind of illness."

To conjure up a conscience in others is tempting to anyone who wishes to extend his control beyond the legal limits. Leaders at the highest level succumb to this temptation. Has any president during the past generation failed to call on labor unions to moderate voluntarily their demands for higher wages, or to steel companies to honor voluntary guidelines on prices? I can recall none. The rhetoric used on such occasions is designed to produce feelings of guilt in noncooperators.

---

[17]G. Bateson, D. D. Jackson, J. Haley, J. Weakland, *Behavioral Science* 1, 251 (1956).

For centuries it was assumed without proof that guilt was a valuable, perhaps even an indispensable, ingredient of the civilized life. Now, in this post-Freudian world, we doubt it.

Paul Goodman speaks from the modern point of view when he says: "No good has ever come from feeling guilty, neither intelligence, policy, nor compassion. The guilty do not pay attention to the object but only to themselves, and not even to their own interests, which might make sense, but to their anxieties."[18]

One does not have to be a professional psychiatrist to see the consequences of anxiety. We in the Western world are just emerging from a dreadful two centuries-long Dark Ages of Eros that was sustained partly by prohibition laws, but perhaps more effectively by the anxiety-generating mechanisms of education. Alex Comfort has told the story well in *The Anxiety Makers*;[19] it is not a pretty one.

Since proof is difficult, we may even concede that the results of anxiety may sometimes, from certain points of view, be desirable. The larger question we should ask is whether, as a matter of policy, we should ever encourage the use of a technique the tendency (if not the intention) of which is psychologically pathogenic. We hear much talk these days of responsible parenthood; the coupled words are incorporated into the titles of some organizations devoted to birth control. Some people have proposed massive propaganda campaigns to instill responsibility into the nation's (or the world's) breeders. But what is the meaning of the word conscience? When we use the word responsibility in the absence of substantial sanctions, are we not trying to browbeat a free man in a commons into acting against his own interest? Responsibility is a verbal counterfeit for a substantial quid pro quo. It is an attempt to get something for nothing.

If the word responsibility is to be used at all, I suggest that it be in the sense Charles Frankel uses it.[20] "Responsibility," says this philosopher, "is the product of definite social arrangements." Notice that Frankel calls for social arrangements—not propaganda.

Mutual Coercion Mutually Agreed Upon

The social arrangements that produce responsibility are arrangements that create coercion, of some sort. Consider bank robbing. The man who takes money from a bank acts as if the bank were a commons. How do we prevent such action? Certainly not by trying to control his behavior solely by a verbal appeal to his sense of responsibility. Rather than rely on propaganda we follow Frankel's lead and insist that a bank is not a commons; we seek the definite social arrangements that will keep it from becoming

---

[18]P. Goodman, *New York Review of Books* 10 (8), 22 (23 May 1968).
[19]A. Comfort, *The Anxiety Makers* (Nelson, London, 1967).
[20]C. Frankel, *The Case for Modern Man* (Harper & Row, New York, 1955), p. 203.

a commons. That we thereby infringe on the freedom of would-be robbers we neither deny nor regret.

The morality of bank robbing is particularly easy to understand because we accept complete prohibition of this activity. We are willing to say, "Thou shalt not rob banks," without providing for exceptions. But temperance also can be created by coercion. Taxing is a good coercive device. To keep downtown shoppers temperate in their use of parking space we introduce parking meters for short periods, and traffic fines for longer ones. We need not actually forbid a citizen to park as long as he wants to; we need merely make it increasingly expensive for him to do so. Not prohibition, but carefully biased options are what we offer him. A Madison Avenue man might call this persuasion; I prefer the greater candor of the word coercion.

Coercion is a dirty word to most liberals now, but it need not forever be so. As with the four-letter words, its dirtiness can be cleansed away by exposure to the light, by saying it over and over without apology or embarrassment. To many, the word coercion implies arbitrary decisions of distant and irresponsible bureaucrats; but this is not a necessary part of its meaning. The only kind of coercion I recommend is mutual coercion, mutually agreed upon by the majority of the people affected.

To say that we mutually agree to coercion is not to say that we are required to enjoy it, or even to pretend we enjoy it. Who enjoys taxes? We all grumble about them. But we accept compulsory taxes because we recognize that voluntary taxes would favor the conscienceless. We institute and (grumblingly) support taxes and other coercive devices to escape the horror of the commons.

An alternative to the commons need not be perfectly just to be preferable. With real estate and other material goods, the alternative we have chosen is the institution of private property coupled with legal inheritance. Is this system perfectly just? As a genetically trained biologist I deny that it is. It seems to me that, if there are to be differences in individual inheritance, legal possession should be perfectly correlated with biological inheritance—that those who are biologically more fit to be the custodians of property and power should legally inherit more. But genetic recombination continually makes a mockery of the doctrine of "like father, like son" implicit in our laws of legal inheritance. An idiot can inherit millions, and a trust fund can keep his estate intact. We must admit that our legal system of private property plus inheritance is unjust—but we put up with it because we are not convinced, at the moment, that anyone has invented a better system. The alternative of the commons is too horrifying to contemplate. Injustice is preferable to total ruin.

It is one of the peculiarities of the warfare between reform and the status quo that it is thoughtlessly governed by a double standard. Whenever a reform measure is proposed it is often defeated when its opponents triumphantly discover a flaw in it. As Kingsley Davis has pointed out,[21] wor-

---

[21] See J. D. Roslansky, *Genetics and the Future of Man* (Appleton-Century-Crofts, New York, 1966), p. 177.

shipers of the status quo sometimes imply that no reform is possible without unanimous agreement, an implication contrary to historical fact. As nearly as I can make out, automatic rejection of proposed reforms is based on one of two unconscious assumptions: (1) that the status quo is perfect; or (2) that the choice we face is between reform and no action; if the proposed reform is imperfect, we presumably should take no action at all, while we wait for a perfect proposal.

But we can never do nothing. That which we have done for thousands of years is also action. It also produces evils. Once we are aware that the status quo is action, we can then compare its discoverable advantages and disadvantages with the predicted advantages and disadvantages of the proposed reform, discounting as best we can for our lack of experience. On the basis of such a comparison, we can make a rational decision which will not involve the unworkable assumption that only perfect systems are tolerable.

Recognition of Necessity

Perhaps the simplest summary of this analysis of man's population problems is this: the commons, if justifiable at all, is justifiable only under conditions of low-population density. As the human population has increased, the commons has had to be abandoned in one aspect after another.

First we abandoned the commons in food gathering, enclosing farmland and restricting pastures and hunting and fishing areas. These restrictions are still not complete throughout the world.

Somewhat later we saw that the commons as a place for waste disposal would also have to be abandoned. Restrictions on the disposal of domestic sewage are widely accepted in the Western world; we are still struggling to close the commons to pollution by automobiles, factories, insecticide sprayers, fertilizing operations, and atomic energy installations.

In a still more embryonic state is our recognition of the evils of the commons in matters of pleasure. There is almost no restriction on the propagation of sound waves in the public medium. The shopping public is assaulted with mindless music, without its consent. Our government has paid out billions of dollars to create a supersonic transport which would disturb 50,000 people for every one person whisked from coast to coast 3 hours faster. Advertisers muddy the airwaves of radio and television and pollute the view of travelers. We are a long way from outlawing the commons in matters of pleasure. Is this because our Puritan inheritance makes us view pleasure as something of a sin, and pain (that is, the pollution of advertising) as the sign of virtue?

Every new enclosure of the commons involves the infringement of somebody's personal liberty. Infringements made in the distant past are accepted because no contemporary complains of a loss. It is the newly proposed infringements that we vigorously oppose; cries of "rights" and "freedom" fill the air. But what does "freedom" mean? When men mutually agreed to pass laws against robbing, mankind became more free, not less so. Individuals locked into the logic of the commons are free only to bring on universal ruin; once they see the necessity of mutual coercion, they become free to pursue other goals. I believe it was Hegel who said, "Freedom is the recognition of necessity."

The most important aspect of necessity that we must now recognize is the necessity of abandoning the commons in breeding. No technical solution can rescue us from the misery of overpopulation. Freedom to breed will bring ruin to all. At the moment, to avoid hard decisions many of us are tempted to propagandize for conscience and responsible parenthood. The temptation must be resisted, because an appeal to independently acting consciences selects for the disappearance of all conscience in the long run, and an increase in anxiety in the short.

The only way we can preserve and nurture other and more precious freedoms is by relinquishing the freedom to breed, and that very soon. "Freedom is the recognition of necessity"—and it is the role of education to reveal to all the necessity of abandoning the freedom to breed. Only so can we put an end to this aspect of the tragedy of the commons.

3   *The Problem of Social Cost**

Ronald Coase

Ronald Coase is Clifton R. Musser Professor Emeritus of Economics at the University of Chicago Law School.

I. The Problem to Be Examined

This paper is concerned with those actions of business firms which have harmful effects on others. The standard example is that of a factory the smoke from which has harmful effects on those occupying neighbouring properties. The economic analysis of such a situation has usually proceeded in terms of a divergence between the private and social product of the factory, in which economists have largely followed the treatment of Pigou in *The Economics of Welfare*. The conclusion to which this kind of analysis seems to have led most economists is that it would be desirable to make the owner of the factory liable for the damage caused to those injured by the smoke, or alternatively, to place a tax on the factory owner varying with the amount of smoke produced and equivalent in money terms to the damage it would cause, or finally, to exclude the factory from residential districts (and presumably from other areas in which the emission of smoke would have harmful effects on others). It is my contention that the suggested courses of action are inappropriate, in that they lead to results which are not necessarily, or even usually, desirable.

II. The Reciprocal Nature of the Problem

The traditional approach has tended to obscure the nature of the choice that has to be made. The question is commonly thought of as one in which A inflicts harm on B and what has to be decided is: how should we restrain A? But this is wrong. We are dealing with a problem of a reciprocal nature. To avoid the harm to B would inflict harm on A. The real question that has to be decided is: should A be allowed to harm B or should B be

"The Problem of Social Cost," by Ronald Coase, from *The Journal of Law and Economics* (October 1969). (Several passages devoted to extended discussions of legal decisions have been omitted.) Reprinted by permission.

*This article, although concerned with a technical problem of economic analysis, arose out of the study of the Political Economy of Broadcasting which I am now conducting. The argument of the present article was implicit in a previous article dealing with the problem of allocating radio and television frequencies ("The Federal Communications Commission," 2 *J. Law & Econ.* [1959]) but comments which I have received seemed to suggest that it would be desirable to deal with the question in a more explicit way and without reference to the original problem for the solution of which the analysis was developed.

allowed to harm A? The problem is to avoid the more serious harm. I in-
stanced in my previous article[1] the case of a confectioner the noise and vi-
brations from whose machinery disturbed a doctor in his work. To avoid
harming the doctor would inflict harm on the confectioner. The problem
posed by this case was essentially whether it was worth while, as a result
of restricting the methods of production which could be used by the confectioner, to secure more doctoring at the cost of a reduced supply of confectionery products. Another example is afforded by the problem of straying cattle which destroy crops on neighbouring land. If it is inevitable that
some cattle will stray, an increase in the supply of meat can only be obtained at the expense of a decrease in the supply of crops. The nature of
the choice is clear: meat or crops. What answer should be given is, of course,
not clear unless we know the value of what is obtained as well as the value
of what is sacrificed to obtain it. To give another example, Professor George
J. Stigler instances the contamination of a stream.[2] If we assume that the
harmful effect of the pollution is that it kills the fish, the question to be
decided is: is the value of the fish lost greater or less than the value of the
product which the contamination of the stream makes possible? It goes almost without saying that this problem has to be looked at in total *and* at
the margin.

III. The Pricing System with Liability for Damage

I propose to start my analysis by examining a case in which most economists would presumably agree that the problem would be solved in a completely satisfactory manner: when the damaging business has to pay for all
damage caused *and* the pricing system works smoothly (strictly this means
that the operation of a pricing system is without cost).

A good example of the problem under discussion is afforded by the
case of straying cattle which destroy crops growing on neighbouring land.
Let us suppose that a farmer and cattle-raiser are operating on neighbouring properties. Let us further suppose that, without any fencing between the properties, an increase in the size of the cattle-raiser's herd increases the total damage to the farmer's crops. What happens to the
marginal damage as the size of the herd increases is another matter. This
depends on whether the cattle tend to follow one another or to roam side
by side, on whether they tend to be more or less restless as the size of the
herd increases and on other similar factors. For my immediate purpose, it
is immaterial what assumption is made about marginal damage as the size
of the herd increases.

---

[1]Coase, "The Federal Communications Commission," 2 *J. Law & Econ.* 26–27 (1959).
[2]G. J. Stigler, *The Theory of Price,* 105 (1952).

To simplify the argument, I propose to use an arithmetical example. I shall assume that the annual cost of fencing the farmer's property is $9 and the price of the crop is $1 per ton. Also, I assume that the relation between the number of cattle in the herd and the annual crop loss is as follows:

Number in Herd (Steers)	Annual Crop Loss (Tons)	Crop Loss per Additional Steer (Tons)
1	1	1
2	3	2
3	6	3
4	10	4

Given that the cattle-raiser is liable for the damage caused, the additional annual cost imposed on the cattle-raiser if he increased his herd from, say, 2 to 3 steers is $3 and in deciding on the size of the herd, he will take this into account along with his other costs. That is, he will not increase the size of the herd unless the value of the additional meat produced (assuming that the cattle-raiser slaughters the cattle) is greater than the additional costs that this will entail, including the value of the additional crops destroyed. Of course, if, by the employment of dogs, herdsmen, aeroplanes, mobile radio and other means, the amount of damage can be reduced, these means will be adopted when their cost is less than the value of the crop which they prevent being lost. Given that the annual cost of fencing is $9, the cattle-raiser who wished to have a herd with 4 steers or more would pay for fencing to be erected and maintained, assuming that other means of attaining the same end would not do so more cheaply. When the fence is erected, the marginal cost due to the liability for damage becomes zero, except to the extent that an increase in the size of the herd necessitates a stronger and therefore more expensive fence because more steers are liable to lean against it at the same time. But, of course, it may be cheaper for the cattle-raiser not to fence and to pay for the damaged crops, as in my arithmetical example, with 3 or fewer steers.

It might be thought that the fact that the cattle-raiser would pay for all crops damaged would lead the farmer to increase his planting if a cattle-raiser came to occupy the neighbouring property. But this is not so. If the crop was previously sold in conditions of perfect competition, marginal cost was equal to price for the amount of planting undertaken and any expansion would have reduced the profits of the farmer. In the new situation, the existence of crop damage would mean that the farmer would sell less on the open market but his receipts for a given production would remain the same, since the cattle-raiser would pay the market price for any crop damaged. Of course, if cattle-raising commonly involved the destruction of crops, the coming into existence of a cattle-raising industry might raise the price of the crops involved and farmers would then extend their planting. But I wish to confine my attention to the individual farmer.

I have said that the occupation of a neighbouring property by a cattle-raiser would not cause the amount of production, or perhaps more exactly the amount of planting, by the farmer to increase. In fact, if the cattle-raising has any effect, it will be to decrease the amount of planting. The reason for this is that, for any given tract of land, if the value of the crop damaged is so great that the receipts from the sale of the undamaged crop are less than the total costs of cultivating that tract of land, it will be profitable for the farmer and the cattle-raiser to make a bargain whereby that tract of land is left uncultivated. This can be made clear by means of an arithmetical example. Assume initially that the value of the crop obtained from cultivating a given tract of land is $12 and that the cost incurred in cultivating this tract of land is $10, the net gain from cultivating the land being $2. I assume for purposes of simplicity that the farmer owns the land. Now assume that the cattle-raiser starts operations on the neighbouring property and that the value of the crops damaged is $1. In this case $11 is obtained by the farmer from sale on the market and $1 is obtained from the cattle-raiser for damage suffered and the net gain remains $2. Now suppose that the cattle-raiser finds it profitable to increase the size of his herd, even though the amount of damage rises to $3; which means that the value of the additional meat production is greater than the additional costs, including the additional $2 payment for damage. But the total payment for damage is now $3. The net gain to the farmer from cultivating the land is still $2. The cattle-raiser would be better off if the farmer would agree not to cultivate his land for any payment less than $3. The farmer would be agreeable to not cultivating the land for any payment greater than $2. There is clearly room for a mutually satisfactory bargain which would lead to the abandonment of cultivation.[3] But the same argument applies not only to the whole tract cultivated by the farmer but also to any subdivision of it. Suppose, for example, that the cattle have a well-defined route, say, to a brook or to a shady area. In these circumstances, the amount of damage to the crop along the route may well be great and if so, it could

---

[3]The argument in the text has proceeded on the assumption that the alternative to cultivation of the crop is abandonment of cultivation altogether. But this need not be so. There may be crops which are less liable to damage by cattle but which would not be as profitable as the crop grown in the absence of damage. Thus, if the cultivation of a new crop would yield a return to the farmer of $1 instead of $2, and the size of the herd which would cause $3 damage with the old crop would cause $1 damage with the new crop, it would be profitable to the cattle-raiser to pay any sum less than $2 to induce the farmer to change his crop (since this would reduce damage liability from $3 to $1) and it would be profitable for the farmer to do so if the amount received was more than $1 (the reduction in his return caused by switching crops). In fact, there would be room for a mutually satisfactory bargain in all cases in which change of crop would reduce the amount of damage by more than it reduces the value of the crop (excluding damage)—in all cases, that is, in which a change in the crop cultivated would lead to an increase in the value of production.

be that the farmer and the cattle-raiser would find it profitable to make a bargain whereby the farmer would agree not to cultivate this strip of land.

But this raises a further possibility. Suppose that there is such a well-defined route. Suppose further that the value of the crop that would be obtained by cultivating this strip of land is $10 but that the cost of cultivation is $11. In the absence of the cattle-raiser, the land would not be cultivated. However, given the presence of the cattle-raiser, it could well be that if the strip was cultivated, the whole crop would be destroyed by the cattle. In which case, the cattle-raiser would be forced to pay $10 to the farmer. It is true that the farmer would lose $1. But the cattle-raiser would lose $10. Clearly this is a situation which is not likely to last indefinitely since neither party would want this to happen. The aim of the farmer would be to induce the cattle-raiser to make a payment in return for an agreement to leave this land uncultivated. The farmer would not be able to obtain a payment greater than the cost of fencing off this piece of land nor so high as to lead the cattle-raiser to abandon the use of the neighbouring property. What payment would in fact be made would depend on the shrewdness of the farmer and the cattle-raiser as bargainers. But as the payment would not be so high as to cause the cattle-raiser to abandon this location and as it would not vary with the size of the herd, such an agreement would not affect the allocation of resources but would merely alter the distribution of income and wealth as between the cattle-raiser and the farmer.

I think it is clear that if the cattle-raiser is liable for damage caused and the pricing system works smoothly, the reduction in the value of production elsewhere will be taken into account in computing the additional cost involved in increasing the size of the herd. This cost will be weighed against the value of the additional meat production and, given perfect competition in the cattle industry, the allocation of resources in cattle-raising will be optimal. What needs to be emphasized is that the fall in the value of production elsewhere which would be taken into account in the costs of the cattle-raiser may well be less than the damage which the cattle would cause to the crops in the ordinary course of events. This is because it is possible, as a result of market transactions, to discontinue cultivation of the land. This is desirable in all cases in which the damage that the cattle would cause, and for which the cattle-raiser would be willing to pay, exceeds the amount which the farmer would pay for use of the land. In conditions of perfect competition, the amount which the farmer would pay for the use of the land is equal to the difference between the value of the total production when the factors are employed on this land and the value of the additional product yielded in their next best use (which would be what the farmer would have to pay for the factors). If damage exceeds the amount the farmer would pay for the use of the land, the value of the additional product of the factors employed elsewhere would exceed the value of the total product in this use after damage is taken into account. It follows that it would be desirable to abandon cultivation of the land and to release the factors employed for production elsewhere. A procedure which merely provided for payment for damage to the crop caused by the cattle but which did not allow for the possibility of cultivation being discontinued would result in too small an employment of factors of production in cattle-raising and too large an employment of factors in cultivation of the crop. But given the possibility of market transactions, a situation in which damage to crops exceeded the rent of the land would not endure. Whether the cattle-raiser pays the farmer to leave the land uncultivated or himself rents the land by paying the landowner an amount slightly greater than the farmer would pay (if the farmer was himself renting the land), the final result would be the same and would maximise the value of production. Even when the farmer is induced to plant crops which it would not be profitable to cultivate for sale on the market, this will be a purely short-term phenomenon and may be expected to lead to an agreement under which the planting will cease. The cattle-raiser will remain in that location and the marginal cost of meat production will be the same as before, thus having no long-run effect on the allocation of resources.

IV. The Pricing System with No Liability for Damage

I now turn to the case in which, although the pricing system is assumed to work smoothly (that is, costlessly), the damaging business is not liable for any of the damage which it causes. This business does not have to make a payment to those damaged by its actions. I propose to show that the allocation of resources will be the same in this case is it was when the damaging business was liable for damage caused. As I showed in the previous case that the allocation of resources was optimal, it will not be necessary to repeat this part of the argument.

I return to the case of the farmer and the cattle-raiser. The farmer would suffer increased damage to his crop as the size of the herd increased. Suppose that the size of the cattle-raiser's herd is 3 steers (and that this is the size of the herd that would be maintained if crop damage was not taken into account). Then the farmer would be willing to pay up to $3 if the cattle-raiser would reduce his herd to 2 steers, up to $5 if the herd were reduced to 1 steer and would pay up to $6 if cattle-raising was abandoned. The cattle-raiser would therefore receive $3 from the farmer if he kept 2 steers instead of 3. This $3 foregone is therefore part of the cost incurred in keeping the third steer. Whether the $3 is a payment which the cattle-raiser has to make if he adds the third steer to his herd (which it would be if the cattle-raiser was liable to the farmer for damage caused to the crop) or whether it is a sum of money which he would have received if he did not keep a third steer (which it would be if the cattle-raiser was not liable to the farmer for damage caused to the crop) does not affect the final result. In both cases $3 is part of the cost of adding a third steer, to be included along with the other costs. If the increase in the value of production in cattle-raising through increasing the size of the herd from 2 to 3 is greater than the additional costs that have to be incurred (including the $3

THE PROBLEM OF SOCIAL COST 29

damage to crops), the size of the herd will be increased. Otherwise, it will not. The size of the herd will be the same whether the cattle-raiser is liable for damage caused to the crop or not.

It may be argued that the assumed starting point—a herd of 3 steers—was arbitrary. And this is true. But the farmer would not wish to pay to avoid crop damage which the cattle-raiser would not be able to cause. For example, the maximum annual payment which the farmer could be induced to pay could not exceed $9, the annual cost of fencing. And the farmer would only be willing to pay this sum if it did not reduce his earnings to a level that would cause him to abandon cultivation of this particular tract of land. Furthermore, the farmer would only be willing to pay this amount if he believed that, in the absence of any payment by him, the size of the herd maintained by the cattle-raiser would be 4 or more steers. Let us assume that this is the case. Then the farmer would be willing to pay up to $3 if the cattle-raiser would reduce his herd to 3 steers, up to $6 if the herd were reduced to 2 steers, up to $8 if one steer only were kept and up to $9 if cattle-raising were abandoned. It will be noticed that the change in the starting point has not altered the amount which would accrue to the cattle-raiser if he reduced the size of his herd by any given amount. It is still true that the cattle-raiser could receive an additional $3 from the farmer if he agreed to reduce his herd from 3 steers to 2 and that the $3 represents the value of the crop that would be destroyed by adding the third steer to the herd. Although a different belief on the part of the farmer (whether justified or not) about the size of the herd that the cattle-raiser would maintain in the absence of payments from him may affect the total payment he can be induced to pay, it is not true that this different belief would have any effect on the size of the herd that the cattle-raiser will actually keep. This will be the same as it would be if the cattle-raiser had to pay for damage caused by his cattle, since a receipt foregone of a given amount is the equivalent of a payment of the same amount.

It might be thought that it would pay the cattle-raiser to increase his herd above the size that he would wish to maintain once a bargain had been made, in order to induce the farmer to make a larger total payment. And this may be true. It is similar in nature to the action of the farmer (when the cattle-raiser was liable for damage) in cultivating land on which, as a result of an agreement with the cattle-raiser, planting would subsequently be abandoned (including land which would not be cultivated at all in the absence of cattle-raising). But such manoeuvres are preliminaries to an agreement and do not affect the long-run equilibrium position, which is the same whether or not the cattle-raiser is held responsible for the crop damage brought about by his cattle.

It is necessary to know whether the damaging business is liable or not for damage caused since without the establishment of this initial delimitation of rights there can be no market transactions to transfer and recombine them. But the ultimate result (which maximises the value of production) is independent of the legal position if the pricing system is assumed to work without cost.

V. The Problem Illustrated Anew

The harmful effects of the activities of a business can assume a wide variety of forms. An early English case concerned a building which, by obstructing currents of air, hindered the operation of a windmill.[4] A recent case in Florida concerned a building which cast a shadow on the cabana, swimming pool and sunbathing areas of a neighbouring hotel.[5] The problem of straying cattle and the damaging of crops which was the subject of detailed examination in the two preceding sections, although it may have appeared to be rather a special case, is in fact but one example of a problem which arises in many different guises. To clarify the nature of my argument and to demonstrate its general applicability, I propose to illustrate it anew by reference to four actual cases.

Let us first reconsider the case of *Sturges v. Bridgman*[6] which I used as an illustration of the general problem in my article on "The Federal Communications Commission." In this case, a confectioner (in Wigmore Street) used two mortars and pestles in connection with his business (one had been in operation in the same position for more than 60 years and the other for more than 26 years). A doctor than came to occupy neighbouring premises (in Wimpole Street). The confectioner's machinery caused the doctor no harm until, eight years after he had first occupied the premises, he built a consulting room at the end of his garden right against the confectioner's kitchen. It was then found that the noise and vibration caused by the confectioner's machinery made it difficult for the doctor to use his new consulting room. "In particular . . . the noise prevented him from examining his patients by auscultation[7] for diseases of the chest. He also found it impossible to engage with effect in any occupation which required thought and attention." The doctor therefore brought a legal action to force the confectioner to stop using his machinery. The courts had little difficulty in granting the doctor the injunction he sought. "Individual cases of hardship may occur in the strict carrying out of the principle upon which we found our judgment, but the negation of the principle would lead even more to individual hardship, and would at the same time produce a prejudicial effect upon the development of land for residential purposes."

The court's decision established that the doctor had the right to prevent the confectioner from using his machinery. But, of course, it would have been possible to modify the arrangements envisaged in the legal ruling by means of a bargain between the parties. The doctor would have been willing to waive his right and allow the machinery to continue in operation if the confectioner would have paid him a sum of money which was greater than the loss of income which he would suffer from having to move

---

[4]See Gale on *Easements* 237–39 (13th ed. M. Bowles 1959).

[5]See *Fontainebleu Hotel Corp. v. Forty-Five Twenty-Five, Inc.,* 114 So. 2d 357 (1959).

[6]11 Ch. D. 852 (1879).

[7]Auscultation is the act of listening by ear or stethoscope in order to judge by sound the condition of the body.

to a more closely or less convenient location or from having to curtail his activities at this location or, as was suggested as a possibility, from having to build a separate wall which would deaden the noise and vibration. The confectioner would have been willing to do this if the amount he would have to pay the doctor was less than the fall in income he would suffer if he had to change his mode of operation at this location, abandon his operation or move his confectionery business to some other location. The solution of the problem depends essentially on whether the continued use of the machinery adds more to the confectioner's income than it subtracts from the doctor's.[8] But now consider the situation if the confectioner had won the case. The confectioner would then have had the right to continue operating his noise and vibration-generating machinery without having to pay anything to the doctor. The boot would have been on the other foot: the doctor would have had to pay the confectioner to induce him to stop using the machinery. If the doctor's income would have fallen more through continuance of the use of this machinery than it added to the income of the confectioner, there would clearly be room for a bargain whereby the doctor paid the confectioner to stop using the machinery. That is to say, the circumstances in which it would not pay the confectioner to continue to use the machinery and to compensate the doctor for the losses that this would bring (if the doctor had the right to prevent the confectioner's using his machinery) would be those in which it would be in the interest of the doctor to make a payment to the confectioner which would induce him to discontinue the use of the machinery (if the confectioner had the right to operate the machinery). The basic conditions are exactly the same in this case as they were in the example of the cattle which destroyed crops. With costless market transactions, the decision of the courts concerning liability for damage would be without effect on the allocation of resources. It was of course the view of the judges that they were affecting the working of the economic system—and in a desirable direction. Any other decision would have had "a prejudicial effect upon the development of land for residential purposes," an argument which was elaborated by examining the example of a forge operating on a barren moor, which was later developed for residential purposes. The judges' view that they were settling how the land was to be used would be true only in the case in which the costs of carrying out the necessary market transactions exceeded the gain which might be achieved by any rearrangement of rights. And it would be desirable to preserve the areas (Wimpole Street or the moor) for residential or professional use (by giving non-industrial users the right to stop the noise, vibration, smoke, etc., by injunction) only if the value of the additional residential facilities obtained was greater than the value of cakes or iron lost. But of this the judges seem to have been unaware.

---

[8]Note that what is taken into account is the change in income after allowing for alterations in methods of production, location, character of product, etc.

The reasoning employed by the courts in determining legal rights will often seem strange to an economist because many of the factors on which the decision turns are, to an economist, irrelevant. Because of this, situations which are, from an economic point of view, identical will be treated quite differently by the courts. The economic problem in all cases of harmful effects is how to maximise the value of production. In the case of *Bass v. Gregory* fresh air was drawn in through the well which facilitated the production of beer but foul air was expelled through the well which made life in the adjoining houses less pleasant. The economic problem was to decide which to choose: a lower cost of beer and worsened amenities in adjoining houses or a higher cost of beer and improved amenities. In deciding this question, the "doctrine of lost grant" is about as relevant as the colour of the judge's eyes. But it has to be remembered that the immediate question faced by the courts is *not* what shall be done by whom *but* who has the legal right to do what. It is always possible to modify by transactions on the market the initial legal delimitation of rights. And, of course, if such market transactions are costless, such a rearrangement of rights will always take place if it would lead to an increase in the value of production.

VI. *The Cost of Market Transactions Taken into Account*

The argument has proceeded up to this point on the assumption (explicit in Sections III and IV and tacit in Section V) that there were no costs involved in carrying out market transactions. This is, of course, a very unrealistic assumption. In order to carry out a market transaction it is necessary to discover who it is that one wishes to deal with, to inform people that one wishes to deal and on what terms, to conduct negotiations leading up to a bargain, to draw up the contract, to undertake the inspection needed to make sure that the terms of the contract are being observed and so on. These operations are often extremely costly, sufficiently costly at any rate to prevent many transactions that would be carried out in a world in which the pricing system worked without cost.

In earlier sections, when dealing with the problem of the rearrangement of legal rights through the market, it was argued that such a rearrangement would be made through the market whenever this would lead to an increase in the value of production. But this assumed costless market transactions. Once the costs of carrying out market transactions are taken into account it is clear that such a rearrangement of rights will only be undertaken when the increase in the value of production consequent upon the rearrangement is greater than the costs which would be involved in bringing it about. When it is less, the granting of an injunction (or the knowledge that it would be granted) or the liability to pay damages may result in an activity being discontinued (or may prevent its being started) which would be undertaken if market transactions were costless. In these conditions the initial delimitation of legal rights does have an effect on the efficiency with which the economic system operates. One arrangement of rights may bring about a greater value of production than any other. But unless this is the arrangement of rights established by the legal system, the costs of reaching the same result by altering and combining rights through the market may be so great that this optimal arrangement of rights, and the greater value of production which it would bring, may never be achieved. The part played by economic considerations in the process of delimiting legal rights will be discussed in the next section. In this section, I will take the initial delimitation of rights and the costs of carrying out market transactions as given.

It is clear that an alternative form of economic organisation which could achieve the same result at less cost than would be incurred by using the market would enable the value of production to be raised. As I explained many years ago, the firm represents such an alternative to organising production through market transactions.[9] Within the firm individual bargains between the various cooperating factors of production are eliminated and for a market transaction is substituted an administrative decision. The rearrangement of production then takes place without the need for bargains between the owners of the factors of production. A landowner who has control of a large tract of land may devote his land to various uses taking into account the effect that the interrelations of the various activities will have on the net return of the land, thus rendering unnecessary bargains between those undertaking the various activities. Owners of a large building or of several adjoining properties in a given area may act in much the same way. In effect, using our earlier terminology, the firm would acquire the legal rights of all the parties and the rearrangement of activities would not follow on a rearrangement of rights by contract, but as a result of an administrative decision as to how the rights should be used.

It does not, of course, follow that the administrative costs of organising a transaction through a firm are inevitably less than the costs of the market transactions which are superseded. But where contracts are peculiarly difficult to draw up and an attempt to describe what the parties have agreed to do or not to do (e.g. the amount and kind of a smell or noise that they may make or will not make) would necessitate a lengthy and highly involved document, and, where, as is probable, a long-term contract would be desirable,[10] it would be hardly surprising if the emergence of a firm or the extension of the activities of an existing firm was not the solution adopted on many occasions to deal with the problem of harmful effects. This solution would be adopted whenever the administrative costs of the firm were less than the costs of the market transactions that it supersedes and the gains which would result from the rearrangement of activities greater than the firm's costs of organising them. I do not need to examine

[9]See Coase, "The Nature of the Firm," 4 *Economica*, New Series, 386 (1937). Reprinted in *Readings in Price Theory*, 331 (1952).

[10]For reasons explained in my earlier article, see *Readings in Price Theory*, n. 14 at 337.

in great detail the character of this solution since I have explained what is involved in my earlier article.

But the firm is not the only possible answer to this problem. The administrative costs of organising transactions within the firm may also be high, and particularly so when many diverse activities are brought within the control of a single organisation. In the standard case of a smoke nuisance, which may affect a vast number of people engaged in a wide variety of activities, the administrative costs might well be so high as to make any attempt to deal with the problem within the confines of a single firm impossible. An alternative solution is direct government regulation. Instead of instituting a legal system of rights which can be modified by transactions on the market, the government may impose regulations which state what people must or must not do and which have to be obeyed. Thus, the government (by statute or perhaps more likely through an administrative agency) may, to deal with the problem of smoke nuisance, decree that certain methods of production should or should not be used (e.g. that smoke preventing devices should be installed or that coal or oil should not be burned) or may confine certain types of business to certain districts (zoning regulations).

The government is, in a sense, a superfirm (but of a very special kind) since it is able to influence the use of factors of production by administrative decision. But the ordinary firm is subject to checks in its operations because of the competition of other firms, which might administer the same activities at lower cost and also because there is always the alternative of market transactions as against organisation within the firm if the administrative costs become too great. The government is able, if it wishes, to avoid the market altogether, which a firm can never do. The firm has to make market agreements with the owners of the factors of production that it uses. Just as the government can conscript or seize property, so it can decree that factors of production should only be used in such-and-such a way. Such authoritarian methods save a lot of trouble (for those doing the organising). Furthermore, the government has at its disposal the police and the other law enforcement agencies to make sure that its regulations are carried out.

It is clear that the government has powers which might enable it to get some things done at a lower cost than could a private organisation (or at any rate one without special governmental powers). But the governmental administrative machine is not itself costless. It can, in fact, on occasion be extremely costly. Furthermore, there is no reason to suppose that the restrictive and zoning regulations, made by a fallible administration subject to political pressures and operating without any competitive check, will necessarily always be those which increase the efficiency with which the economic system operates. Furthermore, such general regulations which must apply to a wide variety of cases will be enforced in some cases in which they are clearly inappropriate. From these considerations it follows that direct governmental regulation will not necessarily give better results than leaving the problem to be solved by the market or the firm. But equally there is no reason why, on occasion, such governmental administrative regulation should not lead to an improvement in economic efficiency. This would seem particularly likely when, as is normally the case with the smoke nuisance, a large number of people are involved and in which therefore the costs of handling the problem through the market or the firm may be high.

There is, of course, a further alternative which is to do nothing about the problem at all. And given that the costs involved in solving the problem by regulations issued by the governmental administrative machine will often be heavy (particularly if the costs are interpreted to include all the consequences which follow from the government engaging in this kind of activity), it will no doubt be commonly the case that the gain which would come from regulating the actions which give rise to the harmful effects will be less than the costs involved in government regulation.

The discussion of the problem of harmful effects in this section (when the costs of market transactions are taken into account) is extremely inadequate. But at least it has made clear that the problem is one of choosing the appropriate social arrangement for dealing with the harmful effects. All solutions have costs and there is no reason to suppose that government regulation is called for simply because the problem is not well handled by the market or the firm. Satisfactory views on policy can only come from a patient study of how, in practice, the market, firms and governments handle the problem of harmful effects. Economists need to study the work of the broker in bringing parties together, the effectiveness of restrictive covenants, the problems of the large-scale real-estate development company, the operation of government zoning and other regulating activities. It is my belief that economists, and policy-makers generally, have tended to over-estimate the advantages which come from governmental regulation. But this belief, even if justified, does not do more than suggest that government regulation should be curtailed. It does not tell us where the boundary line should be drawn. This, it seems to me, has to come from a detailed investigation of the actual results of handling the problem in different ways. But it would be unfortunate if this investigation were undertaken with the aid of a faulty economic analysis. The aim of this article is to indicate what the economic approach to the problem should be.

VII. The Legal Delimitation of Rights and the Economic Problem

The discussion in Section V not only served to illustrate the argument but also afforded a glimpse at the legal approach to the problem of harmful effects. The cases considered were all English but a similar selection of American cases could easily be made and the character of the reasoning would have been the same. Of course, if market transactions were costless, all that matters (questions of equity apart) is that the rights of the various parties should be well-defined and the results of legal actions easy to forecast. But as we have seen, the situation is quite different when market transactions are so costly as to make it difficult to change the arrangement of rights established by the law. In such cases, the courts directly influence economic activity. It would therefore seem desirable that the courts should understand the economic consequences of their decisions and should, insofar as this is possible without creating too much uncertainty about the legal position itself, take these consequences into account when making their decisions. Even when it is possible to change the legal delimitation of rights through market transactions, it is obviously desirable to reduce the need for such transactions and thus reduce the employment of resources in carrying them out.

A thorough examination of the presuppositions of the courts in trying such cases would be of great interest but I have not been able to attempt it. Nevertheless it is clear from a cursory study that the courts have often recognized the economic implications of their decisions and are aware (as many economists are not) of the reciprocal nature of the problem. Furthermore, from time to time, they take these economic implications into account, along with other factors, in arriving at their decisions. The American writers on this subject refer to the question in a more explicit fashion than do the British. Thus, to quote Prosser on Torts, a person may

> make use of his own property or . . . conduct his own affairs at the expense of some harm to his neighbors. He may operate a factory whose noise and smoke cause some discomfort to others, so long as he keeps within reasonable bounds. It is only when his conduct is unreasonable, *in the light of its utility and the harm which results* [italics added], that it becomes a nuisance. . . . As it was said in an ancient case in regard to candle-making in a town, "Le utility del chose excusera le noisomeness del stink."
>
> The world must have factories, smelters, oil refineries, noisy machinery and blasting, even at the expense of some inconvenience to those in the vicinity and the plaintiff may be required to accept some not unreasonable discomfort for the general good.[11]

The standard British writers do not state as explicitly as this that a comparison between the utility and harm produced is an element in deciding whether a harmful effect should be considered a nuisance. But similar views, if less strongly expressed, are to be found.[12] The doctrine that the harmful effect must be substantial before the court will act is, no doubt, in part a reflection of the fact that there will almost always be some gain to offset the harm. And in the reports of individual cases, it is clear that the judges have had in mind what would be lost as well as what would be gained in deciding whether to grant an injunction or award damages. Thus,

---

[11]See W. L. Prosser, *The Law of Torts* 398–99, 412 (2d ed. 1955). The quotation about the ancient case concerning candle-making is taken from Sir James Fitzjames Stephen, *A General View of the Criminal Law of England* 106 (1890). Sir James Stephen gives no reference. He perhaps had in mind *Rex. v. Ronkett*, included in Seavey, Keeton and Thurston, *Cases on Torts* 604 (1950). A similar view to that expressed by Prosser is to be found in F. V. Harper and F. James, *The Law of Torts* 67–74 (1956); *Restatement, Torts* §§826, 827 and 828.

[12]See Winfield on *Torts* 541–48 (6th ed. T. E. Lewis 1954); Salmond on the *Law of Torts* 181–90 (12th ed. R. F. V. Heuston 1957); H. Street, *The Law of Torts* 221–29 (1959).

in refusing to prevent the destruction of a prospect by a new building, the judge stated:

> I know no general rule of common law, which . . . says, that building so as to stop another's prospect is a nuisance. Was that the case, there could be no great towns; and I must grant injunctions to all the new buildings in this town. . . . [13]

The problem which we face in dealing with actions which have harmful effects is not simply one of restraining those responsible for them. What has to be decided is whether the gain from preventing the harm is greater than the loss which would be suffered elsewhere as a result of stopping the action which produces the harm. In a world in which there are costs of rearranging the rights established by the legal system, the courts, in cases relating to nuisance, are, in effect, making a decision on the economic problem and determining how resources are to be employed. It was argued that the courts are conscious of this and that they often make, although not always in a very explicit fashion, a comparison between what would be gained and what lost by preventing actions which have harmful effects. But the delimitation of rights is also the result of statutory enactments. Here we also find evidence of an appreciation of the reciprocal nature of the problem. While statutory enactments add to the list of nuisances, action is also taken to legalize what would otherwise be nuisances under the common law. The kind of situation which economists are prone to consider as requiring corrective government action is, in fact, often the result of government action. Such action is not necessarily unwise. But there is a real danger that extensive government intervention in the economic system may lead to the protection of those responsible for harmful effects being carried too far.

VIII. Pigou's Treatment in "The Economics of Welfare"

The fountainhead for the modern economic analysis of the problem discussed in this article is Pigou's *Economics of Welfare* and, in particular, that section of Part II which deals with divergences between social and private net products which come about because

> one person A, in the course of rendering some service, for which payment is made, to a second person B, incidentally also renders services or disservices to other persons (not producers of like services), or such a sort that payment cannot

---

[13]*Attorney General v. Doughty*, 2 Ves. Sen. 453, 28 Eng. Rep. 290 (Ch. 1752). Compare in this connection the statement of an American judge, quoted in Prosser, *op. cit. supra* n. 16 at 413 n. 54: "Without smoke, Pittsburgh would have remained a very pretty village," Musmanno, J., in *Versailles Borough v. McKeesport Coal & Coke Co.*, 1935, 83 Pitts. Leg. J. 379, 385.

be exacted from the benefited parties or compensation enforced on behalf of the injured parties.[14]

Pigou tells us that his aim in Part II of *The Economics of Welfare* is

to ascertain how far the free play of self-interest, acting under the existing legal system, tends to distribute the country's resources in the way most favorable to the production of a large national dividend, and how far it is feasible for State action to improve upon 'natural' tendencies.[15]

To judge from the first part of this statement, Pigou's purpose is to discover whether any improvements could be made in the existing arrangements which determine the use of resources. Since Pigou's conclusions is that improvements could be made, one might have expected him to continue by saying that he proposed to set out the changes required to bring them about. Instead, Pigou adds a phrase which contrasts "natural" tendencies with State action, which seems in some sense to equate the present arrangements with "natural" tendencies and to imply that what is required to bring about these improvements is State action (if feasible). That this is more or less Pigou's position is evident from Chapter I of Part II.[16] Pigou starts by referring to "optimistic followers of the classical economists"[17] who have argued that the value of production would be maximised if the government refrained from any interference in the economic system and the economic arrangements were those which came about "naturally." Pigou goes on to say that if self-interest does promote economic welfare, it is because human institutions have been devised to make it so. (This part of Pigou's argument, which he develops with the aid of a quotation from Cannan, seems to me to be essentially correct.) Pigou concludes:

But even in the most advanced States there are failures and imperfections. . . . there are many obstacles that prevent a community's resources from being distributed . . . in the most efficient way. The study of these constitutes our present problem. . . . Its purpose is essentially practical. It seeks to bring into clearer light some of the ways in which it now is, or eventually may become, feasible for governments to control the play of economic forces in such ways as to promote the economic welfare, and through that, the total welfare, of their citizens as a whole.[18]

Pigou's underlying thought would appear to be: Some have argued that no State action is needed. But the system has performed as well as it has be-

---

[14]A. C. Pigou, *The Economics of Welfare* 183 (4th ed. 1932). My references will all be to the fourth edition but the argument and examples examined in this article remained substantially unchanged from the first edition in 1920 to the fourth in 1932. A large part (but not all) of this analysis had appeared previously in *Wealth and Welfare* (1912).

[15]*Id.* at xii.

[16]*Id.* at 127–30.

[17]In *Wealth and Welfare*, Pigou attributes the "optimism" to Adam Smith himself and not to his followers. He there refers to the "highly optimistic theory of Adam Smith that the national dividend, in given circumstances of demand and supply, tends 'naturally' to a maximum" (p. 104).

[18]Pigou, *op. cit. supra* n. 35 at 129–30.

cause of State action. Nonetheless, there are still imperfections. What additional State action is required?

If this is a correct summary of Pigou's position, its inadequacy can be demonstrated by examining the first example he gives of a divergence between private and social products.

> It might happen . . . that costs are thrown upon people not directly concerned, through, say, uncompensated damage done to surrounding woods by sparks from railway engines. All such effects must be included—some of them will be positive, others negative elements—in reckoning up the social net product of the marginal increment of any volume of resources turned into any use or place.[19]

The example used by Pigou refers to a real situation. In Britain, a railway does not normally have to compensate those who suffer damage by fire caused by sparks from an engine. Taken in conjunction with what he says in Chapter 9 of Part II, I take Pigou's policy recommendations to be, first, that there should be State action to correct this "natural" situation and, second, that the railways should be forced to compensate those whose woods are burnt. If this is a correct interpretation of Pigou's position, I would argue that the first recommendation is based on a misapprehension of the facts and that the second is not necessarily desirable.

Let us consider the legal position. Under the heading "Sparks from engines," we find the following in Halsbury's *Laws of England*:

> If railway undertakers use steam engines on their railway without express statutory authority to do so, they are liable, irrespective of any negligence on their part, for fires caused by sparks from engines. Railway undertakers are, however, generally given statutory authority to use steam engines on their railway; accordingly, if an engine is constructed with the precautions which science suggests against fire and is used without negligence, they are not responsible at common law for any damage which may be done by sparks. . . . In the construction of an engine the undertaker is bound to use all the discoveries which science has put within its reach in order to avoid doing harm, provided they are such as it is reasonable to require the company to adopt, having proper regard to the likelihood of the damage and to the cost and convenience of the remedy; but it is not negligence on the part of an undertaker if it refuses to use an apparatus the efficiency of which is open to bona fide doubt.

To this general rule, there is a statutory exception arising from the Railway (Fires) Act, 1905, as amended in 1923. This concerns agricultural land or agricultural crops.

> In such a case the fact that the engine was used under statutory powers does not affect the liability of the company in an action for the damage. . . . These provisions, however, only apply where the claim for damage . . . does not exceed £200 [£100 in the 1905 Act], and where written notice of the occurrence of the fire and the intention to claim has been sent to the company within seven days of the oc-

---

[19]*Id.* at 134.

currence of the damage and particulars of the damage in writing showing the amount of the claim in money not exceeding £200 have been sent to the company within twenty-one days.

Agricultural land does not include moorland or buildings and agricultural crops do not include those led away or stacked.[20] I have not made a close study of the parliamentary history of this statutory exception, but to judge from debates in the House of Commons in 1922 and 1923, this exception was probably designed to help the smallholder.[21]

Let us return to Pigou's example of uncompensated damage to surrounding woods caused by sparks from railway engines. This is presumably intended to show how it is possible "for State action to improve on 'natural' tendencies." If we treat Pigou's example as referring to the position before 1905, or as being an arbitrary example (in that he might just as well have written "surrounding buildings" instead of "surrounding woods"), then it is clear that the reason why compensation was not paid must have been that the railway had statutory authority to run steam engines (which relieved it of liability for fires caused by sparks). That this was the legal position was established in 1860, in a case, oddly enough, which concerned the burning of surrounding woods by a railway,[22] and the law on this point has not been changed (apart from the one exception) by a century of railway legislation, including nationalisation. If we treat Pigou's example of "uncompensated damage done to surrounding woods by sparks from railway engines" literally, and assume that it refers to the period after 1905, then it is clear that the reason why compensation was not paid must have been that the damage was more than £100 (in the first edition of *The Economics of Welfare*) or more than £200 (in later editions) or that the owner of the wood failed to notify the railway in writing within seven days of the fire or did not send particulars of the damage, in writing, within twenty-one days. In the real world, Pigou's example could only exist as a result of a deliberate choice of the legislature. It is not, of course, easy to imagine the construction of a railway in a state of nature. The nearest one can get to this is presumably a railway which uses steam engines "without express statutory authority." However, in this case the railway would be obliged to compensate those whose woods it burnt down. That is to say, compensation would be paid in the absence of Government action. The only circumstances in which compensation would not be paid would be those in which there had been Government action. It is strange that Pigou, who clearly thought it desirable that compensation should be paid, should have chosen this particular example to demonstrate how it is possible "for State action to improve on 'natural' tendencies."

Pigou seems to have had a faulty view of the facts of the situation. But it also seems likely that he was mistaken in his economic analysis. It is not

---

[20]See 31 Halsbury, *Laws of England* 474–75 (3d ed. 1960), Article on Railways and Canals, from which this summary of the legal position, and all quotations, are taken.

[21]See 152 H.C. Deb. 2622–63 (1922); 161 H.C. Deb. 2935–55 (1923).

[22]*Vaughan v. Taff Railway Co.*, 3 H. and N. 743 (Ex. 1858) and 5 H. and N. 679 (Ex. 1860).

necessarily desirable that the railway should be required to compensate those who suffer damage by fires caused by railway engines. I need not show here that, if the railway could make a bargain with everyone having property adjoining the railway line and there were no costs involved in making such bargains, it would not matter whether the railway was liable for damage caused by fires or not. This question has been treated at length in earlier sections. The problem is whether it would be desirable to make the railway liable in conditions in which it is too expensive for such bargains to be made. Pigou clearly thought it was desirable to force the railway to pay compensation and it is easy to see the kind of argument that would have led him to this conclusion. Suppose a railway is considering whether to run an additional train or to increase the speed of an existing train or to install spark-preventing devices on its engines. If the railway were not liable for fire damage, then, when making these decisions, it would not take into account as a cost the increase in damage resulting from the additional train or the faster train or the failure to install spark-preventing devices. This is the source of the divergence between private and social net products. It results in the railway performing acts which will lower the value of total production—and which it would not do if it were liable for the damage. This can be shown by means of an arithmetical example.

Consider a railway, which is *not* liable for damage by fires caused by sparks from its engines, which runs two trains per day on a certain line. Suppose that running one train per day would enable the railway to perform services worth $150 per annum and running two trains a day would enable the railway to perform services worth $250 per annum. Suppose further that the cost of running one train is $50 per annum and two trains $100 per annum. Assuming perfect competition, the cost equals the fall in the value of production elsewhere due to the employment of additional factors of production by the railway. Clearly the railway would find it profitable to run two trains per day. But suppose that running one train per day would destroy by fire crops worth (on an average over the year) $60 and two trains a day would result in the destruction of crops worth $120. In these circumstances running one train per day would raise the value of total production but the running of a second train would reduce the value of total production. The second train would enable additional railway services worth $100 per annum to be performed. But the fall in the value of production elsewhere would be $110 per annum; $50 as a result of the employment of additional factors of production and $60 as a result of the destruction of crops. Since it would be better if the second train were not run and since it would not run if the railway were liable for damage caused to crops, the conclusion that the railway should be made liable for the damage seems irresistible. Undoubtedly it is this kind of reasoning which underlies the Pigovian position.

The conclusion that it would be better if the second train did not run is correct. The conclusion that it is desirable that the railway should be made liable for the damage it causes is wrong. Let us change our assumption concerning the rule of liability. Suppose that the railway is liable for damage from fires caused by sparks from the engine. A farmer on lands adjoining the railway is then in the position that, if his crop is destroyed by fires caused by the railway, he will receive the market price from the railway; but if his crop is not damaged, he will receive the market price by sale. It therefore becomes a matter of indifference to him whether his crop is damaged by fire or not. The position is very different when the railway is *not* liable. Any crop destruction through railway-caused fires would then reduce the receipts of the farmer. He would therefore take out of cultivation any land for which the damage is likely to be greater than the net return of the land (for reasons explained at length in Section III). A change from a regime in which the railway is *not* liable for damage to one in which it *is* liable is likely therefore to lead to an increase in the amount of cultivation on lands adjoining the railway. It will also, of course, lead to an increase in the amount of crop destruction due to railway-caused fires.

Let us return to our arithmetical example. Assume that, with the changed rule of liability, there is a doubling in the amount of crop destruction due to railway-caused fires. With one train per day, crops worth $120 would be destroyed each year and two trains per day would lead to the destruction of crops worth $240. We saw previously that it would not be profitable to run the second train if the railway had to pay $60 per annum as compensation for damage. With damage at $120 per annum the loss from running the second train would be $60 greater. But now let us consider the first train. The value of the transport services furnished by the first train is $150. The cost of running the train is $50. The amount that the railway would have to pay out as compensation for damage is $120. It follows that it would not be profitable to run any trains. With the figures in our example we reach the following result: if the railway is not liable for fire-damage, two trains per day would be run; if the railway is liable for fire-damage, it would cease operations altogether. Does this mean that it is better that there should be no railway? This question can be resolved by considering what would happen to the value of total production if it were decided to exempt the railway from liability for fire-damage, thus bringing it into operation (with two trains per day).

The operation of the railway would enable transport services worth $250 to be performed. It would also mean the employment of factors of production which would reduce the value of production elsewhere by $100. Furthermore it would mean the destruction of crops worth $120. The coming of the railway will also have led to the abandonment of cultivation of some land. Since we know that, had this land been cultivated, the value of the crops destroyed by fire would have been $120, and since it is unlikely that the total crop on this land would have been destroyed, it seems reasonable to suppose that the value of the crop yield on this land would have been higher than this. Assume it would have been $160. But the abandonment of cultivation would have released factors of production for employment elsewhere. All we know is that the amount by which the value of production elsewhere will increase will be less than $160. Suppose that it is $150. Then the gain from operating the railway would be $250 (the value of the transport services) minus $100 (the cost of the factors of production) minus $120 (the value of crops destroyed by fire) minus $160 (the fall in the value of crop production due to the abandonment of cultivation) plus $150 (the value of production elsewhere of the released factors of production). Overall, operating the railway will increase the value of total production by $20. With these figures it is clear that it is better that the railway should not be liable for the damage it causes, thus enabling it to operate profitably. Of course, by altering the figures, it could be shown that there are other cases in which it would be desirable that the railway should be liable for the damage it causes. It is enough for my purpose to show that, from an economic point of view, a situation in which there is "uncompensated damage done to surrounding woods by sparks from railway engines" is not necessarily undesirable. Whether it is desirable or not depends on the particular circumstances.

How is it that the Pigovian analysis seems to give the wrong answer? The reason is that Pigou does not seem to have noticed that his analysis is dealing with an entirely different question. The analysis as such is correct. But it is quite illegitimate for Pigou to draw the particular conclusion he does. The question at issue is not whether it is desirable to run an additional train or a faster train or to install smoke-preventing devices; the question at issue is whether it is desirable to have a system in which the railway has to compensate those who suffer damage from the fires which it causes or one in which the railway does not have to compensate them. When an economist is comparing alternative social arrangements, the proper procedure is to compare the total social product yielded by these different arrangements. The comparison of private and social products is neither here nor there. A simple example will demonstrate this. Imagine a town in which there are traffic lights. A motorist approaches an intersection and stops because the light is red. There are no cars approaching the intersection on the other street. If the motorist ignored the red signal, no accident would occur and the total product would increase because the motorist would arrive earlier at his destination. Why does he not do this? The reason is that if he ignored the light he would be fined. The private product from crossing the street is less than the social product. Should we conclude from this that the total product would be greater if there were no fines for failing to obey traffic signals? The Pigovian analysis shows us that it is possible to conceive of better worlds than the one in which we live. But the problem is to devise practical arrangements which will correct defects in one part of the system without causing more serious harm in other parts.

I have examined in considerable detail one example of a divergence between private and social products and I do not propose to make any further examination of Pigou's analytical system. But the main discussion of the problem considered in this article is to be found in that part of Chapter 9 in Part II which deals with Pigou's second class of divergence and it is of interest to see how Pigou develops his argument. Pigou's own description of this second class of divergence was quoted at the beginning of this section. Pigou distinguishes between the case in which a person renders services for which he receives no payment and the case in which a person renders disservices and compensation is not given to the injured parties. Our main attention has, of course, centered on this second case. It is therefore rather astonishing to find, as was pointed out to me by Professor Francesco Forte, that the problem of the smoking chimney—the "stock instance"[23] or "classroom example"[24] of the second case—is used by Pigou as an example of the first case (services rendered without payment) and is never mentioned, at any rate explicitly, in connection with the second case.[25] Pigou points out that factory owners who devote resources to preventing their chimneys from smoking render services for which they receive no payment. The implication, in the light of Pigou's discussion later in the chapter, is that a factory owner with a smokey chimney should be given a bounty to induce him to install smoke-preventing devices. Most modern economists would suggest that the owner of the factor with the smokey chimney should be taxed. It seems a pity that economists (apart from Professor Forte) do not seem to have noticed this feature of Pigou's treatment since a realisation that the problem could be tackled in either of these two ways would probably have led to an explicit recognition of its reciprocal nature.

In discussing the second case (disservices without compensation to those damaged), Pigou says that they are rendered "when the owner of a site in a residential quarter of a city builds a factory there and so destroys a great part of the amenities of neighbouring sites; or, in a less degree, when he uses his site in such a way as to spoil the lighting of the house opposite; or when he invests resources in erecting buildings in a crowded centre, which by contracting the air-space and the playing room of the neighbourhood, tend to injure the health and efficiency of the families living there."[26] Pigou is, of course, quite right to describe such actions as "uncharged disservices." But he is wrong when he describes these actions as "anti-social."[27] They may or may not be. It is necessary to weigh the harm against the good that will result. Nothing could be more "anti-social" than to oppose any action which causes any harm to anyone.

Indeed, Pigou's treatment of the problems considered in this article is extremely elusive and the discussion of his views raises almost insuperable difficulties of interpretation. Consequently it is impossible to be sure that one has understood what Pigou really meant. Nevertheless, it is difficult to resist the conclusion, extraordinary though this may be in an economist of

---

[23]Sir Dennis Robertson, I *Lectures on Economic Principles* 162 (1957).

[24]E. J. Mishan, "The Meaning of Efficiency in Economics," 189, *The Bankers' Magazine* 482 (June 1960).

[25]Pigou, *op. cit. supra* n. 35 at 184.

[26]*Id.* at 185–86.

[27]*Id.* at 186 n. 1. For similar unqualified statements see Pigou's lecture "Some Aspects of the Housing Problem" in B. S. Rowntree and A. C. Pigou, "Lectures on Housing," in 18 *Manchester Univ. Lectures* (1914).

Pigou's stature, that the main source of this obscurity is that Pigou had not thought his position through.

IX. The Pigovian Tradition

It is strange that a doctrine as faulty as that developed by Pigou should have been so influential, although part of its success has probably been due to the lack of clarity in the exposition. Not being clear, it was never clearly wrong. Curiously enough, this obscurity in the source has not prevented the emergence of a fairly well-defined oral tradition. What economists think they learn from Pigou, and what they tell their students, which I term the Pigovian tradition, is reasonably clear. I propose to show the inadequacy of this Pigovian tradition by demonstrating that both the analysis and the policy conclusions which it supports are incorrect.

I do not propose to justify my view as to the prevailing opinion by co-pious references to the literature. I do this partly because the treatment in the literature is usually so fragmentary, often involving little more than a reference to Pigou plus some explanatory comment, that detailed exami-nation would be inappropriate. But the main reason for this lack of refer-ence is that the doctrine, although based on Pigou, must have been largely the product of an oral tradition. Certainly economists with whom I have discussed these problems have shown a unanimity of opinion which is quite remarkable considering the meagre treatment accorded this subject in the literature. No doubt there are some economists who do not share the usual view but they must represent a small minority of the profession.

The approach to the problems under discussion is through an exami-nation of the value of physical production. The private product is the value of the additional product resulting from a particular activity of a business. The social product equals the private product minus the fall in the value of production elsewhere for which no compensation is paid by the busi-ness. Thus, if 10 units of a factor (and no other factors) are used by a busi-ness to make a certain product with a value of $105; and the owner of this factor is not compensated for their use, which he is unable to prevent; and these 10 units of the factor would yield products in their best alternative use worth $100; then, the social product is $105 minus $100 or $5. If the business now pays for one unit of the factor and its price equals the value of its marginal product, then the social product rises to $15. If two units are paid for, the social product rises to $25 and so on until it reaches $105 when all units of the factor are paid for. It is not difficult to see why econ-omists have so readily accepted this rather odd procedure. The analysis fo-cusses on the individual business decision and since the use of certain re-sources is not allowed for in costs, receipts are reduced by the same amount. But, of course, this means that the value of the social product has no so-cial significance whatsoever. It seems to me preferable to use the oppor-tunity cost concept and to approach these problems by comparing the value

of the product yielded by factors in alternative uses or by alternative
arrangements. The main advantage of a pricing system is that it leads to
the employment of factors in places where the value of the product yielded
is greatest and does so at less cost than alternative systems (I leave aside
that a pricing system also eases the problem of the redistribution of income). But if through some God-given natural harmony factors flowed to
the places where the value of the product yielded was greatest without any
use of the pricing system and consequently there was no compensation, I
would find it a source of surprise rather than a cause for dismay.

The definition of the social product is queer but this does not mean
that the conclusions for policy drawn from the analysis are necessarily
wrong. However, there are bound to be dangers in an approach which diverts attention from the basic issues and there can be little doubt that it
has been responsible for some of the errors in current doctrine. The belief
that it is desirable that the business which causes harmful effects should
be forced to compensate those who suffer damage (which was exhaustively
discussed in section VIII in connection with Pigou's railway sparks example) is undoubtedly the result of not comparing the total product obtain-
able with alternative social arrangements.

The same fault is to be found in proposals for solving the problem of
harmful effects by the use of taxes or bounties. Pigou lays considerable
stress on this solution although he is, as usual, lacking in detail and qualified in his support.[28] Modern economists tend to think exclusively in terms
of taxes and in a very precise way. The tax should be equal to the damage
done and should therefore vary with the amount of the harmful effect. As
it is not proposed that the proceeds of the tax should be paid to those suffering the damage, this solution is not the same as that which would force
a business to pay compensation to those damaged by its actions, although
economists generally do not seem to have noticed this and tend to treat the
two solutions as being identical.

Assume that a factory which emits smoke is set up in a district previously free from smoke pollution, causing damage valued at $100 per an-
num. Assume that the taxation solution is adopted and that the factory-
owner is taxed $100 per annum as long as the factory emits the smoke.
Assume further that a smoke-preventing device costing $90 per annum to
run is available. In these circumstances, the smoke-preventing device would
be installed. Damage of $100 would have been avoided at an expenditure
of $90 and the factory-owner would be better off by $10 per annum. Yet
the position achieved may not be optimal. Suppose that those who suffer
the damage could avoid it by moving to other locations or by taking various precautions which would cost them, or be equivalent to a loss in income of, $40 per annum. Then there would be a gain in the value of pro-
duction of $50 if the factory continued to emit its smoke and those now in
the district moved elsewhere or made other adjustments to avoid the damage. If the factory owner is to be made to pay a tax equal to the damage

---

[28]*Id.* 192–4, 381 and *Public Finance* 94–100 (3d ed. 1947).

caused, it would clearly be desirable to institute a double tax system and to make residents of the district pay an amount equal to the additional cost incurred by the factory owner (or the consumers of his products) in order to avoid the damage. In these conditions, people would not stay in the district or would take other measures to prevent the damage from occurring, when the costs of doing so were less than the costs that would be incurred by the producer to reduce the damage (the producer's object, of course, being not so much to reduce the damage as to reduce the tax payments). A tax system which was confined to a tax on the producer for damage caused would tend to lead to unduly high costs being incurred for the prevention of damage. Of course this could be avoided if it were possible to base the tax, not on the damage caused, but on the fall in the value of production (in its widest sense) resulting from the emission of smoke. But to do so would require a detailed knowledge of individual preferences and I am unable to imagine how the data needed for such a taxation system could be assembled. Indeed, the proposal to solve the smoke pollution and similar problems by the use of taxes bristles with difficulties: the problem of calculation, the difference between average and marginal damage, the interrelations between the damage suffered on different properties, etc. But it is unnecessary to examine these problems here. It is enough for my purpose to show that, even if the tax is exactly adjusted to equal the damage that would be done to neighbouring properties as a result of the emission of each additional puff of smoke, the tax would not necessarily bring about optimal conditions. An increase in the number of people living or of businesses operating in the vicinity of the smoke-emitting factory will increase the amount of harm produced by a given emission of smoke. The tax that would be imposed would therefore increase with an increase in the number of those in the vicinity. This will tend to lead to a decrease in the value of production of the factors employed by the factory, either because a reduction in production due to the tax will result in factors being used elsewhere in ways which are less valuable, or because factors will be diverted to produce means for reducing the amount of smoke emitted. But people deciding to establish themselves in the vicinity of the factory will not take into account this fall in the value of production which results from their presence. This failure to take into account costs imposed on others is comparable to the action of a factory owner in not taking into account the harm resulting from his emission of smoke. Without the tax, there may be too much smoke and too few people in the vicinity of the factory; but with the tax there may be too little smoke and too many people in the vicinity of the factory. There is no reason to suppose that one of these results is necessarily preferable.

I need not devote much space to discussing the similar error involved in the suggestion that smoke-producing factories should, by means of zoning regulations, be removed from the districts in which the smoke causes harmful effects. When the change in the location of the factory results in a reduction in production, this obviously needs to be taken into account and weighed against the harm which would result from the factory remaining in that location. The aim of such regulation should not be to eliminate smoke pollution but rather to secure the optimum amount of smoke pollution, this being the amount which will maximise the values of production.

X. A Change of Approach

It is my belief that the failure of economists to reach correct conclusions about the treatment of harmful effects cannot be ascribed simply to a few slips in analysis. It stems from basic defects in the current approach to problems of welfare economics. What is needed is a change of approach.

Analysis in terms of divergencies between private and social products concentrates attention on particular deficiencies in the system and tends to nourish the belief that any measure which will remove the deficiency is necessarily desirable. It diverts attention from those other changes in the system which are inevitably associated with the corrective measure, changes which may well produce more harm than the original deficiency. In the preceding sections of this article, we have seen many examples of this. But it is not necessary to approach the problem in this way. Economists who study problems of the firm habitually use an opportunity cost approach and compare the receipts obtained from a given combination of factors with alternative business arrangements. It would seem desirable to use a similar approach when dealing with questions of economic policy and to compare the total product yielded by alternative social arrangements. In this article, the analysis has been confined, as is usual in this part of economics, to comparisons of the value of production, as measured by the market. But it is, of course, desirable that the choice between different social arrangements for the solution of economic problems should be carried out in broader terms than this and that the total effect of these arrangements in all spheres of life should be taken into account. As Frank H. Knight has so often emphasized, problems of welfare economics must ultimately dissolve into a study of aesthetics and morals.

A second feature of the usual treatment of the problems discussed in this article is that the analysis proceeds in terms of a comparison between a state of laissez faire and some kind of ideal world. This approach inevitably leads to a looseness of thought since the nature of the alternatives being compared is never clear. In a state of laissez faire, is there a monetary, a legal or a political system and if so, what are they? In an ideal world, would there be a monetary, a legal or a political system and if so, what would they be? The answers to all these questions are shrouded in mystery and every man is free to draw whatever conclusions he likes. Actually very little analysis is required to show that an ideal world is better than a state of laissez faire, unless the definitions of a state of laissez faire and an ideal world happen to be the same. But the whole discussion is largely irrelevant for questions of economic policy since whatever we may have in mind as our ideal world, it is clear that we have not yet discovered how to get to it from where we are. A better approach would seem to be to start our analysis with a situation approximating that which actually exists, to examine the effects of a proposed policy change and to attempt to decide whether the new situation would be, in total, better or worse than the original one. In this way, conclusions for policy would have some relevance to the actual situation.

A final reason for the failure to develop a theory adequate to handle the problem of harmful effects stems from a faulty concept of a factor of production. This is usually thought of as a physical entity which the businessman acquires and uses (an acre of land, a ton of fertiliser) instead of as a right to perform certain (physical) actions. We may speak of a person owning land and using it as a factor of production but what the land-owner in fact possesses is the right to carry out a circumscribed list of actions. The rights of a land-owner are not unlimited. It is not even always possible for him to remove the land to another place, for instance, by quarrying it. And although it may be possible for him to exclude some people from using "his" land, this may not be true of others. For example, some people may have the right to cross the land. Furthermore, it may or may not be possible to erect certain types of buildings or to grow certain crops or to use particular drainage systems on the land. This does not come about simply because of Government regulation. It would be equally true under the common law. In fact it would be true under any system of law. A system in which the rights of individuals were unlimited would be one in which there were no rights to acquire.

If factors of production are thought of as rights, it becomes easier to understand that the right to do something which has a harmful effect (such as the creation of smoke, noise, smells, etc.) is also a factor of production. Just as we may use a piece of land in such a way as to prevent someone else from crossing it, or parking his car, or building his house upon it, so we may use it in such a way as to deny him a view or quiet or unpolluted air. The cost of exercising a right (of using a factor of production) is always the loss which is suffered elsewhere in consequence of the exercise of that right—the inability to cross land, to park a car, to build a house, to enjoy a view, to have peace and quiet or to breathe clean air.

It would clearly be desirable if the only actions performed were those in which what was gained was worth more than what was lost. But in choosing between social arrangements within the context of which individual decisions are made, we have to bear in mind that a change in the existing system which will lead to an improvement in some decisions may well lead to a worsening of others. Furthermore we have to take into account the costs involved in operating the various social arrangements (whether it be the working of a market or of a government department), as well as the costs involved in moving to a new system. In devising and choosing between social arrangements we should have regard for the total effect. This, above all, is the change in approach which I am advocating.

4   *Environmental Economics: A Survey**

Maureen L. Cropper

Wallace E. Oates

Maureen L. Cropper is Professor of Economics at the University of Maryland, and Principal Economist, Research Department of the World Bank; and Wallace E. Oates is Professor of Economics at the University of Maryland, and Visiting Scholar at Resources for the Future.

I. Introduction

When the environmental revolution arrived in the late 1960s, the economics profession was ready and waiting. Economists had what they saw as a coherent and compelling view of the nature of pollution with a straightforward set of policy implications. The problem of externalities and the associated market failure had long been a part of microeconomic theory and was embedded in a number of standard texts. Economists saw pollution as the consequence of an absence of prices for certain scarce environmental resources (such as clean air and water), and they prescribed the introduction of surrogate prices in the form of unit taxes or "effluent fees" to provide the needed signals to economize on the use of these resources. While much of the analysis was of a fairly general character, there was at least some careful research underway exploring the application of economic solutions to certain pressing environmental problems (e.g., Allen Kneese and Blair Bower 1968).

The economist's view had—to the dismay of the profession—little impact on the initial surge of legislation for the control of pollution. In fact, the cornerstones of federal environmental policy in the United States, the Amendments to the Clean Air Act in 1970 and to the Clean Water Act in 1972, *explicitly* prohibited the weighing of benefits against costs in the setting of environmental standards. The former directed the Environmental Protection Agency to set maximum limitations on pollutant concentrations

"Environmental Economics: A Survey," by Maureen L. Cropper and Wallace E. Oates, from *Journal of Economic Literature*, 30:675–740 (June 1992).

*We are grateful for many valuable comments on earlier drafts of this paper to a host of economists: Nancy Bockstael, Gardner Brown, Richard Carson, John Cumberlannd, Diane DeWitt, Anthony Fisher, A. Myrick Freeman, Tom Grigalunas, Winston Harrington, Robert Hahn, Charles Howe, Dale Jorgenson, Charles Kolstad, Ray Kopp, Allen Kneese, Alan Krupnick, Randolph Lyon, Ted McConnell, Albert McGartland, Robert Mitchell, Arun Malik, Roger Noll, Raymond Palmquist, John Pezzey, Paul Portney, V. Kerry Smith, Tom Tietenberg, and James Tobey. Finally, we want to thank Jonathan Dunn, Joy Hall, Dan Mussatti, and Rene Worley for their assistance in the preparation of the manuscript.

in the atmosphere "to protect the public health"; the latter set as an objective the "elimination of the discharge of *all* [our emphasis] pollutants into the navigable waters by 1985."[1]

The evolution of environmental policy, both in the U.S. and elsewhere, has inevitably brought economic issues to the fore; environmental regulation has necessarily involved costs—and the question of how far and how fast to push for pollution control in light of these costs has entered into the public debate. Under Executive Order 12291 issued in 1981, many proposed environmental measures have been subjected to a benefit-cost test. In addition, some more recent pieces of environmental legislation, notably the Toxic Substances Control Act (TSCA) and the Federal Insecticide, Fungicide, and Rodenticide Act (FIFRA), call for weighing benefits against costs in the setting of standards. At the same time, economic incentives for the containment of waste discharges have crept into selected regulatory measures. In the United States, for example, the 1977 Amendments to the Clean Air Act introduced a provision for "emission offsets" that has evolved into the Emissions Trading Program under which sources are allowed to trade "rights" to emit air pollutants. And outside the United States, there have been some interesting uses of effluent fees for pollution control.

This is a most exciting time—and perhaps a critical juncture—in the evolution of economic incentives for environmental protection. The Bush Administration proposed, and the Congress has introduced, a measure for the trading of sulfur emissions for the control of acid rain under the new 1990 Amendments to the Clean Air Act. More broadly, an innovative report from within the U.S. Congress sponsored by Senators Timothy Wirth and John Heinz, *Project 88: Harnessing Market Forces to Protect Our Environment* (Robert Stavins 1988) explores a lengthy list of potential applications of economic incentives for environmental management. Likewise, there is widespread, ongoing discussion in Europe of the role of economic measures for pollution control. Most recently in January of 1991, the Council of the Organization for Economic Cooperation and Development (OECD) has gone on record urging member countries to "make a greater and more consistent use of economic instruments" for environmental management. Of particular note is the emerging international concern with global environmental issues, especially with planetary warming; the enormous challenge and awesome costs of policies to address this issue have focused interest on proposals for "Green Taxes" and systems of tradable permits to contain global emissions of greenhouse gases. In short, this seems to be a time when there is a real opportunity for environmental economists to make some valuable contributions in the policy arena—if, as we shall argue, they are willing to move from "purist" solutions to a realistic consideration of the design and implementation of policy measures.

---

[1]Although standards were to be set solely on the basis of health criteria, the 1970 Amendments to the Clean Air Act did not include economic feasibility among its guidelines for setting source-specific standards. Roger Noll has suggested that the later 1977 Amendments were, in fact, more "anti-economic" than any that went before. See Matthew McCubbins, Roger Noll, and Barry Weingast (1989) for a careful analysis of this legislation.

Our survey of environmental economics is structured with an eye toward its policy potential. The theoretical foundations for the field are found in the theory of externalities. And so we begin in Section II with a review of the theory of environmental regulation in which we explore recent theoretical results regarding the choice among the key policy instruments for the control of externalities: effluent fees, subsidies, and marketable emission permits. Section III takes us from the theory of externalities to policy applications with a focus on the structuring and implementation of realistic measures for environmental management. This section reviews the work of environmental economists in trying to move from formal theorems to measures that address the variety of issues confronting an environmental regulator. We describe and evaluate briefly, as part of this treatment, the U.S. and European experiences with economic incentives for pollution control. In addition, we explore a series of regulatory issues—centralization versus decentralization of regulatory authority, international effects of domestic environmental policies, and enforcement— matters on which environmental economists have had something to say.

In Section IV, we turn to the measurement of the benefits and costs of environmental programs. This has been a particularly troublesome area for at least two reasons. First, many of the benefits and costs of these programs involve elements for which we do not have ready market measures: health benefits and aesthetic improvements. Second, policy makers, perhaps understandably, have proved reluctant to employ monetary measures of such things as "the value of human life" in the calculus of environmental policy. Environmental economists have, however, made some important strides in the valuation of "nonmarket" environmental services and have shown themselves able to introduce discussion of these measures in more effective ways in the policy arena.

In a survey in this *Journal* some fifteen years ago, Anthony Fisher and Frederick Peterson (1976) justifiably contended that techniques for measuring the benefits of pollution control are "to be taken with a grain of salt" (p. 24). There has been considerable progress on two distinct fronts since this earlier survey. First, environmental (and other) economists have shown considerable ingenuity in the development of techniques—known as indirect market methods—that exploit the relationships between environmental quality and various marketed goods. These methods allow us to infer the value of improved environmental amenities from the prices of the market goods to which they are, in various ways, related. Second, environmental economists have turned to an approach regarded historically with suspicion in our profession: the direct questioning of individuals about their valuation of environmental goods. Developing with considerable sophistication the so-called "contingent valuation" approach, they have been able to elicit apparently reliable answers to questions involving the valuation of an improved environment. In Section IV, we explore these various methods for the valuation of the benefits and costs of environmental programs and present some empirical findings.

In Section V, we try to pull together our treatment of measuring benefits and costs with a review of cases where benefit-cost analyses have actually been used in the setting of environmental standards. This provides an opportunity for an overall assessment of this experience and also for some thoughts on where such analyses are most needed. We conclude our survey in Section VI with some reflections on the state of environmental economics and its potential contribution to the formulation of public policy.

Before turning to substantive matters, we need to explain briefly how we have defined the boundaries for this survey. For this purpose, we have tried to distinguish between "environmental economics" and "natural resource economics." The distinguishing characteristic of the latter field is its concern with the intertemporal allocation of renewable and nonrenewable resources. With its origins in the seminal paper by Harold Hotelling (1931), the theory of natural resource economics typically applies dynamic control methods of analysis to problems of intertemporal resource usage. This has led to a vast literature on such topics as the management of fisheries, forests, minerals, energy resources, the extinction of species, and the irreversibility of development over time. This body of work is excluded from our survey. The precise dividing line between environmental economics and natural resource economics is admittedly a little fuzzy, but in order to keep our task a manageable one, we have restricted our survey to what we see as the two major issues in environmental economics: the regulation of polluting activities and the valuation of environmental amenities.

II. The Normative Theory of Environmental Regulation

The source of the basic economic principles of environmental policy is to be found in the theory of externalities. The literature on this subject is enormous; it encompasses hundreds of books and papers. An attempt to provide a comprehensive and detailed description of the literature on externalities theory reaches beyond the scope of this survey. Instead, we shall attempt in this section to sketch an outline of what we see as the central results from this literature, with an emphasis on their implications for the design of environmental policy. We shall not address a number of formal matters (e.g., problems of existence) that, although important in their own right, have little to say about the structure of policy measures for protection of the environment.

A. The Basic Theory of Environmental Policy[2]

The standard approach in the environmental economics literature characterizes pollution as a public "bad" that results from "waste discharges" as-

---

[2]For comprehensive and rigorous treatments of the general ideas presented in this section, see, for example, William Baumol (1972), Baumol and Wallace Oates (1988), Paul Burrows (1979), and Richard Cornes and Todd Sandler (1986). We have not included in this survey a literature on conservation and development that has considered issues of irreversibility in the time of development for which the seminal papers are John Krutilla (1967), and Kenneth Arrow and Anthony Fisher (1974). This literature is treated in the Anthony Fisher and Peterson survey (1976) and, more recently, in Anthony Fisher (1981, ch. 5).

sociated with the production of private goods. The basic relationships can be expressed in abbreviated form as:

$$U = U(X,Q) \tag{1}$$

$$X = X(L,E,Q) \tag{2}$$

$$Q = Q(E) \tag{3}$$

where the assumed signs of the partial derivatives are $U_X > 0$, $U_Q < 0$, $X_L > 0$, $X_E > 0$, $X_Q < 0$, and $Q_E > 0$. The utility of a representative consumer in equation (1) depends upon a vector of goods consumed (X) and upon the level of pollution (Q). Pollution results from waste emissions (E) in the production of X, as indicated in (2). Note that the production function in (2) is taken to include as inputs a vector of conventional inputs (L), like labor and capital, the quantity of waste discharges (E), and the level of pollution (Q). In this formulation, waste emissions are treated simply as another factor of production; this seems reasonable since attempts, for example, to cut back on waste discharges will involve the diversion of other inputs to abatement activities—thereby reducing the availability of these other inputs for the production of goods. Reductions in E, in short, result in reduced output. Moreover, given the reasonable assumption of rising marginal abatement costs, it makes sense to assume the usual curvature properties so that we can legitimately draw isoquants in L and E space and treat them in the usual way.

The production function also includes as an argument the level of pollution (Q), since pollution may have detrimental effects on production (such as soiling the output of the proverbial laundry or reducing agricultural output) as well as producing disutility to consumers. The level of pollution is itself some function of the vector of emissions (E) of all the producing units. In the very simplest case, Q might be taken to equal the sum of the emissions over all producers.[3]

One extension of the model involves the explicit introduction of "defensive" activities on the part of "victims." We might, for example, amend the utility function:

$$U = U[X,F(L,Q)] \tag{4}$$

to indicate the individuals can employ a vector of inputs (L) to lessen, in some sense, their exposure to pollution. The level of pollution to which the individual is actually exposed (F) would then depend upon the extent of pollution (Q) and upon the employment of inputs in defensive activities (L). We could obviously introduce such defensive activities for producers as well. We thus have a set of equations which, with appropriate subscripts, would describe the behavior of the many individual households and firms that comprise the system.

---

[3]This highly simplified model, although useful for our analytical purposes, admittedly fails to encompass the complexity of the natural environment. There is an important literature in environmental economics that develops the "materials-balance" approach to environmental analysis (see Kneese, Robert Ayres, and Ralph d'Arge 1970; Karl-Göran Mäler 1974, 1985). This approach introduces explicitly the flows of environmental resources and the physical laws to which they are subject. Some of these matters will figure in the discussion that follows.

It is a straightforward exercise to maximize the utility of our representative individual (or group of individuals) subject to (2) and (3) as constraints along with a further constraint on resource availability. This exercise produces a set of first-order conditions for a Pareto-efficient outcome; of interest here is the condition taking the form:

$$\frac{\partial X}{\partial E} = -\left[\sum\left(\frac{\partial U}{\partial Q}\frac{\partial Q}{\partial E}\right)\bigg/\frac{\partial U}{\partial X} + \sum\left(\frac{\partial X}{\partial Q}\frac{\partial Q}{\partial E}\right)\right] \tag{5}$$

Equation (5) indicates that polluting firms should extend their waste discharges to the point at which the marginal product of these emissions equals the sum of the marginal damages that they impose on consumers [the first summation in (5)] and on producers [the second summation in (5)]. Or, put slightly differently, (5) says that pollution-control measures should be pursued by each polluting agent to the point at which the marginal benefits from reduced pollution (summed over all individuals and all firms) equal marginal abatement cost.

Another of the resulting first-order conditions relates to the efficient level of defensive activities:

$$\frac{\partial U}{\partial F}\frac{\partial F}{\partial L} = \frac{\partial U}{\partial X}\frac{\partial X}{\partial L} \tag{6}$$

which says simply that the marginal value of each input should be equated in its use in production and defensive activities.

The next step is to derive the first-order conditions characterizing a competitive market equilibrium, where we find that competitive firms with free access to environmental resources will continue to engage in polluting activities until the marginal return is zero, that is, until $\partial X/\partial E = 0$. We thus obtain the familiar result that because of their disregard for the external costs that they impose on others, polluting agents will engage in socially excessive levels of polluting activities.

The policy implication of this result is clear. Polluting agents need to be confronted with a "price" equal to the marginal external cost of their polluting activities to induce them to internalize at the margin the full social costs of their pursuits. Such a price incentive can take the form of the familiar "Pigouvian tax," a levy on the polluting agent equal to marginal social damage. In the preceding formulation, the tax would be set equal to the expression in equation (5). Note further that the unit tax (or "effluent fee") must be attached *directly* to the polluting activity, not to some related output or input. Assuming some substitution among inputs in production, the Pigouvian tax would take the form of a levy per unit of waste emissions into the environment—not a tax on units of the firm's output or an input (e.g., fossil fuel associated with pollution).[4]

---

[4]Where it is not feasible to monitor emissions directly, the alternative may be to tax an input or output that is closely related to emissions of the pollutant. This gives rise to a standard sort of second-best problem in taxation.

The derivation of the first-order conditions characterizing utility-max-imizing behavior by individuals yields a second result of interest. Inasmuch as defensive activities in the model provide only private benefits, we find that individual maximizing behavior will satisfy the first-order conditions for Pareto efficiency for such activities. Since they are confronted with a given price for each input, individuals will allocate their spending so that a marginal dollar yields the same increment to utility whether it is spent on consumption goods or defensive activities. There is no need for any extra inducement to achieve efficient levels of defensive activities.

Although this is quite straightforward, there are a couple of matters requiring further comment. First, the Pigouvian solution to the problem of externalities has been the subject of repeated attack along Coasian lines. The Ronald Coase (1960) argument is that in the absence of trans-actions costs and strategic behavior, the distortions associated with ex-ternalities will be resolved through voluntary bargains struck among the interested parties. No further inducements (such as a Pigouvian tax) are needed in this setting to achieve an efficient outcome. In fact, as Ralph Turvey (1963) showed, the introduction of a Pigouvian tax in a Coasian setting will itself be the source of distortions. Our sense, however, is that the Coasian criticism is of limited relevance to most of the major pollu-tion problems. Since most cases of air and water pollution, for example, involve a large number of polluting agents and/or victims, the likelihood of a negotiated resolution of the problem is small—transactions costs are simply too large to permit a Coasian resolution of most major environ-mental problems. It thus seems to us that a Nash or "independent adjustment" equilibrium is, for most environmental issues, the appropriate analytical framework. In this setting, the Pigouvian cure for the externality malady is a valid one.[5]

Second, there has been no mention of any compensation to the victims of externalities. This is an important point—and a source of some confusion in the literature—for Coase and others have suggested that in certain cir-cumstances compensation of victims for damages by polluting agents is nec-essary for an efficient outcome. As the mathematics makes clear, this is not the case for our model above. In fact, the result is even stronger: compen-sation of victims is not permissible (except through lump-sum transfers). Where victims have the opportunity to engage in defensive (or "averting") activities to mitigate the effects of the pollution from which they suffer, com-pensation cannot be allowed. For if victims are compensated for the dam-ages they suffer, they will no longer have the incentive to undertake efficient levels of defensive measures (e.g., to locate away from polluting factories or employ various sorts of cleansing devices). As is clear in the preceding for-mulation, the benefits from defensive activities are private in nature (they accrue solely to the victim that undertakes them) and, as a result, economic

---

[5]For comparative analyses of the bargaining and tax approaches to the control of externalities, see Daniel Bromley (1986), and Jonathan Hamilton, Eytan Sheshinski, and Steven Slutsky (1989).

efficiency requires no incentives other than the benefits they confer on the victim.[6]

The basic theoretical result then (subject to some qualifications to be discussed later) is that the efficient resolution of environmental externalities calls for polluting agents to face a cost at the margin for their polluting activities equal to the value of the damages they produce and for victims to select their own levels of defensive activities with no compensation from polluters. We consider next some policy alternatives for achieving this result.

B. The Choice Among Policy Instruments[7]

The analysis in the preceding section has run in terms of a unit tax on polluting activities. There are, however, other approaches to establishing the proper economic incentives for abatement activities. Two alternative policy instruments have received extensive attention in the literature: unit subsidies and marketable emission permits.

It was recognized early on that a subsidy per unit of emissions reduction could establish the same incentive for abatement activity as a tax of the same magnitude per unit of waste discharges: a subsidy of 10 cents per pound of sulfur emissions reductions creates the same opportunity cost for sulfur emissions as a tax of 10 cents per unit of sulfur discharges. From this perspective, the two policy instruments are equivalent: the regulator can use either the stick or the carrot to create the desired incentive for abatement efforts.

It soon became apparent that there are some important asymmetries between these two policy instruments (e.g., Morton Kamien, Nancy L. Schwartz, and F. Trenery Dolbear 1966; D. Bramhall and Edwin Mills 1966; Kneese and Bower 1968). In particular, they have quite different implications for the profitability of production in a pollution industry: subsidies increase profits, while taxes decrease them. The policy instruments thus have quite different implications for the long-run, entry-exit decisions of firms. The subsidy approach will shift the industry supply curve to the right and result in a larger number of firms and higher industry output, while the Pigouvian tax will shift the supply curve to the left with a consequent contraction in the size of the industry. It is even conceivable that the subsidy approach could result in an increase in the total amount of pollution (Baumol and Oates 1988, ch. 14; Stuart Mestelman 1982; Robert Kohn 1985).

---

[6]There may, of course, exist cases where defensive activities have "publicness" properties—where the actions of one victim to defend himself against pollution also provide defense for others. In such cases, there is clearly an externality present so that individual maximizing behavior will not yield the efficient levels of defensive activities. For a careful and thorough examination of defensive activities, see Richard Butler and Michael Maher (1986). Incidentally, the general issue of compensation of victims from pollution obviously has much in common with the moral hazard problem in insurance.

[7]A further policy instrument not discussed in this section but with some potentially useful applications in environmental policy is deposit-refund systems (Peter Bohm 1981). Such systems can shift some of the responsibility for monitoring and effectively place the burden of proof on the source. For under this approach, the source, to recoup its deposit, must demonstrate that its activities have not damaged the environment. See Robert Costanza and Charles Perrings (1990) for a policy proposal under this rubric.

The basic point is that there is a further condition, an entry-exit condition, that long-run equilibrium must satisfy for an efficient outcome (William Schulze and d'Arge 1974; Robert Collinge and Oates 1982; Daniel Spulber 1985). To obtain the correct number of firms in the long run, it is essential that firms pay not only the cost of the marginal damages of their emissions, but also the total cost arising from their waste emissions. Only if firms bear the total cost of their emissions will the prospective profitability of the enterprise reflect the true social net benefit of entry and exit into the industry.[8] In sum, unit subsidies are not a fully satisfactory alternative to Pigouvian taxes (Donald Dewees and W. A. Sims 1976).

In contrast, in a world of perfect knowledge, marketable emission permits are, in principle, a fully equivalent alternative to unit taxes. Instead of setting the proper Pigouvian tax and obtaining the efficient quantity of waste discharges as a result, the environmental authority could issue emission permits equal in the aggregate to the efficient quantity and allow firms to bid for them. It is not hard to show that the market-clearing price will produce an outcome that satisfies the first-order conditions both for efficiency in pollution abatement activities in the short run and for entry-exit decisions in the long run. The regulator can, in short, set either "price" or "quantity" and achieve the desired result.[9]

This symmetry between the price and quantity approaches is, however, critically dependent upon the assumption of perfect knowledge. In a setting of imperfect information concerning the marginal benefit and cost functions, the outcomes under the two approaches can differ in important ways.

C. Environment Policy Under Uncertainty

In a seminal paper, Martin Weitzman (1974) explored this asymmetry between price and quantity instruments and produced a theorem with important policy implications. The theorem establishes the conditions under which the expected welfare gain under a unit tax exceeds, is equal to, or falls short of that under a system of marketable permits (quotas). In short,

---

[8]In an intriguing qualification to this argument, Martin Bailey (1982) has shown that not only subsidies to polluters, but also compensation to victims, will result in no distortion in resource use where benefits and damages are capitalized into site rents. For a discussion of the Bailey argument, see Baumol and Oates (1988, pp. 230–34). In another interesting extension, Gene Mumy (1980) shows that a combined charges-subsidy scheme can be fully efficient. Under this approach, sources pay a unit tax for emissions above some specified baseline, but receive a unit subsidy for emissions reductions below the baseline. The key provision is that the right to subsidy payments is limited to existing firms (i.e., new sources have a baseline of zero) and that this right can either be sold or be exercised even if the firm chooses to exit the industry. For a useful development of Mumy's insight, see John Pezzey (1990).

[9]The discussion glosses over some quite troublesome matters of implementation. For example, the effects of the emissions of a particular pollutant on ambient air or water quality will often depend importantly on the location of the source. In such cases, the optimal fee must be tailored to the damages per unit of emissions source-by-source. Or, alternatively, in a market for emission permits, the rate at which permits are traded among any two sources will vary with the effects of their respective emissions. In such a setting, programs that treat all sources uniformly can forego significant efficiency gains (Eugene Seskin, Robert Anderson, and Robert Reid 1983; Charles Kolstad 1987). More on all this shortly.

the theorem states that in the presence of uncertainty concerning the costs of pollution control, the preferred policy instrument depends on the *relative* steepness of the marginal benefit and cost curves.[10]

The intuition of the Weitzman proposition is straightforward. Consider, for example, the case where the marginal benefits curve is quite steep but marginal control costs are fairly constant over the relevant range. This could reflect some kind of environmental threshold effect where, if pollutant concentrations rise only slightly over some range, dire environmental consequences follow. In such a setting, it is clearly important that the environmental authority have a close control over the quantity of emissions. If, instead, a price instrument were employed and the authority were to underestimate the true costs of pollution control, emissions might exceed the critical range with a resulting environmental disaster. In such a case, the Weitzman theorem tells us, quite sensibly, that the regulator should choose the quantity instrument (because the marginal benefits curve has a greater absolute slope than the marginal cost curve).

Suppose, next, that it is the marginal abatement cost curve that is steep and that the marginal benefits from pollution control are relatively constant over the relevant range. The danger here is that because of imperfect information, the regulatory agency might, for example, select an overly stringent standard, thereby imposing large, excessive costs on polluters and society. Under these circumstances, the expected welfare gain is larger under the price instrument. Polluters will not get stuck with inordinately high control costs, since they always have the option of paying the unit tax on emissions rather than reducing their discharges further.

The Weitzman theorem thus suggests the conditions under which each of these two policy instruments is to be preferred to the other. Not surprisingly, an even better expected outcome can be obtained by using price and quantity instruments in tandem. As Marc Roberts and Michael Spence (1976) have shown, the regulator can set the quantity of permits at the level that equates expected marginal benefits and costs and then offer a subsidy for emissions reductions in excess of those required by the permits and also a unit tax to provide a kind of "escape hatch" in case control costs turn out to be significantly higher than anticipated. In this way, a combination of price and quantity instruments can, in a setting of imperfect information, provide a larger expected welfare gain than an approach relying on either policy instrument alone (see also Weitzman 1978).[11]

---

[10]This result assumes linearity of the marginal benefit and cost functions over the relevant range and that the error term enters each function additively. Uncertainty in the benefits function, interestingly, is not enough in its own right to introduce any asymmetries; while it is the source of some expected welfare loss relative to the case of perfect information, there is no difference in this loss as between the two policy instruments. For useful diagrammatic treatments of the Weitzman analysis, see Zvi Adar and James Griffin (1976), Gideon Fishelson (1976), and Baumol and Oates (1988, ch. 5).

[11]Butler and Maher (1982) show that in a setting of economic growth, the shifts in the marginal damage and marginal control cost schedules are likely to be such as to increase substantially the welfare loss from a fixed fee system relative to that from a system of marketable permits.

D. Market Imperfections

The efficiency properties of the policy measures we have discussed depend for their validity upon a perfectly competitive equilibrium. This is a suspect assumption, particularly since many of the major polluters in the real world are large firms in heavily concentrated industries: oil refineries, chemical companies, and auto manufacturers. This raises the issue of the robustness of the results to the presence of large firms that are not price takers in their output markets.

James Buchanan (1969) called attention to this issue by showing that the imposition of a Pigouvian tax on a monopolist could conceivably reduce (rather than raise) social welfare. A monopolist restricts output below socially optimal levels, and a tax on waste emissions will lead to yet further contractions in output. The net effect is unclear. The welfare gains from reduced pollution must be offset against the losses from the reduced output of the monopolist.

The first-best response to this conundrum is clear. The regulatory authority should introduce two policy measures: a Pigouvian tax on waste emissions plus a unit subsidy to output equal to the difference between marginal cost and marginal revenue at the socially optimal level of output. Since there are two distortions, two policy instruments are required for a full resolution of the problem. Environmental regulators, however, are unlikely to have the authority (or inclination) to subsidize the output of monopolists. In the absence of such subsidies, the agency might seek to determine the second-best tax on effluents. Dwight Lee (1975) and Andy Barnett (1980) have provided the solution to this problem by deriving formally the rule for the second-best tax on waste emissions. The rule calls for a unit tax on emissions that is somewhat less than the unit tax on a perfectly competitive polluter (to account for the output effect of the tax):

$$t^* = t_c - \left| (P - MC) \frac{dX}{dE} \right| \tag{7}$$

Equation (7) indicates that the second-best tax per unit of waste emissions (t^*) equals the Pigouvian tax on a perfectly competitive firm (t_c) *minus* the welfare loss from the reduced output of the monopolist expressed as the difference between the value of a marginal unit of output and its cost times the reduction in output associated with a unit decrease in waste emissions. It can be shown by the appropriate manipulation of (7) that the second-best tax on the monopolist varies directly with the price elasticity of demand. The rationale is clear: where demand is more price elastic, the price distortion (i.e., the divergence between price and marginal cost) tends to be smaller so that the tax on effluent need not be reduced by so much as where demand is more price inelastic.

It seems unlikely, however, that the regulator will have either the information needed or the authority to determine and impose a set of taxes on waste emissions that is differentiated by the degree of monopoly power. Suppose that the environmental authority is constrained to levying a uniform tax on waste discharges and suppose that it determines this tax in a

Pigouvian manner by setting it equal to marginal social damages from pollution, completely ignoring the issue of market imperfections. How badly are things likely to go wrong? Oates and Diana Strassmann (1984) have explored this question and, using some representative values for various parameters, conclude that the complications from monopoly and other noncompetitive elements are likely to be small in magnitude; the losses from reduced output will typically be "swamped" by the allocative gains from reduced pollution. They suggest that, based on their estimates, it is not unreasonable simply to ignore the matter of incremental output distortions from effluent fees.[12] Their analysis suggests further that the failure of polluting agents to minimize costs because of more complex objective functions (a la Williamson), public agencies of the Niskanan sort, or because of regulatory constraints on profits need not seriously undermine the case for pricing incentives for pollution control. This subject needs further study, especially since many of the principal participants in the permit market for trading sulfur allowances under the new Amendments to the Clean Air Act will be regulated firms.

E. On the Robustness of the Pigouvian Prescription: Some Further Matters

Although the literature has established certain basic properties of the Pigouvian solution to the problem of externalities, there are some remaining troublesome matters. One concerns the information requirements needed to implement the approach. Developing reliable measures of the benefits and costs of environmental amenities is, as we shall see shortly, a difficult undertaking. To determine the appropriate Pigouvian levy, moreover, we not only need measures of existing damages and control costs, but we need to develop measures of the increment costs and benefits over a substantial range. For the proper Pigouvian levy is not a tax equal to marginal social damages at the *existing* level of pollution; it is a tax equal to marginal damages *at the optimal outcome*. We must effectively solve for the optimal level of pollution to determine the level of the tax. As an alternative, we might set the tax equal to the existing level of damages and then adjust it as levels of pollution change in the expectation that such an iterative procedure will lead us to the socially optimal outcome. But even this is not guaranteed (Baumol and Oates 1988, ch. 7).

There is, moreover, a closely related problem. In the discussion thus far, we have examined solely the first-order conditions for efficient outcomes; we have not raised the issue of satisfying any second-order conditions. As Baumol and David Bradford (1972) have shown, this is a particularly dangerous omission in the presence of externalities.[13] In fact, they demonstrate that if a detrimental externality is of sufficient strength, it *must* result in a breakdown of the convexity-concavity conditions required

---

[12]For more on this issue, see Peter Asch and Joseph Seneca (1976), Walter Misiolek (1980), and Burrows (1981).

[13]See also Richard Portes (1970), David Starrett (1972), J. R. Gould (1977), and Burrows (1986).

for an optimal outcome. As a result, there may easily exist a multiplicity of local maxima from which to choose—with no simple rule to determine the first-best outcome.[14] Under such circumstances, equilibrium prices may tell us nothing about the efficiency of current output or the direction in which to seek improvement.

There are thus reasons for some real reservations concerning the direct application of the Pigouvian analysis to the formulation of environmental policy. It is to this issue that we turn next.

III. The Design and Implementation of Environmental Policy

A. Introduction: From Theory to Policy

Problems of measurement and the breakdown of second-order conditions (among other things) constitute formidable obstacles to the determination of a truly first-best environmental policy. In response to these obstacles, the literature has explored some second-best approaches to policy design that have appealing properties. Moreover, they try to be more consistent with the procedures and spirit of decision making in the policy arena.

Under these approaches, the determination of environmental policy is taken to be a two-step process: first, standards or targets for environmental quality are set, and, second, a regulatory system is designed and put in place to achieve these standards. This is often the way environmental decision making proceeds. Under the Clean Air Act, for example, the first task of the EPA was to set standards in the form of maximum permissible concentrations of the major air pollutants. The next step was to design a regulatory plan to attain these standards for air quality.

In such a setting, systems of economic incentives can come into play in the second stage as effective regulatory instruments for the achievement of the predetermined environmental standards. Baumol and Oates (1971) have described such a system employing effluent fees as the "charges and standards" approach. But marketable permit systems can also function in this setting—a so-called "permits and standards" approach (Baumol and Oates 1988, ch. 12).[15]

---

[14]This problem is further compounded by the presence of defensive activities among victims of pollution. The interaction among abatement measures by polluters and defensive activities by victims can be a further source of nonconvexities (Hirofumi Shibata and Steven Winrich 1983; Oates 1983). Yet another source of nonconvexities can be found in the structure of subsidy programs that offer payments for emissions reductions to firms in excess of some minimum size (Raymond Palmquist 1990).

[15]This is admittedly a highly simplified view of the policy process. There is surely some interplay in debate and negotiations between the determination of standards and the choice of policy instruments. More broadly, there is an emerging literature on the political economy of environmental policy that seeks to provide a better understanding of the process of instrument choice—see, for example, McCubbins, Noll, and Weingast (1989), and Robert Hahn (1990).

The chief appeal of economic incentives as the regulatory device for achieving environmental standards is the large potential cost-savings that they promise. There is now an extensive body of empirical studies that estimate the cost of achieving standards for environmental quality under existing command-and-control (CAC) regulatory programs (e.g., Scott Atkinson and Donald Lewis 1974; Seskin, Anderson, and Reid 1983; Alan Krupnick 1983; Adele Palmer et al. 1980; Albert McGartland 1984). These are typically programs under which the environmental authority prescribes (often in great detail) the treatment procedures that are to be adopted by each source. The studies compare costs under CAC programs with those under a more cost effective system of economic incentives. The results have been quite striking: they indicate that control costs under existing programs have often been several times the least-cost levels. (See Thomas Tietenberg 1985, ch. 3, for a useful survey of these cost studies.)

The source of these large cost savings is the capacity of economic instruments to take advantage of the large differentials in abatement costs across polluters. The information problems confronting regulators under the more traditional CAC approaches are enormous—and they lead regulators to make only very rough and crude distinctions among sources (e.g., new versus old firms). In a setting of perfect information, such problems would, of course, disappear. But in the real world of imperfect information, economic instruments have the important advantage of economizing on the need for the environmental agency to acquire information on the abatement costs of individual sources. This is just another example of the more general principles concerning the capacity of markets to deal efficiently with information problems.[16]

The estimated cost savings in the studies cited above result from a more cost effective allocation of abatement efforts within the context of existing control technologies. From a more dynamic perspective, economic incentives promise additional gains in terms of encouraging the development of more effective and less costly abatement techniques. As John Wenders (1975) points out in this context, a system that puts a value on any discharges remaining after control (such as a system of fees or marketable permits) will provide a greater incentive to R&D efforts in control technology than will a regulation that specifies some given level of discharges (see also Wesley Magat 1978, and Scott Milliman and Raymond Prince 1989).

B. The Choice of Policy Instruments Again[17]

Some interesting issues arise in the choice between systems of effluent fees and marketable emission permits in the policy arena (John H. Dales 1968; Dewees 1983; David Harrison 1983). There is, of course, a basic sense in

---

[16]There is also an interesting literature on incentive-compatible mechanisms to obtain abatement cost information from polluters—see, for example, Evan Kwerel (1977).

[17]For a useful, comprehensive survey of the strengths and weaknesses of alternative policy instruments for pollution control, see Bohm and Clifford Russell (1985).

which they are equivalent: the environmental authority can, in principle, set price (i.e., the level of the effluent charge) and then adjust it until emissions are reduced sufficiently to achieve the prescribed environmental standard, or, alternatively, issue the requisite number of permits directly and allow the bidding of polluters to determine the market-clearing price.

However, this basic equivalence obscures some crucial differences between the two approaches in a policy setting; they are by no means equivalent policy instruments from the perspective of a regulatory agency. A major advantage of the marketable permit approach is that it gives the environmental authority direct control over the quantity of emissions. Under the fee approach, the regulator must set a fee, and if, for example, the fee turns out to be too low, pollution will exceed permissible levels. The agency will find itself in the uncomfortable position of having to adjust and readjust the fee to ensure that the environmental standard is attained. Direct control over quantity is to be preferred since the standard itself is prescribed in quantity terms.

This consideration is particularly important over time in a world of growth and inflation. A nominal fee that is adequate to hold emissions to the requisite levels at one moment in time will fail to do so later in the presence of economic growth and a rising price level. The regulatory agency will have to enact periodic (and unpopular) increases in effluent fees. In contrast, a system of marketable permits automatically accommodates itself to growth and inflation. Since there can be no change in the aggregate quantity of emissions without some explicit action on the part of the agency, increased demand will simply translate itself into a higher market-clearing price for permits with no effects on levels of waste discharges.

Polluters (that is, *existing* polluters), as well as regulators, are likely to prefer the permit approach because it can involve lower levels of compliance costs. If the permits are auctioned off, then of course polluters must pay directly for the right to emit wastes as they would under a fee system. But rather than allocating the permits by auction, the environmental authority can initiate the system with a one-time distribution of permits to existing sources—free of charge. Some form of "grandfathering" can be used to allocate permits based on historical performance. Existing firms thus receive a marketable asset, which they can then use either to validate their own emissions or sell to another polluter.[18] And finally, the permit approach has some advantages in terms of familiarity. Regulators have long-standing experience with permits, and it is a much less radical change to make permits effectively transferable than to introduce a wholly new system of regulation based on effluent fees. Marketable permits thus have

---

[18]In an interesting simulation study, Randolph Lyon (1982) finds that the cost of permits to sources under an auction system can be quite high; for one of the auction simulations, he finds that aggregate payments for permits will exceed treatment costs. Lyon's results thus suggest potentially large gains to polluting firms from a free distribution of permits instead of their sale through an auction. These gains, of course, are limited to current sources. Polluting firms that arrive on the scene at a later date will have to purchase permits from existing dischargers.

some quite appealing features to a regulatory agency—features that no doubt explain to some degree the revealed preference for this approach (in the U.S. at least) over that of fees.

Effluent charges have their own appeal. They are sources of public revenue, and, in these days of large budget deficits, they promise a new revenue source to hard-pressed legislators. From an economic perspective, there is much to be said for the substitution of fees for other sources of revenues that carry sizable excess burdens (Lee and Misiolek 1986). In a study of effluent charges on emissions of particulates and sulfur oxides from stationary sources into the atmosphere, David Terkla (1984) estimates, based on assumed levels of tax rates, that revenues in 1982 dollars would range from $1.8 to $8.7 billion and would, in addition, provide substantial efficiency gains ($630 million to $3.05 billion) if substituted for revenues from either the federal individual income tax or corporation income tax.

Moreover, the charges approach does not depend for its effectiveness on the development of a smoothly functioning market in permits. Significant search costs, strategy behavior, and market imperfections can impede the workings of a permit market (Hahn 1984; Tietenberg 1985, ch. 6). In contrast, under a system of fees, no transfers of permits are needed—each polluter simply responds directly to the incentive provided by the existing fee. There may well be circumstances under which it is easier to realize a cost-effective pattern of abatement efforts through a visible set of fees than through the workings of a somewhat distorted permit market. And finally, there is an equity argument in favor of fees (instead of a free distribution of permits to sources). The Organization for Economic Cooperation and Development (OECD), for example, has adopted the "Polluter Pays Principle" on the grounds that those who use society's scarce environmental resources should compensate the public for their use.

There exists a large literature on the design of fee systems and permit markets to attain predetermined levels of environmental quality. This work addresses the difficult issues that arise in the design and functioning of systems of economic incentives—issues that receive little or only perfunctory attention in the purely theoretical literature but are of real concern in the operation of actual policy measures. For example, there is the tricky matter of spatial differentiation. For most pollutants, the effect of discharges on environmental quality typically has important spatial dimensions: the specific location of the source dictates the effects that its emissions will have on environmental quality at the various monitoring points. While, in principle, this simply calls for differentiating the effluent fee according to location, in practice this is not so easy. The regulatory agency often does not have the authority or inclination to levy differing tax rates on sources according to their location. Various compromises including the construction of zones with uniform fees have been investigated (Tietenberg 1978; Seskin, Anderson, and Reid 1983; Kolstad 1987).

Similarly, problems arise under systems of transferable permits where (as is often the case) the effects of the emissions of the partners to a trade are not the same. (The seminal theoretical paper is W. David Montgomery 1972.) Several alternatives have been proposed including zoned systems that allow trades only among polluters within the specified zones, ambient permit systems under which the terms of trade are determined by the relative effects of emissions at binding monitors, and the pollution-offset system under which trades are subject to the constraint of no violations of the prevailing standard at any point in the area (Atkinson and Tietenberg 1982; Atkinson and Lewis 1974; Hahn and Noll 1982; Krupnick, Oates, and Eric Van de Verg 1983; McGartland and Oates 1985; McGartland 1988; Tietenberg 1980, 1985; Walter Spofford 1984; Baumol and Oates 1988, ch. 12). For certain pollutants, these studies make clear that a substantial portion of the cost-savings from economic-incentive approaches will be lost if spatial differentiation is not, at least to some degree, built into the program (Robert Mendelsohn 1986).

The actual design of systems of economic incentives inevitably involves some basic compromises to accommodate the range of complications to the regulatory problem (Albert Nichols 1984). It is instructive to see how some of these issues have been dealt with in practice.

C. Experience with Economic Incentives for Environmental Management[19]

In the United States proposals for effluent fees have met with little success; however, there has been some limited experience with programs of marketable permits for the regulation of air and water quality. In Europe, the experience (at least until quite recently) has been the reverse: some modest use of effluent charges but no experience with transferable permits. We shall provide in this section a brief summary of these measures along with some remarks on their achievements and failures.

Largely for the reasons mentioned in the preceding section, policy makers in the U.S. have found marketable permits preferable to fees as a mechanism for providing economic incentives for pollution control.[20] The major program of this genre is the EPA's Emission Trading Program for the regulation of air quality. But there are also three other programs worthy of note: the Wisconsin system of Transferable Discharge Permits (TDP) for the management of water quality, the lead trading program (known for-

---

[19]The OECD (1989) has recently provided a useful "catalog" and accompanying discussion of the use of economic incentives for environmental protection in the OECD countries.

[20]One case in which there has been some use of fees in the U.S. is the levying of charges on industrial emissions into municipal waste treatment facilities. In some instances these charges have been based not only on the quantity but also on the strength or quality of the effluent. The charges are often related to "average" levels of discharges and have had as their primary objective the raising of funds to help finance the treatment plants. Their role as an economic incentive to regulate levels of emissions has apparently been minor (see James Boland 1986; Baumol and Oates 1979, pp. 258–63). There are also a variety of taxes on the disposal of hazardous wastes, including land disposal taxes in several states.

mally as "interrefinery averaging"), and a recent program for the trading of rights for phosphorus discharges into the Dillon Reservoir in Colorado.[21]

By far the most important of these programs in terms of scope and impact, Emissions Trading has undergone a fairly complicated evolution into a program that has several major components. Under the widely publicized "Bubble" provision, a plant with many sources of emissions of a particular air pollutant is subjected to an overall emissions limitation. Within this limit, the managers of the plant have the flexibility to select a set of controls consistent with the aggregate limit, rather than conforming to specified treatment procedures for each source of discharges with the plant. Under the "Netting" provision, firms can avoid stringent limitations on new sources of discharges by reducing emissions from other sources of the pollutant within the facility. Hahn and Hester (1989b) report that to date there have been over 100 approved Bubble transactions in the U.S. and a much larger number of Netting "trades" (somewhere between 5,000 and 12,000). The estimated cost savings from these trades have been quite substantial; although the estimates exhibit a very wide range, the cost savings probably amount to several billion dollars.

There are provisions under Emissions Trading for external trades across firms—mainly under the Offset provision which allows new sources in nonattainment areas to "offset" their new emissions with reductions in discharges by existing sources. Offsets can be obtained through either internal (within plant) or external trades. Hahn and Hester (1989b) indicate that there have been about 2,000 trades under the Offset policy; only about 10 percent of them have been external trades—the great bulk of offsets have been obtained within the plant or facility.

Emissions Trading, as a whole, receives mixed marks. It has significantly increased the flexibility with which sources can meet their discharge limitations—and this has been important for it has allowed substantial cost savings. The great majority of the trades, however, have been internal ones. A real and active market in emissions rights involving different firms has not developed under the program (in spite of the efforts of an active firm functioning as a broker in this market). This seems to be largely the result of an extensive and complicated set of procedures for external trades that have introduced substantial levels of transactions costs into the market and have created uncertainties concerning the nature of the property rights that are being acquired. In addition, the program has been grafted onto an elaborate set of command-and-control style regulations which effectively prohibit certain kinds of trades. Many potentially profitable trades simply have not come to pass.[22]

---

[21]Tietenberg's book (1985) is an excellent, comprehensive treatment of the Emissions Trading Program. Robert Hahn and Gordon Hester have provided a series of recent and very valuable descriptions and assessments of all four of these programs of marketable permits. See Hahn and Hester (1989a, 1989b), and Hahn (1989). For analyses of the Wisconsin TDP system, see William O'Neil (1983), and O'Neil et al. (1983).

[22]In an interesting analysis of the experience with Emissions Trading, Roger Raufer and Stephen Feldman (1987) argue that some of the obstacles to trading could be circumvented by allowing the leasing of rights.

Likewise, the experience under the Wisconsin TDP system has involved little external trading. The program establishes a framework under which the rights to BOD discharges can be traded among sources. Since the program's inception in 1981 on the Fox River, there has been only one trade: a paper mill which shifted its treatment activities to a municipal wastewater treatment plant transferred its rights to the municipal facility. The potential number of trades is limited since there are only about twenty major sources (paper mills and municipal waste treatment plants) along the banks of the river. But even so, preliminary studies (O'Neil 1983; O'Neil et al. 1983) indicated several potentially quite profitable trades involving large cost savings. A set of quite severe restrictions appears to have discouraged these transfers of permits. Trades must be justified on the basis of "need"—and this does not include reduced costs! Moreover, the traded rights are granted only for the term of the seller's discharge permit (a maximum period of five years) with no assurance that the rights will be renewed. The Wisconsin experience seems to be one in which the conditions needed for the emergence of a viable market in discharge permits have not been established.

In contrast, EPA's "interrefinery averaging" program for the trading of lead rights resulted in a very active market over the relatively short life of the program. Begun in 1982, the program allowed refiners to trade the severely limited rights to lead additives to gasoline. The program expired in 1986, although refiners were permitted to make a use of rights that were "banked" through 1987. Trading became brisk under the program: over the first half of 1987, for example, around 50 percent of all lead added to gasoline was obtained through trades of lead rights, with substantial cost savings reported from these trades. Although reliable estimates of cost-savings for the lead-trading program are not available, Hahn and Hester (1989b) surmise that these savings have run into the hundreds of millions of dollars. As they point out, the success of the program stemmed largely from the absence of a large body of restrictions on trades: refiners were essentially free to trade lead rights and needed only to submit a quarterly report to EPA on their gasoline production and lead usage. There were, moreover, already well established markets in refinery products (including a wide variety of fuel additives) so that refinery managers had plenty of experience in these kinds of transactions.[23]

Finally, there is an emerging program in Colorado for the trading of rights to phosphorous discharges into the Dillon Reservoir. This program is noteworthy in that among those that we have discussed, it is the only one to be designed and introduced by a local government. The plan embodies few encumbrances to trading; the one major restriction is a 2:1 trading ratio for point/nonpoint trading, introduced as a "margin of safety" because of uncertainties concerning the effectiveness of nonpoint source controls. The program is still in its early stages: although no trades have been approved, some have been requested.

---

[23]We should also note that various irregularities and illegal procedures were discovered in this market—perhaps because of lax oversight.

The U.S. experience with marketable permits is thus a limited one with quite mixed results. In the one case where the market was allowed to function free of heavy restrictions, vigorous trading resulted with apparently large cost savings. In contrast, under Emissions Trading and the Wisconsin TDP systems, stringent restrictions on the markets for trading emissions rights appear to have effectively increased transaction costs and introduced uncertainties, seriously impeding the ability of these markets to realize the potentially large cost savings from trading. Even so, the cost savings from Emissions Trading (primarily from the Netting and Bubble provisions) have run into several billion dollars. Finally, it is interesting that these programs seem not to have had any significant and adverse environmental effects; Hahn and Hester (1989a) suggest that their impact on environmental quality has been roughly "neutral."

In light of this experience, the prospects, we think, appear favorable for the functioning of the new market in sulfur allowances that is being created under the 1990 Amendments to the Clean Air Act. This measure, designed to address the acid rain problem by cutting back annual sulfur emissions by 10 million tons, will permit affected power plants to meet their emissions reduction quotas by whatever means they wish, including the purchase of "excess" emissions reductions from other sources. The market area for this program is the nation as a whole so that there should be a large number of potential participants in the market. At this juncture, plans for the structure and functioning of the market do not appear to contain major limitations that would impede trading in the sulfur allowances. There remains, however, the possibility that state governors or public utility commissions will introduce some restrictions. There is the further concern that regulated firms may not behave in a strictly cost-minimizing fashion, thereby compromising some of the cost-effectiveness properties of the trading scheme. But as we suggested earlier, this may not prove to be a serious distortion.

The use of effluent fees is more prevalent in Europe where they have been employed extensively in systems of water quality management and to a limited extent for noise abatement (Ralph Johnson and Gardner Brown, Jr. 1976; Bower et al. 1981; Brown and Hans Bressers 1986; Brown and Johnson 1984; Tietenberg 1990). There are few attempts to use them for the control of air pollution. France, Germany, and the Netherlands, for example, have imposed effluent fees on emissions of various water pollutants for over two decades. It should be stressed that these fee systems are not pure systems of economic incentives of the sort discussed in economics texts. Their primary intent has not been the regulation of discharges, but rather the raising of funds to finance projects for water quality management. As such, the fees have typically been low and have tended to apply to "average" or "expected" discharges rather than to provide a clear cost signal at the margin. Moreover, the charges are overlaid on an extensive command-and-control system of regulations that mute somewhat further their effects as economic incentives.

The Netherlands has one of the oldest and most effectively managed systems of charges—and also the one with relatively high levels of fees.

There is some evidence suggesting that these fees have, in fact, had a measurable effect in reducing emissions. Some multiple regression work by
Hans Bressers (1983) in the Netherlands and surveys of industrial polluters
and water board officials by Brown and Bressers (1986) indicate that firms
have responded to the charges with significant cutbacks in discharges of
water borne pollutants.

In sum, although there is some experience with systems of fees for pollution control, mainly of water pollution, these systems have not, for the
most part, been designed in the spirit of economic incentives for the regulation of water quality. Their role has been more that of a revenue device
to finance programs for water quality management.

These systems, it is worth noting, have addressed almost exclusively
so-called "point-source" polluters. Non-point source pollution (including
agricultural and urban runoff into waterways) has proved much more difficult to encompass within systems of charges or permits. Winston Harrington, Krupnick, and Henry Peskin (1985) provide a useful overview of
the potential role for economic incentives in the management of non-point
sources. This becomes largely a matter of seeking out potentially effective
second-best measures (e.g., fees on fertilizer use), since it is difficult to measure and monitor "discharges" of pollutants from these sources. Kathleen
Segerson (1988) has advanced an ingenious proposal whereby such sources
would be subject to a tax (or subsidy payment) based, not on their
emissions, but on the observed level of environmental quality; although
sources might find themselves with tax payments resulting from circumstances outside their control (e.g., adverse weather conditions), Segerson
shows that such a scheme can induce efficient abatement and entry/exit
behavior on the part of non-point sources.

D. Legal Liability as an Economic Instrument for Environmental Protection

An entirely different approach to regulating sources is to rely on legal liability for damages to the environment. Although we often do not include
this approach under the heading of economic instruments, it is clear that
a system of "strict liability," under which a source is financially responsible for damages, embodies important economic incentives.[24] The imposition of such liability effectively places an "expected price" on polluting
activities. The ongoing suits, for example, following upon the massive
Exxon-Valdez oil spill suggest that such penalties will surely exert pressures
on potential polluters to engage in preventive measures.

Under this approach, the environmental authority, in a setting of uncertainty, need not set the values of any price or quantity instruments, it

---

[24]The major alternative to strict liability is a negligence rule under which a polluter is liable only
if he has failed to comply with a "due standard of care" in the activity that caused the damages. Under strict liability, the party causing the damages is liable irrespective of the care exercised in the polluting activity.

simply relies on the liability rule to discipline polluters. Two issues are of interest here. The first is the capacity, in principle, for strict liability to mimic the effects of a Pigouvian tax. And the second is the likely effectiveness, in practice, of strict liability as a substitute for other forms of economic incentives. There is a substantial literature in the economics of the law that addresses these general issues and a growing number of studies that explore this matter in the context of environmental management (see, for example, Steven Shavell 1984a, 1984b; Segerson 1990).

It is clear that strict liability can, in principle, provide the source of potential damages with the same incentive as a Pigouvian tax. If a polluter knows that he will be held financially accountable for any damages his activities create, then he will have the proper incentive to seek methods to avoid these damages. Strict liability serves to internalize the external costs— just as does an appropriate tax. Strict liability is unlike a tax, however, in that it provides compensation to victims. The Pigouvian tax possesses an important asymmetry in a market sense: it is a charge to the polluter—but not a payment to the victim. And, as noted earlier, such payments to victims can result in inefficient levels of defensive activities. Strict liability thus does not get perfect marks on efficiency grounds, even in principle, for although it internalizes the social costs of the polluter, it can be a source of distortions in victims' behavior.

The more important concern, in practice, is the effectiveness of legal liability in disciplining polluter behavior. Even if the basic rule is an efficient one in terms of placing liability on the source of the environmental damage, the actual "price" paid by the source may be much less than actual damages because of imperfections in the legal system: failures to impose liability on responsible parties resulting from uncertainty over causation, statutes of limitation, or high costs of prosecution.[25] There is the further possibility of bankruptcy as a means of avoiding large payments for damages. The evidence on these matters is mixed (see Segerson 1990), but it seems to suggest that legal liability has functioned only very imperfectly.

An interesting area of application in the environmental arena involves various pieces of legislation that provide strict liability for damages from accidental spills of oil or leakage of hazardous wastes. The Comprehensive Environmental Responses, Compensation, and Liability Act (CERCLA) of 1980 and its later amendments (popularly known as "Superfund") are noteworthy for their broad potential applicability (Thomas Grigalunas and James Opaluch 1988). Such measures may well provide a useful framework for internalizing the external costs of spills (Opaluch and Grigalunas 1984). In particular, the liability approach appears to have its greatest appeal in

---

[25]As one reviewer noted, in these times of heightened environmental sensitivity, liability determinations could easily exceed actual damages in some instances. However, this seems not to have happened in the recent Exxon-Valdez case. The case was settled out of court with Exxon agreeing to pay some $900 million over a period of several years. Some observers believe that this falls well short of the true damages from the Exxon-Valdez oil spill in Alaska.

cases like those under Superfund where damages are infrequent events and for which monitoring the level of care a firm takes under conventional regulatory procedures would be difficult.[26]

E. Environmental Federalism

In addition to the choice of policy instrument, there is the important issue of the locus of regulatory authority. In the case of fees, for example, should a central environmental authority establish a uniform fee applicable to polluters in all parts of the nation or should decentralized agencies set fee levels appropriate to their own jurisdictions? U.S. environmental policy exhibits considerable ambivalence on this matter. Under the Clean Air Act in 1970, the U.S. Congress instructed the Environmental Protection Agency to set uniform national standards for air quality—maximum permissible concentrations of key air pollutants applicable to all areas in the country. But two years later under the Clean Water Act, the Congress decided to let the individual states determine their own standards (subject to EPA approval) for water quality. The basic question is "Which approach, centralized decision making or environmental federalism, is the more promising?

Basic economic principles seem to suggest, on first glance, a straightforward answer to this question. Since the benefits and costs of reduced levels of most forms of pollution are likely to vary (and vary substantially) across different jurisdictions, the optimal level of effluent fees (or quantities of marketable permits) will also vary (Sam Peltman and T. Nicolaus Tideman 1972). The first-best outcome must therefore be one in which fees or quantities of permits are set in accord with local circumstances, suggesting that an optimal regulatory system for pollution control will be a form of environmental federalism.

Some environmental economists have raised an objection to this general presumption. John Cumberland (1981), among others, has expressed the concern that in their eagerness to attract new business and jobs, state or local officials will tend to set excessively lax environmental standards—fees that are too low or quantities of permits that are too high. The fear is that competition among decentralized jurisdictions for jobs and income will lead to excessive environmental degradation. This, incidentally, is a line of argument that has appeared elsewhere in the literature on fiscal federalism under the title of "tax competition." The difficulty in assessing this objection to decentralized policy making is that there exists little systematic evidence on the issue; most of the evidence is anecdotal in character, and, until quite recently, there has been little

---

[26]A more complicated and problematic issue relates to the permission of the courts to sue under Superfund for damages from toxic substances using "the joint and several liability doctrine." Under this provision, *each* defendant is potentially liable for an amount up to the *entire* damage, irrespective of his individual contribution. For an analysis of this doctrine in the Superfund setting, see Tietenberg (1989).

theoretical work addressing the phenomenon of interjurisdictional competition.[27]

In a pair of recent papers, Oates and Robert Schwab (1988a, 1988b)
have set forth a model of such competition in which "local" jurisdictions
compete for a mobile national stock of capital using both tax and environmental policy instruments. Since the production functions are neoclassical in character, an increase in a jurisdiction's capital stock raises the
level of wages through an associated increase in the capital-labor ratio. In
the model, local officials simultaneously employ two policy tools to attract
capital: a tax rate on capital itself which can be lowered or even set negative (a subsidy) to raise the return to capital in the jurisdiction, and a level
of allowable pollutant emissions (or, alternatively, an effluent fee). By
increasing the level of permissible waste discharges either directly or by
lowering the fee on emissions, the local authority increases the marginal
product of capital and thereby encourages a further inflow of capital. The
model thus involves two straightforward tradeoffs: one between wage income and tax revenues, and the other between wage income and local environmental quality. The analysis reveals that in a setting of homogeneous
worker-residents making choices by simple majority rule, jurisdictions select the socially optimal levels of these two policy instruments. The tax rate
on capital is set equal to zero, and the level of environmental quality is chosen so that the willingness to pay for a cleaner environment is equal to
marginal abatement cost. The analysis thus supports the case for environmental federalism: decentralized policy making is efficient in the model.[28]

In one sense, this is hardly a surprising result. Since local residents
care about the level of environmental quality, we should not expect that
they would wish to push levels of pollution into the range where the willingness to pay to avoid environmental damage exceeds the loss in wage
income from a cleaner environment. At the same time, this result is not
immune to various "imperfections." If, for example, local governments
are constrained constitutionally to use taxes on capital to finance various
local public goods, then it is easy to show that not only will the tax rate
on capital be positive, but officials will select socially excessive levels of
pollution. Likewise, if Niskanen bureaucrats run the local public sector,
they will choose excessively lax environmental standards as a mechanism
to attract capital so as to expand the local tax base and public revenues.
Finally, there can easily be conflicts among local groups of residents with
differing interests (e.g., workers vs. nonworkers) that can lead to distorted
outcomes (although these distortions may involve too little or too much
pollution).

---

[27]Two recent studies, one by Virginia McConnell and Schwab (1990), and the other by Timothy
Bartik (1988c), find little evidence of strong effects of existing environmental regulations on the location decisions of firms within the U.S. This, of course, does not preclude the possibility that state
and local officials, in *fear* of such effects, will scale down standards for environmental quality.

[28]Using an alternative analytical framework in which local jurisdictions "bid" against one another for polluting firms in terms of entry fees, William Fischel (1975) likewise finds that local competition produces an efficient outcome.

The basic model does at least suggest that there are some fundamental forces promoting efficient decentralized environmental decisions. If the regions selected for environmental decision making are sufficiently large to internalize the polluting effects of waste discharges, the case for environmental federalism has some force. Exploration of this issue is admittedly in its infancy—in particular, there is a pressing need for some systematic empirical study of the effects of "local" competition on environmental choices.[29]

F. Enforcement Issues

The great bulk of the literature on the economics of environmental regulation simply assumes that polluters comply with existing directives: they either keep their discharges within the prescribed limitation or, under a fee scheme, report accurately their levels of emissions and pay the required fees. Sources, in short, are assumed *both* to act in good faith and to have full control over their levels of discharges so that violations of prescribed behavior do not occur.

Taking its lead from the seminal paper by Gary Becker (1968) on the economics of crime and punishment, a recent literature has addressed enforcement issues as they apply to environmental regulations.[30] As this literature points out, violations of environmental regulations can have two sources: a polluter can willfully exceed his discharge limitation (or underreport his emissions under a fee system) to reduce compliance costs *or* a stochastic dimension to discharges may exist so that the polluter has only imperfect control over his levels of emissions. In such a setting, the regulatory problem becomes a more complicated one. Not only must the regulatory agency set the usual policy parameters (emissions limitations or fees), but it must also decide upon an enforcement policy which involves both monitoring procedures and levels of fines for violations.

The early literature explored these enforcement issues in a wholly static framework. The seminal papers, for example, by Paul Downing and William Watson (1974) and by Jon Harford (1978), established a number of interesting results. Downing and Watson show that the incorporation of enforcement costs into the analysis of environmental policy suggests that optimal levels of pollution control will be less than when these costs are ignored. Harford obtains the especially interesting result that under a system of effluent fees, the level of *actual* discharges is independent both of the level of the fine for underreporting and of the probability of punish-

---

[29]For some other recent theoretical studies of interjurisdictional fiscal competition, see Jack Mintz and Henry Tulkens (1986), John Wilson (1986), David Wildasin (1989), and George Zodrow and Peter Mieszkowski (1986).

[30]Russell, Harrington, and William Vaughan (1986, ch. 4) provide a useful survey of the enforcement literature in environmental economics up to 1985. Harrington (1988) presents a concise, excellent overview both of the more recent literature and of the "stylized facts" of actual compliance and enforcement behavior. See also Russell (1990).

ment (so long as the slope of the expected penalty function with respect to the size of the violation is increasing and the probability of punishment is greater than zero). The polluter sets the level of actual wastes such that marginal abatement cost equals the effluent fee—the efficient level! But he then, in general, underreports his discharges with the extent of underreporting varying inversely with the level of fines and the probability of punishment.

Arun Malik (1990) has extended this line of analysis to the functioning of systems of marketable permits. He establishes a result analogous to Harford's: under certain circumstances, noncompliant polluters will emit precisely the same level of wastes for a given permit price as that discharged by an otherwise identical compliant firm. The conditions, however, for this equivalence are fairly stringent ones. More generally, Malik shows that noncompliant behavior will have effects on the market-clearing price in the permit market—effects that will compromise to some extent the efficiency properties of the marketable permit system.

One implication of this body of work is the expectation of widespread noncompliance on the part of polluters. But as Harrington (1988) points out, this seems not to be the case. The evidence we have from various spot checks by EPA and GAO suggests that most industrial polluters seem to be in compliance most of the time.[31] Substantial compliance seems to exist in spite of modest enforcement efforts: relatively few "notices of violation" have been issued and far fewer polluters have actually been fined for their violations. Moreover, where such fines have been levied, they have typically been quite small. And yet in spite of such modest enforcement efforts, "cheating" is not ubiquitous—violations are certainly not infrequent, but they are far from universal.

This finding simply doesn't square at all well with the results from the static models of polluter behavior.[32] An alternative line of modeling (drawing on the tax-evasion literature) seems to provide a better description of polluter behavior; it also has some potentially instructive normative implications. This approach puts the problem in a dynamic game-theoretic framework. Both polluters and regulators react to the activities of one another in the previous period. In a provocative paper, Harrington (1988) models the enforcement process as a Markov decision problem. Polluters that are detected in violation in one period are moved to a separate group in the next period in which they are subject to more frequent inspection and higher fines. Polluting firms thus have an incentive to comply in order to avoid being moved into the second group (from which they can re-

---

[31]Interestingly, noncompliance seems to be more widespread among municipal waste treatment plants than among industrial sources! (Russell 1990, p. 256). Some of the most formidable enforcement problems involve federal agencies. The GAO (1988), for example, has found the Department of Energy's nuclear weapons facilities to be a source of major concern, the costs of dealing with environmental contamination associated with these facilities are estimated at more than $100 billion.

[32]Perhaps public opprobrium is a stronger disciplinary force than economists are typically inclined to believe!

turn to the original group only after a period during which no violations are detected). In such a framework, firms may be in compliance even though they would be subject to no fine for a violation. Following up on Russell's analysis (Russell, Harrington, and Vaughan 1986, pp. 199–216), Harrington finds that the addition of yet a third group, an absorbing state from which the polluter can never emerge, can result in a "spectacular reduction in the minimum resources required to achieve a given level of compliance" (p. 47). In sum, the dynamic game-theoretic approach can produce compliance in cases in which the expected penalty is insufficient to prevent violations in a purely static model. Moreover, it suggests some potentially valuable guidelines for the design of cost-effective enforcement procedures. Enforcement is an area where economic analysis may make some quite useful contributions.

G. The Effects of Domestic Environmental Policy on Patterns of International Trade

The introduction of policy measures to protect the environment has potential implications not only for the domestic economy but also for international trade. Proposed environmental regulations are, in fact, often opposed vigorously on the grounds that they will impair the "international competitiveness" of domestic industries. The increased costs associated with pollution control measures will, so the argument goes, result in a loss of export markets and increased imports of products of polluting industries.

These potential effects have been the subject of some study. It is clear, for example, that the adoption of costly control measures in certain countries will, in principle, alter the international structure of relative costs with potential effects on patterns of specialization and world trade. These trade effects have been explored in some detail, making use of standard models of international trade (Kazumi Asako 1979; Baumol and Oates 1988, ch. 16; Anthony Koo 1974; Martin McGuire 1982; John Merrifield 1988; Rüdiger Pethig 1976; Pethig et al. 1980; Horst Siebert 1974; James Tobey 1989; Ingo Walter 1975). In particular, there has been a concern that the less developed countries, with their emphasis on economic development rather than environmental protection, will tend over time to develop a comparative advantage in pollution-intensive industries. In consequence, they will become the "havens" for the world's dirty industries; this concern has become known as the "pollution-haven hypothesis" (Walter and Judith Ugelow 1979; Walter 1982).

Some early studies made use of existing macro-econometric models to assess the likely magnitudes of these effects. These studies used estimates of the costs of pollution control programs on an industry basis to get some sense of the effects of these programs on trade and payments flows. Generally, they found small, but measurable, effects (d'Arge and Kneese 1971; Walter 1974).

We are now in a position to examine historically what has, in fact, happened. To what extent have environmental measures influenced the pattern of world trade? Have the LDC's become the havens of the world's dirty industries? Two recent studies, quite different in character, have addressed this issue directly. H. Jeffrey Leonard (1988), in what is largely a case study of trade and foreign-investment flows for several key industries and countries, finds little evidence that pollution-control measures have exerted a systematic effect on international trade and investment. After examining some aggregate figures, the policy stances in several industrialized and developing countries, and the operations of multinational corporations, Leonard concludes that "the differentials in the costs of complying with environmental regulations and in the levels of environmental concern in industrialized and industrializing countries have not been strong enough to offset larger political and economic forces in shaping aggregate international comparative advantage" (p. 231).

Tobey (1989, 1990) has looked at the same issue in a large econometric study of international trade patterns in "pollution-intensive" goods. After controlling for the effects of relative factor abundance and other trade determinants, Tobey cannot find any effects of various measures of the stringency of domestic environmental policies. Tobey estimates two sets of equations that explain, respectively, patterns of trade in pollution-intensive goods and changes in trade patterns from 1970 to 1984. In neither set of equations do the variables measuring the stringency of domestic environmental policy have the predicted effect on trade patterns.

Why have domestic environmental measures not induced "industrial flight;" and the development of "pollution havens?" The primary reason seems to be that the costs of pollution control have not, in fact, loomed very large even in heavily polluting industries. Existing estimates suggest that control costs have run on the order of only 1 to $2^1/_2$ percent of total costs in most pollution-intensive industries; H. David Robison (1985, p. 704), for example, reports that total abatement costs per dollar of output in 1977 were well under 3 percent in all industries with the sole exception of electric utilities where they were 5.4 percent. Such small increments to costs are likely to be swamped in their impact on international trade by the much larger effects of changing differentials in labor costs, swings in exchange rates, etc. Moreover, nearly all the industrialized countries have introduced environmental measures—and at roughly the same time—so that such measures have not been the source of significant cost differentials among major competitors. There seems not to have been a discernible movement in investment in these industries to the developing countries because major political and economic uncertainties have apparently loomed much larger in location decisions than have the modest savings from less stringent environmental controls.

In short, domestic environmental policies, at least to this point in time, do not appear to have had significant effects on patterns of international trade. From an environmental perspective, this is a comforting finding, for it means that there is little force to the argument that we need to relax environmental policies to preserve international competitiveness.

H. Command-and-Control vs. Economic Incentives: Some Concluding Observations

Much of the literature in environmental economics, both theoretical and empirical, contrasts in quite sharp and uncompromising terms the properties of systems of economic incentives with the inferior outcomes under existing systems of command-and-control regulations. In certain respects, this literature has been a bit misleading and, perhaps, unfair. The term command-and-control encompasses a very broad and diverse set of regulatory techniques—some admittedly quite crude and excessively costly. But others are far more sophisticated and cost sensitive. In fact, the dividing line between so-called CAC and incentive-based policies is not always so clear. A program under which the regulator specifies the exact treatment procedures to be followed by polluters obviously falls within the CAC class. But what about a policy that establishes a fixed emissions limitation for a particular source (with no trading possible) but allows the polluter to select the form of compliance? Such flexibility certainly allows the operation of economic incentives in terms of the search for the least-cost method of control.

The point here is that it can be quite misleading to lump together in a cavalier fashion "CAC" methods of regulatory control and to contrast them as a class with the least-cost outcomes typically associated with systems of economic incentives. In fact, the compromises and "imperfections" inherent in the design and implementation of incentive-based systems virtually guarantee that they also will be unable to realize the formal least-cost result.

Empirical studies contrasting the cost effectiveness of the two general approaches have typically examined the cost under each system of attaining a specified *standard* of environmental quality—which typically means ensuring that at no point in an area do pollutant concentrations exceed the maximum level permissible under the particular standard. As Atkinson and Tietenberg (1982) and others have noted, CAC systems typically result in substantial "over-control" relative to incentive-based systems. Since it effectively assigns a zero shadow price to any environmental improvements over and above the standard, the least-cost algorithm attempts to make use of any "excess" environmental capacity to increase emissions and thereby reduce control costs. The less cost-sensitive CAC approaches generally overly restrict emissions (relative to the least-cost solution) and thereby produce pollutant concentrations at nonbinding points that are less than those under the least-cost outcome. In sum, at most points in the area, environmental quality (although subject to the same overall standard) will be higher under a CAC system than under the least-cost solution. So long as there is some value to improved environmental quality beyond the standard, a proper comparison of benefits and costs should give the CAC system credit for this increment to environmental quality. One recent study (Oates, Paul Portney, and McGartland 1989) which does just this for a major air pollutant finds that a relatively sophisticated CAC approach produces results that compare reasonably well to the prospective outcome un der a fully cost effective system of economic incentives.

Our intent is not to suggest that the economist's emphasis on systems of economic incentives has been misplaced, but rather to argue that policy structure and analysis is a good deal more complicated than the usual textbooks would suggest (Nichols 1984). The applicability of systems of economic incentives is to some extent limited by monitoring capabilities and spatial complications. In fact, in any meaningful sense the "optimal" structure of regulatory programs for the control of air and water pollution is going to involve a combination of policy instruments—some making use of economic incentives and others not. Careful economic analysis has, we believe, an important role to play in understanding the workings of these systems. But it can make its best contribution, not through a dogmatic commitment to economic incentives, but rather by the careful analysis of the whole range of policy instruments available, insuring that those CAC measures that are adopted are effective devices for controlling pollution at relatively modest cost (Kolstad 1986).

At the same time, it is our sense that incentive-based systems have much to contribute to environmental protection—and that they have been much neglected in part because of the (understandable) predisposition of regulators to more traditional policy instruments.[33] There are strong reasons for believing, with supporting evidence, that this neglect has seriously impaired our efforts both to realize our objectives for improved environmental quality and to do so at the lowest cost. A general realization of this point seems to be emerging with a consequent renewed interest in many countries in the possibility of integrating incentive-based policies into environmental regulations—a matter to which we shall return in the concluding section.

IV. Measuring the Benefits and Costs of Pollution Control

As we suggested in the previous sections, effluent fees and transferable permits are capable, in principle, of achieving a given pollution standard at least cost. Eventually, however, economists must ask whether environmental standards have been set at appropriate levels: does the marginal cost of achieving the ozone standard in the Los Angeles basin exceed the marginal benefits? The answer to this question requires that we measure the benefits and costs of pollution control.

While the measurement of control costs is itself no simple task, environmental economists have turned most of their attention to the benefit side of the ledger. Of central concern has been the development of methodologies to measure the benefits of goods—such as clean air or water—that

---

[33]See Steven Kelman (1981) for a fascinating—if somewhat dismaying—study of the politics and ideology of economic incentives for environmental protection.

are not sold in markets. These techniques fall into two categories: indirect market methods, which attempt to infer from actual choices, such as choosing where to live, the value people place on environmental goods; and direct questioning approaches, which ask people to make tradeoffs between environmental and other goods in a survey context. We shall review both approaches, and then discuss the application of these methods to valuing the benefits of pollution control. In particular, we will try to highlight areas where benefits have been successfully measured, as well as areas where good benefit estimates are most needed. But first we must be clear about the valuation of changes in environmental quality.

A. Defining the Value of a Change in Environmental Quality

We noted at the beginning of this review that pollution may enter both consumers' utility functions and firms' production functions. (See equations (1) and (2).) To elaborate on how this might occur we introduce a *damage function* that links pollution, Q, to something people value, S,

$$S = S(Q). \tag{8}$$

For a consumer, S might be time spent ill or expected fish catch; for a firm it might be an input into production, such as the stock of halibut. We assume that S replaces Q in the utility and production functions (equations (1) and (2)).

There are two cases of interest here. First, if the consumer (or firm) views S as out of his control, we can define the value of a change in S (which may be easier to measure than the value of a change in Q), and then predict the change in S resulting from a change in Q. For example, if people view reductions in visibility associated with air pollution as beyond their control, one can predict the reduction in visibility from (8) and concentrate on valuing visibility. This is commonly known as the damage function approach to benefit estimation.

The second case is more complicated. It may sometimes be possible to mitigate the effects of pollution through the use of inputs, Z. For example, medicine may exist to alleviate respiratory symptoms associated with air pollution. In this instance, equation (8) must be modified to

$$S = S(Q,Z), \tag{9}$$

and it is Q rather than S that must be valued, because S is no longer exogenous.

For the case of a firm, the value of a change in Q (or S) is the change in the firm's profits when Q (or S) is altered. This amount is the same whether we are talking about the firm's willingness to pay (WTP) for an improvement in environmental quality or its willingness to accept (WTA) compensation for a reduction in environmental quality.

For a consumer, in contrast, the value of a change in Q (or S) depends on the initial assignment of property rights. If consumers are viewed as having to pay for an improvement in environmental quality, for example, from Q^0 to Q^1, the most they should be willing to pay for this change is the reduction in expenditure necessary to achieve their original utility level when Q improves. Formally, if $e(P,S(Q^0),U^0)$ denotes the minimum expenditures necessary to achieve pre-improvement utility U^0 at prices P and environmental quality Q^0, then the most people would be willing to pay (WTP) for the improvement in environmental quality to Q^1 is

$$WTP = e(P,S(Q^0),U^0) - e(P,S(Q^1),U^0). \tag{10}$$

If, on the other hand, consumers are viewed as having rights to the higher level of environmental quality and must be compensated for a reduction in Q, then the smallest amount they would be willing to accept is the additional amount they must spend to achieve their original utility level when Q declines. Formally, willingness to accept (WTA) compensation for a reduction in Q from Q^1 to Q^0 is given by

$$WTA = e(P,S(Q^0),U^1) - e(P,S(Q^1),U^1), \tag{11}$$

where U^1 is the utility level achieved at the higher level of environmental quality.

In general, willingness to accept compensation for a reduction in Q will be higher than willingness to pay for an increase in Q of the same magnitude. As W. Michael Hanemann (1991) has recently shown, the amount by which WTA exceeds WTP varies directly with the income elasticity of demand for S and inversely with the elasticity of substitution between S and private goods. If the income elasticity of demand for S is zero or if S is a perfect substitute for a private good, WTP should equal WTA. If, however, the elasticity of substitution between S and private goods is zero, the difference between WTA and WTP can be infinite. It is therefore important to determine which valuation concept, WTP or WTA, is appropriate for the problem at hand.

The preceding definitions of the value of a change in environmental quality do not by themselves characterize all of the welfare effects of environmental policies. Improvements in environmental quality may alter prices as well as air or water quality, and these price changes must be valued in addition to quality changes.

In contrast to valuing quality changes, valuing price changes is relatively straightforward. WTP for a reduction in price is just the reduction in expenditure necessary to achieve U^0 (the consumer's original utility level) when prices are reduced. As is well known, this is just the area to the left of the relevant compensated demand function (i.e., the one that holds utility at U^0) between the two prices. Willingness to accept compensation for a price increase is the increase in expenditure necessary to achieve U^1, the utility level enjoyed at the lower price, when price is increased.

Unlike the case of a quality change, WTA compensation for a price increase exceeds WTP for a price decrease only by the amount of an income effect. As long as expenditure on the good in question is a small fraction of total expenditure, the difference between the two welfare measures will be small. Moreover, approximating WTP or WTA by consumer surplus—the area to the left of the Marshallian demand function will produce an error of no more than 5 percent in most cases (Robert Willig 1976).[34]

One problem with the definitions of the value of a change in environmental quality (equations (10) and (11)) is that not all environmental benefits can be viewed as certain. Reducing exposure to a carcinogen, for example, alters the probability that persons in the exposed population will contract cancer, and it is this probability that must be valued.

To define the value of a quality change under uncertainty, suppose that the value of S associated with a given Q is uncertain. Specifically, suppose that two values of S are possible: S^0 and S^1. For example, S^0 might be 360 healthy days per year and S^1 no healthy days (death). Q no longer determines S directly, but affects π, the probability that S^0 occurs. If the individual is an expected utility maximizer and if $V(M,S^i)$, $i = 0,1$, denotes his expected utility in each state (M being income), willingness to pay for a change in Q from Q^0 to Q^1 is the most one can take away from the individual and leave him at his original expected utility level (Michael Jones-Lee 1974).

$$\pi(Q^0)V(M,S^0) + [1 - \pi(Q^0)]V(M,S^1)$$
$$= \pi(Q^1)V(M - WTP,S^0)$$
$$+ [1 - \pi(Q^1)]V(M - WTP,S^1). \qquad (12)$$

For a small change in Q, WTP is just the difference in utility between the two states, divided by the expected marginal utility of money.

$$WTP = \frac{[V(M,S^0) - V(M,S^1)]}{\pi V^0{}_M + (1 - \pi)V^1{}_M} \cdot \frac{\partial \pi}{\partial Q} \, dQ. \qquad (13)$$

An important point to note here is that the value of the change in Q is an ex ante value: changes in Q are valued before the outcomes are known. For example, suppose that reducing exposure to an environmental carcinogen is expected to save two lives in a city of 1,000,000 persons. The ex ante approach views this as a 2-in-one-million reduction in the probability of death for each person in the population. The ex post approach, by contrast, would value the reduction in two lives with certainty.

We are now in a position to discuss the principal methods that have been used to value changes in pollution.

---

[34]Sufficient conditions for this to hold are that (1) consumer surplus is no more than 90 percent of income; (2) the ratio of consumer surplus to income, multiplied by one-half the income elasticity of demand, is no more than 0.05.

B. Indirect Methods for Measuring the Benefits of Environmental Quality

Economists have employed three approaches to valuing pollution that rely on observed choices: the averting behavior approach, the weak complementarity approach, and the hedonic price approach.

1. The Averting Behavior Approach. The averting behavior approach relies on the fact that in some cases purchased inputs can be used to mitigate the effects of pollution.[35] For example, farmers can increase the amount of land and other inputs to compensate for the fact that ozone reduces soybean yields. Or, for another, residents of smoggy areas can take medicine to relieve itchy eyes and runny noses.

As long as other inputs can be used to compensate for the effects of pollution, the value of a small change in pollution can be measured by the value of the inputs used to compensate for the change in pollution. If, for example, a reduction in one-hour maximum ozone levels from 0.16 parts per million (ppm) to 0.11 ppm reduces the number of days of respiratory symptoms from 6 to 5, and if an expenditure on medication of $20 has the same effect, then the value of the ozone reduction is $20.

Somewhat more formally, if $S = S(Q,Z)$, willingness to pay for a marginal change in Q may be written as the marginal rate of substitution between an averting good and pollution, times the price of the averting good (Paul Courant and Richard Porter 1981).

$$WTP = -p_1 \frac{\partial S/\partial Q}{\partial S/\partial z_1} \, ,\tag{14}$$

where z_1 is medication. Marginal WTP can thus be estimated from the production function alone.

To value a nonmarginal change in pollution, one must know both the cost function for the good affected by pollution and the marginal value function for that good. For example, in the case of health damages, a large improvement in air quality will shift the marginal cost of healthy days to the right (see Figure 1) and the value of the change is given by the area between the two marginal cost curves, bounded by the marginal value of healthy time. When the good in question is not sold in markets, as is the case for health, estimating the marginal value function is, however, difficult.[36]

An alternative approach, suggested by Bartik (1988a), is to use the change in the cost of producing the original level of S, i.e., the area be-

---

[35]In terms of the notation above, either (9) applies, or other inputs can be substituted for S in production; see equation (2).

[36]If S were sold in markets, estimation of the marginal value function would be simple, assuming one could observe the price of S and assuming that the price was exogenous to any household. The problem is that, for a good produced by the household itself, one cannot observe the price (marginal cost) of the good—it must be estimated from the marginal cost function. Furthermore, the price is endogenous, since it depends on the level of S.

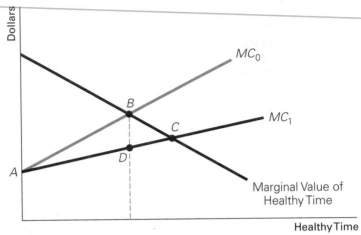

Figure 1 Morbidity Benefits of a Nonmarginal Pollution Reduction

tween the marginal cost functions to the left of S^0 (area ABD in Figure 1), to approximate the value of the environmental quality change. For an improvement in Q, this understates the value of the change because it does not allow the individual to increase his chosen value of S. When the marginal cost of S increases, the relevant area will overstate the value of the welfare decrease. The advantage of this approximation is that it can be estimated from knowledge of the cost function alone.

The usefulness of the averting behavior approach is clearly limited to cases where other inputs can be substituted for pollution. Most pollution damages suffered by firms occur in agriculture, forestry, and fishing. In the case of agriculture, irrigation can compensate for the effects of global warming on crop yields. Likewise, capital (boats and gear) and labor can compensate for fish populations depleted as a result of water pollution.

In the case of pollution damages suffered by households, averting behavior has been used to value health damages and the soiling damages caused by air pollution. Households can avoid health damages either by avoiding exposure to pollution in the first place, or by mitigating the effects of exposure once they occur. For example, the deleterious effects of water pollution can be avoided by purchasing bottled water (V. Kerry Smith and William Desvousges 1986b), and pollutants in outdoor air may be filtered by running an air-conditioner (Mark Dickie and Shelby Gerking 1991).

Two problems, however, arise in applying the averting behavior method in these cases. First, in computing the right-hand-side of (14), the researcher must know what the household imagined the benefit of purchasing water ($\partial S/\partial z_1$) to be, since it is the *perceived* benefits of averting behavior that the household equates to the marginal cost of this behavior. Second, when the averting input produces joint products, as in the case of running an air-conditioner, the cost of the activity cannot be attributed solely to averting behavior. Inputs that mitigate the effects of pollution in-

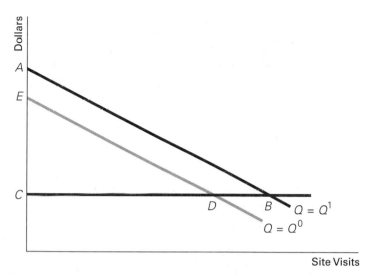

Figure 2 The Effect of a Change in Environmental Quality on the Demand for Visits to a Recreation Site

clude medicine and doctors' visits (Gerking and Linda Stanley 1986); however, use of the latter often runs into the joint product problem—a doctor's visit may treat ailments unrelated to pollution, as well as pollution related illness.

2. The Weak Complementarity Approach. While the averting behavior approach exploits the substitutability between pollution and other inputs into production, the weak complementarity approach values changes in environmental quality by making use of the complementarity of environmental quality, e.g., cleaner water, with a purchased good, e.g., visits to a lake. Suppose that a specified improvement in water quality at a lake resort results in an increase in a household's demand for visits to the resort from ED to AB (see Figure 2). One can view the value of access to the lake at the original quality level Q^0 as the value of being able to visit the lake at a cost of C rather than at some cost E. The value of access to the lake is thus the area EDC.[37] The increase in the value of access when Q changes (area $ABDE$) is the value of the water quality improvement.

For area $ABDE$ to measure the value of the water quality improvement, environmental quality must be weakly complementary to the good in question (Mäler 1974; Nancy Bockstael and Kenneth McConnell 1983). This means that (1) the marginal utility of environmental quality (water quality) must be zero if none of the good is purchased (no visits are made to

---

[37]Strictly speaking EDC should be measured using the consumer's compensated demand function. When measuring the value of access to a good, use of the Marshallian demand function may no longer provide a good approximation to the welfare triangle since the choke prices of the Marshallian and compensated demand functions may vary substantially. The Willig bounds do not apply in this case.

the lake); (2) there is a price above which none of the good is purchased (no visits are made). If (1) did not hold, three would be additional benefits to a change in water quality not reflected in the demand for visits.

In practice, the weak complementarity approach has been used most often to value the attributes of recreation sites—either water quality, or a related attribute, such as fish catch.[38] Although site visits do not have a market price, their cost can be measured by summing the cost of traveling to the site, including the time cost, as well as any entrance fees.

A problem in measuring the demand for site visits as a function of site quality is that there is no variation in site quality among persons who visit a site. A popular solution to this problem is the varying parameters model, which assumes that site quality enters recreation demand functions multiplied by travel cost or income, both of which vary across households.[39] In the first stage of the model, the demand for visits to site i is regressed on the cost of visiting the site and on income. In the second stage the coefficients from stage one are regressed on quality variables at site i. This is equivalent to estimating a set of demand functions in which visits to site i depend on the quality of the ith site, the cost of visiting the ith site, income, and interactions between travel cost and quality, and income and quality.

One drawback of this approach is that it allows visits to a given site to depend only on the cost of visiting that site—the cost of visiting substitute sites is not considered. This is equivalent to assuming that, except for the quality variables that enter the model in stage two, all sites are perfect substitutes. The varying parameters model may, therefore, give misleading results if one wishes to value quality changes at several sites.

A second approach to valuing quality changes is to use a discrete choice model. This approach examines the choice of which site to visit on a given day as a function of the cost of visiting each site, and the quality of each site. If the choice of which site to visit on the first recreation day can be viewed as independent of which site to visit on the ith, a simple discrete choice model, such as the multinomial logit, can be applied to the choice of site, conditional on participation (Clark Binkley and Hanemann 1978; Daniel Feenberg and Mills 1980). The choice of whether to participate and, if so, on how many days, is made by comparing the maximum utility received from taking a trip with the utility of the best substitute activity on that day.[40]

---

[38]Surveys of recreation demand models may be found in Mendelsohn (1987) and also in John Braden and Kolstad (1991). Bockstael, Hanemann, and Catherine Kling (1987) discuss their application to valuing environmental quality at recreation sites.

[39]This solution was first used by Vaughan and Russell (1982) and has also been used by V. Kerry Smith, Desvousges, and Matthew McGivney (1983), and V. Kerry Smith and Desvousges (1986a).

[40]If one estimates a discrete choice model of recreation decisions, the value of a change in environmental quality at site i is no longer measured as indicated in Figure 2 (Hanemann 1984). Because utility is random from the viewpoint of the researcher, compensating variation for a change in quality at a recreation site on a given day equals the change in utility conditional on visiting the site times the probability that the site is visited, plus the change in the probability of visiting the site times the utility received from the site.

The advantage of the discrete choice model is that the probability of visiting any one site depends on the costs of visiting all sites and the levels of quality at all sites. The drawback of the model is that the decision to take a trip or not and, if so, which site to visit, is made independently on each day of the season. The number of trips made to date influence neither which site the individual chooses to go to on a given day, nor whether he takes a trip at all.[41] Thus, these models must be combined with models that predict the total number of trips taken.

3. Hedonic Market Methods. The third method used by economists to value environmental quality, or a related output such as mortality risk, exploits the concept of hedonic prices—the notion that the price of a house or job can be decomposed into the prices of the attributes that make up the good, such as air quality in the case of a house (Ronald Ridker and John Henning 1967), or risk of death in the case of a job (Richard Thaler and Sherwin Rosen 1976). The hedonic price approach has been used primarily to value environmental disamenities in urban areas (air pollution, proximity to hazardous waste sites), which are reflected both in housing prices and in wages. It has also been used to value mortality risks by examining the compensation workers receive for voluntarily assuming job risks. Finally, the hedonic travel cost approach has been used to value recreation sites. We discuss each approach in turn.

Urban Amenities. Air quality and other environmental amenities can be valued in an urban setting by virtue of being tied to residential location: they are part of the bundle of amenities—public schools, police protection, proximity to parks—that a household purchases when buying a house.

The essence of the hedonic approach is to try to decompose the price of a house (or of residential land) into the prices of individual attributes, including air quality. This is done using an hedonic price function, which describes the equilibrium relationship between house price, p, and attributes, $A = (a_1, a_2, \ldots, a_n)$. The marginal price of an attribute in the market is simply the partial derivative of the hedonic price function with respect to that attribute. In selecting a house, consumers equate their marginal willingness to pay for each attribute to its marginal price (S. Rosen 1974; A. Myrick Freeman 1974). This implies that the gradient of the hedonic price function, evaluated at the chosen house, gives the buyer's marginal willingnesses to pay for each attribute.

Somewhat more formally, utility maximization in an hedonic market calls for the marginal price of an attribute to equal the household's mar-

---

[41]One solution to this problem, proposed by Edward Morey (1984), is to estimate a share model, which allocates the recreation budget for a season among different sites. The drawback of this model is that the share of the budget going to each site is assumed to be positive, whereas, in reality, a household may not visit all sites.

ginal willingness to pay for the attribute.

$$\partial p / \partial a_i = \partial \theta / \partial a_i, \tag{15}$$

where θ is the household's bid function, the most one can take away from the household in return for the collection of amenities, A, and keep its utility constant. Equation (15) implies that, in equilibrium, the marginal willingness to pay for an attribute can be measured by its marginal price, computed from the hedonic price function.

If a large improvement in environmental quality is contemplated in one section of a city—an improvement large enough to alter housing prices—the derivative of the hedonic price function no longer measures the value of the amenity change. In the short run, before households adjust to the amenity change and prices are altered, the value of the amenity change is the area under the household's marginal bid function—the right hand side of (15)—between the old and new levels of air quality. To value the amenity change in the long run, however, one must take into account the household's adjustment to the amenity change *and* to any price changes that may result. The area under the marginal bid function (the short-run welfare measure) is, however, a lower bound to the long-run benefits of the amenity change (Bartik 1988b).

Empirical applications of the hedonic approach have typically focused either on valuing marginal amenity changes, which requires estimating only the hedonic price function, or on computing the short-run benefits of nonmarginal amenity changes, which requires estimating marginal bid functions. S. Rosen originally suggested that this be done by regressing marginal attribute price, computed from the gradient of the hedonic price function, on the arguments of the marginal bid function. This procedure, however, may encounter an identification problem which is caused by the fact that the arguments of the marginal attribute bid function determine marginal attribute price as well.

An example of the identification problem, provided by James Brown and Harvey Rosen (1982), occurs when the hedonic price function is quadratic and the marginal value functions are linear in attributes. In the case of a single amenity, a_1,

$$\partial p / \partial a_1 = \beta_0 + \beta_1 a_1 \tag{16}$$

$$\partial \theta / \partial a_1 = b_0 + b_1 a_1 + b_2 M. \tag{17}$$

In this case regression $\beta_0 + \beta_1 a_1$ on a_1 and M will reproduce the parameters of the marginal price function, i.e., $\hat{b}_0 = \beta_0$, $\hat{b}_1 = \beta_1$ and $\hat{b}_2 = 0$. This is illustrated graphically in Figure 3. The problem is that the marginal price function does not shift independently of the marginal bid function. Shifts in the latter, due, say, to differences in income, thus trace out points on the marginal price function.

To achieve identification in this example, one can introduce functional

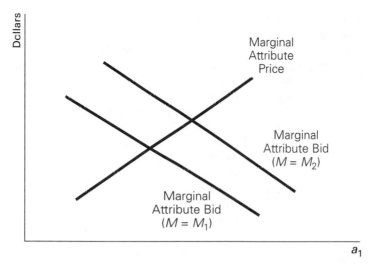

Figure 3 The Identification Problem in an Hedonic Market

form restrictions, such as adding a_1^2 to the marginal price function, but not to the marginal value function, which will cause $\partial p/\partial a_i$ to shift independently of $\partial \theta/\partial a_i$ (Mendelsohn 1984). Another solution is to estimate hedonic price functions for several markets, so that the coefficients of the marginal price function vary across cities (Palmquist 1984; Robert Ohsfeldt and Barton Smith 1985; Ohsfeldt 1988). For this to work, households in all cities must have identical preferences; however, the distribution of measured household characteristics and/or the supply of amenities must vary across cities so that the hedonic price function and its gradient vary from one city to another. In the case of several a_i's, one can impose exclusion restrictions on the a_i's that enter each marginal value function (Dennis Epple 1987) so that marginal prices vary independently of the variables that enter the marginal value function.

In view of the problems in estimating marginal attribute bid functions, it is important to note that an upper bound to the long-run benefits of an amenity improvement can be obtained from the hedonic price function alone. Yoshitsugu Kanemoto (1988) has shown that the change in prices in the improved area predicted by the hedonic price function is an upper bound to the long-run benefits of an amenity improvement. Thus, from knowledge of the hedonic price function alone one can obtain (1) the exact value of a marginal attribute change, and (2) an upper bound to the long-run value of an attribute change.

Wage-Amenity Studies. The analysis of hedonic housing markets, by focusing on housing market equilibrium within a city, implicitly ignores migration among cities. If one takes a long-run view and assumes that workers can move freely from one city to another, then data on compensating wage differentials across cities can be used to infer the value of environmental amenities (Glenn Blomquist, Mark Berger, and John Hoehn 1988; Maureen Cropper and Amalia Arriaga-Salinas 1980; V. Kerry Smith 1983). Intuitively, the value people attach to urban amenities should be reflected in the higher wages they require to live in less desirable cities.

When migration is possible, consumers choose the city in which they live to maximize utility; however, wage income, as well as amenities, vary from one city to another (S. Rosen 1979; Jennifer Roback 1982).[42] Household equilibrium requires that utility be identical in all cities.

The fact that consumers in all cities must enjoy the same level of utility implies that wages and land rents must adjust to compensate for amenity differences. The marginal value of an amenity change to a consumer is thus the sum of the partial derivatives of an hedonic wage function and an hedonic property value function (Roback 1982).

Hedonic Labor Markets. The fact that risk of death is a job attribute traded in hedonic labor markets has provided economists with an alternative to the averting behavior approach as a means of valuing mortality risk (Thaler and S. Rosen 1976). The theory behind this approach is simple: other things equal, workers in riskier jobs must be compensated with higher wages for bearing this risk. As in the case of hedonic housing markets, the worker chooses his job by equating the marginal cost of working in a less risky job—the derivative of the hedonic price function—to the marginal benefit, the value (in dollars) of the resulting increase in life expectancy.

There are three problems in using the compensating wage approach. One is that compensating wage differentials exist only if workers are informed of job risks. Thus, the absence of compensating differentials need not mean that workers do not value reducing the risk of death. A second problem is that compensating differentials appear to exist only in unionized industries (William Dickens 1984; Douglas Gegax, Gerking, and Schulze 1985). This suggests that the wage differential approach may provide estimates of the value of a risk reduction only for certain segments of the population. This problem is compounded by the fact that the least risk averse individuals work in risky jobs. Third, if workers have biased estimates of job risks, or if the objective measures of job risk used in most wage studies over- or understate workers' risk perceptions, market wage premia will yield biased estimates of the value of a risk reduction.

The Hedonic Travel Cost Approach. Yet another area in which the hedonic approach has been applied is in valuing the attributes of recreation sites (G. Brown and Mendelsohn 1984). In valuing sites, the analog to the hedonic price function is obtained by regressing the cost of travelling to a

---

[42]In most models wages, lot size, and amenities vary among, but not within, cities.

recreation site on the attributes of the site, such as expected fish catch, clarity of water, and water color. However, because this relationship is not the result of market forces, there is nothing to guarantee that the marginal cost of an attribute is positive. More desirable sites may be located closer to population centers rather than farther away from them.[43] In this case, the individual's choice of site will not be described by (13), and care must be taken when inferring values from marginal attribute costs (V. Kerry Smith, Palmquist, and Paul Jakus 1990).

C. The Contingent Valuation Method

While the indirect market approaches we have described above can be used to value many of the benefits of pollution reduction, there are important cases in which they cannot be used. When no appropriate averting or mitigating behavior exists, indirect methods cannot be used to estimate the morbidity benefits of reducing air pollution. Recreation benefits may be difficult to measure since there may not be enough variation in environmental quality across sites in a region to estimate the value of water quality using the travel cost approach.

There is, in addition, an entire category of benefits—*nonuse values*—which cannot even in principle be measured by indirect market methods. Nonuse values refer to the benefits received from knowing that a good exists, even though the individual may never experience the good directly. Examples include preserving an endangered species or improving visibility at the Grand Canyon for persons who never plan to visit the Grand Canyon.

This suggests that direct questioning can play a role in valuing the benefits of pollution control. Typically, direct questioning or contingent valuation studies ask respondents to value an output, such as a day spent hunting or fishing, rather than a change in pollution concentrations per se. Examples of commodities that have been valued using the contingent valuation method (CVM) include improvements in water quality to the point where the water is fishable or swimmable (Richard Carson and Robert Mitchell 1988), improvements in visibility resulting from decreased air pollution (Alan Randall, Berry Ives, and Clyde Eastman 1974; Schulze and David Brookshire 1983; Decision Focus 1990), the value of preserving endangered species (James Bowker and John Stoll 1988; Kevin Boyle and Richard Bishop 1987), and days free of respiratory symptoms (George Tolley et al. 1986b; Dickie et al. 1987).

Any contingent valuation study must incorporate (1) a description of the commodity to be valued; (2) a method by which payment is to be made; and (3) a method of eliciting values. In studies that value recre-

---

[43]The problem may be reduced by using only sites actually visited from a given origin in estimating the hedonic travel cost function.

ation-related goods, hypothetical payment may take the form of a user fee or an increase in taxes; in the case of improved visibility, a charge on one's utility bill, since power plant pollution can contribute to air quality degradation. To determine the maximum a person is willing to pay for an improvement in environmental quality, the interviewer may simply ask what this amount is (an open-ended survey), or he may ask whether or not the respondent is willing to pay a stated amount (a closed-ended survey). The yes/no answer does not yield an estimate of each respondent's willingness to pay; however, the fraction of respondents willing to pay at least the stated amount gives a point on the cumulative distribution function of willingness to pay for the commodity (Trudy Cameron and Michelle James 1987).

There seems to be general agreement that closed-ended questions are easier for respondents to answer and therefore yield more reliable information than open-ended questions, especially when the commodity valued is not traded in conventional markets. Asking an open-ended question about a good that respondents have never been asked to value, such as improved visibility, often yields a distribution of responses that has a large number of zero values and a few very large ones. This may reflect the fact that respondents have nothing to which to anchor their responses, and are unwilling to go through the reasoning necessary to discover the value they place on the good. Answering a yes/no question is, by contrast, a much easier task, and one that parallels decisions made when purchasing goods sold in conventional markets.

It must be acknowledged that, despite advances made in contingent valuation methodology during the last 15 years, many remain skeptical of the method. Perhaps the most serious criticism is that responses to contingent valuation questions are hypothetical—they represent professed, rather than actual, willingness to pay. This issue has been investigated in at least a dozen studies that compare responses to contingent valuation questions with actual payments for the same commodity.

How close hypothetical values are to actual ones depends on whether the commodity is a public or private good, on the elicitation technique used, and on whether it is willingness to pay (WTP) for the good or willingness to accept compensation (WTA) that is elicited. Most experiments comparing hypothetical and actual WTP for a private good (strawberries or hunting permits) have found no statistically significant difference between mean values of hypothetical and actual willingness to pay (Dickie, Ann Fisher, and Gerking 1987; Bishop and Thomas Heberlein 1979; Bishop, Heberlein, and Mary Jo Kealy 1983). Such is not the case when hypothetical and actual WTA are compared. In three experiments involving willingness to accept compensation for hunting permits, Bishop and Heberlein (1979) and Bishop, Heberlein, and Kealy (1983) found that actual WTA was statistically significantly lower than hypothetical WTA in two out of three cases. Hypothetical and actual WTP have also been found to differ when the commodity valued is a public good (Kealy, Jack Dovidio, and Mark L. Rockel 1987).

Other criticisms of the CVM have focused on: (1) the possibility that individuals may behave strategically in answering questions—either over-stating WTP if this increases the likelihood that an improvement is made, or understating WTP if it reduces their share of the cost (the free-rider problem); (2) the fact that individuals may not be sufficiently familiar with the commodity to have a well-defined value for it; and (3) the fact that WTP for a commodity is often an order of magnitude less than willingness to accept (WTA) compensation for the loss of the commodity.

The possibility that respondents behave strategically has been tested in laboratory experiments by examining whether announced WTP for a public good varies with the method used to finance the public good. Studies by Bohm (1972), Bruce Scherr and Emerson Babb (1975), and Vernon Smith (1977, 1979) suggest that strategic behavior is not a prob-lem, possibly because of the effort that effective strategic behavior re-quires.

If the commodity to be valued is not well understood, contingent val-uation responses are likely to be unreliable: responses tend to exhibit wide variation, and respondents may even prefer less of a good to more! One in-terpretation of this result is that people really do not have values for the commodity in question—they are created by the researcher in the course of the survey (Thomas Brown and Paul Slovic 1988). This is a serious crit-icism: Do people really know enough about groundwater contamination or biodiversity to place a value on either good?

Fortunately, it is possible to defend against this criticism by seeing how responses vary with the amount of information that is provided about the commodity being valued. If values are well defined, they should not, on av-erage, vary with small changes in the amount of information.

One of the most striking and challenging findings emerging from this work is that willingness to pay for an environmental improvement is usu-ally *many times lower* than willingness to accept compensation to forego the same improvement (Judd Hammack and G. Brown 1974; Bishop and Heberlein 1979; Robert Rowe, d'Arge, and Brookshire 1980; Jack Knetsch and J. A. Sinden 1984). This is sometimes interpreted as evidence that the method of eliciting responses is unsatisfactory; however, as we noted above, there is no reason why WTP for a quality (public good) decrease should not exceed WTP for an increase of the same magnitude, provided that there are few substitutes for the public good.[44] An alternative ex-planation for the WTA/WTP discrepancy that has been offered by some economists (Donald Coursey, John Hovis, and Schulze 1987; Brookshire and Coursey 1987) is that individuals are simply not as familiar with the sale of an item as with its purchase. These authors find that, in experi-ments where individuals were allowed to submit bids or offers for the

---

[44]The explanation of the discrepancy between *WTA* and *WTP* offered by psychologists—that mon-etary losses from some reference point are valued more highly than monetary gains (Daniel Kahne-man and Amos Tversky 1979)—also suggests that this disparity has nothing to do with flaws in the contingent valuation method.

same commodity, WTA approached WTP after several rounds of trans-actions.[45]

D. Applications of Valuation Techniques

Having described the main techniques used to value environmental ameni-ties, we now wish to give the reader a feel for the way in which these tech-niques have been used to value the benefits of pollution control. We shall begin with an overview of the types of benefits associated with the major pieces of environmental legislation. We then turn to a description and as-sessment of actual benefit estimation.

Table 1 lists the major pieces of environmental legislation in the U.S. and the estimated costs of complying with each statute in 1990. With the exception of the Clean Water Act, the primary goal of U.S. environmental legislation is to protect the health of the population. According to the Clean Air Act, ambient standards for the criteria air pollutants are to be set to protect the health of the most sensitive person in the population.[46] The goal of the Safe Drinking Water Act is, similarly, to provide a margin of safety in protecting the country's drinking water supplies from toxic substances, while the goal of the Federal Insecticide, Fungicide, and Rodenticide Act (FIFRA) is to prevent adverse effects to human health and to the environ-ment from the use of pesticides.

Each of the statutes in Table 1 also results in certain nonhealth bene-fits. The Clean Air Act provides important aesthetic benefits in the form of increased visibility, and the 1990 Amendments to the Act, designed to re-duce acid rain, may yield ecological and water quality benefits. The Clean Water Act—whose goal is to make all navigable water bodies fishable and swimmable—yields recreational and ecological benefits. Both Acts yield benefits to firms in agriculture, forestry, and commercial fishing. FIFRA, the primary law governing pesticide usage, is designed to protect animal as well as human health.

In addition to the pollution problem addressed by the major environ-mental statutes, there is increasing concern about the effects of emissions of green house gases, including carbon dioxide, chlorofluorocarbons (CFCs) and methane. Studies suggest that emissions of these gases may contribute to increases in mean temperature, especially in the Northern Hemisphere, changes in precipitation, and sea level rises that could average 65 cm by the end of the next century. The main effects of these changes are likely to be felt in agriculture, in animal habitat, and in human comfort.

---

[45]None of these explanations, however, seems to account for results obtained by Kahneman, Knetsch, and Thaler (1990). They find that, even for common items such as coffee mugs and ball-point pens, sellers have reservation prices that are higher, much higher on average, than buyers' bid prices. This disparity does not appear after several rounds of trading. The initial distribution of prop-erty rights (the "endowment effect") may, therefore, matter, even for goods with many substitutes.

[46]The criteria air pollutants are particulate matter, sulfur oxides, nitrogen oxides, carbon monox-ide, lead, and ozone.

Table 1 Total Annualized Environmental Compliance Costs, by Medium, 1990 (Millions of 1986 dollars)

Medium	Costs	Major Statutes
Air and Radiation, Total	28,029	
Air	27,588	Clean Air Act (CAA)
Radiation	441	Radon Pollution Control Act
Water, Total	42,410	
Water Quality	38,823	Clean Water Act (CWA)
Drinking Water	3,587	Safe Drinking Water Act
Land, Total	26,547	
RCRA	24,842	Resource Conservation and Recovery Act (RCRA)
Superfund	1,704	Comprehensive Environmental Response, Compensation and Liability Act (CERCLA)
Chemicals, Total	1,579	
Toxic Substances	600	Toxic Substances Control Act (TSCA)
Pesticides	979	Federal Insecticide, Fungicide and Rodenticide Act (FIFRA)
Total Costs	100,167	

Note: These represent the costs of complying with all federal pollution control laws, assuming full implementation of the law (USEPA 1990).

In light of the preceding discussion, we review empirical work for four categories of nonmarket benefits: health, recreation, visibility, and ecological benefits. We also discuss the benefits of pollution control to agriculture.

1. The Health Benefits of Pollution Control. The statutes listed in Table 1 contribute to improved human health in several ways. By reducing exposure to carcinogens—in the air, in drinking water, and in food—environmental legislation reduces the probability of death at the end of a latency period—the time that it takes for cancerous cells to develop. Mortality benefits are also associated with control of noncarcinogenic air pollutants, which reduces mortality especially among sensitive persons in the population, e.g., angina sufferers or persons with chronic obstructive lung diseases. Lessening children's exposure to lead in gasoline or drinking water avoids learning disabilities and other neurological problems associated with lead poisoning. Finally, controlling air pollution reduces illness—ranging from minor respiratory symptoms associated with smog (runny nose, itchy eyes) to more serious respiratory infections, such as pneumonia and influenza. Water borne disease (e.g., giardiasis) may also cause acute illness.

Reductions in risk of death have been valued using three methods: averting behavior, hedonic analysis, and contingent valuation. The most common approach to valuing changes in risk of death due to environmental causes is hedonic wage studies. The results of these studies are typically expressed in terms of the value per "statistical life" saved. If reducing exposure to some substance reduces current probability of death by 10^{-5} for each of 200,000 persons in a population, it will save two statistical lives ($10^{-5} \times 200,000$). If each person is willing to pay \$20 for the 10^{-5} risk reduction, then the value of a statistical life is the sum of these willingnesses to pay ($\$20 \times 200,000$), divided by the number of statistical lives saved, or \$2,000,000.

Recent compensating wage studies (Ann Fisher, Daniel Violette, and Lauraine Chestnut 1989) generate mean estimates of the value of a statistical life that fall within an order of magnitude of one another: \$1.6 million to \$9 million (\$1986), with most studies yielding mean estimates between \$1.6 million and \$4.0 million. Contingent valuation studies that value reductions in job-related risk of death (Gerking, Menno DeHaan, and Schulze 1988) or reductions in risk of auto death (Jones-Lee, M. Hammerton, and P. R. Philips 1985) fall in the same range.

Averting behavior studies—based on seat belt use (Blomquist 1979) or the use of smoke detectors (Rachel Dardis 1980)—yield estimates of the value of a statistical life that are an order of magnitude lower than the studies cited above. These studies, however, estimate the value of a risk reduction for the person who just finds it worthwhile to undertake the averting activity. This is because buckling a seat belt or purchasing a smoke detector are 0-1 activities. They are undertaken provided that their marginal benefit equals *or exceeds* their marginal cost, with equality of marginal benefit and marginal cost holding only for the marginal purchaser. If 80 percent of all persons use smoke detectors, the value of the risk reduction to the marginal purchaser may be considerably lower than the mean value.

There are, however, other problems in using the indirect market approaches we have reviewed here to value changes in environmental risks. One problem is that the risks valued in labor market and averting behavior studies are more voluntary than many environmental risks. Work by Slovic, Baruch Fischhoff, and Sarah Lichtenstein (1980, 1982) suggests that willingness to pay estimates obtained in one context may not be transferable to the other. Second, death due to an industrial accident is often instantaneous, whereas death resulting from environmental contaminants may come from cancer and involve a long latency period. Deaths due to cancer thus occur in the future and cause fewer years of life to be lost than deaths in industrial accidents. At the same time, however, cancer is one of the most feared causes of death.

In a study designed to value reductions in chemical contaminants (trihalomethanes) in drinking water, Mitchell and Carson (1986) found that the former effect seems to be important: the value of a statistical life associated with a reduction in risk of death 30 years hence was only \$181,000 (\$1986). This is lower than the value of a statistical life associated with current risk of death for two reasons: (1) the number of expected life years lost is smaller if the risk occurs 20 years hence, and (2) the individual may discount the value of future life years lost (Cropper and Frances Sussman 1990; Cropper and Paul Portney 1990).

In spite of these difficulties, valuing mortality risks is an area in which economists have made important contributions. The notion that, ex ante, individuals are willing to spend only a certain amount to reduce risks to life makes possible rational debate and analysis in the policy arena over tradeoffs in risk reduction. Moreover, estimates of the value of a statistical life are in sufficiently close agreement to permit their use in actual benefit-cost calculations (subject, perhaps, to some sensitivity analysis).

The valuation of morbidity has been less successful. Estimates of the value of reductions in respiratory symptoms come from two sources: averting behavior studies and contingent valuation studies. The averting behavior approach has been used to value illnesses associated with both water and air pollution. It has been more successful in the case of water pollution because an averting behavior exists (buying bottled water) that is closely linked to water pollution (Abdalla 1990; Harrington, Krupnick, and Walter Spofford 1989). By contrast, the averting behaviors used to value air pollution—running an air-conditioner in one's home or car—are in most cases not undertaken primarily because of pollution. The use of doctor visits (purpose unspecified) to mitigate the effects of air pollution suffers from a similar shortcoming.

Contingent valuation studies of respiratory symptoms (coughing, wheezing, sinus congestion) have encountered two problems. The first concerns what is to be valued. Ideally, one would like to value a change in air pollution which, after defensive behavior is undertaken, might cause a change in the level of the symptom experienced. The individual's willingness to pay for the pollution change includes the value of the change in illness after mitigating behavior is undertaken, plus the cost of the mitigating behavior. This suggests that a symptom day be valued after mitigating actions have been taken. A second problem is that the respondent must be encouraged to consider carefully his budget constraint. Failure to handle these problems has led to unbelievably high average values of a symptom day. In more careful studies, mean willingness to pay to eliminate one day of coughing range from $1.39 ($1984) (Dickie et al. 1987) to $42.00 ($1984) (Edna Loehmann et al. 1979); for a day of sinus congestion $1.88 (Dickie et al.) to $52.00 (Loehmann et al.).

An alternative approach to valuing morbidity is to use the cost of illness—the cost of medical treatment plus lost earnings—which, as Harrington and Portney (1976) have shown, is a lower bound to willingness to pay for the change in illness. Mean willingness to pay for symptom reduction is usually three to four times higher than the traditional cost of illness. Berger et al. (1987) report a mean WTP of $27 to eliminate a day of sinus congestion, compared with an average cost of illness of $7. The corresponding figures for throat congestion are $44 and $14.

Studies of willingness to pay to reduce the risk of chronic disease are few (W. Kip Viscusi, Magat, and Joel Huber 1988, is a notable exception), and cost of illness estimates are more prevalent in valuing chronic illness (Ann Bartel and Paul Taubman 1979; Barbara Cooper and Dorothy Rice 1976). Viscusi, Magat, and Huber estimate the value of a statistical case of chronic bronchitis to be $883,000, approximately one-third of the value of a statistical life. This may be contrasted with cost of illness estimates of $200,000 per case of chronic lung disease (Cropper and Krupnick 1989).

As the preceding discussion indicates, more work is needed in the area of both morbidity and mortality valuation. Because of the difficulty in finding activities that mitigate the effects of air pollution, contingent valuation studies would seem to be a more promising approach to valuing morbidity. If new studies are done, they should value combinations of symptoms rather than individual symptoms, since pollution exposures often trigger multiple symptoms, and since the value of jointly reducing several symptoms is generally less than the sum of the values of individual symptom reductions. In the case of mortality risks, more refined estimates are needed that take into account the timing of the risk, the degree of voluntariness, and the cause of death. The timing issue is especially crucial here: the benefits of environmental programs to reduce exposure to carcinogens, such as asbestos, are not realized until the end of a latency period—perhaps 40 years in the case of asbestos. Since the exposed population is 40 years older, fewer life-years are saved, compared with programs that save lives immediately.[47]

2. The Recreation Benefits of Pollution Control. Reductions in water pollution may enhance the quality of recreation experiences by allowing (or improving) swimming, boating, or fishing. Most studies of the recreation benefits of water pollution control have focused on fishing-related benefits, and it is on them that we concentrate our attention.

Travel cost studies have taken one of three approaches to valuing the fishing benefits of improved water quality. In some studies (V. Kerry Smith and Desvousges 1986a), measures of water quality such as dissolved oxygen are valued directly. That is, water quality variables directly enter equations that describe the choice of recreation site or demand functions for site visits.[48] This approach is clearly useful if one wishes to link the valuation study to pollution control policies, such as policies to reduce biochemical oxygen demand (BOD), a measure of the oxygen required to neutralize organic waste. A second approach is to relate site visits (or choice of site) to fish catch. Fish catch is clearly more closely associated with motives for visiting a site than is dissolved oxygen; however, it must be linked to changes in the fish population, which must, in turn, be linked to changes in ambient water quality.

A third approach is to treat changes in water quality as effectively eliminating or creating recreation sites. This approach has been used in valuing the effects of acid rain on fishing in Adirondack lakes: reductions in

---

[47]While some studies have attempted to take the latency period and number of life-years saved into account (Josephine Mauskopf 1987), this is not the general practice (Cropper and Portney 1990).

[48]This approach is also used when the recreation activity studied is swimming or viewing, activities where perceptions of water quality are likely to be linked to water clarity and odor. It has, for example, been applied in studies of beach visits in Boston (Bockstael, Hanemann, and Kling 1987) and lake visits in Wisconsin (George Parsons and Kealy 1990).

pH below certain thresholds have been treated as eliminating acres of surface area for fishing of particular species (John Mullen and Frederic Menz 1985). It is also the approach used by Vaughan and Russell (1982) in valuing the benefits of the Clean Water Act. They treat the benefits of moving all point sources to the Best Practical Control Technology Currently Available (BPT) as an increase in the number of acres of surface water that support game fish (bass, trout) as opposed to rough fish (carp, catfish). The Clean Water Act is thus viewed as increasing the number of recreation sites, rather than raising fish catch at existing sites.

Regardless of the form of water recreation valued, an improvement in water quality has two effects: it increases the utility of people who currently use the resource, and it may increase participation rates (number of days spent fishing). Varying parameter models that value changes in water quality or fish catch using the shift in demand for site visits (see Figure 2) capture both effects. Discrete choice models measure the effect of a quality improvement on a given recreation day, but do not estimate the effect of quality changes on the total number of days spent fishing; however, these models are typically used in conjunction with models that predict the total number of trips. Treating changes in water quality as altering the supply of available sites captures participation effects but not improvements in quality at existing sites.

In addition to travel cost models, contingent valuation studies have been used to value improvements in fish catch or water quality. Because it is difficult to ask consumers to value changes in dissolved oxygen levels or fecal coliform count—another measure of water quality—without linking these water quality measures to the type of activities they support, many CVM studies use the RFF Water Quality Ladder (Vaughan and Russell 1982), which relates a water quality index to the type of water use—boating, fishing (rough fish), fishing (game fish), swimming—that can be supported by various levels of the index. It is these activity levels that are valuated by respondents. The water quality ladder has been used both to value water quality at specific sites (e.g., the Monongahela River, by V. Kerry Smith and Desvousges 1986a) and at all sites throughout the country (Carson and Mitchell 1988).

It is interesting to compare estimates of the value of water quality improvements obtained by the travel cost and contingent valuation approaches. Carson and Mitchell (1988) report that households are, on average, willing to pay $80 per year (in 1983 dollars) for an improvement in water quality throughout the U.S. from boatable to fishable (capable of supporting game fish). V. Kerry Smith and Desvousges (1986a) report a mean value of $25 per household for the same improvement in a five-county region in western Pennsylvania. The difference between these estimates reflects the fact that non-use values are important: households care about clean water in areas where they do not live. Even the $25 estimate for western Pennsylvania reflects nonuse values, since only one-third of the households surveyed engaged in some form of water based recreation.

Because they do not capture nonuse values, travel cost estimates of the value of improving water quality are not directly comparable with those obtained using the CVM. Using a varying parameter model, V. Kerry Smith and Desvousges (1986a) find the value of an improvement in water quality from boatable to fishable to be between $0.06 and $30.00 per person per day ($1983) for 30 Army Corps of Engineers sites. This value may be contrasted with estimates of $5 to $10 per person per day ($1983) obtained by Vaughan and Russell.

The preceding discussion suggests two problems that arise in valuing water quality benefits that do not arise in valuing health effects. The first is an aggregation problem. Suppose that one wishes to value the benefits of water quality improvements in a river basin, and suppose that the travel cost approach is used to measure use values associated with an improvement in dissolved oxygen or fish catch. The nonuse values associated with these improvements could be measured using a contingent valuation study. However, while the responses of nonusers could be added to values obtained from the travel cost approach, it would, in practice, be hard to separate use from nonuse values in the responses of fishermen.

The second problem is one of transferring results from a water quality study done in one geographic area to another area. While one can easily control for differences in willingness to pay in the two regions associated with differences in income and population, the value of water quality improvements is also likely to vary with the particular aesthetic and other characteristics of the region—and such characteristics are intrinsically hard to measure. Thus, whereas one can value a day of coughing independently of location, it is harder to value a generic fishing day.

This raises important questions concerning priorities for research in the area of recreation benefits.[49] Future research can proceed using a contingent valuation approach in which use and nonuse values are elicited simultaneously for sites in the respondent's region. The problem here is to have the respondent value an improvement to recreation that is sufficiently specific that it can be related to changes in pH levels from acid rain or changes in levels of dissolved oxygen associated with the adoption of BPT. The advantage of this approach is that it would capture both use and nonuse values. The advantage of the travel cost approach is that it could use endpoints more closely related to pollution (such as dissolved oxygen); however, it would not yield estimates of nonuse values.

3. The Visibility Benefits of Pollution Control. Reductions in air pollution, by increasing visibility, may improve the quality of life in urban areas as well as at recreation sites. Since the number of persons affected by improvements in visibility is large—at least as great as the number of persons whose health is affected by air pollution—the potential value of such benefits is great.

One can view the results of hedonic property value studies performed in the 1970s and early 1980s as evidence that people value the visibility

---

[49]It should be emphasized that, while there exist several dozen studies of water quality benefits in a recreation context, many studies analyze the same data. Thus, empirical estimates of water quality benefits exist for only a few areas of the country—lakes in Wisconsin and the Adirondacks, beaches in Boston and on the Chesapeake Bay, recreation sites in western Pennsylvania.

benefits of pollution control. In these studies housing prices were regressed on measures of ambient air quality such as particulates or sulfates, which are negatively correlated with visibility. The studies, most of which found significant negative effects of air pollution on housing prices, thus provide indirect evidence that people are willing to pay for improved visibility.[50] For example, John Trijonis et al. (1984) estimated based on differences in housing prices that households in San Francisco were willing, on average, to pay $200 per year for a 10 percent improvement in visibility.

The difficulty in using these studies to estimate benefits, however, is that the coefficient of air pollution (or visibility) captures all reasons why households may prefer to live in nonpolluted areas—including both improved health and reduced soiling. Indeed, the reason why property value studies have become less popular as a method of valuing the benefits of pollution control is that it is difficult to know what the pollution coefficient captures and, therefore, difficult to aggregate benefit estimates obtained from these studies with those obtained from other approaches. Such aggregation is necessary because residential property value studies capture benefits only at home and not at the other locations the household frequents.

For these reasons contingent valuation seems the most promising method for valuing visibility. Because visibility benefits vary regionally, CVM studies can most usefully be classified according to whether they measure urban visibility benefits or benefits at recreation sites, and according to whether the locations studied are in the Eastern or in the Western United States. The former distinction is important because visibility benefits at recreation sites—especially national parks—are likely to have a substantial nonuse component; consequently, the relevant population for which benefits are computed may be considerably larger than for urban visibility benefits. The East/West distinction is important both because of differences in baseline visibility and because of qualitative differences in the nature of visibility impairments, e.g., haze versus brown cloud.

There are two key problems in any contingent valuation study of visibility. One is presenting changes in visibility that are both meaningful to the respondent and that can be related to pollution control polices. The other is separating the respondent's valuation of health effects from his valuation of visibility changes.

Most CVM studies define increased visibility as an improvement in visual range—the distance at which a large, black object disappears from view. Visual range is both correlated with people's perceptions of visibility and with ambient concentrations of certain pollutants (fine nitrate and sulfate aerosols). Differences in visual range are presented in a series of pictures in which all other conditions—weather, brightness, the objects photographed—are, ideally, kept constant.

It has long been recognized (Brookshire et al. 1979) that, in responding to such pictures, people assume that the health effects of pollution diminish as visibility improves. Health effects are therefore inherently diffi-

---

[50]Freeman (1979a) provides an excellent summary of early studies.

cult to separate from visibility changes. The best way to handle this problem is to ask respondents what they assume health effects to be and then to control for these effects.

Unfortunately, existing CVM studies of visibility benefits—especially those for urban areas—have failed to treat the issues raised above in a satisfactory manner. With this limitation in mind, it is nonetheless of interest to contrast the magnitude of benefits associated with improvements in urban air quality with estimates obtained from hedonic property value studies. Studies of visibility improvements in eastern U.S. cities (Tolley et al. 1986a; Douglas Rae 1984) have estimated that households would pay approximately $26 annually for a 10 percent improvement in visibility.[51] Loehmann Boldt, D., and Chaikin, K. (1981) reports an annual average willingness to pay per household of $101 for a 10 percent improvement in visibility in San Francisco. Both figures are considerably lower than estimates implied by property value studies.

Studies in recreation areas have focused on major national parks, including the Grand Canyon (Decision Focus 1990; Schulze and Brookshire 1983), because of the possibility of large nonuse values attached to visibility benefits at these sites. Two conclusions emerge from these studies. First, nonuse values appear to be large relative to use values. Use values associated with an improvement in visibility at the Grand Canyon from 70 to 100 miles are under $2.00 per visitor party per day ($1988) (Schulze and Brookshire 1983; K. K. MacFarland et al. 1983). By contrast, Schulze and Brookshire found that a random sample of households were willing to pay $95 per year ($1988) to prevent a deterioration in visibility at the Grand Canyon from the 50th percentile to the 25th percentile.

Second, the embedding, or superadditivity, problem is potentially quite serious. This refers to the fact that, in general, an individual's willingness to pay for simultaneous improvements in visibility at several sites should be less than the sum of his willingness to pay for isolated improvements at each site (Hoehn and Randall 1989). In a follow-up study to Schulze and Brookshire (1983), Tolley et al. (1986a) found respondents were willing to pay only $22 annually for the same visibility improvement at the Grand Canyon when this was valued at the same time as visibility improvements in Chicago (the site of the interviews) and throughout the East coast.

4. The Ecological Benefits of Pollution Control.[52] By the ecological benefits of pollution control, we mean reduced pollution of animal and plant habitats, such as rivers, lakes, and wetlands. Because the benefits of clean water to recreational fisherman or larger populations of deer to hunters

---

[51]This figure, reported by Chestnut and Rowe (1989), is an average of mean willingness to pay for each city surveyed by Tolley and Rae, based on Chestnut and Rowe's reanalysis of the data.

[52]Outside environmental economics, there is a considerable literature in environmental ethics that explores the issue of nonhuman rights and their policy implications. From this perspective, the economist's benefit-cost calculation with its wholly anthropocentric orientation is an excessively narrow and illegitimate framework for analysis. Kneese and Schulze (1985) provide an excellent treatment of this set of issues.

are captured in recreation studies, the benefits discussed in this section are the nonuse benefits associated with reduced pollution of ecosystems.

It should be clear to the reader that valuing this category of benefits poses serious conceptual problems. One is defining the commodity to be valued. Does one value reductions in pollution concentrations, increases in animal populations, or some more subtle index of the health of an ecosystem? Two approaches can be taken here. The "top down" approach asks the respondent to value the preservation of an ecosystem, such as 100 acres of wetland (John Whitehead and Blomquist 1991). The "bottom up" approach values the preservation of particular species inhabiting the wetland, such as geese and other birds.

Regardless of the approach taken, several problems must be faced. One difficulty is defining what substitutes are assumed to exist, whether for a particular species or for a wetland (Whitehead and Blomquist 1991). Presumably the value placed on the preservation of 10,000 geese depends on the size of the goose population. A related problem arises when programs are valued one at a time; in general, the value attached to preserving several species at the same time is less than the sum of the values attached to preserving each species in isolation. This implies that the totality of what is to be preserved should be valued: one cannot compute this by summing the values attached to individual components.

To date, most studies of endangered species have valued individual species in isolation. For example, Bowker and Stoll (1988) estimate that households are, on average, willing to pay $22 per year ($1983) to preserve the whooping crane, while Boyle and Bishop (1987) find that non-eagle watchers are willing to spend $11 per year to preserve the bald eagle in the state of Wisconsin. These values are appropriate if one is considering a program to preserve either of these species in isolation; however, the values should not be added together if one is contemplating preserving both species.

Even if one decides to value a wetland (of given size) and defines the nature of substitutes, an important question remains: do people really have well-defined, or in the terminology of psychologists, "crystallized" values for these commodities? Since respondents in CVM studies are likely to be less familiar with ecological benefits than with health and recreation benefits, responses are likely to depend critically on the information given to respondents in the survey itself (Karl Samples, John Dixon, and Marcia Gown 1986). This problem, however, is widely recognized and recent studies have taken pains to see how responses are influenced by the amount of information provided.

5. The Agricultural Benefits of Pollution Control. Although we have emphasized the nonmarket benefits of pollution control, some benefits accrue directly to firms, and can be measured by examining shifts in the supply curves for the affected outputs. The industries that are most subject to ambient air and water pollution are forestry, fishing, and agriculture. We focus on agriculture because it is the sector that is likely to experience the largest benefits from pollution control.

Reductions in ozone concentrations and, possibly, in acid rain, should increase the yields of field crops such as soybeans, corn, and wheat. In addition, reductions in greenhouse gases, to the extent that they prevent increases in temperature and decreases in precipitation in certain areas, should also increase crop yields.

In measuring the effects on agricultural output of changes in pollution concentrations or climate, two approaches can be taken. The damage function approach translates a change in environmental conditions into a yield change, assuming that farmers take no action to mitigate the effects of the change. The yield change shifts the supply curve for the crop in question, and the corresponding changes in consumer and producer surpluses are calculated.[53] This is the predominant approach used thus far to analyze the effects of global climate change (Sally Kane, John Reilly, and Tobey 1991). It has also been used in some studies of the effects of ozone on field crops (Richard Adams, Thomas Crocker, and Richard Katz 1984; Raymond Kopp et al. 1985; Kopp and Krupnick 1987).

The averting behavior approach allows farmers to adjust to the change in pollution/climate by altering their input mix and/or by adjusting the number of acres planted. In some applications, a profit function is estimated in which the environmental pollutant enters as a parameter (James Mjelde et al. 1984; Philip Garcia et al. 1986). The value of the change in Q can then be computed directly from the profit function. If the resulting shift in supply is big enough to alter market price, the welfare effects of these price changes must also be computed.

A more common approach is to solve for the effect of the change in pollution on output using a mathematical programming model whose coefficients have not been econometrically estimated (Adams, Scott Hamilton, and Bruce McCarl 1986; Scott Hamilton, McCarl, and Adams 1985). The effect of output changes on price is then computed separately.

While benefit estimates that allow farmers to adjust to changes in pollution are clearly preferable on theoretical grounds to estimates that do not allow such adjustments, it is important to ask how much of a difference this is likely to make empirically, especially as the damage function approach is much easier to implement. For changes in temperature and precipitation, damages are likely to be greatly overstated if opportunities for mitigating behavior (e.g., irrigation) are ignored.[54] On the other hand, mitigating behavior does not seem to make a great deal of difference in the case of ozone damage (Scott Hamilton, McCarl, and Adams 1985).

Estimates of annual damage to field crops from a 25 percent increase in ozone are in the neighborhood of $2 billion ($1980)—not negligible, but

---

[53]In calculating the welfare of a shift in supply, one must be careful to take into account the effects of agricultural price support programs, which distort market prices. See Erik Lichtenberg and David Zilberman (1986).

[54]We base this statement on the results of the RFF MINK project (Norman Rosenberg et al. 1990), which examines damages associated with climate change—specifically, a return to the climate of the dust bowl—in Missouri, Iowa, Nebraska, and Kentucky, under alternate adjustment scenarios.

small relative to estimates of health damages. It is also interesting to note that most of these damages are borne by consumers. Producers in most cases gain from yield decreases due to the resulting increases in prices!

Kane, Reilly, and Tobey (1991) obtain similar results when estimating the welfare effects of global climate change on agriculture: reductions in the yields of field crops (wheat, corn, soybeans, and rice) in the U.S., Canada, China, and the USSR benefit producers worldwide due to increases in commodity prices. Consumers, however, lose. Thus, although the aggregate losses to producers and consumers worldwide are small (about one-half of one percent of world GDP), food-importing countries such as China suffer large welfare losses (equal to 5.5 percent of GDP) while food exporters such as Argentina enjoy welfare gains.

E. Measuring the Costs of Pollution Control

Table 1, which lists the costs of the major environmental statutes, may give the reader the impression that measuring the costs of pollution control is a straightforward matter. Such is not the case.

To begin with, the costs of pollution control must be measured using the same concepts that are used to measure the benefits of pollution control: the change in consumer and producer surpluses associated with the regulations and with any price and/or income changes that may result. The figures in Table 1 represent, for the most part, expenditures on cleaner fuels or abatement control equipment by firms. They do not represent the change in firms' profits, and thus ignore any adjustments firms may make to these expenditures. The figures also ignore the price and output effects associated with reducing emissions. At the very least, one would want to take into account the price changes likely to result within a sector because of environmental regulations—for example, one would want to measure the welfare effects of an increase in electricity prices resulting from the 10 million ton reduction in SO_2 emissions by electric utilities projected under the 1990 Amendments to the Clean Air Act.

We note that, at least in the short run, the effect of ignoring these adjustments is to overstate the cost of environmental regulations. Abatement expenditures overstate the loss in firms' profits if firms can pass on part of their cost increase to consumers. Consumers in turn can avoid some of the welfare effects of price increases of "dirty" goods by substituting "clean" goods for "dirty" ones.

When environmental regulations affect sectors, such as electricity production, that are important producers of intermediate goods, it may be important to measure the impacts that environmental regulations have throughout the economy. Computable general equilibrium models, preferably those in which supply and demand functions have been econometrically estimated, may be needed to measure correctly the social costs of environmental regulation.

Michael Hazilla and Kopp (1990) have used an econometrically estimated CGE model of the U.S. economy to compute the social costs of the

Clean Air and Clean Water Acts, as implemented in 1981. The effects of these regulations on firms are modeled as an upward shift in firms' cost functions, to which firms can adjust by altering their choice of inputs and outputs. It is interesting to contrast the estimates of social costs obtained from this approach with EPA's estimates of compliance costs. The EPA estimated the costs of complying with the Clean Air and Clean Water Acts in 1981 to be $42.5 billion (1981 dollars). Hazill and Kopp estimate the costs to be $28.3 billion; the lower figure reflects the substitution possibilities that the expenditure approach ignores.

In the long run, however, the social costs of the Clean Air and Clean Water Acts exceed simple expenditure estimates because of the effects of decreases in income on saving and investment. In their analysis of the effects of environmental regulation on U.S. economic growth, Dale Jorgenson and Peter Wilcoxen (1990a) measure this effect. Using a CGE model of the U.S. economy, they estimate that mandated pollution controls reduced the rate of GNP growth by .191 percentage points per annum over the period 1973–85.

V. The Costs and Benefits of Environmental Programs

The value of a symptom-day or a statistical life is, of course, only one component in evaluating a pollution control strategy. To translate unit benefit values into the benefits of an environmental program requires three steps: (1) the emissions reduction associated with the program must be related to changes in ambient air or water quality; (2) the change in ambient environmental quality must be related to health or other outcomes through a dose-response function; (3) the health or nonhealth outcomes must be valued. The information required for the first two tasks is considerable, especially if one wants to evaluate a major piece of legislation such as the Clean Air Act or Clean Water Act.

In this section we review attempts to estimate the benefits and costs of environmental programs. Of central interest are cases in which benefit-cost analyses have actually been used in setting environmental standards; in addition, we discuss instances in which such analyses have not been used but should be. This leads naturally to a discussion of priorities for research in the area of benefit and cost measurement.

A. The Use of Benefit-Cost Analysis in Setting Environmental Standards

Executive Order 12291, signed in 1981, requires that benefit-cost analyses be performed for all major regulations (defined as those having annual costs in excess of $100 million). Furthermore, the order requires, *to the extent permitted by law*, that regulations be undertaken only if the benefits to society exceed the costs.

One consequence of Executive Order 12291 is the undertaken of benefit-cost analyses for all major environmental regulations; however, the extent to which benefits and costs can be considered in making regulations is limited by the enabling statutes. Of the major environmental statutes only two, the Toxic Substances Control Act (TSCA) and the Federal Insecticide, Fungicide, and Rodenticide Act (FIFRA) explicitly require that benefits and costs be weighed in setting standards.[55] Some standards—specifically, those pertaining to new sources under the Clean Air Act and to the setting of effluent limitations under the Clean Water Act—allow costs to be taken into account, but do not suggest that benefits and costs be balanced at the margin. In contrast, the National Ambient Air Quality Standards and regulations for the disposal of hazardous waste under RCRA and CERCLA are to be made without regard to compliance costs.

In spite of these limitations, benefit-cost analyses have been used in EPA's rulemaking process since 1981. Between February of 1981 and February of 1986, EPA issued 18 major rules (USEPA 1987), including reviews of National Ambient Air Quality Standards for three pollutants—nitrogen dioxide, particulate matter, and carbon monoxide—effluent standards for water pollutants in the iron and steel and chemicals and plastics industries and regulations to ban lead in gasoline, as well as certain uses of asbestos.[56] Regulatory Impact Analyses (RIAs) were prepared for 15 of these rules.

In five of the RIAs, both benefits and costs were monetized; however, benefits could legally be compared with costs only in the case of lead in gasoline. In this case, the benefits in terms of engine maintenance alone were judged to exceed the costs by $6.7 billion over the period 1985–92, and the regulation was issued. In two other cases—the PM standard and effluent limitations for iron and steel plants—the benefits exceeded the costs of the proposed regulation and the regulation was implemented, although EPA denied that it weighed benefits against costs in reaching its decision. The remaining cases are more difficult to evaluate. The clean water benefits of proposed effluent guidelines for chemicals and plastics manufacturers were judged to exceed regulatory costs in some sections of the country but not in others. EPA recommended that these guidelines be implemented. Of several alternative standards for emissions of particulate matter by surface coal mines, only one was found to yield positive net benefits, and these were small ($300,000). Eventually, no regulation was issued by EPA.

The preceding review suggests that benefit-cost analysis has not entirely been ignored in setting environmental standards, but its use has been selective. In part, this is the result of law—EPA was allowed to weigh benefits against costs for only 5 of the 18 major regulations that its issued be-

---

[55]Some portions of the Clean Air Act, specifically, those pertaining to aircraft emissions, motor vehicle standards and fuel standards, also require that marginal benefits and costs be balanced.

[56]A complete listing of the regulations may be found in USEPA (1987). Also included were regulations governing the disposal of used oil, and standards regarding land disposal of hazardous waste.

tween 1981 and 1986.[57] One could argue that the government should not invest sources in a full blown benefit-cost analysis if the results of such an analysis cannot be used in regulating the polluting activity. But this would be a mistake. Even where the explicit use of a benefit-cost test is prohibited, such studies can be informative and useful. In their own way, they are likely to influence the views of legislators and regulators. In particular, the issue is often one of amending standards—either raising them or lowering them. Benefit-cost information on such adjustments, although not formally admissible, may well have some impact on decisions to revise standards. In addition, simply demonstrating the feasibility and potential application of such studies may lead to their explicit introduction into the policy process at a later time.

B. The Need for Benefit-Cost Analyses of Environmental Standards

We turn now to a set of priorities for benefit-cost analyses of environmental regulation: which of existing environmental programs require closest scrutiny and what benefit techniques must be developed in order to perform these analyses? We begin with an enumeration of these programs, as we see them, and then offer some thoughts on the analysis of each of them.

There are, broadly, two areas in which careful benefit-cost analyses are most needed. One is for statutes whose total costs are thought to exceed their total benefits. A widely cited example is the Clean Water Act (CWA), which will soon be up for renewal. Freeman (1982) suggests that the recreational use values associated with the adoption of BPT are small, relative to the costs presented in Table 1. Justification for these standards must then rest on other grounds. A second example where costs may exceed benefits involves the extent of cleanup of Superfund sites under CERCLA. While the cost of cleaning up these sites is predicted to run into the hundreds of billions of dollars, the health benefits of these cleanups are thought by many to be modest (Curtis Travis and Carolyn Doty 1989). Current law does not require an explicit benefit-cost analysis of remedial alternatives at each Superfund site, but, in our view, it probably should.

The second general class of cases in which careful benefit-cost analyses are needed is where environmental standards are sufficiently stringent to push control efforts onto the steep portion of the marginal cost of abatement curve. Even though the total costs of these standards may exceed their total benefits (see Figure 4), society might experience a gain in welfare from relaxing the standard if the marginal benefits of abatement are considerably below the marginal costs of the level of the standard. In terms of Figure 4, we need to know whether the marginal benefit function is MB_2 or

---

[57]For the other four regulations where a comparison of costs and benefits was allowed—the three toxic substances (TSCA) regulations and the setting of emission standards for light duty trucks—benefits were quantified but not monetized. In the case of PCB's the cost per catastrophe avoided was computed; in the case of asbestos, the cost per life saved.

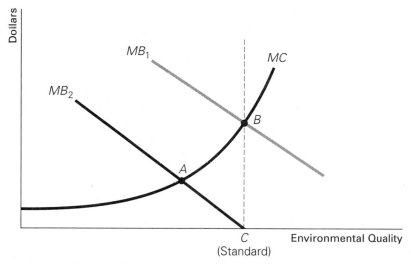

Figure 4 Welfare Loss from Setting Incorrect Standards

MB_1. There are several instances of actual policies that appear to fall within this class: (1) the ground-level ozone standard, in areas that are currently out of compliance with the standard; (2) certain provisions in RCRA for disposal of hazardous waste; and (3) the 1990 acid rain amendments to the Clean Air Act. In addition to these existing laws, proposals for significant reductions in CO_2 emissions may entail high marginal costs, suggesting a close scrutiny of benefits.

Turning first to the Clean Water Act, we note that evaluating the CWA will require computing the use (recreation) and nonuse (ecological) benefits of improved water quality. As we noted above, one can either use a contingent valuation approach that captures both values, or one can attempt to capture use values using travel cost methods and measure nonuse values separately. Whichever approach is used, we emphasize the regional character of the costs and benefits of improved water quality; benefit estimates must, in consequence, be available at this level of disaggregation. The contingent valuation method avoids two problems inherent in the use of travel cost models. First, unless the transferability problem can be solved, travel cost models will have to be estimated for each river or lake throughout the U.S.! And, second, if a contingent valuation survey of nonuse values is to be added to travel cost measures of use values, it may be hard to get users to separate use from nonuse values.

A key issue in valuing the benefits of Superfund cleanups is how to value health risks—usually risks of cancer—that will not occur until the distant future. Many Superfund sites pose very low health risks today, primarily because there is no current route of exposure to toxic waste. People could, however, be exposed to contaminated soils or groundwater if substances were to leak from storage containers in the future. This involves valuing future risks to persons currently alive as well as to persons yet unborn. While some research has been done in this area (Mauskopf 1987; Cropper and Portney 1990; Cropper and Sussman 1990), there are few empirical studies that examine either the value that people place on reducing future risks to themselves or the rate at which they discount lives saved in future generations. Estimates of these values are also crucial if one is to analyze regulations governing the current disposal of hazardous waste under RCRA, as well as other regulations that affect exposure to carcinogens (e.g., air toxics and pesticide regulations).

An additional problem is how to incorporate uncertainty regarding estimates of health risks into the analysis. While most valuation studies treat the probability of an adverse outcome as certain, in reality there is great uncertainty about health risks, especially the risk of contracting cancer from exposure to environmental carcinogens. This uncertainty has two sources: uncertainty about actual exposures received, and uncertainty about the effects of a given exposure.[58] The standard procedure in risk assessments is to "correct" for this uncertainty by presenting a point estimate based on very conservative assumptions (Nichols and Richard Zeckhauser 1986). It would, however, be more appropriate to incorporate the distribution of cancer risk into the analysis.

Existing estimates of the marginal costs and marginal benefits of achieving the one-hour ozone standard in areas that are currently out of attainment suggest that marginal costs exceed marginal benefits (Krupnick and Portney 1991). Estimates of the health benefits of ozone control have, however, focused on the value of reducing restricted-activity or symptom days. There is some evidence that ozone may exacerbate the rate at which lung tissue deteriorates, contributing to chronic obstructive lung disease (COPD). Since, for healthy individuals, the probability of contracting COPD is uncertain, what must be valued is a change in the risk of contracting chronic lung disease corresponding to a change in ozone concentration.

The objective of the provisions of the 1990 Amendments to the Clean Air Act aimed at reducing SO_2 and NO_2 is to reduce acid rain, primarily in the Eastern U.S. and Canada. Although the 10-million-ton reduction in sulfur emissions specified in the amendments is likely to have some health benefits, most of the anticipated benefits are ecological or recreational, resulting from an increase in the pH of lakes.[59] There are also likely to be visibility benefits (reduced haze) in the Eastern U.S. This underscores the need for better estimates of the value of improved visibility, especially in urban areas. It will also be necessary to measure the ecological benefits associated with reduced acid rain, especially as these are likely to differ qualitatively from the ecological benefits associated with the CWA.

---

[58]Estimates of the effect of a given exposure usually come from rodent bioassays, which are used to estimate a dose-response function. In addition to uncertainty regarding the parameters of the dose-response function, there is uncertainty as to how these estimates should be extrapolated from rodents to man.

[59]For a dissenting view see Portney (1990).

Finally, we note that in the area of global climate change, considerable attention has been devoted to measuring the costs of reducing greenhouse gas emissions, especially through the use of a tax on the carbon content of fuels (Jorgenson and Wilcoxen 1990b). Little, however, is known about the benefits of reducing greenhouse gases, even if one assumes that the link between CO_2 and climate change is certain.[60]

The benefits of preventing these climate changes differ from the benefits associated with conventional air and water pollutants in two respects. First, many—though by no means all—of the effects of climate change are likely to occur through markets. These include effects on agriculture and forestry, as well as changes in heating and cooling costs. While this should make benefits easier to measure, the problem is that the effects of CO_2 emissions are not likely to be felt for decades. This implies that valuing such damages is difficult. A damage function approach, which ignores adaptation possibilities, is clearly inappropriate; however, predicting technological possibilities for adaptation is not easy.

Second, the benefits of reducing greenhouse gases will not be felt until the next century. The problem here is that, even at a discount rate of only 3 percent, one dollar of benefits received 100 years from now is worth only 5 cents today. This problem has typically been addressed by suggesting that benefits should be discounted at a very low rate, if at all. An alternative approach is to make transfers to future generations to compensate them for our degradation of the environment, rather than to alter the discount rate.

C. The Distribution of Costs and Benefits

In addition to examining the costs and benefits of environmental legislation, it is of interest to know who pays for pollution abatement and who benefits from it. Typically, studies of the distributional effects of environmental programs emphasize the distribution of benefits and costs by income class.

To determine how the benefits of environmental programs are distributed across different income classes, we must measure how the programs alter the physical environments of different income groups. In one study of the distributional effects of programs aimed at raising the level of national air quality, Leonard Gianessi, Peskin, and Edward Wolff (1979) found striking locational differentials in benefits; not surprisingly, most of the benefits from efforts to improve air quality are concentrated in the more industrialized urban areas (largely the heavily industrialized cities of the East) with fewer benefits accruing to rural residents. Even within metropolitan areas, air quality may differ substantially. Since the poor often live in the most polluted parts of urban areas, they might be thought to be disproportionately large beneficiaries of programs that reduce air pollution—

---

[60]A useful beginning here is the work of William Nordhaus (1990).

and there is evidence that this is, indeed, the case (Asch and Seneca 1978; Jeffrey Zupan 1973). While this may be true, certain indirect effects can follow that offset such benefits. For example, cleaner air in what was a relatively dirty area may increase the demand for residences there and drive up rents, thereby displacing low-income renters. All in all, this is a complicated issue. At any rate, Gianessi, Peskin, and Wolff find that within urban areas the distribution of benefits may be slightly pro-poor, but, as we shall see next, this is likely to be offset (or more than offset) by a regressive pattern of the costs of these programs.[61]

We are on somewhat more solid ground on the distribution of the costs of environmental programs (G. B. Christainsen and Tietenberg 1985). There exist data on the costs of pollution control by industry with which one can estimate how costs have influenced the prices of various classes of products and how, in turn, these increased prices have reduced the real incomes of different income classes. In one early study of this kind, Gianessi, Peskin, and Wolff (1979) examined the distributive pattern of the costs of the Clean Air Act and found that lower-income groups bear costs that constitute a larger fraction of their income than do higher-income classes. (See also Nancy Dorfman and Arthur Snow 1975; Gianessi and Peskin 1980.) Three independent studies of automobile pollution control costs all reach similar findings of regressivity (Dorfman and Snow 1975; Harrison 1975; Freeman 1979b).

In a more recent study, Robison (1985) uses an input-output model to estimate the distribution of costs of industrial pollution abatement. Assuming that the costs of pollution control in each industry are passed on in the form of higher prices, Robison traces these price increases through the input-output matrix to determine their impact on the pattern of consumer prices. Robison's model divides individuals into twenty income classes. For each class, estimates are available of the pattern of consumption among product groups. This information, together with predictions of price increases for each product, is used to estimate the increase in the prices of goods consumed by each income group. Robison finds that the incidence of control costs is quite regressive. Costs as a fraction of income fall over the entire range of income classes; they vary from 0.76 percent of income for the lower income class to 0.16 percent of income for the highest income class.

It is true that these studies relate to existing environmental programs and do not measure directly the potential distributional effects of a system of economic incentives such as effluent fees. But our sense is that the pattern of control costs across industries would be roughly similar under existing and incentive-based programs. It is the same industries under both regimes that will have to undertake the bulk of the abatement measures. Our conjecture thus is that the pattern of costs for our major environmental programs is likely to be distinctly regressive in its incidence, be they of the command-and-control or incentive-based variety.

---

[61]Moreover, there is some persuasive evidence from observed voting patterns on proposed environmental measures (Robert Deacon and Perry Shapiro 1975; Fischel 1979) indicating that higher income individuals are willing to pay more for a cleaner environment than those with lower incomes.

While the distributional effects of environmental programs may not be altogether salutary, we do not wish to exaggerate their importance. We emphasize that the primary purpose of environmental programs is, in economic terms, an efficient allocation of resources. Environmental measures, as Freeman (1972) has stressed, are not very well suited to the achievement of redistributional objectives. But an improved environment provides important benefits for all income classes—and we will be doing no groups a favor by opposing environmental programs on distributional grounds. At the same time, there are opportunities to soften some of the more objectionable redistributive consequences of environmental policies through the use of measures like adjustment assistance for individuals displaced from jobs in heavily polluting industries and the reliance on the more progressive forms of taxation to finance public spending on pollution control programs.

VI. Environmental Economics and Environmental Policy: Some Reflections

As suggested by the lengthy (and only partial) list of references and citations in this survey, environmental economics has been a busy field over the past two decades. Environmental economists have reworked existing theory, making it more rigorous and clearing up a number of ambiguities; they have devised new methods for the valuation of benefits from improved environmental quality; and they have undertaken numerous empirical studies to measure the costs and benefits of actual or proposed environmental programs and to assess the relative efficiency of incentive-based and CAC policies. In short, the "intellectual structure" of environmental economics has been both broadened and strengthened since the last survey of the field by Fisher and Peterson in this *Journal* in 1976.

But what about the contribution of environmental economics to the design and implementation of environmental policy? This is not an easy question to answer. We have seen some actual programs of transferable emissions permits in the United States and some use of effluent charges in Europe. And with the enactment of the 1990 Amendments to the Clean Air Act, the U.S. has introduced a major program of tradable allowances to control sulfur emissions—moving this country squarely into the use of incentive-based approaches to regulation in at least one area of environmental policy.[62] But,

---

[62]Under this provision, the U.S. will address the acid rain problem by cutbacks in sulfur emissions over the next decade of 10 million tons (about a 50 percent reduction). This is to be accomplished through a system of tradable allowances under which affected power plants will be allowed to meet their emissions reductions by whatever means they choose—including the purchase of "excess" emissions reductions from other sources that choose to cut back by more than their required quota. Also noteworthy is the U.S procedure to implement reductions in chlorofluorocarbon emissions under the Montreal Protocol. Under this measure, EPA has effectively grandfathered the U.S. quota among existing producers and importers, from these baselines, firms are allowed to trade allowances (Hahn and McGartland 1989).

at the same time, effluent charge and marketable permit programs are few in number and often bear only a modest resemblance to the pure programs of economic incentives supported by economists. As we noted in the introduction, certain major pieces of environmental legislation prohibit the use of economic tests for the setting of standards for environmental quality, while other directives require them! The record, in short, is a mixed and somewhat confusing one: it reveals a policy environment characterized by a real ambivalence (and, in some instances, an active hostility) to a central role for economics in environmental decision making.[63]

What is the potential and the likelihood of more attention to the use of economic analysis and economic incentives in environmental management? It is easy to be pessimistic on this matter. There is still some aversion, both in the policy arena and across the general public, to the use of "market methods" for pollution control. While we were working on this survey, one of the leading news magazines in the U.S. ran a lengthy feature story entitled "The Environment: Cleaning Up Our Mess—What Works, What Doesn't, and What We Must Do to Reclaim our Air, Land, and Water" (Gregg Easterbrook 1989, in *Newsweek*). A central argument in the article is that the attempt to place environmental policy on a solid "scientific" footing has been a colossal error that has handcuffed efforts to get on with pollution control. Proceeding "on the assumption that environmental protection is a social good transcending cost-benefit calculations" (p. 42), Easterbrook argues that we should not place a high priority on scientific work on the complicated issues of measuring benefits and costs and of providing carefully designed systems of incentives, but should get on with enacting pollution control measures that are technologically feasible. In short, we should control what technology enables us to control without asking too many hard questions and holding up tougher legislation until we know all the answers.

Such a position has a certain pragmatic appeal. As we all know, our understanding of complicated ecological systems and the associated dose-response relationships is seriously incomplete. And as our survey has indicated, our ability to place dollar values on improvements in environmental quality is limited and imprecise. Nevertheless, we have some hard choices to make in the environmental arena—and whatever guidance we can obtain from a careful, if imprecise, consideration of benefits and costs should not be ignored.

We stress, moreover, that the role for economic analysis in environmental policy making is far more important now than in the earlier years of the "environmental revolution." When we set out initially to attack our

---

[63]Some recent studies of actual environmental decision making are consistent with this "mixed" view. Magat, Krupnick, and Harrington (1986), for example, in a study of EPA determination of effluent standards under the Clean Water Act Amendments of 1972, found that "simple rules based either on economic efficiency or the goal of distributional equity did not dominate the rulemaking process" (p. 154). Their analysis did find that standards across industry subcategories reflected to some extent differences in compliance costs among firms. In contrast, Cropper et al. (1992) find that EPA decisions on pesticide regulation have, in fact, reflected a systematic balancing of environmental risks and costs of control. Economic factors, it appears, have mattered in some classes of decisions and not in others.

major pollution problems, there were available a wide array of fairly direct and inexpensive measures for pollution control. We were, in short, operating on relatively low and flat segments of marginal abatement cost (MAC) curves. But things have changed. As nearly all the cost studies reveal, marginal abatement cost functions have the typical textbook shape. They are low and fairly flat over some range and then begin to rise, often quite rapidly. Both the first and second derivatives of these abatement cost functions are positive—and rapidly increasing marginal abatement costs often set in with a vengeance.

We now find ourselves operating, in most instances, along these rapidly rising portions of MAC functions so that decisions to cut pollution yet further are becoming more costly. In such a setting, it is crucial that we have a clear sense of the relative benefits and costs of alternative measures. It will be quite easy, for example, to enact new, more stringent regulations that impose large costs on society, well in excess of the benefits, health or otherwise, to the citizenry. As Portney (1990) has suggested, this may well be true of the new measures to control urban air pollution and hazardous air pollutants under the most recent Amendments to the Clean Air Act. Portney's admittedly rough estimates suggest that the likely range of benefits from these new provisions falls well short of the likely range of their cost.

Economic analysis can be quite helpful in getting at least a rough sense of the relative magnitudes at stake. This is not, we would add, a matter of sophisticated measures of "exact consumer surplus" but simply of measuring as best we can the relevant areas under crude approximations to demand curves (compensated or otherwise). In addition to measurement issues, this new setting for environmental policy places a much greater premium on the use of cost-effective regulatory devices, for the wastes associated with the cruder forms of CAC policies will be much magnified.[64]

In spite of the mixed record, it is our sense that we are at a point in the evolution of environmental policy at which the economics profession is in a very favorable position to influence the course of policy. As we move into the 1990s, the general political and policy setting is one that is genuinely receptive to market approaches to solving our social problems. Not only in the United States but in other countries as well, the prevailing atmosphere is a conservative one with a strong disposition toward the use of market incentives, wherever possible, for the attainment of our social objectives. Moreover, as we have emphasized in this survey, we have learned a lot over the past twenty years about the properties of various policy instruments and how they work (or do not work) under different circumstances. Economists now know more about environmental policy and are

---

[64]Following our earlier discussion of the Weitzman theorem, we note its implication for the issue under discussion here: a preference for price over quantity instruments. So long as there is little evidence of any dramatic threshold effects or other sources of rapid changes in marginal benefits from pollution control, the steepness of the MAC function suggests that regulatory agencies can best protect against costly error by adopting effluent fees rather than marketable emission permits (Hadi Dowlatabadi and Harrington 1989; Oates, Portney, and McGartland 1989).

in a position to offer better counsel on the design of measures for environmental management.

This, as we have stressed, takes us from the abstract world of pure systems of fees or marketable permits. Environmental economists must be (and, we believe, are) prepared to come to terms with detailed, but important, matters of implementation: the determination of fee schedules, issues of spatial and temporal variation in fees or allowable emissions under permits, the life of permits and their treatment for tax purposes, rules governing the transfer of pollution rights, procedures for the monitoring and enforcement of emissions limitations, and so on. In short, economists must be ready to "get their hands dirty."

But the contribution to be made by environmental economists can be a valuable one. And there are encouraging signs in the policy arena of a growing receptiveness to incentive-based approaches to environmental management. As we noted in the introduction, both in the United States and in the OECD countries more generally, there have been recent expressions of interest in the use of economic incentives for protection of the environment. As we were finishing the final draft of this survey, the Council of the OECD issued a strong and lengthy endorsement of incentive-based approaches, urging member countries to "make a greater and more consistent use of economic instruments" for environmental management (OECD 1991).

Finally, we note the growing awareness and concern with global environmental issues. Many pollutants display a troublesome tendency to spill over national boundaries. While this is surely not a new issue (e.g., transnational acid rain), the thinning of the ozone shield and the prospect of global warming are pressing home in a more urgent way the need for a global perspective on the environment. The potential benefits and costs of programs to address these issues, particularly global warming, are enormous— and they present a fundamental policy challenge. The design and implementation of workable and cost-effective measures on a global scale are formidable problems, to put it mildly. And they call for an extension of existing work in the field to the development of an "open economy environmental economics" that incorporates explicitly the issues arising in an international economy linked by trade, financial, *and* environmental flows.[65]

REFERENCES

Abdilla, Charles. "Measuring Economic Losses from Ground Water Contamination: An Investigation of Household Avoidance Cost," *Water Resources Bulletin*, June 1990, *26*(3), pp. 451–63.

---

[65]For a useful effort to develop a research perspective and agenda on the economic analysis of global change, see U.S. National Oceanic and Atmospheric Administration, National Science Foundation and National Aeronautics and Space Administration (1991).

Adams, Richard M.; Crocker, Thomas D. and Katz, Richard W. "Assessing the Adequacy of Natural Science Information: A Bayesian Approach," *Rev. Econ. Statist.*, Nov. 1984, *66*(4), pp. 568–75.

Adams, Richard M.; Hamilton, Scott A. and McCarl, Bruce A. "The Benefits of Pollution Control: the Case of Ozone and U.S. Agriculture," *Amer. J. Agr. Econ.*, Nov. 1986, *68*(4), pp. 886–93.

Adar, Zvi and Griffin, James M. "Uncertainty and the Choice of Pollution Control Instruments," *J. Environ. Econ. Manage.*, Oct. 1976, *3*(3), pp. 178–88.

Arrow, Kenneth J. and Fisher, Anthony C. "Environmental Preservation, Uncertainty, and Irreversibility," *Quart. J. Econ.*, May 1974, *88*(2), pp. 312–19.

Asako, Kazumi. "Environmental Pollution in an Open Economy," *Econ. Rec.*, Dec. 1979, *55*(151). pp. 359–67.

Asch, Peter and Seneca, Joseph J. "Monopoly and External Cost: An Application of Second Best Theory to the Automobile Industry," *J. Environ. Econ. Manage.*, June 1976, *3*(2), pp. 69–79.

———. "Some Evidence on the Distribution of Air quality," *Land Econ.*, Aug. 1978, *54*(3), pp. 478–97.

Atkinson, Scott E. and Lewis, Donald H. "A Cost-Effectiveness Analysis of Alternative Air Quality Control Strategies," *J. Environ. Econ. Manage.*, Nov. 1974, *1*(3), pp. 237–50.

Atkinson, Scott E. and Tietenberg, T.H. "The Empirical Properties of Two Classes of Designs for Transferable Discharge Permit Markets," *J. Environ. Econ. Manage.*, June 1982, *9*(2), pp. 101–21.

Bailey, Martin J. "Externalities, Rents, and Optimal Rules." Sloan Working Paper in Urban Public Economics 16–82, Economics Dept., U. of Maryland College Park, MA, 1982.

Barnett, Andy H. "The Pigouvian Tax Rule Under Monopoly," *Amer. Econ. Rev.*, Dec. 1980, *70*(5), pp. 1037–41.

Bartel, Ann P. and Taubman, Paul. "Health and Labor Market Success: The Role of Various Diseases," *Rev. Econ. Statist.*, Feb. 1979, *61*(1), pp. 1–8.

Bartik, Timothy J. "Evaluating the Benefits of Nonmarginal Reductions in Pollution Using Information on Defensive Expenditures," *J. Environ. Econ. Manage.*, March 1988a, *15*(1), pp. 111–27.

———. "Measuring the Benefits of Amenity Improvements in Hedonic Price Models," *Land Econ.*, May 1988b, *64*(2), pp. 172–83.

———. "The Effects of Environmental Regulation on Business Location in the United States," *Growth Change*, Summer 1988c, *19*(3), pp. 22–44.

Baumol, William J. "On Taxation and the Control of Externalities," *Amer. Econ. Rev.*, June 1972, *62*(3), pp. 307–22.

Baumol, William J. and Bradford, David F. "Detrimental Externalities and Non-Convexity of the Production Set," *Economica*, May 1972, *39*(154), pp. 160–76.

Baumol, William J. and Oates, Wallace E. "The Use of Standards and Prices for Protection of the Environment," *Swedish J. Econ.*, March 1971, *73*(1), pp. 42–54.

———. *Economics, environmental policy, and quality of life.* NY: Prentice-Hall, 1979.

———. *The theory of environmental policy.* Second Edition. Cambridge, England: Cambridge U. Press, 1988.

Becker, Gary S. "Crime and Punishment: An Economic Approach," *J. Polit. Econ.*, Mar./Apr. 1968, *76*(2), pp. 169–217.

Berger, Mark C. et al. "Valuing Changes in Health Risks: A Comparison of Alternative Measures," *Southern Econ. J.*, Apr. 1987, *53*(4), pp. 967–84.

Brinkley, Clark S. and Hanemann, W. Michael. *The recreation benefits of water quality improvement: Analysis of day trips in an urban setting.* EPA-600/5-78-010. Washington, DC: U.S. Environmental Protection Agency, 1978.

Bishop, Richard C. and Heberlein, Thomas A. "Measuring Values of Extramarket Goods: Are Indirect Measures Biased?" *Amer. J. Agr. Econ.*, Dec. 1979, *61*(5), pp. 926–30.

Bishop, Richard C.; Heberlein, Thomas A. and Kealy, Mary Jo. "Contingent Valuation of Environmental Assets: Comparisons with a Simulated Market," *Natural Res. J.*, 1983, *23*(3), pp. 619–34.

Blomquist, Glenn C. "Value of Life Saving: Implications of Consumption Activity," *J. Polit. Econ.*, June 1979, *87*(3), pp. 540–58.

Blomquist, Glenn C.; Berger, Mark C. and Hoehn, John P. "New Estimates of Quality of Life in Urban Areas," *Amer. Econ. Rev.*, Mar. 1988, *78*(1), pp. 89–107.

Bockstael, Nancy E.; Hanemann, W. Michael and Kling, Catherine L. "Estimating the Value of Water Quality Improvements in a Recreational Demand Framework," *Water Resources Res.*, May 1987, *23*(5), pp. 951–60.

Bockstael, Nancy E. and McConnell, Kenneth E. "Welfare Measurement in the Household Production Framework," *Amer. Econ. Rev.*, Sept. 1983, *73*(4), pp. 806–14.

Bohm, Peter. "Estimating Demand for Public Goods: An Experiment," *European Econ. Rev.*, June 1972, *3*(2), pp. 111–30.

———. *Deposit-refund systems: Theory and applications to environmental, conservation, and consumer policy.* Washington, DC: Johns Hopkins U. Press for Resources for the Future, 1981.

Bohm, Peter and Russell, Clifford F. "Comparative Analysis of Alternative Policy Instruments," in *Handbook of natural resource and energy economics.* Volume 1, Eds.: Allen V. Kneese and James L. Sweeney. Amsterdam: North-Holland, 1985, pp. 395–460.

Boland, James "Economic Instruments for Environmental Protection in the United States," ENV/ECO/86.14. Paris, France: Organisation for Economic Cooperation and Development. Sept. 11, 1986.

Bower, Blair et al. *Incentives in water quality management: France and the Ruhr area.* Washington, DC: Resources for the Future, 1981.

Bowker, James and Stoll, John R. "Use of Dichotomous Choice Nonmarket Methods to Value the Whooping Crane Resource," *Amer. J. Agr. Econ.*, May 1988, *70*(2), pp. 372–81.

Boyle, Kevin J. and Bishop, Richard C. "Valuing Wildlife in Benefit-Cost Analyses: A Case Study Involving Endangered Species," *Water Resources Res.*, May 1987, *23*(5), pp. 943–50.

Braden, John B. and Kolstad, Charles D., eds. *Measuring the demand for environmental quality.* Amsterdam, North Holland, 1991.

Bramhall, D. F. and Mills, Edwin S. "A Note on the Asymmetry between Fees and Payments," *Water Resources Res.*, 1966, *2*(3), pp. 615–16.

Bressers, Hans. "The Effectiveness of Dutch Water Quality Policy." Mimeo. The Netherlands: Twente University of Technology, 1983.

Bromley, Daniel W. "Markets and Externalities," in *Natural resource economics: Policy problems and contemporary analysis.* Ed.: Daniel W. Bromley. Hingham, MA: Kluwer Nijhoff, 1986, pp. 37–68.

Brookshire, David D. and Coursey, Don L. "Measuring the Value of a Public Good: An Empirical Comparison of Elicitation Procedures," *Amer. Econ. Rev.*, Sept. 1987, *77*(4), pp. 554–66.

Brookshire, D. S. et al. *Methods development for assessing air pollution control benefits.* Vol. 2: *Experiments in valuing non-market goods: A case study of alternative bene-*

fit measures of air pollution in the south coast air basin of Southern California. Prepared for the U.S. Environmental Protection Agency, Washington, DC, 1979.

Brown, Gardner, Jr. and Bressers, Hans. "Evidence Supporting Effluent Charges." Mimeo. The Netherlands: Twente University of Technology, Sept. 1986.

Brown, Gardner, Jr. and Johnson, Ralph W. "Pollution Control by Effluent Charges: It Works in the Federal Republic of Germany, Why Not in the U.S.," *Natural Res. J.*, Oct. 1984, *24*(4), pp. 929–66.

Brown, Gardner, Jr. and Mendelsohn, Robert. "The Hedonic Travel Cost Method," *Rev. Econ. Statist.*, Aug. 1984, *66*(3), pp. 427–33.

Brown, James N. and Rosen, Harvey S. "On the Estimation of Structural Hedonic Price Models," *Econometrica*, May 1982, *50*(3), pp. 765–68.

Brown, Thomas C. and Slovic, Paul. "Effects of Context on Economic Measures of Value, in *Amenity resource valuation: Integrating economics with other disciplines.* Eds.: G. Peterson, B. Driver, and R. Gregory. State College, PA: Venture Publishing, Inc., 1988.

Buchanan, James M. "External Diseconomies, Corrective Taxes, and Market Structure," *Amer. Econ. Rev.*, Mar. 1969, *59*(1), pp. 174–77.

Burrows, Paul. *The economic theory of pollution control.* Oxford: Martin Robertson, 1979.

Burrows, Paul. "Controlling the Monopolistic Polluter: Nihilism or Eclecticism?" *J. Environ. Econ. Manage.*, Dec. 1981, *8*(4), pp. 372–80.

Burrows, Paul. "Nonconvexity Induced by External Costs on Production: Theoretical Curio or Policy Dilemma?" *J. Environ. Econ. Manage.*, June 1986, *13*(2), pp. 101–28.

Butler, Richard V. and Maher, Michael D. "The Control of Externalities in a Growing Urban Economy," *Econ. Inquiry*, Jan. 1982, *20*(1), pp. 155–63.

———. "The Control of Externalities: Abatement vs. Damage Prevention," *Southern Econ. J.*, Apr. 1986, *52*(4), pp. 1088–1102.

Cameron, Trudy Ann and James, Michelle D. "Efficient Estimation Methods for 'Closed-Ended' Contingent Valuation Surveys," *Rev. Econ. Statist.*, May 1987, *69*(2), pp. 269–76.

Carson, Richard T. and Mitchell, Robert Cameron. "The Value of Clean Water: The Public's Willingness to Pay for Boatable, Fishable, and Swimmable Quality Water." Discussion Paper 88-13. La Jolla, CA: U. of California at San Diego, 1988.

Chestnut, Lauraine and Rowe, Robert D. "Economic Valuation of Changes in Visibility: A State of the Science Assessment for NAPAP" in *Methods for valuing acidic deposition and air pollution effects.* Report 27, 1989, pp. 5-1-5-44.

Christainsen, G. B. and Tietenberg, Thomas H. "Distributional and Macroeconomic Aspects of Environmental Policy," in *Handbook of natural resource and energy economics.* Vol. 1. Eds.: Allen V. Kneese and James L. Sweeney. Amsterdam: North-Holland, 1985, pp. 345–93.

Coase, Ronald H. "The Problem of Social Cost," *J. Law Econ.*, Oct. 1960, *3*, pp. 1–44.

Collinge, Robert A. and Oates, Wallace E. "Efficiency in Pollution Control in the Short and Long Runs: A System of Rental Emission Permits," *Can. J. Econ.*, May 1982, *15*(2), pp. 347–54.

Cooper, Barbara S. and Rice, Dorothy P. "The Economic Cost of Illness Revisited," *Soc. Sec. Bull.*, Feb. 1976, *39*(2), pp. 21–36.

Cornes, Richard and Sandler, Todd. *The theory of externalities, public goods, and club goods.* Cambridge, Eng.: Cambridge U. Press, 1986.

Costanza, Robert and Perrings, Charles. "A Flexible Assurance Bonding System for Improved Environmental Management," *Ecological Economics*, Feb. 1990, *2*, pp. 57–75.

Courant, Paul N. and Porter, Richard. "Averting Expenditure and the Cost of Pollution," *J. Environ. Econ. Manage.*, Dec. 1981, *8*(4), pp. 321–29.

Coursey, Donald L.; Hovis, John L. and Schulze, William D. "The Disparity Between Willingness to Accept and Willingness to Pay Measures of Value," *Quart. J. Econ.*, Aug. 1987, *102*(3), pp. 679–90.

Cropper, Maureen L. and Arriaga-Salinas, Amalia. "Inter-city Wage Differentials and the Value of Air Quality," *J. Urban Econ.*, 1980, *8*(2), pp. 236–54.

Cropper, Maureen L. et al. "The Determinants of Pesticide Regulation: A Statistical Analysis of EPA Decisionmaking," *J. Polit. Econ.*, Feb. 1992, *100*(1), pp. 175–97.

Cropper, Maureen L. and Krupnick, Alan J. "The Social Costs of Chronic Heart and Lung Disease." Quality of the Environment Division Discussion Paper QE89-16. Washington DC: Resources for the Future, 1989.

Cropper, Maureen L. and Portney, Paul R. "Discounting and the Evaluation of Lifesaving Programs," *J. Risk Uncertainty*, Dec. 1990, *3*(4), pp. 369–79.

Cropper, Maureen L. and Sussman, Frances G. "Valuing Future Risks to Life," *J. Environ. Econ. Manage.*, Sept. 1990, *19*(2), pp. 160–74.

Cumberland, John H. "Efficiency and Equity in Interregional Environmental Management," *Rev. Reg. Stud.*, Fall 1981, *10*(2), pp. 1–9.

Dales, John Harkness. *Pollution, property, and prices.* Toronto, Ont.: U. of Toronto Press, 1968.

Dardis, Rachel. "The Value of a Life: New Evidence from the Marketplace," *Amer. Econ. Rev.*, Dec. 1980, *70*(5), pp. 1077–82.

d'Arge, Ralph C. and Kneese, Allen V. "International Trade, Domestic Income, and Environmental Controls: Some Empirical Estimates," in *Managing the environment: International economic cooperation for pollution control.* Eds.: Allen V. Kneese, Sidney E. Rolfe, and Joseph W. Harned. NY: Praeger, 1971, pp. 289–315.

Deacon, Robert T. and Shapiro, Perry. "Private Preference for Collective Goods Revealed Through Voting on Referenda," *Amer. Econ. Rev.*, Dec. 1975, *65*(5), pp. 943–55.

Decision Focus Incorporated. *Development and design of a contingent value survey for measuring the public's value for visibility improvements at the Grand Canyon National Park.* Revised Draft Report, Los Altos, CA, Sept. 1990.

Dewees, Donald N. "Instrument Choice in Environmental Policy," *Econ. Inquiry*, Jan. 1983, *21*(1), pp. 53–71.

Dewees, Donald N. and Sims, W. A. "The Symmetry of Effluent Charges and Subsidies for Pollution Control," *Can. J. Econ.*, May 1976, *9*(2), pp. 323–31.

Dickens, William T. "Differences Between Risk Premiums in Union and Nonunion Wages and the Case for Occupational Safety Regulation," *Amer. Econ. Rev.*, May 1984, *74*(2), pp. 320–23.

Dickie, Mark T. et al. "Reconciling Averting Behavior and Contingent Valuation Benefit Estimates of Reducing Symptoms of Ozone Exposure (draft)," in *Improving accuracy and reducing costs of environmental benefit assessments.* Washington, DC: U.S. Environmental Protection Agency, 1987.

Dickie, Mark; Fisher, Ann and Gerking, Shelby. "Market Transactions and Hypothetical Demand Data: A Comparative Study," *J. Amer. Stat. Assoc.*, Mar. 1987, *82*(397), pp. 69–75.

Dickie, Mark and Gerking, Shelby. "Willingness to Pay for Ozone Control: Inferences From the Demand for Medical Care," *J. Urban Econ.*, forthcoming.

Dorfman, Nancy S., assisted by Snow, Arthur. "Who Will Pay for Pollution Control?—The Distribution by Income of the Burden of the National Environmental Protection Program," *Nat. Tax J.*, Mar. 1975, *28*(1), pp. 101–15.

Dowlatabadi, Hadi and Harrington, Winston. "The Effects of Uncertainty on Policy Instruments: The Case of Electricity Supply and Environmental Regulations." Quality of the Environment Division Discussion Paper QE89-20. Washington, DC: Resources for the Future, 1989.

Downing, Paul B. and Watson, William D., Jr. "The Economics of Enforcing Air Pollution Controls," *J. Environ. Econ. Manage.*, Nov. 1974, *1*(3), pp. 219–36.

Easterbrook, Gregg. "Cleaning Up," *Newsweek*, July 24, 1989, *114*, pp. 26–42.

Epple, Dennis. "Hedonic Prices and Implicit Markets: Estimating Demand and Supply Functions for Differentiated Products," *J. Polit. Econ.*, Feb. 1987, *95*(1), pp. 59–80.

Feenberg, Daniel and Mills, Edwin S. *Measuring the benefits of water pollution abatement*. NY: Academic Press, 1980.

Fischel, William A. "Fiscal and Environmental Considerations in the Location of Firms in Suburban Communities," in *Fiscal zoning and land use controls*. Eds.: Edwin S. Mills and Wallace E. Oates. Lexington, MA: Heath, 1975, pp. 119–73.

———. "Determinants of Voting on Environmental Quality: A Study of a New Hampshire Pulp Mill Referendum," *J. Environ. Econ. Manage.*, June 1979, *6*(2), pp. 107–18.

Fishelson, Gideon. "Emission Control Policies Under Uncertainty," *J. Environ. Econ. Manage.*, Oct. 1976, *3*, pp. 189–97.

Fisher, Ann; Violette, Dan and Chestnut, Lauraine. "The Value of Reducing Risks of Death: A Note on New Evidence," *J. Policy Anal. Manage.*, Winter 1989, *8*(1), pp. 88–100.

Fisher, Anthony C. *Resource and environmental economics*. Cambridge, Eng.: Cambridge U. Press, 1981.

Fisher, Anthony C. and Peterson, Frederick M. "The Environment in Economics: A Survey," *J. Econ. Lit.*, Mar. 1976, *14*(1), pp. 1–33.

Freeman, A. Myrick, III. "Distribution of Environmental Quality," in *Environmental quality analysis: Theory and method in the social sciences*. Eds.: Allen V. Kneese and Blair Bower. Baltimore, MD: John Hopkins University Press for Resources for the Future, 1972, pp. 243–78.

———. "On Estimating Air Pollution Control Benefits from Land Value Studies," *J. Environ. Econ. Manage.*, May 1974, *1*(1), pp. 74–83.

———. *The benefits of environmental improvement*. Baltimore, MD: Johns Hopkins U. Press for Resources for the Future, Inc., 1979a, p. 63.

———. "The Incidence of the Cost of Controlling Automobile Air Pollution," in *The distribution of economic well-being*. Ed.: F. Thomas Juster. Cambridge, MA: Ballinger, 1979b.

———. *Air and water pollution control: A benefit-cost assessment*. NY: John Wiley, 1982.

Garcia, Philip et al. "Measuring the Benefits of Environmental Change Using a Duality Approach: The Case of Ozone and Illinois Cash Grain Farms," *J. Environ. Econ. Manage.*, Mar. 1986, *13*(1), pp. 69–80.

Gegax, Douglas; Gerking, Shelby and Schulze, William. "Perceived Risk and the Marginal Value of Safety." Working paper prepared for the U.S. Environmental Protection Agency, Aug. 1985.

Gerking, Shelby; DeHaan, Menno and Schulze, William. "The Marginal Value of Job Safety: A Contingent Valuation Study," *J. Risk Uncertainty*, June 1988, *1*(2), pp. 185–99.

Gerking, Shelby and Stanley, Linda R. "An Economic Analysis of Air Pollution and Health: The Case of St. Louis," *Rev. Econ. Statist.*, Feb. 1986, *68*(1), pp. 115–21.

Gianessi, Leonard P.; Peskin, Henry M. and Wolff, Edward N. "The Distributional Effects of Uniform Air Pollution Policy in the United States," *Quart. J. Econ.*, May 1979, *93*(2), pp. 281–301.

Gianessi, Leonard P. and Peskin, Henry M. "The Distribution of the Costs of Federal Water Pollution Control Policy," *Land Econ.*, Feb. 1980, *56*(1), pp. 85–102.

Gould, J. R. "Total Conditions in the Analysis of External Effects," *Econ. J.*, Sept. 1977, *87*(347), pp. 558–64.

Grigalunas, Thomas A. and Opaluch, James J. "Assessing Liability for Damages Under CERCLA: A New Approach for Providing Incentives for Pollution Avoidance?" *Natural Res. J.*, Summer 1988, *28*(3), pp. 509–33.

Hahn, Robert W. "Market Power and Transferable Property Rights," *Quart. J. Econ.*, Nov. 1984, *99*(4), pp. 753–65.

———. "Economic Prescriptions for Environmental Problems: How the Patient Followed the Doctor's Orders," *J. Econ. Perspectives*, Spring 1989, *3*(2), pp. 95–114.

———. "The Political Economy of Environmental Regulation: Towards a Unifying Framework," *Public Choice*, Apr. 1990, *65*(1), pp. 21–47.

Hahn, Robert W. and Hester, Gordon L. "Marketable Permits: Lessons for Theory and Practice," *Ecology Law Quarterly*, 1989a, *16*(2), pp. 361–406.

———. "Where Did All the Markets Go? An Analysis of EPA's Emissions Trading Program," *Yale J. Regul.*, Winter 1989b, *6*(1), pp. 109–53.

Hahn, Robert W. and McGartland, Albert M. "The Political Economy of Instrument Choice: An Examination of the U.S. Role in Implementing the Montreal Protocol," *Northwestern U. Law Rev.*, Spring 1989, *83*(3), pp. 592–611.

Hahn, Robert W. and Noll, Roger, G. "Designing a Market for Tradable Emission Permits," in *Reform of environmental regulation*. Ed.: Wesley Magat. Cambridge, MA: Ballinger, 1982, pp. 119–46.

Hamilton, Jonathan H.; Sheshinski, Eytan and Slutsky, Steven M. "Production Externalities and Long-Run Equilibria: Bargaining and Pigovian Taxation," *Econ. Inquiry*, July 1989, *27*(3), pp. 453–71.

Hamilton, Scott A.; McCarl, Bruce A. and Adams, Richard M. "The Effect of Aggregate Response Assumptions on Environmental Impact Analyses," *Amer. J. Agr. Econ.*, May 1985, *67*(2), pp. 407–13.

Hammack, Judd and Brown, Gardner M., Jr. *Waterfowl and wetlands: Toward bioeconomic analysis.* Baltimore, MD: Johns Hopkins U. Press for Resources for the Future, 1974.

Hanemann, W. Michael. "Discrete/Continuous Models of Consumer Demand," *Econometrica*, May 1984, *52*(3), pp. 541–61.

Hanemann, W. Michael. "Willingness to Pay and Willingness to Accept: How Much Can They Differ?" *Amer. Econ. Rev.*, June 1991, *81*(3), pp. 635–47.

Harford, Jon D. "Firm Behavior Under Imperfectly Enforceable Pollution Standards and Taxes," *J. Environ. Econ. Manage.*, Mar. 1978, *5*(1), pp. 26–43.

Harrington, Winston. "Enforcement Leverage When Penalties Are Restricted," *J. Public Econ.*, Oct. 1988, *37*(1), pp. 29–53.

Harrington, Winston; Krupnick, Alan J. and Peskin, Henry M. "Policies for Nonpoint-Source Water Pollution Control," *J. Soil and Water Conservation*, Jan.–Feb. 1985, *40*, pp. 27–32.

Harrington, Winston; Krupnick, Alan J. and Spofford, Walter O., Jr. "The Economic Losses of a Waterborne Disease Outbreak," *J. Urban Econ.*, Jan. 1989, *25*(1), pp. 116–37.

Harrington, Winston and Portney, Paul R. "Valuing the Benefits of Health and Safety Regulations," *J. Urban Econ.*, July 1987, *22*(1), pp. 101–12.

Harrison, David, Jr. *Who pays for clean air: The cost and benefit distribution of federal automobile emissions standards.* Cambridge, MA: Ballinger, 1975.

Harrison, David H. "The Regulation of Aircraft Noise," in *Incentives for environmental protection.* Ed.: Thomas C. Schelling. Cambridge, MA: MIT Press, 1983, pp. 41–143.

IIazilla, Michael and Kopp, Raymond J. "Social Cost of Environmental Quality Regulations: A General Equilibrium Analysis," *J. Polit. Econ.,* Aug. 1990, *98*(4), pp. 853–73.

Hoehn, John P. and Randall, Alan. "Too Many Proposals Pass the Benefit Cost Test," *Amer. Econ. Rev.,* 1989, *789*(3), pp. 544–51.

Hotelling, Harold. "The Economics of Exhaustible Resources," *J. Polit. Econ.,* Apr. 1931, *39*(2), pp. 137–75.

Johnson, Ralph W. and Brown, Gardner M., Jr. *Cleaning up Europe's waters.* NY: Praeger, 1976.

Jones-Lee, Michael W. "The Value of Changes in the Probability of Death or Injury," *J. Polit. Econ.,* July/Aug. 1974, *82*(4), pp. 835–49.

Jones-Lee, Michael W.; Hammerton, M. and Philips, P. R. "The Value of Safety: Results of a National Sample Survey," *Econ. J.,* Mar. 1985, *95*(377), pp. 49–72.

Jorgenson, Dale W, and Wilcoxen, Peter J. "Environmental Regulation and U.S. Economic Growth," *Rand J. Econ.,* Summer 1990a, *21*(2), pp. 314–40.

———. "Reducing U.S. Carbon Dioxide Emissions: The Cost of Different Goals." Harvard U., 1990b.

Kahneman, Daniel; Knetsch, Jack L. and Thaler, Richard H. "Experimental Tests of the Endowment Effect and the Coase Theorem," *J. Polit. Econ.,* Dec. 1990, *98*(6), pp. 1325–48.

Kahneman, Daniel and Tversky, Amos. "Prospect Theory: An Analysis of Decisions Under Risk," *Econometrica,* Mar. 1979, *47*(2), pp. 263–91.

Kamien, Morton I.; Schwartz, Nancy L. and Dolbear, F. T. "Asymmetry between Bribes and Charges," *Water Resources Res.,* 1966, *2*(1), pp. 147–57.

Kane, Sally; Reilly, John and Tobey, James. "An Empirical Study of the Economic Effects of Climate Change on World Agriculture." Mimeo USDA Report, Jan. 1991.

Kanemoto, Yoshitsugu. "Hedonic Prices and the Benefits of Public Prices," *Econometrica,* July 1988, *56*(4), pp. 981–90.

Kealy, Mary Jo; Dovidio, Jack and Rockel, Mark L. "Willingness to Pay to Prevent Additional Damages to the Adirondacks from Acid Rain," *Reg. Sci. Rev.,* 1987, *15*, pp. 118–41.

Kelman, Steven J. *What price incentives? Economists and the environment.* Boston, MA: Auburn House, 1981.

Kneese, Allen V.; Ayres, Robert V. and d'Arge, Ralph C. *Economics and the environment: A materials balance approach.* Washington, DC: Resources for the Future, 1970.

Kneese, Allen V. and Bower, Blair T. *Managing water quality: Economics, technology, institutions,* Baltimore, MD: Johns Hopkins University Press for Resources for the Future, 1968.

Kneese, Allen V. and Schulze, William D. "Ethics and Environmental Economics," in *Handbook of natural resource and energy economics.* Vol. 1. Eds.: Allen V. Kneese and James L. Sweeney. Amsterdam: North-Holland, 1985, pp. 191–220.

Knetsch, Jack L. and Sinden, J. A. "Willingness to Pay and Compensation Demanded: Experimental Evidence of an Unexpected Disparity in Measures of Value," *Quart J. Econ.,* Aug. 1984, *99*(3), pp. 507–21.

Kohn, Robert E. "A General Equilibrium Analysis of the Optimal Number of Firms in a Polluting Industry," *Can. J. Econ.*, May 1985, *18*(2), pp. 347–54.

Kolstad, Charles D. "Empirical Properties of Economic Incentives and Command-and-Control Regulations for Air Pollution Control," *Land Econ.*, Aug. 1986, *62*(3), pp. 250–68.

———. "Uniformity versus Differentiation in Regulating Externalities," *J. Environ. Econ. Manage.*, Dec. 1987, *14*(4), pp. 386–99.

Koo, Anthony Y. C. "Environmental Repercussions and Trade Theory," *Rev. Econ. Statist.*, May 1974, *56*(2), pp. 235–44.

Kopp, Raymond J. and Krupnick, Alan J. "Agricultural Policy and the Benefits of Ozone Control," *Amer. J. Agr. Econ.*, Dec. 1987, *69*(5), pp. 956–62.

Kopp, Raymond J. et al. "Implications of Environmental Policy for U.S. Agriculture: The Case of Ambient Ozone Standards," *J. Environ. Manag.*, June 1985, *20*(4), pp. 321–31.

Krupnick, Alan J. "Costs of Alternative Policies for the Control of NO_2 in the Baltimore Region." Unpub. working paper. Washington, DC: Resources for the Future, 1983.

Krupnick, Alan J.; Oates, Wallace E. and Van De Verg, Eric. "On Marketable Air-Pollution Permits: The Case for a System of Pollution Offsets," *J. Environ. Econ. Manage.*, Sept. 1983, *10*(3), pp. 233–47.

Krupnick, Alan J. and Portney, Paul R. "Controlling Urban Air Pollution: A Benefit-Cost Assessment," *Science*, Apr. 26, 1991, *252*, pp. 522–28.

Krutilla, John V. "Conservation Reconsidered," *Amer. Econ. Rev.*, Sept. 1967, *57*(4), pp. 777–86.

Kwerel, Evan R. "To Tell the Truth: Imperfect Information and Optimal Pollution Control," *Rev. Econ. Stud.*, Oct. 1977, *44*(3), pp. 595–601.

Lee, Dwight R. "Efficiency of Pollution Taxation and Market Structure," *J. Environ. Econ. Manage.*, Sept. 1975, *2*(1), pp. 69–72.

Lee, Dwight R. and Misiolek, Walter S. "Substituting Pollution Taxation for General Taxation: Some Implications for Efficiency in Pollution Taxation," *J. Environ. Econ. Manage.*, Dec. 1986, *13*(4), pp. 338–47.

Leonard, H. Jeffrey. *Pollution and the struggle for the world product.* Cambridge, Eng. Cambridge U. Press, 1988.

Lichtenberg, Erik and Zilberman, David. "The Welfare Economics of Price Supports in U.S. Agriculture," *Amer. Econ. Rev.*, Dec. 1986, *76*(5), pp. 1135–41.

Loehman, Edna T. et al. "Distributional Analysis of Regional Benefits and Cost of Air Quality Control," *J. Environ. Econ. Manage.*, Sept. 1979, *6*(3), pp. 222–43.

Loehman, Edna; Boldt, D. and Chaikin, K. "Measuring the Benefits of Air Quality Improvements in the San Francisco Bay Area." Prepared for the U.S. Environmental Protection Agency by SRI International, Menlo Park, CA, 1981.

Lyon, Randolph M. "Auctions and Alternative Procedures for Allocating Pollution Rights," *Land Econ.*, Feb. 1982, *58*(1), pp. 16–32.

MacFarland, K. K. et al. "An Examination of Methodologies and Social Indicators for Assessing the Value of Visibility," in *Managing air quality and scenic resources at national parks and wilderness areas*. Eds.: Robert D. Rowe and Lauraine G. Chestnut. Boulder, CO: Westview Press, 1983.

Magat, Wesley A. "Pollution Control and Technological Advance: A Dynamic Model of the Firm," *J. Environ. Econ. Manage.*, Mar. 1978, *5*(1), pp. 1–25.

Magat, Wesley A.; Krupnick, Alan J. and Harrington, Winston. *Rules in the making: A statistical analysis of regulatory agency behavior.* Washington, DC: Resources for the Future, 1986.

Mäler, Karl-Göran. *Environmental economics: A theoretical inquiry.* Baltimore, MD: Johns Hopkins U. Press for Resources for the Future, 1974.

———. "Welfare Economics and the Environment," in *Handbook of natural resource and energy economics.* Vol. 1, Eds.: Allen Kneese and James Sweeney. Amsterdam: North-Holland, 1985, pp. 3–60.

Malik, Arun. "Markets for Pollution Control When Firms Are Noncompliant," *J. Environ. Econ. Manage.*, Mar. 1990, *18*(2, Part 1), pp. 97–106.

Mauskopf, Josephine A. "Projections of Cancer Risks Attributable to Future Exposure to Asbestos," *Risk Analysis*, 1987, *7*(4), pp. 477–86.

McConnell, Virginia D. and Schwab, Robert M. "The Impact of Environmental Regulation in Industry Location Decisions: The Motor Vehicle Industry," *Land Econ.*, Feb. 1990, *66*, pp. 67–81.

McCubbins, Matthew D.; Noll, Roger G. and Weingast, Barry R. "Structure and Process, Politics and Policy: Administrative Arrangements and the Political Control of Agencies," *Virginia Law Rev.*, Mar. 1989, *75*(2), pp. 431–82.

McGartland, Albert M. *Marketable permit systems for air pollution control: An empirical study.* Ph.D. Dissertation, U. of Maryland, College Park, MD, 1984.

———. "A Comparison of Two Marketable Discharge Permits Systems," *J. Environ. Econ. Manage.*, Mar. 1988, *15*(1), pp. 35–44.

McGartland, Albert M. and Oates, Wallace E. "Marketable Permits for the Prevention of Environmental Deterioration," *J. Environ. Econ. Manage.*, Sept. 1985, *12*(3), pp. 207–28.

McGuire, Martin. "Regulation, Factor Rewards, and International Trade," *J. Public Econ.*, Apr. 1982, *17*(3), pp. 335–54.

Mendelsohn, Robert. Estimating the Structural Equations of Implicit Markets and Household Production Functions," *Rev. Econ. Statist.*, Nov. 1984, *66*(4), pp. 673–77.

———. "Regulating Heterogeneous Emissions," *J. Environ. Econ. Manage.*, Dec. 1986, *13*(4), pp. 301–12.

———. "Modeling the Demand for Outdoor Recreation," *Water Resources Res.*, May 1987, *23*(5), pp. 961–67.

Merrifield, John D. "The Impact of Selected Abatement Strategies on Translational Pollution, the Terms of Trade, and Factor Rewards: A General Equilibrium Approach," *J. Environ. Econ. Manage.*, Sept. 1988, *15*(3), pp. 259–84.

Mestelman, Stuart. "Production Externalities and Corrective Subsidies: A General Equilibrium Analysis," *J. Environ. Econ. Manage.*, June 1982, *9*(2), pp. 186–93.

Milliman, Scott R. and Prince, Raymond. "Firm Incentives to Promote Technological Change in Pollution Control," *J. Environ. Econ. Manage.*, Nov. 1989, *17*(3), pp. 247–65.

Mintz, Jack M. and Tulkens, Henry. "Commodity Tax Competition between Member States of a Federation: Equilibrium and Efficiency," *J. Public Econ.*, Mar. 1986, *29*(2), pp. 133–72.

Misiolek, Walter S. "Effluent Taxation in Monopoly Markets," *J. Environ. Econ. Manage.*, June 1980, *7*(2), pp. 103–07.

Mitchell, Robert C. and Carson, Richard T. "Valuing Drinking Water Risk Reductions Using the Contingent Valuation Methods: A Methodological Study of Risks from THM and Giardia." Paper prepared for Resources for the Future, Washington, DC, 1986.

———. *Using surveys to value public goods: The contingent valuation method.* Washington, DC: Resources for the Future, 1989.

Mjelde, James W. et al. "Using Farmers' Actions to Measure Crop Loss Due to Air Pollution," *J. Air Pollution Control Association*, Apr. 1984, *34*(4), pp. 360–64.

Montgomery, W. David. "Markets in Licenses and Efficient Pollution Control Programs," *J. Econ. Theory*, Dec. 1972, *5*(3), pp. 395–418.

Morey, Edward R. "The Choice of Ski Areas: A Generalized CES Preference Ordering with Characteristics," *Rev. Econ. Statist.*, Nov. 1984, *66*(4), pp. 584–90.

Mullen, John K. and Menz, Fredric C. "The Effect of Acidification Damages on the Economic Value of the Adirondack Fishery to New York Anglers," *Amer. J. Agr. Econ.*, Feb. 1985, *67*(1), pp. 112–19.

Mumy, Gene E. "Long-Run Efficiency and Property Rights Sharing for Pollution Control," *Public Choice*, 1980, *35*(1), pp. 59–74.

Nichols, Albert L. *Targeting economic incentives for environmental protection.* Cambridge, MA: MIT Press, 1984.

Nichols, Albert L. and Zeckhauser, Richard J. "The Perils of Prudence," *Regulation*, Nov./Dec. 1986, *10*(2), pp. 13–24.

Nordhaus, William D. "To Slow or Not to Slow: The Economics of the Greenhouse Effect." Cowles Foundation Discussion Paper, 1990.

Oates, Wallace E. "The Regulation of Externalities: Efficient Behavior by Sources and Victims," *Public Finance*, 1983, *38*(3), pp. 362–75.

Oates, Wallace E.; Portney, Paul R. and McGartland, Albert M. "The *Net* Benefits of Incentive-based Regulation: A Case Study of Environmental Standard Setting," *Amer. Econ. Rev.*, Dec. 1989, *79*(5), pp. 1233–42.

Oates, Wallace E. and Schwab, Robert M. "Economic Competition Among Jurisdictions: Efficiency Enhancing or Distortion Inducting?" *J. Public Econ.*, Apr. 1988a. *35*(3), pp. 333–54.

Oates, Wallace E. and Schwab, Robert M. "The Theory of Regulatory Federalism: The Case of Environmental Management." Working Paper No. 88-26, Dept. of Economics. U. of Maryland, 1988b.

Oates, Wallace E. and Strassman N., Diana L. "Effluent Fees and Market Structure," *J. Public Econ.*, June 1984, *24*(1), pp. 29–46.

Ohsfeldt, Robert L. "Assessing the Accuracy of Structural Parameter Estimates in Analyses of Implicit Markets," *Land Econ.*, May 1988, *64*(2), pp. 135–46.

Ohsfeldt, Robert L. and Smith, Barton A. Estimating the Demand for Heterogeneous Goods," *Rev. Econ. Statist.*, Feb. 1985, *67*(1), pp. 165–71.

O'Neil, William B. "The Regulation of Water Pollution Permit Trading Under Conditions of Varying Streamflow and Temperature," in *Buying a better environment: Cost-effective regulation through permit trading.* Eds. Erhard F. Joeres and Martin H. David. Madison, WI: U. of Wisconsin Press, 1983, pp. 219–31.

O'Neil, William et al. "Transferable Discharge Permits and Economic Efficiency: The Fox River," *J. Environ. Econ. Manage.*, Dec. 1983, *10*(94), pp. 346–55.

Opaluch, James J. and Grigalunas, Thomas A. "Controlling Stochastic Pollution Events through Liability Rules: Some Evidence from OCS Leasing," *Rand J. Econ.*, Spring 1984, *15*(1), pp. 142–51.

Organization for Economic Cooperation and Development. *The application of economic instruments for environmental protection.* Paris: O.E.C.D., 1989.

———. *Recommendation of the council on the use of economic instruments in environmental policy.* Paris: O.E.C.D., Jan. 1991.

Palmer, Adele R. et al. "Economic Implications of Regulating Chlorofluorocarbon Emissions from Nonaerosol Applications." Report R-2524-EPA. Santa Monica, CA: Rand Corp., 1980.

Palmquist, Raymond B. "Estimating the Demand for the Characteristics of Housing," *Rev. Econ. Statist.*, Aug. 1984, *66*(3), pp. 394–404.

———. "Pollution Subsidies and Multiple Local Optima," *Land Econ.*, Nov. 1990, *66*, pp. 394–401.

Parsons, George R. and Kealy, Mary Jo. "Measuring Water Quality Benefits Using a Random Utility Model of Lake Recreation in Wisconsin." Working Paper No. 90-14, Dept. of Economics, U. of Delaware, 1990.

Peltzman, Sam and Tideman, T. Nicolaus. "Local versus National Pollution Control: Note," *Amer. Econ. Rev.*, Dec. 1972, *62*(5), pp. 959–63.

Pethig, Rüdiger. "Pollution, Welfare, and Environmental Policy in the Theory of Comparative Advantage," *J. Environ. Econ. Manage.*, Feb. 1976, *2*(3), pp. 160–69.

Pethig, Rüdiger et al. *Trade and Environment: A Theoretical Inquiry.* Amsterdam: Elsevier, 1980.

Pezzey, John. "Changes versus Subsidies versus Marketable Permits as Efficient and Acceptable Methods of Effluent Controls: A Property Rights Analysis." Unpub. paper, 1990.

Portes, Richard D. "The Search for Efficiency in the Presence of Externalities," in *Unfashionable economics: Essays in honor of Lord Balogh.* Ed.: Paul Streeten. London: Weidenfeld and Nicholson, 1970, pp. 348–61.

Portney, Paul R. "Policy Watch: Economics and the Clean Air Act," *J. Econ. Perspectives*, Fall 1990, *4*(4), pp. 173–81.

Rae, Douglas A. "Benefits of Visual Air Quality in Cincinnati: Results of a Contingent Ranking Survey." RP-1742, final report prepared by Charles River Associates for Electric Power Research Institute, Palo Alto, CA, 1984.

Randall, Alan; Ives, Berry and Eastman, Clyde. "Bidding Games for Valuation of Aesthetic Environmental Improvements," *J. Environ. Econ. Manage.*, Aug. 1974, *1*(2), pp. 132–49.

Raufer, Roger K. and Feldman, Stephen L. *Acid rain and emissions trading.* Totowa, NJ: Rowman & Littlefield, 1987.

Ridker, Ronald G. and Henning, John A. "The Determinants of Residential Property Values with Special Reference to Air Pollution," *Rev. Econ. Statist.*, May 1967, *49*(2), pp. 246–57.

Roback, Jennifer. "Wages, Rents, and the Quality of Life," *J. Polit. Econ.*, Dec. 1982, *90*(6), pp. 1257–78.

Roberts, Marc J. and Spence, Michael. "Effluent Charges and Licenses Under Uncertainty," *J. Public Econ.*, Apr./May 1976, *5*(3)(4), pp. 193–208.

Robison, H. David. "Who Pays for Industrial Pollution Abatement?" *Rev. Econ. Statist.*, Nov. 1985, *67*(4), pp. 702–06.

Rosen, Sherwin. "Hedonic Prices and Implicit Markets: Product Differentiation in Pure Competition," *J. Polit. Econ.*, Jan./Feb. 1974, *82*(1), pp. 34–55.

Rosen, Sherwin. "Wage-Based Indexes of Urban Quality of Life," in *Current issues in urban economics.* Eds.: Peter Mieszkowski and Mahlon Straszheim. Baltimore, MD: Johns Hopkins U. Press for Resources for the Future, 1979, pp. 74–104.

Rosenberg, Norman J. et al. "Processes for Identifying Regional Influences of and Responses to Increasing Atmospheric CO_2 and Climate Change—the MINK Project." Prepared by Resources for the Future for Pacific Northwest Laboratory, Oct. 1990.

Rowe, Robert D.; d'Arge, Ralph C. and Brookshire, David S. "An Experiment on Economic Value of Visiblity," *J. Environ. Econ. Manage.*, Mar. 1980, *7*(1), pp. 1–9.

Russell, Clifford S. "Monitoring and Enforcement," in *Public policies for environmental protection*, Ed.: Paul Portney. Washington, DC: Resources for the Future, 1990, pp. 243–74.

Russell, Clifford S.; Harrington: Winston and Vaughan, William J. *Enforcing pollution control laws.* Washington DC: Resources for the Future, 1986.

Samples, Karl C.; Dixon, John A. and Gowen, Marcia M. "Information Disclosure and Endangered Species Valuation," *Land Econ.*, Aug. 1986, *62*(3), pp. 306–12.

Scherr, Bruce A. and Babb, Emerson M. "Pricing Public Goods: An Experiment with Two Proposed Pricing Systems," *Public Choice*, Fall 1975, *23*(3), pp. 35–48.

Schulze, William D. and Brookshire, David S. "The Economic Benefits of Preserving Visibility in the National Parklands of the Southwest," *Natural Res. J.*, Jan. 1983, *23*(1), pp. 149–73.

Schulze, William D. and d'Arge, Ralph C. "The Coase Proposition, Information Constraints, and Long-Run Equilibrium," *Amer. Econ. Rev.*, Sept. 1974, *64*(4), pp. 763–72.

Segerson, Kathleen. "Uncertainty and Incentives for Nonpoint Pollution Control," *J. Environ. Econ. Manage.*, Mar. 1988, *15*(1), pp. 87–98.

―――― "Institutional 'Markets': The Role of Liability in Allocating Environmental Resources," in *Proceedings of AERE workshop on natural resource market mechanisms*. Association of Environmental and Resource Economists, June 1990.

Seskin, Eugene P.; Anderson, Robert J., Jr. and Reid, Robert O. "An Empirical Analysis of Economic Strategies for Controlling Air Pollution," *J. Environ. Econ. Manage.*, June 1983, *10*(2), pp. 112–24.

Shavell, Steven. "A Model of the Optimal Use of Liability and Safety Regulations," *Rand J. Econ.*, Summer 1984a, *15*(2), 271–80.

―――― "Liability for Harm versus Regulation of Safety," *J. Legal Stud.*, 1984b, *13*(2), pp. 357–74.

Shibata, Hirofumi and Winrich, J. Steven. "Control of Pollution When the Offended Defend Themselves," *Economica*, Nov. 1983, *50*(200), pp. 425–37.

Siebert Horst. "Environmental Protection and International Specialization," *Weltwirtsch. Arch.*, 1974, *110*(3), pp. 494–508.

Slovic, Paul; Fischloff, Baruch and Lichtenstein, Sarah. "Facts Versus Fears: Understanding Perceived Risk," in *Social risk assessment: How safe is enough*. Ed. Walter A. Albers. NY: Plenum, 1980.

―――― . "Response Mode, Framing, and Information-Processing Effects in Risk Assessment," in *Question framing and response consistency*. Ed.: Robin M. Hogarth. San Francisco, CA: Jossey-Bass, 1982.

Smith, V. Kerry. "The Role of Site and Job Characteristics in Hedonic Wage Models," *J. Urban Econ.*, May 1983, *13*(3), pp. 296–321.

Smith, V. Kerry and Desvousges, William H. "The Generalized Travel Cost Model and Water Quality Benefits: A Reconsideration," *Southern Econ. J.*, Oct. 1985, *52*(2), pp. 371–81.

―――― *Measuring water quality benefits*. Norwell. MA: Kluwer-Nijhoff, 1986a.

―――― "Averting Behavior: Does It Exist?" *Economics Letters*, 1986b, *20*(3), pp. 291–96.

Smith, V. Kerry; Desvousges, William H. and McGivney, Matthew P. "Estimating Water Quality Benefits: An Econometric Analysis," *Land Econ.*, Aug. 1983, *59*(3), pp. 259–78.

Smith, V. Kerry; Palmquist, Raymond B. and Jakus, Paul. "Combining Farrell Frontier and Hedonic Travel Cost Models for Valuing Estuarine Quality." Nov. 15, 1990, second revision.

Smith, Vernon L. "The Principle of Unanimity and Voluntary Consent in Social Choice," *J. Polit. Econ.*, Dec. 1977, *85*(6), pp. 1125–39.

―――― "Incentive Compatible Experimental Processes for the Provision of Public Goods," in *Research in experimental economics*. Ed.: Vernon L. Smith. Greenwich, CT: JAI Press, 1979.

Spofford, Walter O., Jr. "Efficiency Properties of Alternative Control Policies for Meeting Ambient Air Quality Standards: An Empirical Application to the Lower

Delaware Valley." Discussion Paper D-118. Washington, DC: Resources for the Future, Feb. 1984.

Spulber, Daniel F. "Effluent Regulation and Long-Run Optimality," *J. Environ. Econ. Manage.*, June 1985, *12*(2), pp. 103–16.

Starrett, David A. "Fundamental Nonconvexities in the Theory of Externalities," *J. Econ. Theory.* Apr. 1972, *4*(2), pp. 180–99.

Stavins, Robert N., ed. *Project 88—Harnessing market forces to protect our environment: Initiatives for the new president.* A Public Policy Study Sponsored by Senator Timothy E. Wirth, Colorado, and Senator John Heinz, Pennsylvania. Washington, DC. Dec. 1988.

Terkla, David. "The Efficiency Value of Effluent Tax Revenues," *J. Environ. Econ. Manage.*, June 1984, *11*(2), pp. 107–23.

Thaler, Richard and Rosen, Sherwin. "The Value of Life Savings," in *Household production and consumption.* Ed.: Nester Terleckyj. NY: Columbia U. Press, 1976.

Tietenberg, Thomas H. "Spatially Differentiated Air Pollutant Emission Charges: An Economic and Legal Analysis," *Land Econ.*, Aug. 1978, *54*(93), pp. 265–77.

—— "Transferable Discharge Permits and the Control of Stationary Source Air Pollution: A Survey and Synthesis," *Land Econ.*, Nov. 1980, *56*(4), pp. 391–416.

—— *Emissions trading: An exercise in reforming pollution policy.* Washington, DC: Resources for the Future, 1985.

—— "Indivisible Toxic Torts: The Economics of Joint and Several Liability," *Land Econ.*, Nov. 1989, *65*, pp. 305–19.

—— "Economic Instruments for Environmental Regulation," *Oxford Rev. Econ. Policy.* Mar. 1990, *6*.

Tobey, James A. "The Impact of Domestic Environmental Policies on International Trade." Ph.D. Dissertation, Dept. of Economics, U. of Maryland, College Park, 1989.

—— "The Effects of Domestic Environmental Policies on Patterns of World Trade: An Empirical Test," *Kyklos*, 1990, Fasc. 2.

Tolley, George et al. "Establishing and Valuing the Effects of Improved Visibility in Eastern United States." Prepared for the U.S. Environmental Protection Agency, Washington, DC, 1986a.

——. *Valuation of reductions in human health symptoms and risks.* Final Report for the U.S. Environmental Protection Agency. U. of Chicago, 1986b.

Travis, Curtis and Doty, Carolyn. "Superfund: A Program Without Priorities," *Environmental Science and Technology*, 1989, *23*(11), pp. 1333–34.

Trijonis, J. et al. "Air Quality Benefits for Los Angeles and San Francisco Based on Housing Values and Visibility." Final Report for California Air Resources Board, Sacramento, CA, 1984.

Turvey, Ralph. "On Divergences between Social Cost and Private Cost," *Economica*, Aug. 1963, *30*(119), pp. 309–13.

U.S. Environmental Protection Agency. "EPA's Use of Benefit-Cost Analysis: 1981–1986." Aug. 1987, EPA Report 230-05-87-028.

—— "Environmental Investments: The Cost of a Clean Environment." Dec. 1990, EPA Reprot 230-12-90-084.

U.S. General Accounting Office. *Energy issues.* Washington, DC, Nov. 1988.

U.S. National Oceanic and Atmospheric Administration, National Science Foundation, and National Aeronautics and Space Administration. *Economic and global change. New Haven Workshop, May 1990.* Washington, DC, Jan. 1991.

Vaughan, William J. and Russell, Clifford S. "Valuing a Fishing Day: An Application of a Systematic Varying Parameter Model," *Land Econ.*, Nov. 1982, *58*(4), pp. 450–63.

Viscusi, W. Kip; Magat, Wesley A. and Hubert, Joel. "Pricing Environmental Health Risks: Survey Assessments of Risk-Risk and Risk-Dollar Tradeoffs," in *AERE workshop proceedings: Estimating and valuing morbidity in a policy context*, 1988.

Walter, Ingo. "Pollution and Protection: U.S. Environmental Controls as Competitive Distortions," *Weltwirtsch. Arch.*, 1974, *110*(1), pp. 104–13.

────── "Trade, Environment and Comparative Advantage," in *International economics of pollution*. Ed.: Ingo Walter. NY: Wiley, 1975, pp. 77–93.

────── "Environmentally Induced Industrial Relocation in Developing Countries," in *Environment and trade*. Eds.: Seymour J. Rubin and Thomas R. Graham. Totowa, NJ: Allanheld, Osmun, and Co., 1982, pp. 67–101.

Walter, Ingo and Ugelow, Judith. "Environmental Policies in Developing Countries," *Ambio*. 1979, *8*(2,3), pp. 102–09.

Weitzman, Martin L. "Prices vs. Quantities," *Rev. Econ. Stud.*, Oct. 1974, *41*(4), pp. 477–91.

──────. "Optimal Rewards for Economic Regulation," *Amer. Econ. Rev.*, Sept. 1978, *68*(4), pp. 683–91.

Wenders, John T. "Methods of Pollution Control and the Rate of Change in Pollution Abatement Technology," *Water Resources Res.*, 1975, *11*(3), pp. 393–96.

Whitehead, John C. and Blomquist, Glenn C. "Measuring Contingent Values for Wetlands: Effects of Information About Related Environmental Goods," *Water Resources Research*, Oct. 1991, *27*(10), pp. 2523–31.

Wildasin, David E. "Interjurisdictional Capital Mobility: Fiscal Externality and a Corrective Subsidy," *J. Urban Econ.*, Mar. 1989, *25*(2), pp. 193–212.

Willig, Robert D. "Consumer's Surplus Without Apology," *Amer. Econ. Rev.*, Sept. 1976, *66*(4), pp. 589–97.

Wilson, John D. "A Theory of Interregional Tax Competition," *J. Urban Econ.*, May 1086, *19*(3), pp. 296–315.

Zodrow, George R. and Mieszkowski, Peter. "Pigou, Tiebout, Property Taxation and the Under-Provision of Local Public Goods," *J. Urban Econ.*, May 1986, *19*(3), pp. 356–70.

Zupan, Jeffrey. *The distribution of air quality in the New York region*. Washington, DC: Resources for the Future, 1973

5   Sustainability: An Economist's Perspective

Robert M. Solow

Robert M. Solow is Institute Professor of Economics Emeritus at the Massachusetts Institute of Technology.

This talk is different from anything else anyone has heard at Woods Hole; certainly for the last two days. Three people have asked me, "Do you plan to use any transparencies or slides?" Three times I said, "No," and three times I was met with this blank stare of disbelief. I actually have some beautiful aerial photographs of Prince William Sound that I could have brought along to show you, and I also have a spectacular picture of Michael Jordan in full flight that you would have liked to have seen. But in fact I don't need or want any slides or transparencies. I want to talk to you about an idea. The notion of sustainability or sustainable growth (although, as you will see, it has nothing necessarily to do with growth) has infiltrated discussions of long-run economic policy in the last few years. It is very hard to be against sustainability. In fact, the less you know about it, the better it sounds. That is true of lots of ideas. The questions that come to be connected with sustainable development or sustainable growth or just sustainability are genuine and deeply felt and very complex. The combination of deep feeling and complexity breeds buzzwords, and sustainability has certainly become a buzzword. What I thought I might do, when I was invited to talk to a group like this, was to try to talk out loud about how one might think straight about the concept of sustainability, what it might mean and what its implications (not for daily life but for your annual vote or your concern for economic policy) might be.

Definitions are usually boring. That is probably true here too. But here it matters a lot. Some people say they don't know what sustainability means, but it sounds good. I've seen things on restaurant menus that strike me the same way. I took these two parts of a definition from a UNESCO document: " . . . every generation should leave water, air and soil resources as pure and unpolluted as when it came on earth." Alternatively, it was suggested that "each generation should leave undiminished all the species of animals it found existing on earth." I suppose that sounds good, as it is meant to. But I believe that kind of thought is fundamentally the wrong way to go in thinking about this issue. I must also say that there are some

This paper was presented as the Eighteenth J. Seward Johnson Lecture to the Marine Policy Center, Woods Hole Oceanographic Institution, at Woods Hole, Massachusetts, on June 14, 1991.

much more carefully thought out definitions and discussions, say by the U.N. Environment Programme and the World Conservation Union. They all turn out to be vague; in a way, the message I want to leave with you today is that sustainability is an essentially vague concept, and it would be wrong to think of it as being precise, or even capable of being made precise. It is therefore probably not in any clear way an exact guide to policy. Nevertheless, it is not at all useless.

Pretty clearly the notion of sustainability is about our obligation to the future. It says something about a moral obligation that we are supposed to have for future generations. I think it is very important to keep in mind—I'm talking like a philosopher for the next few sentences and I don't really know how to do that—that you can't be morally obligated to do something that is not feasible. Could I be morally obligated to be like Peter Pan and flap my wings and fly around the room? The answer is clearly not. I can't have a moral obligation like that because I am not capable of flapping my arms and flying around the room. If I fail to carry out a moral obligation, you must be entitled to blame me. You could properly say unkind things about me. But you couldn't possibly say unkind things about me for not flying around the room like Peter Pan because you know, as well as I do, that I can't do it.

If you define sustainability as an obligation to leave the world as we found it in detail, I think that's glib but essentially unfeasible. It is, when you think about it, not even desirable. To carry out literally the injunction of UNESCO would mean to make no use of mineral resources; it would mean to do no permanent construction or semi-permanent construction; build no roads; build no dams; build no piers. A mooring would be all right but not a pier. Apart from being essentially an injunction to do something that is not feasible, it asks us to do something that is not, on reflection, desirable. I doubt that I would feel myself better off if I had found the world exactly as the Iroquois left it. It is not clear that one would really want to do that.

To make something reasonable and useful out of the idea of sustainability, I think you have to try a different kind of definition. The best thing I could think of is to say that it is an obligation to conduct ourselves so that we leave to the future the option or the capacity to be as well off as we are. It is not clear to me that one can be more precise than that. Sustainability is an injunction not to satisfy ourselves by impoverishing our successors. That sounds good too, but I want you to realize how problematic it is—how hard it is to make anything precise or checkable out of that thought. If we try to look far ahead, as presumably we ought to if we are trying to obey the injunction to sustainability, we realize that the tastes, the preferences, of future generations are something that we don't know about. Nor do we know anything very much about the technology that will be available to people 100 years from now. Put yourself in the position of someone in 1880 trying to imagine what life would be like in 1980 and you will see how wrong you would be. I think all we can do in this respect is to imagine people in the future being much like ourselves and attributing to them, imputing to them, whatever technology we can "reasonably" extrapolate—whatever that means. I am trying to emphasize the vagueness but not the meaningless of that concept. It is not meaningless, it is just inevitably vague.

We are entitled to please ourselves, according to this definition, so long as it is not at the expense (in the sense that I stated) of future well-being. You have to take into account, in thinking about sustainability, the resources that we use up and the resources that we leave behind, but also the sort of environment we leave behind including the built environment, including productive capacity (plant and equipment) and including technological knowledge. *To talk about sustainability in that way is not at all empty.* It attracts your attention, first, to what history tells us is an important fact, namely, that goods and services can be substituted for one another. If you don't eat one species of fish, you can eat another species of fish. Resources are, to use a favorite word of economists, fungible in a certain sense. They can take the place of each other. That is extremely important because it suggests that we do not owe to the future any particular thing. There is no specific object that the goal of sustainability, the obligation of sustainability, requires us to leave untouched.

What about nature? What about wilderness or unspoiled nature? I think that we ought, in our policy choices, to embody our desire for unspoiled nature as a component of well-being. But we have to recognize that different amenities really are, to some extent, substitutable for one another, and we should be as inclusive as possible in our calculations. It is perfectly okay, it is perfectly logical and rational, to argue for the preservation of a particular species or the preservation of a particular landscape. But that has to be done on its own, for its own sake, because this landscape is intrinsically what we want or this species is intrinsically important to preserve, not under the heading of sustainability. Sustainability doesn't require that any *particular* species of owl or any *particular* species of fish or any *particular* tract of forest be preserved. Substitutability is also important on the production side. We know that one kind of input can be substituted for another in production. There is no reason for our society to feel guilty about using up aluminum as long as we leave behind a capacity to perform the same or analogous functions using other kinds of materials—plastics or other natural or artificial materials. In making policy decisions we can take advantage of the principle of substitutability, remembering that what we are obligated to leave behind is a generalized capacity to create well-being, not any particular thing or any particular natural resource.

If you approach the problem that way in trying to make plans and make policies, it is certain that there will be mistakes. We will impute to the future tastes that they don't have or we will impute to them technological capacities that they won't have or we will fail to impute to them tastes and technological capacities that they do have. The set of possible mistakes is usually pretty symmetric.

That suggests to me the importance of choosing robust policies whenever we can. We should choose policies that will be appropriate over as wide a range of possible circumstances as we can imagine. But it would be wrong for policy to be paralyzed by the notion that one can make mistakes. Liability to error is the law of life. And, as most people around Woods Hole know, you choose policies to avoid potentially catastrophic errors, if you can. You insure wherever you can, but that's it.

The way I have put this, and I meant to do so, emphasizes that sustainability is about distributional equity. It is about who gets what. It is about the sharing of well-being between present people and future people. I have also emphasized the need to keep in mind, in making plans, that we don't know what they will do, what they will like, what they will want. And, to be honest, it is none of our business.

It is often asked whether, at this level, the goal or obligation of sustainability can be left entirely to the market. It seems to me that there is no reason to believe in a doctrinaire way that it can. The future is not adequately represented in the market, at least not the far future. If you remember that our societies live with real interest rates of the order of 5 or 6 percent, you will realize that that means that the dollar a generation from now, thirty years from now, is worth 25 cents today. That kind of discount seems to me to be much sharper than we would seriously propose in our public capacity, as citizens thinking about our obligation to the future. It seems to me to be a stronger discount than most of us would like to make. It is fair to say that those people a few generations hence are not adequately represented in today's market. They don't participate in it, and therefore there is no doctrinaire reason for saying, "Oh well, ordinary supply and demand, ordinary market behavior, will take care of whatever obligation we have to the future."

Now, in principle, government could serve as a trustee, as a representative for future interests. Policy actions, taxes, subsidies, regulations could, in principle, correct for the excessive present-mindedness of ordinary people like ourselves in our daily business. Of course, we are not sure that government will do a good job. It often seems that the rate at which governments discount the future is rather sharper than that at which the bond market does. So we can't be sure that public policy will do a good job. That is why we talk about it in a democracy. We are trying to think about collective decisions for the future, and discussions like this, not with just me talking, are the way in which policies of that kind ought to be thrashed out.

Just to give you some idea of how uncertain both private and public behavior can be in an issue like this, let me ask you to think about the past, not about the future. You could make a good case that our ancestors, who were considerably poorer than we are, whose standard of living was considerably less than our own, were probably excessively generous in providing for us. They cut down a lot of trees, but they saved a lot and they build a lot of railroad rights-of-way. Both private and publicly they probably did better by us than a sort of fair-minded judge in thinking about the equity (whether they got their share and we got our share or whether we profited at their expense) would have required. It would have been okay for them to save a little less, to enjoy a little more and given us a little less of a start than our generation has had. I don't think there is any simple generalization that will serve to guide policy about these issues. There is every reason to discuss economic policy and social policy from this point of view, and anything else is likely to be ideology rather than analysis.

Once you take the point of view that I have been urging on you in thinking about sustainability as a matter of distributional equity between the present and the future, you can see that it becomes a problem about saving and investment. It becomes a problem about the choice between current consumption and providing for the future.

There is a sort of dual connection—a connection that need not be intrinsic but is there—between environmental issues and sustainability issues. The environment needs protection by public policy because each of us knows that by burdening the environment, by damaging it, we can profit and have some of the cost, perhaps most of the cost, borne by others. Sustainability is a problem precisely because each of us knows or realizes that we can profit at the expense of the future rather than at the expense of our contemporaries and the environment. We free-ride on each other and we free-ride on the future.

Environmental policy is important for both reasons. One of the ways we free-ride on the future is by burdening the environment. And so current environmental protection—this is what I meant by a dual connection—will almost certainly contribute quite a lot to sustainability. Although, I want to warn you, not automatically. Current environmental protection contributes to sustainability if it comes at the expense of current consumption. Not if it comes at the expense of investment, of additions to future capacity. So, there are no absolutes. There is nothing precise about this notion but there are perhaps approximate guides to public policy that come out of this way of reasoning about the idea of sustainability. A correct principle, a correct general guide is that when we use up something—and by we I mean our society, our country, our civilization, however broadly you want to think—when we use up something that is irreplaceable, whether it is minerals or a fish species, or an environmental amenity, then we should be thinking about providing a substitute of equal value, and the vagueness comes in the notion of value. The something that we provide in exchange could be knowledge, could be technology. It needn't even be a physical object.

Let me give you an excellent example from the recent past of a case of good thought along these lines and also a case of bad thought along these lines. Commercially usable volumes of oil were discovered in the North Sea some years ago. The two main beneficiaries of North Sea oil were the United Kingdom and Norway. It is only right to say that the United Kingdom dissipated North Sea oil, wasted it, used it up in consumption and on employment. If I meet Mrs. Thatcher in heaven, since that is where I intend to go, the biggest thing I will tax her with is that she blew North Sea oil. Here was an asset that by happenstance the U.K. acquired. If the sort of general approach to sustainability that I have been suggesting to you had been taken by the Thatcher government, someone would have said, "It's okay we are going to use up the oil, that's what it is for, but we will make sure that we provide something else in exchange, that we guide those resources, at least in large part, into investment in capacity in the future." That did not happen. As I said, if you ask where (and by the way the curve of production from the North Sea fields is already on the way down; that asset is on its way to exhaustion) it went, it went into maintaining consumption in the United Kingdom and, at the same time, into unemployment.

Norway, on the other hand, went about it in the typical sober way you expect of good Scandinavians. The Norwegians said, here is a wasting asset. Here is an asset that we are going to use up. Scandinavians are also slightly masochistic, as you know. They said the one thing we must avoid is blowing this; the one thing we must avoid is a binge. They tried very hard to convert a large fraction of the revenues, of the rentals, of the royalties from North Sea oil into investment. I confess I don't know how well they succeeded but I am willing to bet that they did a better job of it than the United Kingdom.

This brings me to the one piece of technical economics that I want to mention. There is a neat analytical result in economics (mainly done by John Hartwick of Queen's University in Canada) which studies an economy that takes what we call the rentals, the pure return to a non-renewable resource, and invests those rentals.[1] That is, it uses up a natural asset like the North Sea oil field, but makes a point of investing whatever revenues intrinsically inhere to the oil itself. That policy can be shown to have neat sustainability properties. In a simple sort of economy, it will guarantee a perpetually constant capacity to consume. By the way, it is a very simple rule, and it is really true only for very simple economies; but it has the advantage, first of all, of sounding right, of sounding like justice, and secondly, of being practical. It is a calculation that could be made. It is a calculation that we don't make and I am going to suggest in a minute that we should be making it. You might want to do better. You might feel so good about your great-grandchildren that you would like to do better than invest the rents on the non-renewable resources that you use up. But in any case, it is, at a minimum, a policy that one could pursue for the sake of sustainability. I want to remind you again that most environmental protection can be regarded as an act of investment. If we were to think that our obligation to the future is in principle discharged by seeing that the return to non-renewable resources is funnelled into capital formation, any kind of capital formation—plant and equipment, research and development, physical oceanography, economics or environmental investment—we could have some feeling that we were about on the right track.

Now I want to mention what strikes me as sort of a paradox—as a difficulty with a concept of sustainability. I said, I kind of insisted, that you should think about it as a matter of equity, as a matter of distributional equity, as a matter of choice of how productive capacity should be shared between us and them, them being the future. Once you think about it that way you are almost forced logically to think about equity not between periods of time but equity right now. There is something inconsistent about people who profess to be terribly concerned about the welfare of future generations but do not seem to be terribly concerned about the welfare of poor people today. You will see in a way why this comes to be a paradox.

---

[1]John M. Hartwick, "Substitution among exhaustible resources and intergenerational equity," *Review of Economic Studies* 45(2): 347–543 (June 1978).

The only reason for thinking that sustainability is a problem is that you think that some people are likely to be shortchanged, namely, in the future. Then I think you really are obligated to ask, "Well, is anybody being shortchanged right now?"

The paradox arises because if you are concerned about people who are currently poor, it will turn out that your concern for them will translate into an increase in current consumption, not into an increase in investment. The logic of sustainability says, "You ought to be thinking about poor people today, and thinking about poor people today will be disadvantageous from the point of view of sustainability." Intellectually, there is no difficulty in resolving that paradox, but practically there is every difficulty in the world in resolving that paradox. And I don't have the vaguest notion of how it can be done in practice.

The most dramatic way in which I can remind you of the nature of that paradox is to think about what it will mean for, say, CO_2 discharge when the Chinese start to burn their coal in a very large way; and, then, while you are interested in moral obligation, I think you should invent for yourself how you are going to explain to the Chinese that they shouldn't burn the coal, even living at their standard of living they shouldn't burn the coal, because the CO_2 might conceivably damage somebody in 50 or 100 years.

Actually the record of the U.S. is not very good on either the intergenerational equity or the intra-generational equity front. We tolerate, for a rich society, quite a lot of poverty, and at the same time we don't save or invest a lot. I've just spent some time in West Germany, and there is considerably less apparent poverty in the former Federal Republic than there is here; and at the same time they are investing a larger fraction of their GNP than we are by a large margin.

It would not be very hard for us to do better. One thing we might do, for starters, is to make a comprehensive accounting of rents on nonrenewable resources. It is something that we do not do. There is nothing in the national accounts of the U.S. which will tell you what fraction of the national income is the return to the using up of non-renewable resources. If we were to make that accounting, then we would have a better idea than we have now as to whether we are at least meeting that minimal obligation to channel those rents into saving and investment. And I also suggested that careful attention to current environmental protection is another way that is very likely to slip in some advantage in the way of sustainability, provided it is at the expense of current consumption and not at the expense of other forms of investment.

I have left out of this talk, as some of you may have noticed until now, any mention of population growth; and I did that on purpose, although it might be the natural first order concern if you are thinking about sustainability issues. Control of population growth would probably be the best available policy on behalf of sustainability. You know that, I know that, and I have no particular competence to discuss it any further; so I won't, except to remind you that rapid population growth is fundamentally a Third

World phenomenon, not a developed country phenomenon. So once again, you are up against the paradox that people in poor countries have children as insurance policies for their own old age. It is very hard to preach to them not to do that. On the other hand, if they continue to do that, then you have probably the largest, single danger to sustainability of the world economy.

All that remains for me is to summarize. What I have been trying to say goes roughly as follows. Sustainability as a moral obligation is a general obligation not a specific one. It is not an obligation to preserve this or preserve that. It is an obligation, if you want to make sense out of it, to preserve the capacity to be well off, to be as well off as we. That does not preclude preserving specific resources, if they have an independent value and no good substitutes. But we shouldn't kid ourselves, that is part of the value of specific resources. It is not a consequence of any interest in sustainability. Secondly, an interest in sustainability speaks for investment generally. I mentioned that directing the rents on non-renewable resources into investment is a good rule of thumb, a reasonable and dependable starting point. But what sustainability speaks for is investment, investment of any kind. In particular, environmental investment seems to me to correlate well with concerns about sustainability and so, of course, does reliance on renewable resources as a substitute for non-renewable ones. Third, there is something faintly phony about deep concern for the future combined with callousness about the state of the world today. The catch is that today's poor want consumption not investment. So the conflict is pretty deep and there is unlikely to be any easy to way resolve it. Fourth, research is a good thing. Knowledge on the whole is an environmentally neutral asset that we can contribute to the future. I said that in thinking about sustainability you want to be as inclusive as you can. Investment in the broader sense and investment in knowledge, especially technological and scientific knowledge, is an environmentally clean an asset as we know. And the last thing I want to say is, don't forget that sustainability is a vague concept. It is intrinsically inexact. It is not something that can be measured out in coffee spoons. It is not something that you could be numerically accurate about. It is, at best, a general guide to policies that have to do with investment, conservation and resource use. And we shouldn't pretend that it is anything other than that.

Thank you very much.

REFERENCES

World Commission on Environment and Development, *Our Common Future* (The Brundtland Report). Oxford: Oxford University Press, 1987.
World Conservation Union, *Caring for the Earth*. Gland, Switzerland, 1991; see especially p. 10.
World Resources Institute, *World Resources 1992–93: Toward Sustainable Development*. New York: Oxford University Press, 1992. See especially Ch. 1.

II

The Costs of Environmental Protection

6   *Environmental Regulation and the Competitiveness of U.S. Manufacturing: What Does the Evidence Tell Us?**

Adam B. Jaffe

Steven R. Peterson

Paul R. Portney

Robert N. Stavins

Adam Jaffe is Associate Professor of Economics at Brandeis University, and Research Associate at the National Bureau of Economic Research; Steven Peterson is Senior Economist at Economics Resource Group; Paul Portney is President and Senior Fellow at Resources for the Future; and Robert Stavins is Albert Pratt Professor of Business and Government, John F. Kennedy School of Government at Harvard University, and University Fellow at Resources for the Future.

1. Introduction

More than two decades ago, the first Earth Day in 1970 marked the beginning of the modern environmental movement. Since that time, the United States has spent more than $1 trillion to prevent or reduce environmental damages created by industrial and commercial activities. During the latter part of this period, the U.S. economy has moved from a position of approximate trade balance on a long-term basis to a position of chronic trade deficit. The coincidence of these two major trends has led many to suspect that environmental regulation may be playing a major causal role in impairing the "competitiveness" of U.S. firms.[1]

"Environmental Regulation and the Competitiveness of U.S. Manufacturing: What Does the Evidence Tell Us?" by Adam B. Jaffe, Steven R. Peterson, Paul R. Portney, and Robert N. Stavins, from *Journal of Economic Literature*, 33:132–163 (March 1995).

*The authors thank Lawrence Goulder, Raymond Kopp, William Nordhaus, Richard Schmalensee, Martin Weitzman, David Wheeler, and participants in seminars at Harvard University and Resources for the Future for helpful comments. Funding for previous work on this subject from the U.S. Department of Commerce is gratefully acknowledged. The authors alone are responsible for any omissions or other errors.

[1]This argument is related but not identical to expressed concerns about the loss of "competitiveness" of the U.S. as a whole. For a trenchant criticism of the notion that countries "compete" in the same ways that individual firms do, see Paul Krugman (1994).

The conventional wisdom is that environmental regulations impose significant costs, slow productivity growth, and thereby hinder the ability of U.S. firms to compete in international markets. This loss of competitiveness is believed to be reflected in declining exports, increasing imports, and a long-term movement of manufacturing capacity from the United States to other countries, particularly in "pollution-intensive" industries.[2]

Under a more recent, revisionist view, environmental regulations are seen not only as benign in their impacts on international competitiveness, but actually as a net *positive* force driving private firms and the economy as a whole to become more competitive in international markets.[3] During the past few years, a heated debate has arisen in the United States revolving around these two views.[4] This paper assembles and assesses the evidence on these hypothetical linkages between environmental regulation and competitiveness.

The terms of the debate and the nature of the problems have not always been clear, but it is possible to sketch the general nature of the concerns. Much of the discussion has revolved around the fear that environmental regulation may reduce net exports in the manufacturing sector, particularly in "pollution-intensive" goods. Such a change in our trade position could have several effects. First, in the short run, a reduction in net exports in manufacturing will exacerbate the overall trade imbalance. Although we are likely to return toward trade balance in the long run, one of the mechanisms through which this happens is a decline in the value of the dollar. This means that imported goods become more expensive, thus reducing the standard of living for many people. Second, if those industries most affected by regulation employ less educated workers, then this portion of the labor force will be particularly hard hit, because those workers may have an especially hard time finding new jobs at comparable wages. Third, a diminishing U.S. share of world capacity in petroleum-refining, steel, autos, and other industries could endanger economic security. Finally, even in the absence of these income distribution or economic security concerns, the rearrangement of production from pollution-intensive to other industries creates a broader set of social costs, at least in the short run. Because the "short run" could last for years or even decades, these transition costs are also a legitimate policy concern.

---

[2]The theoretical argument that ambitious environmental regulations could harm a nation's comparative advantage is well established, but our focus is exclusively on empirical evidence. On the former, see Rudiger Pethig (1975); Horst Siebert (1977); Gary W. Yohe (1979); and Martin C. McGuire (1982).

[3]These ideas, generally associated most with Michael E. Porter (1991), have become widely disseminated among policy makers. For example, a U.S. Environmental Protection Agency (EPA) conference recently concluded that environmental regulations induce "more cost-effective processes that both reduce emissions and the overall cost of doing business . . ." (U.S. Environmental Protection Agency 1992b).

[4]For an overview of the dimensions of this debate, see Richard B. Stewart (1993). Unfortunately, this debate has often been clouded by the very criteria chosen by proponents of alternative views. For example, there has been substantial debate *and* confusion among policy makers about whether environmental regulations create new jobs and whether such "job creation" ought to be considered a regulatory benefit or cost (if either). See Thomas D. Hopkins (1992).

Table 1 U.S. Emissions of Six Major Air Pollutants, 1970–1991[a]

Year	SO_2	NO_x	VOCs	CO	TSPs	Lead
1970	100[b]	100	100	100	100	100
1975	90	107	82	85	58	72
1980	84	124	79	81	48	34
1981	79	113	77	79	45	27
1982	75	107	71	73	40	26
1983	73	104	74	75	41	22
1984	76	106	77	71	43	19
1985	76	102	72	67	41	9
1986	74	99	67	62	38	3
1987	74	100	68	61	39	3
1988	75	104	68	61	42	3
1989	76	102	63	55	40	3
1990	74	102	64	55	39	3
1991	73	99	62	50	39	2

Source: U.S. Environmental Protection Agency (1992a).
[a]The six "criteria air pollutants" listed are: sulfur dioxide (SO_2); nitrogen oxides (NO_x); reactive volatile organic compounds (VOCs); carbon monoxide (CO); total suspended particulates (TSPs); and lead.
[b]Indexed to 1970 emissions, set equal to 100. Note that these are aggregate national emissions, not emissions per capita or emissions per unit of GNP; the latter two statistics would, of course, exhibit greater downward trends.

There are a number of reasons to believe that the link between environmental regulation and competitiveness could be significant. First, environmental regulation has grown significantly in the United States since 1970, and substantial gains have been achieved in reducing pollutant emissions (Table 1).

But according to the U.S. Environmental Protection Agency (EPA), the annual cost of complying with environmental regulation administered by EPA now exceeds $125 billion in the United States, or about 2.1 percent of gross domestic product (GDP).[5] Furthermore, EPA has projected that annual environmental compliance spending may reach $190 billion by the end of this decade. If that happens, the United States will be devoting nearly 2.6 percent of its GDP to environmental compliance by the year 2000.[6]

---

[5]As we discuss later in some detail, these direct compliance costs represent only a share of the overall social costs of environmental regulation. For example, Weitzman (1994) estimates that the total "environmental drag" on the U.S. economy may be two to three times greater than these fractions of GNP dedicated to compliance spending would suggest.

[6]Figures are in constant 1992 dollars (throughout the paper, unless otherwise specified), assuming a seven percent cost of capital (U.S. Environmental Protection Agency 1990). These estimates include both capital and operating costs. Projections for compliance costs of existing regulations are based on historical extrapolations. Projections for the costs of new and proposed regulations are based on EPA regulatory analyses. EPA actually makes its projections in terms of gross national product (GNP), rather than gross domestic product (GDP), but any difference between the two is small compared to uncertainty over compliance costs.

Table 2 Pollution Abatement and Control Expenditures for Selected OECD Countries as a Percentage of Gross Domestic Product

	1981	1982	1983	1984	1985	1986	1987	1988	1989	1990
United States	1.5	1.5	1.5	1.4	1.4	1.4	1.4	1.3	1.4	1.4
France	0.9	0.9	0.9	0.8	0.9	0.8	1.0	1.0	1.0	1.0
West Germany	1.5	1.5	1.4	1.4	1.5	1.5	1.6	1.6	1.6	1.6
Netherlands	—	1.2	—	—	1.3	1.5	1.5	—	1.5	—
United Kingdom	1.6	—	—	—	1.3	1.3	—	—	—	1.5

Sources: Organization for Economic Cooperation and Development (1990, p. 40), for years 1981–1985; Organization for Economic Cooperation and Development (1993b, p. 11) for years 1986–1990.

It is extremely difficult to compare this compliance cost burden with that borne by competing firms in other countries. Environmental requirements throughout most of the developing world are less stringent than ours, and related compliance costs are hence generally lower. On the other hand, some data suggest that other countries, such as Germany, have regulatory programs that give rise to regulatory costs roughly comparable to those imposed on U.S. firms (Table 2).[7]

Putting aside the potential effect of differences in regulatory stringency, there are other ways in which environmental regulations may affect competitiveness. Holding constant the *stringency* of environmental standards, the *form* these rules take can potentially affect business location. For instance, U.S. environmental regulations often go beyond specifying numerical discharge standards for particular sources or source categories, and mandate, instead, specific control technologies or processes. If other countries tend to avoid such technological mandates and thus allow more flexibility in compliance, manufacturing abroad may be relatively attractive because sources will have the ability to use new, innovative, and low-cost ways to meet discharge standards.

Another difference between U.S. and foreign environmental regulation should also be recognized: namely, the adversarial approach to regulation typically taken in the United States. Regulatory decisions in the United States are time-consuming and characterized by litigation and other legal wrangling. By way of contrast, a more cooperative relationship is said to exist between regulator and regulatee in some other countries, with the United Kingdom offered as the definitive example (David Vogel 1986). Un-

---

[7]It is indicative of the data problems in this area that the OECD numbers in Table 2 differ in both level *and* trend from the EPA numbers cited above and presented in Table 4. It is our view that the data in the latter table more accurately reflect annual expenditures in the United States to comply with federal environmental regulations. It would be helpful if the environmental agencies of other nations made the same effort as the U.S. Environmental Protection Agency to keep track of and regularly report estimated compliance expenditures.

fortunately, data on these aspects of respective costs are essentially unavailable.

In general, the studies that attempt to analyze directly the effects of environmental regulations on trade and competitiveness are limited in number. If one casts a wide enough net, however, by defining competitiveness rather broadly and by searching for indirect as well as direct evidence, it is possible to identify more than one hundred studies potentially capable of shedding some light on the relationship.[8] It is nearly the case, however, that no two of these studies ask the same question or even examine the same problem. This is one of the challenges of trying to assess the competing hypotheses of the environment-competitiveness linkage.

Despite our relatively broad focus with regard to competitiveness, the scope of this review is somewhat limited in another respect. Specifically, we limit our attention here to studies shedding light on the effects of environmental regulation on manufacturing firms. This is not because of an absence of such regulation in natural resource industries such as forestry, agriculture, mining, and commercial fishing. Indeed, the controversy over the Northern Spotted Owl, the Endangered Species Act in general, and the effects of habitat preservation on the location of timber production is among the most visible U.S. environmental issues of recent times. Similarly, regulations pertaining to pesticide use in agriculture, the reclamation of land mined for coal or non-fuel minerals, or the equipment that can be used by commercial fishing fleets can clearly affect the costs faced by (and hence the international competitiveness of) U.S. firms in these industries.

Rather, we concentrate our attention on manufacturing industries for two reasons. First, that is where the research has been done. With a few exceptions, economists have paid little attention to the effects of environmental regulation on competitiveness in the natural resources sector. By way of contrast, there is a substantial and growing literature focused on the manufacturing sector, as suggested above. Second, the political and policy debate has centered around the possible "flight" of manufacturing from the U.S. to other countries with less stringent environmental standards.

To some extent, this distinction is a peculiar one. To be sure, environmental restrictions on pesticide use or habitat destruction cannot induce someone to move a farm or commercial forest to another country. Such natural capital is immobile, even in the long run. But if concern about competitiveness is primarily a "jobs" issue—and, to many, at least, it is—then it is relevant that environmental regulations pertaining to natural resource industries can affect *where* crops are grown, timber is harvested, fish are caught, or minerals are mined. Nevertheless, because the overwhelming share of attention by policy makers and academics has been devoted to the competitiveness of manufacturing, we concentrate our attention there, as well.

---

[8]For a comprehensive review of the literature, see Jaffe et al. (1993). An earlier survey is provided by Judith M. Dean (1992). See, also U.S. Office of Technology Assessment (1992).

The remainder of this paper is organized as follows. Section 2 outlines an analytical framework for identifying the effects of environmental regulation on international trade in manufactured goods, discusses how different notions of competitiveness fit into that framework, and examines the major categories of environmental regulatory costs. In Section 3, we draw on the available evidence to examine the effects of environmental regulations on international trade in manufacturing. In Section 4, we turn to the empirical evidence regarding the linkage between environmental regulation and investment; and in Section 5, we look at links between regulation and more broadly defined economic growth. Finally, in Section 6, we draw some conclusions.

2. Framework for Analyzing Regulation and Competitiveness

2.1 A Theoretically Desirable Indicator of Competitiveness

The standard theory of international trade is based on the notion that trade is driven by comparative advantage—that countries export those goods and services that they make relatively (but not necessarily absolutely) more efficiently than other nations, and import those goods and services they are relatively less efficient at producing. Because of the anticipated international adjustments that occur when relative costs change, we could measure—in theory, at least—the real effects of regulation (or any other policy change, for that matter) on competitiveness by identifying the effect that the policy would have on net exports *holding real wages and exchange rates constant.*[9] We would wish to measure the reduction in net exports "before" any adjustments in the exchange rate (and hence in net exports of other goods) have taken place, because other industries whose net exports increase to balance a fall in exports should not be thought of as having become more competitive if their export increase is brought about solely by a fall in exchange rates. Similarly, we should not construe an increase in exports brought about solely by a fall in real wages as an increase in "competitiveness."

The unfortunate problem with this analytically clean definition of competitiveness is that it is essentially impossible to implement in practice. We simply are not presented with data generated by the hypothetical experiment in which regulations are imposed while everything else is held constant. In principle, one could formulate a structural econometric model in which net exports by industry, wages, and exchange rates are determined jointly as a function of regulatory costs and resource endowments. We have identified no study that has attempted to do so, and it is not clear that

---

[9]This definition is closely related to those suggested by Laura D'Andrea Tyson (1988), and Organization of Economic Cooperation and Development (1993a).

available data would support such an effort.[10] As a result, we are left with indicators of the effects on competitiveness that are not wholly satisfactory because they fail to take account of the complicated adjustment mechanisms that operate when regulations are imposed. Nevertheless, these indicators can be useful to sort through many of the policy debates regarding the environment-competitiveness linkage.

2.2 Alternative Indicators of "Competitiveness"

The indicators of "competitiveness" that are used in the existing literature can be classified into three broad categories.[11] One set of measures has to do with the change in net exports of certain goods, the production of which is heavily regulated, and with comparisons between net exports of these goods and others produced under less regulated conditions. For example, stringent environmental regulation of the steel industry should, all else equal, cause the net exports of steel to fall *relative* to the net exports of goods the production of which is more lightly regulated. Thus, the magnitude and significance of an econometric parameter estimate that captures the effect of regulatory stringency in a regression explaining changes in net exports across industries could be taken as an indicator of the strength of the effects of regulation on competitiveness.

A second potential indicator is the extent to which the locus of *production* of pollution-intensive goods has shifted from countries with stringent regulations toward those with less. After all, the policy concern about competitiveness is that the United States is losing world market share in regulated industries to countries with less stringent regulations. If this is so, then there should be a general decrease in the U.S. share of world production of highly regulated goods and an increase in the world share of production of these goods by countries with relatively light regulation.

Third, if regulation is reducing the attractiveness of the United States as a locus for investment, then there should be a relative increase in investment by U.S. firms overseas in highly regulated industries. Similarly, all else equal, new plants in these industries would be more likely to be located in jurisdictions with lax regulation.

Finally, in addition to research focusing on these aspects of competitiveness, there exists one other set of important analytical approaches that can shed light on the environment-competitiveness debate. These are analyses focused on the more fundamental link between environmental compliance costs, productivity, investment, and the ultimate social costs of regulation. These analyses, including investigations of the productivity effects of regulation as well as general-equilibrium studies of long-term, social costs of regulation, have implications for both the conventional and the revisionist hypotheses concerning environmental regulation and competitiveness.

---

[10]Later we discuss the quantity and quality of available cross-country compliance-cost data.

[11]We henceforth drop the quotation marks around our use of the term "competitiveness" for convenience of presentation.

Because the economic adjustment to regulation is highly complex, and because there are a multiplicity of issues wrapped up in the term "competitiveness," it is not possible to combine estimates of these different aspects of the process into a single, overall quantification of the effects of regulation on competitiveness.[12] The best that can be done is to assess somewhat qualitatively the magnitude of estimated effects, based on multiple indicators. We return to that assessment shortly.

2.3 A Framework for Analysis

These diverse sets of indicators reflect the various routes through which regulation can conceivably affect competitiveness. First, environmental regulations of affect a firm's costs of production, both directly through its own expenditures on pollution reduction and indirectly through the higher prices it must pay for certain factors of production that are affected by regulation. Both direct and indirect costs will affect competitiveness, including measures of trade and investment flows.[13]

It is also true that environmental regulations can reduce costs for some firms or industries, by lowering input prices or by increasing the productivity of their inputs. Such "benefits to industry" could take the form, for example, of reduced costs to the food processing industry when its supplies of intake water are less polluted; likewise, workers may become more productive if health-threatening air pollution is reduced (see Bart D. Ostro 1983). Such benefits would have positive effects on U.S. trade and investment through the same mechanisms by which increased costs would have negative effects. Additionally, firms in the environmental services sector typically benefit from stricter regulations affecting their clients and/or potential clients.[14]

In any case, the degree to which domestic regulatory costs (and benefits) affect trade will depend also on the magnitude of the costs (and ben-

---

[12]Having highlighted a theoretically desirable measure and a set of empirically practical means of assessing the link between environmental protection and economic competitiveness, we should also note the multiplicity of *inappropriate* means of examining this link. Indeed, the amount of published, muddled thinking on this subject seems to exceed the norm. Numerous studies have focused exclusively on "jobs created in the environmental services sector" and taken this to be a measure of net positive economic benefits of regulation (apart from any environmental benefits). A recent example of this approach is provided by Roger H. Bezdek (1993), with numerous citations to other such studies. See Hopkins (1992) and Portney (1994) for critiques of this approach.

[13]For the economy as a whole, there is, of course, no distinction between direct and indirect costs. To measure total industry expenditures for pollution compliance, it would be incorrect to add the increased costs of the steel industry resulting from higher steel prices; to do so would result in obvious double-counting. The necessity of tracking indirect costs arises, however, when the analyst wishes to estimate the impact of regulation on a particular industry, or to compare effects on different industries. We postpone discussion of another notion of "indirect costs," including transition costs and reduced investment, which we refer to for semantic clarity as "other social costs" of regulation. See Section 5, below.

[14]There are, of course, additional benefits of environmental regulation that accrue to society at large rather than to industry. We exclude these here, not because they are unimportant, but because they do not bear on the issue of competitiveness.

Table 3 A Taxonomy of Costs of Environmental Regulation

Government Administration of Environmental
  Statutes and Regulations
    Monitoring
    Enforcement

Private Sector Compliance Expenditures
  Capital
  Operating

Other Direct Costs
  Legal and Other Transactional
  Shifted Management Focus
  Disrupted Production

Negative Costs
  Natural Resource Inputs
  Worker Health
  Innovation Stimulation

General Equilibrium Effects
  Product Substitution
  Discouraged Investment
  Retarded Innovation

Transition Costs
  Unemployment
  Obsolete Capital

Social Impacts
  Loss of Middle-Class Jobs
  Economic Security Impacts

efits) that other countries impose on the firms operating within their borders. Likewise, other nations' policies will also affect the investment decisions of their indigenous firms and of foreign firms, as well. Any changes in investment patterns that do occur ultimately affect trade flows as well, and both trade and investment effects interact with exchange rates.

2.4 Measuring the Costs of Environmental Regulation

In Table 3, we provide a taxonomy of the costs of environmental regulation, beginning with the most obvious and moving toward the least direct.[15] First, many policy makers and much of the general public would identify the on-budget costs to government of administering (monitoring and enforcing) environmental laws and regulations as *the* cost of environmental regulation. Most analysts, on the other hand, would identify the capital and operating expenditures associated with regulatory compliance as the fun-

---

[15]For a very useful decomposition and analysis of the full costs of environmental regulation, see Schmalensee, (1994). Conceptually, the cost of an environmental regulation is equal to "the change in consumer and producer surpluses associated with the regulations and with any price and/or income changes that may result" (Maureen L. Cropper and Wallace E. Oates 1992, p. 721).

damental part of the overall costs of regulation, although a substantial share of compliance costs for some federal regulations fall on state and local governments rather than private firms—the best example being the regulation of contaminants in drinking water. Additional direct costs include legal and other transaction costs, the effects of refocused management attention, and the possibility of disrupted production.

Next, one should also consider potential "negative costs" (in other words, nonenvironmental benefits) of environmental regulation, including the productivity impacts of a cleaner environment and the potential innovation-stimulating effects of regulation (linked with the so-called Porter hypothesis, which we discuss later). General equilibrium effects associated with product substitution, discouraged investment,[16] and retarded innovation constitute another important layer of costs, as do the transition costs of real-world economies responding over time to regulatory changes. Finally, there is a set of potential social impacts that is given substantial weight in political forums, including impacts on jobs and economic security.

Within the category of direct compliance costs, expenditures for pollution abatement in the United States have grown steadily over the past two decades, both absolutely and as a percentage of GNP (Table 4), reaching $125 billion (2.1 percent of GNP) by 1990. EPA estimates these costs will reach 2.6 percent of GNP by 2000.[17]

Even estimates of direct, compliance expenditures vary greatly. For example, Gary L. Rutledge and Mary L. Leonard (1992) estimate that pollution abatement costs for 1990 were $94 billion, rather than $125 billion as estimated by EPA.[18]

There are a number of potential problems of interpretation associated with these data. The questionnaire used by the U.S. Department of Commerce (1993) to collect data for its *Pollution Abatement Costs and Expenditures (PACE)* survey asks corporate or government officials how capital expenditures compared to what they would have been in the absence of environmental regulations. This creates two problems. The first involves the determination of an appropriate baseline. Absent any regulation, firms might still engage in some—perhaps a great deal of—pollution control to limit tort liability, stay on good terms with communities in which they are located, maintain a good environmental image, etc. Should such expenditures be included or excluded in the no-regulation baseline?

---

[16]For example, if a firm chooses to close a plant because of a new regulation (rather than installing expensive control equipment), this would be counted as zero cost in typical compliance-cost estimates.

[17]Recall that these estimates capture, at most, only what we have labelled private sector compliance expenditures in Table 4. As is shown in Table 5, business pollution-abatement expenditures represented about 61 percent of total *direct* costs in 1990. The remainder consisted of: personal consumption abatement (11%); government abatement (23%); government regulation and monitoring (2%); and research and development (3%).

[18]The primary difference between the estimates is due to the fact that EPA includes the cost of all solid waste disposal, while Rutledge and M. L. Leonard exclude some of these costs. See, also: Rutledge and Leonard 1993. The EPA data, however, exclude a significant portion of other expenditures mandated at the state and local level.

Table 4 Total Costs of Pollution Control[a] (millions of 1992 dollars)

	1972	1973	1974	1975	1976	1977	1978	1979	1980	1981	1982
Total Air & Radiation	9,915	11,995	12,725	13,942	15,854	18,071	19,993	21,413	22,313	22,992	23,550
Total Water	12,387	14,352	16,795	18,940	21,769	24,234	26,342	28,707	30,925	33,149	34,832
Total Land	10,543	11,120	11,683	12,235	12,984	14,160	14,897	16,223	17,011	17,660	⁻6,502
Total Chemicals	115	179	229	226	436	510	729	1,056	1,111	989	890
Multi-Media	135	174	576	734	911	1,149	1,129	1,107	1,085	869	757
Total Costs	33,094	37,818	42,009	46,043	51,954	58,124	63,089	68,156	72,446	75,658	76,530
Percentage of GNP	0.88	0.96	1.07	1.19	1.28	1.37	1.41	1.49	1.58	1.62	1.68

	1983	1984	1985	1986	1987	1988	1989	1990	1991	1992	2000
Total Air & Radiation	25,970	27,899	31,885	31,782	33,751	34,482	35,326	35,029	36,852	37,763	46,859
Total Water	37,199	39,099	41,418	44,197	46,904	48,104	50,317	52,604	55,114	57,277	72,705
Total Land	17,034	18,711	19,881	21,884	23,860	25,392	28,760	33,177	37,184	41,186	57,673
Total Chemicals	762	856	966	1,027	1,024	1,137	1,531	1,973	2,356	2,662	3,614
Multi-Media	865	821	859	1,147	1,052	1,475	1,853	2,003	2,493	2,486	2,872
Total Costs	81,829	87,388	92,507	100,037	106,590	110,590	117,826	124,787	133,999	141,375	184,342
Percentage of GNP	1.74	1.74	1.78	1.87	1.92	1.91	1.98	2.13	2.24	2.32	2.61

Source: U.S. Environmental Protection Agency (1990, pp. 8-20 to 8-21).
[a]Assuming present implementation annualized at 7 percent.

Table 5 Expenditures for Pollution Abatement and Control by Section[a] (millions of 1992 dollars)

Sector	1981	1982	1983	1984	1985	1986	1987	1988	1989	1990
Personal Consumption Abatement	10,278	10,307	12,119	13,270	14,254	15,349	13,159	14,316	12,278	10,485
Business Abatement	48,969	45,726	46,031	49,825	51,314	52,994	53,846	55,615	57,784	60,122
Government Abatement	16,446	15,912	15,504	16,760	17,684	18,974	20,727	20,559	21,560	23,122
Regulation & Monitoring	2,190	2,068	1,946	1,823	1,647	1,923	1,838	1,988	2,005	1,980
Research & Development	2,626	2,484	3,115	2,998	3,107	3,186	3,204	3,216	3,303	3,303
Total	80,509	76,495	78,713	84,677	87,914	92,425	92,773	95,694	96,928	99,024

Source: Rutledge and Leonard (1992), pp. 35–38.
[a]Excludes expenditures for solid waste collection and disposal; excludes agricultural production except feedlot operations.

Second, when additional capital expenditures are made for end-of-the-pipe abatement equipment, respondents have relatively little difficulty in calculating these expenditures. But when new capital equipment is installed, which has the effect of both reducing emissions and improving the final product or enhancing the efficiency with which it is produced, it is far more difficult to calculate how much of the expenditures are attributable to environmental standards. Furthermore, it is not always clear whether a regulation is an "environmental regulation." The *PACE* data do not include expenditures for worker health and safety (U.S. Department of Commerce 1993, p. A4), but some expenditures for health and safety essentially control the working environment. Determining precisely which regulatory costs should be included in the costs of environmental regulations is ultimately somewhat arbitrary.[19]

The most striking feature of either annual capital or annual total expenditures for pollution abatement is the degree of variation across industries.[20] For all manufacturing industries combined, 7.5 percent of new capital expenditures in 1991 were for pollution control equipment, and gross annual operating costs for pollution control were 0.62 percent of the total value of shipments. For the highest abatement-cost industries, however, the costs of complying with environmental regulations were dramatically higher (Table 6).

In particular, for the chemicals, petroleum, pulp and paper, and primary metals industries, new capital expenditures for pollution abatement

---

[19]For a detailed discussion of environmental compliance cost measurement problems, see U.S. Congressional Budget Office (1985).

[20]Gross annual costs for pollution abatement are equal to the sum of operating costs attributable to pollution abatement and payments to the government for sewage services and solid waste collection and disposal.

Table 6 Pollution Abatement Expenditures for Selected Industries, 1991 (Monetary amounts are in millions of 1992 dollars.)

Industry	Total Capital Expenditures	Pollution Abatement Cap. Exp. (PACE)	PACE as Percentage of Total Cap. Exp.	Total Value of Shipments	Abatement Gross Annual Cost (GAC)	GAC as Percentage of Value of Shipments
All Industries	$101,773	$7,603	7.47%	$2,907,848	$17,888	0.62%
Industries with High Abatement Costs						
Paper and Allied Products	$9,269	$1,269	13.68%	$132,545	$1,682	1.27%
Chemical and Allied Products	$16,471	$2,126	12.91%	$300,770	$4,164	1.38%
Petroleum and Coal Products	$6,066	$1,505	24.81%	$162,642	$2,931	1.80%
Primary Metal Industries	$6,049	$692	11.45%	$136,674	$2,061	1.51%
Industries with Moderate Abatement Costs						
Furniture and Fixtures	$750	$25	3.29%	$41,183	$140	0.34%
Fabricated Metal Products	$4,190	$182	4.35%	$161,614	$867	0.54%
Electric, Electronic Equipment	$8,356	$241	2.88%	$203,596	$857	0.42%
Industries with Low Abatement Costs						
Printing and Publishing	$5,187	$38	0.73%	$161,211	$235	0.15%
Rubber, Misc. Plastics Products	$4,337	$84	1.95%	$103,576	$454	0.44%
Machinery, except Electrical	$7,546	$132	1.75%	$250,512	$591	0.24%

Source: U.S. Department of Commerce (1993), pp. 12–13.

range from 11 to 25 percent of overall capital expenditures, and annual abatement (operating) costs ranged from 1.3 to 1.8 percent of the total value of shipments.

3. Environmental Regulations and International Trade

3.1 Effects of Regulation on Net Exports

Natural resource endowments have been a particularly important determinant of trading patterns (see, for example, Edward E. Leamer 1984). Having recognized this, we note that when a firm pollutes, it is essentially using a natural resource (a clean environment), and when a firm is compelled or otherwise induced to reduce its pollutant emissions, that firm has, in effect, seen its access to an important natural resource reduced. Industries that lose the right to pollute freely may thus lose their comparative advantage, just as the copper industry in developed countries lost its comparative advantage as copper resources dwindled in those regions. The result is a fall in exports.

This suggests an analytical approach to investigating the environmental protection-competitiveness connection. The primary difficulty in implementing this approach, however, is the limited availability of data on environmental regulatory compliance expenditures, particularly for foreign (and especially for developing) countries. Because such comparative data are generally unavailable, we must rely instead on studies that either examine the effect of environmental controls on U.S. net exports (without considering more general trading patterns) or those that examine international trading patterns (but rely on qualitative measures of environmental control costs in different countries).

First, we can ask whether (all else equal) net exports have been systematically lower in U.S. industries subject to relatively stringent environmental regulations. The evidence pertaining to this question is not conclusive (Table 7). Employing a Heckscher-Ohlin model of international trade, Joseph P. Kalt (1988) regressed changes in net exports between the years 1967 and 1977 across 78 industrial categories on changes in environmental compliance costs and other relevant variables, and found a statistically insignificant inverse relationship. On the other hand, when the sample was restricted to manufacturing industries, the predicted negative effect of compliance costs on net exports became significant. It is troubling, however, that the magnitude and significance of the effect was increased even further when the chemical industry was excluded from the sample, because this is an industry with relatively high environmental compliance costs (Table 6).[21]

Gene M. Grossman and Alan B. Krueger (1993) found that pollution abatement costs in industries in the United States have apparently not af-

---

[21]The explanation appears to be the relatively strong net export performance of the chemical industry (at the same time that it was heavily regulated).

Table 7 Effects of Environmental Regulations on Net Exports

Study	Time Period of Analysis	Industrial Scope	Geographic Scope	Results[a]
Grossman and Krueger 1993	1987	Manufacturing	U.S.-Mexico Trade	Insignificant
Kalt 1988	1967–1977	78 industry categories	U.S. Trade	Insignificant
		Manufacturing		Significant
		Manufacturing w/o Chemicals		More Significant
Tobey 1990	1977	Mining, Paper, Chemicals, Steel, Metals	23 Nations	Insignificant

[a]See the text for descriptions of the results of each study.

fected imports from Mexico or activity in the maquiladora sector[22] along the U.S.-Mexico border.[23] Using 1987 data across industry categories and three different measures of economic impacts—total U.S. imports from Mexico, imports under the offshore assembly provisions of the U.S. tariff codes, and the sectoral pattern of maquiladora activity—they examined possible statistical relationships with: industry factor intensities, tariff rates, and the ratio of pollution abatement costs to total value-added in respective U.S. industries. With all three performance measures, they found that "traditional determinants of trade and investment patterns"—in particular, labor intensity—were very significant, but that cross-industry differences in environmental costs were both quantitatively small and statistically insignificant.[24] Given the physical proximity of Mexico, the large volume of trade between the two countries, and the historically significant differences between Mexican and U.S. environmental laws, these findings cast doubt on the hypothesis that environmental regulations have significant adverse effects on net exports.

---

[22]The maquiladora program was established by Mexico in the 1960s to attract foreign investment. Under the program, qualified firms are exempt from national laws that require majority Mexican ownership and prohibit foreign ownership of border and coastline property. Also inputs for production processes can be imported duty-free, as long as 80 percent of the output is re-exported. For further discussion of the maquiladoras sector in the context of the environmental protection—competitiveness debate, see Robert K. Kaufmann, Peter Pauly, and Julie Sweitzer (1993).

[23]As Grossman and Krueger (1993) point out, however, there is evidence from one government survey suggesting that a number of U.S. furniture manufacturers relocated their California factories across the Mexican border as a result of increases in the stringency of California state air pollution standards affecting paints and solvents (U.S. General Accounting Office 1991).

[24]As we discuss later, this result is consistent with something else the data reveal—international differences in environmental costs (as a fraction of total production costs) are trivial compared with apparent differences in labor costs and productivity.

Finally, environmental regulations in other nations are, of course, also important in determining trade patterns, but here the available evidence again indicates that the relative stringency of environmental regulations in different countries has had no effect on net exports (James A. Tobey 1990). Using a qualitative measure of the stringency of national environmental policies (Ingo Walter and J. Ugelow 1979), Tobey applied what is otherwise a straightforward Hecksher-Ohlin framework to test empirically for the sources of international comparative advantage. In an examination of five pollution-intensive industries—mining, paper, chemicals, steel, and metals—Tobey found that environmental stringency was in no case a statistically significant determinant of net exports. The results could theoretically be due to no more than the failure of the ordinal measure of environmental stringency to be correlated with true environmental control costs,[25] but Tobey's results are essentially consistent with those from other, previous analyses that employed direct cost measures (Walter 1982; Charles S. Pearson 1987; and H. Jeffrey Leonard 1988).

3.2 International Trade in Pollution-Intensive Goods

We can also search for evidence on the impact of environmental regulations on international competitiveness by examining temporal shifts in the overall pattern of trade in pollution-intensive goods.[26] Defining such goods as those produced by industries that incur the highest levels of pollution abatement and control expenditures in the United States, shifts in trade flows can be examined to determine whether a growing proportion of these products in world trade originate in developing countries, where regulatory standards are often (but not always) relatively lax (Patrick Low and Alexander Yeats 1992). The results for the period 1965–1988 show that: (i) the share of pollution-intensive products in total world trade fell from 19 to 16 percent; (ii) the share of pollution-intensive products in world trade originating in North America fell from 21 to 14 percent;[27] (iii) the share of pollution-intensive products originating in Southeast Asia rose from 3.4 to 8.4 percent; and (iv) developing countries gained a comparative advantage in pollution-intensive products at a greater rate than developed countries.[28]

---

[25]For example, a nation might have strict regulations but not enforce them.

[26]Unfortunately, a major constraint faced by any such analysis is a lack of sufficient data on environmental costs and regulations in foreign countries to permit a direct link to be established between observed changes in trade flows and differences in environmental regulations across various countries. Not only are data on environmental regulations sparse, but a further difficulty is separating the impact of environmental costs on trade from shifts in natural resource advantages or other factor endowments, such as labor costs.

[27]This result is consistent with a parallel finding by Kalt (1988) that in 1967 U.S. exports were more pollution-intensive than its imports while the opposite was true by 1977.

[28]These results are consistent with the findings of Robert E. B. Lucas, Wheeler, and Hemamala Hettige (1992), who also found evidence that pollution-intensive industries had migrated from the United States to developing countries, in a study of 15,000 plants (from Census Bureau data) for the period, 1986–1987.

These results may be less meaningful than they may seem at first glance. First of all, Low and Yeats found that industrialized countries accounted for the lion's share of the world's exports of pollution-intensive goods from 1965 to 1988, contradicting the notion that pollution-intensive industries have fled to developing countries. Second, to the extent pollution-intensive industries *have* moved from industrialized to industrializing countries, this may be due simply to increased demand within the latter for the products of pollution-intensive industries. Third, natural resource endowments may partly or largely explain the pattern of pollution-intensive exports.[29]

In general, it would be preferable to examine individual nations' production of pollution-intensive goods relative to world production rather than their share of world trade or the proportion of their exports that are pollution intensive. This is because as world demand grows for pollution-intensive goods, production facilities will be built in new locations close to sources of product demand, and trade in these goods may shrink. A declining volume of world trade in such goods would result in a drop in U.S. exports, even if the United States maintained its *share* of such trade. The drop in overall trade could indicate that other countries were developing expertise in making these goods for domestic consumption, and that the U.S. competitive advantage was shrinking.

The evidence that developing countries are more likely to gain a comparative advantage in the production of pollution-intensive goods than in clean ones[30] is consistent with the change in U.S. trading patterns identified by H. David Robison (1988; see also Ralph D'Arge 1974 and Organization for Economic Cooperation and Development 1985). He found that the abatement content of U.S. imports[31] has risen more rapidly than the abatement content of exports as U.S. environmental standards have grown relatively more stringent than those in the rest of the world. However, the U.S.-Canadian trade pattern has not shifted in this way, presumably because of the similarity of Canadian and U.S. environmental standards and costs. While this result suggests that U.S. environmental regulations have had an affect on trading patterns, Robison's model indicates that, relative to domestic consumption, the effects of increased abatement costs of U.S. trade are quite small, even when no mitigating general equilibrium effects are taken into account.

Observed changes in international trading patterns over the past thirty years thus indicate that pollution-intensive industries have migrated, but

---

[29]The data suggest that countries that export a high proportion of pollution-intensive goods may do so because their natural resource base makes them efficient producers of particular pollution-intensive products. Finland exports paper products, while Venezuela and Saudi Arabia export refined petroleum products.

[30]This result is based primarily on an analysis of one industry, iron and steel pipes and tubes (Low and Yeats 1992).

[31]The abatement content of imported goods is the cost of abatement that would be embodied in those goods had they been produced in the United States.

Table 8 Effects of Environmental Regulations on Trade Patterns in Abatement-Intensive Goods

Study	Time Period of Analysis	Industrial Scope	Geographic Scope	Results[a]
Low and Yeats 1992	1965–1988	"Dirty" industries[b]	World Trade	Generally consistent with migration of dirty industries
Robison 1988	1973–1982	78 industry categories	U.S. Trade	Increased U.S. imports of relatively abatement-intensive goods
			Canadian Trade	No change in relative abatement-intensity of trade

[a]See the text for descriptions of the results of each study.
[b]Dirty industries are those incurring the highest level of abatement expenditure in the U.S.

the observed changes are small in the overall context of economic development (Table 8). Furthermore, it is by no means clear that the changes in trade patterns were caused by increasingly strict environmental regulations in developed countries. The observed changes in international trading patterns are consistent with the general process of development in the Third World. As countries develop, manufacturing accounts for a larger portion of their economic activity.

4. Environmental Regulations and Investment

The spatial pattern of economic activity is party a function of resource endowments and the location of markets; but, to some degree, it is also an accident of history. Although firms may locate where production costs are low and market access is good, there are benefits to firms that locate where other firms have previously located (in terms of existing infrastructure, a trained work force, potential suppliers, and potential benefits from specialization).[32] Under this latter view, productivity and competitiveness arise, at least in part, from the existence of a large industrial base; the ability to attract capital is also an important determinant of competitiveness.

In any case, the choice of a new plant location is obviously a complex one. When choosing between domestic and foreign locations, firms con-

---

[32]See Wheeler and Ashoka Mody (1992) for a brief discussion of these issues in the context of the effects of regulation. For a more general discussion of agglomeration effects, see Krugman (1991).

sider the market the plant will serve, the quality of the work force available, the risks associated with exchange rate fluctuations, the political stability of foreign governments, and the available infrastructure, among other factors. Hence, isolating the effect of environmental regulations on the decision will inevitably be difficult. Two sources of evidence can be used to investigate the sensitivity of firms' investment patterns to environmental regulations: changes in direct foreign investment and siting decisions for domestic plants.

4.1 Direct Foreign Investment

Although there has been little focus on the direct effects of environmental regulations on foreign investment decisions,[33] the results from more general studies can be informative. Wheeler and Mody (1992) found that multinational firms appear to base their foreign investment decisions primarily upon such things as labor costs and access to markets, as well as upon the presence of a developed industrial base. On the other hand, corporate tax rates appear to have little or no appreciable effect on these investment decisions. To the extent that environmental regulations impose direct costs similar to those associated with taxes, one could infer that concerns about environmental regulations will be dominated by the same factors that dominate concerns about taxes in these investment decisions.[34]

General trends in direct investment abroad (DIA) can also provide insights into the likely effects of environmental regulations. If environmental regulations cause industrial flight from developed countries, then direct foreign investment by pollution-intensive industries should increase over time, particularly in developing nations. In fact, from 1973 to 1985, overall direct foreign investment by the U.S. chemical and mineral industries *did* increase at a slightly greater rate than that for all manufacturing industries.[35] Over the same period, however, there was an increase in the proportion of DIA made by all manufacturing industries in developing countries, while the proportion of DIA made by the chemicals industry in developing countries actually fell.[36]

---

[33]There is abundant anecdotal evidence in the press and at least one survey of 1,000 North American and Western European corporations regarding their attitudes toward investing in Eastern and Central Europe (Anthony Zamparutti and Jon Klavens 1993).

[34]Wheeler and Mody (1992) included a composite variable in their analysis designed to measure the effects of a variety of risks associated with various countries. One of the ten components of this composite variable reflects the bureaucratic "hassle" associated with doing business in the countries examined. If this variable had been entered separately, the analysis might have shed more light on the nonpecuniary effects of regulation on location decisions.

[35]Direct investment abroad (DIA) made by the chemical and mineral industries as a proportion of DIA by all manufacturing industries increased from 25.7 percent to 26.5 percent between 1973 and 1985 (H. J. Leonard 1988). Of course, this statistic may simply indicate that markets for these products were growing in developing countries.

[36]The proportion of DIA made by mineral processing industries in developing countries increased from 22.8 to 24.4 percent between 1973 and 1985. This shift could have been caused by changes in comparative advantage due to natural resource endowments (Leonard 1988).

Information is also available on the capital expenditures of (majority-owned) foreign affiliates of U.S. firms. The evidence indicates that those affiliates in pollution intensive industries, such as chemicals, did not undertake capital expenditures at a rate greater than manufacturing industries in general. Majority-owned affiliates in pollution-intensive industries in developing countries, however, did increase their capital expenditures at a slightly greater rate than did all manufacturing industries (H. J. Leonard 1988).[37] Overall, the evidence of industrial flight to developing countries is weak, at best.[38]

4.2 Domestic Plant Location

As suggested above, data on required pollution-control expenditures in foreign countries are insufficient to permit plant-level analyses of the effects of environmental regulations on international siting of plants. Nevertheless, such analyses have been conducted for plant location decisions in the United States in an effort to link such decisions to environmental regulatory factors. Despite the fact that new environmental regulations typically will not cause firms to relocate *existing* plants (due to significant relocation costs), firms have more flexibility in making decisions about the siting of new plants. Indeed, some environmental regulations are particularly targeted at new plants—so-called, "new source performance standards."

There appears to be widespread belief that environmental regulations have a significant effect on the siting of new plants in the United States. The public comments and private actions of legislators and lobbyists, for example, certainly indicate that they believe that environmental regulations affect plant location choices. Indeed, there is evidence that the 1970 Clean Air Act and the 1977 Clean Water Act Amendments were designed in part to limit the ability of states to compete for businesses through lax enforcement of environmental standards (Portney 1990). The House Committee Report on the 1970 Clean Air Act amendments claims that "the promulgation of Federal emission standards for new sources . . . will preclude efforts on the part of States to compete with each other in trying to attract

---

[37]A preliminary study by Charles D. Kolstad and Yuqing Xing (1994) has examined the relationship between the laxity of various countries' environmental regulations and the level of investment by the U.S. chemical industry in those nations. The authors used two proxies for the laxity of environmental regulation: emissions of sulphur dioxide (SO_2) per dollar of GDP, and the growth rate of SO_2 emissions. They found that both measures were positively and significantly related to the amount of inbound direct investment by the chemical industry, and they interpreted this as evidence that strict regulation discourages investment. It seems equally likely, however, that these empirical results are due to omitted variables or causality running in the opposite direction, from investment to pollution.

[38]It has been suggested in the popular press that multinational companies install pollution control equipment in their foreign plants for a variety of reasons—including public relations and stockholders demands—even where and when not required by local laws and regulations (see, for example, "The Supply Police," Newsweek, Feb. 15, 1993, pp. 48–49). If true, this could help explain why investment patterns have been relatively unaffected by regulatory stringency.

new plants and facilities without assuming adequate control of large scale emissions therefrom" (U.S. Congress 1979). Likewise, environmental standards became a major obstacle to ratification of the North American Free Trade Agreement (NAFTA) in 1993, largely because of concerns that U.S. companies would move to Mexico to take advantage of relatively lax environmental standards there.

The evidence from U.S. studies suggests that these concerns may not be well founded. Timothy J. Bartik (1985) examined business location decisions as influenced by a variety of factors. While he did not take the stringency of states' environmental regulations into account, his findings are helpful in identifying factors that can affect business location decisions. First, Bartik found that both state taxes and public services are important determinants of location choice;[39] second, he found that unionization of a state's labor force has a strongly negative effect on the likelihood that firms will locate new plants within a given state. Third, he found that the existing level of manufacturing activity in a state seems to have a positive effect on the decision to locate a new plant, consistent with other findings in the international context (Low and Yeats 1992).

While these results indicate that firms are sensitive, in general, to cost variations among states when deciding where to locate new facilities, there is little direct evidence of a relationship between stringency of environmental regulations and plant location choices (although the fact that state taxes were significant could be taken to infer that environmental regulations ought to be significant as well).[40] In a more recent analysis that included measures of environmental stringency, Bartik (1988) found that state government air and water pollution control expenditures, average costs of compliance, and allowed particulate emissions all had small[41] and insignificant effects on plant location decisions.[42] In a subsequent analysis, Bartik (1989) detected a significant, negative impact of state-level environmental regulations on the start-up rate of small businesses, but the effect was substantively small.[43] These results are essentially consistent with those of Arik Levinson (1992), who found that large differences in the stringency of environmental regulations among states had no effect on the locations of most new plants; but the locations of new branch plants of large

---

[39]The effect of state taxes was statistically significant, but not particularly large in Bartik's (1985) analysis. A 10 percent increase in the corporate tax rate (from 5 to 5.5%, for example) will cause a 2 to 3 percent decline in the number of new plants.

[40]In any event, the magnitude of the two effects could be dramatically different, because state taxes may impose a burden that is large relative to the monetary-equivalent regulatory burden.

[41]In the case of highly polluting industries, Bartik (1988) could not reject the possibility of a substantively large effect of environmental regulation, although the estimated effect was statistically not significant.

[42]State spending on pollution control is meant to be a proxy for the likelihood that a plant will face inspection. Bartik experimented with a variety of variables and specifications, and the general results were quite robust to these changes.

[43]A change of one standard deviation in the environmental stringency variable—the Conservation Foundation's rating of state environmental laws and regulations (from Christopher Duerksen 1983)—yielded a 0.01 standard deviation change in the state start-up rate of small businesses.

Table 9 Effects of Environmental Regulations on Domestic Plant Location Decisions

Study	Time Period of Analysis	Industrial Scope	Results[a]
Bartik 1988	1972–1978	Manufacturing branch plants of Fortune 500 companies	No significant effects[b]
Bartik 1989	1976–1982	New small businesses in 19 manufacturing industries	Significant but small effects[c]
Friedman, Gerlowski, and Silberman 1992	1977–1988	Foreign multinational corporations	No significant effects[d]
Levinson 1992	1982–1987	U.S. manufacturing	No significant effects[e]
McConnell and Schwab 1990	1973, 1975, 1979, 1982	Motor-vehicle assembly plants (SIC 3711)	Most insignificant effects[f]

[a]See the text for descriptions of the results of each study.
[b]In a previous study, Bartik (1985) found significant impacts of state corporate tax rates, suggesting that differences in the costs of doing business matter.
[c]A one standard deviation change in environmental stringency yielded a 0.01 standard deviation change in the start-up rate of small businesses.
[d]An exception is that when the sample was restricted to new branch plants built by Japanese firms alone, the environmental variable was both negative and significant.
[e]Although the results are insignificant when the entire sample is considered, state-level environmental regulations exhibit significant effects when the sample is restricted to firms in the most pollution-intensive industries (chemicals, plastics, and electronics).
[f]The insignificance of regional differences in environmental regulation held across a substantial number of alternative measures of environmental regulatory stringency. They found significant effects in the case of countries that were exceptionally far out of compliance with air quality standards.

multi-plant companies in pollution-intensive industries were found to be somewhat sensitive to differences in pollution regulations.[44]

In another plant-location study, Virginia D. McConnell and Robert M. Schwab (1990) found no significant effects of regional differences in environmental regulation on the choice of location of automobile industry branch plants.[45] This finding held across a variety of alternative measures of environmental stringency. Finally, Joseph Friedman, Daniel A. Gerlowski, and Jonathan Silberman (1992) analyzed the determinants of new manufacturing branch plant location in the United States by foreign multi-

[44]In work in progress, Wayne B. Gray (1993) uses data from six Censuses of Manufacturing between 1963 and 1987 to examine how the births and deaths of plants are related to a set of state characteristics, including: factor prices, population density, unionization, taxes, education, and various measures of environmental regulation, such as enforcement activity by state and federal regulators, pollution abatement costs, and indices of state-level environmental policy stringency. In this preliminary work, Gray finds significant effects for two of his measures of regulatory stringency—air pollution enforcement and state-level laws—but the respective parameters have opposite signs.

[45]An exception was found in the case of counties that were exceptionally far out of compliance with air quality standards.

national corporations. Among the independent variables they used to explain location choice was a measure of regulatory intensity—the ratio of pollution abatement capital expenditures in a state to the gross product in the state originating in manufacturing. When the investment decisions of all foreign companies were considered together, the measure of environmental stringency—while negative—did not exert a statistically significant effect on new plant investment (Table 9).[46]

5. Environmental Regulations and Economic Growth

The evidence reviewed above does not provide much support for the proposition that environmental regulation has significant adverse effects on competitiveness. This can be placed in perspective by scrutinizing what may be more fundamental, though possibly less direct, evidence related to the overall social costs of environmental regulation.[47]

5.1 Productivity Effects

If firms are operating efficiently before environmental regulations are imposed, new regulations will theoretically cause firms to use more resources in the production process. We can posit five ways in which environmental regulations could negatively affect productivity (see Robert H. Haveman and Gregory B. Christiansen 1981; Robert W. Crandall 1981; and U.S. Office of Technology Assessment 1994). First, by definition, the *measured* productivity of the affected industry will fall because measured inputs of capital, labor, and energy are being diverted to the production of an additional output—environmental quality—that is not included in conventional measures of output and hence productivity (Robert Repetto 1990; Robert M. Solow 1992). Second, when and if firms undertake process or management changes in response to environmental regulations, the new practices may be less efficient than old ones (although, as we discuss below, there are those who suggest that this factor operates in the opposite direction, i.e., regulation-induced process and management shake-ups may increase productive efficiency). Third, environmental investments could conceivably

---

[46]When the sample was restricted to new branch plants built by Japanese firms alone, however, the environmental variable was both negative and significant. In other words, ceteris paribus, states with more stringent regulation were less likely to attract new Japanese-owned branch plants in manufacturing.

[47]One way to gain a perspective on this issue is to ask: Are environmental regulations more costly to a society with an open economy or one with a closed economy? On the simplest possible level, the existence of trade *reduces* the social cost of regulation. Rather than invest in pollution control equipment for its pollution-intensive industries, a country might specialize in the production of cleaner goods and stop producing pollution-intensive goods, choosing to import these goods rather than produce them domestically. Essentially, a country open to international trade has available a means of cleaning up its environment that is not available to countries closed to trade.

crowd out other investments by firms.[48] Fourth, many environmental regulations exempt older plants from requirements, in effect mandating higher
standards for new plants. This "new-source bias" can be particularly harmful by discouraging investment in new, more efficient facilities. Fifth, requirements that firms use the "best available control technology" for pollution abatement may increase the adoption of these new technologies *at
the time* regulations go into effect, but subsequently blunt firms' incentives
to develop new pollution control or prevention approaches over time. This
is because their emission standard may be tightened each time the firm in-
novates with a cost-saving approach.

Empirical analyses of these productivity effects have found modest adverse impacts on environmental regulation. A number of studies focused on
the 1970s, a period of productivity decline in the United States (Table 10), attempting to determine what portion of the decline in productivity growth
rates could be attributed to increased regulatory costs. When the scope of the
analysis is most or all manufacturing sectors, the estimates of the fraction of
the decline in the total factor productivity growth rate due to environmental
regulations range from 8 percent to 16 percent (Edward Denison 1979; Gray
1987; Haveman and Christiansen 1981;[49] and J. R. Norsworthy, Michael J.
Harper, and Kent Kunze 1979). Thus, regulation cannot be considered the
primary cause of the productivity slowdown. There is, however, substantial
variation by industrial sector: 10 percent for the chemical industry; 30 percent for paper producers (Anthony J. Barbera and McConnell 1990); and 44
percent for electric utilities (Frank M. Gallop and Mark J. Roberts 1983).

Gray and Shadbegian (1993) merged plant-level input and output data
from the Census and Survey of Manufactures with plant-level data from
the PACE surveys. They estimated equations for productivity at the plant
level as a function of pollution control expenditures. If the only effect of
pollution control expenditures on productivity were that they do not contribute to measured output, then their coefficient in such a regression ought
to be minus one, because, holding inputs (including pollution control expenditures) constant, there ought to be $1 less output for every $1 diverted
to pollution control. They found, however, that output fell by $3–$4 for
every dollar of PACE spending, suggesting extremely large adverse productivity effects. In subsequent work (Gray and Shadbegian 1994), however, the same authors showed that these results were extremely sensitive
to econometric specification, and that the large negative effects in the first
paper were largely an artifact of measurement error in output.[50] In a spec-

---

[48]The empirical evidence here is mixed. Adam Rose (1983) finds that pollution-control investments reduce other investments by firms, but on less than a one-for-one basis; Gray and Ronald J.
Shadbegian (1993) actually found a positive correlation of environmental investments and "productive investments" for some sectors, such as pulp and paper mills.

[49]Haveman and Christiansen (1981) examine the contribution of environmental regulation to
the observed decline in labor productivity, not total factor productivity.

[50]The specification in Gray and Shadbegian (1993) is to regress productivity levels (the ratio of
value-added to a weighted average of inputs) on the ratio of PACE expenditures to value-added. If
value-added is measured with error, this introduces a downward bias in the coefficient on the
PACE/Value-added ratio.

Table 10 Effects of Environmental Regulations on Total Factor Productivity Decline[a]

Study	Time Period of Analysis	Industrial Scope	Results[b] Percentage Share Due to Environmental Regulation
Barbera and McConnell 1990	1970–1980	Chemicals; Stone, Clay, and Glass; Iron and Steel	10%–12%
Barbera and McConnell 1990	1970–1980	Paper	30%
Denison 1979	1972–1975	Business sector	16%
Gallop and Roberts 1983	1973–1979	Electric utilities	44%
Gray 1987	1973–1978	240 manufacturing sectors	12%
Haveman and Christainsen 1981	1973–1975	Manufacturing	8%–12%
Norsworthy, Harper, and Kunze 1979	1973–1978	Manufacturing	12%[c]

[a]Based upon Table A-1 in U.S. Office of Technology Assessment 1994.
[b]See the text for descriptions of the results of each study.
[c]Share of labor productivity decline due to environmental regulation.

ification that is robust to the measurement error problem, they found that the coefficient on PACE expenditures fell to about 1.5 in pooled time-series/cross section regressions, and was not significantly greater than one in fixed-effect regressions. Thus, there remains some evidence of a productivity penalty, but it has to be regarded as weak because the pooled regression is likely to be subject to spurious negative correlation between productivity levels and pollution control expenditures.[51]

Any discussion of the productivity impacts of environmental protection efforts should recognize that not all environmental regulations are created equal in terms of their costs or their benefits.[52] So-called market-based or economic-incentive regulations, such as those based on tradeable permits or pollution charges, will tend to be more cost-effective than regulations requiring technological adoption or establishing conventional performance standards. This is because under the market-based regulatory regime, firms are likely to abate up to the point they find it profitable, and firms that find it cheapest to reduce their levels of pollution will clean up the most. With

---

[51]If some plants are generally inefficient relative to others, then it would not be surprising if they had both higher control costs and lower productivity, even if there were no causal relationship between the two.

[52]Stewart (1993) attributes observed differences in the productivity effects of environmental regulations in the U.S., Canada, and Japan (U.S. Congressional Budget Office 1985) to differences in legal and administrative systems, although he notes that the CBO study did not attempt to control for regulatory stringency.

such incentive-based regulatory systems, regulators can thus achieve a given level of pollution control more cheaply than by imposing fixed technological or performance standards on firms (Robert W. Hahn and Stavins 1991). Furthermore, market-based environmental policy instruments provide ongoing incentives for firms to adopt new and better technologies and processes, because under these systems, it always pays to clean up more if a sufficiently cheap way of doing so can be identified and adopted.[53]

5.2 General Equilibrium Effects

To quantify the overall, long-run social costs of regulation (where costs are measured by the compensation required to leave individuals as well off after a regulation as before—ignoring environmental benefits), a general equilibrium perspective is essential, in order to incorporate interindustry interactions and cumulative effects of changes in investment levels. In general, the overall social costs of environmental regulation will exceed direct compliance costs because regulations can cause reductions in output, inhibit investments in productive capital, reduce productivity, and bring about transitional costs (Schmalensee 1994).

Michael Hazilla and Kopp (1990) compared projected costs for compliance with the Clean Air and Clean Water Acts, with and without allowing for general equilibrium adjustments in labor input and investment by industry. They found that the annual social costs allowing for general equilibrium adjustments were smaller than projected pollution control expenditures in early years, but eventually came to exceed greatly the partial equilibrium projection (because of reductions in investment and labor supply).

Dale W. Jorgenson and Peter J. Wilcoxen (1990) used a model with 35 industry sectors (including government enterprises), a representative consumer, and an exogenous current account balance. Each sector's demand for inputs responds to prices according to econometrically estimated demand functions. There is a single malleable capital good, whose quantity is based on past investment and whose service price is determined endogenously. Investment is determined by the consumer's savings, which is given by the solution to a perfect foresight intertemporal optimization of consumption. They model the dynamic effects of operating costs associated with pollution control, pollution control investment, and compliance with motor vehicle emissions standards. They find that over the period 1974–1985, the combined effect of these mandated costs was to reduce the average growth rate of real GNP by about 0.2 percentage points per year, with required investment having the biggest effect and operating costs the smallest.[54] By 1985, the cumulative effect of this reduced growth is that

---

[53]See Jaffe and Stavins, forthcoming. Some types of market-based instruments can raise special problems in the context of international trade, however, if the policy instruments are not harmonized across nations (Harmen Verbruggen 1993).

[54]Because the compliance expenditures are included in GNP, this reduction in growth is a cost over and above the direct costs.

simulated GNP without environmental regulation would be about 1.7 percent more than the actual historical value. This lost output is of roughly the same magnitude as the direct costs of compliance (Table 4).[55]

The results of any simulation model are, of course, somewhat sensitive to the structure and parameter values employed. This can be a particular concern with computable general equilibrium models because of their size and complexity. Nevertheless, the results examined in this section suggest that there are significant dynamic impacts of environmental regulation in the form of costs associated with reduced investment.

5.3 Economic Growth Enhancement

The vast majority of economic analyses of regulation and competitiveness are based upon the assumption that regulations increase production costs. Nevertheless, there have been some recent suggestions in the literature that regulations may actually stimulate growth and competitiveness. This argument—articulated recently by Porter (1991)[56]—has generated a great deal of interest and enthusiasm among some influential policy makers (see, for example, Senator Al Gore 1992).

There are several levels on which the so-called Porter hypothesis may be interpreted. First of all, it can be taken simply to mean that some sectors of private industry, in particular, environmental services, will benefit directly from more stringent environmental regulations *on their customers* (but not on themselves). Thus, the acid-rain reduction provisions of the Clean Air Act amendments of 1990, which call for significant reductions in sulfur dioxide (SO_2) emissions from electric utilities, are unambiguously good news for the manufacturers of flue-gas purification equipment (scrubbers) and producers of low-sulfur coal.

To push this argument slightly further, it would also not be surprising if environmental regulation induced innovation with respect to technologies to achieve compliance. Surely, catalytic converter technology today is superior to what it would have been if auto emissions had never been regulated. Internationally, it has been suggested that German firms possess some competitive advantage in water-pollution control technology and U.S. firms dominate hazardous waste management, because of relatively stricter regulations (Organization for Economic Cooperation and Development 1992; U.S. Environmental Protection Agency 1993). Jean Lanjouw and Mody (1993) looked at patients originating from inventors in different countries, in patent classes deemed to be environmental technologies, and found that increases in environmental compliance costs were related to increases in patenting of such technologies with a one to two year lag. The existence

---

[55]Jorgenson and Wilcoxen (1992) estimate that the 1990 amendments to the Clean Air Act will impose incremental losses in economic growth that are approximately one-fifth as large as the losses they estimated for regulation in place during the 1974–1985 period.

[56]The idea goes back, at least, to Nicholas A. Ashford, C. Ayers, and R.F. Stone (1985). For a recent explication, see Claas van der Linde (1993).

of such "induced innovation" suggests that projections of compliance costs made *before* regulatory implementation may be biased upwards, because they will inevitably take existing technology as given to some extent. On the other hand, this effect does *not* necessarily suggest that measured compliance costs overstate actual costs, because measured costs will reflect technology as it actually evolved.[57]

Second, putting aside the obvious gainers in the environmental services sector, the Porter hypothesis can be taken to imply that, under stricter environmental regulations, *some* regulated firms will benefit competitively, at the expense of *other* regulated firms. If, for example, larger firms find it less costly to comply than smaller firms, then the former might actually benefit from regulation, if higher prices from reduced competition more than offset *their* increased costs. Similarly, the Chrysler Corporation may have benefitted—relative to General Motors and Ford—from the imposition of automobile fuel-efficiency standards[58] in 1975, because its fleet consisted of smaller-sized models. Somewhat related to this, the hypothesis can be thought of as referring dynamically to the reality that environmental regulation can provide some firms with "early mover" advantages by pushing them to produce products that will in the future be in demand in the marketplace.

The proponents of the Porter hypothesis—in public policy circles—have asserted some significantly stronger interpretations, however, namely that the competitiveness of the U.S. as a whole can be enhanced by stricter regulation.[59] It has been suggested that induced innovation can create lasting comparative advantage for U.S. firms, if other countries eventually follow our lead to stricter regulations and there are strong "first-mover" advantages enjoyed by the first firms to enter the markets for control equipment (see, for example, David Gardiner 1994). Even ignoring export possibilities, it has been suggested that environmental regulation can increase domestic efficiency, either by wringing inefficiencies out of the production process as firms struggle to meet new constraints or by spurring innovation in the long term through "outside-of-the-box thinking."[60] The notion is that the imposition of regulations impels firms to reconsider their production processes, and hence to discover innovative approaches to reduce pollution *and* decrease costs or increase output. If this happened widely enough, total social costs of regulation could be no greater than measured compliance costs. Indeed, if the innovation-stimulating effect of regulation were large enough, then regulation would

---

[57]One could argue that measured costs understate the social cost, because they generally do not include the cost of R&D to develop new control technologies. On the other hand, if, as discussed further below, R&D has large positive externalities, then the next mismeasurement is ambiguous.

[58]Energy Policy and Conservation Act of 1975 (89 Stat. 902), amending the Motor Vehicle Information and Cost Savings Act (86 Stat. 947).

[59]Scott Barrett (forthcoming) calls this notion "strategic standard-setting."

[60]Porter (1990) emphasizes that a number of industrial sectors subject to the most stringent domestic environmental regulations have become more competitive internationally: chemicals, plastics, and paints.

offer the possibility of a "free lunch," that is, improvements in environ-mental quality without any costs.[61]

Economists generally have been unsympathetic to these stronger ar-guments, because they depend upon firms being systematically ignorant of profitable production improvements or new technologies that regulations bring forth. (For a more detailed explication of economists' skepticism, see Karen L. Palmer and R. David Simpson 1993, and Oates, Palmer, and Port-ney 1993.) Nevertheless, specific instances of "cheap" or even "free lunches" may occur. For example, Barbera and McConnell (1990) found that lower production costs in the nonferrous metals industry were brought about by new environmental regulations that led to the introduction of new, low-polluting production practices that were also more efficient.[62] One way in which environmental regulation could theoretically have a positive impact on measured productivity at the industry level is by forcing exceptionally inefficient plants to close. To the degree that production is shifted to other domestic plants with higher productivity, the industry's overall productiv-ity could actually increase. One study suggests that this is what happened when environmental regulations in the 1970s unintentionally accelerated the "modernization" of the U.S. steel industry (U.S. Office of Technology Assessment 1980).[63]

Even if firms are systematically ignorant of potential new processes that are both cleaner and more profitable than current methods of pro-duction, there is considerable doubt as to whether regulators would know more about these better methods of production than firm managers, or that continually higher regulatory standards would lead firms regularly to dis-cover new clean and profitable technologies.[64] Moreover, one must be care-ful when claiming that firms are not operating on their production fron-tiers: if there are managerial costs to investigating new production

---

[61]Note that the suggestion of proponents of the Porter hypothesis is *not* that the benefits of en-vironmental regulation (in terms of reduced health and ecological damages) exceed the costs of en-vironmental protection. This is obviously possible, and it is an empirical issue. Rather, the notion of a "free lunch" is that—putting aside the benefits of environmental protection—the costs of regulatory action can be zero or even negative (a "paid lunch"). For an example of "free lunch" arguments—both theoretical and empirical—in the context of energy efficiency and global climate change, see Robert Ayers (1993).

[62]Two of five industries studied experienced induced savings in conventional capital costs and operating costs as a result of stricter environmental regulations and consequent increases in envi-ronmental capital investment. But, even for these two industries, the indirect effects were not suffi-cient to offset the direct cost increases. In the other three industries studied, environmental regula-tions caused both direct increases in environmental capital investments *and* increases in conventional capital costs and operating costs.

[63]While the premature scrapping of "obsolete" capital will raise measured industry productiv-ity, this does not mean that it is socially beneficial. Such plants were, presumably, producing output whose value exceeded variable production costs.

[64]The optimal timing of the adoption of a new technology is obviously a complicated issue. Al-though early adoption can be better than waiting, if technology advances quickly, it may be optimal for firms to wait to invest until even better processes are available. Regulation may cause firms to in-vest in clean technologies today, but then discourage investment in still cleaner technologies later. See Jaffe and Stavins (1994).

technologies, then firms may be efficient even if they do not realize that new, more efficient processes exist until regulations necessitate their adoption.[65] In other words, there may be many efficiency-enhancing ideas that firms could implement if they invested the resources required to search for them. If firms do successfully search in a particular area for beneficial ideas, it will appear ex post that they were acting sub-optimally by not having investigated this area sooner. But with limited resources, the real question is not whether searching produces new ideas, but whether particular searches that are generated by regulation system-atically lead to more or better ideas than searches in which firms would otherwise engage.[66]

Finally, one could argue that regulation, by forcing a re-examination of products and processes, will induce an overall increase in the resources devoted to "research," broadly defined. Even if firms were previously choos-ing the (privately) optimal level of research investment, this inducement could be (socially) desirable, if the social rate of return to research activi-ties is significantly greater than the private return.[67] Jaffe and Palmer (1994) examined the PACE expenditure data, R&D spending data, and patent data, in a panel of industries between 1976 and 1989. They found some evidence that increases in PACE spending were associated with increases in R&D spending, but no evidence that this increased spending produced greater innovation as measured by successful patent applications.

One empirical analysis that is frequently cited in support of the Porter hypothesis is Stephen M. Meyer (1992), which examines whether states with strict environmental laws demonstrate poor economic performance relative to states with more lax standards. Meyer (1992, p. iv) finds that

> *at a minimum* the pursuit of environmental quality does not hinder economic growth and development. Furthermore, there appears to be a moderate yet consis-tent positive association between environmentalism and economic growth.

---

[65]As contrary anecdotal evidence, we should recognize that many business people find econo-mists' skepticism about businesses not operating on their frontiers to be, at best, an indication of the naivete of academic economists, and, at worst, a special case of the joke about the economist who fails to pick up a twenty-dollar bill from the sidewalk because he assumes that if it were not coun-terfeit someone else would surely have taken it.

[66]As noted above, environmental regulations may lower some firms' costs and increase their pro-ductivity by cleaning the environment. Some studies find that environmental regulations are pro-ductive when one takes into account the cost of the "environmental inputs" into the production process (Repetto 1990). Studies of this type are tangential to the "Porter hypothesis," because such studies focus on situations where the benefits of environmental regulations are not sufficient to make indi-vidual firms undertake cleanup, but are substantial enough that industry as a whole may benefit. For example, it is unlikely that any single firm has an incentive to reduce its smokestack emissions solely to improve its own workers' health, but if every firm lowered its emissions, industry might find that, as a result of the change, fewer work days were lost due to illness. See Lester B. Lave and Eugene Seskin (1977); U.S. Environmental Protection Agency (1982); and Douglas W. Dockery et al. (1993).

[67]A priori, private incentives to engage in research could be either too low (because research gener-ates knowledge externalities enjoyed by other firms) or too high (because research creates negative exter-nalities by destroying quasi-rents being earned by other firms). Empirical evidence seems to confirm that social returns exceed private returns (Edwin Mansfield et al. 1977; Jaffe 1986; and Zvi Griliches 1990).

Unfortunately, his statistical analysis sheds very little light on a possible causal relationship between regulation and economic performance.[68] His approach does not control for factors other than the stringency of a state's environmental laws that could affect the state's economic performance. Consequently, it is quite possible that he has merely found a spurious positive correlation between the stringency of a state's environmental standards and its economic performance. His results are consistent with the hypothesis that poor states with no prospect for substantial growth will not enact tough environmental regulations, just as developing countries are less likely than rich countries to enact tough environmental regulations.[69]

Thus, overall, the literature on the "Porter hypothesis" remains one with a high ratio of speculation and anecdote to systematic evidence. While economists have good reason to be skeptical of arguments based on nonoptimizing behavior where the only support is anecdotal, it is also important to recognize that if we wish to persuade others of the validity of our analysis we must go beyond tautological arguments that rest solely on the postulate of profit-maximization. Systematic empirical analysis in this area is only beginning, and it is too soon to tell if it will ultimately provide a clear answer.

6. Conclusions

Overall, there is relatively little evidence to support the hypothesis that environmental regulations have had a large adverse effect on competitiveness, however that elusive term is defined. Although the long-run social costs of environmental regulation may be significant, including adverse effects on productivity, studies attempting to measure the effect of environmental regulation on net exports, overall trade flows, and plant-location decisions have produced estimates that are either small, statistically insignificant, or not robust to tests of model specification.

---

[68]This has not kept a number of authors from describing Meyer's analysis as absolutely conclusive: "Meyer's study does repudiate the hypothesis that environmental regulations reduce economic growth and job creation" (Bezdek 1993, p. 10).

[69]For some environmental problems, such as inadequate sanitation and unsafe drinking water, there is a monotonic and *inverse* relationship between the level of the environmental threat and per capita income (International Bank for Reconstruction and Development 1992). This relationship holds both cross-sectionally (across nations) and for single nations over time. For other environmental problems, the relationship with income level is not monotonic at all, but an inverted *u*-shaped function in which at low levels of income, pollution increases with per capita income, but then at some point begins to decline with further increases in income. This is true of most forms of air and water pollution (Grossman and Krueger 1994), some types of deforestation, and habitat loss. Pollution increases from the least developed agricultural countries to those beginning to industrialize fully—such as Mexico and the emerging market economies of Eastern Europe and parts of the former Soviet Union. After peaking in such nations, pollution is found to decline in the wealthier, industrialized nations that have both the demand for cleaner air and water and the means to provide it. Finally, for another set of environmental pollutants, including carbon dioxide emissions, there is an *increasing* monotonic relationship between per capita income and emission levels, at least within the realm of experience.

There are a number of reasons why the effects of environmental regulation on competitiveness may be small and difficult to detect. First, the existing data are severely limited in their ability to measure the relative stringency of environmental regulation, making it difficult to use such measures in regression analyses of the effects of regulation on economic performance. Second, for all but the most heavily regulated industries, the cost of complying with federal environmental regulation is a relatively small fraction of total cost of production. According to EPA, that share for U.S. industry as a whole averages about two percent, although it is certainly higher for some industries, such as electric utilities, chemical manufacturers, petroleum refiners, and basic metals manufacturers. This being the case, environmental regulatory intensity should not be expected to be a significant determinant of competitiveness in *most* industries. Labor cost differentials, energy and raw materials cost differentials, infrastructure adequacy, and other factors would indeed overwhelm the environmental effect.

Third, although U.S. environmental laws and regulations are generally the most stringent in the world, the difference between U.S. requirements and those in other western industrial democracies is not great, especially for air and water pollution control.[70] Fourth, even where there are substantial differences between environmental requirements in the United States and elsewhere, U.S. firms (and other multinationals, as well) are reluctant to build less-than-state-of-the-art plants in foreign countries. If such willingness existed before the accident at the Union Carbide plant in Bhopal, India, it does not now. Thus, even significant differences in regulatory stringency may not be exploited. Fifth and finally, it appears that even in developing countries where environmental standards (and certainly enforcement capabilities) are relatively weak, plants built by indigenous firms typically embody more pollution control—sometimes substantially more— than is required. To the extent this is true, even significant *statutory* differences in pollution control requirements between countries may not result in significant effects on plant location or other manifestations of competitiveness.

Having stated these conclusions, it is important to emphasize several caveats. First, in many of the studies, differences in environmental regulation were measured by environmental control costs as a percentage of value-added, or some other measure that depends critically on accurate measurement of environmental spending. Even for the United States, where data on environmental compliance costs are relatively good, compliance expenditure data are notoriously unreliable. The problem is more pronounced in other OECD countries, whose environmental agencies have not typically tracked environmental costs. Thus, we may have found little relationship between environmental regulations and competitiveness simply because the data are of poor quality.

---

[70]See Kopp, Diane Dewitt, and Portney (1990) for empirical evidence, and Barrett (1992) for a theoretical argument of why governments should *not* be expected to adopt relatively weak pollution standards for competitive reasons.

In an era of increasing reliance on incentive-based and other performance-based environmental regulations, accurate accounting for pollution control will become an even more pronounced problem. This is because pollution control expenditures increasingly are taking the form of process changes and product reformulations, rather than installation of end-of-pipe control equipment. It will be increasingly difficult (perhaps even impossible) to allocate accurately that part of the cost of a new plant that is attributable to environmental control (Hahn and Stavins 1992). Ironically, in ten years we may know less about total annual pollution control costs than we do now, in spite of increased concern about these expenditures and their possible effects on competitiveness.

A second caveat is that only two of the studies we reviewed controlled for differences in "regulatory climate" between jurisdictions. If the delays and litigation surrounding regulation are the greatest impediments to exporting or to new plant location, these effects will not be picked up by studies that look exclusively at source discharge standards or traditional spending for pollution control equipment as measures of regulatory intensity, unless these direct compliance costs are highly correlated with the costs of litigation and delay.

A third factor that tempers our findings is the difficulty of measuring the effectiveness of enforcement efforts. Subtle differences in enforcement strategies are very difficult to measure, but these differences can lead to variations from country to country that *could* influence competitiveness. Finally, it is important to recall that any comprehensive effort to identify the competitiveness effects associated with regulation must look at both the costs *and* benefits of regulation. To the extent that air or water pollution control effects reduce damages, they may reduce costs for some businesses and thus make them more competitive. Similarly, pollution control can reduce labor costs and enhance competitiveness in some locations under certain conditions.

Just as we have found little consistent empirical evidence for the conventional hypothesis regarding environmental regulation and competitiveness, there is also little or no evidence supporting the revisionist hypothesis that environmental regulation stimulates innovation and improved international competitiveness. Given the large direct and indirect costs that regulation imposes, economists' natural skepticism regarding this free regulatory lunch is appropriate, though further research would help to convince others that our conclusions are well grounded in fact.

Overall, the evidence we have reviewed suggests that the truth regarding the relationship between environmental protection and international competitiveness lies in between the two extremes of the current debate. International differences in environmental regulatory stringency pose insufficient threats to U.S. industrial competitiveness to justify substantial cutbacks in domestic environmental regulations. At the same time, such regulation clearly imposes large direct and indirect costs on society, and there is no evidence supporting the enactment of stricter domestic environmental regulations to stimulate economic competitiveness. Instead, policy makers should do what they can to establish environmental priorities and goals that are consistent with the real tradeoffs that are inevitably required by regulatory activities; that is, our environmental goals should be based on careful balancing of benefits and costs. At the same time, policy makers should seek to reduce the magnitude of these costs by identifying and implementing flexible and cost-effective environmental policy instruments, whether they be of the conventional type or of the newer breed of market-based approaches.

REFERENCES

Ayres, Robert U. "On Economic Disequilibrium and Free Lunch." Working Paper. Centre for the Management of Environmental Resources, INSEAD, Fontainebleau, France, June 1993.

Ashford, Nicholas A.; Ayers, C. and Stone, R. F. "Using Regulation to Change the Market for Innovation," *Harvard Environ. Law Rev.*, 1985, 9, pp. 419–66.

Barbera, Anthony J. and McConnell, Virginia D. "The Impact of Environmental Regulations on Industry Productivity: Direct and Indirect Effects," *J. Environ. Econ. Manage.*, Jan. 1990, 18(1), pp. 50–65.

Barrett, Scott. "Strategy and Environment," *Columbia J. World Bus.*, Fall/Winter 1992, 27, pp. 202–08.

———. "Strategic Environmental Policy and International Trade," *J. Public Econ.*, forthcoming.

Bartik, Timothy J. "Business Location Decisions in the United States: Estimates of the Effects of Unionization, Taxes, and Other Characteristics of States," *J. Bus. Econ. Statist.*, Jan. 1985, 3(1), pp. 14–22.

———. "The Effects of Environmental Regulation on Business Location in the United States," *Growth Change*, Summer 1988, 19(3), pp. 22–44.

———. "Small Business Start-Ups in the United States: Estimates of the Effects of Characteristics of States," *Southern Econ. J.*, Apr. 1989, 55(4), pp. 1004–18.

Bezdek, Roger H. "Environment and Economy: What's the Bottom Line?" *Environment*, Sept. 1993, 35(7), pp. 7–11, 25–32.

Crandall, Robert W. "Pollution Controls and Productivity Growth in Basic Industries," in *Productivity measurement in regulated industries*. Eds.: Thomas G. Cowing and Rodney F. Stevenson. New York, NY: Academic Press, Inc. 198, pp. 347–68.

Cropper, Maureen L. and Oates, Wallace E. "Environmental Economics: A Survey," *J. Econ. Lit.*, June 1992, 30(2), pp. 675–740.

D'arge, Ralph. "International Trade, Domestic Income, and Environmental Controls: Some Empirical Estimates" in *Managing the environment: International economic cooperation for pollution control.* Ed.: Allen Kneese. New York: Praeger, 1974, pp. 289–315.

Dean, Judith M. "Trade and the Environment: A Survey of the Literature," in *International trade and the environment.* Ed.: Patrick Low. Washington, DC: International Bank for Reconstruction and Development/World Bank, 1992.

Denison, Edward F. *Accounting for slower economic growth: The U.S. in the 1970's.* Washington, DC: Brookings Institution, 1979.

Dockery, Douglas W. et al. "An Association Between Air Pollution and Mortality in Six U.S. Cities," *New Eng. J. Medicine*, 1993, 329, pp. 1753–59.

Duerksen, Christopher. *Environmental regulation of industrial plant siting.* Washington, DC: Conservation Foundation, 1983.

Friedman, Joseph; Gerlowski, Daniel A. and Silberman, Jonathan. "What Attracts Foreign Multinational Corporations? Evidence from Branch Plant Location in the United States," *J. Reg. Sci.*, Nov. 1992, *32*(4), pp. 403–18.

Gallop, Frank M. and Roberts, Mark J. "Environmental Regulations and Productivity Growth: The Case of Fossil-Fueled Electric Power Generation," *J. Polit. Econ.*, 1983, *91*, pp. 654–74.

Gardiner, David. "Does Environmental Policy Conflict with Economic Growth?" *Resources*, Spring 1994, (115), pp. 20–21.

Gore, Senator AL. *Earth in the balance: Ecology and the human spirit.* New York: Houghton Mifflin Company, 1992.

Gray, Wayne B. "The Cost of Regulation: OSHA, EPA, and the Productivity Slowdown," *Amer. Econ. Rev.*, Dec. 1987, 77(5), pp. 998–1006.

———. "Cross-State Differences in Environmental Regulation and the Births and Deaths of Manufacturing Plants," 1993, work in progress.

Gray, Wayne B. and Shadbegian, Ronald J. "Environmental Regulation and Manufacturing Productivity At The Plant Level." Discussion Paper, U.S. Department of Commerce, Center for Economic Studies, Washington, DC, 1993.

———. "Pollution Abatement Costs, Regulation, and Plant-Level Productivity." Forthcoming working paper, National Bureau of Economic Research, Cambridge, MA, July 1994.

Griliches, Zvi. "Patent Statistics as Economic Indicators: A survey," *J. Econ. Lit.*, Dec. 1990, *28*(4), pp. 1661–1707.

Grossman, Gene M. and Krueger, Alan B. "Environmental Impacts of a North American Freed Trade Agreement," in *The U.S.-Mexico free trade agreement.* Ed.: Peter Garber. Cambridge, MA: MIT Press, 1993, pp. 13–56.

———. "Economic Growth and the Environment." Working Paper No. 4634. Cambridge, MA: National Bureau of Economic Research, 1994.

Hahn, Robert W. and Stavins, Robert N. "Incentive-Based Environmental Regulation: A New Era from an Old Idea," *Ecology Law Quart.*, 1991, *18*, pp. 1–42.

———. "Economic Incentives for Environmental Protection: Integrating Theory and Practice," *Amer. Econ. Rev.*, May 1992, *82*(2), pp. 464–68.

Haveman, Robert H. and Christiansen, Gregory B. "Environmental Regulations and Productivity Growth," in *Environmental regulation and the U.S. economy.* Eds.: Henry M. Peskin, Paul R. Portney, and Allen V. Kneese. Washington, DC: Resources for the Future, 1981, pp. 55–75.

Hazilla, Michael and Kopp, Raymond J. "Social Cost of Environmental Quality Regulations: A General Equilibrium Analysis," *J. Polit. Econ.*, Aug. 1990, *98*(4), pp. 853–73.

Hopkins, Thomas D. "Regulation and Jobs—Sorting Out the Consequences." Prepared for the American Petroleum Institute, Washington, DC, Oct. 1992.

International Bank for Reconstruction and Development/the World Bank. *World development report 1992: Development and the environment.* New York: Oxford U. Press, 1992.

Jaffe, Adam B. "Technological Opportunity and Spillovers of R&D: Evidence from Firms' Patents, Profits, and Market Value," *Amer. Econ. Rev.*, Dec. 1986, 76(5), pp. 984–1001.

Jaffe Adam B. and Palmer, Karen L. "Environmental Regulation and Innovation: A Panel Data Study." Paper prepared for the Western Economic Association Meetings, June 1994.

Jaffe, Adam B. et al. "Environmental Regulations and the Competitiveness of U.S. Industry." Report prepared for the Economics and Statistics Administration, U.S. Department of Commerce. Cambridge, MA: Economics Resource Group, 1993.

Jaffe, Adam B. and Stavins, Robert N. "The Energy Paradox and the Diffusion of Conservation Technology," *Resource Energy Econ.*, May 1994, *16*(2), pp. 91–122.

———. "Dynamic Incentives of Environmental Regulation: The Effects of Alternative Policy Instruments on Technology Diffusion," *J. Environ & Econ. Manage.* July 1995, *29*(1), forthcoming.

Jorgenson, Dale W. and Wilcoxen, Peter J. "Environmental Regulation and U.S. Economic Growth," *Rand J. Econ.*, Summer 1990, *21*(2), pp. 314–40.

———. "Impact of Environmental Legislation on U.S. Economic Growth, Investment, and Capital Costs," in *U.S. environmental policy and economic growth: How do we fare?* Ed.: Donna L. Brodsky. Washington, DC: American Council for Capital Formation, 1992.

Kalt, Joseph P. "The Impact of Domestic Environmental Regulatory Policies on U.S. International Competitiveness," in *International competitiveness.* Eds.: A. Michael Spence and Heather A. Hazard. Cambridge, MA: Harper and Row, Ballinger, 1988, pp. 221–62.

Kaufmann, Robert K.; Pauly, Peter and Sweitzer, Julie. "The Effects of NAFTA on the Environment," *Energy J.*, 1993, *14*(3), pp. 217–40.

Kolstad, Charles D. and Xing, Yuqing. "Do Lax Environmental Regulations Attract Foreign Investment?" Working Paper, Department of Economics and Institute for Environmental Studies, U. of Illinois, Urbana, Illinois, February 1994.

Kopp, Raymond J. Dewitt, Diane and Portney, Paul R. "International Comparison of Environmental Regulation," in *Environmental policy and the cost of capital.* Washington, DC: American Council for Capital Formation, 1990.

Krugman, Paul. *Geography and trade.* Cambridge, MA: MIT Press, 1991.

———. "Competitiveness: A Dangerous Obsession," *Foreign Affairs*, Mar./Apr. 1994, *73*(2), pp. 28–44.

Lanjouw, Jean and Mody, Ashok. "Stimulating Innovation and the International Diffusion of Environmentally Responsive Technology: The Role of Expenditures and Institutions." mimeo, World Bank, 1993.

Lave, Lester B. and Seskin, Eugene. *Air pollution and human health.* Washington, DC: John Hopkins U. Press for Resources for the Future, 1977.

Leamer, Edward E. *Sources of international comparative advantage.* Cambridge: MIT Press, 1984.

Leonard, H. Jeffrey. *Pollution and the struggle for the world product.* Cambridge, UK: Cambridge U. Press, 1988.

Levinson, Arik. "Environmental Regulations and Manufacturers' Location Choices: Evidence from the Census of Manufactures." New York: Columbia U., 1992.

van der Linde, Claas. "The Micro-Economic Implications of Environmental Regulation: A Preliminary Framework," in *Environmental policies and industrial competitiveness.* Paris: Organization of Economic Cooperation and Development (OECD), 1993, pp. 69–77.

Low, Patrick and Yeats, Alexander. "Do 'Dirty' Industries Migrate?" in *International trade and the environment.* Washington, DC: The World Bank, 1992.

Lucas, Robert E.B.; Wheeler, David and Hettige, Hemamala. "Economic Development, Environmental Regulation and the International Migration of Toxic Industrial Pollution: 1960–1988," in *International trade and the environment.* Ed.: Patrick Low. Washington, DC: World Bank, 1992, pp. 67–86.

Mansfield, Edwin et al. "Social and Private Rates of Return from Industrial Innovations," *Quart. J. Econ.*, May 1977, *91*(2), pp. 221–40.
McConnell, Virginia D. and Schwab, Robert M. "The Impact of Environmental Regulation on Industry Location Decisions: The Motor Vehicle Industry," *Land Econ.*, Feb. 1990, *66*(1), pp. 67–81.
McGuire, Martin C. "Regulation, Factor Rewards, and International Trade," *J. Public Econ.*, Apr. 1982, *17*(3), pp. 335–54.
Meyer, Stephen M. "Environmentalism and Economic Prosperity: Testing the Environmental Impact Hypothesis." M.I.T. Mimeo, 1992. Cambridge, MA, Updated 1993.
Norsworthy, J. R.; Harper, Michael J. and Kunze, Kent. "The Slowdown in Productivity Growth: Analysis of Some Contributing Factors," *Brookings Pap. Econ. Act.*, 1979, 2, pp. 387–421.
Oates, Wallace; Palmer, Karen and Portney, Paul, "Environmental Regulation and International Competitiveness: Thinking About The Porter Hypothesis." Mimeo, 1993.
Organization for Economic Cooperation and Development. *The macro-economic impacts of environmental expenditures.* Paris, France: Organization for Economic Cooperation and Development, 1985.
———. *OECD environment data compendium.* Paris, France: Organization for Economic Cooperation and Development, 1990.
———. *The OECD environment industry: Situation, prospects, and government policies.* Paris, France: Organization of Economic Cooperation and Development, 1992.
———. *Summary report of the workshop on environmental policies and industrial competitiveness, 28–29 January 1993.* Paris, France: Organization of Economic Cooperation and Development, 1993a.
———. *Pollution abatement and control expenditure in OECD countries.* OECD Environment Monograph No. 75. Paris, France: Organization of Economic Cooperation and Development, 1993b.
Ostro, Bart D. "The Effects of Air Pollution on Work Loss and Morbidity," *J. Environ. Econ. Manage.*, Dec. 1983, *10*(4), pp. 371–82.
Palmer, Karen L. and Simpson, R. David. "Environmental Policy as Industrial Policy," *Resources*, Summer 1993, (112), pp. 17–21.
Pearson, Charles S., ed. *Multinational corporations, environment, and the Third World.* Durham, NC: Duke U. Press and World Resources Institute, 1987.
Pethig, Rudiger. "Pollution, Welfare, and Environmental Policy in the Theory of Comparative Advantage," *J. Environ. Econ. Manage.*, 1975, 2, pp. 160–69.
Porter, Michael E. *The competitive advantage of nations.* New York: Free Press, 1990.
———. "America's Green Strategy," *Sci. Amer.*, Apr. 1991, p. 168.
Portney, Paul R. "Economics and the Clean Air Act," *J. Econ. Perspectives*, Fall 1990, *4*(4), pp. 173–81.
———. "Does Environmental Policy Conflict with Economic Growth?" *Resources*, Spring 1994, (115), pp. 21–23.
Repetto, Robert. "Environmental Productivity and Why It Is So Important," *Challenge*, Sept.–Oct. 1990, *33*(5), pp. 33–38.
Robison, H. David. "Industrial Pollution Abatement: The Impact on Balance of Trade," *Can. J. Econ.*, Feb. 1988, *21*(1), pp. 187–99.
Rose, Adam. "Modeling the Macroeconomic Impact of Air Pollution Abatement," *J. Reg. Sci.*, Nov. 1983, *23*(4), pp. 441–59.
Rutledge, Gary L. and Leonard, Mary L. "Pollution Abatement and Control Expenditures, 1972–90," *Surv. Curr. Bus.*, June 1992, *72*(6), pp. 25–41.

———. "Pollution Abatement and Control Expenditures, 1987–91," *Surv. Curr. Bus.*, May 1993, *73*(5), pp. 55–62.

Schmalensee, Richard. "The Costs of Environmental Protection," in *Balancing economic growth and environmental goals.* Ed.: Mary Beth Kotowski. Washington, DC: American Council for Capital Formation Center for Policy Research, 1994, pp. 55–75.

Siebert, Horst. "Environmental Quality and the Gains from Trade," *Kyklos*, 1977, *30*(4), pp. 657–73.

Solow, Robert M. *An almost practical step toward sustainability.* Washington, DC: Resources for the Future, 1992.

Stewart, Richard B. "Environmental Regulation and International Competitiveness," *Yale Law J.*, June 1993, *102*(8), pp. 2039–2106.

Tobey, James A. "The Effects of Domestic Environmental Policies on Patterns of World Trade: An Empirical Test," *Kyklos*, 1990, *43*(2), pp. 191–209.

Tyson, Laura D'andrea. "Competitiveness: An Analysis of the Problem and a Perspective on Future Policy," in *Global competitiveness: Getting the U.S. back on track.* Ed.: Martin K. Starr. New York, NY: Norton, 1988, pp. 95–120.

U.S. Congress. *Legislative history of the Clean Air Act.* Part 3. Washington, DC: U.S. GPO, 1979.

U.S. Congressional Budget Office. *Environmental regulation and economic efficiency.* Washington, DC: U.S. GPO, 1985.

U.S. Department of Commerce. *Pollution abatement costs and expenditures, 1991.* Economics and Statistics Administration, Bureau of the Census. Washington, DC: U.S. GPO, 1993.

U.S. Environmental Protection Agency. *Air quality criteria for particulate matter and sulfur oxides.* Research Triangle Park, North Carolina: U.S. Environmental Protection Agency, 1982.

———. *Environmental investments: The cost of a clean environment.* Washington, DC: U.S. Environmental Protection Agency, 1990.

———. *National air quality and emissions trends report.* Office of Air Quality Planning and Standards, EPA-450-R-92-001. Research Triangle Park, North Carolina: U.S. Environmental Protection Agency, 1992a.

———. "The Clean Air Marketplace: New Business Opportunities Created by the Clean Air Act Amendments—Summary of Conference Proceedings." Washington, DC, Office of Air and Radiation, July 24, 1992b.

———. *International trade in environmental protection equipment.* Washington, DC: U.S. Environmental Protection Agency, 1993.

U.S. General Accounting Office. *U.S.—Mexico Trade: Some U.S. wood furniture firms relocated from Los Angeles area to Mexico.* Report Number GAO/NSIAD-91-191. Washington, DC: U.S. General Accounting Office, 1991.

U.S. Office of Technology Assessment. *Technology and steel industry competitiveness.* OTA-M-122. Washington, DC: U.S. GPO, 1980.

———. *Trade and the environment: Conflicts and opportunities.* Washington, DC: U.S. GPO, 1992.

———. *Industry, technology, and the environment: Competitive challenges and business opportunities.* OTA-ITE-586. Washington, DC: U.S. GPO, 1994.

Verbruggen, Harmen. "The Trade Effects of Economic Instruments," in *Environmental policies and industrial competitiveness.* Paris: Organization of Economic Cooperation and Development (OECD), 1993, pp. 55–62.

Vogel, David. *National styles of regulation: Environmental policy in Great Britain and the United States.* Ithaca, NY: Cornell U. Press, 1986.

Walter, Ingo. "Environmentally Induced Industrial Relocation to Developing Countries," in *Environment and trade: The relation of international trade and environmental policy.* Eds.: Seymour J. Rubin and Thomas R. Graham. Totowa, NJ: Allanheld, Osmun, 1982, pp. 67–101.

Walter, Ingo and Ugelow, J. "Environmental Policies in Developing Countries," *Ambio*, 1979, *8*, pp. 102–09.

Weitzman, Martin L. "On the 'Environmental' Discount Rate." *J. Environ. Econ. Manage.*, Mar. 1994, *26*(2), pp. 200–09.

Wheeler, David and Mody, Ashoka. "International Investment Location Decisions: The Case of U.S. Firms," *J. Int. Econ.*, Aug. 1992, *33*(1,2), pp. 57–76.

Yohe, Gary W. "The Backward Incidence of Pollution Control—Some Comparative Statics in General Equilibrium," *J. Environ. Econ. Manage.*, Sept. 1979, *6*(3), pp. 187–98.

Zamparutti, Anthony and Jon Klavens. "Environment and Foreign Investment in Central and Eastern Europe: Results from a Survey of Western Corporations," in *Environmental policies and industrial competitiveness.* Paris: Organization of Economic Cooperation and Development (OECD), 1993, pp. 120–27.

7 Toward a New Conception of the Environment-Competitiveness Relationship*

Michael E. Porter
Claas van der Linde

Michael E. Porter is the C. Roland Christensen Professor of Business Administration, Harvard Business School; and Claas van der Linde is on the faculty of the International Management Research Institute of St. Gallen University, Switzerland.

The relationship between environmental goals and industrial competitiveness has normally been thought of as involving a tradeoff between social benefits and private costs. The issue was how to balance society's desire for environmental protection with the economic burden on industry. Framed this way, environmental improvement becomes a kind of arm-wrestling match. One side pushes for tougher standards; the other side tries to beat the standards back.

Our central message is that the environmental-competitiveness debate has been framed incorrectly. The notion of an inevitable struggle between ecology and the economy grows out of a static view of environmental regulation, in which technology, products, processes and customer needs are all fixed. In this static world, where firms have already made their cost-minimizing choices, environmental regulation inevitably raises costs and will tend to reduce the market share of domestic companies on global markets.

However, the paradigm defining competitiveness has been shifting, particularly in the last 20 to 30 years, away from this static model. The new paradigm of international competitiveness is a dynamic one, based on innovation. A body of research first published in *The Competitive Advantage of Nations* has begun to address these changes (Porter, 1990). Competitiveness at the industry level arises from superior productivity, either in terms of lower costs than rivals or the ability to offer products with supe-

"Toward a New Conception of the Environmental-Competitiveness Issue," by Michael E. Porter and Claas van der Linde, from *Journal of Economic Perspectives*, 9(4):97–118 (Fall 1995).

*The authors are grateful to Alan Auerbach, Ben Bonifant, Daniel C. Esty, Ridgway M. Hall, Jr., Donald B. Marron, Jan Rivkin, Nicolaj Siggelkow, R. David Simpson and Timothy Taylor for extensive valuable editorial suggestions. We are also grateful to Reed Hundt for ongoing discussions that have greatly benefitted our thinking.

rior value that justify a premium price.[1] Detailed case studies of hundreds of industries, based in dozens of countries, reveal that internationally competitive companies are not those with the cheapest inputs or the largest scale, but those with the capacity to improve and innovate continually. (We use the term innovation broadly, to include a product's or service's design, the segments it serves, how it is produced, how it is marketed and how it is supported.) Competitive advantage, then, rests not on static efficiency nor on optimizing within fixed constraints, but on the capacity for innovation and improvement that shift the constraints.

This paradigm of dynamic competitiveness raises an intriguing possibility: in this paper, we will argue that properly designed environmental standards can trigger innovation that may partially or more than fully offset the costs of complying with them. Such "innovation offsets," as we call them, can not only lower the net cost of meeting environmental regulations, but can even lead to absolute advantages over firms in foreign countries not subject to similar regulations. Innovation offsets will be common because reducing pollution is often coincident with improving the productivity with which resources are used. In short, firms can actually benefit from properly crafted environmental regulations that are more stringent (or are imposed earlier) than those faced by their competitors in other countries. By stimulating innovation, strict environmental regulations can actually enhance competitiveness.

There is a legitimate and continuing controversy over the social benefits of specific environmental standards, and there is a huge benefit-cost literature. Some believe that the risks of pollution have been overstated; others fear the reverse. Our focus here is not on the social benefits of environmental regulation, but on the private costs. Our argument is that whatever the level of social benefits, these costs are far higher than they need to be. The policy focus should, then, be on relaxing the tradeoff between competitiveness and the environment rather than accepting it as a given.

The Link from Regulation to Promoting Innovation

It is sometimes argued that companies must, by the very notion of profit seeking, be pursuing all profitable innovations. In the metaphor economists often cite, $10 bills will never be found on the ground because someone would have already picked them up. In this view, if complying with environmental regulation can be profitable, in the sense that a company can more than offset the cost of compliance, then why is such regulation necessary?

---

[1]At the industry level, the meaning of competitiveness is clear. At the level of a state or nation, however, the notion of competitiveness is less clear because no nation or state is, or can be, competitive in everything. The proper definition of competitiveness at the aggregate level is the average *productivity* of industry or the value created per unit of labor and per dollar of capital invested. Productivity depends on both the quality and features of products (which determine their value) and the efficiency with which they are produced.

The possibility that regulation might act as a spur to innovation arises because the world does not fit the Panglossian belief that firms always make optimal choices. This will hold true only in a static optimization framework where information is perfect and profitable opportunities for innovation have already been discovered, so that profit-seeking firms need only choose their approach. Of course, this does not describe reality. Instead, the actual process of dynamic competition is characterized by changing technological opportunities coupled with highly incomplete information, organizational inertia and control problems reflecting the difficulty of aligning individual, group and corporate incentives. Companies have numerous avenues for technological improvement, and limited attention.

Actual experience with energy-saving investments illustrates that in the real world, $10 bills are waiting to be picked up. As one example, consider the "Green Lights" program of the Environmental Protection Agency. Firms volunteering to participate in this program pledge to scrutinize every avenue of electrical energy consumption. In return, they receive advice on efficient lighting, hearing and cooling operations. When the EPA collected data on energy-saving lighting upgrades reported by companies as part of the Green Lights program, it showed that nearly 80 percent of the projects had paybacks of two years or less (DeCanio, 1993). Yet only after companies became part of the program, and benefitted from information and cajoling from the EPA, were these highly profitable projects carried out. This paper will present numerous other examples of where environmental innovation produces net benefits for private companies.[2]

We are currently in a transitional phase of industrial history where companies are still inexperienced in dealing creatively with environmental issues. The environment has not been a principal area of corporate or technological emphasis, and knowledge about environmental impacts is still rudimentary in many firms and industries, elevating uncertainty about innovation benefits. Customers are also unaware of the costs of resource inefficiency in the packaging they discard, the scrap value they forego and the disposal costs they bear. Rather than attempting to innovate in every direction at once, firms in fact make choices based on how they perceive their competitive situation and the world around them. In such a world, regulation can be an important influence on the discretion of innovation, either for better or for worse. Properly crafted environmental regulation can serve at least six purposes.

First, regulation signals companies about likely resource inefficiencies and potential technological improvements. Companies are still inexperienced in measuring their discharges, understanding the full costs of incomplete utilization of resources and toxicity, and conceiving new ap-

---

[2]Of course, there are many nonenvironmental examples of where industry has been extremely slow to pick up available $10 bills by choosing new approaches. For example, total quality management programs only came to the United States and Europe decades after they had been widely diffused in Japan, and only after Japanese firms had devastated U.S. and European competitors in the marketplace. The analogy between searching for product quality and for environmental protection is explored later in this paper.

proaches to minimize discharges or eliminate hazardous substances. Regulation rivets attention on this area of potential innovation.[3]

Second, regulation focused on information gathering can achieve major benefits by raising corporate awareness. For example, Toxics Release Inventories, which are published annually as part of the 1986 Superfund reauthorization, require more than 20,000 manufacturing plants to report their releases of some 320 toxic chemicals. Such information gathering often leads to environmental improvement without mandating pollution reductions, sometimes even at lower costs.

Third, regulation reduces the uncertainty that investments to address the environment will be valuable. Greater certainty encourages investment in any area.

Fourth, regulation creates pressure that motivates innovation and progress. Our broader research on competitiveness highlights the important role of outside pressure in the innovation process, to overcome organizational inertia, foster creative thinking and mitigate agency problems. Economists are used to the argument that pressure for innovation can come from strong competitors, demanding customers or rising prices of raw materials; we are arguing that properly crafted regulation can also provide such pressure.

Fifth, regulation levels the transitional playing field. During the transition period to innovation-based solutions, regulation ensures that one company cannot opportunistically gain position by avoiding environmental investments. Regulations provide a buffer until new technologies become proven and learning effects reduce their costs.

Sixth, regulation is needed in the case of incomplete offsets. We readily admit that innovation cannot always completely offset the cost of compliance, especially in the short term before learning can reduce the cost of innovation-based solutions. In such cases, regulation will be necessary to improve environmental quality.

Stringent regulation can actually produce greater innovation and innovation offsets than lax regulation. Relatively lax regulation can be dealt with incrementally and without innovation, and often with "end-of-pipe" or secondary treatment solutions. More stringent regulation, however, focuses greater company attention on discharges and emissions, and compliance requires more fundamental solutions, like reconfiguring products and processes. While the cost of compliance may rise with stringency, then, the potential for innovation offsets may rise even faster. Thus the *net* cost of compliance can fall with stringency and may even turn into a net benefit.

How Innovation Offsets Occur

Innovation in response to environmental regulation can take two broad forms. The first is that companies simply get smarter about how to deal with pollution once it occurs, including the processing of toxic materials

---

[3]Regulation also raises the likelihood that product and process in general will incorporate environmental improvements.

and emissions, how to reduce the amount of toxic or harmful material generated (or convert it into salable forms) and how to improve secondary treatment. Molten Metal Technology, of Waltham, Massachusetts, for example, has developed a catalytic extraction process to process many types of hazardous waste efficiently and effectively. This sort of innovation reduces the cost of compliance with pollution control, but changes nothing else.

The second form of innovation addresses environmental impacts while simultaneously improving the affected product itself and/or related processes. In some cases, these "innovation offsets" can exceed the costs of compliance. This second sort of innovation is central to our claim that environmental regulation can actually increase industrial competitiveness.

Innovation offsets can be broadly divided into product offsets and process offsets. Product offsets occur when environmental regulation produces not just less pollution, but also creates better-performing or higher-quality products, safer products, lower product costs (perhaps from material substitution or less packaging), products with higher resale or scrap value (because of ease in recycling or disassembly) or lower costs of product disposal for users. Process offsets occur when environmental regulation not only leads to reduced pollution, but also results in higher resource productivity such as higher process yields, less downtime through more careful monitoring and maintenance, materials savings (due to substitution, reuse or recycling of production inputs), better utilization of by-products, lower energy consumption during the production process, reduced material storage and handling costs, conversion of waste into valuable forms, reduced waste disposal costs or safer workplace conditions. These offsets are frequently related, so that achieving one can lead to the realization of several others.

As yet, no broad tabulation exists of innovation offsets. Most of the work done in this area involves case studies, because case studies are the only vehicle currently available to measure compliance costs and both direct and indirect innovation benefits. This journal is not the place for a comprehensive listing of available case studies. However, offering some examples should help the reader to understand how common and plausible such effects are.

Innovation to comply with environmental regulation often improves product performance or quality. In 1990, for instance, Raytheon found itself required (by the Montreal Protocol and the U.S. Clean Air Act) to eliminate ozone-depleting chlorofluorocarbons (CFCs) used for cleaning printed electronic circuit boards after the soldering process. Scientists at Raytheon initially thought that complete elimination of CFCs would be impossible. However, they eventually adopted a new semiaqueous, terpene-based cleaning agent that could be reused. The new method proved to result in an increase in average product quality, which had occasionally been compromised by the old CFC-based cleaning agent, as well as lower operating costs (Raytheon, 1991, 1993). It would not have been adopted in the absence of environmental regulation mandating the phase-out of CFCs. Another example is the move by the Robbins Company (a jewelry company based in Attleboro, Massachusetts) to a closed-hoop, zero-discharge system for handling the water used in plating (Berube, Nash, Maxwell and Ehrenfeld, 1992). Robbins was facing closure due to violation of its existing discharge permits. The water produced by purification through filtering and ion exchange in the new closed-loop system was 40 times cleaner than city water and led to higher-quality plating and fewer rejects. The result was enhanced competitiveness.

Environmental regulations may also reduce product costs by showing how to eliminate costly materials, reduce unnecessary packaging or simplify designs. Hitachi responded to a 1991 Japanese recycling law by redesigning products to reduce disassembly time. In the process, the number of parts in a washing machine fell 16 percent, and the number of parts on a vacuum cleaner fell 30 percent. In this way, moves to redesign products for better recyclability can lead to fewer components and thus easier assembly.

Environmental standards can also lead to innovation that reduces disposal costs (or boost scrap or resale value) for the user. For instance, regulation that requires recyclability of products can lead to designs that allow valuable materials to be recovered more easily after disposal of the product. Either the customer or the manufacturer who takes back used products reaps greater value.

These have all been examples of product offsets, but process offsets are common as well. Process changes to reduce emissions frequently result in increases in product yields. At Ciba-Geigy's dyestuff plant in New Jersey, the need to meet new environmental standards caused the firm to reexamine its wastewater streams. Two changes in its production process—replacing iron with a different chemical conversion agent that did not result in the formation of solid iron sludge and process changes that eliminated the release of potentially toxic product into the wastewater stream—not only boosted yield by 40 percent but also eliminated wastes, resulting in annual cost savings of $740,000 (Dorfman, Muir and Miller, 1992).[4]

Similarly, 3M discovered that in producing adhesives in batches that were transferred to storage tanks, one bad batch could spoil the entire contents of a tank. The result was wasted raw materials and high costs of hazardous waste disposal. 3M developed a new technique to run quality tests more rapidly on new batches. The new technique allowed 3M to reduce hazardous wastes by 10 tons per year at almost no cost, yielding an annual savings of more than $200,000 (Sheridan, 1992).

Solving environmental problems can also yield benefits in terms of reduced downtime. Many chemical production processes at DuPont, for example, require start-up time to stabilize and bring output within specifications, resulting in an initial period during which only scrap and waste is produced. Installing higher-quality monitoring equipment has allowed

---

[4]We should note that this plant was ultimately closed. However, the example described here does illustrate the role of regulatory pressure in process innovation.

DuPont to reduce production interruptions and the associated wasteful production start-ups, thus reducing waste generation as well as downtime (Parkinson, 1990).

Regulation can trigger innovation offsets through substitution of less costly materials or better utilization of materials in the process. For example, 3M faced new regulations that will force many solvent users in paper, plastic and metal coatings to reduce its solvent emissions 90 percent by 1995 (Boroughs and Carpenter, 1991). The company responded by avoiding the use of solvents altogether and developing coating products with safer, water-based solutions. At another 3M plant, a change from a solvent-based to a water-based carrier, used for coating tablets, eliminated 24 tons per year of air emissions. The $60,000 investment saved $180,000 in unneeded pollution control equipment and created annual savings of $15,000 in solvent purchases (Parkinson, 1990). Similarly, when federal and state regulations required that Dow Chemical close certain evaporation ponds used for storing and evaporating wastewater resulting from scrubbing hydrochloric gas with caustic soda, Dow redesigned its production process. By first scrubbing the hydrochloric acid with water and then caustic soda, Dow was able to eliminate the need for evaporation ponds, reduce its use of caustic soda, and capture a portion of the waste stream for reuse as a raw material in other parts of the plant. This process change cost $250,000 to implement. It reduced caustic waste by 6,000 tons per year and hydrochloric acid waste by 80 tons per year, for a savings of $2.4 million per year (Dorfman, Muir and Miller, 1992).

The Robbins Company's jewelry-plating system illustrates similar benefits. In moving to the closed-loop system that purified and recycled water, Robbins saved over $115,000 per year in water, chemicals, disposal costs, and lab fees and reduced water usage from 500,000 gallons per week to 500 gallons per week. The capital cost of the new system, which completely eliminated the waste, was $220,000, compared to about $500,000 for a wastewater treatment facility that would have brought Robbins' discharge into compliance only with current regulations.

At the Tobyhanna Army Depot, for instance, improvements in sandblasting, cleaning, plating and painting operations reduced hazardous waste generation by 82 percent between 1985 and 1992. That reduction saved the depot over $550,000 in disposal costs, and $400,000 in material purchasing and handling costs (PR Newswire, 1993).

Innovation offsets can also be derived by converting waste into more valuable forms. The Robbins Company recovered valuable precious metals in its zero discharge plating system. At Rhone-Poulenc's nylon plant in Chalampe, France, diacids (by-products that had been produced by an adipic acid process) used to be separated and incinerated. Rhone-Poulenc invested Fr 76 million and installed new equipment to recover and sell them as dye and tanning additives or coagulation agents, resulting in annual revenues of about Fr 20.1 million. In the United States, similar by-products from a Monsanto Chemical Company plant in Pensacola, Florida, are sold to utility companies who use them to accelerate sulfur dioxide removal during flue gas desulfurization (Basta and Vagi, 1988).

A few studies of innovation offsets do go beyond individual cases and offer some broader-based data. One of the most extensive studies is by IN-FORM, an environmental research organization. INFORM investigated activities to prevent waste generation—so-called source reduction activities—at 29 chemical plants in California, Ohio and New Jersey (Dorfman, Muir and Miller, 1992). Of the 181 source-reduction activities identified in this study, only one was found to have resulted in a net cost increase. Of the 70 activities for which the study was able to document changes in product yield, 68 reported yield increases; the average yield increase for the 20 initiatives with specific available data was 7 percent. These innovation offsets were achieved with surprisingly low investments and very short payback periods. One-quarter of the 48 initiatives with detailed capital cost information required no capital investment at all; of the 38 initiatives with payback period data, nearly two-thirds were shown to have recouped their initial investments in six months or less. The annual savings per dollar spent on source reduction averaged $3.49 for the 27 activities for which this information could be calculated. The study also investigated the motivating factors behind the plant's source-reduction activities. Significantly, it found that waste disposal costs were the most often cited, followed by environmental regulation.

To build a broader base of studies on innovation offsets to environmental regulation, we have been collaborating with the Management Institute for Environment and Business on a series of international case studies, sponsored by the EPA, of industries and entire sectors significantly affected by environmental regulation. Sectors studied include pulp and paper, paint and coatings, electronics manufacturing, refrigerators, dry cell batteries and printing inks (Bonifant and Ratcliffe, 1994; Bonifant 1994a,b; van der Linde, 1995a,b,c). Some examples from that effort have already been described here.

A solid body of case study evidence, then, demonstrates that innovation offsets to environmental regulation are common.[5] Even with a generally hostile regulatory climate, which is not designed to encourage such innovation, these offsets can sometimes exceed the cost of compliance. We expect that such examples will proliferate as companies and regulators become more sophisticated and shed old mindsets.

Early-Mover Advantage in International Markets

World demand is moving rapidly in the direction of valuing low-pollution and energy-efficient products, not to mention more resource-efficient products with higher resale or scrap value. Many companies are using innovation to command price premiums for "green" products and open

---

[5]Of course, a list of case examples, however long, does not prove that companies can always innovate or substitute for careful empirical testing in a large cross-section of industries. Given our current ability to capture the true costs and often multifaceted benefits of regulatory-induced innovation, reliance on the weight of case study evidence is necessary. As we discuss elsewhere, there is no countervailing set of case studies that shows that innovation offsets are unlikely or impossible.

up new market segments. For example, Germany enacted recycling standards earlier than in most other countries, which gave German firms an early-mover advantage in developing less packaging-intensive products, which have been warmly received in the marketplace. Scandinavian pulp and paper producers have been leaders in introducing new environmentally friendly production processes, and thus Scandinavian pulp and paper equipment suppliers such as Kamyr and Sunds have made major gains internationally in selling innovative bleaching equipment. In the United States, a parallel example is the development by Cummins Engine of low-emissions diesel engines for trucks, buses and other applications in response to U.S. environmental regulations. Its new competence is allowing the firm to gain international market share.

Clearly, this argument only works to the extent that national environmental standards anticipate and are consistent with international trends in environmental protection, rather than break with them. Creating expertise in cleaning up abandoned hazardous waste sites, as the U.S. Superfund law has done, does little to benefit U.S. suppliers if no other country adopts comparable toxic waste cleanup requirements. But when a competitive edge is attained, especially because a company's home market is sophisticated and demanding in a way that pressures the company to further innovation, the economic gains can be lasting.

Answering Defenders of the Traditional Model

Our argument that strict environmental regulation can be fully consistent with competitiveness was originally put forward in a short *Scientific American* essay (Porter, 1991; see also van der Linde, 1993). This essay received far more scrutiny than we expected. It has been warmly received by many, especially in the business community. But it has also had its share of critics, especially among economists (Jaffe, Peterson, Portney and Stavins, 1993, 1994; Oates, Palmer and Portney, 1993; Palmer and Simpson, 1993; Simpson, 1993; Schmalensee, 1993).

One criticism is that while innovation offsets are theoretically possible, they are likely to be rare or small in practice. We disagree. Pollution is the emission or discharge of a (harmful) substance or energy form into the environment. Fundamentally, it is a manifestation of economic waste and involves unnecessary, inefficient or incomplete utilization of resources, or resources not used to generate their highest value. In many cases, emissions are a sign of inefficiency and force a firm to perform non-value-creating activities such as handling, storage and disposal. Within the company itself, the costs of poor resource utilization are most obvious in incomplete material utilization, but are also manifested in poor process control, which generates unnecessary stored material, waste and defects. There are many other hidden costs of resource inefficiencies later in the life cycle of the product. Packaging discarded by distributors or customers, for example, wastes resources and adds costs. Customers bear additional costs when they use polluting products or products that waste energy. Resources are also wasted when customers discard products embodying unused materials or when they bear the costs of product disposal.[6]

As the many examples discussed earlier suggest, the opportunity to reduce cost by diminishing pollution should thus be the rule, not the exception. Highly toxic materials such as heavy metals or solvents are often expensive and hard to handle, and reducing their use makes sense from several points of view. More broadly, efforts to reduce pollution and maximize profits share the same basic principles, including the efficient use of input, substitution of less expensive materials and the minimization of unneeded activities.[7]

A corollary to this observation is that scrap or waste or emissions can carry important information about flaws in product design or the production process. A recent study of process changes in 10 printed circuit board manufacturers, for example, found that 13 of 33 major changes were initiated by pollution control personnel. Of these, 12 resulted in cost reduction, eight in quality improvements and five in extension of production capabilities (King, 1994).

Environmental improvement efforts have traditionally overlooked the systems cost of resource inefficiency. Improvement efforts have focused on *pollution control* through better identification, processing and disposal of discharges or waste, an inherently costly approach. In recent years, more advanced companies and regulators have embraced the concept of *pollution prevention*, sometimes called source reduction, which uses material substitution, closed-loop processes and the like to limit pollution before it occurs.

But although pollution prevention is an important step in the right direction, ultimately companies and regulators must learn to frame environmental improvement in terms of *resource productivity*, or the efficiency and effectiveness with which companies and their customers use resources.[8] Improving resource productivity within companies goes beyond eliminating pollution (and the cost of dealing with it) to lowering true economic cost and raising the true economic value of products. At the level of resource productivity, environmental improvement and competitiveness come together. The imperative for resource productivity rests on the private costs that companies bear because of pollution, not on mitigating pollution's social costs. In addressing these private costs, it highlights the opportunity costs of pollution—wasted resources, wasted efforts and diminished product value to the customer—not its actual costs.

---

[6]At its core, then, pollution is a result of an intermediate state of technology or management methods. Apparent exceptions to the resource productivity thesis often prove the rule by highlighting the role of technology. Paper made with recycled fiber was once greatly inferior, but new de-inking and other technologies have made its quality better and better. Apparent tradeoffs between energy efficiency and emissions rest on incomplete combustion.

[7]Schmalensee (1993) counters that NO_x emissions often result from thermodynamically efficient combustion. But surely this is an anomaly, not the rule, and may represent an intermediate level of efficiency.

[8]One of the pioneering efforts to see environmental improvement this way is Joel Makower's (1993) book, *The E-Factor: The Bottom-Line Approach to Environmentally Responsible Business.*

This view of pollution as unproductive resource utilization suggests a helpful analogy between environmental protection and product quality measured by defects. Companies used to promote quality by conducting careful inspections during the production process, and then by creating a service organization to correct the quality problems that turned up in the field. This approach has proven misguided. Instead, the most cost-effective way to improve quality is to build it into the entire process, which includes design, purchased components, process technology, shipping and handling techniques and so forth. This method dramatically reduces inspection, rework and the need for a large service organization. (It also leads to the oft-quoted phrase, "quality is free.") Similarly, there is reason to believe that companies can enjoy substantial innovation offsets by improving resource productivity throughout the value chain instead of through dealing with the manifestations of inefficiency like emissions and discharges.

Indeed, corporate total quality management programs have strong potential also to reduce pollution and lead to innovation offsets.[9] Dow Chemical, for example, has explicitly identified the link between quality improvement and environmental performance, by using statistical process control to reduce the variance in processes and lower waste (Sheridan, 1992).

A second criticism of our hypothesis is to point to the studies finding high costs of compliance with environmental regulation, as evidence that there is a fixed tradeoff between regulation and competitiveness. But these studies are far from definitive.

Estimates of regulatory compliance costs prior to enactment of a new rule typically exceed the actual costs. In part, this is because such estimates are often self-reported by industries who oppose the rule, which creates a tendency to inflation. A prime example of this type of thinking was a statement by Lee Iacocca, then vice president at the Ford Motor Company, during the debate on the 1970 Clean Air Act. Iacocca warned that compliance with the new regulations would require huge price increases for automobiles, force U.S. automobile production to a halt after January 1, 1975, and "do irreparable damage to the U.S. economy" (Smith, 1992). The 1970 Clean Air Act was subsequently enacted, and Iacocca's predictions turned out to be wrong. Similar dire predictions were made during the 1990 Clean Air Act debate; industry analysts predicted that burdens on the U.S. industry would exceed $100 billion. Of course, the reality has proven to be far less dramatic. In one study in the pulp and paper sector, actual costs of compliance were $4.00 to $5.50 per ton compared to original industry estimates of $16.40 (Bonson, McCubbin and Sprague, 1988).

Early estimates of compliance cost also tend to be exaggerated because they assume no innovation. Early cost estimates for dealing with regula-

---

[9]A case study of pollution prevention in a large multinational firm showed those units with strong total quality management programs in place usually undertake more effective pollution prevention efforts than units with less commitment to total quality management. See Rappaport (1992), cited in U.S. Congress, Office of Technology Assessment (1994).

tions concerning emission of volatile compounds released during paint application held everything else constant, assuming only the addition of a hood to capture the fumes from paint lines. Innovation that improved the paint's transfer efficiency subsequently allowed not only the reduction of fumes but also paint usage. Further innovation in waterborne paint formulations without any VOC-releasing solvents made it possible to eliminate the need for capturing and treating the fumes altogether (Bonifant, 1994b). Similarly, early estimates of the costs of complying with a 1991 federal clean air regulation calling for a 98 percent reduction in atmospheric emissions of benzene from tar-storage tanks used by coal tar distillers initially assumed that tar-storage tanks would have to be covered by costly gas blankets. While many distillers opposed the regulations, Pittsburgh-based Aristech Chemical, a major distiller of coal tar, subsequently developed an innovative way to remove benzene from tar in the first processing step, thereby eliminating the need for the gas blanket and resulting in a saving of $3.3 million instead of a cost increase (PR Newswire, 1993).

Prices in the new market for trading allowances to emit SO_2 provide another vivid example. At the time the law was passed, analysts projected that the marginal cost of SO_2 controls (and, therefore, the price of an emission allowance) would be on the order of $300 to $600 (or more) per ton in Phase I and up to $1000 or more in Phase II. Actual Phase I allowance prices have turned out to be in the $170 to $250 range, and recent trades are heading lower, with Phase II estimates only slightly higher (after adjusting for the time value of money). In case after case, the differences between initial predictions and actual outcomes—especially after industry has had time to learn and innovate—are striking.

Econometric studies showing that environmental regulation raises costs and harms competitiveness are subject to bias, because net compliance costs are overestimated by assuming away innovation benefits. Jorgenson and Wilcoxen (1990), for example, explicitly state that they did not attempt to assess public or private benefits. Other often-cited studies that solely focus on costs, leaving out benefits, are Hazilla and Kopp (1990) and Gray (1987). By largely assuming away innovation effects, how could economic studies reach any other conclusion than they do?

Internationally competitive industries seem to be much better able to innovate in response to environmental regulation than industries that were uncompetitive to begin with, but no study measuring the effects of environmental regulation on industry competitiveness has taken initial competitiveness into account. In a study by Kalt (1988), for instance, the sectors where high environmental costs were associated with negative trade performance were ones such as ferrous metal mining, nonferrous mining, chemical and fertilizer manufacturing, primary iron and steel and primary nonferrous metals, industries where the United States suffers from dwindling raw material deposits, very high relative electricity costs, heavily subsidized foreign competitors and other disadvantages that have rendered them uncompetitive quite apart from environmental costs.[10] Other sectors identified by Kalt as having incurred very high environmental costs can actually be interpreted as supporting our hypothesis. Chemicals, plastics and synthetics, fabric, yarn and thread, miscellaneous textiles, leather tanning, paints and allied products, and paperboard containers all had high environmental costs but displayed positive trade performance.

A number of studies have failed to find that stringent environmental regulation hurts industrial competitiveness. Meyer (1992, 1993) tested and refuted the hypothesis that U.S. states with stringent environmental policies experience weak economic growth. Leonard (1988) was unable to demonstrate statistically significant offshore movements by U.S. firms in pollution-intensive industries. Wheeler and Mody (1992) failed to find that environmental regulation affected the foreign investment decisions of U.S. firms. Repetto (1995) found that industries heavily affected by environmental regulations experienced slighter reductions in their share of world exports than did the entire American industry from 1970 to 1990. Using U.S. Bureau of Census Data of more than 200,000 large manufacturing establishments, the study also found that plants with poor environmental records are generally not more profitable than cleaner ones in the same industry, even controlling for their age, size and technology. Jaffe, Peterson, Portney and Stavins (1993) recently surveyed more than 100 studies and concluded there is little evidence to support the view that U.S. environmental regulation had a large adverse effect on competitiveness.

Of course, these studies offer no proof for our hypothesis, either. But it is striking that so many studies find that even the poorly designed environmental laws presently in effect have little adverse effect on competitiveness. After all, traditional approaches to regulation have surely worked to stifle potential innovation offsets and imposed unnecessarily high costs of compliance on industry (as we will discuss in greater detail in the next section). Thus, studies using actual compliance costs to regulation are heavily biased toward finding that such regulation has a substantial cost.[11] In

---

[10]It should be observed that a strong correlation between environmental costs and industry competitiveness does not necessarily indicate causality. Omitting environmental benefits from regulation, and reporting obvious (end-of-pipe) costs but not more difficult to identify or quantify innovation benefits can actually obscure a reverse causal relationship: industries that were uncompetitive in the first place may well be less able to innovate in response to environmental pressures, and thus be prone to end-of-pipe solutions whose costs are easily measured. In contrast, competitive industries capable of addressing environmental problems in innovative ways may report a lower compliance cost.

[11]Gray and Shadbegian (1993), another often-mentioned study, suffers from several of the problems discussed here. The article uses industry-reported compliance costs and does not control for plant technology vintage or the extent of other productivity-enhancing investments at the plant. High compliance costs may well have been borne in old, inefficient plants where firms opted for secondary treatment rather than innovation. Moreover, U.S. producers may well have been disadvantaged in innovating given the nature of the U.S. regulatory process—this seems clearly to have been the case in pulp and paper, one of the industries studied by the Management Institute for Environment and Business (MEB).

no way do such studies measure the potential of well-crafted environmental regulations to stimulate competitiveness.

A third criticism of our thesis is that even if regulation fosters innovation, it will harm competitiveness by crowding out other potentially more productive investments or avenues for innovation. Given incomplete information, the limited attention many companies have devoted to environmental innovations and the inherent linkage between pollution and resource productivity described earlier, it certainly is not obvious that this line of innovation has been so thoroughly explored that the marginal benefits of further investment would be low. The high returns evident in the studies we have cited support this view. Moreover, environmental investments represent only a small percentage of overall investment in all but a very few industries.[12]

A final counterargument, more caricature than criticism, is that we are asserting that any strict environmental regulation will inevitably lead to innovation and competitiveness. Of course, this is not our position. Instead, we believe that if regulations are properly crafted and companies are attuned to the possibilities, then innovation to minimize and even offset the cost of compliance is likely in many circumstances.

Designing Environmental Regulation to Encourage Innovation

If environmental standards are to foster the innovation offsets that arise from new technologies and approaches to production, they should adhere to three principles. First, they must create the maximum opportunity for innovation, leaving the approach to innovation to industry and not the standard-setting agency. Second, regulations should foster continuous improvement, rather than locking in any particular technology. Third, the regulatory process should leave as little room as possible for uncertainty at every stage. Evaluated by these principles, it is clear that U.S. environmental regulations have often been crafted in a way that deters innovative solutions, or even renders them impossible. Environmental laws and regulations need to take three substantial steps: phrasing environmental rules as goals that can be met in flexible ways; encouraging innovation to reach and exceed those goals; and administering the system in a coordinated way.

---

[12]In paints and coatings, for example, environmental investments were 3.3 percent of total capital investment in 1989. According to Department of Commerce (1991) data (self-reported by industry), capital spending for pollution control and abatement outside of the chemical, pulp and paper, petroleum and coal, and primary metal sectors made up just 3.15 percent of total capital spending in 1991.

Clear Goals, Flexible Approaches

Environmental regulation should focus on outcomes, not technologies.[13] Past regulations have often prescribed particular remediation technologies—like catalysts or scrubbers to address air pollution—rather than encouraging innovative approaches. American environmental law emphasized phrases like "best available technology," or "best available control technology." But legislating as if one particular technology is always the "best" almost guarantees that innovation will not occur.

Regulations should encourage product and process changes to better utilize resources and avoid pollution early, rather than mandating end-of-pipe or secondary treatment, which is almost always more costly. For regulators, this poses a question of where to impose regulations in the chain of production from raw materials, equipment, the producer of the end product, to the consumer (Porter, 1985). Regulators must consider the technological capabilities and resources available at each stage, because it affects the likelihood that innovation will occur. With that in mind, the governing principle should be to regulate as late in the production chain as practical, which will normally allow more flexibility for innovation there and in upstream stages.

The EPA should move beyond the single medium (air, water and so on) as the principal way of thinking about the environment, toward total discharges or total impact.[14] It should reorganize around affected industry clusters (including suppliers and related industries) to better understand a cluster's products, technologies and total set of environmental problems. This will foster fundamental rather than piecemeal solutions.[15]

Seeding and Spreading Environmental Innovations

Where possible, regulations should include the use of market incentives, including pollution taxes, deposit-refund schemes and tradable permits.[16] Such approaches often allow considerable flexibility, reinforce resource

---

[13]There will always be instances of extremely hazardous pollution requiring immediate action, where imposing a specific technology by command and control may be the best or only viable solution. However, such methods should be seen as a last resort.

[14]A first step in this direction is the EPA's recent adjustment of the timing of its air rule for the pulp and paper industry so that it will coincide with the rule for water, allowing industry to see the dual impact of the rules and innovate accordingly.

[15]The EPA's regulatory cluster team concept, under which a team from relevant EPA offices approaches particular problems for a broader viewpoint, is a first step in this direction. Note, however, that of the 17 cluster groups formed, only four were organized around specific industries (petroleum refining, oil and gas production, pulp and paper, printing), while the remaining 13 focused on specific chemicals or types of pollution (U.S. Congress, Office of Technology Assessment, 1994).

[16]Pollution taxes can be implemented as effluent charges on the quantity of pollution discharges, as user charges for public treatment facilities, or as product charges based on the potential pollution of a product. In a deposit-refund system, such product charges may be rebated if a product user disposes of it properly (for example, by returning a lead battery for recycling rather than sending it to a landfill). Under a tradable permit system, like that included in the recent Clean Air Act Amendments, a maximum amount of pollution is set, and rights equal to that cap are distributed to firms. Firms must hold enough rights to cover their emissions; firms with excess rights can sell them to firms who are short.

productivity, and also create incentives for ongoing innovation. Mandating outcomes by setting emission levels, while preferable to choosing a particular technology, still fails to provide incentives for continued and ongoing innovation and will tend to freeze a status quo until new regulations appear. In contrast, market incentives can encourage the introduction of technologies that exceed current standards.

The EPA should also promote an increased use of preemptive standards by industry, which appear to be an effective way of dealing with environmental regulation. Preemptive standards, agreed to with EPA oversight to avoid collusion, can be set and met by industry to avoid government standards that might go further or be more restrictive on innovation. They are not only less costly, but allow faster change and leave the initiative for innovation with industry.

The EPA should play a major role in collecting and disseminating information on innovation offsets and their consequences, both here and in other countries. Limited knowledge about opportunities for innovation is a major constraint on company behavior. A good start can be the "clearinghouse" of information on source-reduction approaches that EPA was directed to establish by the Pollution Prevention Act (PPA) of 1990. The Green Lights and Toxics Release Inventories described at the start of this paper are other programs that involve collecting and spreading information. Yet another important initiative is the EPA program to compare emissions rates at different companies, creating methodologies to measure the full internal costs of pollution and ways of exchanging best practices and learning on innovative technologies.

Regulatory approaches can also function by helping create demand pressure for environmental innovation. One example is the prestigious German "Blue Angel" eco-label, introduced by the German government in 1977, which can be displayed only by products meeting very strict environmental criteria. One of the label's biggest success stories has been in oil and gas heating appliances: the energy efficiency of these appliances improved significantly when the label was introduced, and emissions of sulfur dioxide, carbon monoxide and nitrogen oxides were reduced by more than 30 percent.

Another point of leverage on the demand side is to harness the role of government as a demanding buyer of environmental solutions and environmentally friendly products. While there are benefits of government procurement of products such as recycled paper and retreaded tires, the far more leveraged role is in buying specialized environmental equipment and services.[17] One useful change would be to alter the current practice of requiring bidders in competitive bid processes for government projects to only bid with "proven" technologies, a practice sure to hinder innovation.

---

[17]See Marron (1994) for a demonstration of the modest productivity gains likely from government procurement of standard items, although in a static model.

The EPA can employ demonstration projects to stimulate and seed innovative new technologies, working through universities and industry associations. A good example is the project to develop and demonstrate technologies for super-efficient refrigerators, which was conducted by the EPA and researchers in government, academia and the private sector (United States Environmental Protection Agency, 1992). An estimated $1.7 billion was spent in 1992 by the federal government on environmental technology R&D, but only $70 million was directed toward research on pollution prevention (U.S. Congress, Office of Technology Assessment, 1994).

Incentives for innovation must also be built into the regulatory process itself. The current permitting system under Title V of the Clean Air Act Amendments, to choose a negative example, requires firms seeking to change or expand their production process in a way that might impact air quality to revise their permit extensively, *no matter how little the potential effect on air quality may be.* This not only deters innovation, but drains the resources of regulators away from timely action on significant matters. On the positive side, the state of Massachusetts has initiated a program to waive permits in some circumstances, or promise an immediate permit, if a company takes a zero-discharge approach.

A final priority is new forums for settling regulatory issues that minimize litigation. Potential litigation creates enormous uncertainty; actual litigation burns resources. Mandatory arbitration, or rigid arbitration steps before litigation is allowed, would benefit innovation. There is also a need to rethink certain liability issues. While adequate safeguards must be provided against companies that recklessly harm citizens, there is a pressing need for liability standards that more clearly recognize the countervailing health and safety benefits of innovations that lower or eliminate the discharge of harmful pollutants.

Regulatory Coordination

Coordination of environmental regulation can be improved in at least three ways: between industry and regulators, between regulators at different levels and places in government, and between U.S. regulators and their international counterparts.

In setting environmental standards and regulatory processes to encourage innovation, substantive industry participation in setting standards is needed right from the beginning, as is common in many European countries. An appropriate regulatory process is one in which regulations themselves are clear, who must meet them is clear, and industry accepts the regulations and begins innovating to address them, rather than spending years attempting to delay or relax them. In our current system, by the time standards are finally settled and clarified, it is often too late to address them fundamentally, making secondary treatment the only alternative. We need to evolve toward a regulatory regime in which the EPA and other regulators make a commitment that standards will be in place for, say, five years, so that industry is motivated to innovate rather than adopt increment solutions.

Different parts and levels of government must coordinate and organize themselves so that companies are not forced to deal with multiple parties with inconsistent desires and approaches. As a matter of regulatory structure, the EPA's proposed new Innovative Technology Council, being set up to advocate the development of new technology in every field of environmental policy, is a step in the right direction. Another unit in the EPA should be responsible for continued reengineering of the process of regulation to reduce uncertainty and minimize costs. Also, an explicit strategy is needed to coordinate and harmonize federal and state activities.[18]

A final issue of coordination involves the relationship between U.S. environmental regulations and those in other countries. U.S. regulations should be in sync with regulations in other countries and, ideally, be slightly ahead of them. This will minimize possible competitive disadvantages relative to foreign competitors who are not yet subject to the standard, while at the same time maximizing export potential in the pollution control sector. Standards that lead world developments provide domestic firms with opportunities to create valuable early-mover advantages. However, standards should not be too far ahead of, or too different in character from, those that are likely to apply to foreign competitors, for this would lead industry to innovate in the wrong directions.

Critics may note, with some basis, that U.S. regulators may not be able to project better than firms what type of regulations, and resultant demands for environmental products and services, will develop in other nations. However, regulators would seem to possess greater resources and information than firms for understanding the path of regulation in other countries. Moreover, U.S. regulations influence the type and stringency of regulations in other nations, and as such help define demand in other world markets.

Imperatives for Companies

Of course, the regulatory reforms described here also seek to change how companies view environmental issues.[19] Companies must start to recognize the environment as a competitive opportunity—not as an annoying cost or a postponable threat. Yet many companies are ill-prepared to carry out a strategy of environmental innovation that produces sizable compensating offsets.

---

[18]The cluster-based approach to regulation discussed earlier should also help eliminate the practice of sending multiple EPA inspectors to the same plant who do not talk to one another, make conflicting demands and waste time and resources. The potential savings from cluster- and multimedia-oriented permitting and inspection programs appear to be substantial. During a pilot multimedia testing program called the Blackstone Project, the Massachusetts Department of Environmental Protection found that multimedia inspections required 50 percent less time than conventional inspections—which at that time accounted for nearly one-fourth of the department's operating budget (Roy and Dillard, 1990).

[19]For a more detailed perspective on changing company mindsets about competitiveness and environmentalism, see Porter and van der Linde (1995) in the *Harvard Business Review*.

For starters, companies must improve their measurement and assessment methods to detect environmental costs and benefits.[20] Too often, relevant information is simply lacking. Typical is the case of a large producer of organic chemicals that retained a consulting firm to explore opportunities for reducing waste. The client thought it had 40 waste streams, but a careful audit revealed that 497 different waste streams were actually present (Parkinson, 1990). Few companies analyze the true cost of toxicity, waste, discharges and the second-order impacts of waste and discharges on other activities. Fewer still look beyond the out-of-pocket costs of dealing with pollution to investigate the opportunity costs of the wasted resources or foregone productivity. How much money is going up the smokestack? What percentage of inputs are wasted? Many companies do not even track environmental spending carefully, or subject it to evaluation techniques typical for "normal" investments.

Once environmental costs are measured and understood, the next step is to create a presumption for innovation-based solutions. Discharges, scrap and emissions should be analyzed for insights about beneficial product design or process changes. Approaches based on treatment or handling of discharges should be accepted only after being sent back several times for reconsideration. The responsibility for environmental issues should not be delegated to lawyers or outside consultants except in the adversarial regulatory process, or even to internal specialists removed from the line organization, residing in legal, government or environmental affairs departments. Instead, environmental strategies must become a general management issue if the sorts of process and product redesigns needed for true innovation are to even be considered, much less be proposed and implemented.

Conclusion

We have found that economists as a group are resistant to the notion that even well-designed environmental regulations might lead to improved competitiveness. This hesitancy strikes us as somewhat peculiar, given that in other contexts, economists are extremely willing to argue that technological change has overcome predictions of severe, broadly defined environmental costs. A static model (among other flaws) has been behind many dire predictions of economic disaster and human catastrophe: from the predictions of Thomas Malthus that population would inevitably outstrip food

---

[20]Accounting methods that are currently being discussed in this context include "full cost accounting," which attempts to assign all costs to specific products or processes, and "total cost accounting," which goes a step further and attempts both to allocate costs more specifically and to include cost items beyond traditional concerns, such as indirect or hidden costs (like compliance costs, insurance, on-site waste management, operation of pollution control and future liability) and less tangible benefits (like revenue from enhanced company image). See White, Becker and Goldstein (1991), cited in U.S. Congress, Office of Technology Assessment (1994).

supply; to the *Limits of Growth* (Meadows and Meadows, 1972), which predicted the depletion of the world's natural resources; to *The Population Bomb* (Ehrlich, 1968), which predicted that a quarter of the world's population would starve to death between 1973 and 1983. As economists are often eager to point out, these models failed because they did not appreciate the power of innovations in technology to change old assumptions about resource availability and utilization.

Moreover, the static mindset that environmentalism is inevitably costly has created a self-fulfilling gridlock, where both regulators and industry battle over every inch of territory. The process has spawned an industry of litigators and consultants, driving up costs and draining resources away from real solutions. It has been reported that four out of five EPA decisions are currently challenged in court (Clay, 1993, cited in U.S. Congress, Office of Technology Assessment, 1994). A study by the Rand Institute for Civil Justice found that 88 percent of the money paid out between 1986 and 1989 by insurers on Superfund claims went to pay for legal and administrative costs, while only 12 percent were used for actual site cleanups (Acton and Dixon, 1992).

The United States and other countries need an entirely new way of thinking about the relationship between environment and industrial competitiveness—one closer to the reality of modern competition. The focus should be on relaxing the environment-competitiveness tradeoff rather than accepting and, worse yet, steepening it. The orientation should shift from pollution control to resource productivity. We believe that no lasting success can come from policies that promise that environmentalism will triumph over industry, nor from policies that promise that industry will triumph over environmentalism. Instead, success must involve innovation-based solutions that promote both environmentalism and industrial competitiveness.

REFERENCES

Acton, Jan Paul, and Lloyd S. Dixon, *Superfund and Transaction Costs: The Experiences of Insurers and Very Large Industrial Firms.* Santa Monica: Rand Institute for Civil Justice, 1992.

Amoco Corporation and United States Environmental Protection Agency, "Amoco-U.S. EPA Pollution Prevention Project: Yorktown, Virginia, Project Summary," Chicago and Washington, D.C., 1992.

Basta, Nicholas and David Vagi, "A Casebook of Successful Waste Reduction Projections," *Chemical Engineering*, August 15, 1988, 95:11, 37.

Berube, M., J. Nash, J. Maxwell, and J. Ehrenfeld, "From Pollution Control to Zero Discharge: How the Robbins Company Overcame the Obstacles," *Pollution Prevention Review*, Spring 1992, 2:2, 189–207.

Bonifant, B., "Competitive Implications of Environmental Regulation in the Electronics Manufacturing Industry," Management Institute for Environment and Business, Washington, D.C., 1994a.

Bonifant, B., "Competitive Implications of Environmental Regulation in the Paint and Coatings Industry," Management Institute for Environment and Business, Washington, D.C., 1994b.

Bonifant, B., and I. Ratcliffe, "Competitive Implications of Environmental Regulation in the Pulp and Paper Industry," Management Institute for Environment and Business, Washington, D.C., 1994.

Bonson, N. C., Neil McCubbin, and John B. Sprague, "Kraft Mill Effluents in Ontario." Report prepared for the Technical Advisory Committee, Pulp and Paper Sector of MISA, Ontario Ministry of the Environment, Toronto, Ontario, Canada, March 29, 1988, Section 6, p. 166.

Boroughs, D. L., and B. Carpenter, "Helping the Planet and the Economy," U.S. News & World Report, March 25, 1991, 110:11, 46.

Clay, Don, "New Environmentalist: A Cooperative Strategy," Forum for Applied Research and Public Policy, Spring 1993, 8, 125–28.

DeCanio, Stephen J., "Why Do Profitable Energy-Saving Investment Projects Languish?" Paper presented at the Second International Research Conference of the Greening of Industry Network, Cambridge, Mass., 1993.

Department of Commerce, "Pollution Abatement Costs and Expenditures," Washington, D.C., 1991.

Dorfman, Mark H., Warren R. Muir, and Catherine G. Miller, Environmental Dividends: Cutting More Chemical Wastes. New York: INFORM, 1992.

Ehrlich, Paul, The Population Bomb. New York: Ballantine Books, 1968.

Freeman, A. Myrick, III, "Methods for Assessing the Benefits of Environmental Programs." In Kneese, A. V., and J. L. Sweeney, eds., Handbook of Natural Resource and Energy Economics. Vol. 1. Amsterdam: North-Holland, 1985, pp. 223–70.

Gray, Wayne B., "The Cost of Regulation: OSHA, EPA, and the Productivity Slowdown," American Economic Review, 1987, 77:5, 998–1006.

Gray, Wayne B., and Ronald J. Shadbegian, "Environmental Regulation and Productivity at the Plant Level," discussion paper, U.S. Department of Commerce, Center for Economic Studies, Washington, D.C., 1993.

Hartwell, R. V., and L. Bergkamp, "Eco-Labelling in Europe: New Market-Related Environmental Risks?," BNA International Environment Daily, Special Report, Oct. 20, 1992.

Hazilla, Michael, and Raymond J. Kopp, "Social Cost of Environmental Quality Regulations: A General Equilibrium Analysis," Journal of Political Economy, 1990, 98:4, 853–73.

Jaffe, Adam B., S. Peterson, Paul Portney, and Robert N. Stavins, "Environmental Regulations and the Competitiveness of U.S. Industry," Economics Resource Group, Cambridge, Mass., 1993.

Jaffe, Adam B., S. Peterson, Paul Portney, and Robert N. Stavins, "Environmental Regulation and International Competitiveness: What Does the Evidence Tell Us," draft, January 13, 1994.

Jorgenson, Dale W., and Peter J. Wilcoxen, "Environmental Regulation and U.S. Economic Growth," Rand Journal of Economics, Summer 1990, 21:2, 314–40.

Kalt, Joseph P., "The Impact of Domestic Environmental Regulatory Policies on U.S. International Competitiveness." In Spence, A. M., and H. Hazard, eds., International Competitiveness, Cambridge, Mass: Harper and Row, Ballinger, 1988, pp. 221–62.

King, A., "Improved Manufacturing Resulting from Learning-From-Waste: Causes, Importance, and Enabling Conditions," working paper, Stern School of Business, New York University, 1994.

Leonard, H. Jeffrey, *Pollution and the Struggle for World Product*. Cambridge, U.K.: Cambridge University Press, 1988.

Makower, Joel, *The E-Factor: The Bottom-Line Approach to Environmentally Responsible Business*. New York: Times Books, 1993.

Marron, Donald B., "Buying Green: Government Procurement as an Instrument of Environmental Policy," mimeo, Massachusetts Institute of Technology, 1994.

Massachusetts Department of Environmental Protection, Daniel S. Greenbaum, Commissioner, interview, Boston, August 8, 1993.

Meadows, Donella H., and Dennis L. Meadows, *The Limits of Growth*. New York: New American Library, 1972.

Meyer, Stephen M., *Environmentalism and Economic Prosperity: Testing the Environmental Impact Hypothesis*. Cambridge, Mass.: Massachusetts Institute of Technology, 1992.

Meyer, Stephen M., *Environmentalism and Economic Prosperity: An Update*. Cambridge, Mass.: Massachusetts Institute of Technology, 1993.

National Paint and Coatings Association, *Improving the Superfund: Correcting a National Public Policy Disaster*. Washington, D.C., 1992.

Palmer, Karen L., and Ralph David Simpson, "Environmental Policy as Industrial Policy," *Resources*, Summer 1993, *112*, 17–21.

Parkinson, Gerald, "Reducing Wastes Can Be Cost-Effective," *Chemical Engineering*, July 1990, 97:7, 30.

Porter, Michael E., *Competitive Advantage: Creating and Sustaining Superior Performance*. New York: Free Press, 1985.

Porter, Michael E., *The Competitive Advantage of Nations*. New York: Free Press, 1990.

Porter, Michael E., "America's Green Strategy," *Scientific American*, April 1991, *264*, 168.

Porter, Michael E., and Claas van der Linde, "Green *and* Competitive: Breaking the Stalemate," *Harvard Business Review*, September-October 1995.

PR Newswire, "Winners Announced for Governor's Waste Minimization Awards," January 21, 1993, State and Regional News Section.

Oates, Wallace, Karen L. Palmer, and Paul Portney, "Environmental Regulation and International Competitiveness: Thinking About the Porter Hypothesis." Resources for the Future Working Paper 94-02, 1993.

Rappaport, Ann, "Development and Transfer of Pollution Prevention Technology Within a Multinational Corporation," dissertation, Department of Civil Engineering. Tufts University, May 1992.

Raytheon Inc., "Alternative Cleaning Technology." Technical Report Phase II. January-October 1991.

Raytheon Inc., J. R. Pasquariello, Vice President Environmental Quality; Kenneth J. Tierney, Director Environmental and Energy Conservation; Frank A. Marino, Senior Corporate Environmental Specialist; interview, Lexington, Mass., April 4, 1993.

Repetto, Robert, "Jobs, Competitiveness, and Environmental Regulation: What are the Real Issues?," Washington, D.C.: World Resources Institute, 1995.

Roy, M., and L. A. Dillard, "Toxics Use in Massachusetts: The Blackstone Project," *Journal of Air and Waste Management Association*, October 1990, *40*:10, 1368–71.

Schmalensee, Richard, "The Costs of Environmental Regulation." Massachusetts Institute of Technology, Center for Energy and Environmental Policy Research Working Paper 93-015, 1993.

Sheridan, J. H., "Attacking Wastes and Saving Money . . . Some of the Time," *Industry Week*, February 17, 1992, *241*:4, 43.

Simpson, Ralph David, "Taxing Variable Cost: Environmental Regulation as Industrial Policy." Resources for the Future Working Paper ENR93-12, 1993.

Smith, Zachary A, *The Environmental Policy Paradox*. Englewood Cliffs, N.J.: Prentice Hall, 1992.

United States Environmental Protection Agency, "Multiple Pathways to Super Efficient Refrigerators," Washington, D.C., 1992.

U.S. Congress, Office of Technology Assessment, "Industry, Technology, and the Environment: Competitive Challenges and Business Opportunities," OTA-ITE-586, Washington, D.C., 1994.

van der Linde, Claas, "The Micro-Economic Implications of Environmental Regulation: A Preliminary Framework." In *Environmental Policies and Industrial Competitiveness*. Paris: Organization of Economic Co-Operation and Development, 1993, pp. 69–77.

van der Linde, Claas, "Competitive Implications of Environmental Regulation in the Cell Battery Industry," Hochschule St. Gallen, St. Gallen, forthcoming 1995a.

van der Linde, Claas, "Competitive Implications of Environmental Regulation in the Printing Ink Industry," Hochschule St. Gallen, St. Gallen, forthcoming 1995b.

van der Linde, Claas, "Competitive Implications of Environmental Regulation in the Refrigerator Industry," Hochschule St. Gallen, St. Gallen, forthcoming 1995c.

Wheeler, David, and Ashoka Mody, "International Investment Location Decisions: The Case of U.S. Firms," *Journal of International Economics*, August 1992, *33*, 57–76.

White, A. L., M. Becker, and J. Goldstein, "Alternative Approaches to the Financial Evaluation of Industrial Pollution Prevention Investments," prepared for the New Jersey Department of Environmental Protection, Division of Science and Research, November 1991.

8   *Tightening Environmental Standards: The Benefit-Cost or the No-Cost Paradigm?**

Karen Palmer

Wallace E. Oates

Paul R. Portney

Karen Palmer is Senior Fellow at Resources for the Future; Wallace Oates is Professor of Economics at the University of Maryland, and Visiting Scholar at Resources for the Future; and Paul Portney is President and Senior Fellow at Resources for the Future.

Michael Porter and Claas van der Linde have written a paper that is interesting and, to us at least, somewhat astonishing. It is a defense of environmental regulation—indeed, an invitation to more stringent regulation—that makes essentially no reference to the *social* benefits of such regulation. This approach contrasts starkly with the methods that economists and other policy analysts have traditionally used when assessing environmental or other regulatory programs.

The traditional approach consists of comparing the beneficial effects of regulation with the costs that must be borne to secure these benefits. For environmental regulation, the social benefits include the reductions in morbidity or premature mortality that can accompany cleaner air, the enhanced recreational opportunities that can result from water-quality improvements, the increased land values that might attend the cleanup of a hazardous waste site, the enhanced vitality of aquatic ecosystems that might follow reductions in agricultural pesticide use or any of the other potentially significant benefits associated with tighter standards. From this benefit-cost approach emerges the standard tradeoff discussed in virtually every economics textbook.

Porter and van der Linde deny the validity of this approach to the analysis of environmental regulation, claiming it to be an artifact of what they see as a "static mindset." In their view, economists have failed to appreciate the capacity of stringent environmental regulations to induce innova-

"Tightening Environmental Standards: The Benefit-Cost or the No-Cost Paradigm?" by Karen Palmer, Wallace E. Oates, and Paul R. Portney, from *Journal of Economic Perspectives*, 9(4):119–132 (Fall 1995).

*We are grateful for helpful comments on earlier drafts to Albert McGartland, Richard Schmalensee and the editors of this journal. We wish to thank the Environmental Protection Agency, the National Science Foundation and the Sloan Foundation for support that made this work possible.

tion, and this failure has led them to a fundamental misrepresentation of the problem of environmental regulation. There is no tradeoff, Porter and van der Linde suggest; instead, environmental protection, properly pursued, often presents a free or even a paid lunch. As they put it, there are lots of $10 bills lying around waiting to be picked up.

We take strong issue with their view. If this were simply a matter of intellectual sparring, it would be inconsequential outside academe. But their view has found a ready audience in some parts of the policymaking community. For example, Vice President Gore (1992, p. 342) writes that "3M, in its Pollution Prevention Pays program, has reported significant profit improvement as a direct result of its increased attention to shutting off all the causes of pollution it could find." If environmental regulations are essentially costless (or even carry a negative cost!), then it is unnecessary to justify and measure with care the presumed social benefits of environmental programs. Stringent environmental measures (of the right kind) are good for business as well as the environment; in the Washington parlance, we have ourselves a "win-win situation." Not surprisingly, this view has also been warmly received by environmentalists and by regulators eager to avoid being seen as imposing unwanted costs on businesses or lower levels of government. At a time of burgeoning interest in Congress in the economic justification for federal regulations, Porter and van der Linde suggest the cost of environmental regulation may be negligible or even nonexistent.

To clarify the points that are in dispute, we should state at the outset that we agree with Porter and van der Linde on a number of matters. First, we share their enthusiasm for a heavier reliance on incentive-based regulation in lieu of command-and-control. Early returns suggest, for example, that tradable permits for sulfur dioxide emissions will reduce the cost of the 1990 acid rain control program by at least 50 percent when measured against the most likely command-and-control alternative (Burtraw, 1995; U.S. General Accounting Office, 1994; Rico, 1995). Second, we agree that early estimates of regulatory compliance costs are likely to be biased upward because of unforeseen technological advances in pollution control or prevention. Third, we accept that providing information, such as in EPA's "Green Lights" program (through which the agency provides technical assistance concerning energy-efficient lighting), may well help disseminate new technologies. Fourth, we acknowledge that regulations have sometimes led to the discovery of cost-saving or quality-improving innovation; in other words, we do *not* believe that firms are ever-vigilantly perched on their efficiency frontiers.

On this last point, however, we do not find Porter and van der Linde at all convincing concerning the pervasiveness of inefficiencies. The major empirical evidence that they advance in support of their position is a series of case studies. With literally hundreds of thousands of firms subject to environmental regulation in the United States alone, it would be hard *not* to find instances where regulation has seemingly worked to a polluting firm's advantage. But collecting cases where this has happened in no way establishes a general presumption in favor of this outcome. It would be an easy matter for us to assemble a matching list where firms have found their costs increased and profits reduced as a result of (even enlightened) environmental regulations, not to mention cases where regulation has pushed firms over the brink into bankruptcy.

What is needed, we believe, is a more systematic approach to the issue. Following a general observation to put things in context, we begin with a model in which increasing the stringency of incentive-based environmental regulations *must* result in reduced profits for the firm. This model is incomplete in various ways, but it provides a useful baseline for the succeeding discussion. From this baseline, we can then explore the sorts of changes in the model that could produce the result that regulation leads to higher profits—the outcome that Porter and van der Linde seem to suggest is the norm. We are then in a better position to assess the evidence and the weight of their case.

Innovation and Environmental Regulation: An Observation

Porter and van der Linde accuse mainstream environmental economics, with its "static mindset," of having neglected innovation. This charge is puzzling. For several decades now, environmental economists have made their case for incentive-based policy instruments (such as effluent charges or tradable emission permits) precisely by emphasizing the incentives that these measures provide for innovation in abatement technology (Kneese and Bower, 1968, p. 139). Virtually every standard textbook in environmental economics makes the point that incentive-based approaches are perhaps more attractive for reasons of dynamic efficiency than for their ability to minimize the costs of attaining environmental standards at any particular point in time. A substantial literature has developed in recent years that explores the effects of various policy instruments on research and development decisions concerning abatement technology, a literature on which we shall draw in this discussion.[1]

What distinguishes the Porter and van der Linde perspective from neoclassical environmental economics is *not* the "static mindset" of the latter. It is two other presumptions. First, they see a private sector that systematically overlooks profitable opportunities for innovation.[2] Second, and equally important, they envision a regulatory authority that is in a position to correct this "market failure."[3] With properly designed measures, regu-

---

[1]The reader interested in exploring this literature might begin with Magat (1978), Downing and White (1986), Malueg (1989), Milliman and Prince (1989), Parry (1992), Biglaiser and Horowitz (1995) and Simpson (1995).

[2]This, incidentally, seems a rather odd and sad commentary on the private sector to be coming from one of the country's eminent business professors and consultants.

[3]This "market failure," incidentally, is quite different in character from the usual public goods argument that private firms underinvest in research and development because they will have difficulty appropriating enough of the social benefits. What Porter and van der Linde have in mind is a failure of private decision makers to respond to *private* profit opportunities.

lators can set in motion innovative activities through which firms can realize these overlooked opportunities. Their vision thus suggests a new role for regulatory activity in bringing about dynamic efficiency: enlightened regulators provide the needed incentives for cost-saving and quality-improving innovations that competition apparently fails to provide. Regulators can, as Porter and van der Linde put it, help firms "to overcome organizational inertia and to foster creative thinking," thereby increasing their profits.[4] We find this view hard to swallow, and suspect that most regulated firms would share our difficulty.

Environmental Regulation and Competitiveness: A Proposition

Drawing on some of the early literature on innovation in abatement technology, we now present a model in which even incentive-based environmental regulation results in reduced profits for the regulated firm. The model essentially formalizes the basic point that the addition (or tightening) of constraints on a firm's set of choices cannot be expected to result in an increased level of profits. Readers uninterested in the analytics may wish to skip to the next section.

We emphasize that this model is static in character and fails to address the inherent uncertainty in research and development (R&D) decisions. In this sense, it is subject to precisely the sort of criticism that Porter and van der Linde level in their paper. However, for the same reason, it provides a useful point of entry into the issue. The model is premised on the assumption that the polluting firm maximizes profits and operates in a perfectly competitive market; the firm takes competitors' outputs and R&D expenditures as given and also takes any regulations as exogenously determined. Given these assumptions, the model does not allow for any sort of strategic interaction. The possible effects of relaxing these assumptions and allowing game-theoretic strategic interactions among firms, or between the polluting firm and the regulator, will be discussed in the next section of this paper.

Figure 1 depicts the polluting firm's options. The horizontal axis shows the "abatement level," so that the reduction in pollution increases as one moves from left to right. The vertical axis is measured in dollars, which means that one can graph both the firm's cost of various levels of pollution abatement and compare those costs with market-oriented effluent

---

[4]It is unclear whether Porter and van der Linde view this expanded role for regulation as a general proposition, or whether it is limited to environmental regulation. They appear to suggest the latter when they contend that as waste emissions into the environment, "[Pollution] is a manifestation of economic waste and involves unnecessary, inefficient or incomplete utilization of resources. . . ." This we also find puzzling. Whether it is efficient to recycle wastes, to discharge them into the environment or to adopt an entirely new technology that employs fewer polluting inputs depends on the costs (meaning, of course, the full social costs) of the various alternatives.

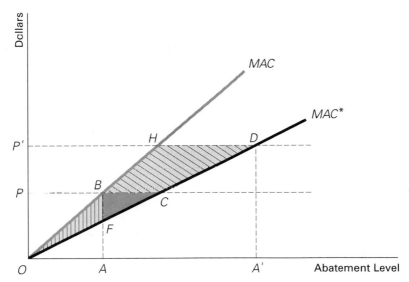

Figure 1 The Incentive to Innovate under an Emission Fee

charges imposed by environmental regulators. The MAC curve (without a star) is the firm's present "marginal abatement cost" function; it indicates the marginal cost incurred by the firm to reduce pollution by an additional unit. The upward slope of the curve implies that the marginal cost of reducing pollution is rising.

Let us now assume that the firm could, if it chooses, reduce its marginal abatement cost function from the curve MAC to MAC*. Notice that with MAC*, a given marginal expenditure has a greater effect on pollution abatement than it would have with MAC. However, to move from MAC to MAC*, the firm must spend money to research and develop new pollution abatement technology. To simplify the problem, we will assume that the R&D expenditure necessary to move from MAC to MAC* is known completely—there is no risk or uncertainty.

This model will presume market-oriented regulators who use effluent charges to encourage pollution abatement. As long as a profit-maximizing firm can abate pollution itself for less than the effluent charge, it will choose to do so. However, after the point where the cost of abating pollution exceeds the effluent charge, the firm will prefer to pay the charge. Let us assume that the firm is initially confronted by an effluent charge of P. It chooses its profit-maximizing level of abatement activity, A, corresponding to the point B, where marginal abatement cost equals the effluent charge.

If the firm has been operating at abatement level A, an implication is that the (annualized) cost of the R&D effort to reduce MAC to MAC* must exceed the gains to the firm. The R&D investment in additional pollution-abatement technology won't pay off; thus outcome B must produce more profits for the firm than does the attainable point C. Figure 1 also depicts the gains to the polluting firm from undertaking the R&D effort, which can be divided into two parts. The source of the first part is that the earlier level of abatement activity becomes cheaper; the amount of gain here is given by the triangle *OFB*. The second part comes from the new technology. The company will choose to abate a greater amount of pollution and thus avoid paying the pollution charge on that additional pollution; the gain here is the triangle *BCF*.

The total gains to the polluting firm from innovation would thus be the area bounded by *OFCB*. Since the firm has not chosen this option, it must be that the cost of the R&D program that would move the firm from MAC to MAC* exceeds the area of the profit that would be gained, *OFCB*.

Now, assume that the environmental authority introduces a new, more stringent market-oriented environmental standard, taking the form of an increase in the effluent fee to P'. Without further assumptions, one cannot say whether the firm will respond to the higher effluent charge by sticking with the old technology and ending up at *H* or by investing in the new one and ending up at *D*.[5] But we will prove that both *H* and *D* generate lower profits than *B*. Therefore, it will be unambiguously true in this model that the higher effluent standard reduces profits for the firm.

It is straightforward to show that if the firm sticks with its old technology, the higher effluent charge must reduce its profits. In this case, the firm moves from *B* to *H*, and while this higher level of pollution abatement may be better for society, the firm is unambiguously worse off. It is paying the same amount to abate pollution up to *B* as it was before. Between *B* and *H*, it is paying more to abate pollution than under the previous, lower effluent charge. And above *H*, it is paying the higher effluent charge rather than the previously lower one.[6]

It is only a bit trickier to demonstrate that profits at *D*, where the firm faces a higher effluent charge with the new technology, must be lower than profits at *B*, where the firm chose to face the lower effluent charge with its existing technology. Notice first that along the MAC* frontier, profits at

---

[5]What are some of the factors determining whether the firm chooses to respond to a higher effluent charge by investing in new technology? Overall, of course, the question is whether the cost-savings from the new technology exceed the R&D expenditures. Recent work offers some further insights. Ulph (1994) shows that an increase in an emission tax rate may increase a firm's incentive to engage in environmental R&D, but is likely to decrease its incentive to engage in R&D of a general unit-cost-reducing nature, leading to an ambiguous effect on overall R&D expenditures and on the firm's costs. Simpson (1995) suggests that when R&D is both cost reducing and emission reducing, the incentive effects of an increase in the emissions tax for R&D are lower the more R&D reduces marginal cost and the more competitive are rival firms.

[6]This is an application of a more general principle that for a given technology, profit is decreasing in input prices. In the environmental economics literature, waste emissions are typically treated as an input (along with labor, capital and so on) in the production function. This is reasonable, since attempts to cut back on waste emissions will involve the diversion of other inputs to abatement activities, thereby reducing the availability of these other inputs for the production of goods. Reductions in emissions, in short, result in reduced output. Moreover, given the reasonable assumption of rising marginal abatement costs, it makes sense to assume the usual curvature properties so that we can legitimately construct isoquants in emissions and another input and treat them in the usual way. In this framework, the emissions fee becomes simply the price of an input called "waste emissions."

choice D (given the higher effluent charge) must be lower than profits at point C, given the lower previous effluent charge. As already explained, if technology is constant, the higher effluent charge unambiguously reduces profits. But the basis of this model was that at the lower effluent charge, the firm didn't find it worthwhile to invest in the new technology; that is, profits were lower at C than at B. By transitivity, if profits at B exceed C, and profits at C exceed D, then it must be true that the higher effluent charge reduces profits for the firm, even if it adopts a new technology.

Thus, in this model of innovation in abatement technology, an increase in the stringency of environmental regulations unambiguously makes the polluting firm worse off. Even if the firm can invest and adopt a new, more efficient abatement technology, if that technology wasn't worth investing in before, its benefits won't be enough to raise the company's profits after the environmental standards are raised, either.

This leads us naturally to ask how one might amend the simple model to alter this basic result. We point out that simply making the model dynamic and/or introducing uncertainty will not overturn this result. It is straightforward to show that our basic proposition likewise applies to a firm that maximizes the expected present value of future profits. What elements, then, are missing from this simplified model that could give rise to an *increase* in profits following the imposition of tighter standards?

We can identify two such elements of potential importance. One possibility is strategic behavior, perhaps involving interactions between polluting firms, or between these firms and the regulating agency, or between regulatory agencies in different countries. The second possibility (the one emphasized by Porter and van der Linde) is the existence of opportunities for profitable innovation in the production of the firm's output that for some reason have been overlooked and that would be realized in the wake of new and tougher environmental regulations. The next two sections take up these extensions to the basic model and present some of the relevant empirical evidence.

Strategic Interaction Among Polluters and Regulators

In the basic model, the polluting firm was operating in a competitive environment, taking as given both the behavior of competing firms and the standards set by the regulator. One important line of extension of the analysis is the introduction of strategic interaction among the various participants. There is some recent and ongoing work along these lines. For example, Barrett (1994) has explored a series of models in which regulators and polluting firms behave strategically. He finds that, in the spirit of the Porter-van der Linde thesis, there are indeed cases in which the government can actually improve the international competitive position of domestic exporters by imposing environmental standards upon them. One such case occurs if each firm takes the price of its competitor as fixed and then competes by setting its own profit-maximizing price. If the government sets a strong emission standard—by which Barrett means a standard beyond the point where the marginal benefits of pollution control equal marginal abatement costs—the domestic firm's marginal cost, and therefore its price, will rise. Recognizing that the domestic firm must charge a higher price to comply with the new standard, foreign competitors raise their prices without fear of retaliation. However, an increase in the foreign price raises demand for the output of the domestic firm with a resulting increase in its profits. This result holds when the domestic industry is an oligopoly as well as when it is a monopoly competing in an oligopolistic international market. It *may* also hold under Cournot competition—where each firm takes the quantity produced by its competitors as given and competes by altering the quantity it produces—if the domestic industry is an oligopoly, although this need not be the case.

In general, however, this result is not robust to other changes in the nature of the strategic behavior. For instance, if the domestic firm is a monopolist in its home country and the domestic and foreign firm are Cournot competitors, then the home government can improve the domestic firm's competitive position by reducing its environmental standards below the efficient level. Kennedy (1994) obtains a similar finding in a model with Cournot competition.

In another treatment of the issue, Simpson and Bradford (1996) develop a strategic trade model that explicitly includes R&D expenditures by firms. In this model, firms behave strategically both in setting levels of spending on R&D and in selecting output levels. The government regulates pollution through an emission fee. Simpson and Bradford find that for certain specifications of the cost and demand functions, increasing the emission fee can increase domestic R&D investment, reduce foreign R&D spending and increase domestic welfare (composed of domestic profits plus pollution fee revenues). However, they note that slight variations in the form of the cost function can reverse these results. Ulph (1994) surveys a number of recent papers that explicitly incorporate strategic R&D investment behavior by firms. This body of work indicates that the effect of environmental regulation on R&D is ambiguous and that even in the cases where higher emissions standards lead to higher domestic R&D spending, governments may still be better off selecting a lower-than-social-cost emission tax rate to shift profits from foreign firms to domestic firms.

Overall, this literature suggests that while it is possible to get results like those that Porter and van der Linde suggest are the norm from models that incorporate strategic behavior, such results are special cases. In many instances, these same strategic trade models suggest that the domestic authority should employ *weak* environmental regulations to promote international competitiveness. Moreover, as Barrett (1994) and Simpson and Bradford (1996) suggest, there are typically other sorts of measures that are more effective at improving international competitiveness than strategic environmental regulatory policy. This bottom line does not deny the Porter-van der Linde argument entirely; certain kinds of strategic models can produce outcomes of the type they describe. But it does seem to us that strategic models are unlikely to establish anything close to a general presumption that stringent environmental measures will enhance competitiveness. In addition, such strategic behavior is not what Porter and van der Linde have in mind. We turn to their basic contention now.

Regulation and "Offsets"

Their claim is that technologies exist of which the firm is unaware until prodded into discovering them by stringent environmental regulations. They go on to contend that such regulation will spur firms to innovate and that the newly discovered technologies will generally offset, or more than offset, the costs of pollution abatement or prevention. Our response takes two very different tacks.

First, we spoke with the vice presidents or corporate directors for environmental protection at Dow, 3M, Ciba-Geigy and Monsanto—all firms mentioned by Porter and van der Linde in their discussion of innovation or process offsets. While each manager acknowledged that in certain instances a particular regulatory requirement may have cost less than had been expected, or perhaps even paid for itself, each also said quite emphatically that, on the whole, environmental regulation amounted to a significant *net* cost to his company.

We have little doubt about the general applicability of this conclusion. Fortunately, we need not confine ourselves to speculation and anecdotes about the pervasiveness or the significance of pollution or innovation offsets. There are data available on this matter, and they indicate that such offsets pale in comparison to expenditures for pollution abatement and control.

Each year the Environmental Economics Division of the Commerce Department's Bureau of Economic Analysis (BEA) makes estimates of pollution abatement and control expenditures in the United States. One source for these estimates are Bureau of the Census surveys of manufacturing establishments, state and local governments, electric utilities, petroleum refiners and mining operations. Other information is gathered on federal government expenditures on pollution control, the cost of solid waste disposal, individual spending for motor vehicle pollution control equipment and operating costs and other environmental spending, as well. In 1992, according to BEA, pollution abatement and control expenditures in the United States came to $102 billion (Rutledge and Vogan, 1994, p. 47).

In addition to estimates of environmental spending, BEA also estimates the magnitude of the "offsets" that Porter and van der Linde claim are so pervasive. In fact, the Census Bureau survey of manufacturers (upon which BEA relies for most of its information about offsets) specifically asks respondents to report "cost offsets," which are defined in such a way as seemingly to encompass both the "product" and "process" offsets that

Porter and van der Linde describe (U.S. Commerce Department, 1994).[7]
For 1992, BEA estimates that cost offsets for the U.S. amounted to $1.7
billion, less than 2 percent of estimated environmental expenditures. This
implies *net* spending for environmental protection in excess of $100 bil-
lion in 1992.

Net spending on protecting the environment may be greater than that,
however, because there is reason to believe that the BEA estimates of environmental costs are on the low side. According to the Environmental Protection Agency (1990), the total cost associated with federal environmental regulation in the United States in 1992 was $135 billion.[8] EPA's estimates
differ from those of BEA for a variety of reasons, some of which are difficult to discern. But some of the difference is due to the fact that EPA counts
certain expenditures that BEA ignores (like those associated with measures
to improve indoor air quality); because EPA apparently includes some opportunity costs in addition to out-of-pocket expenditures; and because the
two agencies use different approaches occasionally even when focusing on
the same category of pollution control. Some of the additional costs the
EPA includes may give rise to their own offsets, but it is unlikely they will
increase in proportion to these added costs. This is especially true where
the difference between EPA's estimates and BEA's estimates involve imputed or opportunity costs.

One possible criticism of these estimates of offsets is that certain kinds
of offsets in response to more stringent environmental regulation are not
easily reportable on the Census Bureau survey form, and hence do not find
their way into the Census or BEA estimates. For instance, a manufacturing firm that dropped a product line altogether because it wished to avoid
environmental regulations, and entered what instead turned out to be a
more profitable product line, would be hard-pressed to report this as an
"offset" according to the definition provided in the Census Bureau survey.
But even if one doubled or tripled or even quadrupled the estimated offsets that are reported by Census and included in BEA's estimates, the total offsets would be less than $10 billion per year, leaving net annual en-
vironmental compliance costs in the range of $100 billion or more.

---

[7]It is worth including one of the examples from the Census Bureau survey to illustrate how closely
the survey conforms to the Porter and van der Linde vision of offsets. The survey (U.S. Commerce Department, 1994, p. A-11) contains the following wording: "A manufacturer installs a closed loop recovery system in the production process so as to prevent the dumping of the chemicals into the water system. Since the closed loop recovery system recaptures and reuses the chemicals in the production
process, it reduces expenses for chemicals. The pollution abatement portion of the capital expenditure
pertaining to the closed loop recovery system is reported in Item 7 [the section of the survey where
new capital expenditures are reported]. The operating expenses to maintain the system are reported
in Item 3 [the analogous section for operating costs]. The value of recovered chemicals is reported as
a cost offset." This example matches perfectly the example of the Robbins Company given by Porter
and van der Linde, hence suggesting a close connection between the "offsets" described by Porter and
van der Linde and the BEA estimates of offsets based on the Census Bureau survey.

[8]To this must be added the costs of additional control measures introduced by states (like California) that have, in some instances, gone beyond the federal statutes. We know of no estimates of
these additional costs, but they may be substantial.

It is impossible to escape the conclusion that the U.S. devotes significant resources, *net of cost savings*, to environmental protection each year. Moreover, we reach this conclusion without making reference to the work of either Jorgenson and Wilcoxen (1990) or Hazilla and Kopp (1990), both of whom showed that the social costs of environmental regulation are *greater* when viewed in a dynamic general equilibrium context than in a static, partial equilibrium setting, because of the manner in which environmental regulations depress "productive" investment and the consequent reduction in the rate of economic growth. Porter and van der Linde deny the validity of this work on the grounds that it fails to factor offsets into account. Since these offsets appear to be quite small—based on both the reports of those who make environmental investments, as well as on hard data—this is hardly a liability of the general equilibrium approach.

One more word about offsets. Suppose that every single dollar a firm spent on pollution control or prevention was matched by a dollar of savings in the form of product or process offsets described by Porter and van der Linde. Would it then be the case that environmental regulation is free? Of course not. The sacrifice would be measured by other opportunities foregone. Firms can and do invest in changing the size and skill mix of their labor force, in their capital base, in the sources and term structure of their financing, their research and development strategies and other things, as well. Each of these investments is expected to do more than return one dollar for each dollar spent—typically firms must project returns that exceed a "hurdle rate" of 20 percent or more before undertaking an investment. Thus, even if environmental compliance produced offsets on a dollar-for-dollar basis—rather than one dollar for every 50 spent, as the data suggest—the foregone return on invested capital would still be a significant cost of regulation.

The International Setting

The original question prompting this debate concerned the impact of environmental regulations on the competitiveness of U.S. industry in the international arena. In a much shorter essay that appeared several years ago in *Scientific American*, Porter (1991) argued that the perverse command-and-control character of most U.S. regulation has seriously handicapped American firms in competitive with foreign rivals. Making the case (with which we enthusiastically agree) for incentive-based policy measures, Porter argued that U.S. firms were losing out to competition from German and Japanese companies, which benefit from more enlightened regulatory regimes.[9]

---

[9]For a more detailed treatment of these particular issues, see our response (Oates et al., 1993) to the Porter (1991) paper.

However, we believe the truth of the matter is rather different. It is not the case that other countries, including Germany or Japan, have made better use of incentive-based approaches than the United States. While other countries appear to have put in place regulatory programs that are less adversarial (and therefore less time consuming) than certain U.S. programs, most environmental regulation in Europe looks every bit as proscriptive as does the U.S. version. In fact, visitors from OECD and developing countries pour through Washington on a regular basis, trying to learn about the sulfur dioxide trading program put in place here five years ago.

Moreover, it is not clear that environmental regulation is harming the competitiveness of U.S. firms. In fact, Porter and van der Linde acknowledge as much, citing Jaffe et al. (1995, p. 157), who conclude in their survey paper that "overall, there is relatively little evidence to support the hypothesis that environmental regulations have had a large adverse effect on competitiveness, however that elusive term is defined."

This finding is important, but it has little to do with innovation offsets. As Jaffe et al. (1995) point out, there are several reasons why the relative stringency of U.S. environmental regulation to date has not been found to have adverse effects on competitiveness. First, for all but the most heavily polluting industries, the cost of complying with federal environmental regulations is a small fraction of total costs, sufficiently small (in most instances) to be swamped by international differentials in labor and material costs, capital costs, swings in exchange rates and so on. Second, although U.S. environmental regulations are arguably the most stringent in the world, the *differentials* between U.S. standards and those of our major industrialized trading partners are not very great, especially for air and water pollution control. Third, U.S. firms (as well as other multinationals) appear inclined to build modern, state-of-the-art facilities abroad, irrespective of the stringency of environmental statutes in the host country. Thus, even a significant difference in environmental standards between, say, the United States and a developing country will mean little to firms not willing to take advantage of lax standards.[10]

This is not to say that cost differentials stemming from international variations in environmental regulations are nonexistent. But as Jaffe et al. (1995, p. 159) conclude, these differentials "pose insufficient threats to U.S. industrial competitiveness to justify substantial cutbacks in domestic environmental regulations." More basically, the case for redesigning environmental programs to make more effective use of market incentives has little to do with international competitiveness; it's a much more straightforward issue of getting environmental value for the expenditures of social resources.

---

[10]The rationale for this behavior appears to be two-fold. First, there is a widespread perception that tighter environmental regulations in the developing countries are inevitable, and that it is less expensive to invest initially in state-of-the-art abatement technology than it will be to retrofit later. Second, the aftermath of certain disasters, notably the Union Carbide catastrophe in Rhopal, India, has made management aware of the dangers inherent in the adoption of less than state-of-the-art control technologies in developing countries.

Conclusion

The underlying message from Porter and van der Linde about environmental regulation is not to worry, because it really won't be all that expensive. But it will. Annual U.S. expenditures for environmental protection, net of any offsets, currently are at least $100 billion, and probably considerably more. From *society's* standpoint, with the benefits of a cleaner environment figures into the balance, every dime of this money may be well spent; the literature is replete with examples of environmental programs that pass a benefit-cost test. But a comparison of the benefits and costs is exactly how one should determine the economic attractiveness of specific programs—not on the false premise of cost-free controls.

REFERENCES

Barrett, Scott, "Strategic Environmental Policy and International Trade," *Journal of Public Economics*, 1994, *54*:3, 325–38.

Biglaiser, Gary, and John K. Horowitz, "Pollution Regulation and Incentives for Pollution-Control Research," *Journal of Economics and Management Strategy*, Winter 1995, *3*, 663–840.

Burtraw, Dallas, "Efficiency Sans Allowance Traders?: Evaluating the SO2 Emission Trading Program to Date." Resources for the Future Discussion Paper No. 95–30, 1995.

Downing, Paul B., and Lawrence J. White, "Innovation in Pollution Control," *Journal of Environmental Economics and Management*, March 1986, *13*, 18–29.

Gore, Albert, *Earth in the Balance*. Boston: Houghton Mifflin Co., 1992.

Hazilla, Michael, and Raymond Kopp, "Social Cost of Environmental Quality Regulations: A General Equilibrium Analysis," *Journal of Political Economy*, August 1990, *98*, 853–73.

Jaffe, Adam B., Steven R. Peterson, Paul R. Portney, and Robert N. Stavins, "Environmental Regulations and the Competitiveness of U.S. Manufacturing: What Does the Evidence Tell Us?," *Journal of Economic Literature*, March 1995, *33*, 132–63.

Jorgenson, Dale W., and Peter J. Wilcoxen, "Environmental Regulation and U.S. Economic Growth," *Rand Journal of Economics*, Summer 1990, *21*, 314–40.

Kennedy, Peter, "Equilibrium Pollution Taxes in Open Economies with Imperfect Competition," *Journal of Environmental Economics and Management*, July 1994, *27*, 49–63.

Kneese, Allen V., and Blair T. Bower, *Managing Water Quality: Economics, Technology, Institutions*. Baltimore, Md.: Johns Hopkins University Press, 1968.

Magat, Wesley A., "Pollution Control and Technological Advance: A Dynamic Model of the Firm," *Journal of Environmental Economics and Management*, March 1978, *5*, 1–25.

Malueg, David A., "Emission Credit Trading and the Incentive to Adopt New Pollution Abatement Technology," *Journal of Environmental Economics and Management*, January 1989, *16*, 52–7.

Milliman, Scott R., and Raymond Prince, "Firm Incentives to Promote Technological Change in Pollution Control," *Journal of Environmental Economics and Management*, November 1989, *17*, 247–65.

Oates, Wallace E., Karen Palmer, and Paul R. Portney, "Environmental Regulation and International Competitiveness: Thinking About the Porter Hypothesis." Resources for the Future Discussion Paper No. 94–02, 1993.

Parry, Ian, "Environmental R&D and the Choice Between Pigouvian Taxes and Marketable Emissions Permits," unpublished Ph.D. dissertation, University of Chicago, 1992.

Porter, Michael E., "America's Green Strategy," *Scientific American*, April 1991, *264*, 168.

Rico, Renee, "The U.S. Allowance Trading System for Sulfer Dioxide: An Update on Market Experience," *Energy and Resource Economics*, March 1995, *5*:2, 115–29.

Rutledge, Gary L., and Christine R. Vogan, "Pollution Abatement and Control Expenditures, 1972–92," *Survey of Current Business*, May 1994, *74*, 36–49.

Simpson, David, "Environmental Policy, Innovation and Competitive Advantage." Resources for the Future Discussion Paper No. 95–12, 1995.

Simpson, David, and Robert L. Bradford, "Taxing Variable Cost: Environmental Regulation as Industrial Policy," *Journal of Environmental Economics and Management*, forthcoming 1996.

Ulph, Alistair, "Environmental Policy and International Trade: A Survey of Recent Economic Analysis," Milan, Italy: Nota di Lavoro 53:94, Fondazione Eni Enrico Mattei, 1994.

U.S. Department of Commerce (Bureau of the Census), "Pollution Abatement Costs and Expenditures, 1993," Current Industrial Reports; MA200(93)-1, Washington, D.C.: U.S. Government Printing Office, 1994.

U.S. Environmental Protection Agency, *Environmental Investments: The Cost of a Clean Environment*. Washington, D.C.: U.S. Environmental Protection Agency, 1990.

U.S. General Accounting Office, "Allowance Trading Offers an Opportunity to Reduce Emissions at Less Cost," document, GAO/RCED-95–30, 1994.

III

The Benefits of Environmental Protection

9 Nonmarket Valuation of Environmental Resources: An Interpretive Appraisal*

V. Kerry Smith

Kerry Smith is Arts and Sciences Professor of Environmental Economics at Duke University.

I. Introduction

Methods for valuing nonmarketed environmental resources were first proposed forty-five years ago, but applications were slow to develop until the early 1970s. Dramatic progress has been realized in the last two-and-a-half decades as these applications have multiplied. Until recently, however, most of this progress attracted little attention outside of a narrow group of economists. Beginning in 1981 with Executive Order 12291 (which required benefit-cost analyses of major regulations in the United States) and somewhat later in Western Europe (symbolized by the so-called "greening" of Margaret Thatcher),[1] interest has increased in considering estimated values for environmental resources as part of public investment, management, and regulatory decisions. Today, demands for this type of valuation information come from diverse sources for different reasons. The courts need valuation information for assessing natural resource damages, public utility commissions use it in environmental costing, and trade

"Nonmarket Valuation of Environmental Resources: An Interpretive Appraisal," by V. Kerry Smith, from *Land Economics*, 69(1):1–26 (February 1993).

*Partial support for this research was provided by the University of North Carolina Sea Grant Program, Project Number R/MRD-21. An earlier version of this paper was presented in 1991 at the Australian Agricultural Economic Society's annual meetings. Thanks are due Jeff Bennett, Richard Bishop, Tony Chisholm, Michael Hanemann, Alan Randall, and two anonymous referees for their most constructive comments on several earlier drafts and to Barbara Scott for substantially improving the exposition.

[1]Cairncross (1992) recently described a metaphor used by Margaret Thatcher in 1988 that symbolized her transformation to environmentalism. Cairncross quotes the metaphor as follows: "No generation has a freehold on the earth. All we have is a life tenancy—*with a full repairing lease*" (p. 6, emphasis added). Thatcher's greening is usually associated with her recognition of the need for government to set the terms of this lease.

negotiators want to evaluate whether environmental policies are being used as trade barriers.[2]

The slowdown in many economies of the developed world is unlikely to diminish demands for valuation estimates for environmental resources. People are convinced that industrialized societies, as well as developing economies, are transforming regional environments on an unprecedented scale. Environmental resources are increasingly recognized as assets providing services that are no longer readily available. Indeed, demands to measure their values and incorporate them into our decisions is precisely what we would expect as their scarcity increases.

This paper provides an interpretive review of what has been learned from research on nonmarket valuation. It focuses on the performance of modeling strategies rather than on estimates of specific resources' values. Taking stock of what has been learned from nonmarket valuation research is important for at least three reasons. First, it helps to gauge whether available methods and estimates will be capable of meeting the current demands on them. Second, it identifies the new research required to keep pace with policy needs. Finally, it may help in understanding why (despite the sustained research in this area) it has taken so long for nonmarket valuation to be taken seriously.

The remainder of this review is organized as follows. Sections II and III describe the indirect and direct approaches for measuring people's values for environmental services and summarize what we know about their performance. Section IV considers a controversial area of nonmarket valuation—the measurement of nonuse values. It reviews the theoretical foundations and prospects for estimating nonuse values that differ from some recent critiques. Section V identifies an area requiring significant conceptual advances that largely has been neglected in the literature—the extent of the relevant market for environmental resources. The last section describes elements that should comprise any protocol designed to coordinate nonmarket valuation studies.

II. Extending Revealed Preference: The Indirect Approaches

The revealed preference approach for describing consumer behavior relies on the idea that an individual's choice of a consumption bundle of marketed goods (given their prices) conveys information. The bundle that a consumer with given income purchases must (because of its selection) be preferred to all others at that particular set of prices. Indirect approaches

---

[2]Breen (1989) discusses the evolution of natural resource damage assessment liability under U.S. statutes. Kopp, Portney, and Smith (1990) discuss the implications of the Court of Appeals ruling for economic analyses of damage assessments. Pearce, Markanyda, and Barbier (1989) are generally credited with raising awareness of the role of economic analysis as part of environmental policy in the United Kingdom.

for measuring the values of nonmarketed commodities also rely on consumers' choices. However, because the objectives extend beyond deriving restrictions to conventional demand functions to recovering valuation information, more detailed assumptions are required.

Of course, this should not be surprising. It is equally true in deriving welfare measures for price changes. As Diewert (1976) demonstrated, Harberger-type welfare indicators can be interpreted as displaying the effects of revealed preferences through indexes that yield correctly signed measures of the welfare changes associated with prices changes for a wide class of true, underlying preference functions. However, it is important to acknowledge that these measures do not have the same properties when considering a *proposed* price change. The early Diewert analysis as well as his more recent (1989) derivation of ideal welfare indicators require that the change under evaluation has taken place. Only then can we assume that all prices and corresponding quantities are known. In most policy analysis, the endpoint is *not* known, so prediction is necessary. This means additional assumptions must be made so demands can be estimated and predictions developed. For the values of nonmarket resources, the required assumptions are more detailed because we also must specify the technical indicators of quality that are hypothesized to influence observed behavior.

To appreciate the features of the indirect approaches, we need do little more than focus on the marginal rate of substitution (MRS) between the nonmarketed environmental service and some numeraire as an economic measure of an individual's real value for the last unit he or she consumed of a commodity. Consider the exchange of goods on markets. Under these conditions, we know that each commodity's relative price reveals the consumers' real (marginal) values. In developing measures of people's values for goods and services, the focus shifts to the typical (or representative) individual and the fact that real values are known once we have the relative prices associated with the consumption bundles selected. If the amounts purchased are also known, then with sufficient variation in these pairs (i.e., prices and quantities), we can develop conventional valuation measures. That is, Hicksian measures of consumer surplus for single price changes (see Hausman 1981 and Värtia 1983), and in some cases for multiple price changes (see LaFrance and Hanemann 1989), can be recovered from Marshallian demand functions derived from this information.

These procedures do not necessarily imply that we can value other changes in the quality or conditions of access to marketed goods. Even if we can observe behavioral responses to quality changes, we may not be able to recover Hicksian measures of the value of a quality change (see Bockstael and McConnell 1991). Integrating a Marshallian demand function over price to recover a quasi-expenditure function implies a constant of integration that may depend on quality. Weak complementarity of quality with the commodity used in the integration provides one type of information to describe how this constant must respond to quality changes (see Larson 1991). Indeed, this issue directly parallels the questions posed in using indirect methods for valuing environmental services. In this case, by maintaining that individual preferences exhibit weak complementarity between the environmental resource and some commodity where we can observe a Marshallian demand (and that this linkage forms the only contribution the resource makes to utility), we also assume that the environmental resource will not have nonuse values.

The travel cost recreation demand model is the most straightforward of the indirect methods. Initially proposed in 1947 by Harold Hotelling, the model is one of the "success stories" of nonmarket valuation and occupies a major place in the applied research programs of resource and environmental economists. The model recognizes that visitors to a recreation site pay an implicit price—the cost of traveling to it (including the opportunity costs of their time). By observing an appropriate quantity measure and these costs for individuals at different distances (along with any entrance fees and related charges), we obtain information comparable to that provided by market transactions. Of course, this description assumes that the implicit price can be treated as a parameter and that the quantity measure is straightforward. Once either of these assumptions is modified, the correspondence to marketed goods becomes less direct.

Numerous variations in the basic model have been considered. Two changes illustrate the sensitivity of the model's ability to recover a simple demand relationship from observed choices. First, discretion in either how time can be allocated (i.e., multiple time constraints; see Smith, Desvousges, and McGivney 1983) or in the prices available for added working time (i.e., kinked budget constraints; see Bockstael, Strand, and Hanemann 1987) will influence the opportunity cost of time and therefore the nature of the "implicit prices." Second, most early studies treated trips to the site as the basic unit of consumption, implicitly assuming a fixed time-on-site during each trip. When on-site time per trip is a choice variable, MRSs (for trips during a season and the time on site during each of them relative to the numeraire) will respond to different sets of relative prices. The exact pattern will depend on how the budget constraint is defined. In some cases (see McConnell 1990), we can separate the decisions, but this requires that we simplify the description to consider the number of trips and time on site per trip as the two choice variables with both implicit prices as parameters.

These complexities aside, most evaluators conclude that the travel cost methodology has "worked well." (See Bockstael, McConnell, and Strand 1991; Smith 1989; or Ward and Loomis 1986.) Reviewers of an earlier draft of this paper appropriately asked what this observation meant. I believe it is based on four features of the hundreds of estimates accumulated using the travel cost model. First, the estimates uphold rudimentary predictions of consumer theory (such as having the quality negatively related to the own price). Second, when the model is applied to comparable sites, the estimates reveal a broad consistency in the relative size of price and income elasticities (as well as in the estimated consumer surplus per unit of site usage). Likewise, estimates across different types of recreation sites reveal plausible differences in these economic characteristics. For example, we would expect wilderness areas to behave more like luxury goods than freshwater boating sites, and this is what the estimates imply. Demand functions for recreation sites in areas with numerous substitute facilities are more elastic than those for sites with few comparable alternatives.

Third, meta-analyses of both surplus per unit of use and price elasticities indicate that modeling judgments affect the estimates as theory would suggest. Moreover, both measures vary with the type of recreation site being studied. While some observers might argue that the first finding weakens the method, I do not agree. When a method relies on connecting decisions to underlying preferences using prior assumptions about what motivates and constrains people's behavior, we should expect these judgments to matter. What is important is that the impact of each judgment agrees with a priori expectations and that we can develop methods for testing the assumptions and judgments that are most relevant to recreationists' circumstances. Finally, controlled experiments suggest that when the assumptions underlying the model are upheld, the model does perform reasonably well in characterizing underlying consumer preferences.[3]

There is an important caveat to these observations that I return to below. Most of this evidence relates to using the model to describe the demand for and value of services provided by specific types of reaction sites and not to estimating the value people place on changes in the sites' quality features. Attempts to value changes in site quality are the newest area of applications, and we do not have the same basis for evaluating these estimates.

A second class of indirect valuation methods uses averting behavior or household production function (HPF) models to infer an individual's value for some aspect of environmental quality when private actions can influence how it is experienced. Like Hostelling's insight in the travel cost model, the HPF framework uses people's actions to isolate features of their values. In this case, the choices observed in the HPF framework involve reallocating expenditures on marketed commodities or time to adjust to a change in the amount of some nonmarketed resource. The HPF framework alone does not add information. Rather, it offers a rationale for imposing restrictions on preferences (or what is referred to as the household technology) so observable decisions can provide the necessary valuation information.

A number of different applications linking a pollution measure to some observable response are classified as versions of the HPF method. Physical damage functions may well be the most common. A second empirical model often suggested as based on the HPF framework involves models for reported mitigating behavior, such as purchasing a filter to remove water pollutants (see Smith and Desvousges 1986). Neither of these provides sufficient information to recover valuation information.

---

[3]Kling's (1988) and Kling and Weinberg's (1990) research provides an ideal example of such evaluations. More recently, Adamowicz, Fletcher, and Graham-Tomasi (1989) examined the sensitivity of consumer surplus estimates to mis-specifications of the travel cost demand function.

A third class of HPF applications does permit a link between observable decisions and a valuation estimate. In these applications, the HPF is specifically restricted to exhibit certain properties. For example, perfect substitution underlies using expenditures for a commodity that is assumed to be a perfect substitute for the services of an environmental resource to value that resource. Another possibility involves maintaining the equivalent of weak complementarity by assuming that one factor input is an essential input in the household production technology (Bockstael and McConnell 1983). Other combinations of features of the HPF also can be interpreted as functional restrictions imposed on consumer preferences. (See Neill 1987 and Larson 1990 as examples.) A unifying principle connects each of these strategies: taken together with a general specification for preferences, they restrict the factors motivating individual choice so the desired MRS can be linked to an *observable* set of relative prices (whether actual prices or implicit costs).

Finally, the HPF framework can be applied when nonmarket services are included as arguments in full expenditure/cost models for individual purchases of marketed commodities. This type of application imposes restrictions that can be as limiting as perfect substitution. It requires that the role of nonmarketed inputs be completely specified by identifying how they contribute to the expenditure function. Because it is often difficult to use intuition in formulating these hypotheses, the HPF argument has sometimes been used to motivate how "price" indexes for sets of marketed commodities are likely to be affected by the nonmarketed service. (See MathTech 1982 and Gilbert 1985 as examples.) Of course, these strategies involve imposing separability restrictions together with a specific functional structure on the role of the nonmarketed service.[4]

The marginal rate of substitution is also the preference information recovered from the last type of indirect method to be reviewed—hedonic price functions. Their story is now well known. By specifying characteristics that distinguish heterogeneous commodities and by recognizing that equilibrium means an absence of incentives for arbitrage, the hedonic model describes how a set of prices for each of the commodities will define the equilibrium. With a large enough number of different commodities, this equilibrium is characterized by a price function that describes how prices change with the characteristics of the commodities involved. This insight can be used in nonmarket valuation because some of these characteristics are site specific. Market participants must be aware of this site connection and share a common basis for recognizing it if these characteristics are to influence the prices.

Household production models have been limited by the information available. Damage functions linking air pollution to mortality or morbidity rates have been reasonably successful when their goal is interpreted as establishing a linkage between exposure to pollutants and health responses.

---

[4]For further discussion of the assumptions underlying HPF models, see Smith (1991).

However, measures of the extent of their effects remain controversial. This is partly because the outcome measures usually require subjective judgments (e.g., restricted activity days to describe a health effect). They also can be the result of an underlying physical relationship coupled with the incentives provided by fringe benefit programs, as in the case of work-loss days.

The reduced form averting models had fewer applications, largely because data on these types of decisions are limited. Nonetheless, in several different situations where information could be collected about mitigation decisions, we found that the conventional model (which focuses on a view of consumer behavior that emphasizes the intensive margin of choice) is *not* well suited to what households report. For example, in a panel study of households' decisions to reduce radon concentrations in their homes, the respondents sought "safety." They wanted the problem "fixed" and did not seem to evaluate incremental gains in comparison with costs as our models hypothesized (see Smith, Desvousges and Payne 1992). Similarly, in a study of mitigation decisions involving gypsy moths, limitations in what households recalled about their expenditures and what was accomplished reduced the usefulness of the model to estimate the values motivating these choices (Jakus and Smith 1992). If these conclusions are supported in additional studies, they would imply that mitigation models will require a different set of assumptions that recognize the discrete nature of the way people evaluate their options and the factors that constrain them in order to recover valuation estimates.

The record with hedonic property value applications is somewhat more extensive than the averting models, but not as well developed as with travel cost recreation demand analyses. While a number of hedonic property value models include environmental amenities (and disamenities), studies investigating the influence of air pollution comprise most of this literature. Beginning with Ridker and Henning's study (1967), thirty-seven applications (including both published and unpublished studies) were reviewed in a recent meta-analysis of hedonic estimates of the effect of air pollution on property values (see Smith and Huang 1991). This empirical summary considered two issues:

1. Does the evidence support a negative and statistically significant relationship between air pollution and property values? and

2. Given an affirmative answer to the first question, can the evidence be used to estimate the representative household's marginal valuation of reductions in air pollution?

Over 75 percent of the studies reported a negative and significant (using a 10 percent p-value) relationship. While this may seem to provide fairly decisive support for a negative relationship, a selection effect is probably influencing the available evidence. Published studies are more likely to support a linkage because the evidence for an effect makes them "worthy" of

publication. As a result, it is not clear what threshold proportion of negative and significant estimates we should expect by "chance." Testing our
sample proportion against the null hypothesis of 50 percent leads to an
easy rejection of this null hypothesis.

A more convincing case for an affirmative answer to the first question is
found by examining whether the data characteristics and modeling practices
in these studies influenced their ability to uncover the significant relationship. Probit estimates for the sample of estimates as a whole or in subsets intended to reduce the prospects for correlation across studies (and hence the
impact of nonspherical errors for inference with the summary models) clearly
indicate that our outcome measure—finding the hypothesized linkage—is influenced by the overall level of air pollution in the city studied, the number
of observations available for the primary analysis, the type of housing price
measure, and other indicators of the empirical model's "quality."

We found the second question more difficult to answer because most
of the available studies did not attempt to provide valuation estimates. They
merely sought to investigate whether the connection between air pollution
and property values could be detected. Nonetheless, the estimates of a marginal rate of substitution for particulate matter do support a robust, positive relationship between estimates of the MRS for air pollution improvements and income.

While this is encouraging, it does not mean the estimates offer a plausible basis for benefit measurement. Moreover, the models' ability to isolate important influences on the MRS estimates is more limited than that
found for an earlier meta-analysis of travel cost estimates (see Smith and
Kaoru 1990a, 1990b). There are a number of potential explanations, including the fact that fewer hedonic studies were involved. Equally important, because those completed included very different measures for the pollutants involved, it is more difficult to define a common increment to the
valued "commodity." Finally, the theoretical structure underlying the MRS
link to the slope of the hedonic price function is more complex than generally assumed for benefit measures based on travel cost demand models.
Except under special conditions, an individual's value for a change in air
pollution cannot be measured from hedonic estimates alone.[5]

Overall experience with the indirect methods confirms Freeman's
(1979) early appraisal—nonmarket values can be measured with observed
choices even though they are made outside of direct markets for the commodities being valued. Having argued that these methods can work, we
should also evaluate the available estimates based on how well they meet
current and emerging policy needs. In the case of recreation sites and the
travel cost recreation demand framework (whether conventional demand
functions or random utility models), the record is reasonably good. The

[5]See Palmquist (1988) for a discussion suggesting that we conceptualize the second-stage models for site attributes as pseudo demand functions and Palmquist (1991) for a detailed review for the
hedonic model.

large number of studies and the similarities between modeling strategies for implicit price and quantity pairs with prices and quantities from market transactions may explain why this class of studies is closer to having a set of value estimates for a wide range of different recreation sites.

With hedonic models, the empirical record is very limited. While the evidence clearly supports a relationship between air pollution and property values that parallels theoretical expectations, few studies have investigated the properties of hedonic estimates of the marginal value of air quality improvements. (Graves et al. 1988 is one recent exception.) The sparse evidence from averting behavior models simply reflects limited opportunities do observe (or collect) information on these types of responses. For some physical damage functions, especially those related to important agricultural crops, reasonable linkages between air pollutants and yield have been established.

Nonetheless, the overall empirical record is quite limited when compared to current policy needs—whether benefit-cost analyses, environmental costing, natural resource damage assessments, environmental accounting, or other emerging topics. Moreover, in some cases, the available estimates are quite old. For example, the most recent set of hedonic property values estimates for evaluating the effects of air pollution are for transactions and air quality conditions in 1980. This disparity between what is available and what is being requested to meet policy needs has focused attention on three activities:

- *benefits transfer*—the methods for adapting existing models or value estimates to construct valuations for resources that are different in type or location from the one originally studied;

- *generalized empirical models*—newly estimated models capable of being used in a wide range of applications;

- *special purpose data collection*—new information to develop estimates for the most important resource questions.

If we conducted a benefit-cost analysis of the decision to attempt a new empirical effort for every new policy question, it would almost certainly yield negative net benefits even though the available empirical evidence is limited. Attention needs to be shifted to identifying the types of resources where transfers can be performed and those where they cannot. Addressing this task seems to be the first step in specifying a protocol for benefits transfer. Where transfers are possible, valuation functions play a role similar to price indexes and need to be developed and maintained as an ongoing activity to meet policy needs. Where the resources involved have a large number of substitutes but empirical estimates of value functions are especially limited, it seems reasonable to argue for developing estimates of more easily generalized valuation functions. Special resources with few substitutes will require individual analyses.

Finally, two methodological aspects of the "next steps" in applying indirect methods to respond to current policy needs are important. First, because more than one method can be used to value the services involved for some environmental resources, we should exploit these theoretical connections. Second (and perhaps more important to evaluating whether the measures accurately reflect people's values for these resources), averting behavior, hedonic property value, and travel cost models measure what might be described as the privately "capturable" aspects of the environmental services being valued. Each method must "link" the nonmarket service to a private choice. To the extent that environmental services have public good aspects and that this "publicness" has value in addition to the private aspects, *none* of the available indirect methods will reflect these values. These public good services offer another way of describing the role of nonuse values as I discuss below.

III. Structured Conversations:
The Direct Approaches

The fastest growing literature in nonmarket valuation involves using contingent valuation surveys (designated as CVM for the contingent valuation method) to elicit how people would respond to hypothetical changes in some environmental resources. These surveys can involve direct valuation questions; discrete take-it-or-leave-it questions; and matching, ranking, quantity, bidding, or double-bounded formulations. While the initial suggestion to use surveys was made about the same time as Hotelling's proposal for the travel cost approach by Ciriacy-Wantrup (1947), concerted applications of the method did not begin until nearly twenty-five years later.

CVM research has proceeded through several phases of activities. After Davis's thesis (1964), the early research can be distinguished into two groups. One set of applications with well-defined populations adopted the CVM method without attempting to evaluate its properties and sought to estimate the values for nonmarket resources or changes in the quality of recreational experiences.[6] The second group of applications had a dual objective: to evaluate the properties of CVM as a methodology and to estimate consumers' values for changes in the quantity or quality of specific environmental resources. Studies in this second group often had small samples that tended to focus on the potential for biases due to the strategic incentives, the information presented, the hypothetical nature of the task, the bidding approach to questioning, and other methodological issues. Nonetheless, a reasonable degree of success and persistence focused increasing attention on CVM findings.

Because mainstream economists remain skeptical of the insights derived from people's responses to hypothetical questions, initial objec-

---

[6]Examples of these early studies include Matthews and Brown (1970) for salmon fishing; Hammack and Brown (1974) for migratory waterfowl; Cicchetti and Smith (1973) for congestion effects in wilderness recreations; and Randall, Ives, and Eastman (1974) for aesthetic damage arising from a coal-electricity plant in the Four Corners region. This last study appears to have been the first to use modern survey techniques to draw a stratified random sample. The other studies relied on previous surveys or recreation licenses to define the population contacted as part of subsequent CVM research.

tions to CVM crystallized around two general questions: is CVM reliable, and is it accurate? The next stage in CVM research sought to address these questions in a variety of ways. The current stage in CVM research is derivative of both of these efforts. It recognizes the need to integrate the psychological and economic dimensions of framing CVM questions with conventional practices in survey design, implementation, and analysis. (See Mitchell and Carson 1989 for a comprehensive treatment.)

Before considering the reliability and accuracy issues, we must recognize that neither issue can be answered completely without controlled experiments. Moreover, it should also be acknowledged that the ability to exercise this control limits the types of commodities and decisions that can be included in the CVM analysis. Therefore there always remains the possibility for questioning whether the findings are relevant to those situations that could not be considered. As a result, research has focused on evaluating a wide range of indirect gauges of the validity and reliability of CVM findings. Seven types of evaluations have been undertaken, including:

1. comparison of indirect and CVM estimates of the value of some change in an environmental resource;

2. use of constructed markets in which commodities not usually sold were offered for sale and the results compared with CVM estimates for the same commodity;

3. evaluation of CVM for measuring the demand for actual marketed commodities of programs in comparison with actual demands;

4. test/retest comparisons of the stability of CVM estimates from the same sample over time;

5. creation of laboratory experiments in which hypothetical and actual sales of commodities were undertaken;

6. surveys of purchase intentions and actual sales of commodities; and

7. nonparametric "tests" of the consistency of CVM and travel cost estimates with the strong axioms of revealed preference theory.

Table 1 cites examples of each type of study and summarizes their overall findings. For the most part, they support the CVM estimates as being "comparable" in performance to the alternative approach providing the reference point (or standard) in each case. In some cases, the two estimates might be judged to be significantly different but still exhibit a strong causal relationship. Why have analysts been content with an apparently weak level of correspondence? The answer can be found in the specifics of each comparison. I will use studies from three types of comparisons described in Table 1 as examples.

The first comparison of direct versus indirect estimates of the values of some nonmarketed good by Brookshire et al. (1982) used a hedonic prop-

Table 1 Evaluation of CVM's Performance: Some Initial and Current Examples

Approach	Methods	Environmental Resource	Conclusion
Comparison—Direct vs. Indirect			
Brookshire, Thayer, Schulze, and d'Arge (1982)	Hedonic property value vs. itertive bidding CVM.	Air quality measured for CVM with pictures displaying visibility differences; for property value using particulated matter and nitrogen dioxide; analyst judgment for match.	Rent gradient exceeded CVM estimate of WTP as hypothesized from theory.
Seller, Stoll, and Chavas (1985)	Travel cost vs. direct question CVM and take-it-or-leave-it CVM.	Value of 4 lakes for boating.	No clear relation between travel cost and CVM; but close correspondence to discrete CVM.
Smith, Desvousges, and Fisher (1986)	Generalized and simple travel cost for water quality vs. direct, payment card, and iterative bidding versions of CVM.	Water quality measured by dis-solved oxygen for travel cost and RFF water quality ladder with CVM.	No clear correspondence with generalized travel cost (GTC), but likely to be fault of GTC model; simple TC for river and user values same order of magnitude; regression results reject 45° line, but indicate link.
Cummings, Schulze, Gerking, and Brookshire (1986)	Hedonic wage vs. CVM with direct question format.	Value of municipal infrastructure measured by construction, machinery and equipment per capita and in CVM by percentage increases in community's stock—described using specific allocation among fire, police, recreation, water supply, sewage, streets, and roads and general government that respondents were allowed to reallocate.	No significant difference between the two elasticity measures.

Simulated Markets

Study	Commodity	Method	Findings
Bohm (1972)	Public television programs.	Actual payments to evaluate free-riding behavior and hypothetical experiments.	Bohm's comparison concluded differences between actual and hypothetical; Mitchell and Carson re-analysis contradicts this when focusing on comparison of individual actual payments to hypothetical.
Bishop and Heberlein (1990)	Deer hunting permits; purchase and sale of permits in 1983 and 1984 seasons.	1983 auction used with 4 different frameworks for accepting bids and changes in them; 1984 single price-offer, take-it-or-leave-it.	Some differences depending on designs of auction mechanism; over all judgments was close correspondence.
Dickie, Fisher, and Gerking (1987)	Strawberries offered at different prices.	Actual *vs.* hypothetical demand functions.	No significant difference in estimated demands; predicted amounts of strawberries different by more than 100% unless adjusted for outliers and interviewer effects.
Kealy, Montgomery, and Dovido (1990)	Cadbury chocolate bars as private good and reduction in acidic deposition in Adirondack Lakes as public good.	Discrete choice models and changes in stated and actual purchase decisions.	Significant differences in proportions with stated intentions to purchase and those with actual purchase decisions.
Actual Markets vs. CVM Smith et al. (1991)	Piped water supply in rural Pakistan; varied implementation to induce strategic effects in some of the villages used for CVM.	Random utility model (RUM) to describe the actual connection decisions to public water systems and double-bounded CVM in different areas using some payment vehicle.	Comparison of estimated values RUM vs. CVM satisfy convergent validity criteria; also WTP function from CVM data predicted connection frequency in areas with available supplies.
Test/Retest Loomis (1989, 1990)	Maintain the ecological character of Mono Lake in California by preserving water level.	Comparison using t-tests and regression models of WTP bids and discrete CVM responses when some individuals questioned at nine-month intervals.	Both general population survey and sample of on-site visitors exhibited stable CVM responses over time.

231

Table 1 *(continued)*

Approach	Methods	Environmental Resource	Conclusion
Laboratory Experiments			
Brookshire and Coursey (1987)	Comparison of different elicitation methods for CVM question with laboratory experiments; considered both WTP and WTA.	Density of trees in an urban park in Fort Collins, Colorado.	Median bids from laboratory comparable to CVM but uniformly smaller with WTP, regardless of CVM elicitation question.
Purchase Intention/Actual			
Seip and Strand (1992)	Comparison of percent stating will-ingness to purchase membership with actual membership purchases.	Commodity described as membership in prominent Norwegian environmental group.	Little correspondence, actual membership decisions much smaller than intentions but significant problems with research design.
Duffield and Patterson (1992)	Comparison of means responses between three samples: actual donations; Dillman-type CVM survey sent by University researchers; CVM survey sent by Nature Conservancy.	Instream water flows for tributaries of two rivers that provide spawning habitat for arctic grayling and cutthroat trout in Montana.	Correspondence depends on how the average CVM-based WTP is compared with actual donations. If samples confined to respondents or contributors, University CVM, and actual contributions not significantly different Dramatically lower response rates for actual contributions.
Revealed Preference			
Adamowicz and Graham-Tomasi (1991)	Violations of strong axiom of re-revealed preference for commodities closely related to travel costs and then travel costs plus CVM-based WTP per day; compared with violations in a randomly generated set of "prices" and quantities.	Bighorn sheep hunting trips in Alberta; assumed each trip is independent.	Exceptionally low rate of violations for both travel cost and travel cost plus CVM evaluations.

erty value model and contingent valuation for valuing air quality.[7] In their study, both methods are assumed to be capturing exactly the same reasons for valuing air quality improvements, so the estimates derived from the hedonic should provide an *upper bound* on the CVM results. While their findings are consistent with these a priori expectations and the motivation for the comparison was to "evaluate" CVM, we can argue that the methods do *not* measure the same concept of benefits and would not perform equally well in capturing all the benefits realized by respondents (or home buyers) from improvements in air quality. The CVM analysis described the alternative air pollution levels with photos, while the property value models used changes in concentrations of particulate matter and nitrogen dioxide that were argued to offer comparable visibility changes. The CVM described the change as affecting the entire area, while the pollution measures in the hedonic model were intended to characterize concentrations at each housing location.

Equally important, the CVM elicited annual payments, while the hedonic used sales prices for homes as assets. Annualizing the change in asset value requires assuming how each individual perceives the discount rate and time horizon involved in this contract. Finally, we would expect that each person's MRS for air quality relative to the numeraire would be related to *all* the ways it is experienced and *not* simply the exposure at home. Thus, the extrapolation from a point estimate of this MRS to the value of an incremental change in air pollution will depend upon how other sources of exposure enter this utility function.

These types of concerns are not confined to the Brookshire et al. study. They can be identified with most comparisons of CVM and indirect methods. For example, my evaluation of CVM versus travel cost with Desvousges and Fisher (see Smith, Desvousges, and Fisher 1986) exhibits a comparable set of judgments in connecting the water quality ladder used for the CVM to the dissolved oxygen levels that served as the water quality measure for the travel cost model.

Changing the commodity from environmental amenities like water quality to private goods does not alter the general point. It will influence how assumptions affect outcomes. For example, the Dickie, Fisher, and Gerking (1987) study of strawberry sales found that demand curves based on hypothetical sales did not differ significantly from models using actual sales. *But,* this conclusion was somewhat sensitive to how the analysis treated interviewer effects and one outlier. Moreover, if the criteria were changed to the predicted demands for strawberries from the two models, the conclusions would depend on the treatment of outliers. Their analysis does not mention that the relevant variance in the random variables being compared also changes, so large numerical differences in predicted quantities may not indicate statistically significant differences. All of these is-

---

[7]Actually, Knetsch and Davis (1966) first reported a comparison of aggregate valuation estimates for recreation sites from travel cost, willingness-to-travel, and contingent valuation analyses.

sues are not the result of the design (i.e., asking quantities) or the specific commodity used (i.e., pints of strawberries). They illustrate the role of judgment in the analysis.

My analysis with Whittington and several coauthors (see Smith et al. 1991) used the need to value public drinking water supplies in rural Pakistan to compare the results derived from experience with past connection decisions for earlier systems versus that derived from a double-bounded CVM survey designed to elicit maximum annual tariffs for the water system. After developing economic models relevant to each type of data, we estimated the implied values for comparable water systems and evaluated their correspondences. Estimates based on CVM were closely related to those from the indirect model (in this case a random utility model, RUM, describing connections). However, the CVM estimates were 1.71 times the values derived with the RUM framework when alternative water supplies were good and 2.97 when they were poor.

These differences surely seem "large." It is important to put them in some perspective. How much would we expect prices for the same commodity to vary in the same city across stores? over ten years ago, Pratt, Wise, and Zeckhauser (1979) reported evidence on this issue as part of a study of information and market equilibria. The ratios of maximum to minimum prices for the same commodity or service range from 1.11 to 6.67 for the thirty-nine commodities they investigated. Eighteen have ratios of 2.0 or greater. Of course, this does not prove that CVM estimates are "as good as" a market price.[8] Instead, it highlights the importance of modeling judgments in interpreting any economic data.

Another type of comparison attempted to reduce the influence of judgment by dealing with the same commodities and the same people. Three studies fit this description—the Kealy, Montgomery, and Dovidio (1990) comparison of purchase intentions with actual decisions for chocolate bars and prevention of additional damages to the Adirondack region aquatic system from acid rain; the Seip and Strand (1992) evaluation of membership decisions in a prominent environmental group in Norway; and Duffield and Patterson's (1992) valuation of Montana Rivers. While the Kealy et al. study makes several types of comparisons, the one relevant here is its comparison of respondents' first-period stated intentions with their second-period choices when confronted with the same decision. The study discusses two different types of tests. The first considers coefficients from discrete choice models estimated using responses to the hypothetical questions along with the simulated markets outcomes for each good. The second test relies on the degree of agreement in reported and actual decisions (as measured by correlation coefficients). The initial test indicates significant differences, but must be interpreted cautiously

---

[8]Carlson and Pescatrice (1980) also found wide variation in the retail prices for some thirty-four products in New Orleans after controlling for brand and type of product. Thus, the Pratt et al. (1979) evidence seems to be observed with some regularity and has led to models of market behavior where markedly different prices can persist for long periods.

for several reasons. The authors acknowledge that their discrete choice models did not isolate the effects of variables other than price. Equally important, their design introduces a dependency between the models being compared. Subjects included in the sample for hypothetical questions (in the first period) also appear in the sample with a simulated market and hence in its discrete choice model. The test used assumes that the samples are independent. Finally, the specific hypothesis tested in the authors' first comparison is not equality of valuation measures but equality in *all* the coefficients from the two probit models (one for the hypothetical and a second for the actual responses) for each of the two commodities. Estimates of the values for each commodity will depend on how variables that are not significant determinants of the hypothetical and actual choices are treated in estimating the willingness to pay, as well as the approximation used to construct a variance estimate for the calculated willingness to pay.

These comments illustrate the difficulty in evaluating welfare measures. Because an individual's willingness to pay is not a parameter and we expect it to vary with many of the factors that constrain individual behavior, comparisons of hypothetical and simulated markets must strive to compare estimates of the functions for the conditional means defined under consistent conditions.

Seip and Strand (1992) report the results of three types of contacts with progressively smaller subsets of a sample of Norwegian adults. The first contact involved in-person interviews that defined the sample to include 101 adults. During this initial interview, respondents were asked about environmental attitudes and given different information about the purpose of the study. Then each respondent was asked about: (a) their willingness to join a prominent Norwegian environmental group with an annual membership fee of 200 Krona and (b) the maximum annual amount they would pay to support the group. A month later, those who indicated they would join (about 64 of the original 101 in the sample) were solicited by mail to join. After two mailings, only six responded by agreeing to join. The last contact was conducted about a year later to a subset of those who expressed values exceeding the membership fee (i.e., 25 of the original 58 adults) to investigate why they had not responded. The authors interpret their findings as indicating substantial upward biases in CVM's estimates. Even if we ignore a number of serious problems with the study's design, their basic conclusion is not necessarily warranted.[9] Virtually all of the discrepancy could be argued to arise from either the inadequate commodity definition or a change in respondents' economic circumstances.

---

[9]These include a lack of clarity in the commodity offered in the CVM and simulated markets and a change in the survey approach from in-person to mail contacts between the hypothetical and actual components of their study. Because the sample sizes are so small, the analysis could not attempt to control for the effects of socioeconomic variables in explaining the progressive selection effects.

Duffield and Patterson's (1992) recent study of the value of in-stream flow (to enhance the stream as a habitat for two species of fish listed as "Species of Special Concern" in Montana) illustrates the issue that Seip and Strand attempted to raise. How should nonrespondents to cash solicitations be treated in estimating the willingness to pay for the specific environmental resource offered? Estimates of willingness to pay would be judged as comparable when conventional contingent valuation and cash surveys were compared on a per-respondent or per-contributor basis, but *not* if all nonrespondents are treated as having zero willingness to pay. Large differences in the response rates between the hypothetical and actual solicitation surveys lead to a question. If these programs are important to a large fraction of the sample receiving the CVM survey, why isn't a comparable fraction of the sample responding to the actual solicitation? This might be explained as an example of free riding. Under this view, the values derived from an actual solicitation might be biased because of strategic behavior and therefore not provide the desired standard for evaluating CVM.

What conclusions can we draw from comparing CVM with other alternatives? I believe the record indicates that some forms of CVM can provide theoretically consistent and plausible measures of individuals' values for some types of environmental resources. The types of commodities need not be limited to the narrow set defined by Cummings, Brookshire, and Schulze's (1986) reference operating conditions. However, we are far from identifying how the characteristics of the commodities to be valued, the attributes of the people whose values are to be measured, and the features of the survey influence the reliability of CVM estimates.

Before closing this discussion, it is appropriate to consider a highly publicized evaluation of CVM developed as part of Exxon's litigation effort for the natural resource damage case provoked by the Exxon-Valdez oil spill. Four of the studies reported at the Exxon-sponsored symposium have been argued to be especially relevant to judgments about CVM. They focused on cases where CVM would elicit total values that are likely (in their authors' judgment) to be primarily composed of nonuse values. Any review of evaluations of CVM could easily appear to explain away the problems that evaluation uncovers after the fact. Because that is not my intention, I have focused my discussion on the criterion the authors of each study argue should be used to evaluate how CVM performed in their particular case study. While the specifics associated with the design, framing, implementation, and analysis of CVM studies are also important to whether findings should be interpreted to be representative of how the method performs, I will not attempt to discuss these issues here.

Two studies (Diamond et al. 1992 and Desvousges et al. 1992) sought to evaluate CVM by testing whether survey responses were consistent with behavior implied by well-behaved preferences. While similar in general strategy to that of Adamowicz and Graham-Tomasi (1991), the specific hypotheses tested were primarily associated with how the values for larger amounts of environmental commodities should behave when elicited in different ways. Diamond et al. approached their test by posing different questions to separate subsamples that asked about timber harvesting in varying numbers of specific wilderness areas. Respondents were told that there were 57 wilderness areas in the four states where the telephone survey took place (i.e., Colorado, Idaho, Montana, and Wyoming).

Timber harvesting was described as being proposed for between seven and ten areas with as many as three specifically identified. Respondents were offered the opportunity to pay to prevent harvesting in the identified area(s). Willingness-to-pay (WTP) values (elicited using a direct CVM question) were not significantly different across the three areas offered individually. While I stated that it is not my intention to deal with the specific empirical analyses, it should be noted that there is some controversy about two of the three empirical papers. For example, Carson and Hanemann (1992) have suggested that this first conclusion is sensitive to how the test is conducted. Pairwise tests do not yield the same conclusions for a subset of the areas evaluated. The sum of the values for either two or three areas (when each area's value was elicited individually) was significantly greater than the WTP elicited for the cases when the same two or three were offered as a group to independent subsamples. The authors conclude that CVM surveys are not measuring consumer preferences for these environmental resources.

Desvousges et al. (1992) approached the question of how an individual's willingness to pay behaves with variations in the amount of the environmental commodity somewhat differently. They considered two situations—avoiding migratory bird kills and preventing damage from small versus "all" oil spills. The first situation posed to respondents described a regulation to cover 250,000 waste-oil holding ponds that cause deaths of migratory waterfowl. The estimated means for WTPs for the regulation (across independent subsamples) did not vary when the impacts were described as 2,000, 20,000, and 200,000 bird kills. However, in describing these effects, the questionnaire told respondents that all impacts were less than either 1 percent (for 2,000 and 20,000) or less than 2 percent (for 200,000) of the migratory waterfowl population in the central flyway.

The second situation offered independent subsamples two different oil spill response plans. The first involved local response efforts and was described as follows: "Experts think that these measures **will prevent** 90 percent of the environmental damage from oil spills of **less than** 50,000 gallons." This small-spill scenario suggested that action would be taken for larger spills, but the response would not be capable of "containing or cleaning up most of the oil from large spills **more than** 50,000 gallons." The large-spill scenario described regional (as opposed to local) response centers, which experts thought would prevent 75 percent of any environmental damage. As with the Diamond et al. (1992) analysis, these authors expected to find that larger amounts of the amenities posed would be more highly valued, and the means from independent subsamples generally were not (based on parametric and nonparametric tests relying on only the WTP responses).

Neither study investigated whether people would in fact *perceive* the proposed differences in environmental commodities as appreciably larger amounts. In the case of wilderness areas, there are any number of ways one might describe how respondents conceive of changes in one or more wilderness areas. Each implies a different pattern of expectations for their valuation of changes in the areas available. For example, if respondents were interested in maintaining some minimum capacity, the Diamond et al. premise that preventing harvesting on more areas provides a greater quantity of environmental services would not be correct. In this case, the aggregate of the WTPs elicited for single sites should *not* equal the value of avoiding timber harvests on multiple sites. The relevant public good underlying the nonuse value would be this minimum capacity, which does not change across the commodities offered to their respondents.

A similar argument applies to the Desvousges et al. (1992) migratory waterfowl results. The effects are *all* small in relation to the population. Indeed, by reporting the percentages to respondents, the authors may have contributed to perceptions that these were small. A step function (or other specification relying on the minimum function as proposed by Hirschleifer 1983 for some public goods) has appeared to be consistent in focus groups with how people seem to perceive injuries to some types of environmental resources. The oil spill scenarios elicited the equivalent of option prices for different amounts of protection. The values will depend on how people conceive of the set of services provided by these programs. This set includes the likelihood of large spills in relationship to small ones, as well as on how they perceive the effectiveness of response activities. Because small spills are described as the most likely and the effectiveness of each type of response center is presented as a judgment, it is difficult to evaluate how people perceived the change implied by comparisons of the two commodities. To select any one feature arguing that economic theory requires valuation responses to change in a particular way with respect to variations in that single dimension is simply not a correct interpretation of theory.

Both studies highlight how little we know about measuring the amounts of environmental amenities (or services), and therefore how important qualitative analysis of people's perceptions of the problem can be to the framing of the commodity in a CVM study. However, the same types of problems are equally relevant to measuring the amounts of environmental quality using indirect methods. In these situations, technical proxy variables such as dissolved oxygen or turbidity (for water quality) and ambient concentration of particulates (for air quality) do not directly translate into people's perceptions of environmental service measures. The general nature of the problem is important, because both papers report specific case studies and seek to draw very broad conclusions about the contingent valuation methodology as it might be applied to any situation for measuring total values including nonuse components. Diamond et al. conclude that "responses to CV [contingent valuation] surveys are not economic preferences" (1992, 2). Likewise, Desvousges et al. conclude from their two case studies that "we do not think that CV provides either valid or reliable estimates of nonuse damages" (1992, 40). Neither judgment would be warranted from single case studies.

Two other empirical studies of CVM sponsored by Exxon considered the budget context (Kemp and Maxwell 1992) and the properties of models for open-ended and discrete choice CVM responses (McFadden and Leonard 1992). Kemp and Maxwell compared values elicited using a "top-down," progressive disaggregation from all social programs through over twenty-seven subcomponents versus a "single-focus" value elicited for minimizing the risk of oil spills off Alaska's coast. The authors found that the "single-focus" value was 290 times larger than the "top-down" aggregation. Unfortunately, they are not theoretically compatible.

The single-focus question elicits a Hicksian WTP for a change in *one* commodity. The top-down approach elicits a value for the same commodity *along with simultaneous increases in twenty-seven other commodities* (after adjusting for the nesting in their sequence of questions). The two WTP measures *should be different*. Their results would be subject to further criticism even without this inconsistency in how each approach implicitly defines the WTP. This second class of problems arises because the commodity is not well defined. Respondents are likely to have different perceptions about the amounts of the twenty-seven goods they currently experience. (This is part of the framing issue described in detail by Fischhoff and Furby 1988.) Thus, increments to these levels may imply different responses across people simply because of their initial perceptions.

McFadden and Leonard (1992) analyzed open-ended and discrete choice responses to the Diamond et al. (1992) questions about preventing timber harvesting in a single wilderness area. They found significant differences between the open-ended and discrete choice estimates of WTP, low precision in WTP estimates, and "implausible" responsiveness of WTP to income and household size. While this study raises a number of interesting econometric issues, its overall conclusion that this sensitivity is unique to CVM and therefore the methodology fails to provide a reliable approach for measuring nonuse values should be questioned. The potential for extreme observations with open-ended questions is documented in the literature, along with proposals to use selection models to adjust for screening such observations from the sample used in analysis. Approaches that attempt to explain the source of extreme responses in the open-ended questions were apparently not considered. Moreover, differences between open-ended and calculated responses (for a discrete choice model) arise from *both* the responses people make and the model used to interpret them. McFadden and Leonard drop covariates (other than income) from most of their analysis. Because their questions seek a total value (including use values) and because about one-third of their sample had visited the area posed, price effects associated with respondents' travel costs to the areas of interest may be important. We cannot assume that a representative sample will account for price (i.e., travel cost) effects. Consequently the differences between measures of WTP could easily arise from the model specification used with the discrete choice analysis. Ideally, comparisons between the two should be based on the specification of theoretically consistent multivariate relationships describing the conditional means for the WTP each question implied.

If we ignore these concerns and the problems raised earlier about people's understanding (and acceptance) of the Diamond et al. (1992) questions, the observed sensitivity may not be inconsistent with discrete choice models' performance under controlled conditions. Experimental studies report substantial sensitivity in consumer surplus with travel cost models when "true" values are known. This is also true of marginal values from hedonic property models. (The specifics are summarized below.) Moreover, recent sampling experiments comparing the WTP estimates for total value (composed of existence and use values derived from discrete choice models) by Huang, Nychka, and Smith (1992) suggest that both logit and probit can exhibit extreme performance (comparing the estimated conditional WTP with their respective true values over 100 replications using sample sizes of 200 observations). Moreover, the magnitude of the mean squared error (and its distribution across respondents) depends on the importance of the environmental resource, the functional form for the "true" underlying utility function, *and* the model specification used in estimating the discrete choice relationships.

Because sensitivity can arise from the model under controlled conditions (where there are existence values by definition), this sensitivity alone does not provide a reason for rejecting CVM. Comparable patterns can be found with controlled experiments based on indirect utility functions proposed by Madriaga and McConnell (1987) and Cameron (1992) for describing a role for environmental amenities.

The last source of McFadden and Leonard's criticism arises from implausibly small estimates of the responsiveness of WTP to income derived from their CVM samples. Two issues should be considered in evaluating this criticism. First, the Diamond et al. CVM questions emphasize the availability of abundant substitutes for the wilderness area(s) involved in timber harvesting. Because McFadden and Leonard's measure of WTP's responsiveness to income can be interpreted using Hanemann's (1991) expressions for the price flexibility of income, they need not be inconsistent with income elasticities of demand for wilderness services (for all motives—use and nonuse) that exceed one, provided the elasticity of substitution for these services is high. Second, McFadden and Leonard appear to be interpreting their estimates as relating to a more general commodity of "resource preservation." This is not the case. Their questions focus on specifically identified wilderness areas that could well contribute to resource preservation services, but the question's framing assures that many other wilderness areas are already available as close substitutes. Overall, these new studies do not change my cautiously optimistic judgment based on the literature that preceded them.

One reason for this judgment follows from what we know about methods based on actual choices in comparison to CVM. With indirect methods, we model how people make these types of decisions. When controlled evaluations of the influence of modeling judgments have been conducted, the results indicate that models applied with the "conventional" approximations *do* reflect people's values for nonmarketed goods and services, but often with fairly large errors. For example, Kling's (1988) and Kling and Weinberg's (1990) sampling studies found that the performance of travel cost demand or RUM estimates (both as approximations of some unknown underlying set of preferences) depends on the nature of people's decisions as reflected in the samples involved. The average error as a fraction of the measure of consumer surplus ranged from 9 percent to 107 percent. Cropper, Deck, and McConnell's (1988) analysis of the performance of alternative specifications for hedonic price functions in estimating the marginal prices for housing characteristics also exhibits a widely dispersed range of errors with the ratio of the average error to the mean true marginal price ranging from under 1 percent to over 150 percent.

Thus, in both cases, the estimated errors with indirect methods could easily be as large as the discrepancies observed in comparing estimates from CVM and indirect methods. Skepticism about CVM arises because economists retain a fundamental distrust of asking people about their choices (or values) in hypothetical situations. A test of their concerns would require: (a) knowing the "true" values people place on a commodity in specific circumstances and (b) understanding how people answer questions about hypothetical situations. Because we will never know people's "true" values for any commodity and are unlikely in the near future to have anything resembling a model of how they answer CVM questions, it seems reasonable to ask whether standards for testing the current view of how people answer CVM questions are too stringent. As Plott (1991) recently observed in addressing similar issues with respect to the usefulness of experimental methods," ". . . a theory is viewed as being of the form 'if x then y.' Following this belief, the proper way to test a theory is to create a circumstance in which all of the assumptions of the theory are satisfied, the x part of the statement, and then conduct the experiment to see if y is the result. . . . the problem is that the assumptions of economic theories are seldom stated in operational terms, and the theories themselves can be so vague that tests in the sense above are practically impossible" (p. 906). Resolving these issues in experimental economics, he suggests, requires analysts to formulate tests in different ways, as "contests among competing models."

This perspective offers some opportunities for understanding debates about the usefulness of CVM. Advocates of CVM tend to consider a "contest" between the conventional model of consumer behavior (i.e., people answer hypothetical questions in the same way as actual behavior) with a model suggesting purely hypothetical responses (i.e., random answers). In this contest, when they find studies demonstrating that values or choices in hypothetical situations are influenced by the quality attributes of the commodity offered, respondents' incomes, available substitutes, and other economically relevant variables, they conclude that CVM findings "win" because they do adhere to conventional consumer models in general terms.

In contrast, critics pose the idealized test concept of what would be required before CVM findings should be taken seriously. A more constructive dialogue requires a change in the terms of reference. This change would define a clear set of external criteria to evaluate models of CVM responses and consider a wider range of alternative explanations for these responses. The "contests" could then focus on the relative degree of correspondence offered by these alternative explanations for CVM compared to the correspondence CVM responses have when used in models based on the conventional economic description of consumer choice. Of course, regardless of the underlying model of CVM responses, understanding how people perceive environmental commodities is essential for obtaining plausible responses to any questions asked of them.

IV. How Do Existence Values Affect the Verdict on Nonmarket Valuation?

When Krutilla (1967) first identified the possibility of existence values, he developed the argument in terms of decisions that might irretrievably alter a unique natural environment. He recognized that we could conceptualize the ways these assets contribute to people's well-being by describing the services they provide. Some of them are used through in situ consumption. Other types of services do not require consumers to visit the site or otherwise "reveal" their preferences.

Early conceptual literature in this area sought to develop Krutilla's arguments in three ways. First, these values are *from* people *for* elements of their natural environment. They are *not* inherent to the resources being valued, as suggested by some ecologists. Second, because they are not confined to people who never use a resource, analytical research has focused on defining existence values in ways that distinguish them from use values. (See McConnell 1983; Boyle and Bishop 1987; Smith 1987; Freeman forthcoming; and Randall 1991.) Third, because these values initially were regarded as fundamentally different from use-generated benefits, some of the early discussion focused on the motives (i.e., bequest and stewardship) that might assist in understanding them. In some respects, all of this discussion has missed a fundamental insight into existence values independently identified by Plourde (1975) and then somewhat later by McConnell (1983) in his analytical definition of existence values. We can envision them as arising from *pure public good* services provided by environmental assets. This is not simply a semantic distinction. It implies that we do not need to rethink our descriptions of consumption to justify existence (or equivalently nonuse) values. Instead, research must explore how to describe the public good services underlying nonuse values, both analytically and to respondents in surveys (in the context of CVM applications).

To date the analytical literature begins with a very general characterization using an indirect utility function, such as equation [1].

$$V(Y, P, Q) = U. \tag{1}$$

Y designates the individual's income, P a vector of prices for private goods available on markets (or through defined conditions of access such as recreation sites), and Q a measure (or a vector of measures) of the service(s) of the environmental resource(s). Distinctions between use and nonuse values are described by introducing constraints that link one or more of the goods rationed by prices to Q. (See Madriaga and McConnell 1987, Boyle and Bishop 1987, Smith 1987, or Randall 1991 as examples.) One such constraint might suggest that when Q falls below some level, it is equivalent to driving the prices for some types of uses to infinity (Boyle and Bishop 1987, 945). Others distinguish the pure existence values associated with losing a resources or species from changes in its quality or quantity.

Hanemann (1988) represents these concepts somewhat more directly by rewriting [1] with a separate subfunction, $v(\cdot)$, as in equation [2].

$$\tilde{V}(v(Y, P, Q), Q) = U. \tag{2}$$

Use value for Q is then defined by the increment to Y that would hold the level of the subfunction $v(\cdot)$ constant as Q changed. Total value is the increment to Y that holds the function $\tilde{V}(\cdot)$ constant when Q changes. The difference between these increments to Y is a measure of nonuse value. What is missing in this analytical treatment is a description of why Q should have these two roles in preferences and how they might relate to the issues involved in applications. A diverse set of research provides some insights into how these questions might be answered.

First, Randall and Stoll (1983) and Bishop (1986) suggest that closer scrutiny of individuals' motives for valuing Q should identify attitudes consistent with the contributions we hypothesize underlie Q's separate contribution to $\tilde{V}(\cdot)$. This argument and the formulation in equation [2] is somewhat similar to Andreoni's (1989) description of multiple influences on charitable donations. There are, however, differences. My point here is that there is an analytical similarity between these modeling structures with an important amendment to equation [2]. The Q in $v(\cdot)$ must be replaced by the individual's donation. q_i, and Q in $\tilde{V}(\cdot)$ is represented as

$$q_i + \sum_{j \neq i} q_j,$$

where the second term accounts for all others' donations (i.e., the q_j's represent others' contributions). This definition specifies a link between private satisfaction arising from increases in private donations (or "warm glow"), $(\partial \tilde{V}/\partial v) \cdot (\partial v/\partial q_i)$, and their role through more generalized motives for altruism, $(\partial V/\partial Q) \cdot (\partial Q/\partial q_i)$, (with $(\partial Q/\partial q_i) = 1$ from the definition of the connection between private donations and the "public" effect). With this change, arguments that people have "warm glow" and altruisitic motives for donations can be seen as nothing more than suggestions that charity is a mixed public/private good (see Cornes and Sandler 1986). q_i is completely analogous to a private good, and the simple additive form determining Q is one form of Hirshleifer's (1983) social composition function. When the argument is applied to the case of use/nonuse values, it has no specific implications about how many resources provide equivalent services to those underlying the nonuse (or existence) values. Unfortunately, some discussions of the Andreoni model seem to argue that this similarity in analytical structure implies that charitable contributions for any activity are a substitute source for the services underlying the nonuse values of a specific environmental resource. The issues involved in identifying those resources that provide substitute services for the private contribution (i.e., q_i) to utility versus the public component pose empirical questions that have not been carefully addressed.

What can be said at this stage is that these types of connections parallel the definitions used for mixed public/private goods and seem likely to provide opportunities for enhancing our understanding of the connections between the private (or use-related) services of an environmental resource and the public for nonuse) services. For example, retaining the Hanemann formulation, the Q in $v(\cdot)$ could be replaced by the services (or quality) of a resource experienced during the in situ consumption underlying use values. This could be specified as an argument in the function defining the Q appearing in $\tilde{V}(\cdot)$. Other arguments determining the Q appearing in $\tilde{V}(\cdot)$ could include other people's experiences with the resource or measures of the services available from other resources (reflecting Randall and Stoll's 1983 Q altruism). The function describing Q must satisfy some restrictions. Nothing in Hanemann's (1988) description or the present more restricted version of it requires Q to have public good characteristics. Both treatments focus on the features of an individual's preference function. For Q to represent services underlying nonuse values, it must be capable of changing without an individual undertaking any actions. Thus, including others' consumption of q_j's in the function or levels of other resources not experienced through any actions by the individual are ways of accomplishing this objective. They are not the only ones. In order for this type of change in Q to occur, the factors altering Q must be nonappropriable and nonexcludable—in other words they must satisfy the requirements of a public good.

The function describing Q can be quite general. For example, if the nonuse services are described as the minimum of the amounts of environmental services from a specific resource available to all citizens, then the services of Q available to any one person would not be disturbed so long as that minimum remained unaffected. Losses experienced by reductions in services for those who previously enjoyed greater use levels would not influence the services underlying this specification of the source of nonuse value, provided they did not affect this minimum. Of course, the arguments could also be perceived as services from other resources. These examples are not intended to promote any specific formulation. Instead, they suggest that greater attention to available insights on how private and public aspects of the goods influence behavior (i.e., incentives for free riding) may yield insights for representing nonuse services. A focus on the source of services underlying nonuse values highlights an issue overlooked by attempts in the current analytical literature to partition use and nonuse values. Use values may well depend on the level of services attributed to nonuse values. This is recognized in the earlier literature only at the point where the threshold level of the resource precludes any use-related services.

V. Heterogenous Preferences and the Geographic Extent of the Market

Several factors contribute to making the available information on the values people place on services from nonmarketed resources inadequate for measuring the value of natural resources as assets. Refining the indirect methods for measuring the values people place on nonmarketed resources highlighted the importance of beginning the analysis at the micro level. As a consequence, our attention shifted from aggregated models hypothesized to describe some population's "rate-of-use" to specific descriptions of individuals' patterns of use. With this reorientation, we began to focus on the representative individual's value for a resource's services. To acquire the necessary data (within existing research budgets), our analyses concentrated on surveys of in situ users. Thus, we have little basis for knowing how changes in the resource will affect aggregate levels of use.

The process of translating per-unit values for an asset's services to the value of the asset itself requires that the analyst define the geographic extent of the market. I borrowed this term from the literature of applied industrial organization. With nonmarket resources, however, we do not have the co-movements in prices (across related commodities or geographic locations) to assist in defining market boundaries. Instead we must complete a specific analysis that answers these questions: (a) who cares about the change? and (b) how do their values vary both with what is changed *and* with their individual characteristics?

We have a pragmatic motivation for paying more attention to this problem. Definitions of the extent of the market are probably more important to the values attributed to environmental resources as assets than any changes that might arise from refining our estimates of per-unit values. While the greatest attention on evaluating CVM versus indirect methods focuses on whether they are within 50 or 100 percent of each other, what separates different analysts' evaluations of the values for environmental resources is more likely to be their assumptions about who holds these "representative" values.

Kopp and I recently undertook a detailed appraisal of the assumptions distinguishing plaintiff's and defendant's estimates of the natural resource damages associated with the contamination of a five-mile stretch of a river by mine wastes (see Kopp and Smith 1989). Estimates by the plaintiff's analysts were about one hundred times greater than those of the defendant's analysts (i.e., $15 million versus $140,000). Yet closer inspection of the models underlying each aggregate value (as well as the constituent assumptions required to estimate the present value of the losses) revealed fairly close correspondence in assumptions. Indeed, one analyst for the plaintiff used CVM surveys and estimated that each household would place an annual value of $5.60 on restoring this section of the river. By contrast, estimates by the defendant's analysts were either large or comparable on a per-household basis: $8.34 annually for fishing and $5.50 for non-water-based activities. The differences are largely explained by the assumptions each side made about the geographic extent of the market.

For use values, answers to these questions seem reasonably straightforward. Economists simply have not had the proper data to investigate the question. The problems are more complex for nonuse values, and they must be resolved if a total value framework is to be used for estimating the values generated by each environmental resource as an asset. While analysts increasingly recognize the importance of developing an analytical framework for describing why people value the public good services of environmental resources, a common theoretical structure is not yet available. Instead definitions of the relevant market must rely on inductive methods that use survey research to understand why some people have appreciable nonuse values and others do not.

VI. A Valuation Protocol

Analysts now generally recognize that economic methods can be used to estimate values for some types of environmental services. Especially important, the accumulated empirical experience has provided a reasonably good inventory of the features of travel cost, hedonic, and CVM analyses that are likely to be important to the reliability of their valuation estimates for environmental resources. However, moving from a literature consisting of diverse valuation case studies to a more systematic set of benefit measures capable of being consistently aggregated or disaggregated will require a standardized set of definitions of the "commodities" (i.e., services) provided by environmental resources. These definitions do not require that we treat similar resources as indistinguishable. We routinely encounter heterogeneity problems in defining marketable commodities because diverse arrays of varieties are available for most products. In these cases, we rely on prices to facilitate the measurement of aggregates. We could, in principle, rely on differences in the value functions across similar nonmarket resources. First we must develop a definitional structure to organize the commodities into classes. Any classification is arbitrary to some degree. What must be recognized and accepted is that we are already constructing analyses using implicit taxonomies for the services of environmental resources, either in terms of effects or in terms of classifications of the resources. Sometimes both are used.

Because these classifications define an aggregation structure for environmental services, research should be directed at evaluating whether the candidate systems are:

- consistent with people's perceptions of the resources' services;
- compatible with the constraints and interrelationships between the natural assets supporting these services; and
- responsive to policy needs for valuation information.

Resource-related agencies are taking some steps in these directions through the development of databases to document benefit studies and guidelines for short-term (Type A) and more extensive (Type B) natural resource damage assessments. What we need is a methodology for valuing and quantifying nonmarketed environmental resources that is comparable to what one finds on the theory and implementation of price and quantity indexes. Progress on these issues will require closer coordination of research to link the insights available from contingent valuation with what can be learned from indirect methods.

REFERENCES

Adamowicz, Viktor L., and Theodore Graham-Tomasi. 1991. "Revealed Preference Tests of Nonmarket Goods Valuation Methods." *Journal of Environmental Economics and Management* 1 (Jan.):29–45.

Adamowicz, Viktor L., Gerald L. Fletcher, and Theodore Graham-Tomasi. 1989. "Functional Form and the Statistical Properties of Welfare Measures." *American Journal of Agricultural Economics* 7 (May):414–21.

Andreoni, James. 1989. "Giving With Impure Altruism: Applications to Charity and Ricardian Equivalence." *Journal of Political Economy* 97 (Dec.):1447–58.

Bishop, Richard C. 1986. "Resource Valuation Under Uncertainty: Theoretical Principles for Empirical Research." In *Advances in Applied Micro Economics*, ed. V. Kerry Smith. Greenwich, CT: JAI Press.

Bishop, Richard C., and Thomas A. Heberlein. 1990. "The Contingent Valuation Method," In *Economic Valuation of Natural Resources. Issues, Theory and Applications*, eds. R. L. Johnson and G. V. Johnson. Boulder, CO: Westview Press.

Bockstael, Nancy E., and Kenneth E. McConnell. 1983. "Welfare Measurement in the Household Production Framework." *American Economic Review* 73 (Sept.):806–14.

———. 1991. "The Demand for Quality Differentiated Goods: A Synthesis." Working paper, Department of Agricultural and Resource Economics, University of Maryland, College Park, January.

Bockstael, Nancy E., Kenneth E. McConnell, and Ivar E. Strand, Jr. 1991. "Recreation." In *Measuring the Demand for Environmental Quality*, ed. John Braden and Charles D. Kolstad. Amsterdam: North Holland.

Bockstael, Nancy E., Ivar E. Strand, Jr., and W. Michael Hanemann. 1987. "Time and the Recreational Demand Model." *American Journal of Agricultural Economics* 69 (May):293–302.

Bohm, Peter. 1972. "Estimating Demand for Public Goods: An Experiment." *European Economic Review* 3:111–30.

Boyle, K. J., and R. C. Bishop. 1987. "The Total Value of Wildlife: A Case Study Involving Endangered Species." *Water Resources Research* 23 (May):943–50.

Breen, Barry. 1989. "Citizen Suits for Natural Resource Damages: Closing a Gap in Federal Environmental Law." *Wake Forest Law Review* 24:851–80.

Brookshire, David S., and Don L. Coursey. 1987. "Measuring the Value of a Public Good: An Empirical Comparison of Elicitation Procedures." *American Economic Review* 77 (Sept.):554–66.

Brookshire, David S., Mark A. Thayer, William D. Schulze, and Ralph C. d'Arge. 1982. "Valuing Public Goods: A Comparison of Survey and Hedonic Approaches." *American Economic Review* (Mar.):165–77.

Cairncross, Frances. 1992. *Costing the Earth*. Boston: Harvard Business School Press.

Cameron, Trudy Ann. 1992. "Combining Contingent Valuation and Travel Cost Data for the Valuation of Nonmarket Goods." *Land Economics* 68 (Aug.):302–17.

Carlson, John A., and Don R. Pescatrice. 1980. "Persistent Price Distributions." *Journal of Economics and Business* 33 (Fall):21–27.

Carson, Richard T., and W. Michael Hanemann. 1992. "The Exxon Valdez Damage Assessment Process." Presented at the American Association of Agricultural Economists annual meetings, Baltimore, August 10.

Cicchetti, Charles J., and V. Kerry Smith. 1973. "Congestion, Quality Deterioration and Optimal Use: Wilderness Recreation in the Spanish Peaks Primitive Area." *Social Science Research* 2 (Mar.):15–30.

Ciriacy-Wantrup, S. V. 1947. "Capital Returns from Soil-Conservation Practices." *Journal of Farm Economics* 29:1181–96.

Cornes, Richard, and Todd Sandler. 1986. *The Theory of Externalities, Public Goods, and Club Goods*. Cambridge: Cambridge University Press.

Cropper, Maureen L., Leland B. Deck, and K. E. McConnell. 1988. "On the Choice of Functional Form for Hedonic Price Functions." *Review of Economics and Statistics* 70 (Nov.):668–75.

Cummings, Ronald G., David S. Brookshire, and William D. Schulze, eds. 1986. *Valuing Public Goods: A State of the Arts Assessment of the contingent Valuation Method*. Totowa, NJ: Rowman and Allanheld.

Cummings, Ronald G., William D. Schulze, Shelby Gerking, and David Brookshire. 1986. "Measuring the Elasticity of Substitution of Wages for Municipal Infrastructure: A Comparison of the Survey and Wage Hedonic Approaches." *Journal of Environmental Economics and Management* 13 (Sept.):269–76.

Davis, Robert K. 1964. *The Value of Outdoor Recreation: An Economic Study of the Maine Woods*. Ph.D. thesis, Harvard University.

Desvousges, W. H., F. R. Johnson, R. W. Dunford, K. J. Boyle, S. P. Hudson, and K. N. Wilson. 1992. "Measuring Natural Resource Damages with Contingent Valuation: Tests of Validity and Reliability." Presented at symposium, Contingent Valuation: A Critical Assessment, Washington, DC, April 2–3. Cambridge, MA: Cambridge Economics, Inc.

Diamond, P. A., J. A. Hausman, G. K. Leonard, and M. A. Denning. 1992. "Does Contingent Valuation Measure Preferences? Experimental Evidence." Presented at symposium, Contingent Valuation: A Critical Assessment, Washington, DC, April 2–3. Cambridge, MA: Cambridge Economics, Inc.

Dickie, Mark, Ann Fisher, and Shelby Gerking. 1987. "Market Transactions and Hypothetical Demand Data: A Comparative Study." *Journal of the American Statistical Association* 82 (Mar.):69–75.

Diewert, W. Erwin. 1976. "Harberger's Welfare Indicator and Revealed Preference Theory." *American Economic Review* 66 (Mar.):143–52.

———. 1989. "Exact and Superlative Welfare Change Indicators." Discussion paper No. 89–27, Department of Economics, University of British Columbia, November.

Duffield, John W., and David A. Patterson. 1992. "Field Testing Existence Values: An Instream Flow Trust Fund for Montana Rivers." Paper presented at Association of Environmental and Resource Economists meeting, New Orleans, January.

Fischhoff, Baruch, and Lita Furby. 1988. "Measuring Values: A Conceptual Framework for Interpreting Transactions with Special Reference to Contingent Valuation of Visibility." *Journal of Risk and Uncertainty* 1 (June):147–84.

Freeman, A. Myrick, III. 1979. *The Benefits of Environmental Improvement: Theory and Practice*. Baltimore: Johns Hopkins University.

———. Forthcoming. "Nonuse Values in Natural Resource Damage Assessment." In *Valuing Natural Resources*, ed. R. J. Kopp and V. K. Smith. Washington, DC: Resources for the Future.

Gilbert, Carol C. S. 1985. *Household Adjustment and the Measurement of Benefits from Environmental Quality*. Ph.D. thesis, University of North Carolina, Chapel Hill.

Graves, Phil, James C. Murdoch, Mark A. Thayer, and Don Waldman. 1988. "The Robustness of Hedonic Price Estimation: Urban Air Quality." *Land Economics* 64 (Aug.):220–33.

Hammack, Judd, and Gardner M. Brown, Jr. 1974. *Waterfowl and Wetlands: Toward Bioeconomic Analysis*. Washington, DC: Johns Hopkins University Press for Resources for the Future.

Hanemann, W. Michael. 1988. "Three Approaches to Defining 'Existence' or Nonuse Values Under Certainty." Department of Agricultural and Resource Economics, University of California, Berkeley, July.

———. 1991. "Willingness to Pay versus Willingness to Accept: How Much Can They Differ?" *American Economic Review* 81 (June):635–47.

Hausman, Jerry A. 1981. "Exact Consumer's Surplus and Deadweight Loss." *American Economic Review* 71 (Sept.):662–76.

Hirshleifer, Jack. 1983. "From Weakest-Link to Best Shot: The Voluntary Provision of Public Goods." *Public Choice* 41 (3):371–86 and correction in *Public Choice* (1985).

Hotelling, Harold. Dated 1947. Letter to National Park Service in *An Economic Study of the Monetary Evaluation of Recreation in the National Parks* (U.S. Department of the Interior, National Park Service and Recreational Planning Division, 1949).

Huang, Ju Chin, Douglas W. Nychka, and V. Kerry Smith. 1992. "Parametric and Nonparametric Estimates of Willingness to Pay with Discrete Choice Random Utility Models." Paper in preparation, Resource and Environmental Economics Program, North Carolina State University.

Jakus, Paul M., and V. Kerry Smith. 1992. "Measuring Use and Nonuse Values for Landscape Amenities: A Contingent Behavior Analysis of Gypsy Moth Control." Paper presented at annual meetings of the Association of Environmental and Resource Economists, New Orleans, January.

Kealy, Mary Jo, Mark Montgomery, and John F. Dovido. 1990. "Reliability and Predictive Validity of Contingent Values: Does the Nature of the Good Matter? *Journal of Environmental Economics and Management* 19 (Nov.):244–63.

Kemp, M. A., and C. Maxwell. 1992. "Exploring a Budget Context for Contingent Valuation Estimates." Presented at symposium, Contingent Valuation: A Critical Assessment, Washington, DC, April 2–3. Cambridge, MA: Cambridge Economics, Inc.

Kling, Catherine L. 1988. "Comparing Welfare Estimates of Environmental Quality Changes from Recreation Demand Models." *Journal of Environmental Economics and Management* 15 (Sept.):331–40.

Kling, Catherine L., and Marcia Weinberg. 1990. "Evaluating Estimates of Environmental Benefits Based on Multiple Site Demand Models: A Simulation Approach." In *Advances in Applied Micro-Economics*, Vol. V, eds. V. K. Smith and A. N. Link. Greenwich, CT: JAI Press.

Knetsch, Jack L., and Robert K. Davis. 1966. "Comparison of Methods for Recreation Evaluation." In *Water Research*, eds. A. V. Kneese and S. C. Smith. Baltimore: Johns Hopkins Press.

Kopp, Raymond J., Paul R. Portney, and V. Kerry Smith. 1990. "The Economics of Natural Resource Damages after Ohio v. U.S. Department of the Interior." *Environmental Law Reporter* 20 (Apr.):10127–31.

Kopp, Raymond J., and V. Kerry Smith. 1989. "Benefit Estimation Goes to Court: The Case of Natural Resource Damage Assessments." *Journal of Policy Analysis and Management* 8 (Fall):593–612.

Krutilla, John V. 1967. "Conservation Reconsidered." *American Economic Review* 47 (Sept.):777–86.

LaFrance, Jeffrey L., and W. Michael Hanemann. 1989. "The Dual Structure of Incomplete Demand Systems." *American Journal of Agricultural Economics* 71 (May):262–74.

Larson, Douglas M. 1990. "Measuring Willingness to Pay for Nonmarket Goods." Paper presented at American Agricultural Economics Association Meetings, Vancouver, August 4–8.

———. 1991. "Recovering Weakly Complementary Preferences." *Journal of Environmental Economics and Management* 21 (Sept.):97–108.

Loomis, John B. 1989. "Test-Retest Reliability of Contingent Valuation Method: A Comparison of General Population and Visitor Response." *American Journal of Agricultural Economics* 71 (Feb.):76–84.

———. 1990. "Comparative Reliability of the Dichotomous Choice and Open-Ended Contingent Valuation Techniques." *Journal of Environmental Economics and Management* 18 (Jan.):78–85.

Madriaga, Bruce, and K. E. McConnell. 1987. "Exploring Existence Values." *Water Resources Research* 23 (May):936–42.

Math-Tech Inc. 1982. *Benefits Analysis of Alternative Secondary National Ambient Air Quality Standards for Sulfur Dioxide and Total Suspended Particulates*, Vol. II. Report to U.S. Environmental Protection Agency. Research Triangle Park, NC: Office of Air Quality Planning and Standards, U.S. EPA, August.

Matthews, Stephen B., and Gardner M. Brown. 1970. *Economic Evaluation of the 1967 Sport Salmon Fisheries of Washington*. Technical Report No. 2, Olympia: Washington Department of Fisheries.

McConnell, Kenneth E. 1983. "Existence and Bequest Value." In *Managing Air Quality and Scenic Resources at National Parks and Wilderness Areas*, eds. R. D. Rowe and L. G. Chestnut, Boulder, CO: Westview Press.

———. 1990. "On Site Time in the Demand for Recreation." Department of Agricultural and Resource Economics. University of Maryland, College Park.

McFadden, D. L., and G. K. Leonard. 1992. "Issues in the Contingent Valuation of Environmental Goods: Methodologies for Data Collection and Analysis." Presented at symposium, Contingent Valuation: A Critical Assessment, Washington, DC, April 2–3. Cambridge, MA: Cambridge Economics, Inc.

Mitchell, R. C., and R. T. Carson. 1989. *Using Surveys to Value Public Goods—The Contingent Valuation Method.* Washington, DC: Resources for the Future, Inc.

Neill, Jon R. 1987. "Another Theorem on Using Market Demands to Determine Willingness to Pay for Non-Traded Goods," *Journal of Environmental Economics and Management* 15 (June):224–32.

Palmquist, Raymond B. 1988. "Welfare Measurement in the Hedonic Model: The Case of Nonparametric Prices." *Journal of Environmental Economics and Management* 15 (Sept.):297–312.

———. 1991. "Hedonic Methods," In *Measuring the Demand for Environmental Quality*, eds. John Braden and Charles D. Kolstad. Amsterdam: North Holland.

Pearce, David W., Anil Markanyda, and Edward B. Barbier. 1989. *Blueprint for a Green Economy.* London: Earthscan Publications Ltd.

Plott, Charles R. 1991. "Will Economics Become an Experimental Science?" *Southern Economic Journal* 57 (Apr.):901–19.

Plourde, Charles. 1975. "Conservation of Extinguishable Species." *Natural Resources Journal* 15 (Oct.):791–97.

Pratt, John W., David A. Wise, and Richard Zeckhauser. 1979. "Price Differences in Almost Competitive Markets. *The Quarterly Journal of Economics* 93 (May):189–212.

Randall, Alan. 1991. "Nonuse Benefits." In *Measuring the Demand for Environmental Improvement*, eds. John B. Braden and Charles D. Kolstad. Amsterdam: North Holland.

Randall, Alan, Berry Ives, and Clyde Eastman. 1974. "Bidding Games for Valuation of Aesthetic Environmental Improvements." *Journal of Environmental Economics & Management* 1 (Aug.):132–49.

Randall, Alan, and John R. Stoll. 1983. Existence Value in a Total Valuation Framework. In *Managing Air Quality and Scenic Resources at National Parks and Wilderness Areas*, eds. R. D. Rowe and L. G. Chestnut. Boulder, CO: Westview Press.

Ridker, R. G., and J. A. Henning. 1967. "The Determinants of Residential Property Values with Special Reference to Air Pollution." *Review of Economics and Statistics* 49:246–57.

Seip, Kalle, and Jon Strand. 1992. "Willingness to Pay for Environmental Goods in Norway: A Contingent Valuation Study with Real Payment." *Environmental and Resource Economics* 2(1):91–106.

Seller, Christine, John R. Stoll, and Jean-Paul Chavas. 1985. "Validation of Empirical Measures of Welfare Change: A Comparison of Non-Market Techniques." *Land Economics* 61 (Dec.):926–30.

Smith, V. Kerry. 1987. "Nonuse Values in Benefit Cost Analysis." *Southern Economic Journal* 54 (July):19–26.

———. 1989. "Taking Stock of Progress with Travel Cost Recreation Demand Methods: Theory and Implementation." *Marine Resource Economics* 6:279–310.

———. 1991. "Household Production Functions and Environmental Benefit Measurement." In *Measuring the Demand for Environmental Quality*, ed. John Braden and Charles D. Kolstad. Amsterdam: North Holland.

Smith, V. Kerry, and William H. Desvousges. 1986. "Averting Behavior: Does it Exist?" *Economic Letters* 20:291–96.

Smith, V. Kerry, William H. Desvousges, and Ann Fisher. 1986. "A Comparison of Direct and Indirect Methods for Estimating Environmental Benefits." *American Journal of Agricultural Economics* 68 (May):280–89.

Smith, V. Kerry, William H. Desvousges, and Matthew P. McGivney. 1983. "The Opportunity Cost of Travel Time in Recreation Demand Models." *Land Economics* 59 (Aug.):259–78.

Smith, V. Kerry, William H. Desvousges, and John Payne. 1992. "Does the Framing of Risk Information Influence Mitigating Behavior." Resource and Environmental Economics Program. North Carolina State University, April.

Smith, V. Kerry, and Ju Chin Huang. 1991. "Meta Analyses for Nonmarket Valuation: Can Hedonic Models Value Air Quality?" Presented at the National Bureau of Economic Research Conference, Resource and Environmental Economics Program, North Carolina State University, December.

Smith, V. Kerry, and Yoshiaki Kaoru. 1990a. "What Have We Learned Since Hotelling's Letter? A Meta Analysis." *Economic Letters* 32:267–72.

———. 1990b. "Signals or Noise? Explaining the Variation in Recreation Benefit Measurement." *American Journal of Agricultural Economics* 72 (May):419–33.

Smith, V. Kerry, Jin Long Liu, Mir Anjum Altaf, Haroon Jamal, and Dale Whittington. 1991. "How Reliable are Contingent Valuation Surveys for Policies in Developing Economies." Draft under revision, Resource and Environmental Economics Program, North Carolina State University.

Värtia, Y. O. 1983. "Efficient Methods of Measuring Welfare Changes and Compensated Income in Terms of Orderly Demand Functions." *Econometrica* 51 (Jan.):79–98.

Ward, Frank A., and John B. Loomis. 1986. "The Travel Cost Demand Model as an Environmental Policy Assessment Tool: A Review of Literature." *Western Journal of Agricultural Economics* 11(2):164–78.

10 *The Contingent Valuation Debate: Why Economists Should Care* *

Paul R. Portney

Paul Portney is President and Senior Fellow at Resources for the Future.

The contingent valuation method involves the use of sample surveys (questionnaires) to elicit the willingness of respondents to pay for (generally) hypothetical projects or programs. The name of the method refers to the fact that the values revealed by respondents are contingent upon the constructed or simulated market presented in the survey. A spirited (and occasionally mean-spirited) battle over such methods is currently being waged, involving competing factions within the federal government, economists and lawyers representing business and environmental groups, and interested academics as well. At issue is a seemingly quite specific question: should environmental regulations currently under development at both the Department of the Interior and the Department of Commerce sanction the use of the contingent valuation method in estimating the damage done by spills of oil, chemicals, or other substances covered by federal law? More generally, the debate raises broad questions about what economists have to say about the values that individuals place on public or private goods.

The two papers that follow this one make cases for and against the use of the contingent valuation method. My aim here is to provide an overview of the technique and the debate surrounding it. I also want to suggest why this debate should matter to economists, both professionally and in their roles as citizens and consumers.

"The Contingency Valuation Debate: Why Economists Should Care," by Paul R. Portney, from *Journal of Economic Perspectives*, 8(4):3–17 (Fall 1994).

*For helpful comments on earlier drafts of this paper, thanks are due Kenneth Arrow, Richard Carson, Ronald Cummings, Peter Diamond, Rick Freeman, Michael Hanemann, Glen Harrison, Barbara Kanninen, Raymond Kopp, Alan Keuger, Edward Leamer, Robert Mitchell, Richard Schmalensee, Howard Schuman, Carl Shapiro, Robert Solow, and especially Kerry Smith and Timothy Taylor. Taylor's many editorial suggestions improved the paper greatly. Any errors are the author's responsibility alone.

The Origins of the Contingent Valuation Method

As is often the case, it is useful to start with a bit of history.[1]

The first published reference to the contingent valuation method apparently occurred in 1947, when Ciriacy-Wantrup wrote about the benefits of preventing soil erosion (Ciriacy-Wantrup, 1947). He observed that some of these favorable effects (like reduced siltation of streams) were public goods, and suggested that one way to obtain information on the demand for these goods would be to ask individuals directly how much they would be willing to pay for successive increments. However, he never attempted to implement this idea directly.

It wasn't until almost two decades later that the contingent valuation method began to be applied in academic research. In his efforts to determine the value to hunters and wilderness lovers of a particular recreational area, Davis (1963) designed and implemented the first contingent valuation survey that attempted to elicit these values directly.

As a test for the reasonableness of his findings, Davis compared them with an estimate of willingness-to-pay that was based on the "travel cost" approach. The notion here, first suggested by Hotelling in a letter to the National Park Service in 1947, is that the "price" for visiting a park or other recreational area (even one for which entry is free) will vary according to the travel costs of visitors coming from different places (see also Clawson, 1959). Thus, a natural experiment exists where one can measure the quantity of visits to the park demanded by people at a range of prices (that is, coming from different distances) and estimate a demand curve, consumer surplus, and so on. Davis found that the travel cost method of estimating willingness to pay for visits to a recreation area provided a quite similar answer to his contingent valuation survey.

Natural resource and environmental economics then took an enormous jump when John Krutilla published "Conservation Reconsidered," arguably the most influential paper ever written in that subdiscipline (Krutilla, 1967). In less than ten pages, Krutilla identified the importance of the essentially irreversible nature of the development of natural environments, suggested that the divergence between willingness-to-pay and willingness-to-accept compensation for what he called "grand scenic wonders" may be especially large,[2] pointed to the potentially large economic value of preserving genetic variation, and foreshadowed the apparently growing value of outdoor recreation and wilderness preservation relative to what he referred to as "fabricated goods." Most important for our purposes here, Krutilla raised the possibility in this paper of what is now known as "existence value." This is the value that individuals may attach to the mere knowledge that rare and diverse species, unique natural environments, or other "goods" exist, even

---

[1]For a more elegant and detailed history, see Hanemann (1992).
[2]Hanemann (1991) explores this question in a rigorous way.

if these individuals do not contemplate ever making active use of or bene-fitting in a more direct way from them. Existence value is sometimes re-ferred to as nonuse or passive use value to suggest that the utility derived does not depend on any direct or indirect interaction with the resource or good in question.

Since then, researchers in natural resource and environmental eco-nomics (and other branches of economics as well) have made increasing use of contingent valuation techniques to estimate existence values and many other things, as well.[3] For instance, surveys were used to elicit indi-viduals' willingness to pay for such things as a reduction in household soil-ing and cleaning (Ridker, 1967), the rights to hunt waterfowl (Hammack and Brown, 1974), reduced congestion in wilderness areas (Cicchetti and Smith, 1973), improved visibility in the Southwest (Randall, Ives, and East-man, 1974), and the value of duck hunting permits (Bishop and Heberlein, 1979), to name but a few. Moreover, contingent valuation methods have been used for the valuation of a large number of non-environmental poli-cies or programs, such as reduced risk of death from heart attack (Acton, 1973), reduced risk of respiratory disease (Krupnick and Cropper, 1992), and improved information about grocery store prices (Devine and Marion, 1979).

But while such studies formed a sort of academic industry, none of them were designed or implemented with litigation in mind. It was not until the late 1980s that contingent valuation studies began to receive the kind of scrutiny routinely devoted to the evidence in high-stakes legal proceedings.

Describing the Methodology

There is no standard approach to the design of a contingent valuation sur-vey. Nevertheless, virtually every application consists of several well-defined elements.[4]

First, a survey must contain a scenario or description of the (hypo-thetical or real) policy or program the respondent is being asked to value or vote upon. Sticking to environmental issues, this might be a regulatory program that will reduce air pollution concentrations, a land acquisition program to protect wildlife habitats, or a program to reduce the likelihood of oil spills, to name but a few. In some cases, these scenarios are quite de-tailed, providing information on the expected effects of the program as well as the likely course of events should the program not be adopted. For in-stance, the scenario might contain an estimate of the reduction in annual

---

[3]For an extraordinary bibliography of papers and studies related to the contingent valuation method, a bibliography that includes 1674 entries, see Carson et al. (1994).

[4]For a thorough description of the contingent valuation method, see Mitchell and Carson (1989).

mortality risk that would be expected to accompany an improvement in air quality; or it might explain the rate at which an endangered species would be expected to recover if it was given additional protection. In other words, the scenario is intended to give the respondent a clear picture of the "good" that the respondent is being asked to value.

Next, the survey must contain a mechanism for eliciting value or a choice from the respondent. These mechanisms can take many forms, including such things as open-ended questions ("What is the maximum amount you would be willing to pay for . . . ?"), bidding games ("Would you pay $5 for this program? Yes? Would you pay $10? What about . . . ?") or referendum formats ("The government is considering doing X. Your annual tax bill would go up by Y if this happens. How would you vote?").

Finally, contingent valuation surveys usually elicit information on the socioeconomic characteristics of the respondents (age, race, sex, income, education, marital status, and so on), as well as information about their environmental attitudes and/or recreational behavior, usually with an eye toward estimating a willingness-to-pay function that includes these characteristics as possible explanatory variables. They may also include follow-up questions to see if the respondent both understood and believed the information in the scenario and took the hypothetical decision-making exercise seriously.

Moving to the Policy Arena

When economists attempt to infer values, we prefer evidence based on actual market behavior, whether directly or indirectly revealed. Thus, a technique like the contingent valuation method—wherein values are inferred from individuals' stated responses to hypothetical situations—could readily be expected to stir lively debate in academic seminars and in the pages of economics journals. But why has the controversy over the contingent valuation method spilled over into the "real world," and why has it become so heated?

The answer lies in two federal laws and one very unfortunate accident. These three things have resulted in government agencies bringing lawsuits against a variety of parties in which the former are attempting to recover large sums of money from the latter for lost existence values (among other types of damages) resulting from damages to natural resources. Many regard the contingent valuation method as being the only technique currently capable of providing monetary estimates of the magnitudes of these losses.

The first law is the Comprehensive Environmental Response, Compensation and Liability Act of 1980, also referred to as CERCLA or, more commonly, as the Superfund law. Its primary purposes were to create a mechanism for identifying sites at which hazardous materials posed a threat to human health or the environment, and to establish procedures through which parties that were deemed responsible for the contamination could be identified and made to pay for the cleanup.

But the Superfund law also contains a sleeper provision: it gave government agencies the right to sue for damages to the natural resources for which they were trustees (including lakes, streams, forests, bays, bayous, marshes, land masses, and so on) resulting from discharges of hazardous substances. The Department of the Interior was subsequently directed to write regulations spelling out what kinds of damages were compensable under this section of Superfund and what kinds of techniques would be admissible for damage estimation. Thus did existence values and the contingent valuation method come to meet the real world.

In 1986, the Department of the Interior (DOI) issued these regulations.[5] Oversimplifying somewhat, the regulations specified that lost nonuse values (largely lost existence values) were recoverable under Superfund only if use values were not measurable, and—in a very qualified way—sanctioned the use of the contingent valuation technique to measure damages. In response to a number of legal challenges, in 1989 a federal court of appeals directed DOI to redraft its regulations, specifically instructing the department to give equal weight to use and nonuse values in damage assessments and to treat the contingent valuation method much more seriously as a valuation technique.[6]

To some extent, however, events overtook the Department of the Interior regulations. In March 1989, the supertanker Exxon Valdez ran aground on Bligh Reef in Prince William Sound, Alaska, spilling 11 million gallons of crude oil into the sea. Although a number of natural resource damage cases had been brought by individual states and the federal government up to that time, none of the incidents precipitating the suits had nearly the visibility and impact of that spill. Among other things, that accident dramatized the potential economic impact of the DOI regulations. Indeed, if in addition to the out-of-pocket losses suffered by fishermen, resort owners, tour guides, recreationists and others directly and indirectly harmed by the accident, Exxon would be forced to pay also for lost nonuse or existence values, the ante would be raised substantially. This possibility focused the attention of Exxon and many other companies on existence values and the contingent valuation method.

The Exxon Valdez spill also caught the attention of Congress. It promptly passed an altogether new law, the Oil Pollution Act of 1990, aimed at reducing the likelihood of future oil spills and providing for damage recovery for any spills that should occur. Under the new law, the Department of Commerce—acting through the National Oceanic and Atmospheric Administration, or NOAA—was directed to write its own regulations governing damage assessment. This became the next battlefield on which to fight about the legitimacy of existence values and the contingent valuation method.

---

[5]See 51 *Federal Register* 27674 (August 1, 1986).
[6]*State of Ohio v. United States Department of Interior*, 880 F. 2d 432 (D.C. Circuit 1989).

The NOAA Panel

The Department of the Interior had worked in relative obscurity when drafting its damage assessment regulations under Superfund. By contrast, NOAA began its parallel task under a spotlight. Environmentalists insisted that the NOAA rules parallel those of Interior, embracing lost existence values as fully compensable damages and identifying the contingent valuation method as the appropriate way to measure them. Not surprisingly, those upon whom these assessments might one day fall—led by the oil companies—pushed hard to exclude existence values and the contingent valuation method from the regulations. Amidst these conflicting pressures, and in recognition of the technical economic nature of the questions at debate, the General Counsel of NOAA, Thomas Campbell, took an unusual step. He asked Nobel laureates Kenneth Arrow and Robert Solow if they would chair a panel of experts to provide advice to NOAA on the following question: is the contingent valuation method capable of providing estimates of lost nonuse or existence values that are reliable enough to be used in natural resource damage assessments?[7]

It is important to note that the panel was *not* asked its opinion on the legitimacy of existence values *per se*. This may have been because the court of appeals had earlier ruled, in the case of the Department of the Interior regulations, that lost existence values were to be treated the same as other economic losses in damage assessments; whatever the reason, the panel was asked to confine its attention solely to the potential reliability of the contingent valuation method.

The NOAA panel met eight times between June and November of 1992. This included an extraordinary all-day hearing in August during which it heard statements from 22 experts, including several of the most prominent names in the economics profession, who either extolled the virtues of the contingent valuation method or condemned it. The panel completed its deliberations in December and, on January 11, 1993, submitted its report to NOAA. The report was published in the *Federal Register* on January 15, 1993.[8]

The NOAA panel may have managed to upset everyone with its report. Those opposed to the use of the contingent valuation method were disappointed by what many took to be the "bottom line" of the panel report. This was the phrase, " . . . the Panel concludes that CV studies [applications of the contingent valuation method] can produce estimates reliable enough to be the starting point of a judicial process of damage assessment, including lost passive-use values." Not surprisingly, this conclusion cheered those government agencies, academic researchers, and others wishing to make continued application of the contingent valuation method in their work.

Nevertheless, the panel reached this conclusion with some reluctance. I believe it fair to say that none of its members would have been comfortable with the use of any of the previous applications of the contingent valuation

---

[7]In addition to Arrow and Solow, the panel included Edward Leamer, Roy Radner, Howard Schuman (a professor of sociology and survey research expert), and myself.

[8]See 58 *Federal Register* 4601 (January 15, 1993).

THE CONTINGENT VALUATION DEBATE: WHY ECONOMISTS SHOULD CARE ~ 259

method as the basis for actual monetary damage awards. (To reiterate, none of these studies was intended for this purpose.) For this reason, the panel established a set of guidelines to which it felt future applications of the contingent valuation method should adhere, if the studies are to produce reliable estimates of lost existence values for the purposes of damage assessment or regulation. Although these guidelines are too numerous to reproduce in their entirety here, seven of the most important are summarized here.

First, applications of the contingent valuation method should rely upon personal interviews rather than telephone surveys where possible, and on the telephone surveys in preference to mail surveys.

Second, applications of the contingent valuation method should elicit willingness to pay to prevent a future incident rather than minimum compensation required for an incident that has already occurred. (Note that the latter would be the theoretically correct measure of damages for an accident that has already taken place.)

Third, applications of the contingent valuation method should utilize the referendum format; that is, the respondents should be asked how they would vote if faced with a program that would produce some kind of environmental benefit in exchange for higher taxes or product prices. The panel reasoned that because individuals are often asked to make such choices in the real world, their answers would be more likely to reflect actual valuations than if confronted with, say, open-ended questions eliciting maximum willingness to pay for the program.

Fourth, applications of the contingent valuation method must begin with a scenario that accurately and understandably describes the expected effects of the program under consideration.

Fifth, applications of the contingent valuation method must contain reminders to respondents that a willingness to pay for the program or policy in question would reduce the amount they would have available to spend on other things.

Sixth, applications of the contingent valuation method must include reminders to respondents of the substitutes for the "commodity" in question. For example, if respondents are being asked how they would vote on a measure to protect a wilderness area, they should be reminded of the other areas that already exist or are being created independent of the one in question.

Seventh, applications of the contingent valuation method should include one or more follow-up questions to ensure that respondents understood the choice they were being asked to make and to discover the reasons for their answer.

These guidelines made a number of proponents of the contingent valuation method quite unhappy. In their view, strict adherence to the panel's guidelines—especially the suggestion that in-person interviews be used to elicit values—would make it very expensive to use the contingent valuation method for damage estimation or regulatory purposes. Moreover, a number of the guidelines seem intended to ensure that applications of the contingent valuation method result in "conservative" estimates of lost existence values—that is, estimates that were more likely to underestimate than to overestimate these values.

The NOAA panel created its long list of requirements because it felt strongly that casual applications of the contingent valuation method should not be used to justify large damage awards, especially in cases where the likelihood of significant lost existence values was quite small. By establishing a series of hurdles for contingent valuation studies to meet, the panel hoped to elevate considerably the quality of future studies and thereby increase the likelihood that these studies would produce estimates that could be relied on for policy purposes.

It should be noted in closing that the NOAA panel report had no special legal standing in NOAA's deliberations. Instead, it was one of literally hundreds of submissions pertaining to the contingent valuation method that NOAA received during the time it was drafting its proposed regulations. Nevertheless, when NOAA published its long-awaited proposed rules on January 7, 1994, it said: "In proposing its standards for the use of CV [contingent valuation] in the damage assessment context, NOAA has relied heavily on the recommendations of the Panel."[9] For instance, the proposed regulations encourage trustees conducting contingent valuation studies to consider using the referendum format, and in-person interviews, as the panel had suggested. In addition, the proposed regulations include a requirement that contingent valuation studies test for the sensitivity of responses to the scope of the damage described in the scenario. The NOAA panel had suggested that if respondents were not willing to pay more to prevent more serious accidents, say, other things being equal, the contingent valuation survey was unlikely to produce reliable results. Interestingly, when the Department of the Interior re-proposed its regulations pertaining to contingent valuation on May 4, 1994, it too included a requirement that contingent valuation studies test for sensitivity to scope.[10] The papers by Diamond and Hausman and also Hanemann in this issue discuss "scope tests" in some detail.

The Importance of the Contingent Valuation Debate

Economists should have a strong interest in the debate surrounding the contingent valuation method. The most obvious reasons have to do with the economic stakes involved; but these are not the only reasons.

Natural Resource Damage Assessments

Currently, the Department of Commerce (acting through NOAA) is involved in approximately 40 lawsuits in which it is seeking to recover damages for

---

[9]See 59 *Federal Register* 1062 (January 7, 1994), p. 1143.
[10]See 59 *Federal Register* 2309 (May 4, 1994).

injury to the natural resources for which it is trustee. The Department of the Interior is involved in roughly another 20 cases. The contingent valuation method figures into no more than a dozen of these 60 or so cases, though it could prove to be quite influential in those cases.

To illustrate, consider the case of the Exxon Valdez. In late 1991, Exxon settled the natural resource damage suits brought against it by both the federal government and the State of Alaska for $1.15 billion, payable over 11 years. Yet, a state-of-the-art study done for the State in Alaska in the wake of the accident—one using the contingent valuation method to estimate lost existence values nationally—concluded that these losses alone amounted to nearly $3 billion (Carson et al., 1992). Because the case involving the Exxon Valdez was settled out of court, as have all cases involving the contingent valuation method to this point, it is impossible to know whether this study affected the size of the settlement.

It seems highly likely, however, that applications of the contingent valuation method will influence future damage awards or out-of-court settlements. Several of the most heavily regulated industries in the United States are among those affected by either Superfund or the Oil Pollution Act; the chemical and petroleum refining industries are potentially affected by both statutes. This in turn has implications for the amount of deterrence they and others will undertake. If existing state and federal environmental regulations, coupled with the specter of tort liability, already induce something close to the "right" amount of preventive activity by firms in these industries, the possibility of additional liability for lost existence values will push firms beyond the social optimum. On the other hand, if lost existence values are widely accepted as real economic losses that these firms have been ignoring heretofore, the imposition of liability for these losses may move firms closer to the optimum.

These cases alluded to earlier do not provide the only opportunity for damage recovery under Superfund. Currently, there are more than 1,200 sites on EPA's National Priorities List—the list of sites which can be cleaned up using money from the trust fund created for that purpose. Once the appropriate remedy has been selected and implemented at each of these sites, and once liability for the cost of this cleanup has been affixed, the trustees for any damaged resources, such as contaminated groundwater, can bring natural resource damage suits against the responsible parties. In these cases, contingent valuation could be used to estimate possible lost existence values.

New Regulations

Virtually all of the attention that the contingent valuation method has attracted in the policy world has been in the context of natural resource damage assessments under Superfund and the Oil Pollution Act. Nevertheless, I believe that the most significant applications of the contingent valuation method will involve the estimation of the benefits and costs of proposed regulations under Superfund and particularly other environmental laws.

Regulated entities in the United States—private firms, agencies at the federal, state, and local levels, and individuals—currently spend an estimated $130 billion annually to comply with federal environmental regulations alone (EPA, 1990). This is about 2.2 percent of GDP, a larger fraction than is devoted to environmental compliance expenditures anywhere else in the world. Much less is known about the annual compliance expenditures necessitated by other federal regulatory agencies. However, based on a comprehensive review of previous analyses, Hopkins (1992) cautiously estimated that annual compliance expenditures for all federal regulation, environmental and otherwise, were in the vicinity of $400 billion.

Under Executive Order 12044 issued by President Carter, Executive Order 12291 issued by President Reagan, and Executive Order 12866 issued by President Clinton, all federal regulatory agencies must make an effort to quantify as many of the benefits and costs of their proposed actions as possible.[11] This is where applications of the contingent valuation method will likely become important.

Imagine, for example, a proposed regulation that would cost a great deal of money but would provide relatively little in the way of direct benefits in the areas where environmental quality would improve. In such a case, it may be tempting for the regulatory agency to justify its proposed action by alleging that individuals throughout the country derive a psychological benefit (an existence value) from knowing that environmental quality has been improved in the affected areas—even though there will be no environmental improvements in the areas in which they live. A contingent valuation study might be produced to support this assertion, and might make the difference as to whether the proposal passes a benefit-cost test.

There is no reason why existence values should be unique to environmental policy, either. For instance, I might derive utility from knowing that factories are safer as a result of Occupational Safety and Health Administration regulations, that pharmaceuticals carry less risk because of the oversight of the Food and Drug Administration, and that swimming pool slides are safer because of the vigilance of the Consumer Product Safety Commission. All this may be so even though I do not work in a factory, take prescription drugs, or have a swimming pool. In other words, individuals may have existence values for many different "goods," and the inclusion of such values in a regulatory analysis could markedly alter the decision-making calculus.

Which leads me to what I believe has been an important and largely overlooked point in the debate about existence values and the contingent valuation method. To this point, proponents of the technique have envisioned its being used to estimate lost existence values and other *benefits* of

---

[11]Strangely enough, this requirement holds true even when the agency is not allowed to engage in benefit-cost balancing in setting certain kinds of standards. For example, the key sections of many environmental statutes forbid balancing benefits and costs, although such trade-offs are permitted in other parts of these laws and are even required in some other laws (Portney, 1990).

proposed regulatory programs. Thus, the business community tends to oppose such methods because it believes the methods will only be used to support expansive regulation and large damage awards.

But sauce for the goose is surely sauce for the gander. Since costs are the duals of benefits, I see no reason why the contingent valuation method cannot or should not be used for the estimation of regulatory costs as well as benefits.

Consider a hypothetical regulation that would increase costs for a number of petroleum refineries and would force several others to shut down. For the purposes of the required benefit-cost analysis, the EPA would usually count as costs the annual capital cost of the equipment installed by the refineries that would remain in operation, plus any additional annual operating and maintenance costs they would incur. An unusually thorough analysis might occasionally include the (generally temporary) loss of or reduction in income of the workers whose jobs would be lost as a result of the regulation. But typically, the extent of the cost analysis is limited to out-of-pocket expenditures for new pollution control equipment or cleaner fuels.

With contingent valuation available to measure lost existence values, the matter is surely more complicated than this.[12] If I derive some utility from the mere existence of certain natural environments I never intend to see (which I do), might I not also derive some satisfaction from knowing that refineries provide well-paying jobs for hard-working people, even though neither I nor anyone I know will ever have such a job? I believe I do. Thus, any policy change that "destroys" those jobs imposes a cost on me—a cost that, in principle, could be estimated using the contingent valuation method.

Since regulatory programs will always impose costs on someone—taking the form of higher prices, job losses, or reduced shareholder earnings—lost existence values may figure every bit as prominently on the cost side of the analytic ledger as the benefit side. To my knowledge, however, no business organization has commissioned an application of the contingent valuation method to ascertain the empirical significance of these potential additional costs, nor has any academic independently undertaken one.

If the concept of existence value comes to be more broadly interpreted in economics, as I have suggested above that it should, and *if* the contingent valuation method comes to be regarded as a reliable way to measure these values, then applied benefit-cost analysis may be forever changed. It is already difficult to conduct such analyses for government programs that

---

[12]Even without the concern raised by contingent valuation, a number of questions can be raised about the very straightforward cost analysis described here. For example, Hazilla and Kopp (1990) have shown that if one takes a general equilibrium approach to social cost estimation, very different results are obtained when compared to those from a traditional partial equilibrium analysis. This calls into question previous estimates of regulatory compliance costs (see also Jorgenson and Wilcoxen, 1990).

impose hard-to-value, non-pecuniary costs on individuals, that change the distribution of income (either at a point in time or between generations), that affect mortality or morbidity, and that involve the preservation of genetic resources.

Imagine now the difficulty of doing applied benefit-cost analysis when virtually every citizen in the United States is potentially benefitted or injured by virtually every possible program. In principle, at least, it will become extraordinarily difficult to draw bounds around those likely to gain and lose so as to facilitate valuation.

In practice, this problem may be somewhat less daunting. Perhaps it will turn out that existence values apply on the benefit side only in cases of truly unique natural environments like the Grand Canyon, irreplaceable "assets" like the Declaration of Independence, or programs that substantially improve the lives of many beneficiaries. On the other side of the ledger, perhaps only policy changes that inflict massive economic harm on certain groups of people or certain regions will generate losses among those not directly affected by the policy. If so, applied benefit-cost analysis may survive intact, but this empirical question is one that economists ought to be interested in answering.

Putting Theory Into Practice

A final set of reasons for economists to care about the contingent valuation debate have less to do with policy consequences, and more to do with how contingent valuation is affecting economic theory and the practice of empirical economics.

Whatever its shortcomings, the contingent valuation method would appear to be the only method capable of shedding light on potentially important values. Some environmental benefits can be measured in indirect ways. For example, the benefits of air quality improvements can manifest themselves in residential property values; enhanced workplace health and safety may be reflected in wage rates; improvements in recreational opportunities may be revealed in reduced travel costs. But there is simply no behavioral trace through which economists can glean information about lost existence values.

The only likely candidate for such information that I am aware of is voluntary contributions to national or international conservation organizations. But these groups typically provide their contributions with a mixture of public and private goods (an attractive magazine or calendar, for example), which makes it almost impossible to determine how much of one's contribution represents a willingness to pay for the pure preservation of unique natural area or genetic resources. In addition, many contributors to these organizations visit (make *active* use of) the protected areas, thus making it difficult to separate active from passive use values. Finally, the public good nature of the benefits of preservation means that there will be a tendency to underprovide on account of free riding.

According to proponents of the contingent valuation method, asking people directly has the potential to inform about the nature, depth, and economic significance of these values. Economists who hold this position readily admit that direct elicitation of these values will require the skills of other social scientists, including survey research specialists, cognitive psychologists, political scientists, marketing specialists, sociologists, and perhaps even philosophers. In fact, the critical scrutiny directed at the contingent valuation method has led some economists to think more deeply about cognitive processes, rationality, and the nature of preferences for *all* goods, public or private. We may, in other words, come out of this debate with an improved theory of preference and choice.

Another (and related) reason to care about the contingent valuation method debate has to do with the importance of encouraging the development of new analytical techniques. Here the parallels to experimental economics seem to me to be instructive. It was not so long ago that Vernon Smith, Charles Plott and a handful of other economists began to create artificial markets in "laboratory" settings. One purpose was to see whether hypotheses about market equilibration derived from theoretical models were borne out in laboratory settings. Since that time, experimental methods have been used to inform real-word policy-making, including, among other cases, the allocation of airport landing slots by the Civil Aeronautics Board, the auction of T-bills by the Department of Treasury, the sale of air pollution emission allowances by the Environmental Protection Agency, and the design of natural gas contracts by the Federal Energy Regulatory Commission.

Yet despite its increasing acceptance in the economics profession, and its apparent usefulness to decision makers, experimental economics has not had an easy go. Its early critics claimed that the "artificiality" of the laboratory setting rendered meaningless the findings of experimental studies. And it is my impression (but only that) that some journal editors have been reluctant to embrace papers based on experimental studies. To this day, some critics still have grave doubts about its utility.

This seems to me not unlike the state of play regarding the contingent valuation method today. Its detractors have argued that the technique is not only currently unable to provide reliable estimates of lost existence values, but also that it will never be able to do so. On the other hand, at least some proponents of the contingent valuation method appear to believe that even casual applications can produce results reliable enough to be used as the basis for potentially significant damage awards. Both views were rejected by the NOAA panel.

The present struggle is over whether some middle ground exists. There do exist quite careful and thorough applications of the contingent valuation method, with the work of Carson et al. (1992) on the Exxon Valdez oil spill being the best example. I am reluctant to assert that even this study is sufficient to justify monetary penalties. But the estimates from that study are convincing enough to me to suggest that the contingent valuation method should be the object of further research and lively intellectual debate.

Conclusion

Whether the economics profession likes it or not, it seems inevitable to me that contingent valuation methods are going to play a role in public policy formulation. Both regulatory agencies and governmental offices responsible for natural resource damage assessment are making increasing use of it in their work. This has now been reinforced by the Department of the Interior and NOAA–proposed regulations sanctioning the use of the contingent valuation method. Surely, it is better for economists to be involved at all stages of the debate about the contingent valuation method, than to stand by while others dictate the way this tool will be used.

REFERENCES

Acton, Jan, "Evaluating Public Progress to Save Lives: The Case of Heart Attacks," RAND Research Report R-73-02. Santa Monica: RAND Corporation, 1973.

Bishop, Richard, and Thomas Heberlein, "Measuring Values of Extramarket Goods: Are Indirect Measures Biased?," *American Journal of Agricultural Economics*, December 1979, *61*, 926–30.

Carson, Richard, et al., *A Contingent Valuation Study of Lost Passive Use Values Resulting From the Exxon Valdez Oil Spill*, Report to the Attorney General of the State of Alaska, prepared by Natural Resource Damage Assessment, Inc., La Jolla, California, 1992.

Carson, Richard, et al., *A Bibliography of Contingent Valuation Studies and Papers*. La Jolla, California: Natural Resources Damage Assessment, Inc., 1994.

Cicchetti, Charles J., and V. Kerry Smith, "Congestion, Quality Deterioration, and Optimal Use: Wilderness Recreation in the Spanish Peaks Primitive Area," *Social Science Research*, 1973, *2*, 15–30.

Ciriacy-Wantrup, S. V., "Capital Returns from Soil Conservation Practices," *Journal of Farm Economics*, November 1947, *29*, 1181–96.

Clawson, Marion, "Methods of Measuring the Demand for and Value of Outdoor Recreations," Reprint no. 10, Resources for the Future, Washington, D.C., 1959.

Davis, Robert, *The Value of Outdoor Recreation: An Economic Study of the Maine Woods*, doctoral dissertation in economics, Harvard University, 1963.

Devine, D. Grant, and Bruce Marion, "The Influence of Consumer Price Information on Retail Pricing and Consumer Behavior, *American Journal of Agricultural Economics*, May 1979, *61*, 228–37.

Environmental Protection Agency, *Environmental Investments: The Cost of a Clean Environment*, Report no. EPA-230-12-90-084, 1990.

Hammack, Judd, and Gardner Brown, *Waterfowl and Wetlands: Toward Bioeconomic Analysis*. Baltimore: Johns Hopkins University Press, 1974.

Hanemann, W. Michael, "Willingness to Pay and Willingness to Accept: How Much Can They Differ?," *American Economic Review*, June 1991, *81*, 635–47.

Hanemann, W. Michael, "Preface: Notes on the History of Environmental Valuation in the U.S." In Navrud, Stale, ed., *Pricing the Environment: The European Experience*. London: Oxford University Press, 1992, 9–35.

Hazilla, Michael, and Raymond Kopp, "Social Cost of Environmental Quality Regulations: A General Equilibrium Analysis," *Journal of Political Economy*, August 1990, *98*, 853–73.

Hopkins, Thomas, "The Costs of Federal Regulation," *Journal of Regulation and Social Costs*, March 1992, *2*, 5–31.

Jorgenson, Dale, and Peter Wilcoxen, "Environmental Regulation and U.S. Economic Growth," *RAND Journal of Economics*, Summer 1990, *21*, 314–40.

Krupnick, Alan, and Maureen Cropper, "The Effect of Information on Health Risk Valuation," *Journal of Risk and Uncertainty*, February 1992, *2*, 29–48.

Krutilla, John, "Conservation Reconsidered," *American Economic Review*, September 1967, *356*, 777–86.

Mitchell, Robert, and Richard Carson, *Using Surveys to Value Public Goods: The Contingent Valuation Method*. Washington, D.C.: Resources for the Future, 1989.

Portney, Paul, *Public Policies for Environmental Protection*. Washington, D.C.: Resources for the Future, 1990.

Randall, Alan, Berry Ives, and Clyde Eastman, "Bidding Games for Valuation of Aesthetic Environmental Improvements," *Journal of Environmental Economics and Management*, 1974, *1*, 132–49.

Ridker, Ronald, *The Economic Cost of Air Pollution*. New York: Praeger, 1967.

11 Valuing the Environment through Contingent Valuation*

W. Michael Hanemann

W. Michael Hanemann is Professor of Agricultural and Resuorce Economics, University of California, Berkeley.

The ability to place a monetary value on the consequences of pollution discharges is a cornerstone of the economic approach to the environment. If this cannot be done, it undercuts the use of economic principles, whether to determine the optimal level of pollution or to implement this via Pigouvian taxes or Coase-style liability rules. Sometimes, the valuation involves a straightforward application of methods for valuing market commodities, as when sparks from a passing train set fire to a wheat field. Often, however, the valuation is more difficult. Outcomes such as reducing the risk of human illness or death, maintaining populations of native fish in an estuary, or protecting visibility at national parks are not themselves goods that are bought and sold in a market. Yet, placing a monetary value on them can be essential for sound policy.

The lack of a market to generate prices for such outcomes is no accident. Markets are often missing in such cases because of the nonexcludable or nonrival nature of the damages: for those affected by it, pollution may be a public good (or bad). The public good nature of the damages from pollution has several consequences. It explains, for example, why the damages are sometimes large—only a few people may want to own a sea otter pelt, say, but many may want this animal protected in the wild. It also explains why market prices are inappropriate measures of value. In the presence of externalities, market transactions do not fully capture preferences. Collective choice is the more relevant paradigm.

This is precisely what Ciriacy-Wantrup (1947) had in mind when he first proposed the contingent valuation method. Individuals should be interviewed and "asked how much money they are willing to pay for successive additional quantities of a collective extra-market good." If the individual values are aggregated, "the result corresponds to a market-demand schedule" (p.

"Valuing the Environment Through Contingent Value," by W. Michael Hanemann, from *Journal of Economic Perspectives*, 8(4):19–43 (Fall 1994).

*I want to thank Richard Carson, Jon Krosnick, Robert Mitchell, Stanley Presser and Kerry Smith for their helpful comments, and Nicholas Flores and Sandra Hoffmann for excellent assistance. I also thank the editors, without whom this paper would be far longer.

1189). Thus, surveys offered a way to trace the demand curve for a public good that could not otherwise be gleaned from market data. Schelling (1968) made a similar point in his paper on valuing health. While the price system is one way to find out what things are worth to people, he wrote, another way is to ask people, whether through surveys or votes. Answering surveys may be hypothetical, but no more than buying unfamiliar or infrequent commodities. "In any case, relying exclusively on market valuations and denying the value of direct enquiry in the determination of government programs would depend on there being for every potential government service, a close substitute available in the market at a comparable price. It would be hard to deduce from first principles that this is bound to be the case" (pp. 143–4).

Schelling's point was not that indirect methods using market transactions have no role, but rather that they cannot always be counted on to provide a complete measure of value. Analysts can often capture some effects of a change in air quality or a change in risk to human health through a hedonic analysis that looks for evidence to property values or wage rates (Rosen, 1974). But people may also value those items in ways not reflected in wages or property values. Similarly with averting expenditures and household production models (Freeman, 1993), which rely on the demand for market commodities that are complements to, or surrogates for, the nonmarket good. If people value that good at least partly for reasons unrelated to their consumption of the complementary private goods, those methods capture just part of people's value—what is called the "use value" component, following Krutilla (1967).[1] They fail to measure the "non-use value" or "existence value" value component, which contingent valuation can capture.

An alternative is to turn to the political system, for example using collective choice models to estimate demands for local public goods (Oates, 1994). However, Cropper (1994) suggests this is unlikely to be useful for the environment because, in the United States, there are few cases where local governments actually set environmental quality. Moreover, as Chase (1968) noted, the method contains an element of circularity: a major reason for the spread of benefit-cost analysis is legislators' desire to obtain information on the public's value for government programs. While it may sometimes be desirable to leave the assessment of value to the legislative process, it is not obvious that this is always so. Measuring liability for damages from pollution is an example. In some cases one wants to ascertain how the public values something, and contingent valuation may be the only way to measure this short of a plebiscite.

Ciriacy-Wantrup (1947) recognized that surveys are not foolproof. The degree of success depends on the skill with which the survey is designed and implemented. But it was time, he felt, that economics took advantage of developments in social psychology and the newly emerging academic field of survey research: "Welfare economics could be put on a more realistic foundation if a closer cooperation between economics

---

[1] For a formal definition, see Hanemann (1994a).

and certain young branches of applied psychology could be established" (p. 1190). This finally occurred in the 1980s, and contingent valuation came of age. Two landmarks were an EPA conference in 1984 that brought together leading practitioners, other economists, and psychologists to assess the state-of-the-art (Cummings et al., 1986), and the publication of what has become the standard reference on contingent valuation, Mitchell and Carson (1989), which puts it in a broader context involving elements from economics, psychology, sociology, political science, and market research.

Contingent valuation is now used around the world (Navrud, 1992; Bateman and Willis, forthcoming), both by government agencies and the World Bank for assessing a variety of investments. A recent bibliography lists 1600 studies and papers from over 40 countries on many topics, including transportation, sanitation, health, the arts and education, as well as the environment (Carson et al., 1994c). Some notable examples are Randall, Ives and Eastman (1974) on air quality in the Four Corners area, the first major non-use value study; Brookshire et al. (1982) on air pollution in Southern California; Carson and Mitchell (1993) on national water quality benefits from the Clean Water Act; Smith and Desvousges (1986) on cleaning up the Monongahela River, Jones-Lee, Hammerton and Phillips (1985) on highway safety; Boyle, Welsh and Bishop (1993) on rafting in the Grand Canyon; Briscoe et al. (1990) on drinking water supply in Brazil; and the study on the *Exxon Valdez* oil spill I helped conduct for the State of Alaska (Carson et al., 1992).

This paper focuses generally on the use of contingent valuation to measure people's values for environmental resources, rather than specifically on natural resource damages. It will describe how researchers go about conducting reliable surveys. It then addresses some common objections to surveys and, lastly, considers the compatibility between contingent valuation and economic theory.

Conducting Reliable Surveys

In all research, details matter. How a contingent valuation survey is conducted is crucial. While there is no panacea, various procedures have been developed in recent years that enhance the credibility of a survey and make it more likely to produce reliable results. These touch all aspects, including sampling, instrument development, formulation of the valuation scenario, questionnaire structure, and data analysis. The main ways of assuring reliability are summarized here.

Suppose one approached people in a shopping mall, made them put their bags down for a moment, and asked them what was the most they would be willing to pay for a sea otter in Alaska or an expanse of wilderness in Montana. This is how the President of American Petroleum Institute and other critics have characterized contingent valuation (DiBona,

1992). The essence of their argument is summarized in titles such as "Ask a Silly Question" and "Pick a Number" (Anon., 1991; Bate, 1994). it does not require any unusual perspicacity to see that this approach is unlikely to produce reliable results. For precisely this reason, it is *not* what good contingent valuation researchers do, and it is *not* what was recommended by the NOAA Panel on Contingent Valuation (Arrow et al., 1993) described in Portney's paper in this issue.

Serious surveys of the general public avoid convenience sampling, such as stopping people in the street; they employ statistically based probability sampling.[2] They also avoid self-administered surveys, such as mail surveys or questionnaires handed out in a mall, because of the lack of control over the interview process. For a major study, the NOAA Panel recommended in-person interviews for their superior reliability. Furthermore, interviews should occur in a setting that permits respondents to reflect and give a considered opinion, such as their home. Unless the study deals with consumer products, shopping malls are a poor choice. Indeed, the only contingent valuation study where people were stopped for a few minutes in a mall was one performed for Exxon (Desvousges et al., 1992).

The crux is how one elicits value. The two key developments have been to confront subjects with a specific and realistic situation rather than an abstraction, and to use a closed-ended question which frames the valuation as voting in a referendum.

A common temptation is to characterize the object of valuation in rather general terms: "What would you pay for environmental safety?" "What would you pay for wilderness?" The problem is that these are abstractions. People's preferences are not measured in the abstract but in terms of specific items. "Paying for wilderness" is meaningless; what is meaningful is paying higher taxes or prices to finance particular actions by somebody to protect a particular wilderness in some particular manner. Therefore, one wants to confront respondents with something concrete. Moreover, one should try to avoid using counterfactuals. "What would you pay not to have had the *Exxon Valdez* oil spill?" is utterly hypothetical because one cannot undo the past. By contrast, "What would you pay for this new program that will limit damage from any future oil spills in Prince William Sound?" offers something that is tangible.

The goal in designing a contingent valuation survey is to formulate it around a specific commodity that captures what one seeks to value, yet is plausible and meaningful. The scenario for providing the commodity may be real; if not, the key is to make it seem real to respondents. They are not actually making a payment during the interview, but they are expressing their intention to pay. The vaguer and less specific the commodity and payment mechanism, the more likely respondents are to treat the valuation as

---

[2]DiBona's scenario actually was the practice in the 1930s when most surveys were "brief encounters" on the street or in stores (Smith, 1987). The 1940s saw the adoption of probability sampling, standardized survey techniques, longer and more complex survey instruments, and in-depth focused interviews (Merton and Kendall, 1946).

symbolic. To make the payment plausible, one needs to specify the details and tie them to provision of the commodity so this cannot occur without payment. There should be a clear sense of commitment; for example, if the program is approved, firms will raise prices, or the government taxes, so there is no avoiding payment once a decision is made.[3]

Until the mid-1980s, most contingent valuation surveys used some version of an open-ended question, like "What is the most you would be willing to pay for . . . ?" Since then, most major contingent valuation studies have used closed-ended questions like "If it cost x, would you be willing to pay this amount?" or "If it cost x, would you vote for this?" Different people are confronted with different dollar amounts. Plotting the proportion of "yes" responses against the dollar amount traces out the cumulative distribution function of willingness-to-pay.[4]

Of course, if people carried utility functions engraved in their brains, the question format would not matter. But they don't, and it does matter. In this country, posted prices are the norm rather than bargaining. In market transactions people usually face discrete choices: here is an item, it costs x, will you take it? Similarly in voting. Moreover, there is abundant evidence that respondents find the open-ended willingness-to-pay question much more difficult to answer than the closed-ended one; for market and nonmarket goods alike, people can generally tell you whether they would pay some particular amount, but they find it much harder to know what is the *most* that they would possibly pay. Indeed, the experience with open-ended willingness-to-pay questions for market goods is that people are more likely to tell you what the good costs than what it is worth to them. In addition to being less realistic and harder to answer, the open-ended format creates incentives which are different from those in the closed-ended format. With the open-ended format, as with an oral auction, there are strategic reasons for stating less than one's full value—a theoretical result strongly supported by experimental evidence. This is not so with a closed-ended format; there, the NOAA Panel held, there is no strategic reason for the respondent to do other than answer truthfully.[5]

For these reasons, the NOAA Panel considered the closed-ended format combined, where possible, with a voting context the most desirable for contingent valuation: "The simplest way to approach the valuation problem," it held, "is to consider a contingent valuation survey as essentially a self-contained referendum in which respondents vote to tax themselves for a particular purpose" (p. 20). This is a rather different conception of contingent valuation from asking silly questions of passers-by.

---

[3]To underscore this, the interviewer may tell respondents that the government uses surveys like this to find out whether taxpayers are willing to pay for new programs it is considering.

[4]The methodology here is to assume a random utility model for individual preferences. This can be estimated using standard techniques for binary choices. Bishop and Heberlein (1979) were the first to use this format; the link with utility theory was developed in Hanemann (1984).

[5]With auctions, it is well documented that formal matters and that oral auctions generate lower prices than posted-price auctions. Why the surprise when the same holds true for open- versus closed-ended payment questions?

In his introduction to this symposium, Portney describes other ways to make a contingent valuation questionnaire more reliable: providing adequate and accurate information; making the survey balanced and impartial; insulating it from any general dislike of big business; reminding respondents of the availability of substitutes, and of their budget constraint; facilitating "don't know" responses; allowing respondents to reconsider at the end of the interview. Several steps can be taken to eliminate any perception of interviewer pressure. At the outset, the interviewer can assure respondents that there are no "right" answers. Before asking the voting question, to legitimate a negative response, the interviewer could say something like: "We have found that some people vote for the program and others vote against. Both have good reasons for voting that way," and then list some reasons for saying "no."[6] Another possibility is if the interviewer does not actually see the respondents' votes, for example by having them write on a ballot placed in a sealed box.

A recent innovation, considered essential by the NOAA Panel, is a "debriefing" section at the end of the survey. This checks respondents' understanding and acceptance of key parts of the contingent valuation scenario. For example, was the damage as bad as described? Did you think the program would work? Did you think you really would have to pay higher taxes if the program went through? This also probes the motives for their answer to the willingness-to-pay question. What was it about the program that made you decide to vote for it? Why did you vote no? Moreover, throughout the survey, all spontaneous remarks by the respondent are recorded verbatim as they occur. After the survey, the interviewer is debriefed and asked about the circumstances of the interview, how attentive the respondent was, whether the respondent seemed to understand the questions and appeared confident in his responses. In this way, one creates a rich portrait of the interview. This information can be exploited in the data analysis. One can monitor for the misunderstandings, measure statistically how they affected respondents' willingness-to-pay, and adjust accordingly. For example, if a subject who voted "yes" appeared to be valuing something different than the survey intended, this case can be dropped or the "yes" converted to a "no."

With any data, different statistical procedures can produce different results. The closed-ended format raises several statistical issues, for example, one might summarize the willingness-to-pay distribution by using its mean, or its median, or another quantile. The mean is extremely sensitive to the right tail of the distribution; that is, to the responses of the higher bidders. For this reason, if the mean is to be used, a nonparametric or bounded influence approach is highly recommended for fitting the willingness-to-pay distribution. The median, by contrast, is usually very ro-

---

[6]For example, the interviewer might note that some people prefer to spend the money on other social or environmental problems instead, or they find the cost is more than they can afford or than the program is worth, or they cannot support the program because it would benefit only one area (Carson et al., 1992).

bust (Hanemann, 1984). Another issue is that the choice of dollar bids affects the precision with which the parameters of the willingness-to-pay distribution are estimated; significant improvements can be achieved by using optimal experimental designs (Kanninen, 1993). Statistical techniques can also be used to probe for yea-saying or other response effects, and correct for them if they are present (Hanemann and Kanninen, forthcoming).

While none of these alone is decisive, taken together they are likely to produce a reliable measure of value. Apart from the expense of in-person interviews, they are all eminently feasible.[7] Other essential ingredients are relentless attention to detail and rigorous testing of the instrument, usually in collaboration with survey experts, so that the researcher understands exactly how it works in the field and is sure it communicates what was intended.

It is no coincidence that the handful of studies that Diamond and Hausman select from the contingent valuation literature in their companion paper in this issue violate most of these precepts, as do the Exxon surveys reported in Hausman (1993). None uses in-person interviews. Many are self-administered. Most use open-ended questions. None is cast as voting.[8] Many ask questions with a remarkable lack of detail.[9] Several seem designed to highlight the symbolic aspects of valuation at the expense of substance.[10] The Exxon surveys were designed and fielded in great haste, with little pretesting, just at a time when federal agencies were gearing up for natural resource damage regulations.[11] The only way to justify this is to make the tacit assumption that, if contingent valuation is valid, details of its implementation should not matter. This is fundamentally wrong: measurement results are not invariant with respect to measurement practice in *any* science.

---

[7]Is there an acceptable alternative to in-person surveys? The NOAA Panel felt mail surveys have significant problems rendering them unsuitable. Telephone surveys avoid these problems, but preclude the use of visual aids and need to be short. The most promising alternative is a mail/telephone combination in which an information package is mailed to respondents who are then interviewed by phone (Hanemann, Loomis and Kanninen, 1991). This permits an extensive phone interview which seems to provide many of the benefits of an in-person survey at much lower cost.

[8]Two studies Diamond and Hausman cite as showing a lack of commitment in contingent valuation, Seip and Strand (1992) and Duffield and Patterson (1991), used open-ended questions about payment to an environmental charity. Most of Seip and Strand's subjects who were followed up afterwards said that they had been expressing their willingness-to-pay for environmental problems generally, rather than the particular environmental group. Careful pretesting would have discovered this beforehand.

[9]This is notably a problem in Diamond et al. (1993).

[10]Including Kahneman and Ritov (1993), Kahneman and Knetsch (1992), and Kemp and Maxwell (1993). The last two employs a "top-down" procedure in which respondents are given details of the item only *after* they value it. They are first confronted with something broad, like "preparedness for disasters." After stating their willingness-to-pay for the broad category, they are told what it comprises and asked their willingness-to-pay for *one* of those components. Then, they are told what *this* comprises, and so on. The *change* in the *quantity* of any item is never specified.

[11]Hanemann (1994a,b) critiques these studies.

Objections to Surveys

McCloskey (1985, p. 181) observes that economists generally dislike surveys: "Economists are so impressed by the confusions that might possibly arise from questionnaires that they have turned away from them entirely, and prefer the confusions resulting from external observation." In this section, I discuss four common objections to surveys.

Surveys Are Vulnerable to Response Effects

Small changes in question wording or order sometimes cause significant changes in survey responses (Schuman and Presser, 1981). Since virtually all data used in economics come from surveys (including experiments, which are a form of survey), and all surveys are vulnerable to response effects, it is important to understand why these arise and how they can be controlled. A consensus is beginning to emerge based on insights from psychology and linguistics. Answering survey questions requires some effort, usually for no apparent reward. Respondents must interpret the meaning of the question, search their memory for pertinent information, integrate this into a judgment, and communicate the judgment to the interviewer. Although some are motivated to make the effort, others may become impatient, disinterested, or tired. Instead of searching for an accurate and comprehensive answer, they satisfice, just aiming for some response that will be accepted. Furthermore, interviews are interactions governed by social and linguistic norms that shape assumptions and expectations. Viewing respondents as satisficing agents following norms of conversation has proved helpful in interpreting survey data, explaining response effects, and designing more effective surveys (Groves, 1989; Krosnick, 1991).

Not all response phenomena are equally intractable. Some, such as order effects (for example, bias towards the first item in a list), can be detected and controlled, either by choosing the sequence that produces a conservative result or by randomizing the order of items across interviews.

A second type of effect is where there is a shift in meaning. This is substance, not noise. For example, similar words turn out to mean different things: "allow" is not the same as "not forbid," nor "higher prices" the same as "higher taxes."[12] Or there are framing effects, where subjects respond differently to situations the researcher saw as equivalent. It has been shown through debriefings that the subject perceived the situations as substantively different, because either the researcher induced an unintended change in meaning or context, or the subjects made inferences that went beyond the in-

---

[12]And different words can mean the same thing, as in the movie *Annie Hall* where Woody Allen and Diane Keaton are asked by their psychiatrists how often they have sex. He says: "Hardly ever, maybe three times a week." She says: "Constantly, I'd say three times a week." With consumer expenditure surveys, Miller and Guin (1990) attest that life imitates art.

formation given (Frisch, 1993).[13] In each case, the shift in meaning is a source
of error only if the researcher is unaware of it. Through rigorous testing with
cognitive techniques, the researcher can come to understand exactly what the
instrument means to people, and what they mean in response.[14]

A third phenomenon arises from the inherent difficulty of the task assigned the respondent. In recalling past events or behavior, for example,
respondents resort to rounding, telescoping (time compression) and other
inferential strategies that yield inaccurate reports of magnitudes and frequencies.[15] Bradburn et al. (1987) emphasize that factual and attitudinal
surveys share many similar cognitive processes and errors. There is no easy
solution for recall errors. This continues to be a problem for many data
used by economists,[16] though not for contingent valuation data since there
is no recall.

One cannot avoid the fact that surveys, like all communication, are sensitive to nuance and context and are bound by constraints of human cognition. One tries to detect discrepancies and repair them, but they cannot
be entirely ruled out. It is important to keep a sense of proportion. As far
as I know, nobody has stopped using data from the Current Population
Survey, Consumer Expenditure Survey, Monthly Labor Survey, or Panel
Study on Income Dynamics because there are response effects in such surveys. The same should apply to contingent valuation surveys.

The Survey Process Creates the Values

It has been asserted that contingent valuation respondents have no real
value for the item, but just make one up during the course of the interview:
the process creates the values that it seeks to measure. Debriefings can
identify whether subjects were inattentive or unfocused and offered hasty
or ill-considered responses, and these can be discarded if desired. But, the
issue raised here is more fundamental. Diamond and Hausman feel they

---

[13]When there is incomplete information in a survey, respondents may go ahead and make their
own assumptions. Consequently, the researcher loses control over his instrument. Diamond et al.
(1993) is a contingent valuation example.

[14]On testing by federal survey agencies, see Tanur (1992). Lack of adequate testing can explain
some notable violations of procedural invariance—respondents saw cues or meaning which the researcher didn't intend and failed to detect. An example is the base rate fallacy where "when no specific information was given, prior probabilities are properly utilized; when worthless evidence is given
prior probabilities are ignored" (Tversky and Kahneman, 1974). A norm of conservation is to present
information one believes relevant. That this was the expectation of subjects could have been detected
through debriefings. On violations of conversational norms in base-rate experiments, see Krosnick,
Li and Lehman (1990).

[15]Some pronounced telescoping errors are to be found in the Alaska recreation survey conducted
by Hausman, Leonard and McFadden (1993).

[16]Juster and Stafford (1991) and Mathiowetz and Duncan (1988) discuss biases in labor supply
estimates due to problems with bunching and misreporting in Current Population Survey data. Atkinson and Micklewright (1983) discuss errors in Family Expenditure Survey reports of income and its
components. Other inconsistencies between micro- and macro-data sets for the household sector are
discussed in Maki and Nishiyama (1993).

know real preferences when they see them, and they do not see them in contingent valuation. Based on the debriefing statements in Schkade and Payne (1993) that show most subjects, faced with an open-ended willingness-to-pay question, think about either what the item could cost or what they have spent on something remotely similar, Diamond and Hausman conclude that these people are just making up their answer rather than evincing "true economic preferences." But, what are "true economic preferences?" If a subject responds thoughtfully to a question about voting to raise taxes for a public good, by what criterion is that not a valid preference?

It is true that economists often assume consumer choice reflects an individual's global evaluation of alternatives, a "top-down" or "stored-rule" decision process. The stored-rule notion traces back to Hobbes and the English empiricists who conceived of cognition in terms of storing and retrieving " slightly faded copies of sensory experiences" (Neisser, 1967). Wilson and Hodges (1992) call this the "filing cabinet" concept of the mind. It long dominated not only economics but also psychology. But it is now being abandoned in the face of accumulating evidence from the neurosciences (Rose, 1992) and elsewhere that all cognition is a constructive process—people construct their memories, their attitudes, and their judgments. The manner of construction varies with the person, the item, and the context. A general principle is that people are cognitive misers: they tend to resolve problems of reasoning and choice in the simplest way possible. This is the emerging consensus not only in survey research, but also in social psychology, political psychology, and market research (Martin and Tesser, 1992; Sniderman, Brody and Tetlock, 1991; Payne, Bettman and Johnson, 1988).

For non-habituated and complex consumer choices, people often make "bottom-up" decisions; that is, they make up a decision rule at the moment they need to use it (Bettman, 1988). Olshavsky and Granbois (1979, p. 98) found that "for many purchases a decision process never exists, not even on first purchase." Bettman and Zins (1977) found that grocery shoppers construct a choice heuristic "on the spot" about 25 percent of the time; bottom-up construction of preferences occurred especially for meat and produce "as might be expected, since consumers cannot really rely on brand name for most choices of this type," less often for beverages and dairy products "where either strong taste preferences may exist or only a limited number of brands are available" (p. 81). This calls to mind a remark by Robert Solow that the debriefings in Schkade and Payne "sound an awful lot like Bob Solow in the grocery store." I suppose critics of contingent valuation would consider that Solow does not have true economic preferences, or that he has true economic preferences when buying milk but not meat.

The real issue is not whether preferences are a construct but whether they are a *stable* construct. While this surely varies with circumstances, the evidence for contingent valuation is quite strong. There is now a number of test-retest studies in the contingent valuation literature, and these show both consistency in value over time and a high correlation at the individual level (Carson et al., 1994b). These levels of consistency are comparable to the most stable social attitudes such as political party identification.

Ordinary People Are Ill-Trained for Valuing the Environment

If, as the NOAA Panel suggests, the goal of a contingent valuation survey is to elicit people's preferences as if they were voting in a referendum, then prior experience or training are irrelevant. These are not a criterion for voting.[17] Nor is their absence an argument against contingent valuation per se. Through direct questioning, one can readily identify which respondents knew of the issue before the interview, or before the oil spill, and determine whether they hold different values from those who did not. How one proceeds in calculating aggregate willingness-to-pay is something that can be decided separately from the survey. Who has standing, and whose values should count, are questions that we as economists have no special competence to judge.

Survey Response Can't Be Verified

There are three ways to validate contingent valuation results: replication, comparison with estimates from other sources, and comparison with actual behavior where this is possible. Replication is useful even on a small scale both to see if results hold up and to check whether the instrument is communicating as intended. This is the single best way for a researcher to determine whether somebody's survey instrument works as claimed.

When contingent valuation measures direct use values, it may be possible to make a comparison with estimates obtained through indirect methods. Knetsch and Davis (1966) conducted the first test, comparing contingent valuation and travel demand estimates (a method described in Portney's paper) of willingness-to-pay for recreation in the Maine woods. The difference was less than 3 percent. There are now over 80 studies, of-

---

[17]Voter ignorance is a constant refrain for Diamond and Hausman. They use it to form a syllogism: voters are ill-informed, contingent valuation is like a referendum, therefore contingent valuation respondents are ill-informed. Both parts are false. Contingent valuation researchers take pains to ensure their samples are representative and their questionnaires intelligible, informative, and impartial, thus avoiding the vagaries of turnout and biased advertising in election campaigns. This is why political scientists are becoming interested in "deliberate polling"—in effect, extended contingent valuation surveys (Fishkin, 1991). Many analysts see a substantial core of rationality in voter behavior. Cronin (1989) finds Magleby's (1984) assessment of voter ignorance in referenda overblown. Fiorina (1981) and McKelvey and Ordeshook (1986) emphasize how campaign protagonists use signals to inform voters. Lupia (1993) analyzes the insurance reform battle in the 1988 California ballot and finds that informational "short cuts" enabled poorly informed voters to act as though they were well informed. What Sniderman (1993) calls "the new look in public opinion research" stresses how ordinary citizens use the information at hand to make sense of politics.

fering several hundred comparisons between contingent valuation and in direct methods. The results are often fairly close; overall, the contingent valuation estimates are slightly *lower* than the revealed preference estimates and highly correlated with them (Carson et al., 1994a).

The ideal is direct testing of contingent valuation predictions against actual behavior. There are about ten such tests in the literature. Diamond and Hausman mention only five of these. The ones not mentioned yield results quite favorable to contingent valuation.

Bohm (1972) conducted the first test, where subjects in Stockholm were asked their willingness-to-pay to see a new TV program. In five treatments, the program was shown if the group raised 500 Kr, with actual payment based in various ways on stated willingness-to-pay. A sixth treatment asked subjects what was the highest amount they would have given *if* they had been asked to pay an individual admission fee. The mean response was 10.2 Kr (about $2) when the group was asked a hypothetical question, versus an overall average of 8.1 Kr when the group actually paid. The difference between contingent valuation and non-contingent valuation means was not statistically significant in four of the five cases.

Bishop and Heberlein (1990) conducted a series of experiments with hunters who had applied for a deer-hunting permit in a favored game preserve run by the state of Wisconsin. The most relevant for current practice is an experiment in which they wrote to two groups of hunters offering to sell them a permit at a specified price. In one case, this was a real offer; in the other, it was asked as a hypothetical question. Estimated willingness-to-pay was $31 in the real sale versus $35 in the hypothetical sale, a statistically insignificant difference.

Dickie, Fisher and Gerking (1987) offered boxes of strawberries door-to-door at different prices. One treatment was a real offer—the household could buy any number of boxes at this price. The other asked how many boxes they *would* buy if these were offered at the given price. The resulting two demand curves were not significantly different. The parameter estimates were actually more robust over alternative model specifications for the hypothetical than the actual data (Smith, 1994).

Carson, Hanemann and Mitchell (1986) tested the accuracy of voting intentions in a water quality bond election in California in 1985. Closed-ended contingent valuation questions were placed on the Field California Poll a month before the vote, using different figures for the household cost. Adjust for "don't know" responses, the predicted proportion of yes votes at the actual cost was 70–75 percent. The ballot vote in favor was 73 percent.

Cummings, Harrison and Rutstrom (1993) offered subjects small commodities at various prices. For one group, it was a real sale. A second group was first asked a hypothetical contingent valuation question—this item is not actually for sale but, if it were, would you buy it now? The experimenter then announced that, after all, she *would* sell the item, but they should feel free to revise their answer. When juicers were the item, 11 percent actually bought them in the real sale; with the second treatment, 41 percent said they would but it if it were on sale, but then only 16 percent did. The 41 percent and 11 percent are significantly different. With calculations, 21 percent would buy in the hypothetical sale, versus 8 percent in the real sale. One wonders whether some respondents interpreted the question as "*if you needed a juicer*, would you buy this one?" Smith (1994) shows that the calculator responses do not generate a downward sloping demand curve for either the actual or hypothetical data. The experimental procedure contained nothing to emphasize commitment or counteract yea-saying in the hypothetical treatment. Cummings and his colleagues have recently added wording like the "reasons to say no" mentioned earlier. In one case, this reduced the hypothetical yes for calculators from 21 percent to 10 percent, not significantly different from the real 8 percent; in another there was no effect (Cummings, 1994).

Other contingent valuation tests have used open-ended payment questions, with predictable difficulties. Boyce et al. (1989) measured willingness-to-pay and willingness-to-accept for a house plant, with mixed results; Neill et al. (1994) measured willingness-to-pay for a map and a picture, with negative results. Both confound the issue by comparing contingent valuation responses to an experimental auction, begging the question of whether auction behavior understates willingness-to-pay. Duffield and Patterson (1991) and Seip and Strand (1992) compare actual and hypothetical contributions to an environmental cause. Diamond and Hausman focus on these studies because they showed a significant difference. But, soliciting an intention to make a charitable donation is a poor test of contingent valuation, because it invites less commitment than soliciting an intention to vote for higher taxes. To make things worse, Seip and Strand used members of the environmental group as the interviewers in their hypothetical treatment, thus increasing pressures for compliance. They compared hypothetical phone responses with responses to an actual mail solicitation. Duffield and Patterson compared hypothetical mail solicitations from the University of Montana with actual mail solicitations from the Nature Conservancy. In both studies, the difference in survey administration introduces a confounding factor which undermines the comparison.[18]

A cleaner test is provided by Sinden (1988) who conducted a series of 17 parallel experiments soliciting actual and hypothetical monetary donations to a fund for assisting soil conservation or controlling eucalypt dieback. In all 17 cases, there was no statistical difference between actual and hypothetical willingness-to-pay.

---

[18]The problem with mail surveys is that people may think the survey is junk mail and throw it out unopened. Duffield and Patterson made no allowance for the difference in sponsor identity on the envelope, which could explain the difference in response rates (Schuman, 1992). Response rates apart, the pattern of contributions was similar in the two treatments. Seip and Strand made no allowance for the fact that phone and mail solicitations generally have different response rates. Infosino (1986) found a sales rate three times higher with telephone than mail in an AT&T marketing effort.

Thus, there is some substantial evidence for the validity of contingent valuation survey responses, although more studies are certainly needed. Many existing studies do not incorporate the refinements in contingent valuation method, described earlier, that emphasize realism and commitment. In this respect, the test by Carson, Hanemann and Mitchell (1986) points in the right direction because it deals directly with expression of voting intentions. The positive results in that study are consistent with other evidence showing that polls in this country reliably indicate public sentiment at the time they are taken, and polls close to an election are generally accurate predictors of the outcome.[19] Kelley and Mirer (1974) found voting intentions correctly predicted the actual vote in four presidential elections for 83 percent of those respondents who voted.[20] Surveys of purchase intentions in market research may not be accurate predictors of subsequent purchase behavior, but surveys of voting intentions are.[21]

Contingent Valuation and Economic Theory

Critics of contingent valuation like Diamond and Hausman, and their coauthors in Hausman (1993), reject contingent valuation as a method of economic valuation because the results of contingent valuation studies are inconsistent with economic theory as they see it. These assertions have become quite widely known. However, careful examination shows that in some cases the claims are not supported by the findings in the contingent valuation literature, and in others they rest on unusual notions about what economic theory does or does not prescribe. I briefly review these issues here, leaving a more detailed treatment to Hanemann (1994a).

Diamond and Hausman, and Milgrom (1993), make a number of statements about what is a permissible argument in a utility function. They ar-

---

[19]Diamond and Hausman seem troubled that voters change their minds during the course of an election campaign. They cite a 1976 electricity rate proposition in Massachusetts where support went from 71 percent in February to 25 percent in the November ballot. They fail to mention the reasons. Magleby (1984, p. 147) identifies opposition spending as the chief cause of such opinion reversals, and that certainly occurred in 1976—opponents outspent supporters more than threefold. In May, the Dukakis administration came out against it, as eventually did businesses, the unions, hospitals, colleges, and major newspapers.

[20]Ajzen and Fishbein (1980) offer some reasons to expect a high level of attitude-behavior correspondence for voting in terms of their theory of reasoned action.

[21]One reason for the difference is timing: unlike elections, people generally control the timing of their market purchases. The result is they may end up buying the commodity, but later than they said (Juster, 1964). This is especially likely for durables, the focus of much literature, since their durability permits delay in replacement. This is consistent with findings that purchase intentions are significantly more accurate for nondurables than durables (Ferber and Piskie, 1965); intentions *not* to purchase durables are highly accurate (Theil and Kosobud, 1968); and predictions of the brand selected when the purchase *does* occur tend to be highly accurate (Ajzen and Fishbein, 1980; Warshaw, 1980).

gue that people should care about outcomes, not about the process whereby
these are generated. People should not care whether animals are killed by
man or die naturally. They should not care about details of provision or
payment for a commodity, only price. Above all, they should value things
for purely selfish motives. In their accompanying piece, Diamond and Hausman phrase this argument by saying that respondents should not contemplate "what they think is good for the country," because that reflects "warm
glow" rather than "true economic preferences."[22] From this perspective,
contingent valuation is unacceptable because it picks up existence values;
for those to be allowed in a benefit-cost analysis, Milgrom (1993, p. 431)
argues, "it would be necessary for people's individual existence values to
reflect only their own personal economic motives and not altruistic motives, or sense of duty, or moral obligation."[23]

This criticism hardly comports with the standard view in economics
that decisions about what people value should be left up to them. For example, Kenneth Arrow (1963, p. 17) wrote: "It need not be assumed here
that an individual's attitude toward different social states is determined exclusively by the commodity bundles which accrue to his lot under each.
The individual may order all social states by whatever standards he deems
relevant." Or as Gary Becker (1993, p. 386) writes: "[I]ndividuals maximize
welfare *as they conceive it*, whether they be selfish, altruistic, loyal, spite-
ful, or masochistic." When estimating demand functions for fish prior to
Vatican II, no economist ever proposed removing Catholics because they
were eating fish out of a sense of duty. Nor, when estimating collective
choice models, do we exclude childless couples who vote for school bonds
because they lack a personal economic motive.

A more substantive matter is how willingness-to-pay varies with factors that could reasonably be expected to influence it. This has been raised
in connection with the embedding effect and the income elasticity of willingness-to-pay. Regarding the latter, Diamond and Hausman assert in this
issue that the income effects measured in typical contingent valuation surveys are lower than would be expected if true preferences are measured.
McFadden and Leonard (1993, p. 185) make the more specific claim that
an income elasticity of willingness-to-pay less than unity constitutes
grounds for doubting the validity of the contingent valuation method. There
is no basis for either assertion. In the literature on the demand for state
and local government services in the United States, the income elasticities

---

[22]"Warm glow" is simply a red herring. I have seen no empirical evidence that people get a warm
glow from voting to raise their own taxes, whether in real life or in a contingent valuation study.

[23]Milgrom (1993) also asserts that using contingent valuation to measure altruistic preferences
creates double counting. His analysis has three flaws. First, it depends on the particular specification
of the utility function, as Johansson (1992) notes; if the argument of the utility function is another's
consumption rather than his utility, there is no double counting. Second, it derives its force from the
auxiliary assumption that the respondent *does not realize* that the other people for whom he cares
will have to pay, too; this is not a problem in a referendum format. Third, in many contingent valuation studies the object of the altruism is often wildlife—sea otters, for example. Since those crea-
tures are *not* surveyed, the issue of double counting is moot.

generally fall in the range 0.3 to 0.6 (Cutler, Elmendorf and Zeckhauser, 1993). With charitable giving by individuals, the income elasticities generally fall in the range of 0.4 to 0.8 (Clotfelter, 1985). The income elasticities in the contingent valuation literature vary with the item being valued, but are generally in the same range (Kristrom and Riera, 1994).

The term "embedding effect," introduced by Kahneman and Knetsch (1992), has come to mean several different things. The general notion is captured in the (mis)conception that, with contingent valuation, you get the same willingness-to-pay if you value one lake, two lakes, or ten lakes.[24] This combines three distinct notions. One assertion, which arises when the object of preference is thought to be simply the number of lakes, is that willingness-to-pay varies inadequately with changes in the scale or scope of the item being valued. This is a scope effect. Alternatively, if each lake is seen as a separate argument in the utility function, then the assertion is that a given lake has quite different value if it is first, second or tenth in a set of items to be valued—it gets a high value when the first, but it adds little or nothing to total value when second or tenth. This is a sequencing effect. Thirdly, with either preference structure, the willingness-to-pay for a composite change in a group of public goods may be less than the sum of the willingness-to-pay for the individual changes separately. This is a sub-additivity effect.

The question of how willingness-to-pay varies with the scale or scope of the item being valued in a contingent valuation survey has long been considered, starting with Cicchetti and Smith (1973) who elicited hiker's values for trips in a Montana wilderness area and found that the willingness-to-pay for trips where other hikers were encountered on two nights was 34 percent lower than the willingness-to-pay for trips with no encounters. Many other studies have since reported comparable findings using both internal (within-subject) and external (split-sample) scope tests, including meta-analyses by Walsh, Johnson and McKean (1992) covering over 100 contingent valuation studies of outdoor recreation, and Smith and Osborne (1994) on 10 contingent valuation studies of air quality. Carson (1994) reviews 27 papers with split-sample tests of scope and finds a statistically significant effect of scope on willingness-to-pay in 25 of them.

The two exceptions are Kahneman and Knetsch (1992) and Desvousges et al. (1992). Critics of contingent valuation rely heavily on these two studies when asserting the absence of scope effects in contingent valuation.[25] Some of the problems with these two studies have already been noted, including

---

[24]Though widely believed, this is a myth. It may be traced to Kahneman (1986), which is usually cited as showing that respondents were willing to pay the same amount to clean up fishing lakes in one region of Ontario as in all of Ontario. His data actually show a 50 percent difference. Moreover, the survey involved a brief telephone interview using an open-ended willingness-to-pay question. It provided no detail on how and when the cleanup would occur. Respondents may not have seen cleaning up *all* the lakes as something likely to happen soon.

[25]Also, in their contingent valuation survey, Diamond et al. (1993, pp. 45–46) mention that, using a Kruskal-Wallis test, they found no difference in willingness-to-pay for three wilderness areas ranging in size from 700,000 to 1.3 million acres. If they had run a simple regression of willingness-to-pay on acreage, they would have found a significant scope effect.

their failure to use a closed-ended voting format, the after-the-fact provision of information in Kahneman and Knetsch's "top-down" procedure, and the use of brief shopping mall intercepts by Desvousges et al.[26] The latter elicited people's willingness-to-pay for preventing the deaths of migratory waterfowl. Three separate versions of the questionnaire said that 2,000, 20,000, and 200,000 out of 85 million birds die each year from exposure to waste-oil holding ponds that could be sealed under a new program. Respondents were told that the deaths amounted to *much less than* 1 *percent* of the bird population, to *less than* 1 *percent*, and to *about* 2 *percent*. If respondents focused on the relative impact on the population, it is hard to believe that they would have perceived any real difference among these percentages. The results of the scope test depend crucially on how much one trims the data to remove what are clearly outliers. With a 10 percent trim, one obtains a highly significant scope effect.[27] At any rate, even if one regards these two studies as highly credible evidence that respondents were insensitive to scope, they certainly do not represent the majority finding in the contingent valuation literature regarding the variation of willingness-to-pay with scope.

How much should willingness-to-pay vary with scope? Diamond (1993) asserts that economic theory requires it to increase *more than proportionately* with the number of bird deaths. The variables in his model are the number of birds originally in the population, q_0, the number at risk of dying, q_R, and the number of those that are saved, q_s. Let $q_F \equiv q_0 - q_R + q_s$. Diamond assumes that people should care only about q_F, the ultimate number of birds, not how many were alive initially, at risk, or saved. He also assumes preferences are quasiconcave in q_0. The two assumptions together imply *quasiconvexity* in q_R, which is what makes the elasticity of willingness-to-pay with respect to q_R greater than unity. The conclusion depends critically on the assumption of perfect substitution between q_0, q_s, and $-q_R$. When contingent valuation data disconfirm this, Diamond dismisses the method. Others might be more inclined to believe the data and drop the assumption.[28]

---

[26]Other questions about Kahneman and Knetsch are raised by Harrison (1992) and Smith (1992).

[27]How the survey was administered clearly affected the results. Schkade and Payne (1993) used the same questionnaire as Desvouges et al., but slowed respondents down and made them think about their answer. Their data show a different pattern of willingness-to-pay responses, and a significant relationship between willingness-to-pay and the percentage of birds killed (Haneman, 1994b).

[28]Some, while not sharing Diamond's extreme position on the elasticity of willingness-to-pay, still hold that contingent valuation responses vary inadequately with scale. People's perceptions undoubtedly differ from objective measures of attributes. But this is not just a feature of contingent valuation. In psychophysics, it has been known since the 1880s that there is a general tendency for judgments of magnitude to vary inadequately. Observers standing at a distance overestimate the height of short posts, and underestimate that of tall ones; people reaching quickly for an object overestimate small distances and angles, and underestimate large ones, subjects matching loudness of a tone to a duration overestimate the loudness of short tones, and underestimate the loudness of long ones; people overestimate infrequent causes of death, and underestimate frequent ones; small probabilities are overestimated, large ones underestimated (Poulton, 1989). This "response contraction bias" in judgment or rating is an authentic feature of how people perceive the world, not an artifact of contingent valuation.

With regard to sequencing and sub-additivity effects, these effects are certainly present in contingent valuation responses, but one expects them to occur, and they can be explained in terms of substitution effects and diminishing marginal rates of substitution. When the quality of one lake improves, you value an improvement in a second lake *less* if the lakes are what Madden (1991) calls *R*-substitutes, and *more* if they are *R*-complements. Far from being inconsistent with economic preferences (Diamond et al., 1993, pp. 48–49), sub-additivity is likely to be the norm: while all goods cannot be *R*-complements, Madden shows they *can* all be *R*-substitutes.[29] Similarly, *R*-substitution explains sequence effects: if the lakes are *R*-substitutes, the willingness-to-pay for an improvement in one lake is *lower* when it comes at the end of a sequence of changes in lake improvements than at the beginning while the willingness-to-accept for the change in the lake is *higher* when it comes later in a sequence (Carson, Flores and Hanemann, 1992).[30] It should come as no surprise that the value of one commodity changes when the quantity of another varies: in other words, that willingness-to-pay depends on economic context.[31]

For many economists, the ultimate argument against contingent valuation is that it violates the habitual commitment of the profession to revealed preference. Three points should be noted. First, one must distinguish between private market goods and public goods. Revealed preference is harder to apply to the latter, especially when they are national rather than local public goods (Cropper, 1994). Second, revealed preference is not foolproof, either. It involves an extrapolation from observation of particular choices to general conclusions about preference. One relies on various auxiliary assumptions to rule out factors that might invalidate the extrapolation. Those assumptions are not themselves verifiable if one is restricted to observed behavior. This can sometimes make revealed preference a rel-

---

[29]If the intention of the Diamond et al. (1993) contingent valuation survey was to test the adding-up of willingness-to-pay, it was strangely designed for the purpose. The survey stated that there were 57 federal wilderness areas in the Rocky Mountain states, without identifying them, and said that there now was a proposal to open these to commercial development. In one version, respondents were told that seven unidentified areas had already been earmarked for development, and were asked their willingness-to-pay to protect an eighth area, identified as the Selway Bitterroot Wilderness. In another, respondents were told that eight unnamed areas had been earmarked for development and asked their willingness-to-pay to protect a ninth area, identified as the Washakie Wilderness. In a third version, respondents were told that seven unnamed areas had been earmarked for development and asked their willingness-to-pay to protect two areas identified as Selway and Washakie. In all three cases, respondents were not told the identity or fate of the other 48 or 49 areas. Given that respondents were not indifferent among wilderness areas, as evidenced by the regression mentioned in note 25, I leave it to the reader to decide whether the surveys constitute a sensible basis for testing the adding up of willingness-to-pay.

[30]In natural resource damages, where willingness-to-accept is the relevant welfare measure, this implies that the usual practice of taking the injured resource as the first item in any possible valuation sequence is a conservative procedure.

[31]The practical implications are that, when one values a program, it be placed in whatever sequence applies under the circumstances, and that one take care when extrapolating results in a benefits transfer exercise because the values might change with the difference in circumstances (Hoehn and Randall, 1989).

atively hypothetical undertaking.[32] Third, there is no reason why observing people's behavior and asking them about behavioral intentions and motives should be mutually exclusive. Fathoming human behavior is never easy; one should utilize every possible source of information.

Above all, one should take a balanced view of the difficulties with each approach. As Sen (1973, p. 258) wrote, "we have been too prone, on the one hand, to overstate the difficulties of introspection and communication and, on the other, to underestimate the problems of studying preferences revealed by observed behavior." In the debate on contingent valuation, critics have shown a tendency to employ simplistic dichotomies. Surveys of attitudes are fallible and subject to the vagaries of context and interpretation; surveys of behavior are unerring. In the market place, people are well informed, deliberate, and rational. Outside it, they are ignorant, confused, and illogical. As consumers, people can be taken seriously; as voters, they cannot. In particular instances, these assertions may be correct. As generalizations, however, they are a caricature.

Conclusions

When cost-benefit analysis started in the United States in the 1930s, economic valuation was generally perceived in terms of market prices. To value something, one ascertained an appropriate market price, adjusted for market imperfections if necessary, and then used this to multiply some quantity. Two things changed this. The first was the recognition, prompted by the "new welfare economics" of the 1940s and especially Hotelling's paper on public utility pricing, that the appropriate welfare criterion is maximization of aggregate consumers' plus producers' surplus. While market prices can safely be used to value marginal changes for market commodities, the impact of nonmarginal changes is measured by the change in areas under demand and supply curves. The second development was Samuelson's theory of public goods and his finding that their valuation must be based on vertical aggregation of individual demand curves.

Together, these developments led to an important paradigm shift—one that contributed directly to the emergence of nonmarket valuation and is

---

[32]Revealed preference estimates are sensitive to the measurement of price, which is often uncertain and precarious for disaggregated commodities (Pratt, Wise and Zeckhauser, 1979; Randall, 1994). The price at which demand falls to zero, needed to estimate consumer's surplus, may lie outside the range of the observed data and be estimated inaccurately (for example, one knows travel cost only for participants, or one believes that participants and nonparticipants have different preferences). This can cause revealed preference to produce a less reliable estimate of use value than contingent valuation (Hanemann, Chapman and Kanninen, 1993). With other variables there may be inadequate variation in the data (for example, attributes are correlated across brands). Hence, revealed preference data alone may yield a less reliable estimate of demand functions than contingent valuation choice data, and one may need to combine both types of data for best results (Adamowicz, Louviere and Williams, 1994).

still evident in the current debate on contingent valuation.[33] This shift changed the focus of valuation away from market prices towards demand and supply functions as the underlying repositories of value. These functions are behavioral relations, and the implication of the paradigm shift was that economics is not just the study of markets, but more generally the study of human preferences and behavior.

The conceptual link to nonmarket valuation is the recognition that, while a demand curve is not observable if there is no market for a commodity, there still exists a latent demand curve that perhaps can be teased out through other means. Indirect methods are one approach to doing this, and contingent valuation is another. In both cases, the details of implementation have a large impact on the quality of the results.

Faced with the assertion that contingent valuation surveys can *never* be a reliable source of information either for benefit cost analysis or for damage assessment, the NOAA Panel rejected this as unwarranted. Two years later, there is now even more evidence from recent studies and literature analyses to support the Panel's conclusion. However, it would be misleading for me to suggest that contingent valuation surveys can be made to work well in all circumstances. I am sure situations could exist where a contingent valuation researcher might be unable to devise a plausible scenario for the item of interest. Nor would I wish to argue that all contingent valuation surveys are of high quality. The method, though simple in its directness, is in fact difficult to implement without falling into various types of design problems that require effort, skill and imagination to resolve. Each particular study needs to be scrutinized carefully. But the same is true of any empirical study.

While I believe in the feasibility of using contingent valuation to measure people's value for the environment, I do not mean to advocate a narrow benefit-cost analysis for all environmental policy decisions, nor to suggest that everything can or should be quantified. There will be cases where the information is inadequate, the uncertainties too great, or the consequences too profound or too complex to be reduced to a single number. I am well aware of the fallacy of misplaced precision. But this cuts both ways. It also applies to those who suggest that it is better not to measure nonuse values at all than to measure them through contingent valuation. I reply to such critics by quoting Douglass North: "The price you pay for precision is an inability to deal with real-world issues" (*Wall Street Journal*, 7/29/94).

Is expert judgment an alternative to contingent valuation? Experts clearly play the leading role in determining the physical injuries to the environment and in assessing the costs of clean-up and restoration. Assessing what things *are worth* is different. How the experts know the value that the public places on an uninjured environment, without resort to measurement involving some sort of survey, is unclear. When that public val-

---

[33]For an account of the development of nonmarket valuation generally, see Hanemann (1992).

uation is the object of measurement, a well-designed contingent valuation survey is one way of consulting the relevant experts—the public itself.

REFERENCES

Adamowicz, W., J. Louviere, and M. Williams, "Combining Revealed and Stated Preference Methods for Valuing Environmental Amenities," *Journal of Environmental Economics and Management*, 1994, *26*, 271–92.

Ajzen, Icek, and Martin Fishbein, *Understanding Attitudes and Predicting Social Behavior*. New Jersey: Prentice-Hall, Inc., 1980.

Anonymous, "'Ask a Silly Question . . .' Contingent Valuation of Natural Resource Damages," *Harvard Law Review*, June 1992, *105*, 1981–2000.

Arrow, Kenneth, J., *Social Choice and Individual Values*, 2nd ed., New Haven: Yale University Press, 1963.

Arrow, Kenneth et al., *report of the NOAA Panel on Contingent Valuation*, Washington, D.C.: January 1993, p. 41.

Atkinson, A. B., and J. Micklewright, "On the Reliability of Income Data in the Family Expenditure Survey, 1970–1977," *Journal of the Royal Statistical Society* (A), 1983, *146(1)*, 33–53.

Bate, Roger, "Pick a Number: A Critique of Contingent Valuation Methodology and Its Application in Public Policy." Competitive Enterprise Institute, Environmental Studies Program, Washington, D.C., January 1994.

Bateman, Ian, and Ken Willis (eds.), *Valuing Environmental Preferences: Theory and Practice of the Contingent Valuation Method in the US, EC and Developing Countries*. Oxford, UK: Oxford University Press, forthcoming.

Becker, Gary S., "Nobel Lecture: The Economic Way of Looking at Behavior." *Journal of Political Economy*, June 1993, *101(3)*, 385–409.

Bettman, James R., "Processes of Adaptivity in Decision Making," *Advances in Consumer Research*, 1988, *15*, 1–4.

Bettman, J. R., and M. A. Zins, "Constructive Processes in Consumer Choice," *Journal of Consumer Research*, September 1977, *4*, 75–85.

Bishop, Richard C., and Thomas A. Heberlein, "Measuring Values of Extramarket Goods: Are Indirect Measures Biased?" *American Journal of Agricultural Economics*, December 1979, *61*, 926–30.

Bishop, Richard C., and Thomas A. Heberlein, "The Contingent Valuation Method." In Johnson, Rebecca L., and Gary V. Johnson, eds., *Economic Valuation of Natural Resources: Issues, Theory, and Applications*, Boulder: Westview Press, 1990, 81–104.

Bohm, Peter, "Estimating Demand for Public Goods: An Experiment," *European Economic Review*, 1972, *3*, 111–30.

Boyce, R. R., et al., "Experimental Evidence of Existence Value in Payment and Compensation Contexts." Paper presented at the USDA W-133 Annual Meeting, San Diego, California, February 1989.

Boyle, Kevin J., Michael P. Welsh, and Richard C. Bishop, "The Role of Question Order and Respondent Experience in Contingent-Valuation Studies," *Journal of Environmental Economics and Management*, 1993, *25*, S-80-S-99.

Bradburn, Norman M., Lance J. Rips, and Steven K. Shevell, "Answering Autobiographical Questions: The Impact of Memory and Inference on Surveys," *Science*, April 1987, *236*, 157–161.

Briscoe, John, et al., "Toward Equitable and Sustainable Rural Water Supplies: A Contingent Valuation Study in Brazil," *World Bank Economic Review*, May 1990, 4, 115–34.

Brookshire, David S., Mark A. Thayer, William D. Schulze, and Ralph C. d'Arge, "Valuing Public Goods: A Comparison of Survey and Hedonic Approaches," *American Economic Review*, 1982, 72, 165–77.

Carson, Richard T., "Contingent Valuation Surveys and Tests of Insensitivity to Scope." Paper presented at the International Conference on Determining the Value of Nonmarketed Goods: Economic Psychological, and Policy Relevant Aspects of Contingent Valuation Methods, Bad Hamburg, Germany, July 1994.

Carson, Richard T., and Nicholas E. Flores, "Another Look at 'Does Contingent Valuation Measure Preferences: Experimental Evidence'—How Compelling is the Evidence?" Economics Department, University of California, San Diego, December 1993.

Carson, R., N. Flores, and W. M. Hanemann, "On the Creation and Destruction of Public Goods: The Matter of Sequencing," working paper 690, Agricultural and Resource Economics, University of California, Berkeley, 1992.

Carson, Richard T., Nicholas E. Flores, Kerry Martin and Jennifer Wright, "Contingent Valuation and Revealed Preference Methodologies: Comparing the Estimates for Quasi-Public Goods," Discussion Paper 94-07, University of California, San Diego, May 1994a.

Carson, Richard T., W. Michael Hanemann, and Robert Cameron Mitchell, "The Use of Simulated Political Markets to Value Public Goods," Economics Department, University of California, San Diego, October 1986.

Carson, Richard T., Kerry Martin, Jennifer Wright," A Note on the Evidence of the Temporal Reliability of Contingent Valuation Estimates," working paper, University of California, San Diego, Economics Department, July 1994b.

Carson, Richard T., and Robert Cameron Mitchell, "The Value of Clean Water: The Public's Willingness to Pay for Boatable, Fishable, and Swimmable Quality Water," *Water Resources Research*, 1993, 29, 2445–54.

Carson, R., et al., *A Contingent Valuation Study of Lost Passive Use Values Resulting from the Exxon Valdez Oil Spill*, Report to the Attorney General of Alaska, Natural Resource Damage Assessment, Inc. La Jolla, CA, November 1992.

Carson, Richard T., et al., *A Bibliography of Contingent Valuation Studies and Papers*, Natural Resource Damage Assessment, Inc., La Jolla, CA, March 1994c.

Chase, S. B., ed., *Problems in Public Expenditure Analysis*, Washington, D.C.: Brookings Institution, 1968.

Cicchetti, Charles J., and V. Kerry Smith, "Congestion, Quality Deterioration, and Optimal Use: Wilderness Recreation in the Spanish Peaks Primitive Area," *Social Science Research*, 1973, 2, 15–30.

Ciriacy-Wantrup, S. V., "Capital Returns from Soil-Conservation Practices," *Journal of Farm Economics*, November 1947, 29, 1188–90.

Clotfelter, Charles T., *Federal Tax Policy and Charitable Giving*. Chicago: The University of Chicago Press, 1985.

Cronin, Thomas E., *Direct Democracy: The Politics of Initiative, Referendum, and Recall*. Cambridge: Harvard University Press, 1989.

Cropper, Maureen L., "Comments on Estimating the Demand for Public Goods: The Collective Choice and Contingent Valuation Approaches." Paper presented at the DOE/EPA Workshop on "Using Contingent Valuation to Measure Non-Market Values," Herndon, VA, May 19–20, 1994.

Cummings, Ronald G., "Relating Stated and Revealed Preferences: Challenges and Opportunities." Paper presented at the DOE/EPA Workshop on "Using Contingent Valuation to Measure Non-Market Values," Herndon, VA, May 19–20, 1994.

Cummings, Ronald G., David S. Brookshire, and William D. Schulze, et al., eds. *Valuing Environmental Goods: An Assessment of the Contingent Valuation Method*. Totowa, New Jersey: Rowman and Allanheld, 1986.

Cummings, Ronald G., Glenn W. Harrison, and E. E. Ruström, "Homegrown Values and Hypothetical Surveys: Is the Dichotomous Choice Approach Incentive Compatible?" Economics Working Paper Series, B-92-12, Division of Research, College of Business Administration, The University of South Carolina, February 1993.

Cutler, David, Douglas W. Elmendorf, and Richard J. Zeckhauser, "Demographic Characteristics and the Public Bundle," National Bureau of Economic Research, Cambridge, NBER Working Paper No. 4283, February 1993.

Desvousges, William H., et al., *Measuring Nonuse Damages Using Contingent Valuation: An Experimental Evaluation of Accuracy*. North Carolina: Research Triangle Institute Monograph, 1992.

Diamond, Peter A., Jerry Hausman, Gregory K. Leonard, and Mike A. Denning, "Does Contingent Valuation Measure Preferences? Experimental Evidence." In Hausman, J. A., ed., *Contingent Valuation: A Critical Assessment*. New York: North-Holland, 1993, 41–89.

DiBona, Charles J., "Assessing Environmental Damage," *Issues in Science and Technology*, Fall 1992, *8*, 50–54.

Dickie, M. A. Fisher, and S. Gerking, "Market Transactions and Hypothetical Demand Data: A Comparative Study," *Journal of American Statistical Association*, March 1987, *82*, 69–75.

Duffield, John W., and David A. Patterson, "Field Testing Existence Values: An Instream Flow Trust Fund for Montana Rivers." Presented at the American Economics Association Annual Meeting, New Orleans, Louisiana, January 4, 1991.

Ferber, Robert, and Robert A. Piskie, "Subjective Probabilities and Buying Intentions," *Review of Economics and Statistics*, August 1965, *47*, 322–25.

Fiorina, Morris P., *Retrospective Voting in American National Elections*. New Haven: Yale University Press, 1981.

Fishkin, J. S., *Democracy and Deliberation: New Directions for Democratic Reform*. New Haven: Yale University Press, 1991.

Freeman, A. Myrick, *The Measurement of Environment and Resource Values: Theory and Method*. Washington, D.C.: Resources for the Future, 1993.

Frisch, Deborah, "Reasons for Framing Effects," *Organizational Behavior and Human Decision Processes*, 1993, *54*, 399–429.

Groves, Robert M., *Survey Errors and Survey Costs*. New York: John Wiley and Sons, 1989.

Hanemann, W. Michael, "Welfare Evaluations in Contingent Valuation Experiments with Discrete Responses," *American Journal of Agricultural Economics*, August 1984, *66*, 332–41.

Hanemann, W. Michael, "Preface: Notes on the History of Environmental Valuation in the USA." In Navrud, Stale, ed., *Pricing the Environment: The European Experience*. Oxford, UK: Oxford University Press, 1992.

Hanemann, W. Michael, "Contingent Valuation and Economics," Working Paper No. 697, Giannini Foundation of Agricultural and Resource Economics, University of California, Berkeley, February 1994a. To appear in Willis, Ken, and John Corkindale, eds., *Environmental Valuation: Some New Perspectives*, Wallingford, Oxon, UK: CAB International, forthcoming.

Hanemann, W. Michael, "Strictly For the Birds: A Re-examination of the Exxon Tests of Scope in CV," working paper, Giannini Foundation of Agricultural and Resource Economics, University of California, Berkeley, August 1994b.

Hanemann, W. Michael, and B. J. Kanninen, "Statistical Analysis of CV Data." In Bateman, I., and K. Willis, eds. *Valuing Environmental Preferences: Theory and Practice of the Contingent Valuation Method in the US, EC and Developing Countries.* Oxford: Oxford University Press, forthcoming.

Hanemann, W. Michael, David Chapman, and Barbara Kanninen, "Non-Market Valuation Using Contingent Behavior: Model Specification and Consistency Tests." Presented at the American Economic Association Annual Meeting, Anaheim, California, January 6, 1993.

Hanemann, W. M., J. Loomis, and B. Kanninen, "Statistical Efficiency of Double-Bounded Dichotomous Choice Contingent Valuation," *American Journal of Agricultural Economics*, 1991, 73, 1255–63.

Harrison, Glenn W., "Valuing Public Goods with the Contingent Valuation Method: A Critique of Kahneman and Knetsch," *Journal of Environmental Economics and Management*, 1992, 23, 248–57.

Hausman, J. A., ed., *Contingent Valuation: A Critical Assessment.* New York: North-Holland, 1993.

Hoehn, J. P., and A. Randall, "Too Many Proposals Pass the Benefit Cost Test," *American Economic Review*, June 1989, 79, 544–51.

Infosino, William J., "Forecasting New Product Sales from Likelihood of Purchase Ratings," *Marketing Science*, Fall 1986, 5, 372–384.

Johansson, Per-Olov, "Altruism in Cost-Benefit Analysis," *Environmental and Resource Economics*, 1992, 2, 605–13.

Jones-Lee, Michael W., M. Hammerton, and P. R. Philips, "The Value of Safety: Results of a National Sample Survey," *Economic Journal*, March 1985, 95, 49–72.

Juster, F. Thomas, *Anticipations and Purchases: An Analysis of Consumer Behavior.* Princeton: Princeton University Press, 1964.

Juster, F. Thomas, and Frank P. Stafford, "The Allocation of Time: Empirical Findings, Behavioral Models, and Problems of Measurement," *Journal of Economic Literature*, 1991, 29, 471–522.

Kahneman, Daniel, "Valuing Environmental Goods: An Assessment of the Contingent Valuation Method: The Review Panel Assessment." In Cummings, R. G., D. S. Brookshire, W. D. Schulze, et al., eds., *Valuing Environmental Goods: An Assessment of the Contingent Valuation Method.* Totowa, New Jersey: Rowman & Allanheld, 1986, 185–94.

Kahneman, Daniel, and Jack L. Knetsch, "Valuing Public Goods: The Purchase of Moral Satisfaction," *Journal of Environmental Economics and Management*, 1992, 22, 57–70.

Kahneman, Daniel, and Ilana Ritov, "Determinants of Stated Willingness to Pay for Public Goods: A Study in the Headline Method," unpublished, Department of Psychology, University of California, Berkeley, 1993.

Kanninen, B. J., "Optimal Experimental Design for Double-Bounded Dichotomous Choice Contingent Valuation," *Land Economics*, May 1993, 69, 128–46.

Kelly, S., and T. W. Mirer, "The Simple Act of Voting," *American Political Science Review*, 1974, 68, 572–91.

Kemp, Michael A., and Christopher Maxwell, "Exploring a Budget Context for Contingent Valuation Estimates." In Hausman, J. A., ed., *Contingent Valuation: A Critical Assessment.* New York: North-Holland, 1993, 217–69.

Knetsch, J. L., and R. K. Davis, Comparisons of Methods for Recreation Evaluation." In Kneese A. V., and S. C. Smith, eds., *Water Research*, Baltimore: Resources for the Future Inc., Johns Hopkins Press, 1966, 125–42.

Kriström, Bengt, and Pere Riera, "Is the Income Elasticity of Environmental Improvements Less Than One?" Paper presented at the Second Conference on Environmental Economics, Ulvöng, Sweden, June 2–5, 1994.

Krosnick, Jon A., "Response Strategies for Coping with the Cognitive Demands of Attitude Measures in Surveys," *Applied Cognitive Psychology*, 1991, *5*, 213–36.

Krosnick, Jon A., Fan Li, and Darrin R. Lehman, "Conservational Conventions, Order of Information Acquisition, and the Effect of Base Rates and Individuating Information on Social Judgments," *Journal of Personality and Social Psychology*, 1990, *59*, 1140–52.

Krutilla, John V., "Conservation Reconsidered," *American Economic Review*, September 1967, *57*, 777–86.

Lupia, Arthur, "Short Cuts versus Encyclopedias: Information and Voting Behavior in California Insurance Reform Elections," working paper, Department of Political Science, University of California, San Diego, April 1993.

Madden, Paul, "A Generalization of Hicksian *q* Substitutes and Complements with Application to Demand Rationing," *Econometrica*, September 1991, *59*, 1497–1508.

Magleby, David B., *Direct Legislation, Voting on Ballot Propositions in the United States*. Baltimore and London: The John Hopkins University Press, 1984.

Maki, Atsushi, and Shigeru Nishiyama, "Consistency Between Macro- and Micro-Data Sets in the Japanese Household Sector," *Review of Income and Wealth*, 1993, *39*, 195–207.

Martin, Leonard L., and Abraham Tesser, eds., *The Construction of Social Judgments*. New Jersey: Lawrence Erlbaum Associates, chapter 2, 1992, 37–65.

Mathiowetz, Nancy A., and Greg J. Duncan, "Out of Work, Out of Mind: Response Errors in Retrospective Reports of Unemployment," *Journal of Business & Economic Statistics*, 1988, *6*, 221–29.

McCloskey, Donald, *The Rhetoric of Economics*. Madison: The University of Wisconsin Press, 1985.

McFadden, Daniel, and Gregory K. Leonard, "Issues in the Contingent Valuation of Environmental Goods: Methodologies for Data Collection and Analysis." In Hausman, J. A., ed., *Contingent Valuation: A Critical Assessment*. New York: North-Holland, 1993, 165–215.

McKelvey, Richard D., and Peter C. Ordeshook, "Information, Electoral Equilibria and the Democratic Ideal," *Journal of Politics*, 1986, *48*, 909–37.

Merton, Robert K., and Patricia L. Kendall, "The Focused Interview," *American Journal of Sociology*, 1946, *51*, 541–57.

Milgrom, Paul, "Is Sympathy an Economic Value? Philosophy, Economics, and the Contingent Valuation Method." In Hausman, J. A., ed., *Contingent Valuation: A Critical Assessment*. New York: North-Holland, 1993, 417–41.

Miller, Leslie A., and Theodore Downes-Le Guin, "Reducing Response Error in Consumers' Reports of Medical Expenses: Application of Cognitive Theory to the Consumer Expenditure Interview Survey," *Advances in Consumer Research*, 1990, *17*, 193–206.

Mitchell, Robert Cameron, and Richard T. Carson, *Using Surveys to Value Public Goods: The Contingent Valuation Method*. Washington, D. C.: Resources for the Future, 1989.

Navrud, Ståle, *Pricing the European Environment*. New York: Oxford University Press, 1992.

Neill, Helen R., et al., "Hypothetical Surveys and Real Economic Commitments," *Land Economics*, May 1994, *70*, 145–54.

Neisser, Urlic, *Cognitive Psychology*. Appleton-Century-Crofts, Educational Division, New York: Meredith Corporation, 1967.

Oates, W., "Comments on Estimating the Demand for Public Goods: The Collective Choice and Contingent Valuation Approaches." Paper presented at the DOE/EPA Workshop on Using Contingent Valuation to Measure Non-Market Values, Hemdon, VA, May 19–20, 1994.

Olshavsky, Richard W., and Donald H. Granbois, "Consumer Decision Making— Fact or Fiction?" *Journal of Consumer Research*, September 1979, *6*, 93–100.

Payne, J. W., J. R. Bettman, and E. J. Johnson, "Adaptive Strategy Selection in Decision Making," *Journal of Experimental Psychology Learning, Memory, and Cognition*, 1988, *14*, 534–52.

Poulton, E. C., *Bias in Quantifying Judgments*. Hove, UK: Lawrence Erlbaum Associates, 1989.

Pratt, John W., David A. Wise, and Richard Zeckhauser, "Price Differences in Almost Competitive Markets," *Quarterly Journal of Economics*, May 1979, *93*, 189–212.

Randall, Alan, "A Difficulty with the Travel Cost Method," *Land Economics*, February 1994, *70*, 88–96.

Randall, Alan, Berry C. Ives, and Clyde Eastman, "Bidding Games for Valuation of Aesthetic Environmental Improvements," *Journal of Environmental Economics and Management*, 1974, *1*, 132–49.

Rose, Steven, *The Making of Memory: From Molecules to Mind*. New York: Anchor Books, Doubleday, 1992.

Rosen, S., "Hedonic Prices and Implicit Markets: Product Differentiation in Pure Competition," *Journal of Political Economy*, January-February 1974, *82*, 34–55.

Schelling, Thomas, "The Life You Save May Be Your Own." In Chase, S., ed., *Problems in Public Expenditure Analysis*. Washington, D.C.: Brookings Institution, 1968, 143–4.

Schkade, David A., and John W. Payne, "Where Do the Numbers Come From? How People Respond to Contingent Valuation Questions." In Hausman, J. A., ed., *Contingent Valuation: A Critical Assessment*. New York: North-Holland, 1993, 271–303.

Schuman, H., remarks in transcript of Public Meeting of the National Oceanic and Atmospheric Administration, Contingent Valuation Panel, Washington, D.C.: NOAA, Department of Commerce, August 12, 1992, p. 101.

Schuman, H., and S. Presser, *Questions and Answers in Attitude Surveys*. New York: Academic Press, 1981.

Seip, K., and J. Strand, "Willingness to Pay for Environmental Goods in Norway: A Contingent Valuation Study with Real Payment," *Environmental and Resource Economics*, 1992, *2*, 91–106.

Sen, A. K., "Behavior and the Concept of Preference," *Economica*, August 1973, *40*, 241–59.

Sinden, J. A., "Empirical Tests of Hypothetical Biases in Consumers' Surplus Surveys," *Australian Journal of Agricultural Economics*, 1988, *32*, 98–112.

Smith, Tom W., "The Art of Asking Questions, 1936–1985," *Public Opinion Quarterly*, 1987, *51*, 21–36.

Smith, V. Kerry, "Arbitrary Values, Good Causes, and Premature Verdicts," *Journal of Environmental Economics and Management*, 1992, *22*, 71–89.

Smith, V. Kerry, "Lightning Rods, Dart Boards and Contingent Valuation," *Natural Resources Journal*, forthcoming 1994.

Smith, V. Kerry, and William H. Desvousges, *Measuring Water Quality Benefits*. Boston: Kluwer-Nijhoff Publishing, 1986.

Smith, V. Kerry, and Laura Osborne, "Do Contingent Valuation Estimates Pass a 'Scope' Test?: A Preliminary Meta Analysis." Presented at the American Economics Association Annual Meeting, Boston MA, January 5, 1994.

Sniderman, Paul M., "The New Look in Public Opinion Research." In Finifter, Ada W., ed., *Political Science: The State of the Discipline II*. Washington, D.C.: The American Political Science Association, 1993, 219–45.

Sniderman, Paul M., Richard A. Brody, and Phillip E. Tetlock, *Reasoning and Choice, Explorations in Political Psychology*. Cambridge: Cambridge University Press, 1991.

Tanur, Judith M., ed., *Questions about Questions: Inquiries into the Cognitive Bases of Surveys*. New York: Russell Sage Foundation, 1992.

Theil, Henri, and Richard F. Kosobud, "How Informative Are Consumer Buying Intentions Surveys?" *Review of Economics and Statistics*, February 1968, *50*, 50–59.

Tversky, Amos, and Daniel Kahneman, "Judgment under Uncertainty: Heuristics and Biases," *Science*, 1974, *185*, 124–31.

Walsh, Richard G., Donn M. Johnson, and John R. McKean, "Benefits Transfer of Outdoor Recreation Demand Studies: 1968–1988," *Water Resources Research* 1992, *28*, 707–13.

Warshaw, Paul R., "Predicting Purchase and Other Behaviors from General and Contextually Specific Intentions," *Journal of Marketing Research*, February 1980, *17*, 26–33.

Wilson, Timothy D., and Sara D. Hodges, "Attitudes as Temporary Constructions." In Martin L., and A. Tesser, eds., *The Construction of Social Judgments*. New Jersey: Lawrence Erlbaum Associates, chapter 2, 1992, 37–65.

12 _Contingent Valuation: Is Some Number Better than No Number?*_

Peter A. Diamond

Jerry A. Hausman

Peter Diamond is Institute Professor, Department of Economics at the Massachusetts Institute of Technology; and Jerry Hausman is John and Jennie S. MacDonald Professor, Department of Economics at the Massachusetts Institute of Technology.

Most economic analyses aim at explaining market transactions. Data on transactions, or potentially collectible data on transactions, are the touchstone for recognizing interesting economic analyses. However loose the connection between a theoretical or empirical analysis and transactions, this connection is the basis of the methodology of judging the credibility and reliability of economic analyses. Generally, individuals do not purchase public goods directly. Lack of data on transactions implies that economists must find other methods to assess surveys asking for valuations of public goods.

To address this problem, we begin with a discussion of the methodology of evaluating contingent valuation surveys. While there is some experimental evidence about small payments for public goods, we work with the assumption that we do not have data on actual transactions for interesting environmental public goods to compare with survey responses of hypothetical willingness-to-pay. This situation creates the need for other standards for evaluating survey responses. Evaluation involves the credibility, bias (also referred to as reliability in the literature), and precision of responses. Credibility refers to whether survey respondents are answering the question the interviewer is trying to ask. If respondents are answering the right question, reliability refers to the size and direction of the biases that may be present in the answers. Precision refers to the variability in responses. Since precision can usually be increased by the simple expedient of increasing the sample size, we will not discuss precision further in this paper. Problems of credibility or of bias are not reduced by increases in

"Contingent Value: Is Some Number Better than No Number?" by Peter A. Diamond and Jerry A. Hausman, from _Journal of Economic Perspectives_, 8(4):45–64 (Fall 1994).

*The authors want to thank Bernard Saffran and four editors for helpful comments.

sample size. Thus credibility and bias must be evaluated when considering the use of such surveys—in benefit-cost analyses, in the determination of damages after a finding of liability, or as general information to affect the legislative process.[1]

We discuss how to judge the content in contingent valuation surveys together with evidence from surveys that have been done. Surveys designed to test for consistency between stated willingness-to-pay and economic theory have found that contingent valuation responses are not consistent with economic theory. The main contingent valuation anomaly that we discuss is called the "embedding effect," and was first analyzed systematically by Kahneman and Knetsch (1992).[2] The embedding effect is the name given to the tendency of willingness-to-pay responses to be highly similar across different surveys, even where theory suggests (and sometimes requires) that the responses be very different.[3] An example of embedding would be a willingness-to-pay to clean up one lake roughly equal to that for cleaning up five lakes, including the one asked about individually. The embedding effect is usually thought to arise from the nonexistence of individual preferences for the public good in question and from the failure of survey respondents, in the hypothetical circumstances of the survey, to consider the effect of their budget constraints. Because of these embedding effects, different surveys can obtain widely variable stated willingness-to-pay amounts for the same public good, with no straightforward way for selecting one particular method as the appropriate one.

In short, we think that the evidence supports the conclusion that to date, contingent valuation surveys do not measure the preferences they attempt to measure. Moreover, we present reasons for thinking that changes in survey methods are not likely to change this conclusion. Viewed alternatively as opinion polls on possible government actions, we think that these surveys do not have much information to contribute to informed policy-making. Thus, we conclude that reliance on contingent valuation surveys in either damage assessments or in government decision making is basically misguided.

---

[1]With two estimates of an economic value, one can analyze directly whether one is a biased estimate of the other. With nonuse value, the lack of an alternative direct estimate of willingness-to-pay makes it relevant to consider credibility directly, as well as the differences between survey results and behavior in other contexts where transactions data are available.

[2]Another failure of contingent valuation surveys to be consistent with economic preferences is that stated willingness-to-pay is usually found to be much less than stated willingness-to-accept. From economic theory, willingness-to-pay differs from willingness-to-accept only by an income effect. Thus, their values should be extremely close in typical contingent valuation circumstances, where the stated willingness-to-pay is a small share of the consumer's overall budget, and willingness-to-pay amounts show a small income elasticity. For further discussion of this problem with contingent valuation surveys and other problems, see Diamond and Hausman (1993) and Milgrom (1993).

[3]The term embedding came from the research approach of "embedding" a particular good in a more inclusive good, and contrasting the stated willingness-to-pay for the good with that obtained by allocating the willingness-to-pay for the more inclusive good among its components (Kahneman, personal communication).

Judging Surveys of Willingness-To-Pay for Public Goods

A number of bases exist for forming judgments about whether particular respondents are answering the right question and whether the response is roughly correct. One widely accepted basis is by reaching the conclusion that a particular response is simply not credible as an answer to the question the interviewer is trying to ask. It is standard practice in the contingent valuation literature to eliminate some responses as being unreasonably large to be the true willingness-to-pay. Thus trimming responses that are more than, say, 5 percent of income for an environmental public good that contains only nonuse value may be criticized for having an arbitrary cutoff, but not for omitting answers that are believed to be credible. Similarly, it is standard practice to eliminate some responses of zero on the basis that these are "protest zeros," that answers to other questions in the survey indicate that individuals do put a positive value on changes in the level of the public good, and thus zero is not a credible answer.

A widely accepted incredibility test indicates that it is not automatic that the response given is an answer to the question that the interviewer wants answered. But we need to go further in considering how to form a judgment on the survey responses; it is not adequate to assume that any response that is not obviously wrong is an accurate response to the question the survey designer had in mind.

A number of additional bases have been used by people arguing that responses are or are not acceptable. The methods we shall discuss include verbal protocol analysis, the patterns of willingness-to-pay responses across individuals, and across surveys.

In considering the relevance of this evidence for the question of whether survey responses are accurate measures of true preferences, it is useful to have in mind some possible alternative hypotheses of how people respond to such surveys, since the responses are not simply random numbers. Several hypotheses have been put forward as alternatives to the hypothesis that the responses are measures of true economic preferences. Individuals may be expressing an attitude toward a public good (or class of public goods), expressed in a dollar scale because they are asked to express it in a dollar scale (Kahneman and Ritov, 1993). Individuals may receive a "warm glow" from expressing support for good causes (Andreoni, 1989).[4] Individuals may be describing what they think is good for the country, in a sort of casual benefit-cost analysis (Diamond and Hausman, 1993). Individuals may be expressing a reaction to actions that have been taken (for example, allowing an oil spill) rather than evaluating the state of a resource.

Under all of these alternative hypotheses, responses are not an attempt by an individual to evaluate his or her own preference for a public good.

---

[4]This approach was developed for actual charitable contributions, not survey responses. Kahneman and Knetsch (1992) call it the purchase of moral satisfaction.

For example, people doing casual benefit-cost analyses may be reflecting how much they think people generally care about the issue. We think that different hypotheses are likely to be appropriate for different people. Thus the question is not whether the hypothesis of an accurate measurement of preferences is the single best hypothesis, but whether the fraction of the population for whom the hypothesis of accuracy is reasonable is sufficiently large to make the survey as a whole useful for policy purposes.

All of these alternatives are based on what individuals are trying to do; there are further questions of standard survey biases (such as interviewer bias, framing bias, hypothetical bias) and whether people have enough information to express a preference with any accuracy, even if they are attempting to express a preference. Insofar as this understanding is faulty, expressed preferences are not an expression of true economic preferences.

Verbal Protocol Analysis

For verbal protocol analysis, individuals are asked to "think aloud" as they respond to a questionnaire, reporting everything that goes through their minds. Everything the subjects say is recorded on audio tapes that are transcribed and coded for the types of considerations being mentioned. Schkade and Payne (1993) have done such an analysis using a contingent valuation survey that asks for willingness-to-pay to protect migratory waterfowl from drowning in uncovered waste water holding ponds from oil and gas operations.

The transcripts show the inherent difficulty in selecting a willingness-to-pay response and the extent to which people refer to elements that ought to be irrelevant to evaluating their own preferences. If people are trying to report a preference, we would expect them to consider inputs into the forming of their preferences, such as how much they care about birds, how important the number of killed birds are relative to the numbers in the species. Conversely, we would not expect them to report a willingness-to-pay just equal to what they think the program will cost. Respondents verbalized many diverse considerations. Perhaps the most common strategy involved first acknowledging that something should be done and then trying to figure out an appropriate amount. About one-fourth of the sample mentioned the idea that if everyone did his part then each household would not have to give all that much. About one-sixth of the sample made comparisons with donations to charities. About one-fifth of the sample said they just made up a number or guessed an answer. Many respondents seemed to wish to signal concern for a larger environmental issue. This pattern may reflect the unfamiliarity of the task the respondents faced.

These findings strongly suggest that people are not easily in touch with underlying preferences about the type of commodity asked about. The findings do not lend support to the hypothesis that responses are an attempt to measure and express personal preferences. To the extent that individuals consider costs to everyone, the analysis supports the hypothesis of casual benefit-cost analysis. To the extent that individuals look to their own charitable contributions for a guide, the analysis is consistent with hypotheses that explain actual contributions, such as the warm glow hypothesis.

Variation in Willingness-To-Pay Across Individuals

If stated willingness-to-pay is a reflection of true preferences, then we would expect certain patterns of answers across different individuals (other things equal). We would expect self-described environmentalists to have larger willinesses-to-pay. We would expect individuals with higher incomes to have larger willingnesses-to-pay. Both results do occur. However, such results do not distinguish among the various hypotheses that were spelled out above since we would expect roughly similar results from any of them. Thus this potential basis for evaluation does not have much bite.[5] We do observe that the income effects that are measured in typical surveys are lower than we would expect if true preferences are measured, lower for example than measured income elasticities for charitable giving.[6]

Variation in Willingness-To-Pay Across Surveys

Another approach to forming a judgment is to compare willingness-to-pay responses to different questions, whether in the same or in different surveys.

Multiple Questions. If a survey question reveals a true valuation, it should not matter whether the question is asked by itself or with other questions, nor if asked with any other questions, what the order of questioning is. However, when Tolley et al. (1983) asked for willingness-to-pay to preserve visibility at the Grand Canyon, the response was five times higher when this was the only question, as compared to its being the third such question. Attempts to claim this result to be consistent with preferences have relied on income effects and substitution effects. Neither of these rationalizations for the anomalous results is compelling, as we explain in a moment.

The importance of question order was also shown in a study by Samples and Hollyer (1990) asking for the values of preserving seals and whales. Some respondents were asked for willingness-to-pay to preserve seals first, followed by a question about whales. Others were asked for willingness-to-pay in the reverse order. Seal value tended to be lower when asked after whale value, while whale value was not affected by the sequence of ques-

---

[5]The importance of the lack of bite of such considerations comes, in part, from the fact that the contingent valuation study of the Exxon Valdez spill that was done for the state of Alaska (Carson et al., 1992) included such analyses, but none of the more powerful split-sample consistency tests that we discuss below.

[6] The empirical finding of low income elasticities is also inconsistent with the typical finding of a large divergence between willingness-to-pay and willingness-to-accept, discussed in footnote 2.

tions.[7] Thus the sum of willingness-to-pay depended on the sequence of the questions asked. The authors offer an explanation (p. 189) "based on debriefing sessions held with the interviewer."

> Apparently, when respondents valued seals first, they used their behavior in this market situation to guide their responses to whale valuation questions. Since whales are generally more popular than seals, respondents were reluctant to behave more benevolently toward seals compared with humpback whales. Consequently, whale values were inflated in the S-W questionnaire version to maintain a relatively higher value for the humpbacks. This behavioral anchoring effect did not exist in the W-S version, where whales were valued first.

To have the value of preserving both seals and whales depend on the sequence in which the questions are asked is not consistent with the hypothesis that stated willingness-to-pay accurately measures preferences. These results can be interpreted in two ways. One interpretation is that contingent valuation studies that ask two questions rather than one are unreliable. The other interpretation is that the warm glow hypothesis is supported, since having expressed support for the environment in the first question permits a sharp fall in the second response. This effect is not present, however, when such a response would seem illogical to the respondent. More generally, one needs to decide whether a given pattern of responses is a result of survey design issues or a result of the underlying bases of response. This distinction is especially important when the pattern of results appears anomalous with or contradictory to the hypothesis that preferences are accurately measured.

Single Questions and the Embedding Effect. Alternatively, one can ask a single willingness-to-pay question each to different samples. For example, assume that one group is asked to evaluate public good X; a second is asked to evaluate Y; and a third is asked to evaluate X and Y. What interpretations could we make if the willingness-to-pay for X and Y (together) is considerably less than the sum of the willingness-to-pay for X and the willingness-to-pay for Y?[8] One interpretation is that we are seeing an income effect at work. That is, having "spent" for X, one has less income left to purchase Y. Given that the stated willingness-to-pay amounts are very small relative to income and that measured income elasticities are very small, the attempted income effect argument does not explain the differences found.

A second interpretation is to assume that individual preferences have a large substitution effect between X and Y. In some settings the assumption on preferences needed to justify the results is implausible. For example, Diamond et al. (1993) asked for willingness-to-pay to prevent logging

---

[7]Samples and Hollyer used dichotomous choice surveys. They estimated that whales were valued at $125 when asked about first, and $142 when second. Seals were valued at $103 when asked about first and $62 when second. When they asked about both (together) in a single question, the estimated values were $131 and $146 in two surveys.

[8]This approach is similar to the work that was initiated by Kahneman (1986) and done recently by Kahneman and Knetsch (1992), Kemp and Maxwell (1993), Desvousges et al. (1993), Diamond et al. (1993), McFadden and Leonard (1993), Loomis, Hoehn and Hanemann (1990).

in one, two, and three particular wilderness areas. Stated willingness-to-pay to preserve two (and three) areas was less than the sum of willingness-to-pay to preserve each of them separately.

At first look, this result appears to be an appropriate substitution effect, since protecting one area results in being less willing to protect another. However, preferences should be defined over wilderness remaining, not over proposals for development that are defeated. If preferences are concave over the amount of wilderness available (or, more generally, if different wilderness areas are substitutes), then willingness-to-pay is larger the smaller the quantity of wilderness remaining. This implies that the willingness-to-pay to preserve two threatened areas should be larger than the sum of willingness-to-pay to preserve each as the lone area threatened with development.[9] Instead, stated willingness-to-pay was roughly the same for preserving one, two or three threatened areas, making the amount for several areas together significantly less than the sum of the amounts for the areas separately. Note that these surveys vary both the number of areas threatened and the number to be preserved. Neither the income effect nor the substitution effect can plausibly explain the embedding effect in this experiment. The hypothesis that this survey is eliciting individual preferences is not consistent with individuals having reasonably behaved preferences. However, from the point of view of the warm glow hypothesis, this pattern makes sense. That is, the warm glow hypothesis is that individuals are primarily reporting an expression of support for the environment, an expression that does not vary much with small changes in the precise environmental change being described.

A similar variation in responses across surveys appears in the study of Desvousges et al. (1993). They described a problem killing 2000, 20,000 and 200,000 birds. The willingness-to-pay to solve this problem was roughly the same in all three cases. Since the number of surviving birds is smaller the larger the problem, concave preferences over surviving birds should have resulted in more than a 100-fold variation in willingness-to-pay across this range.[10] Thus this study shows a contradiction between stated willingness-to-pay and the usual economic assumptions on preferences. Again, the study

---

[9]For derivation of the convexity of willingness-to-pay when preferences are concave and the scenario is varied in this way, see Diamond (1993). That paper also contains a number of other implications of preferences for willingness-to-pay that can be used for internal consistency tests.

[10]Proponents of contingent valuation have made several critiques of this study. One critique is that it was a mall stop survey. But similar results followed when the questionnaire was used for the verbal protocol study cited above, which involved subjects coming to be interviewed. Another criticism is that in addition to the absolute numbers, the survey questions described the number of birds at risk as "much less than 1%" of the population, "less than 1%," and "about 2%." Thus, one can wonder whether respondents were paying attention to the absolute numbers which varied 100-fold or the percentages which varied from "much less than 1%" to "about 2%." Interpreting "much less than" as less than half, about 2% is at least a four-fold increase over less than half of 1%. If some people were paying attention to the percentages and some to the absolute numbers, the range should have been between four-fold and 100-fold. If, as Hanemann suggests, respondents did not perceive any real difference between "much less than 1%" and "about 2%," it is noteworthy that they perceived a large difference between zero and "much less than 1%." Moreover, these percentages were selected by the authors since they were the percentages in three actual oil spills: Arthur Kill, Nestucca, *Exxon Valdez*. This pattern of results is consistent with the responses being dominated by a "warm glow."

is consistent with the hypothesis that the responses are primarily warm glow, and so need not vary noticeably over moderate differences in the resource.

Adding-up Test. One difficulty in the approach described above is that the plausibility of the willingness-to-pay patterns depends on assumptions on the plausible (concave) structure of preferences. Another approach to tests of consistency that does not rely on an assumption of concave preferences is to attempt to measure the same preference in two different ways. This test can be constructed by varying the background scenario as well as varying the commodity to be purchased. For example, assume that one group is asked to evaluate public good X; a second group is told that X will be provided and is asked to evaluate also having Y; and a third is asked to evaluate X and Y (together). Now the willingness-to-pay for X and Y (together) should be the same as the sum of the willingness-to-pay for X and the willingness-to-pay for Y, having been given X (the same up to an income effect that can be measured in the survey and that empirically is small).[11] Thus, Diamond et al. (1993) varied the number of wilderness areas being developed as well as the number that could be protected. In this way the sum of two areas separately evaluated (with different degrees of development) should be the same as the value of preserving two areas (apart from a very small income effect). Again, the results of the survey are inconsistent with the responses being a measure of preferences.[12]

Embedding still infects even very recent work done by experienced contingent valuation analysts who were well aware of the problem. Schulze et al. (1993) asked for willingness-to-pay for partial and complete cleanup of contamination of the Clark Fork National Priorities List sites in Montana. After removing protest zeroes and high responses, the mean stated

---

[11]Willingness-to-pay is a function of the two vectors giving alternative levels of public goods and the level of income. Thus the willingness-to-pay to improve the environment from z to z'' of someone with income I can be written WTP(z, z'', I). The change from z to z'' can be broken into two pieces, a change from z to z' and a change from z' to z''. From the definition of willingness-to-pay, one has WTP(z, z'', I) = WTP(z, z', I) + WTP(z', z'', I-WTP(z, z', I)).

This adding-up test makes no use of an assumption on the magnitude or sign of income or substitution effects. One could do an adding-up test without the adjustment of income shown in the equation by comparing WTP(z, z'', I) with WTP(z, z', I) + WTP(z', z'', I). This comparison would involve a deviation from exact adding-up because of the income effect. With a willingness-to-pay on the order of $30 and a household income level of $30,000, even an income elasticity of one—higher than the elasticity typically measured in contingent valuation surveys—would lead to a $.03 deviation from exact adding-up. For a formal derivation, see the revised version of Diamond (1993).

[12]In brief response to Hanemann's criticisms of our analysis, we note that he does not address this adding-up test and seems comfortable accepting the idea that the less wilderness preserved, the less people care about any particular area of wilderness. These two tests do not rely on any assumption of different wilderness areas being interchangeable, as indicated by the vector interpretation of z in the previous footnote. In terms of Hanemann's test mentioned in his note 25 of whether willingness-to-pay to protect each of the areas is the same, we note that he did not do the statistical test correctly. Moreover, this reference is an example of Hanemann's trait of ignoring the central criticism while attacking a side issue. In Diamond et al., the focus is on the adding-up test, not a scope test. The adding-up test was clearly rejected.

willingness-to-pay for complete cleanup was $72.46 (standard error of $4.71) while the mean response for a considerably smaller partial cleanup was $72.02 (s.e. $5.10). As part of the survey, respondents were asked whether their responses were just for this cleanup or partly to cleanup other sites or basically as a contribution for all environmental or other causes (or other). Only 16.9 percent reported their answers as just for this cleanup; that is, a vast majority of respondents recognized an embedding effect in their own responses. These respondents were asked what percentage of their previous answer was for this cleanup, and the willingness-to-pay responses were adjusted by these percentages. After this adjustment, the mean stated willingness-to-pay for complete cleanup was $40.00 (s.e. $2.62) while the mean response for partial cleanup was $37.15 (s.e. $2.71).

These numbers (and the large fraction of people recognizing that they are embedding) support the hypothesis that the responses are dominated by a warm glow. No reason is offered by the authors for the conclusion that the adjustment they do removes the dominance of warm glow. Neither do they perform an adding-up test such as that described above. This adding-up test could have been done by asking a third sample for willingness-to-pay to extend a "planned" partial cleanup to a complete cleanup. In short, the embedding problem does not appear to be one that contingent valuation practitioners know how to solve.

With a pattern of results that are inconsistent with the usual economic assumptions, two interpretations are always possible: the surveys were defective or the contingent valuation method as currently practiced does not measure with accuracy. One should consider all the surveys that attempt to test for consistency in order to judge which interpretation is likely to be correct. The studies we have described have been criticized as not done well enough to be an adequate test.[13] However, they are the only quantitative tests we are aware of. No comparable comparison tests have been done by proponents of the accuracy of contingent valuation, although the embedding effect has long been recognized.

Differing Payment Vehicles. It is interesting to note what two contingent valuation proponents, Mitchell and Carson (1989), have written about the question that respondents are trying to answer. In discussing the sensitivity of responses to the payment vehicle (the way in which the hypothetical payment is to be collected), they write (pp. 123–24):

> It was earlier assumed that only the nature and amount of the amenity being valued should influence the WTP [willingness-to-pay] amounts; all other scenario components, such as the payment vehicle and method of provision, should be neutral in effect . . . More recently, Arrow (1986), Kahneman (1986), and Randall (1986) have argued against that view, holding that important conditions of a sce-

---

[13]One can ask whether the patterns of thought reflected in the responses to the questions in any particular survey also occur in other survey settings. Cognitive psychology has found a number of such patterns that are robust. We think that the patterns reflected in these surveys are similarly robust.

nario, such as the payment vehicle, should be expected to affect the WTP amounts. In their view, which we accept, respondents in a CV [contingent valuation] study are not valuing levels of provision of an amenity in the abstract; they are valuing a policy which includes the conditions under which the amenity will be provided, and the way the public is likely to be asked to pay for it.

In other words, Mitchell and Carson appear to accept the idea (consistent with the findings about some respondents by Schkade and Payne, 1993) that individuals' responses arise from casual benefit-cost analyses, not solely from an examination of their own preferences over resources. For welfare analysis and damage measurement, benefit-cost studies may be different from preferences. We will return to this issue.

Evaluation of Bias: Calibration

Surveys about behavior often have systematic biases relative to the behavior they ask about. Thus, it is common to "calibrate" the responses—that is, adjust for the biases—as part of using them for predictive purposes. In particular, when using surveys to estimate demand for new products, it is standard practice to use a calibration factor to adjust survey responses in order to produce an estimate of actual demand (Urban, Katz, Hatch, and Silk, 1983). As Mitchell and Carson (1989, p. 178) have written: "Such 'calibration' is common in marketing designed to predict purchases. If a systematic divergence between actual and CV [contingent valuation] survey existed and could be actual and CV [contingent valuation] survey behavior existed and could be quantified, calibration of CV results could be undertaken."

As some evidence on the need for calibration, comparisons of hypothetical surveys and actual offers often find large and significant differences. These comparisons have been done for private goods (Bishop and Heberlein, 1979; Dickie, Fisher and Gerking, 1987; Neill et al., 1993).[14] Comparisons have also been done for charitable donations (Duffield and Patterson, 1992; Seip and Strand, 1992). These studies find a need to calibrate, with calibration factors involving dividing stated willingness-to-pay by a number ranging from 1.5 to 10.

How this calibration should be extended to the public good context is unclear, since the public good context includes both unfamiliar commodities and unfamiliar transactions. But the lack of study of appropriate calibration factors is not a basis for concluding that the best calibration is one-for-one.[15]

---

[14]On the Dickie, Fisher and Gerking (1987) study, see also the critique by Hausman and Leonard (1992).

[15]In its proposed rules for damage assessment, the National Oceanic and Atmospheric Administration (1994) has proposed a default calibration of dividing by two, in the absence of direct arguments by trustees of natural resources for a different calibration factor.

Welfare Analysis

If an accurate measure of willingness-to-pay for the pure public good of the existence of an environmental amenity were available, the measured willingness-to-pay would belong in benefit-cost analysis, just like a pure public good based on resource use. Similarly, the measure should be included in the incentives government creates (through fines and damage payments) to avoid damaging an environmental amenity. As we know from the pure theory of public goods, we would simply add individual willingness-to-pay across the population.[16] In this section, we consider the welfare implications of using stated willingness-to-pay as if it were an accurate measure of preferences in the case that the responses are generated by the alternative hypotheses given above.

One set of problems arises even if willingness-to-pay is being measured accurately, if measured willingness-to-pay contains an altruism component. That is, individuals may be willing to pay to preserve an environmental amenity because of their concerns for others (who may be users or also nonusers). Consider what happens if society adds up everyone's willingness-to-pay and compares the sum with the cost of some action. As a matter of social welfare evaluation we might conclude that such altruistic externalities are double counting, since a utility benefit shows up in the willingness-to-pay of both the person enjoying the public good and the people who care about that person. For example, consider the income distribution problem in a three-person economy. If two of the people start to care about each other, is this change in preferences a reason for a government to increase the level of incomes allocated to the two of them? Similarly, we can ask if the government should devote more taxes to cleaning up lakes where neighbors are friendly with each other than to lakes where neighbors do not know (or care about) each other.

Moreover, if altruistic externalities are thought to be appropriately included in the analysis, it is necessary to include all such externalities for accurate evaluation. In particular, if people care about each other's utilities, they care about the costs borne by others as well as the benefits received by others. An adjustment for altruism must include external costs as well as external benefits if we are to avoid the possibility of a Pareto worsening from an action based on a calculation that appears to be a Pareto improvement (Milgrom, 1993).

A second general problem arises when stated willingness-to-pay may be a poor guess, even though it may be the best guess individuals have of their true willingness-to-pay. Individuals often face the problem of trying to form judgments about the gains from a purchase in settings where the

---

[16]For the correct use of a benefit-cost calculation, we need to be considering the marginal project for finding the optimum. With many projects under consideration, and a nonoptimal starting point, one does not get the right answer by asking about many projects independently and carrying out all that pass the test (Hoehn and Randall, 1989).

link between the commodity and utility is hard to evaluate. One example is the grade of gasoline to buy, assuming that one wants to minimize cost per mile. In the case of environmental amenities, individuals may have a derived demand based on their beliefs about the relationship between the amenity and variables they really care about. For example, they may care about the survival of a species and not know about the range of natural variation in population size, about the probability of survival as a function of population size, nor about the effect of environmental damage on population size. Such derived preferences may be a poor guide to policy; it may be more informative to have expert evaluation of the consequences of an environmental change than to consult the public directly about environmental damage.

The issues just discussed were based on the hypothesis that stated willingness-to-pay is a measure of an individual preference over an outcome. Under the hypothesis that responses reflect casual benefit-cost evaluations rather than preferences, it would be inappropriate to add any other benefits to those coming from a contingent valuation survey since such benefits are presumably included by the respondents, however imperfectly, in their benefit-cost analyses. But if contingent valuation is just a survey of benefit-cost estimates, rather than preferences, it might be better to have a more careful analysis done by people knowing more about environmental issues and about the principles of benefit-cost analysis. Moreover, if responses are benefit-cost estimates rather than preferences, they do not measure a compensable loss in damage suits.

The embedding effect is supportive of the hypothesis that responses are primarily determined by warm glow. If respondents get pleasure from thinking of themselves as supportive of the environment, the willingness-to-pay for this warm glow is not part of the gain from a *particular* environmental project—unless there are no cheaper ways of generating the warm glow. That is, if an individual wants to see the government do at least one environmental project (or n projects) a year in order to feel "environmentally supportive," the person should support one project, but not any particular project. Moreover, if different samples are asked about different projects, the responses will appear to support many projects, even though the warm glow comes from the desire to support a single project.

An illustration of this view comes from the fact that when individuals are asked simultaneously about many projects, stated willingness-to-pay is far below the sum of stated willingness-to-pay from asking about the projects separately. For example, Kemp and Maxwell (1993) asked one group for willingness-to-pay to minimize the risk of oil spills off the coast of Alaska, and found a mean stated willingness-to-pay of $85 (with a 95 percent confidence interval of ±$44). Then they asked a different sample for willingness-to-pay for a broad group of government programs, followed by asking these people to divide and subdivide their willingness-to-pay among the separate programs. By the time they reached minimizing the risk of oil spills off the coast of Alaska, they found a mean of $0.29 (with a 95 percent confidence interval of ±$0.21).

These findings make little sense if responses are measures of preferences, and considerable sense if the response is primarily a warm glow effect from a desire to express support for protecting the environment. In the latter circumstance, we would expect little warm glow for any single project in a context where respondents are asked about many government projects affecting the environment. Therefore warm glow may need to be purged from stated willingness-to-pay even if (as witnessed by charitable contributions) people really are willing to pay for some warm glow.[17]

A different complication arises if people do not really care about the resource, but care about the activity that might harm a resource. For example, the stated willingness-to-pay to clean up a natural oil seepage might be zero while the stated willingness-to-pay to clean up a man-made oil spill is positive. This outcome is the flip side of the "protest zero," where people state no willingness-to-pay to repair environmental damage that they feel is someone else's responsibility. As noted earlier, it is standard practice to consider this zero not to be an accurate measure of preferences, on the assumption that people care about the resource.

Survey results suggest that many answers are heavily influenced by concern about actions, not resources. For example, Desvousges et al. (1993) find a large stated willingness-to-pay to save small numbers of common birds. The finding seems much more likely to reflect a feeling that it is a shame that people do things that kill birds rather than a preference over the number of birds. Concern over the actions of others is different from concern about the state of the environment. Concern about actions is conventionally part of the basis of punitive damages, but not compensatory damages. That is, deliberately or recklessly destroying the property of others opens one up to liability for compensatory damages for the value of the property destroyed and also punitive damages. On the other hand, the legal system does not compensate people who are upset that others engage in actions such as reading *Lady Chatterley's Lover*. When and how such concerns should affect public policy is a complex issue, one not explored here.

One complication from the perspective of benefit-cost analysis is that preferences over acts (as opposed to states of the world) do not provide the consistency that is necessary for consistent economic policy. For example, if people are willing to pay to offset an act, then proposing and not doing an act appears to generate a welfare gain. For example, consider the warm glow from blocking development of a wilderness area. If one proposes two projects and has one blocked, are people better off (from the warm glow) than if one project is proposed and happens? Does this imply that the gov-

---

[17]In the context of the bird study by Desvousges et al. (1993), Kahneman (personal communication) has proposed to purge the warm glow by extrapolating willingness-to-pay as a function of birds saved back to zero and then subtracting this amount from the estimate of willingness-to-pay at any particular level of birds. This approach involves a curve-fitting extrapolation and the assumption that warm glow is totally insensitive to the magnitude of the problem, an assumption that is probably not completely correct.

ernment would do good by proposing projects that it does not mind seeing blocked? More generally, the relationship of benefit-cost analysis and Pareto optimality has been developed and is understood in a setting where preferences are defined over resources.

We note that under the hypothesis of Kahneman and Ritov (1993), responses to contingent valuation surveys are expressions of attitudes toward public goods that the respondents are required to state in dollar terms. Responses are then not measures of willingness-to-pay and provide no quantitative basis for estimates of environmental damages, although like polls generally, they do alert the government about concerns of the public.

The "Some Number Is Better than No Number" Fallacy

We began this essay by arguing that stated willingness-to-pay from contingent valuation surveys are not measures of nonuse preferences over environmental amenities. We then considered some of the welfare implications of treating the responses as if they were a measure of nonuse preferences when they were generated by different considerations. We concluded that such welfare analysis would not be a guide to good policy. Our conclusion is often challenged by the common Washington fallacy that even if stated willingness-to-pay is inaccurate, it should be used because no alternative estimate exists for public policy purposes. Put more crudely, one hears the argument that "some number is better than no number."[18] This argument leads to the claim that it is better to do benefit-cost studies with stated willingness-to-pay numbers, despite inaccuracy and bias, rather than use zero in the benefit-cost analysis and adjust for this omission somewhere else in the decision-making process.

To evaluate this argument, one needs a model of the determination of government policy.[19] Ideally, one would like to carry out a number of government decisions twice: once using zero in the benefit-cost study, and a second time using stated willingness-to-pay, with associated adjustments of the decision process in recognition of the inclusion or omission of a contingent valuation number. Such a comparison would rec-

---

[18]The history of economic policy awaits an investigation, similar to the famous study of the sociologist R. K. Merton on the history of Newton's "on the shoulders of giants" remark, to trace the lineage of the "some number is better than no number" fallacy.

[19]One can also consider how a social welfare maximizing planner might use the information in contingent valuation surveys. There is useful information if people are expressing preferences that are not otherwise accessible to the planner. However, if the other hypotheses are the correct description of the bases of willingness-to-pay responses, then the planner would not be receiving useful information. Treating the responses as measures of what they do not measure would mislead such a planner.

ognize that much more input goes into government decisions than just the benefit-cost study. That is, the comparison is not between relying on contingent valuation and relying on Congress, but between relying on Congress after doing a contingent valuation study and relying on Congress without doing a contingent valuation study.[20] Thus one is asking whether inclusion of such survey results tends to improve the allocation process, even if the numbers are not reliable estimates of the preferences called for by the theory. Similarly, one can ask whether the combination of fines and damage payments will result in more efficient decisions to avoid accidents with or without a contingent valuation estimate of nonuse value.

Judge Stephen Breyer (1993) has recently reviewed government responses to public perceptions of risk. Since he feels that public perceptions of risk are inaccurate and that Congress is responsive to these public perceptions, Breyer wants to increase the role of administrative expertise in designing public policy to deal with risks. A similar situation seems to exist with respect to contingent valuations of nonuse value. If we conclude that contingent valuation is really an opinion poll on concern about the environment in general, rather than a measure of preferences about specific projects, public policy is likely to do better if the concern is noted but expert opinion is used to evaluate specific projects and to set financial incentives to avoid accidents. One could hope for a more consistent relative treatment of alternative natural resources in this way.

In both economic logic and politics, we expect that using contingent valuation in decision making about the environment would soon be extended to other policy arenas where existence values are equally plausible. We do not expect that policy would be improved by using contingent valuation to affect the levels and patterns of spending for elementary school education, foreign aid, Medicaid, Medicare, AFDC, construction of safer highways, medical research, airline safety, or police and fire services. Yet people have concerns for others in all of these areas that parallel their concern for the environment.

Concern for other people naturally includes concern about their jobs. Thus, in considering rules that limit economic activity to protect the environment, it is as appropriate to include a contingent valuation of existence value for destroyed jobs as the one for protection of the environment. The fact that jobs may be created elsewhere in the economy does not rule out concern about job destruction per se. These possible extensions of the use of contingent valuation increase the importance of considering the "some number is better than no number" fallacy.

---

[20]The results of a contingent valuation survey are not binding. Thus a respondent who was behaving strategically would select a response that reflected his or her belief in how the results of the survey would affect actual outcomes. Thus we do not understand how the NOAA Panel could conclude that with a dichotomous choice question there is no strategic reason for the respondent to do otherwise than answer truthfully.

Referenda

We have heard the argument that if referenda are legitimate, so too is contingent valuation. That is, one can consider a contingent valuation survey to be a forecast of how voters would respond to a binding referendum. This perspective raises the same issues considered above. How should we decide how to interpret the bases of how people vote in referenda? Since different bases imply different appropriate uses of the responses, how should voting responses be used for economic analysis? Moreover, the necessity of calibration remains, since no obvious reason exists for people necessarily to vote the same in binding and nonbinding referenda. And, as in the previous section, we can ask whether we think we get better policies with or without such surveys.

It is interesting to consider issues raised by polls about actual referenda, as well as by the referenda themselves. Sometimes polls are accurate predictors of voting outcomes; sometimes, they are not, even when they are taken close to election day. Sometimes, repeated polls about the same referendum find very large changes in expressed intentions as a referendum campaign proceeds.

Magleby (1984) has analyzed statewide polls in California and Massachusetts for which at least three separate surveys were done. In some cases, the polls show roughly the same margin over time. Magleby calls these "standing opinions" and believes that this stability comes from the deep attachment to their opinions that voters hold on some controversial issues such as the death penalty and the equal rights amendment. In some cases, the polls show significant changes in the margin of preferences, but no change in the side that is ahead. Magleby calls these "uncertain opinions." Examples of such votes involve handgun registration and homosexual teachers. In some cases, significant changes in voting intentions occur as the campaign proceeds, with victory in the actual election going to the side that had at one time been far behind. Magleby calls these outcomes "opinion reversals." For example, in a referendum for flat rate electricity, a February poll showed 71 percent in favor, 17 percent opposed, and 12 percent undecided. The actual vote was 23 percent in favor, 69 percent opposed and 7 percent skipping this question. Other examples of such votes are a state lottery and a tax reduction measure. In his analysis of 36 propositions in California, Magleby found that on 28 percent of the issues, voters held standing opinions, on 19 percent voters had uncertain opinions, and on 53 percent he found opinion reversals. That is, in a majority of cases, early opinion polls were not good predictors of election outcomes. Moreover, they were not even good predictors of later opinion polls, after the campaign had run for some time.

It seems to us that responses to contingent valuation questionnaires for a single environmental issue are likely to be based on little information, since there is limited time for presentation and digestion of information during a contingent valuation survey. This conclusion suggests that the results of such surveys are unlikely to be accurate predictors of informed opinions on the same issues if respondents had more information and further time for reflection, including learning of the opinions of others. Such surveys are therefore unlikely to be a good basis for either informed policy-making or accurate damage assessment.

Even if a contingent valuation survey were a good predictor of an actual referendum, one can also question the use of actual referenda to obtain economic values. Considerable skepticism exists about the extent to which voting on a referendum represents informed decision making (see, for example, Magleby, 1984). In the functioning of a democracy, it may be more important to place some powers directly with the voters, rather than with their elected representatives, than to worry about the quality of decision making by voters.[21] However, incorporating contingent valuation survey responses in benefit-cost analyses or judicial proceedings does not seem to have a special role in enhancing democracy. In the looser context of legislative debate, such opinion polls may have a role to play, although the net value of that role is unclear.

NOAA Panel Evaluation of Contingent Valuation

In light of the controversy and the stakes involved, the National Oceanic and Atmospheric Administration recently appointed a prestigious panel to consider the reliability of contingent valuation studies of nonuse values in damage suits.[22] The panel's Report (NOAA, 1993) begins with criticisms of contingent valuation. In discussing the alleged inconsistency of some results with rational choice, the Report states (p. 4604) that: "some form of internal consistency is the least we would need to feel some confidence that the verbal answers correspond to some reality." The Report also addresses the need for rationality (p. 4604).

> It could be asked whether rationality is indeed needed. Why not take the values found as given? There are two answers. One is that we do not know yet how to reason about values without some assumption of rationality, if indeed it is possible at all. Rationality requirements impose a constraint on the possible values, without which damage judgments would be arbitrary. A second answer is that, as discussed above, it is difficult to find objective counterparts to verify the values obtained in the response to questionnaires.

In discussing "warm glow" effects, the Report recognizes the claim that contingent valuation responses include a warm glow. They write (p. 4605):

---

[21]The allocation of a decision directly to the voters, rather than indirectly through the choice of elected representatives, and the form in which referenda are put to voters are both methods of agenda control. In many settings, design of the agenda has large effects on voting outcomes.

[22]Kenneth Arrow (co-chair), Robert Solow (co-chair), Edward Leamer, Paul Portney, Roy Radner, and Howard Schuman.

"If this is so, CV [contingent valuation] responses should not be taken as reliable estimates of true willingness to pay."

The Report states that the burden of proof of reliability must rest on the survey designers. It states (p. 4609) that a survey would be unreliable if there were "[i]nadequate responsiveness to the scope of the environmental insult," as occurred in the embedding examples we have discussed. Unfortunately, the Panel did not elaborate on how to test for reliability.[23] We interpret the view they express to call for testing of the internal consistency of responses to the same survey instrument with different levels of environmental problem and policy successes. The Report cites no existing study that has passed such internal consistency tests.

The Report presents a set of guidelines which would define an "ideal" contingent valuation survey (and are summarized in Portney's paper in this issue). The Report asserts (p. 4610) that studies meeting such guidelines can produce estimates "reliable enough to be the starting point" of a judicial process of damage assessment. The Report offers no reason for reaching this conclusion, although the finding that surveys that do not meet their guidelines may be biased is not a basis for concluding that surveys that do meet their guidelines are not biased. In particular, they state no reason for reaching the conclusion that following their guidelines implies that responses are not dominated by a "warm glow." The Panel does not explicitly call for testing whether a survey done according to their guidelines is reliable. In particular, they do not mention a need to check the internal consistency of responses. Nor do they explain their conclusion that the inconsistencies between stated willingness-to-pay and economic theory come from survey design issues and would go away if the survey had followed their guidelines.

Conclusion

We believe that contingent valuation is a deeply flawed methodology for measuring nonuse values, one that does not estimate what its proponents claim to be estimating. The absence of direct market parallels affects both the ability to judge the quality of contingent valuation responses and the ability to calibrate responses to have usable numbers. It is precisely the lack of experience both in markets for environmental commodities and in the consequences of such decision that makes contingent valuation questions so hard to answer and the responses so suspect.

We have argued that internal consistency tests (particularly adding-up tests) are required to assess the reliability and validity of such surveys. When these tests have been done, contingent valuation has come up short. Contingent valuation proponents typically claim that the surveys used for these tests were not done well enough. Yet they have not subjected their

---

[23]Nor, we add, do Portney or Hanemann in this symposium.

own surveys to such tests. (We note that Hanemann does not address the question of which split-sample internal consistency tests, if any, he thinks a contingent valuation survey needs to pass.) There is a history of anomalous results in contingent valuation surveys that seems closely tied to the embedding problem. Although this problem has been recognized in the literature for over a decade, it has not been solved. Thus, we conclude that current contingent valuation methods should not be used for damage assessment or for benefit cost analysis.

It is impossible to conclude definitely that surveys with new methods (or the latest survey that has been done) will not pass internal consistency tests. Yet, we do not see much hope for such success. This skepticism comes from the belief that the internal consistency problems come from an absence of preferences, not a flaw in survey methodology. That is, we do not think that people generally hold views about individual environmental sites (many of which they have never heard of); or that, within the confines of the time available for survey instruments, people will focus successfully on the identification of preferences, to the exclusion of other bases for answering survey questions. This absence of preferences shows up as inconsistency in responses across surveys and implies that the survey responses are not satisfactory bases for policy.

REFERENCES

Andreoni, James, "Giving with Impure Altruism: Applications to Charity and Ricardian Equivalence," *Journal of Political Economy*, December 1989, *97*, 1447–58.

Bishop, R. C., and T. A. Heberlein, "Measuring Values of Extramarket Goods: Are Indirect Measures Biased?," *American Journal of Agricultural Economics*, December 1979, *61*, 926–30.

Breyer, Stephen, *Breaking the Vicious Circle: Toward Effective Risk Regulation*. Cambridge: Harvard University Press, 1993.

Carson, Richard T., et al., "A Contingent Valuation Study of Lost Passive Use Values Resulting From the Exxon Valdez Oil Spill," A Report to the Attorney General of the State of Alaska, 1992.

Desvousges, W. H., et al., "Measuring Natural Resource Damages with Contingent Valuation: Test of Validity and Reliability. In Hausman, J., ed., *Contingent Valuation: A Critical Assessment*. Amsterdam: North Holland Press, 1993, 91–164.

Diamond, P. A., "Testing the Internal Consistency of Contingent Valuation Surveys," working paper, MIT, 1993.

Diamond, P. A., and J. A. Hausman, "On Contingent Valuation Measurement of Nonuse Values" In Hausman, J., Ed., *Contingent Valuation: A Critical Assessment*. Amsterdam: North Holland Press, 1993, 3–38.

Diamond, P. A., J. A. Hausman, G. K. Leonard, and M. A. Denning, "Does Contingent Valuation Measure Preferences? Experimental Evidence." In Hausman, J., ed., *Contingent Valuation: A Critical Assessment*. Amsterdam: North Holland Press, 1993.

Dickie, Mark, Ann Fisher, and Shelby Gerking, "Market Transactions and Hypothetical Demand Data: A Comparative Study," *Journal of the American Statistical Association*, March 1987, *82*, 69–75.

Duffield, John W., and David A. Patterson, "Field Testing Existence Values: An In-stream Flow Trust Fund for Mountain Rivers," mimeo, University of Montana, 1992.

Hausman, J. A., *Contingent Valuation: A Critical Assessment*. Amsterdam: North Holland Press, 1993.

Hausman, J. A., and G. Leonard, *Contingent Valuation and the Value of Marketed Commodities*. Cambridge: Cambridge Economics, 1982.

Hoehn, John, and Alan Randall, "Too Many Proposals Pass the Benefit Cost Test," *American Economic Review*, June 1989, *79*, 544–51.

Kahneman, Daniel, "Comments on the Contingent Valuation Method." In Cummings, Ronald G., David S. Brookshire, and William D. Schulze, eds., *Valuing Environmental Goods: A State of the Arts Assessment of the Contingent Valuation Method*. Totowa: Rowman and Allanheld, 1986, 185–94.

Kahneman, Daniel, and Jack L. Knetsch, "Valuing Public Goods: The Purchase of Moral Satisfaction," *Journal of Environmental Economics and Management*, January 1992, *22*, 57–70.

Kahneman, Daniel and Ilana Ritov, "Determinants of Stated Willingness to Pay for Public Goods: A Study in the Headline Method," mimeo, Department of Psychology, University of California, Berkeley, 1993.

Kemp, M. A. and Maxwell, "Exploring a Budget Context for Contingent Valuation Estimates," In Hausman, J., ed., *Contingent Valuation: A Critical Assessment*, Amsterdam: North Holland Press, 1993, 217–70.

Loomis, John, John Hoehn, and Michael Hanemann, "Testing the Fallacy of Independent Valuation and Summation in Multi-part Policies: An Empirical Test of Whether 'Too Many Proposals Pass the Benefit Cost Test,'" mimeo, University of California, Davis, 1990.

Magleby, David B., *Direct Legislation, Voting on Ballot Propositions in the United States*. Baltimore and London: The Johns Hopkins University Press, 1984.

McFadden, Daniel, and Gregory K. Leonard, "Issues in the Contingent Valuation of Environmental Goods: Methodologies for Data Collection and Analysis." In Hausman, J., ed., *Contingent Valuation: A Critical Assessment*, Amsterdam: North Holland Press, 1993.

Milgrom, P., "Is Sympathy an Economic Value?," In Hausman, J., ed., *Contingent Valuation: A Critical Assessment*. Amsterdam: North Holland Press, 1993, 417–42.

Mitchell, Robert Cameron and Richard T. Carson, *Using Surveys to Value Public Goods*. Washington D. C.: Resources for the Future, 1989.

National Oceanic and Atmospheric Administration, 1993, "Report of the NOAA Panel on Contingent Valuation," *Federal Register*, 1993, *58*, 10, 4602–14.

National Oceanic and Atmospheric Administration, "National Resource Damage Assessments; Proposed Rules," *Federal Register*, 1994, *59*, 5, 1062–191.

Neill, Helen, R., et al., "Hypothetical Surveys and Real Economic Commitments," Economics Working Paper B-93-01, Department of Economics, College of Business Administration, University of South Carolina, 1993.

Samples, Karl C., and James R. Hollyer, "Contingent Valuation and Wildlife Resources in the Presence of Substitutes and Complements," In Johnson, Rebecca L., and Gary V. Johnson, eds., *Economic Valuation of Natural Resources: Issues, Theory and Applications*. Boulder: Westview Press, 1990, 177–192.

Schkade, D. A., and J. W. Payne, "Where do the numbers come from? How people respond to Contingent Valuation Questions." In Hausman, J., ed., *Contingent Valuation: A Critical Assessment*. Amsterdam: North Holland Press, 1993, 271–304.

Schulze, William, D., et al., "Contingent Valuation of Natural Resource Damages Due to Injuries to the Upper Clark Fork River Basin," State of Montana, Natural Resource Damage Program, 1993.

Seip, Kalle, and Jon Strand, "Willingness to Pay For Environmental Goods in Norway: A Contingent Valuation Study With Real Payment," *Environmental and Resource Economics*, 1992, *2*, 91–106.

Tolley, George S., et al., "Establishing and Valuing the Effects of Improved Visibility in the Eastern United States," Report to the U.S. Environmental Protection Agency, Washington, D.C., 1983.

Urban, Glen L., Gerald M. Katz, Thomas E. Hatch, and Alvin J. Silk, "The ASSESSOR Pre-Test Market Evaluation System," *Interfaces*, 1983 *13*, 38–59.

IV

The Goals of Environmental Policy: Economic Efficiency and Benefit-Cost Analysis

13 Is There a Role for Benefit-Cost Analysis in Environmental, Health, and Safety Regulation?

Kenneth J. Arrow   Paul R. Portney

Maureen L. Cropper   Milton Russell

George C. Eads   Richard Schmalensee

Robert W. Hahn   V. Kerry Smith

Lester B. Lave   Robert N. Stavins

Roger G. Noll

Kenneth J. Arrow is Joan Kenney Professor of Economics Emeritus at Stanford University; Maureen L. Cropper is Professor of Economics at the University of Maryland, and Principal Economist in the Research Department of the World Bank; George C. Eads is Vice President of Charles River Associates, Washington, D.C.; Robert W. Hahn is Resident Scholar at the American Enterprise Institute, and Director of the AEI-Brookings Joint Center for Regulatory Studies; Lester B. Lave is James Higgins Professor of Economics and Finance, Professor of Urban and Public Affairs, and Professor of Engineering and Public Policy at Carnegie-Mellon University; Roger G. Noll is Morris M. Doyle Centennial Professor, Department of Economics at Stanford University; Paul R. Portney is President and Senior Fellow at Resources for the Future; Milton Russell is Senior Fellow at the Joint Institute for Energy and Environment, and Professor Emeritus of Economics at the University of Tennessee; Richard Schmalensee is Dean of the Sloan School of Management at the Massachusetts Institute of Technology; V. Kerry Smith is Arts and Sciences Professor of Environmental Economics at Duke University; and Robert N. Stavins is Albert Pratt Professor of Business and Government, John F. Kennedy School of Government at Harvard University, and University Fellow at Resources for the Future.

The growing impact of regulations on the economy has led both Congress and the Administration to search for new ways of reforming the regulatory process. Many of these initiatives call for greater reliance on the use of economic analysis in the development and evaluation of regulations. One specific approach being advocated is benefit-cost analysis, an economic tool for comparing the desirable and undesirable impacts of proposed policies.

For environmental, health, and safety regulation, benefits are typically defined in terms of the value of having a cleaner environment or a safer workplace. Ideally, costs should be measured in the same terms: the losses implied by the increased prices that result from the costs of meeting a regulatory objective. In practice, the costs tend to be measured on the basis of direct compliance costs, with secondary consideration given to indirect costs, such as the value of time spent waiting in a motor vehicle inspection line.

The direct costs of federal environmental, health, and safety regulation appear to be on the order of $200 billion annually, or about the size of all domestic nondefense discretionary spending (1). The benefits of the regulations are less certain, but evidence suggests that some but not all recent regulations would pass a benefit-cost test (2). Moreover, a reallocation of expenditures on environmental, health, and safety regulations has the potential to save significant numbers of lives while using fewer resources (3). The estimated cost per statistical life saved has varied across regulations by a factor of more than $10 million (4), ranging from an estimated cost of $200,000 per statistical life saved with the Environmental Protection Agency's (EPA's) 1979 trihalomethane drinking water standard to more than $6.3 trillion with EPA's 1990 hazardous waste listing for wood-preserving chemicals (3, 5). Thus, a reallocation of priorities among these same regulations could save many more lives at the given cost, or alternatively, save the same number of lives at a much lower cost (6).

Most economists would argue that economic efficiency, measured as the difference between benefits and costs, ought to be one of the fundamental criteria for evaluating proposed environmental, health, and safety regulations. Because society has limited resources to spend on regulation, benefit-cost analysis can help illuminate the trade-offs involved in making different kinds of social investments. In this regard, it seems almost irresponsible to not conduct such analyses, because they can inform decisions about how scarce resources can be put to the greatest social good. Benefit-cost analysis can also help answer the question of how much regulation is enough. From an efficiency standpoint, the answer to this question is simple: regulate until the incremental benefits from regulation are just offset by the incremental costs. In practice, however, the problem is much more difficult, in large part because of inherent problems in measuring marginal benefits and costs. In addition, concerns about fairness and process may be important noneconomic factors that merit consideration. Regulatory policies inevitably involve winners and losers, even when aggregate benefits exceed aggregate costs (7).

Over the years, policy-makers have sent mixed signals regarding the use of benefit-cost analysis in policy evaluation. Congress has passed several statutes to protect health, safety, and the environment that effectively preclude the consideration of benefits and costs in the development of certain regulations, even though other statutes actually require the use of benefit-cost analysis (8). Meanwhile, former presidents Carter, Reagan, and Bush and President Clinton have all introduced formal processes for reviewing economic implications of major environmental, health, and safety regulations. Apparently the Executive Branch, charged with designing and implementing regulations, has seen a need to develop a yardstick against which the efficiency of regulatory proposals can be assessed. Benefit-cost analysis has been the yardstick of choice (9).

We suggest that benefit-cost analysis has a potentially important role to play in helping inform regulatory decision-making, although it should not be the sole basis for such decision-making. We offer the following eight principles on the appropriate use of benefit-cost analysis (10).

1. Benefit-cost analysis is useful for comparing the favorable and unfavorable effects of policies. Benefit-cost analysis can help decision-makers better understand the implications of decisions by identifying and, where appropriate, quantifying the favorable and unfavorable consequences of a proposed policy change, even when information on benefits and costs, is highly uncertain. In some cases, however, benefit-cost analysis cannot be used to conclude that the economic benefits of a decision will exceed or fall short of its costs, because there is simply too much uncertainty.

2. Decision-makers should not be precluded from considering the economic costs and benefits of different policies in the development of regulations. Agencies should be allowed to use economic analysis to help set regulatory priorities. Removing statutory prohibitions on the balancing of benefits and costs can help promote more efficient and effective regulation. Congress could further promote more effective use of resources by explicitly asking agencies to consider benefits and costs in formulating their regulatory priorities.

3. Benefit-cost analysis should be required for all major regulatory decisions. Although the precise definition of "major" requires judgment (11), this general requirement should be applied to all government agencies. The scale of a benefit-cost analysis should depend on both the stakes involved and the likelihood that the resulting information will affect the ultimate decision. For example, benefit-cost analyses of policies intended to retard or halt depletion of stratospheric ozone were worthwhile because of the large stakes involved and the potential for influencing public policy.

4. Although agencies should be required to conduct benefit-cost analyses for major decisions and to explain why they have selected actions for which reliable evidence indicates that expected benefits are significantly less than expected costs, those agencies should not be bound by strict benefit-cost tests. Factors other than aggregate economic benefits and costs, such as equity within and across generations, may be important in some decisions.

5. Benefits and costs of proposed policies should be quantified wherever possible. Best estimates should be presented along with a description of the uncertainties. In most instances, it should be possible to describe the effects of proposed policy changes in quantitative terms; however, not all impacts can be quantified, let alone be given a monetary value. Therefore, care should be taken to assure that quantitative factors do not dominate important qualitative factors in decision-making. If an agency wishes to introduce a "margin of safety" into a decision, it should do so explicitly (*12*).

Whenever possible, values used to quantify benefits and costs in monetary terms should be based on trade-offs that individuals would make, either directly or, as is often the case, indirectly in labor, housing, or other markets (*13*). Benefit-cost analysis is premised on the notion that the values to be assigned to program effects—favorable or unfavorable—should be those of the affected individuals, not the values held by economists, moral philosophers, environmentalists, or others.

6. The more external review that regulatory analyses receive, the better they are likely to be. Historically, the U.S. Office of Management and Budget has played a key role in reviewing selected major regulations, particularly those aimed at protecting the environment, health, and safety. Peer review of economic analyses should be used for regulations with potentially large economic impacts (*14*). Retrospective assessments of selected regulatory impact analyses should be carried out periodically.

7. A core set of economic assumptions should be used in calculating benefits and costs. Key variables include the social discount rate, the value of reducing risks of premature death and accidents, and the values associated with other improvements in health. It is important to be able to compare results across analyses, and a common set of economic assumptions increases the feasibility of such comparisons. In addition, a common set of appropriate economic assumptions can improve the quality of individual analyses. A single agency should establish a set of default values for typical benefits and costs and should develop a standard format for presenting results.

Both economic efficiency and intergenerational equity require that benefits and costs experienced in future years be given less weight in decision-making than those experienced today. The rate at which future benefits and costs should be discounted to present values will generally not equal the rate of return on private investment. The discount rate should instead be based on how individuals trade off current for future consumption. Given uncertainties in identifying the correct discount rate, it is appropriate to use a range of rates. Ideally, the same range of discount rates should be used in all regulatory analyses.

8. Although benefit-cost analysis should focus primarily on the overall relation between benefits and costs, a good analysis will also identify

important distributional consequences. Available data often permit reliable estimation of major policy impacts on important subgroups of the population (15). On the other hand, environmental, health, and safety regulations are neither effective nor efficient tolls for achieving redistributional goals.

Conclusion. Benefit-cost analysis can play an important role in legislative and regulatory policy debates on protecting and improving health, safety, and the natural environment. Although formal benefit-cost analysis should not be viewed as either necessary or sufficient for designing sensible public policy, it can provide an exceptionally useful framework for consistently organizing disparate information, and in this way, it can greatly improve the process and, hence, the outcome of policy analysis. If properly done, benefit-cost analysis can be of great help to agencies participating in the development of environmental, health, and safety regulations, and it can likewise be useful in evaluating agency decision-making and in shaping statutes.

REFERENCES AND NOTES

1. T. D. Hopkins, "Cost of Regulation: Filling in the Gaps" (report prepared for the Regulatory Information Service Center, Rochester, NY, 1992); Office of Management and Budget, *Budget of the United States Government, Fiscal Year 1996* (Government Printing Office, Washington, DC, 1995).
2. R. W. Hahn, in *Risks, Costs, and Lives Saved: Getting Better Results from Regulation.* R. W. Hahn, Ed. (Oxford Univ. Press, Oxford, and AEI Press, Washington, DC, in press).
3. J. F. Morrall, *Regulation 10*, 25 (November–December 1986).
4. These figures represent the incremental direct cost of part or all of proposed regulations relative to specified baselines. For examinations of issues associated with estimating the full costs of environmental protection, see (16).
5. Office of Management and Budget, *Regulatory Program of the United States Government: April 1, 1992–March 31, 1993* (Government Printing Office, Washington, DC, 1993).
6. If the goals of a program or the level of a particular standard have been specified, economic analysis can still play an important role in evaluating the costs of various approaches for achieving these goals. Too frequently, regulation has used a one-size-fits-all or command-and-control approach to achieve specified goals. Cost-effectiveness analysis, which identifies the minimum-cost means to achieve a given goal, can aid in designing more flexible approaches, such as using markets and performance standards that reward results.
7. L. Lave, in (2).
8. Several statutes have been interpreted to restrict the ability of regulators to consider benefits and costs. Examples include the Federal Food, Drug, and Cosmetic Act (Delaney Clause); health standards under the Occupational Safety and Health Act; safety regulations from the National Highway and Transportation Safety Agency; the Clean Air Act; the Clean Water Act; the Resource Conservation and Recovery Act; the Safe Drinking Water Act; and the Comprehensive Environmental Response, Compensation, and Liability Act. On the other hand,

the Consumer Product Safety Act, the Toxic Substances Control Act, and the Federal Insecticide, Fungicide, and Rodenticide Act explicitly allow regulators to consider benefits and costs.

9. In particular cases, such as the phasing out of lead in gasoline and the banning of certain asbestos products, benefit-cost analysis has played an important role in decision-making (17).

10. For a more extended discussion, see (18).

11. In this context, "major" has traditionally been defined in terms of annual economic impacts on the cost side.

12. For example, potentially irreversible consequences are not outside the scope of benefit-cost analysis. The combination of irreversibilities and uncertainty can have significant effects on valuation.

13. For a conceptual overview of methods of estimating the benefits of environmental regulation and a brief survey of empirical estimates, see (19). For examinations of regulatory costs, see (16).

14. For a description of problems that arise when benefit-cost analysis is used in the absence of standardized peer review, see (20).

15. G. B. Christiansen and T. H. Tietenberg, in *Handbook of Natural Resource and Energy Economics*, A. V. Kneese and J. L. Sweeney, Eds. (North-Holland, Amsterdam, 1985), vol. 1, pp. 345–393.

16. R. Schmalensee, in *Balancing Economic Growth and Environmental Goals*, M. B. Kotowski, Ed. (American Council for Capital Formation, Center for Policy Research, Washington, DC, 1994), pp. 55–75; A. B. Jaffe, S. R. Peterson, P. R. Portney, R. N. Stavins, *J. Econ. Lit. 33*, 132 (1995).

17. A. Fraas, *Law Contemp. Probl. 54*, 113 (1991).

18. K. J. Arrow et al., *Benefit-Cost Analysis in Environmental, Health, and Safety Regulation* (AEI Press, Washington, DC, 1996).

19. M. L. Cropper and W. E. Oates, *J. Econ. Lit. 30*, 675 (1992); A. M. Freeman, *The Measurement of Environmental and Resource Values* (Resources for the Future, Washington, DC, 1993).

20. W. N. Grubb, D. Whittington, M. Humphries, in *Environmental Policy Under Reagan's Executive Order: The Role of Benefit-Cost Analysis*. V. K. Smith, Ed. (Univ. of North Carolina Press, Chapel Hill, 1984), pp. 121–164.

21. This work was sponsored by the American Enterprise Institute, the Annapolis Center, and Resources for the Future, with funding provided by the Annapolis Center. The manuscript benefited from comments from an editor and a referee, but the authors alone are responsible for the final product.

14   *Regulating the Regulators*

W. Kip Viscusi

W. Kip Viscusi is John F. Cogan, Jr. Professor of Law amd Economics, Harvard Law School.

I. Oversight in a World of Financial Limits

Since the 1970s, there has been a tremendous growth in government regulation pertaining to risk and the environment. These efforts have emerged quite legitimately because market processes alone cannot fully address risk-related concerns.[1] Without some kind of regulation or liability, for example, firms lack appropriate incentives to restrict their pollution. Similarly, when products or activities are extremely risky, if people are not cognizant of the risks they face, the firms generating the hazards may not have adequate incentives to issue warnings. To solve these problems, regulatory agencies have mounted a wide variety of efforts to improve the quality of the air we breathe, the water we drink, the products we use, and the workplaces where we toil.

Notwithstanding the legitimate impetus for these regulatory activities, government agencies sometimes overstep their bounds. The presence of market failure creates a potential role for government action, but this action must be well conceived. A clearly misguided and unduly burdensome regulation certainly would not be in society's best interest even if it were intended to address a legitimate social problem. As in other policy contexts, the task is to structure regulatory efforts to promote society's welfare as effectively as possible.

The importance of this task stems from the need to ensure that the substantial overall cost of regulatory policies is justified. Estimates suggest that total annual regulatory costs are in the vicinity of $400 to $500 billion.[2] Of this amount, approximately $100 billion comprises transfers that do not create a net efficiency loss. The remaining $300 to $400 billion is divided between paperwork costs and other regulatory expenses. It is particularly noteworthy that the estimated annual cost of environmental regulations alone is $124 billion.[3]

"Regulating the Regulators," by W. Kip Viscusi, from *University of Chicago Law Review*, 63:1423–1461 (1996).

[1] See generally W. Kip Viscusi, John M. Vernon, and Joseph E. Harrington, Jr., *Economics of Regulation and Antitrust* (MIT 2d ed 1995).

[2] Id at 34.

[3] Thomas D. Hopkins, *The Costs of Federal Regulation*, 2 J Reg & Soc Costs 16 (1992).

Although these estimates show that regulatory costs are not trivial, the price tag could become even greater. Unfortunately, much more remains to be done if our objective is a risk-free society. Indeed, even if the entire gross domestic product were allocated to preventing accidental deaths, we would have available less than $60 million per fatality to be prevented.[4] Moreover, if we allocated all of our resources to preventing accidental deaths, we would have nothing left to spend to prevent cancer, or to provide food, housing, medical care, and so on. In short, regulatory expenditures could easily outstrip society's ability to pay. Eventually we must draw the line on how much we wish to allocate, for risk regulation, environmental protection, and other regulatory programs. The questions are: how far should we go in these efforts, and how should we choose among them?

In some cases, an absolutist commitment to a zero-risk level may not only be unduly expensive, but it may also prove counterproductive. In specifying the requirements for an updated computerized air traffic control system, the Federal Aviation Administration ("FAA") insisted that such a system have a reliability of 99.99999 percent ("seven nines" reliability). This system would only fail three seconds per year on average. Some observers believe that the contractual requirements the FAA stipulated for IBM, the system's designer, violated the laws of physics.[5] The commitment to perfection paralyzed the updating of the air traffic control system and led to the old system's remaining in place, thereby leading to a higher risk than would have existed had a more flexible approach been adopted.[6]

Although the Executive Office of the President has long exercised formal oversight to foster sounder regulation, these efforts have not been entirely successful because they have occasionally conflicted with agencies' legislative mandates. In hopes of establishing a consistent basis for assessing and selecting regulations, the current Congress has considered a series of bills designed to promote more effective regulations.[7] In some instances, these were omnibus bills that pertained to regulatory policy in general. Such broad-based reforms would supersede agencies' legislative mandates, impose benefit-cost tests, and alter the manner in which risks are assessed. Other more narrowly framed bills either would leave existing legislative mandates intact or else would simply reform the regulatory approach to a specific class of policies, such as the Environmental Protection Agency's ("EPA") hazardous waste cleanup programs under Superfund.[8] Which directions should be selected for regulatory policy and which tests are most important will be the focus of this Essay.

---

[4]W. Kip Viscusi, *Fatal Tradeoffs: Public and Private Responsibilities for Risk* 5 (Oxford 1992).

[5]For a full description of this policy approach and its limitations, see Matthew L. Wald, *Ambitious Update of Air Navigation Becomes a Fiasco*, NY Times A1, A11 (Jan 29, 1996).

[6]The F.A.A. is so risk averse, it is shod with this idea, "We can't field anything until it's absolutely perfect.'" Id (reporting statement of Thomas C. Richards, an FAA Administrator under President Bush).

[7]For discussion of these bills, see notes 89–94 and accompanying text.

[8]The legislation also could, for example, impose benefit-cost tests in the setting of drinking water standards or other narrowly defined environmental objectives rather than an omnibus approach that revamps all EPA activities.

The guiding principle underlying the policy prescriptions advocated here is that government agencies should select those policies that are in society's best interest. Honest risk assessment and benefit-cost balancing should be our guides. After reviewing the existing legislative mandates of regulatory agencies and the role of government oversight, this Essay will explore several techniques for assessing regulatory policies, including benefit-cost analysis, cost-effectiveness tests, risk assessment, and risk-risk analysis. Each of these methodological approaches provides a different perspective on the merits of regulatory policies. These techniques are reflected in various current oversight guidelines and in guidelines proposed by various bills.

Many reformers have encountered political difficulties. Perhaps this is because many of their proposals are overly excessive grab bags of institutional and substantive reforms, while other proposals have failed to recognize the underlying deficiencies in agencies' legislative mandates. Improving regulatory efficiency will remain a salient policy objective so long as society devotes considerable resources to these efforts, and the fate of any current or future piece of legislation will not affect its underlying importance.

II. The Effect of Legislative Mandates on Regulatory Policy

It is somewhat ironic that Congress has taken the initiative in putting regulatory policies on sounder footing. Many of the problems are of Congress's own making. The underlying difficulties stem primarily from past congressional actions and legislation that circumscribed the character of regulatory policies and limited attempts to balance regulation equitably. Congress, of course, has not assumed the responsibility for drafting specific regulations, though there are some exceptions, such as the cigarette labeling requirements.[9] For the most part, the role of Congress has been to define broadly the legislative objectives of regulatory agencies. The agencies then implement these objectives subject to judicial review and the review process established within the Executive Office of the President.

One potential check on excessive regulation is judicial review. However, the success of a legal challenge to a regulation is not based on its overall economic merits but rather on whether the agency adhered to its legislative mandate in promulgating the regulation. In many instances the legislation has defined the mission of the agency so narrowly that trade-offs between regulatory costs and risk reduction objectives are not permitted. The Clean Air Act, for example, specifically precludes the consideration of costs in the setting of national ambient air quality standards.[10] Indeed, no legislative mandates specifically require that an agency show that the economic benefits exceed the costs of a regulation, and in most

---

[9]15 USC § 1333 (1994) (specifying exact wording and format of warning labels).

[10]See *Lead Industries Association v EPA*, 647 F2d 1130, 1148–51 (DC Cir 1980) (interpreting 42 USC § 7409 (1988) to prohibit consideration of feasibility in setting air quality standards).

instances there are specific provisions that could give the agency administrator the leeway to avoid such explicit balancing. Even if balancing is not
required, if tradeoffs were explicitly permitted, administrators would have
the option of promulgating more reasonable policies. Perhaps more important, OMB could better pressure them into doing so.

Most of the original controversy surrounding legislative mandates to
regulatory agencies derived from litigation over proposed Occupational
Safety and Health Administration ("OSHA") regulations. The restrictive
terms of the Occupational Safety and Health Act of 1970 are similar to
those of other agency legislative mandates in that the Act does not urge the
agency to balance the benefits and costs of its safety regulations and adopt
those regulations that achieve the greatest net gain to society. Rather, the
Act sets the agency on a single-minded mission "to assure so far as possible every working man and woman in the Nation safe and healthful working conditions."[11] The agency, of course, does not have unbridled discretion. For example, the Act also requires that the tasks imposed by OSHA
regulations be "feasible."[12] Nevertheless, nothing establishes any necessary
relationship between the benefits derived from the regulation and the costs
imposed on society.

The first major challenge to OSHA's narrow interpretation of its legislative mandate was the 1980 Supreme Court decision involving the OSHA
benzene standard.[13] Although that decision did not resolve the benefit-cost
tradeoff issue, it did hold that the agency cannot require employers to take
costly measures that merely eliminate trivial hazards but instead must show
that the hazards pose a significant risk to human health and thus the standards are "reasonably necessary or appropriate to provide safe or healthful employment."[14] The Court specifically noted that it may not be socially
desirable to eliminate trivial risks:

> But "safe" is not the equivalent of "risk-free." There are many activities that we
> engage in every day—such as driving a car or even breathing city air—that entail
> some risk of accident or material health impairment; nevertheless, few people
> would consider these activities "unsafe." Similarly, a workplace can hardly be con-
> sidered "unsafe" unless it threatens the workers with a significant risk of harm.[15]

How small is too small to merit regulation is still an unresolved issue.
From an economic-efficiency standpoint, it may be desirable to regulate
even a minuscule risk if the cost of reducing the risk is correspondingly
small. What matters is the balance between risks and costs, not necessarily the magnitude of the risk. Nevertheless, how we think about the magnitude of the risk and how we estimate this magnitude are also important.
Much of the recent regulatory reform legislation before Congress is specif-

---

[11]Occupational Safety and Health Act of 1970, Pub L No 91-596, 84 Stat 1590, codified at 29
USC § 651(b) (1994).

[12]29 USC § 655(b)(5) (1994).

[13]*Industrial Union Department, AFL-CIO v American Petroleum Institute*, 448 US 607 (1980).

[14]Id at 642.

[15]Id.

ically concerned with this risk-assessment issue since distortions in the assessment of risk produce a misleading index of the merits of the regulatory policy.

The next principal Supreme Court case on regulatory authority was the 1981 decision regarding the OSHA cotton dust standard.[16] That standard had been challenged by the textile industry as unduly burdensome and not reflecting an appropriate balance of benefits and costs. The Court ruled that the agency was not required to adopt a benefit-cost test. It interpreted the agency's legislative mandate in terms of whether the regulation was "capable of being done" rather than interpreting feasibility in terms of obtaining an appropriate safety payoff from regulatory costs.[17]

Although OSHA is not required to adopt a benefit-cost test, a 1991 decision of the D.C. Circuit indicated that OSHA may nevertheless have the leeway to incorporate more balancing in the setting of regulatory standards than it has in the past.[18] The court interpreted one provision of the Occupational Safety and Health Act permissively, finding that it could reasonably be read to require the balancing of benefits and costs.[19] In a concurring opinion, Judge Stephen Williams outlined a new test for regulatory policy—risk-risk analysis—that suggests that some regulations that are inordinately burdensome and that do not produce very substantial benefits in return for substantial costs may in fact have a net adverse effect on public health.[20] Risk-risk analysis will be considered in greater detail below.

The primary message from the various relevant court decisions is that administrative agencies enjoy wide discretion to set regulations in whatever manner they choose, since their legislative mandates usually neither prescribe nor forbid specific economic-policy tests. For example, *Chevron U.S.A. Inc. v Natural Resources Defense Council, Inc.*[21] concerned a challenge to the EPA's "bubble policy," which permitted firms to treat air pollution as if an artificial bubble surrounded the plant. Rather than complying with specific air pollution requirements for each smokestack at the plant, firms could, in effect, examine the total emissions within the bubble and then select the most cost-effective means of reaching a specific air pollution target. Although the applicability of the bubble policy was limited to situations specifically approved by the agency, the Natural Resources Defense Council ("NRDC") nevertheless challenged the flexibility offered by EPA. Whereas previous court challenges had suggested that regulatory agencies had interpreted their legislative mandates too narrowly, the NRDC's challenge suggested that the EPA had interpreted its mandate too broadly, in too balanced a fashion. In particular, it gave firms flexibility in selecting the most cost-effective means

---

[16]*American Textile Manufacturers Institute, Inc. v Donovan*, 452 US 490 (1981).

[17]Id at 508–09.

[18]See *International Union, UAW v OSHA*, 938 F2d 1310 (DC Cir 1991).

[19]Id at 1318–21.

[20]*International Union*, 938 F2d at 1326 (Williams concurring). This approach is also called health-health analysis. See, for example, Cass R. Sunstein, *Health-Health Tradeoffs*, 63 U Chi L Rev 1533 (1996).

[21]467 US 837 (1984).

for reducing pollution rather than requiring that every emissions source meet a stringent pollution standard. In *Chevron*, the Supreme Court ruled that agencies may interpret ambiguities in their legislative mandates in a reasonable manner, and so long as they are doing so, courts will not interfere with the agencies' interpretations.[22]

Because *Chevron* mandates this deferential standard of review, those attempting to reform regulatory policy cannot rely on existing legislative mandates to constrain agency action. As I will demonstrate below by examining specific regulatory policies, agencies have largely used their restrictive legislative mandates as shields to prevent judicial challenges to regulations as well as to resist internal administration efforts to achieve reasonable benefit-cost balancing. The regulatory reform bills before the 104th Congress consequently can serve as a mechanism for placing regulatory policies on more solid footing.

III. The Regulatory Oversight Process

Regulatory agencies respond to their own constituencies within the constraints imposed by their legislative mandates and the statutes they enforce. Because agencies' parochial interests do not necessarily reflect national interests, the past six presidents have launched formal efforts to monitor and influence regulatory policies. President Nixon instituted "quality of life" reviews to examine the economic costs of regulations, a process that was formalized under the Ford administration.[23] President Ford established a new agency within the Executive Office of the President, the Council on Wage and Price Stability, that would oversee new regulatory policies and file comments in the public record on behalf of the Administration.[24] This oversight group did not, however, have any formal veto power over regulatory policy. President Carter continued this process, adding a requirement that regulations must be cost-effective.[25] In their inflationary impact analyses, agencies had to show that the "least burdensome of the acceptable alternatives has been chosen."[26]

These tests did not require that the benefits of regulations exceed the costs. President Reagan, however, did impose such a requirement and altered the institutional mechanism for regulatory review, shifting responsibility to the Office of Information and Regulatory Affairs ("OIRA") in the Office of Management and Budget ("OMB"), where it remains.[27] The Reagan approach stipulated that "[r]egulatory actions shall not be undertaken unless the potential benefits to society for the regulation outweigh the potential costs to society."[28]

---

[22]Id at 842–45.

[23]See Exec Order No 11821, 3 CFR 926 (1974).

[24]See Council on Wage and Price Stability Act, Pub L No 93-387, 88 Stat 750 (1974), codified as amended at 12 USC § 1904 (1976).

[25]See Exec Order No 12044, 3 CFR 152 (1978).

[26]Id § 2(d)(3), 3 CFR at 154.

[27]Exec Order No 12291, 3 CFR 127 (1981).

[28]Id § 2(b), 3 CFR at 128.

This requirement was not, however, binding in instances where the agency's legislative mandate ruled out a benefit-cost test,[29] which unfortunately is the norm for most risk- and environmental-regulation agencies.

This structure remained intact under the Bush administration and has continued in place with only slight modification under the Clinton administration. The Clinton administration changed the wording of the Executive Order, making it clear that not all regulatory benefits and costs can be monetized and that nonmonetary consequences should be influential as well.[30] President Clinton also greatly expanded the openness of the review process and increased the disclosure requirements.[31]

The degree to which these benefit-cost tests lack binding force is exemplified in the profile of regulatory policies in Table 1. Let us take as our reference point for desirable regulatory policies an implicit value of $5 million per life saved, which is the wage-risk tradeoff reflected in worker decisions.[32] Put somewhat differently, if a worker is facing an average annual job risk of 1:10,000, such a worker will demand a wage premium of $500 to incur the risk. A group of ten thousand such workers, one of whom is expected to die, consequently will receive $5 million in return for this additional risk. This kind of value-of-life calculation goes well beyond the monetary loss associated with the risk of mortality and is generally accepted in the economics literature as the appropriate measure of society's willingness to pay for risk reduction.[33] Moreover, this methodology has been explicitly endorsed by the OMB for purposes of valuing risk reduction in regulatory policies.[34] A value-of-life figure of $5 million falls in the midpoint of the estimated range; most studies in the literature have estimated the value of life anywhere from $3 million to $7 million.[35]

For concreteness, let us take as an appropriate cutoff for regulatory policy the cost per statistical life saved of $5 million. Regulatory policies that save statistical lives are those addressed at preventing very small risks of death. For example, a worker safety program that reduced job risks by 1/10,000 for 10,000 workers would save one statistical life on average. The attractiveness of these efforts is quite different from those that save identified lives, such as the child trapped in a well or workers trapped in a coal mine. If the OMB succeeded in approving only those policies whose benefits exceeded the costs, the no policies with a cost per life saved in excess of $5 million would be adopted. As the statistics presented in Table 1 demonstrate, policies that meet this benefit-cost threshold are the exception rather than the norm. Indeed, very few policies actually pass the test.

---

[29]Id § 2, 3 CFR at 128.

[30]See Exec Order No 12866 § 1(a), (b)(6), 3 CFR 638, 638–39 (1993).

[31]For a description of these provisions, see Richard H. Pildes and Cass R. Sunstein, *Reinventing the Regulatory State*, 62 U Chi L Rev 1, 22–24 (1995).

[32]See generally Viscusi, *Fatal Tradeoffs* at 34–74 (cited in note 4).

[33]For a survey of the literature, see id at 57–74.

[34]See Office of Management and Budget, *Regulatory Program of the United States Government, April 1, 1988–March 31, 1989* 570 (US GPO 1989); Office of Management and Budget, *Regulatory Program of the United States Government, April 1, 1990–March 31, 1991* 662–63 (US GPO 1990).

[35]Viscusi, *Fatal Tradeoffs* at 51–74 (cited in note 4).

Table 1 The Cost of Various Risk-Reducing Regulations Per Life Saved

Pass Benefit-Cost Test

Regulation	Year & Status[a]	Agency	Initial Annual Risk[b]	Annual Lives Saved	Cost per Life Saved (millions of 1984 dollars)
Unvented Space Heaters	1980 F	CPSC	2.7 in 10^5	63.000	.10
Oil & Gas Well Service	1983 P	OSHA-S	1.1 in 10^3	50.000	.10
Cabin Fire Protection	1985 F	FAA	6.5 in 10^8	15.000	.20
Passive Restraints/Belts	1984 F	NHTSA	9.1 in 10^5	1,850.000	.30
Underground Construction	1989 F	OSHA-S	1.6 in 10^3	8.100	.30
Alcohol & Drug Control	1985 F	FRA	1.8 in 10^6	4.200	.50
Servicing Wheel Rims	1984 F	OSHA-S	1.4 in 10^5	2.300	.50
Seat Cushion Flammability	1984 F	FAA	1.6 in 10^7	37.000	.60
Floor Emergency Lighting	1984 F	FAA	2.2 in 10^8	5.000	.70
Crane Susp Persnl Platf	1988 F	OSHA-S	1.8 in 10^3	5.000	1.20
Cncrte & Masonry Constr	1988 F	OSHA-S	1.4 in 10^5	6.500	1.40
Hazard Communication	1983 F	OSHA-S	4.0 in 10^5	200.000	1.80
Benzene/Fugtve Emissions	1984 F	EPA	2.1 in 10^5	0.310	2.80

Fail Benefit-Cost Test

Regulation	Year & Status[a]	Agency	Initial Annual Risk[b]	Annual Lives Saved	Cost per Life Saved (millions of 1984 dollars)
Grain Dust	1987 F	OSHA-S	2.1 in 10^4	4.000	5.30
Radionuclides/Urnm Mines	1984 F	EPA	1.4 in 10^4	1.100	6.90
Benzene	1987 F	OSHA-H	8.8 in 10^4	3.800	17.10
Arsenic/Glass Plant	1986 F	EPA	8.0 in 10^4	0.110	19.20
Ethylene Oxide	1984 F	OSHA-H	4.4 in 10^5	2.800	25.60
Arsenic/Copper Smelter	1986 F	EPA	9.0 in 10^4	0.060	26.50
Urnium Mill Tlngs Inactive	1983 F	EPA	4.3 in 10^4	2.100	27.60
Urnium Mill Tlngs Active	1983 F	EPA	4.3 in 10^4	2.100	53.00
Asbestos	1986F	OSHA-H	6.7 in 10^5	74.700	89.30
Asbestos	1989 F	EPA	2.9 in 10^5	10.000	104.20
Arsenic/Glass Mfrg	1986 R	EPA	3.8 in 10^5	0.250	142.00
Benzene/Storage	1984 R	EPA	6.0 in 10^7	0.043	202.00
Radionuclides/DOE Faclts	1984 R	EPA	4.3 in 10^6	0.001	210.00
Radionuclides/Elm Phsphrs	1984 R	EPA	1.4 in 10^5	0.046	270.00
Benzene/Ethylbnznl Styrne	1984 R	EPA	2.0 in 10^6	0.006	483.00
Arsenic/Low-Arsnc Copper	1986 R	EPA	2.6 in 10^4	0.090	764.00
Benzene/Maleic Anhydride	1984 R	EPA	1.1 in 10^6	0.029	820.00
Land Disposal	1988 F	EPA	2.3 in 10^8	2.520	3,500.00
EDB	1989 R	OSHA-H	2.5 in 10^4	0.002	15,600.00
Formaldehyde	1987 F	OSHA-H	6.8 in 10^7	0.010	72,000.00

[a]P, R, or F—Proposed, rejected or final rule.

[b]Annual deaths per exposed population. An exposed population of 10^3 is 1,000, 10^4 is 10,000, etc.

Source: Viscusi, *Fatal Tradeoffs* at 264 table 14-5 (cited in note 4). Based on information presented in John F. Morrall III, *A Review of the Record,* 10 Reg 25, 30 (Nov–Dec 1986). These statistics were updated by John F. Morrall III, via unpublished communication with the author, July 10, 1990.

It is noteworthy that all of the listed regulations from the Department of Transportation ("DOT"), which is unusual in that it uses a benefit-cost approach, do meet the benefit-cost test. In particular, DOT traditionally valued lives at the present value of lost earnings and did not pursue policies when the cost per life saved exceeded that amount. Subsequently, DOT moved to a willingness-to-pay approach and currently values life in the vicinity of $3 million per statistical life.[36]

The costs of most of the regulations in Table 1 exceed the $5 million-per-lost-life threshold. It should be emphasized that Table 1 includes only specific regulatory policies and does not include agency actions and programs that do not result in actual regulations. For example, the Superfund program prevents cases of cancer at a cost per case avoided of almost $4 billion, but this program is not captured in the statistics reported here.[37] Table 1 includes both proposed and rejected regulations. If in fact the regulatory oversight process eliminated all regulations that did not pass a benefit-cost test, then, assuming that there were no other major categories of unquantified benefits, one would expect all regulations with a cost per life saved in excess of $5 million to be rejected. However, it is noteworthy that the agencies have not rejected all such ineffective programs. Indeed, the lowest cost-per-life-saved amount for a regulation rejected by the OMB is the one associated with the EPA's arsenic/glass manufacturing standard, for which the cost per life saved was $142 million. Thus, the OMB has succeeded in eliminating only extremely ineffective regulations. This result has not arisen because the OMB failed to implement the terms of the Executive Orders. Rather, it is a consequence of the strict nature of agencies' legislative mandates, which require or permit them to foster narrowly defined objectives, such as risk reduction or environmental protection, irrespective of maintaining a reasonable benefit-cost tradeoff.

IV. Alternative Regulatory Policy Tests

A. Benefit-Cost Analysis

The most comprehensive regulatory test from an economic efficiency standpoint is benefit-cost analysis.[38] The overall concept is straightforward and quite intuitively appealing. In particular, government agencies should adopt

---

[36]The author served as a consultant to the FAA and prepared a report to the agency on value-of-life issues to facilitate the agency's recent selection of a value-of-life figure. See W. Kip Viscusi, *The Value of Risk to Life and Health*, 31 J Econ Lit 1912 (1993) (study based on FAA report).

[37]The Superfund cost estimate of $4 billion per case of cancer is discussed in W. Kip Viscusi and James T. Hamilton, *Cleaning up Superfund*, Pub Int 52 (Summer 1996). This research was prepared under a cooperative agreement with the EPA.

[38]See generally Edith Stokey and Richard Zeckhauser, *A Primer for Policy Analysis* (Norton 1978).

regulatory policies that best advance society's interests, or those that provide the greatest amount of benefits, less costs. In addition, no regulatory policy should be pursued unless the benefits exceed the costs. In the case of a regulation targeted at mortality risks, the expected number of live saved multiplied by the value of life must exceed the regulatory costs for the policy to be desirable on this view.

Much of the controversy over this test arises from the frequent concern that not all benefit components are adequately considered. This difficulty is particularly great with respect to policy outcomes that lack both readily available market prices and market-based techniques to infer such prices. For example, attaching a dollar value to scarce natural resources or endangered species is not a straightforward process.

The practical alternative to market-based pricing is a contingent valuation approach in which respondents to survey questions assume hypothetical markets for these commodities and indicate their willingness to pay for the commodities' preservation.[39] As the debate over the Exxon *Valdez* oil spill valuation indicated, there is no clear-cut basis for establishing these values in a noncontroversial manner.[40]

Even when what is at stake is individuals' lives, regulatory policy debates are subject to a variety of uncertainties. To assess the statistical lives lost from a given danger, one must assess the risk probability as well as the total population exposed. Moreover, one must attach a value to the lives at stake. All three of these enterprises are, to say the least, tricky. The scientific evidence pertaining to risk-probability values is often hotly debated.[41] As a result, government agencies frequently assess the magnitude of the risk in broad terms, reflecting the conflicting scientific evidence. That is, agencies have responded to this uncertainty by using "conservative" risk assessments that focus on upper-bound values, a controversial step that will be considered in greater detail below.[42]

The second component of the risk assessment is the magnitudes of the populations exposed. In the case of risk assessment for Superfund sites, the EPA considers not only current populations but also potential future populations in currently unpopulated areas.[43] Hypothetical future populations should not receive the same weight as current populations actually exposed to the risk since there may never be such residents exposed to toxic

---

[39]See generally W. Michael Hanemann, *Valuing the Environment Through Contingent Valuation*, 8 J Econ Persp 19 (Fall 1994).

[40]The main debate was over whether public opinion surveys could yield reliable estimates of the value of nonuse environmental damages. The plaintiffs had confidence in these techniques, whereas Exxon challenged their validity. See generally id.

[41]See generally Kenneth R. Foster, David E. Bernstein, and Peter W. Huber, eds, *Phantom Risk: Scientific Inference and the Law* (MIT 1993).

[42]Albert L. Nichols and Richard J. Zeckhauser, *The Perils of Prudence: How Conservative Risk Assessments Distort Regulation*, 10 Reg 13 (Nov–Dec 1986) (describing the distortions in regulatory policy caused by the use of "conservative" risk assessments).

[43]See James T. Hamilton and W. Kip Viscusi, *Human Health Risk Assessments for Superfund*, 21 Ecol L Q 573, 586–88 (1994).

hazards. Ideally, one should weigh future exposed groups by the probability that such groups will in fact exist to be exposed. Moreover, other policy actions, such as the imposition of deed restrictions and the capping and fencing of hazardous waste sites, might prevent these hypothetical exposures.

Surprisingly, the third aspect of risk assessment—valuing the lives that will be lost—may be the most precisely estimated component of the regulatory analysis.[44] Difficulties arise, however, in making judgments regarding people whose durations of future lifetime differ. For example, should society be willing to spend more to save the life of a twenty-three-year-old than someone who is ninety-five? This problem is simplified to some extent when one realizes that regulatory policies do not confer immortality but rather simply extend lifetimes.[45] Adjusting for the quality and quantity of lives saved is, however, a degree of refinement that no doubt will continue to be problematic. However, given the failure of policymakers even to incorporate first principles of efficient targeting, as exemplified by the regulatory expenditure levels in Table 1, nuances such as distinguishing among populations in valuing life need not be resolved at the outset.

A typical assumption in benefit-cost analysis is that the agencies' assessment of benefits is most uncertain, whereas the costs are fixed. However, closer examination reveals that even the cost components are quite uncertain. For example, Superfund cleanup costs have considerably exceeded EPA's original estimates,[46] and in the case of the controversial cotton dust regulation, OSHA greatly misestimated both the costs and benefits of the regulation.[47]

What then should policymakers do when benefits and costs are highly uncertain? One possibility is to do nothing at all until further information clarifies these values. Deferring decisions is sometimes an appropriate strategy, particularly when information is likely forthcoming and when correcting an erroneous regulatory decision is expensive. However, inaction may also have major costs of its own. If government agencies were to wait until all scientific uncertainties were fully resolved, they would seldom undertake any initiatives. The extent of the risks associated with health hazards, such as the risks posed by airborne carcinogens, remains a matter of debate. Should these be ignored? Safety hazards, such as the risk of an automobile accident, are known with much greater precision. However, even for accident risks, particular information crucial to regulatory policy may not be known. What, for example, will be the safety benefit of installing

---

[44]See Viscusi, *Fatal Tradeoffs* at 34–74 (cited in note 4).

[45]See generally Richard Zeckhauser and Donald Shepard, *Where Now for Saving Lives?*, 40 L & Contemp Probs 5 (Autumn 1976).

[46]See generally Milton Russell, E. William Colglazier, and Mary R. English, *Hazardous Waste Remediation: The Task Ahead* (Tennessee 1991).

[47]See Viscusi, *Fatal Tradeoffs* at 161–77 (cited in note 4); see generally Paul W. Kolp and W. Kip Viscusi, *Uncertainty in Risk Analysis: A Retrospective Assessment of the OSHA Cotton Dust Standard*, 4 Advances in Applied Microeconomics 105 (1986).

side air bags in cars? Scientists are unlikely to be able to estimate these mortality reductions with precision, as was shown by their highly inaccurate predictions regarding the effect of seat belts on auto safety.[48]

In general, a lack of information should not cause policy paralysis. We make decisions daily involving substantial uncertainties, and the government should do likewise.[49] By a similar token, the existence of uncertainties is not a rationale for ignoring the known benefit and cost consequences of policy. Policymakers should not, in effect, abandon rational thought about policy impacts and rely on their instincts simply because they have encountered complexities and uncertainties. Indeed, one might well argue that policy analysis is particularly useful when the ramifications of the policy are sufficiently complicated that the policy choice is not obvious.[50]

B. Cost-Effectiveness Analysis

A weaker variant of benefit-cost analysis is cost-effectiveness analysis. Under this approach the agency must show that it has adopted the cheapest way of achieving a specific objective, such as a pollution reduction. Under benefit-cost analysis the agency must do more. It must also show that achieving the specified objective makes sense, that is, the benefits of doing so exceed the costs.

Cost-effectiveness analysis takes as given that the policy objective is worthwhile. Such an assumption may not be warranted if, for all policy options, the costs of meeting that objective exceed the benefits, or if there are other possible policy objectives that are preferable. An agency may select the cheapest method for reducing benzene emissions to a particular level, but the level chosen may be excessively stringent. Until we have some mechanism for ascertaining the wisdom of the underlying policy objective, then mere cost-effectiveness is not a sufficient test of policy adequacy.

Nevertheless, promoting cost-effective achievement of policy objectives remains a salient policy concern. Policymakers have employed cost-effectiveness as a guide in developing performance-oriented standards. Traditionally, government regulatory agencies such as EPA and OSHA have promulgated technology-forcing standards that specify particular means of compliance that must be adopted by the firm. The disadvantage of the technology-forcing approach is that it eliminates the firm's discretion to choose the least-cost mechanism of compliance. By specifying a performance objective and giving firms leeway to select the means to achieve this

---

[48]For a review of these policy assessments and their divergence from actual accident-rate patterns, see Sam Peltzman, *The Effects of Automobile Safety Regulation*, 83 J Pol Econ 677 (1975).

[49]Indeed, in many cases one could argue that the government should be bolder than we are as individuals, since at least in terms of cost uncertainties it can often spread these uncertainties across the entire United States population.

[50]The importance of dealing with uncertainty from the standpoint of government policy and using policy analysis are major themes in the principal textbook in the field. See Stokey and Zeckhauser, *Primer for Policy Analysis* (cited in note 38).

objective (instead of specifying a particular means of compliance), agencies can enable firms to reduce their costs.

Two examples illustrate this phenomenon. First, the OSHA grain dust standard gave firms several specific options for cleaning up grain dust levels in grain elevators to prevent risks of explosion.[51] If sweeping up the grain dust whenever it exceeded one-eighth of an inch were cheaper than using pneumatic dust-control equipment, then firms could reduce their compliance costs by choosing the sweeping route. It is noteworthy, however, that despite this flexibility, the grain dust standard still fails (albeit barely) a benefit-cost test.[52] Perhaps the greatest success story for a performance-oriented standard is the EPA bubble policy. Rather than requiring that each smokestack at a firm meet a particular emission level, the EPA permitted firms to operate as if surrounded by an artificial bubble.[53] The question then became whether the total emissions from the plant were excessive, thus permitting the firm to choose which emission sources to reduce. This flexibility enabled firms to adopt the most cost-effective mechanism for pollution reduction, leading to over $400 million in cost savings.[54] The more recent extensions of flexible policy options such as the bubble policy and tradeable permits increase this discretion by enabling firms to effectively bid for pollution rights, producing annual savings of compliance costs estimated at approximately $1 billion.[55]

C. Risk Assessment

Rather than become embroiled in economic controversies such as the appropriate amount to spend on risk reduction, why not simply focus on risks alone? As indicated earlier, society lacks the resources to eliminate all risks. Nevertheless, it is feasible to prioritize policies based on risk by focusing our regulatory energies first on the riskiest areas and then turning to less risky activities.

In thinking about this approach, it is important to reiterate what we mean by a risk level. Risk is the product of both the probability and the severity of harm as well as the number of people exposed. Unfortunately, in many instances, government agencies simply focus on the probability and overlook the risk exposure. In the case of the Superfund program, there are two critical risk triggers.[56] For Superfund sites with chemical

---

[51]For a description of this regulation, see Viscusi, *Fatal Tradeoffs* at 275 (cited in note 4).

[52]See Table 1.

[53]For a description of the EPA bubble policy, see Robert W. Crandall, *Controlling Industrial Pollution: The Economics and Politics of Clean Air* 83–84 (Brookings 1983).

[54]The cost savings from the EPA bubble policy are documented in Robert W. Hahn and Gordon L. Hester, *Where Did All the Markets Go? An Analysis of EPA's Emissions Trading Program*, 6 Yale J Reg 109, 138 (1989).

[55]See Alan Carlin, *The United States Experience with Economic Incentives to Control Environmental Pollution* 5-6, 5-12 to 5-13 (US EPA 1992).

[56]See Hamilton and Viscusi, 21 Ecol L Q at 578–81 (cited in note 43).

risk pathways that pose a cancer risk exceeding 10-4,[57] EPA regulations suggest that cleanup is warranted. For risk levels smaller than 10-6, cleanup is not warranted, and for risk levels in the intermediate range between 10-4 and 10-6, cleanup is the subject of a discretionary decision by EPA officials.[58]

What is noteworthy about this precision with respect to risks is the total absence of population considerations. EPA assesses risk levels to current populations now and in the future (designated current risk pathways), as well as risk levels to hypothetical future populations resulting from a change in land use, such as vacant land becoming residential (designated future risk pathways). Real and potential risks are treated symmetrically, and in each case the size of the population exposed to the risk does not enter the calculations.

Even if population exposures were considered, risk alone is not a sufficient guide. Consider the risk information in Table 2. A risk of death of one in a million arises every time we spend one hour in a coal mine (black lung disease), spend two days in Boston (air pollution), travel six minutes by canoe, eat forty tablespoons of peanut butter, or drink Miami drinking water for one year. Which risk is most deserving of regulation? Should we target environmental exposures and give them higher priority than recreational risks?

One approach might be to look at total body counts rather than risk probabilities. If our concern is with accidental deaths, then the leading candidate for regulation would be automobiles, as motor vehicles now account for roughly forty-two thousand of the ninety thousand accidental deaths per year.[59] However, we have already expended considerable resources for a variety of automobile safety devices, so our willingness to redesign automobiles to improve safety or our willingness to abandon automobiles altogether is likely to be quite limited.

If instead we wish to focus on all causes of death in the United States, the three leading candidates would be personal consumption decisions—tobacco, diet/activity patterns, and alcohol. Together, these activities contribute to 38 percent of all deaths.[60] Yet, are we willing to abandon smoking and drinking and undertake a vigorous exercise program to reduce these risks substantially? Or, alternatively, would we prefer the government to target toxic agents? Toxic agents are estimated to account for only 3 percent of all deaths—less than one-tenth of the amount caused by the three leading risky consumption activities.[61]

In his recent book, Justice Stephen Breyer advocates using a variety of reference points, such as the risk level posed by cigarettes or automobiles,

[57]Risk levels are expressed as the likelihood of one person developing cancer over a lifetime. A risk level of "10-4" would predict one additional cancer case per ten thousand exposed individuals; "10-6" would predict one additional case per one million exposed individuals.

[58]Hamilton and Viscusi, 21 Ecol L Q at 578–81 (cited in note 43).

[59]See National Safety Council, *Accident Facts, 1994 Edition* 1 (1994).

[60]See J. Michael McGinnis and William H. Foege, *Actual Causes of Death in the United States*, 270 JAMA 2207, 2207–08 (1993).

[61]Id at 2208–09.

Table 2 Risks That Increase the Annual Death Risk by One in One Million

Activity	Cause of Death
Smoking 1.4 cigarettes	Cancer, heart disease
Drinking 0.5 liter of wine	Cirrhosis of the liver
Spending 1 hour in a coal mine	Black lung disease
Spending 3 hours in a coal mine	Accident
Living 2 days in New York or Boston	Air pollution
Traveling 6 minutes by canoe	Accident
Traveling 10 minutes by bicycle	Accident
Traveling 150 miles by car	Accident
Flying 1000 miles by jet	Accident
Flying 6000 miles by jet	Cancer caused by cosmic radiation
Living 2 months in Denver	Cancer caused by cosmic radiation
Living 2 months in average stone or brick building	Cancer caused by natural radioactivity
One chest X-ray taken in a good hospital	Cancer caused by radiation
Living 2 months with a cigarette smoker	Cancer, heart disease
Eating 40 tablespoons of peanut butter	Liver cancer caused by aflatoxin B
Drinking Miami drinking water for 1 year	Cancer caused by chloroform
Drinking 30 12-oz. cans of diet soda	Cancer caused by saccharin
Living 5 years at site boundary of nuclear power plant in the open	Cancer caused by radiation
Drinking 1000 24-oz. soft drinks from banned plastic bottles	Cancer from acrylonitrile monomer
Living 20 years near PVC plant	Cancer caused by vinyl chloride (1976 standard)
Living 150 years within 20 miles of nuclear power plant	Cancer caused by radiation
Eating 100 charcoal-broiled steaks	Cancer from benzopyrene
Risk of accident by living within 5 miles of nuclear reactor for 50 years	Cancer caused by radiation

Source: Richard Wilson, *Analyzing the Daily Risks of Life, 81* Tech Rev 41, 45 table (1979).

to help policymakers think more sensibly about risk.[62] However, his most compelling comparisons emphasize costs. He observes that expenditure levels for asbestos removal would only be consistent with our other private expenditures on safety if we were willing to spend much more than we now do for automobile safety:

> We can translate the [asbestos removal] figure into a more intuitively accessible number by recalling that auto accidents kill about fifty thousand people each year. We might then imagine how much we would willingly pay for a slightly safer car, a car that would reduce auto deaths by, say, 5 percent, to 47,500. Would we pay an extra $1,000 for such a car? An extra $5,000 for that added contribution to safety? To spend $100 billion as a nation to save ten lives annually assumes we value safety so much that each of us would pay $48,077 extra for any such new, slightly safer car.[63]

Ultimately, some comparison of risks and costs is necessary to assess whether the beneficial aspects of the regulatory policy warrant the cost. Making such comparisons is not necessarily detrimental to regulatory policy. The FAA decided not to require wing modifications for the DC-10 because the risk reduction achieved would decrease the risk of a plane crash by only one chance in a billion. However, the cost of the modification—two thousand dollars—was small enough that on a benefit-cost basis over the life of the plane it would have been worthwhile to require the necessary changes.[64]

Risk levels alone are not a sufficient guide to policy. Probabilities of the hazard and numbers of people exposed to the risk are surely consequential. However, our unwillingness to forego all risky personal consumption activities, whether it be slothfulness or eating red meat, and our similar unwillingness to invest in risk-free but very fuel-efficient cars that might resemble tanks, suggests that ultimately we do wish to select the risks we face in a manner that recognizes tradeoffs.

The magnitude of a risk is, however, potentially instructive, particularly as an input to benefits analysis—provided that the risk is properly assessed. Unfortunately, current risk assessment practices throughout the federal government typically do not yield unbiased risk judgments. Rather, current practices emphasize upper bounds of the possible risk values, or what has been designated a "conservatism" bias.[65] In the case of the EPA Superfund program, there is a focus on upper bounds of the potential risk. EPA analysts often use parameter estimates from the ninety-fifth percentile of the parameter distribution. Thus, the emphasis in each stage of the calculations is on how bad the risk could be under a worst-case scenario that

---

[62]See Stephen Breyer, *Breaking the Viscious Circle: Toward Effective Risk Regulation* 3–10 (Harvard 1993).

[63]Id at 13–14.

[64]See W. Kip Viscusi, *Rick by Choice: Regulating Health and Safety in the Workplace* 112–13 (Harvard 1983).

[65]For a more detailed discussion of this bias, see generally Nichols and Zeckhauser, 10 Reg at 13 (cited in note 42).

might occur 5 percent of the time rather than on the expected consequences.[66] If, however, one uses the ninety-fifth percentile for each component of a calculation and then compounds these risk-parameter estimates when calculating the total risk, the degree of conservatism will be much greater. EPA calculations of groundwater ingestion risks, for example, use upper-bound values for ingestion rate, exposure frequency, exposure duration, chemical concentration, and toxicity. The net effect of compounding these upper-bound values for five different parameter estimates is that the overall degrees of conservatism for the total risk assessed at Superfund sites is beyond the ninety-ninth percentile of the risk distribution.

Consider how these biases could become compounded within the context of a simple example. Suppose that EPA assumes that the concentration of hazardous chemicals at a site is at the upper bound of what it could possibly be so that there is only one chance in twenty that the chemicals could be this risky. Also assume that we make worst-case scenario assumptions regarding the total amount of the hazardous chemicals that will be ingested through ground water contamination, where this ingestion will also occur with a probability of 1 in 20. Then the probability that we will have a worst-case scenario in terms of the concentration of the chemical, as well as the amount of the chemical that is ingested will be 1 in 400, or the product of these two 1 in 20 probabilities if the events are independent. By focusing on the worst-case scenario for every parameter that is used to assess the risk, EPA is in effect assuming that everything that could possibly go wrong will go wrong simultaneously, which is much more unlikely than any one thing going wrong individually.

Focusing on upper-bound values creates a variety of distortions. First, the exact extent of the conservatism is generally not known to policymakers. The degree of conservatism varies by parameter and across policy-decision contexts, making comparative judgments difficult. We know that the risk assessments are "conservative," but not how conservative or whether the degree of conservatism is the same in every instance. Second, focusing on conservative risk parameters creates a bias in favor of regulating uncertain risks. Consider two different chemical hazards. Chemical A poses a known risk of cancer of 2 in 100,000. Chemical B has uncertain properties. Scientists have differing opinions over the relative risk of the two chemicals, as nine scientists out of ten believe that chemical B is without risk and one out of ten believes that the risk may be as high as 6 in 100,000. Adopting the conservative approach, government officials would focus on chemical B since it poses the greatest *potential* risk. However, we would save a greater expected number of lives if we focused on chemical A, for which the mean predicted risk is greater.[67]

---

[66]W. Kip Viscusi, James T. Hamilton, and P. Christen Dockins, *Policy Consequences of Conservative Risk Assessments for Hazardous Waste Sites*, Duke University Working Paper (on file with U Chi L Rev).

[67]For a defense of using conservative risk values, see James E. Krier, *Rick and Design*, 19 J Legal Stud 781 (1990).

The third, more general problem with a conservatism bias is that it institutionalizes an irrational form of economic behavior. A well known form of irrationality in economics is the Ellsberg paradox.[68] Suppose that you win a prize if you draw a red ball from urn 1, which contains 50 red balls and 50 white balls. Similarly, suppose that you win an identical prize if you can draw a ball of the color you named from urn 2, which contains an unspecified mixture of 100 red and white balls. Which urn do you prefer? Respondents generally prefer the urn offering the known probability of success even though the risk probabilities are equivalent.[69] Similarly, when faced with the prospect of losses, individuals would rather face a known probability of incurring a loss rather than an imprecise probability.[70] These various forms of ambiguity aversion comprise a well known class of anomalies in economics that contradicts usual models of expected utility theory.[71] The government should not mimic these shortcomings in individual behavior, but rather it should make the kinds of rational and balanced decisions that people would make if they could understand risk sensibly. Paying excessive attention to the worst possible outcome while ignoring much more probable risk levels distorts policy-making and diverts our risk reduction resources from truly substantial hazards to minuscule risks that are not well understood.

Some of the impetus for conservative risk assessment may stem from past unfavorable experiences with risks that were underestimated. In the case of the space shuttle program, NASA authorities estimated the risk of a disaster before the *Challenger* explosion as 1 flight in 100,000.[72] In 1988, the agency had raised the estimated risk of a catastrophe over the entire mission to 1 in 50. Recent safety investments have led to a midpoint risk estimate of 1 in 145, with the risk range extending from 1 in 76 to 1 in 230 missions.

The main message from this experience is not that we should undertake risk assessments as if Murphy's Law (if anything can go wrong it will) operates. Rather, the experience should highlight the dangers that may arise from excessive optimism, particularly when overly optimistic assumptions are compounded. In responding to this experience, however, we should not necessarily adopt the opposite approach of compounding overly pessimistic assumptions. The proper task for risk assessors is to use the best information currently available to assess the true range of the risk, and then to determine which risk level is the most reliable mean estimate of the actual risk. If our risk assessments are truly unbiased, then we should expect an equal number of overestimations and underestimations. Thus, there is no danger of systematic underestimation.

---

[68]For a description of this paradox as well as the counterpart of ambiguity aversion in the case of losses, see Viscusi, *Fatal Tradeoffs* at 135–36, 143–45 (cited in note 4).

[69]One can, for example, turn the "soft" probability of urn 2 into a "hard" probability by flipping a fair coin and then selecting the ball color based on the outcome.

[70]See Viscusi, *Fatal Tradeoffs* at 143–45 (cited in note 4).

[71]For a review of this literature, see Colin Camerer and Martin Weber, *Recent Developments in Modeling Preferences: Uncertainty and Ambiguity*, 5 J Risk & Uncertainty 325 (1992).

[72]These statistics as well as the subsequent statistics in this paragraph are drawn from William J. Broad, *Risks Remain Despite NASA's Rebuilding*, NY Times 1, 12 (Jan 28, 1996).

D. Risk-Risk Analysis

A single-minded commitment to risk reduction is not only an overly narrow approach to evaluating a regulatory policy, but it is also potentially harmful even from the standpoint of reducing risk. Perhaps somewhat paradoxically, overzealous policies can actually increase societal risk rather than decrease it.

This observation formed the basis of a judicial commentary on an expensive OSHA regulation in which Judge Williams of the D.C. Circuit observed that excessive regulatory expenditures would make society poorer, potentially worsening individual health.[73] Perhaps inspired by this opinion, the OMB raised with agencies the issue of the potentially counterproductive effects of excessive regulatory expenditures.[74] This Section will explore the different variants of what has come to be known as risk-risk analysis,[75] indicating how even if risk reduction is the only objective of a regulatory policy, we must do more than focus on the direct risk effects of the policy alone.

The first form of risk-risk tradeoff to appear in the economics literature pertains to risk offsets associated with regulatory policies, or what recent proposed legislation refers to as "substitution risks."[76] Regulations that ban activities or products almost invariably create substitution risks. This occurs when the commodities that replace those that are banned carry their own risks, so that the net risk change is not as great as it might seem initially. If, for example, we require that infants riding in airplanes not sit in their parents' laps but rather have their own seat and safety belt, then the cost of an additional ticket will lead some parents to drive, which is a riskier mode of travel. Similarly, eliminating pesticides from our diet by eating organic produce will reduce the risk of cancer from pesticides, but if the result is that we eat fewer fruits and vegetables, our overall cancer risk may increase.[77] To prevent the risk of fire-related burns, the Consumer Product Safety Commission ("CPSC") required that children's sleepwear be coated with the flame retardant. Tris, but later discovered that this chemical was potentially carcinogenic.[78] This risk-risk tradeoff is a type of substitution risk.

---

[73]See *International Union, UAW v OSHA*, 938 F2d 1310, 1326–27 (DC Cir 1991) (Williams concurring).

[74]The opening salvo in this administrative battle was a March 10, 1992, letter from James B. MacRae, Jr., Acting Administrator of OIRA, to Nancy Risque-Rohrbach, Assistant Secretary for Policy, United States Department of Labor. For a discussion of this letter and the ensuing controversy, see Ralph L. Keeney, *Mortality Risks Induced by the Costs of Regulations*, 8 J Risk & Uncertainty 96, 96–97 (1994).

[75]See generally Lester B. Lave, *The Strategy of Social Regulation: Decision Frameworks for Policy* (Brookings 1981); John D. Graham and Jonathan Baert Wiener, eds, *Risk versus Risk: Tradeoffs in Protecting Health and the Environment* (Harvard 1995).

[76]HR 1022 contains a particularly extensive treatment of substitution risk, requiring that agencies recognize this phenomenon and incorporate analyses of substitution risks in their assessments of regulatory policies. See Risk Assessment and Cost-Benefit Act of 1995, HR 1022 § 105(4), 104th Cong, 1st Sess (Feb 23, 1995), in 141 Cong Rec H2261, H2263 (Feb 27, 1995).

[77]For a discussion of this tradeoff, see Bruce N. Ames and Lois Swirsky Gold, *Environmental Pollution and Cancer: Some Misconceptions*, in Kenneth R. Foster, David E. Bernstein, and Peter W. Huber, eds, *Phantom Risk: Scientific Inference and the Law* 153, 176–78 (MIT 1993).

[78]See W. Kip Viscusi, *Regulating Consumer Product Safety* 111 (American Enterprise Institute 1984).

The class of risk-offset effects that has particularly captured the attention of economists involves product users' diminished safety precautions in response to regulatory protections. If the government regulates products or activities in a way that makes them less dangerous, then users will have diminished incentives to take care. Initial research on the safety effects resulting from seat belt use suggested that the use of these belts may have led drivers to go faster, thus partially offsetting some of the safety gains.[79] Debate over the magnitude of this phenomenon continues, as researchers remain uncertain as to whether the diminished care is sufficient to offset the beneficial effect of seat belts. Nevertheless, broad evidence indicates at least some diminished precaution taking, as reflected in the increased risk to pedestrians and motorcyclists in the aftermath of the seat belt regulations.[80]

Although people might quite rationally choose to take fewer precautions after safety technologies have reduced the risks, diminished care also may result from the public's overassessment of the adequacy of these safety efforts. One possibility, which I have termed the "lulling effect," is that consumers may be lulled into a false sense of security and diminish their care by too great an extent.[81] CPSC officials frequently refer to child-resistant caps as being child-proof. But the introduction of these caps did not result in the expected diminishing in poisonings. Because of the difficulty of grappling with the caps, many parents left the caps off the bottles; indeed, almost 50 percent of poisonings resulted from open bottles.[82] In addition, some parents may permit children greater access to the products because of an apparent belief that the products are safer, a phenomenon consistent with the observed failure of safety caps to decrease poisoning rates below the level expected in the absence of the regulation.

The "lulling effect" is visible in parental behavior following the recent regulation mandating child-resistant cigarette lighters.[83] Parents report that the child-resistant mechanism gives them greater peace of mind and decreases their safety concerns. There is also evidence, based on actual placements of lighters in households, that the introduction of the child-resistant mechanism has led parents to leave lighters in locations more accessible to children. In this instance, the net prediction is that on balance the child-resistant mechanism will enhance safety since the safety benefits of the

---

[79]See Peltzman, 83 J Pol Econ at 703–05 (cited in note 48).

[80]See Glenn C. Blomquist, *The Regulation of Motor Vehicle and Traffic Safety* 55–74 (Kluwer 1988).

[81]For a discussion of this phenomenon, see W. Kip Viscusi, *The Lulling Effect: The Impact of Child-Resistant Packaging on Aspirin and Analgesic Ingestions*, 74 Am Econ Rev 324 (May 1984); Viscusi, *Fatal Tradeoffs* at 224–27 (cited in note 4).

[82]In particular, the open-bottle share of poisonings in 1978, the last year for which data are available, was 49 percent for aspirin and 47 percent for aspirin and analgesics. See Viscusi, *Fatal Tradeoffs* at 238 (cited in note 4).

[83]See W. Kip Viscusi and Gerald O. Cavallo, *The Effect of Product Safety Regulation on Safety Precautions*, 14 Risk Analysis 917 (1994).

lighter feature outweigh the consequences of the diminished care. Nevertheless, there is clear-cut evidence that the diminished precaution taking will decrease the extent of the risk improvement that would otherwise occur. These responses highlight the importance of alerting consumers and workers to the continued need for precautionary behavior even in the presence of safety regulations.

A second type of risk-risk tradeoff is an inevitable consequence of all economic activity. Quite simply, all economic activity is risky. Workers are injured daily in construction, manufacturing, and even in white-collar work. Regulatory requirements trigger a variety of economic activities, whether it be producing scrubbers for the reduction of air pollution, removing asbestos from schools, or driving a car back to the dealer after an automobile recall. Inquiries and deaths resulting from these activities are inevitable. If we place a dollar value of $50,000 on each statistical injury and $5 million on each statistical fatality, then 3 to 4 percent of all industry expenditures comprise the costs associated with worker injuries.[84] If our only concern is with risk, we should surely be cognizant of the fact that regulatory expenditures will generate economic activity, which itself will be risky. If the regulations are extremely ineffective, then these expenditure-related risks alone would render the regulatory effort counterproductive.

For concreteness, suppose that a regulation saves one statistical life through its direct effect on safety. At what expenditure level will the regulation generate economic activity that will lead to more health risks than the regulation prevents? Suppose that the safety improvement resulting from the regulation is valued at $5 million. Then the health risk arising from regulatory expenditures will just equal this amount if the cost per statistical life saved is $167 million (if injuries comprise 3 percent of regulatory costs) or $125 million (if injuries comprise 4 percent of regulatory costs).

Applying this approach to the regulatory cost levels in Table 1, the expenditure-related health costs of regulation imply that all regulations at or below the arsenic/glass manufacturing standard will be counterproductive at the lower end of this cost range, and all regulations below the benzene storage regulations will be counterproductive at the upper end.

The third form of risk-risk analysis was the focus of Judge William's concurrence and has been the focus of efforts by the OMB. The underlying idea is that regulatory expenditures represent opportunity costs to so-

[84]These estimates are derived by W. Kip Viscusi and Richard Zeckhauser, *The Fatality and Injury Costs of Expenditures*, 8 J Risk & Uncertainty 19 (1994). That article also presents industry-specific estimates of both the injury costs and the fatality costs of regulatory expenditures. In many respects these estimates are simply the flip side of the estimates of compensating differentials that workers receive for incurring risks. The fact that workers are compensated for many of these risks may affect how society views them from a benefit-cost standpoint. To the extent that markets provide for compensation of these risks, the rationale for regulation will not be good. However, if our only concern is with health effects, to be consistent agencies should consider all health effects of policies, both good and bad.

ciety that divert resources from other uses. These funds could have provided for greater health care, food, housing, and other goods and services that promote individual longevity. The economics behind this relationship is not controversial.[85] Being richer is safer than being poorer.

Estimating the magnitude of the tradeoff is more difficult. Table 3 summarizes a recent set of studies that have identified this linkage. For the most part, researchers have used regression analyses to assess the role of individual and family income on mortality. Some of these studies focus on specific events that led to decreases in income, such as recessions, whereas others utilize national or international data over a longer period. The range reflected in these estimates is quite broad; the income drop needed to generate one expected death has been placed at anywhere between $1.9 million and $33.2 million.

Perhaps the greatest limitation of these studies is the correlation between income and health. Higher income levels promote healthy consumption patterns and individual longevity. On the other hand, improved health enhances one's earning capabilities. Disentangling this linkage may be particularly difficult, especially given that income is correlated with other health-enhancing variables, such as knowledge of how to decrease health risks.

To eliminate these statistical controversies, I developed an alternative approach that does not utilize direct estimates of the mortality-income relationship.[86] Instead, it exploits the theoretical linkage between the amount of money that people are willing to spend to save a statistical life—approximately $5 million on average—and the amount of expenditures that will lead to the loss of a statistical life. Surely individuals would not be willing to undertake expenditures that are counterproductive with respect to risk. Thus, it is implausible that workers could reveal a value of life of $5 million in their job safety decisions, while at the same time society loses a statistical life every time $1.9 million (the lowest estimate in Table 3) is spent. If that were the case, firms investing $5 million per statistical life in improved safety conditions would kill more than two workers in doing so because spending $5 million on the usual mix of goods would save more than two lives. Using the theoretical linkage between the value of saving a statistical life and the regulatory expenditure that will lead to the loss of a statistical life, I showed that this amount will be approximately ten times the implicit value of saving a statistical life, or $50 million.[87] Thus, for every regulatory policy in Table 1 below the uranium mill tailings-inactive standard, the income loss-mortality linkage suggests that the regulation will produce a net health loss.

There are consequently three risk-risk effects that cut across regulatory policies and limit their effectiveness. The first effect, substitution risk,

[85]For derivation of these relationships, see W. Kip Viscusi, *Mortality effects of regulatory costs and policy evaluation criteria*, 25 RAND J Econ 94 (1994).

[86]This approach was originally developed for the Executive Office of the President in the Bush Administration. The 1992 Report by the author to OMB, *Wealth, Health Investments, and the Value of Life*, was refined in Viscusi, 25 RAND J Econ at 94 (cited in note 85).

[87]See Viscusi, 25 RAND J Econ at 105–07 (cited in note 85).

Table 3 Summary of Income-Mortality Studies

Study	Nature of Relationship	Income Loss Per Statistical Death $ millions (Nov 1992 dollars)
Hadley and Osei (1982)	1 percent increase in total family income for white males age 45–64 leads to .07 present decline in mortality.	33.2
U.S. Joint Economic Committee (1984)	3 percent drop in real per capital income in 1973 recession generated 2.3 percent increase in mortality.	3.0
Anderson and Burkhauser (1985)	Longitudinal survey, Social Security Administration Retirement History Survey, 1969–79. $1 difference in hourly wage levels in 1969 generates 4.2 percent difference in mortality rates over next 10 years.	1.9
Duleep (1986)	Social Security mortality data 1973–78 for men aged 36–65 imply a higher mortality rate of .023 for income group $3,000–$6,000 compared to income group $6,000–$9,000.	2.7
Keeney (1990), based on Kitagawa and Hauser (1973)	Mortality rate-income level data fit expositional curve relating mortality rates to income, employing 1959 data on mortality of whites, age 25–64, death certificate information.	12.5
Lutter and Morrall (1994)	International data on mortality-income relationship from the World Bank, 1965 and 1986.	9.3
Chapman and Hariharan (1994)	Social Security Administration Retirement History Survey, 1969–1979, controlling for initial health status; tradeoff of $12.2 million per life in 1969 dollars.	13.3

varies from context to context and cannot be assessed on any general level. However, an overall assessment of the other two risk-risk effects is possible. The bad news for government regulators is that both of these risk-risk offsets are at work. Suppose that the regulators are considering a $100 billion regulatory program. Using a midpoint estimate that the direct health costs of expenditures are 3.5 percent of the total expenditure, there will be $3.5 billion in direct health losses. The second adverse consequence— income loss-mortality effect—will be the loss of two thousand statistical lives when the government spends $100 billion. Using a value of $5 million to assess the value of each life lost leads to a total cost of $10 billion. In all, there will be $13.5 billion in health losses from $100 billion in regulatory costs. Unless the regulation generates at least $13.5 billion in health benefits, individual health will be made worse off by the regulation.

This result can be used to calculate the critical cost per life threshold that must be met for a regulation to have beneficial effects on individual health. For any regulatory expenditure of $37 million or more per statistical life, there will be a net loss of life and health due to the combined effect of the expenditure-health linkage and the income loss-mortality linkage. In terms of Table 1, the counterproductive range of regulatory policies begins just below the uranium mill tailings-inactive regulation.

A regulation that increases risk is not in society's interest. Such a regulation is extremely counterproductive in that it does not even meet the narrow test of enhancing society's health. Surely regulatory agencies should be concerned with this broader effect of regulatory policy since their mandate is to improve the health and welfare of citizens generally, not simply within the narrow confines of a particular regulatory policy. If a policy unduly harms individual health in ways not considered by the regulators, it should not be pursued.

As a practical matter, much of the appeal of risk-risk analysis stems from its ability to provide a quantitative test for regulatory policy in a world in which strict benefit-cost analysis is not always feasible. Should this approach ever gain widespread acceptance within the government, it could potentially eliminate some of the most counterproductive regulations. However, it is not a substitute for a more comprehensive benefit-cost analysis that takes into account the fuller implications of regulatory policy.[88]

V. Regulatory Reform Legislation

The 104th Congress has considered a variety of regulatory reform bills in 1995 and 1996. These bills seek to restructure the way in which government agencies approach regulations. In some instances, the proposed leg-

---

[88]The existence of the risk-risk relationship does, however, require that one modify the traditional benefit-cost test. For a discussion of the necessary modifications, see generally Viscusi, 25 RAND J Econ at 94 (cited in note 85).

islation consists of omnibus bills applying to all regulatory agencies.[89] In other instances, the bills are more narrowly focused and address only a single regulatory area, such as Superfund[90] or energy risk management.[91]

The content of these bills is quite diffuse, as they include not only numerous guidelines for policy analysis but many institutional reforms as well. Three components, present in all the bills, seem most critical to improving economic efficiency in regulatory policy: inclusion of a supermandate, imposition of a benefit-cost test requirement, and a stipulation that risk assessments be honest and unbiased.

The supermandate assumption is perhaps most important. The provisions of some of the bills (for example, S 343) would not be binding on an agency if they were inconsistent with the agency's existing legislative mandate. However, since most of the risk and environmental regulatory agency legislation either expressly precludes a benefit-cost test or else gives the agency administrator leeway to interpret the mission-oriented nature of its mandate as if it did, there may be a great many cases in which the reform bill provisions simply will not be binding. The practical advantage of a sweeping reform bill is that it can impose a broadly accepted criterion for policy assessment in all domains of regulatory policy, eliminating the need to revise legislation on a case-by-case basis, which is less politically feasible. The potential disadvantage is that such legislation may not give special consideration to particular problem areas that might arise; these areas, however, can best be addressed within the substantive provisions of the legislation discussed below.

The second provision common to all of the regulatory reform legislation, and the most important of the substantive provisions, is a benefit-cost requirement. In particular, the focal point of all these bills is a stipulation that the agency demonstrate that the benefits of the regulation exceed the costs. For this standard to work in all policy contexts, however, it is necessary to include the appropriate qualifier that not all benefit and cost components may be quantifiable in monetary terms. Particular difficulties arise with respect to endangered species and passive-use environmental benefits. However, requiring that the agency administrator find that the benefits to society exceed the costs, including both monetized and nonmonetized variables, would at least cast the regulatory policy decision in an appropriate light. True, such a standard loses the bright-line status of a monetary benefit-cost test. However, the advantage gained is that the

---

[89]Bills of this type include the Risk Assessment and Cost-Benefit Act of 1995, HR 1022 (cited in note 76); Risk Assessment and Cost-Benefit Analysis Act of 1995, HR 690, 104th Cong, 1st Sess (Jan 25, 1995); Restructuring a Limited Government Act, HR 1923, 104th Cong, 1st Sess (June 22, 1995); Comprehensive Regulatory Reform Act of 1995, S 343, 104th Cong, 1st Sess (Feb 2, 1995) in 141 Cong Rec S2056 (Feb 2, 1995).

[90]See Superfund Reform Act of 1995, HR 228, 104th Cong, 1st Sess (Jan 4, 1995) (comprehensive reform of Superfund, including provisions for ranking hazards).

[91]See Department of Energy Risk Management Act of 1995, S 333, 104th Cong, 1st Sess (Feb 2, 1995) (requiring risk assessment procedures).

benefit-cost analysis will indeed be truly comprehensive and reflect all the pertinent effects on society.[92]

The third critical provision of the regulatory reform legislation pertains to risk assessment. Rather than relying on upper-bound risk assessment values, agencies would be required to present information regarding mean levels of risks. Moreover, if agencies nevertheless supplied upper-bound values, they would also be required to provide lower-bound values so that policymakers could assess the extent of the risk range.[93] Since the lower bound of the risk range is frequently zero risk, policymakers could better distinguish the hazards that are truly present from those that are more speculative.[94]

These three components alone could constitute a sweeping regulatory reform bill that would put regulatory policy on sound analytic footing. However, the current regulatory reform proposals go well beyond these simple provisions, as various members of Congress pursue complex analytical and institutional changes. Certain provisions are more attractive than others, but apparently no combination has yet done the trick; the new Congress has yet to pass a regulatory reform bill.

VI. The Failure of Legislative Reform

Congress's inability to pass a regulatory reform bill to date may reflect the proposed legislation's overly ambitious scale and its inclusion of some provisions designed, perhaps in part, to obstruct rather than reform regulation. In many respects, this experience is reminiscent of that at the start of the Reagan administration, when regulatory reform became synonymous with cost relief for industry.[95] Whereas the Reagan reforms were often case-specific and generally did not alter the structure of regulatory policy, the more recent reform efforts have had a more structural focus. However, in many cases, these institutional reforms are neither essential nor compelling from an economic standpoint.

Consider, for example, HR 1022, the Risk Assessment and Cost-Benefit Act of 1995.[96] This bill is one of the more ambitious omnibus regulatory reform proposals. It includes a supermandate provision and re-

---

[92]Including nonmonetized effects in the benefit-cost analysis may make court challenges to regulatory decisions more difficult, but the OMB can provide a countervailing influence to promote sound judgments. The OMB has fostered a benefit-cost approach throughout its existence, and restructuring the regulatory legislation to strengthen the OMB's role would promote greater balance in regulatory policies.

[93]These provisions are included, for example, in HR 1022 § 105(1) at H2263 (cited in note 76).

[94]A prominent example of an agency including zero within the risk range is the risk reported by the CPSC from urea formaldehyde foam insulation exposures. See Viscusi, *Regulating Consumer Product Safety* at 99–101 (cited in note 78).

[95]For a critique and review of the Reagan regulatory reform efforts, see Viscusi, *Fatal Tradeoffs* at 248–92 (cited in note 4).

[96]See generally HR 1022 (cited in note 76).

quires benefit-cost tests and unbiased risk assessments. However, the bill also includes a great deal more.

Some of the provisions simply elaborate on the substantive aspects of the analysis to be undertaken. For example, the bill requires that the agency consider substitution risks in assessing a regulation's total net effect on risk.[97] In other instances, the bill imposes requirements that would appear to be self-evident given the legislation itself, such as provisions pertaining to research and training in risk assessment.[98]

Perhaps most striking are the provisions that are unnecessary given the existence of a benefit-cost test. If benefit-cost guidelines are followed, an approach that focuses on the risk level alone—at best a partial test—is inferior to the more comprehensive approach that considers both risks and costs. Given this fact, two components of the legislation seem both redundant and second-best alternatives to the included benefit-cost test: the first requires that agencies provide risk comparisons to put the risk level in context;[99] the second requires the agency to undertake a comparative risk analysis in its effort to set priorities.[100] Such efforts are misguided because agencies should not necessarily select the regulation that addresses the greatest risks. Rather, they should select those targets of regulation that offer the greatest spread between benefits and costs.

One of the main reasons why agency critics have targeted policies that address minor risks is that if legislative mandates make risk the main currency of interest, policy debates will follow that dimension. However, once the policy debate is broadened to include a reasoned balancing of benefits and costs, myopic attention to risk levels alone seems overly narrow.

Other possibly burdensome features of the current regulatory reform legislation include process reforms. Regulatory agencies would be required to prepare plans on how they were generating new risk information,[101] to provide reports to Congress on priority setting,[102] and to provide more general reports to Congress on their regulatory efforts.[103] Comprehensive thinking about regulatory performances and policies is potentially instructive, but frequently these efforts involve little more than symbolic exercises that needlessly divert agency resources from the tasks at hand. The key issue is whether Congress would use this information constructively. If the benefits of regulatory policies in fact exceed costs, as documented in the regulatory impact analyses and reviewed by the OMB, then there is greater reason for confidence that new regulations will be much more cost-justified than those adopted to date.

---

[97]Id § 105(4) at H2263.
[98]Id § 108 at H2263.
[99]Id § 105(3) at H2263.
[100]Id § 109 at H2263–64.
[101]Id § 501 at H2265.
[102]Id § 601 at H2265.
[103]Id § 107(B) at H2263.

Perhaps the greatest controversy concerns the proposed new stages of regulatory policy review. The first stage is peer review by panels of scientific experts; such review would be required for regulations imposing major costs.[104] Introducing another layer of regulatory review will, however, delay new regulations.[105] By increasing the OMB's scientific capabilities and creating a permanent institutional base with such expertise, a thorough scientific review of regulatory proposals would be possible under the current system. Avoiding formal peer review would also address concerns that society will suffer environmental or risk costs during the delays occasioned by the review.

The final set of provisions, pertaining to judicial review, is particularly controversial and raises the prospect that the courts may delay many regulatory proposals.[106] To the extent that nonmonetary benefit-cost components are included in the analysis, judicial review may focus on ambiguous policy criteria. Turning the courts into venues of economic inquiry also presumes a degree of economic expertise that courts currently lack. Instead of dealing with these issues in the courts, the OMB and its staff of regulatory overseers could provide the needed institutional check on misguided regulatory policies once the criteria for regulations were altered.[107] It should also be noted that adding judicial review provisions may encourage legal challenges. However, even without these provisions, which are a red flag to opponents, one can always challenge regulatory actions in court if they violate the agency's legislative mandate. Therefore, highlighting the potential for judicial challenges through special provisions in reform legislation may be unnecessary.

Conclusion

In recent years, analysts have devoted considerable attention to devising policy analysis approaches that would enable policymakers to eliminate the most undesirable regulations without violating legislative prohibitions against benefit-cost balancing. Risk-risk analysis and its variants that consider the mortality consequences of regulatory expenditures are perhaps the most visible policy assessment techniques of this type. Such circuitous mechanisms for eliminating undesirable regulations are potentially useful in trimming the least productive efforts. However, until an assessment of

---

[104]See, for example, id § 301 at H2264–65.

[105]Based on the author's current experience in serving on two EPA Science Advisory Boards, he does not have a great deal of confidence in the expeditiousness of the peer review process.

[106]The judicial review provisions are the subject of HR 1022 § 401 at H2265 (cited in note 76).

[107]Justice Breyer, for example, advocates establishing an elite civil service corps who would develop expertise in regulatory analysis issues, including both science and economics. Such a professional group committed to regulatory analysis and review is likely to be better positioned than courts to make other policy judgments. See Breyer, *Breaking the Vicious Circle* at 59–81 (cited in note 62).

the overall beneficial and adverse effects of regulation becomes the guideline for regulatory policy decisions, these choices will necessarily fall short of what is attainable.

A single comprehensive bill could eliminate the inefficiencies stemming from a variety of restrictive legislative mandates. Legislation that includes benefit-cost tests, principles of honest risk assessment, and a supermandate provision would provide the necessary legislative counterpart to augment the OMB's regulatory oversight. Including extraneous features and imposing expanded institutional requirements that could delay vital regulatory improvements may distract attention from the central task of revamping the fundamental criteria for setting regulatory policy.

Society currently commits hundreds of billions of dollars each year to risk and environmental regulations. It is time that we demand an honest return on our risk reduction investment.

15   *Cost-Benefit Analysis: An Ethical Critique (with replies)**

Steven Kelman

Steven Kelman is Albert J. Weatherhead III and Richard W. Weatherhead Professor of Public Management at the John F. Kennedy School of Government, Harvard University.

At the broadest and vaguest level, cost-benefit analysis may be regarded simply as systematic thinking about decision-making. Who can oppose, economists sometimes ask, efforts to think in a systematic way about the consequences of different courses of action? The alternative, it would appear, is unexamined decision-making. But defining cost-benefit analysis so simply leaves it with few implications for actual regulatory decision-making. Presumably, therefore, those who urge regulators to make greater use of the technique have a more extensive prescription in mind. I assume here that their prescription includes the following views:

(1) There exists a strong presumption that an act should not be undertaken unless its benefits outweigh its costs.

(2) In order to determine whether benefits outweigh costs, it is desirable to attempt to express all benefits and costs in a common scale or denominator, so that they can be compared with each other, even when some benefits and costs are not traded on markets and hence have no established dollar values.

(3) Getting decision-makers to make more use of cost-benefit techniques is important enough to warrant both the expense required to gather the data for improved cost-benefit estimation and the political efforts needed to give the activity higher priority compared to other activities, also valuable in and of themselves.

My focus is on cost-benefit analysis as applied to environmental, safety, and health regulation. In that context, I examine each of the above propositions from the perspective of formal ethical theory, that is, the study of what actions it is morally right to undertake. My conclusions are:

"Cost-Benefit Analysis: An Ethical Critique," by Steven Kelman, from *AEI Journal on Government and Society Regulation* (January/February 1981) pp. 33–40. Reprinted with permission of the American Enterprise Institute for Public Policy Research, Washington, D.C.

*Including replies printed in the *AEI Journal*, March/April 1981 issue.

(1) In areas of environmental, safety, and health regulation, there may be many instances where a certain decision might be right even though its benefits do not outweigh its costs.

(2) There are good reasons to oppose efforts to put dollar values on non-marketed benefits and costs.

(3) Given the relative frequency of occasions in the areas of environmental, safety, and health regulation where one would not wish to use a benefits-outweigh-costs test as a decision rule, and given the reasons to oppose the monetizing of non-marketed benefits or costs that is a prerequisite for cost-benefit analysis, it is not justifiable to devote major resources to the generation of data for cost-benefit calculations or to undertake efforts to "spread the gospel" of cost-benefit analysis further.

I

How do we decide whether a given action is morally right or wrong and hence, assuming the desire to act morally, why it should be undertaken or refrained from? Like the Molière character who spoke prose without knowing it, economists who advocate use of cost-benefit analysis for public decisions are philosophers without knowing it: the answer given by cost-benefit analysis, that actions should be undertaken so as to maximize net benefits, represents one of the classic answers given by moral philosophers—that given by utilitarians. To determine whether an action is right or wrong, utilitarians tote up all the positive consequences of the action in terms of human satisfaction. The act that maximizes attainment of satisfaction under the circumstances is the right act. That the economists' answer is also the answer of one school of philosophers should not be surprising. Early on, economics was a branch of moral philosophy, and only later did it become an independent discipline.

Before proceeding further, the subtlety of the utilitarian position should be noted. The positive and negative consequences of an act for satisfaction may go beyond the act's immediate consequences. A facile version of utilitarianism would give moral sanction to a lie, for instance, if the satisfaction of an individual attained by telling the lie was greater than the suffering imposed on the lie's victim. Few utilitarians would agree. Most of them would add to the list of negative consequences the effect of the one lie on the tendency of the person who lies to tell other lies, even in instances when the lying produced less satisfaction for him than dissatisfaction for others. They would also add the negative effects of the lie on the general level of social regard for truth-telling, which has many consequences for future utility. A further consequence may be added as well. It is sometimes said that we should include in a utilitarian calculation the feeling of dissatisfaction produced in the liar (and perhaps in others) because, by telling a lie, one has "done the wrong thing." Correspondingly, in this view, among the positive consequences to be weighed into a utilitarian calculation of truth-telling is satisfaction arising from "doing the right thing." This view rests on an error, however, because it *assumes* what it is the purpose of the calculation to *determine*—that telling the truth in the instance in question is indeed the right thing to do. Economists are likely to object to this point, arguing that no feeling ought "arbitrarily" to be excluded from a complete cost-benefit calculation, including a feeling of dissatisfaction at doing the wrong thing. Indeed, the economists' cost-benefit calculations would, at least ideally, include such feelings. Note the difference between the economist's and the philosopher's cost-benefit calculations, however. The economist may choose to include feelings of dissatisfaction in his cost-benefit calculation, but what happens if somebody asks the economist, "Why is it right to evaluate an action on the basis of a cost-benefit test?" If an answer is to be given to that question (which does not normally preoccupy economists but which does concern both philosophers and the rest of us who need to be persuaded that cost-benefit analysis is right), then the circularity problem reemerges. And there is also another difficulty with counting feelings of dissatisfaction at doing the wrong thing in a cost-benefit calculation. It leads to the perverse result that under certain circumstances a lie, for example, might be morally right if the individual contemplating the lie felt no compunction about lying and morally wrong only if the individual felt such a compunction!

This error is revealing, however, because it begins to suggest a critique of utilitarianism. Utilitarianism is an important and powerful moral doctrine. But it is probably a minority position among contemporary moral philosophers. It is amazing that economists can proceed in unanimous endorsement of cost-benefit analysis as if unaware that their conceptual framework is highly controversial in the discipline from which it arose— moral philosophy.

Let us explore the critique of utilitarianism. The logical error discussed before appears to suggest that we have a notion of certain things being right or wrong that *predates* our calculation of costs and benefits. Imagine the case of an old man in Nazi Germany who is hostile to the regime. He is wondering whether he should speak out against Hitler. If he speaks out, he will lose his pension. And his action will have done nothing to increase the chances that the Nazi regime will be overthrown: he is regarded as somewhat eccentric by those around him, and nobody has ever consulted his views on political questions. Recall that one cannot add to the benefits of speaking out any satisfaction from doing "the right thing," because the purpose of the exercise is to determine whether speaking out *is* the right thing. How would the utilitarian calculation go? The benefits of the old man's speaking out would, as the example is presented, be nil, while the costs would be his loss of his pension. So the costs of the action would outweigh the benefits. By the utilitarians' cost-benefit calculation, it would be *morally wrong* for the man to speak out.

Another example: two very close friends are on an Arctic expedition together. One of them falls very sick in the snow and bitter cold, and sinks quickly before anything can be done to help him. As he is dying, he asks his friend one thing, "Please, make me a solemn promise that ten years from today you will come back to this spot and place a lighted candle here to remember me." The friend solemnly promises to do so, but does not tell a soul. Now, ten years later, the friend must decide whether to keep his promise. It would be inconvenient for him to make the long trip. Since he told nobody, his failure to go will not affect the general social faith in promise-keeping. And the incident was unique enough so that it is safe to assume that his failure to go will not encourage him to break other promises. Again, the costs of the act outweigh the benefits. A utilitarian would need to believe that it would be *morally wrong* to travel to the Arctic to light the candle.

A third example: a wave of thefts has hit a city and the police are having trouble finding any of the thieves. But they believe, correctly, that punishing someone for theft will have some deterrent effect and will decrease the number of crimes. Unable to arrest any actual perpetrator, the police chief and the prosecutor arrest a person whom they know to be innocent and, in cahoots with each other, fabricate a convincing case against him. The police chief and the prosecutor are about to retire, so the act has no effect on any future actions of theirs. The fabrication is perfectly executed, so nobody finds out about it. Is the *only* question involved in judging the act of framing the innocent man that of whether his suffering from conviction and imprisonment will be greater than the suffering avoided among potential crime victims when some crimes are deterred? A utilitarian would need to believe that it is *morally right to punish the innocent man* as long as it can be demonstrated that the suffering prevented outweighs his suffering.

And a final example: imagine two worlds, each containing the same sum total of happiness. In the first world, this total of happiness came about from a series of acts that included a number of lies and injustices (that is, the total consisted of the immediate gross sum of happiness created by certain acts, minus any long-term unhappiness occasioned by the lies and injustices). In the second world the same amount of happiness was produced by a different series of acts, none of which involved lies or injustices. Do we have any reason to prefer the one world to the other? A utilitarian would need to believe that the choice between the two worlds is a *matter of indifference*.

To those who believe that it would not be morally wrong for the old man to speak out in Nazi Germany or for the explorer to return to the Arctic to light a candle for his deceased friend, that it would not be morally right to convict the innocent man, or that the choice between the two worlds is not a matter of indifference—to those of us who believe these things, utilitarianism is insufficient as a moral view. We believe that some acts whose costs are greater than their benefits may be morally right and, contrariwise, some acts whose benefits are greater than their costs may be morally wrong.

This does not mean that the question whether benefits are greater than costs is morally irrelevant. Few would claim such. Indeed, for a broad range of individual and social decisions, whether an act's benefits outweigh its costs is a sufficient question to ask. But not for all such decisions. These may involve situations where certain duties—duties not to lie, break promises, or kill, for example—make an act wrong, even if it would result in an excess of benefits over costs. Or they may involve instances where people's rights are at stake. We would not permit rape even if it could be demonstrated that the rapist derived enormous happiness from his act, while the victim experienced only minor displeasure. We do not do cost-benefit analyses of freedom of speech or trial by jury. The Bill of Rights was not RARGed. As the United Steelworkers noted in a comment on the Occupational Safety and Health Administration's economic analysis of its proposed rule to reduce worker exposure to carcinogenic coke-oven emissions, the Emancipation Proclamation was not subjected to an inflationary impact statement. The notion of human rights involves the idea that people may make certain claims to be allowed to act in certain ways or to be treated in certain ways, even if the sum of benefits achieved thereby does not outweigh the sum of costs. It is this view that underlies the statement that "workers have a right to a safe and healthy work place" and the expectation that OSHA's decisions will reflect that judgment.

In the most convincing versions of nonutilitarian ethics, various duties or rights are not absolute. But each has a *prima facie* moral validity so that, if duties or rights do not conflict, the morally right act is the act that reflects a duty or respects a right. If duties or rights do conflict, a moral judgment, based on conscious deliberation, must be made. Since one of the duties non-utilitarian philosophers enumerate is the duty of beneficence (the duty to maximize happiness), which in effect incorporates all of utilitarianism by reference, a nonutilitarian who is faced with conflicts between the results of cost-benefit analysis and nonutility-based considerations will need to undertake such deliberation. But in that deliberation, additional elements, which cannot be reduced to a question of whether benefits outweigh costs, have been introduced. Indeed, depending on the moral importance we attach to the right or duty involved, cost-benefit questions may, within wide ranges, become irrelevant to the outcome of the moral judgment.

In addition to questions involving duties and rights, there is a final sort of question where, in my view, the issue of whether benefits outweigh costs should not govern moral judgment. I noted earlier that, for the common run of questions facing individuals and societies, it is possible to begin and end our judgment simply by finding out if the benefits of the contemplated act outweigh the costs. This very fact means that one way to show the great importance, or value, attached to an area is to say that decisions involving the area should not be determined by cost-benefit calculations. This applies, I think, to the view many environmentalists have of decisions involving our natural environment. When officials are deciding what level of pollution will harm certain vulnerable people—such as asthmatics or the elderly—while not harming others, one issue involved may be the right of those people not to be sacrificed on the altar of somewhat higher living standards for the rest of us. But more broadly than this, many environmentalists fear that subjecting decisions about clean air or water to the cost-benefit tests that determine the general run of decisions removes those matters from the realm of specially valued things.

II

In order for cost-benefit calculations to be performed the way they are supposed to be, all costs and benefits must be expressed in a common measure, typically dollars, including things not normally bought and sold on markets, and to which dollar prices are therefore not attached. The most dramatic example of such things is human life itself; but many of the other benefits achieved or preserved by environmental policy—such as peace and quiet, fresh-smelling air, swimmable rivers, spectacular vistas—are not traded on markets either.

Economists who do cost-benefit analysis regard the quest after dollar values for nonmarket things as a difficult challenge—but one to be met with relish. They have tried to develop methods for imputing a person's "willingness to pay" for such things, their approach generally involving a search for bundled goods that *are* traded on markets and that vary as to whether they include a feature that is, *by itself*, not marketed. Thus, fresh air is not marketed, but houses in different parts of Los Angeles that are similar except for the degree of smog are. Peace and quiet is not marketed, but similar houses inside and outside airport flight paths are. The risk of death is not marketed, but similar jobs that have different levels of risk are. Economists have produced many often ingenious efforts to impute dollar prices to non-marketed things by observing the premiums accorded homes in clean air areas over similar homes in dirty areas or the premiums paid for risky jobs over similar nonrisky jobs.

These ingenious efforts are subject to criticism on a number of technical grounds. It may be difficult to control for all the dimensions of quality other than the presence or absence of the non-marketed thing. More important, in a world where people have different preferences and are subject to different constraints as they make their choices, the dollar value imputed to the non-market things that most people would wish to avoid will be lower than otherwise, because people with unusually weak aversion to those things or usually strong constraints on their choices will be willing to take the bundled good in question at less of a discount than the average person. Thus, to use the property value discount of homes near airports as a measure of people's willingness to pay for quiet means to accept as a proxy for the rest of us the behavior of those least sensitive to noise, of airport employees (who value the convenience of a near-airport location) or of others who are susceptible to an agent's assurances that "it's not so bad." To use the wage premiums accorded hazardous work as a measure of the value of life means to accept as proxies for the rest of us the choices of people who do not have many choices or who are exceptional risk-seekers.

A second problem is that the attempts of economists to measure peo-ple's willingness to pay for non-marketed things assume that there is no difference between the price a person would require for *giving up* some-thing to which he has a preexisting right and the price he would pay to *gain* something to which he enjoys no right. Thus, the analysis assumes no difference between how much a homeowner would need to be paid in or-der to give up an unobstructed mountain view that he already enjoys and how much he would be willing to pay to get an obstruction moved once it is already in place. Available evidence suggests that most people would in-sist on being paid far more to assent to a worsening of their situation than they would be willing to pay to improve their situation. The difference arises from such factors as being accustomed to and psychologically attached to that which one believes one enjoys by right. But this creates a circularity problem for any attempt to use cost-benefit analysis to determine *whether* to assign to, say, the homeowner the right to an unobstructed mountain view. For willingness to pay will be different depending on whether the right is assigned initially or not. The value judgment about whether to as-sign the right must thus be made first. (In order to set an upper bound on the value of the benefit, one might hypothetically assign the right to the person and determine how much he would need to be paid to give it up.)

Third, the efforts of economists to impute willingness to pay invariably involve bundled goods exchanged in *private* transactions. Those who use figures garnered from such analysis to provide guidance for *public* deci-sions assume no difference between how people value certain things in pri-vate individual transactions and how they would wish those same things to be valued in public collective decisions. In making such assumptions, economists insidiously slip into their analysis an important and contro-versial value judgment, growing naturally out of the highly individualistic microeconomic tradition—namely, the view that there should be no dif-ference between private behavior and the behavior we display in public so-cial life. An alternative view—one that enjoys, I would suggest, wide reso-nance among citizens—would be that public, social decisions provide an opportunity to give certain things a higher valuation than we choose, for one reason or another, to given them in our private activities.

Thus, opponents of stricter regulation of health risks often argue that we show by our daily risk-taking behavior that we do not value life infi-nitely, and therefore our public decisions should not reflect the high value of life that proponents of strict regulation propose. However, an alterna-tive view is equally plausible. Precisely because we fail, for whatever rea-sons, to give life-saving the value in everyday personal decisions that we in some general terms believe we should give it, we may wish our social de-cisions to provide us the occasion to display the reverence for life that we espouse but do not always show. By this view, people do not have fixed un-ambiguous "preferences" to which they give expression through private ac-tivities and which therefore should be given expression in public decisions. Rather, they may have what they themselves regard as "higher" and "lower" preferences. The latter may come to the fore in private decisions, but people may want the former to come to the fore in public decisions. They may sometimes display racial prejudice, but support antidiscrimination laws. They may buy a certain product after seeing a seductive ad, but be skeptical enough of advertising to want the government to keep a close eye on it. In such cases, the use of private behavior to impute the values that should be entered for public decisions, as is done by using willingness to pay in private transactions, commits grievous offense against a view of the behavior of the citizen that is deeply engrained in our democratic tradition. It is a view that denudes politics of any independent role in society, reducing it to a mechanistic, mimicking recalculation based on private behavior.

Finally, one may oppose the effort to place prices on a non-market thing and hence in effect incorporate it into the market system out of a fear that the very act of doing so will reduce the thing's perceived value. To place a price on the benefit may, in other words, reduce the value of that benefit. Cost-benefit analysis thus maybe like the thermometer that, when placed in a liquid to be measured, itself changes the liquid's temperature.

Examples of the perceived cheapening of a thing's value by the very act of buying and selling it abound in everyday life and language. The disgust that accompanies the idea of buying and selling human beings is based on the sense that this would dramatically diminish human worth. Epithets such as "he prostituted himself," applied as linguistic analogies to people who have sold something, reflect the view that certain things should not be sold because doing so diminishes their value. Praise that is bought is worth little, even to the person buying it. A true anecdote is told of an economist who retired to another university community and complained that he was having difficulty making friends. The laconic response of a critical colleague—"If you want a friend why don't you buy yourself one"—illustrates in a pithy way the intuition that, for some things, the very act of placing a price on them reduces their perceived value.

The first reason that pricing something decreases its perceived value is that, in many circumstances, non-market exchange is associated with the production of certain values not associated with market exchange. These may include spontaneity and various other feelings that come from personal relationships. If a good becomes less associated with the production of positively valued feelings because of market exchange, the perceived value of the good declines to the extent that those feelings are valued. This can be seen clearly in instances where a thing may be transferred both by market and by non-market mechanisms. The willingness to pay for sex bought from a prostitute is less than the perceived value of the sex consummating love. (Imagine the reaction if a practitioner of cost-benefit analysis computed the benefits of sex based on the price of prostitute services.)

Furthermore, if one values in a general sense the existence of a non-market sector because of its connection with the production of certain valued feelings, then one ascribes added value to any non-marketed good simply as a repository of values represented by the non-market sector one wishes to preserve. This seems certainly to be the case for things in nature, such as pristine streams or undisturbed forests: for many people who value them, part of their value comes from their position as repositories of values the non-market sector represents.

The second way in which placing a market price on a thing decreases its perceived value is by removing the possibility of proclaiming that the thing is "not for sale," since things on the market by definition are for sale. The very statement that something is not for sale affirms, enhances, and protects a thing's value in a number of ways. To begin with, the statement is a way of showing that a thing is valued for its own sake, whereas selling a thing for money demonstrates that it was valued only instrumentally. Furthermore, to say that something cannot be transferred in that way places it in the exceptional category—which requires the person interested in obtaining that thing to be able to offer something else that is exceptional, rather than allowing him the easier alternative of obtaining the thing for money that could have been obtained in an affinity of ways. This enhances its value. If I am willing to say "You're a really kind person" to whoever pays me to do so, my praise loses the value that attaches to it from being exchangeable only for an act of kindness.

In addition, if we have already decided we value something highly, one way of stamping it with a cachet affirming its high value is to announce that it is "not for sale." Such an announcement does more, however, than just reflect a preexisting high valuation. It signals a thing's distinctive value to others and helps us persuade them to value the thing more highly than they otherwise might. It also expresses our resolution to safeguard that distinctive value. To state that something is not for sale is thus also a source of value for that thing, since if a thing's value is easy to affirm or protect, it will be worth more than an otherwise similar thing without such attributes.

If we proclaim that something is not for sale, we make a once-and-for-all judgment of its special value. When something is priced, the issue of its perceived value is constantly coming up, as a standing invitation to reconsider that original judgment. Were people constantly faced with questions such as "how much money could get you to give up your freedom of speech?" or "how much would you sell your vote for if you could?", the perceived value of the freedom to speak or the right to vote would soon become devastated as, in moments of weakness, people started saying "maybe it's not worth *so much* after all." Better not to be faced with the constant questioning in the first place. Something similar did in fact occur when the slogan "better red than dead" was launched by some pacifists during the Cold War. Critics pointed out that the very posing of this stark choice—in effect, "would you *really* be willing to give up your life in exchange for not living under communism?"—reduced the value people attached to freedom and thus diminished resistance to attacks on freedom.

Finally, of some things valued very highly it is stated that they are "priceless" or that they have "infinite value." Such expressions are reserved for a subset of things not for sale, such as life or health. Economists tend to scoff at talk of pricelessness. For them, saying that something is price-less is to state a willingness to trade off an infinite quantity of all other goods for one unit of the priceless good, a situation that empirically ap-pears highly unlikely. For most people, however, the word priceless is preg-nant with meaning. Its value-affirming and value-protecting functions can-not be bestowed on expressions that merely denote a determinate, albeit high, valuation. John Kennedy in his inaugural address proclaimed that the nation was ready to "pay any price [and] bear any burden . . . to assure the survival and the success of liberty." Had he said instead that we were will-ing to "pay a high price" or "bear a large burden" for liberty, the statement would have rung hollow.

III

An objection that advocates of cost-benefit analysis might well make to the preceding argument should be considered. I noted earlier that, in cases where various non-utility-based duties or rights conflict with the maxi-mization of utility, it is necessary to make a deliberative judgment about what act is finally right. I also argued earlier that the search for commen-surability might not always be a desirable one, that the attempt to go be-yond expressing benefits in terms of (say) lives saved and costs in terms of dollars is not something devoutly to be wished.

In situations involving things that are not expressed in a common mea-sure, advocates of cost-benefit analysis argue that people making judgments "in effect" perform cost-benefit calculations anyway. If government regu-lators promulgate a regulation that saves 100 lives at a cost of $1 billion, they are "in effect" valuing a life at (a minimum of) $10 million, whether or not they say that they are willing to place a dollar value on a human life. Since, in this view, cost-benefit analysis "in effect" is inevitable, it might as well be made specific.

This argument misconstrues the real difference in the reasoning processes involved. In cost-benefit analysis, equivalencies are established in *advance* as one of the raw materials for the calculation. One determines costs and benefits, one determines equivalencies (to be able to put various costs and benefits into a common measure), and then one sets to toting things up—waiting, as it were, with bated breath for the results of the cal-culation to come out. The outcome is determined by the arithmetic; if the outcome is a close call or if one is not good at long division, one does not know how it will turn out until the calculation is finished. In the kind of deliberative judgment that is performed without a common measure, no establishment of equivalencies occurs in advance. Equivalencies are not aids to the decision process. In fact, the decision-maker might not even be aware of what the "in effect" equivalencies were, at least before they are revealed to him afterwards by someone pointing out what he had "in effect" done. The decision-maker would see himself as simply having made a deliberate judgment; the "in effect" equivalency number did not play a causal role in the decision but at most merely reflects it. Given this, the argument against making the process explicit is the one discussed earlier in the discussion of problems with putting specific quantified values on things that are not normally quantified—that the very act of doing so may serve to reduce the value of those things.

My own judgment is that modest efforts to assess levels of benefits and costs are justified, although I do not believe that government agencies ought to sponsor efforts to put dollar prices on non-market things. I also do not believe that the cry for more cost-benefit analysis in regulation is, on the whole, justified. If regulatory officials were so insensitive about regulatory costs that they did not provide acceptable raw material for deliberative judgments (even if not of a strictly cost-benefit nature), my conclusion might be different. But a good deal of research into costs and benefits already occurs—actually, far more in the U.S. regulatory process than in that of any other industrial society. The danger now would seem to come more from the other side.

Replies to Steven Kelman

From James V. DeLong, Vice President at the National Legal Center for the Public Interest

Steven Kelman's "Cost-Benefit Analysis—An Ethical Critique" presents so many targets that it is difficult to concentrate one's fire. However, four points seem worth particular emphasis:

(1) The decision to use cost-benefit analysis by no means implies adoption of the reductionist utilitarianism described by Kelman. It is based instead on the pragmatic conclusion that any value system one adopts is more likely to be promoted if one knows something about the consequences of the choices to be made. The effort to put dollar values on noneconomic benefits is nothing more than an effort to find some common measure for things that are not easily comparable when, in the real world, choice must be made. Its object is not to write a computer program but to improve the quality of difficult social choices under conditions of uncertainty, and no sensible analyst lets himself become the prisoner of the numbers.

(2) Kelman repeatedly lapses into "entitlement" rhetoric, as if an assertion of a moral claim closes an argument. Even leaving aside the fundamental question of the philosophical basis of those entitlements, there

are two major problems with this style of argument. First, it tends naturally toward all-encompassing claims.

Kelman quotes a common statement that "workers have a right to a
safe and healthy workplace," a statement that contains no recognition that
safety and health are not either/or conditions, that the most difficult questions involve gradations of risk, and that the very use of entitlement language tends to assume that a zero-risk level is the only acceptable one. Second, entitlement rhetoric is usually phrased in the passive voice, as if the
speaker were arguing with some omnipotent god or government that is ma-
liciously withholding the entitlement out of spite. In the real world, one
persons' right is another's duty, and it often clarifies the discussion to focus more precisely on who owes this duty and what it is going to cost him
or her. For example, the article posits that an issue in government decisions about acceptable pollution levels is "the right" of such vulnerable
groups as asthmatics or the elderly "not to be sacrificed on the altar of
somewhat higher living standards for the rest of us." This defends the entitlement by assuming the costs involved are both trivial and diffused. Suppose, though, that the price to be paid is not "somewhat higher living standards," but the jobs of a number of workers?

Kelman's counter to this seems to be that entitlements are not firm rights,
but only presumptive ones that prevail in any clash with nonentitlements,
and that when two entitlements collide the decision depends upon the "moral
importance we attach to the right or duty involved." So the above collision
would be resolved by deciding whether a job is an entitlement and, if it is,
by then deciding whether jobs or air have greater "moral importance."

I agree that conflicts between such interests present difficult choices,
but the quantitative questions, the cost-benefit questions, are hardly irrelevant to making them. Suppose taking X quantity of pollution from the air
of a city will keep one asthmatic from being forced to leave town and cost
1,000 workers their jobs? Suppose it will keep 1,000 asthmatics from being forced out and cost one job? These are not equivalent choices, economically or morally, and the effort to decide them according to some abstract idea of moral importance only obscures the true nature of the moral
problems involved.

(3) Kelman also develops the concept of things that are "specially valued," and that are somehow contaminated if thought about in monetary
terms. As an approach to personal decision making, this is silly. There are
many things one specially values—in the sense that one would find the effort to assign a market price to them ridiculous—which are nonetheless affected by economic factors. I may specially value a family relationship, but
how often I phone is influenced by long-distance rates. I may specially value
music, but be affected by the price of records or the cost of tickets at the
Kennedy Center.

When translated to the realm of government decisions, however, the
concept goes beyond silliness. It creates a political grotesquerie. People specially value many different things. Under Kelman's assumptions, people

must, in creating a political coalition, recognize and accept as legitimate everyone's special value, without concern for cost. Therefore, everyone becomes entitled to as much of the thing he specially values as he says he specially values, and it is immoral to discuss vulgar questions of resource limitations. Any coalition built on such premises can go in either of two directions: It can try to incorporate so many different groups and interests that the absurdity of its internal contradictions becomes manifest. Or it can limit its membership at some point and decide that the special values of those left outside are not legitimate and should be sacrificed to the special values of those in the coalition. In the latter case, of course, those outside must be made scapegoats for any frustration of any group member's entitlement, a requirement that eventually leads to political polarization and a holy war between competing coalitions of special values.

(4) The decisions that must be made by contemporary government indeed involve painful choices. They affect both the absolute quantity and the distribution not only of goods and benefits, but also of physical and mental suffering. It is easy to understand why people would want to avoid making such choices and would rather act in ignorance than with knowledge and responsibility for the consequences of their choices. While this may be understandable, I do not regard it as an acceptable moral position. To govern is to choose, and government officials—whether elected or appointed—betray their obligations to the welfare of the people who hired them if they adopt a policy of happy ignorance and nonresponsibility for consequences.

The article concludes with the judgment that the present danger is too much cost-benefit analysis, not too little. But I find it hard to believe, looking around the modern world, that its major problem is that it suffers from an excess of rationality. The world's stock of ignorance is and will remain quite large enough without adding to it as a matter of deliberate policy.

From Robert M. Solow, Institute Professor of Economics Emeritus at the Massachusetts Institute of Technology

I am an economist who has no personal involvement in the practice of cost-benefit analysis, who happens to think that modern economics underplays the significance of ethical judgments both in its approach to policy and its account of individual and organizational behavior, and who once wrote in print:

> It may well be socially destructive to admit the routine exchangeability of certain things. We would prefer to maintain that they are beyond price (although this sometimes means only that we would prefer not to know what the price really is).

You might expect, therefore, that I would be in sympathy with Steven Kelman's ethical critique of cost-benefit analysis. But I found the article profoundly, and not entirely innocently, misleading. I would like to say why.

First of all, it is not the case that cost-benefit analysis works, or must work, by "monetizing" everything from mother love to patriotism. Cost-benefit analysis is needed only when society must give up some of one good thing in order to get more of another good thing. In other cases the decision is not problematical. The underlying rationale of cost-benefit analysis is that the cost of the good thing to be obtained is precisely the good thing that must or will be given up to obtain it. Wherever he reads "willingness to pay" and balks, Kelman should read "willingness to sacrifice" and feel better. In a choice between hospital beds and preventive treatment, lives are traded against lives. I suppose it is only natural that my brethren should get into the habit of measuring the sacrifice in terms of dollars forgone. In the typical instance in which someone actually does a cost-benefit analysis, the question to be decided is, say, whether the public should be taxed to pay for a water project—a context in which it does not seem far-fetched to ask whether the project will provide services for which the public would willingly pay what it would have to give up in taxes. But some less familiar unit of measurement could be used.

Let me add here, parenthetically, that I do agree with Kelman that there are situations in which the body politic's willingness to sacrifice may be badly measured by the sum of individuals' willingnesses to sacrifice in a completely "private" context. But that is at worst an error of technique, not a mistaken principle.

Second, Kelman hints broadly that "economists" are so morally numb as to believe that a routine cost-benefit analysis could justify killing widows and orphans, or abridging freedom of speech, or outlawing simple evidences of piety or friendship. But there is nothing in the theory or the practice of cost-benefit analysis to justify that judgment. Treatises on the subject make clear that certain ethical or political principles may irreversibly dominate the advantages and disadvantages capturable by cost-benefit analysis. Those treatises make a further point that Kelman barely touches on: since the benefits and the costs of a policy decision are usually enjoyed and incurred by different people, a distributional judgment has to be made which can override any simple-minded netting out. In addition, Kelman's point that people may put different values on the acquisition of a good for the first time and on the loss of a preexisting entitlement to the same good is not exactly a discovery. He should look up "compensating variation" and "equivalent variation" in a good economics textbook.

Third, Kelman ends by allowing that it is not a bad thing to have a modest amount of cost-benefit analysis going on. I would have supposed that was a fair description of the state of affairs. Do I detect a tendency to eat one's cost-benefit analysis and have it too? If not, what is the point of all the overkill? As a practical matter, the vacuum created by diminished reliance on cost-benefit analysis is likely to be filled by a poor substitute for ethically informed deliberation. Is the capering of Mr. Stockman more to Mr. Kelman's taste?

From Gerard Butters, Assistant Director for Consumer
Protection at the Bureau of Economics, Federal Trade
Commission; John Calfee, Resident Scholar at the
American Enterprise Institute; and Pauline Ippolito,
Associate Director for Special Projects at the Bureau
of Economics, Federal Trade Commission

In his article, Steven Kelman argues against the increased use of cost-benefit analysis for regulatory decisions involving health, safety, and the environment. His basic contention is that these decisions are moral ones, and
that cost-benefit analysis is therefore inappropriate because it requires the
adoption of an unsatisfactory moral system. He supports his argument with
a series of examples, most of which involve private decisions. In these situations, he asserts, cost-benefit advocates must renounce any moral qualms
about lies, broken promises, and violations of human rights.

We disagree (and in doing so, we speak for ourselves, not for the Federal Trade Commission or its staff). Cost-benefit analysis is not a means
for judging private decisions. It is a guide for decision making involving
others, especially when the welfare of many individuals must be balanced.
It is designed not to dictate individual values, but to take them into account when decisions must be made collectively. Its use is grounded on the
principle that, in a democracy, government must act as an agent of the
citizens.

We see no reason to abandon this principle when health and safety are
involved. Consider, for example, a proposal to raise the existing federal
standards on automobile safety. Higher standards will raise the costs, and
hence the price, of cars. From our point of view, the appropriate policy
judgment rests on whether customers will value the increased safety sufficiently to warrant the costs. Any violation of a cost-benefit criterion would
require that consumers purchase something they would not voluntarily purchase or prevent them from purchasing something they want. One might
argue, in the spirit of Kelman's analysis, that many consumers would want
the government to impose a more stringent standard than they would
choose for themselves. If so, how is the cost-safety trade-off that consumers
really want to be determined? Any objective way of doing this would be a
natural part of cost-benefit analysis.

Kelman also argues that the process of assigning a dollar value to things
not traded in the marketplace is rife with indignities, flaws, and biases. Up
to a point, we agree. It *is* difficult to place objective dollar values on certain intangible costs and benefits. Even with regard to intangibles which
have been systematically studied, such as the "value of life," we know of
no cost-benefit advocate who believes that regulatory staff economists
should reduce every consideration to dollar terms and simply supply the
decision maker with the bottom line. Our main concerns are twofold: (1)
to make the major costs and benefits explicit so that the decision maker

makes the trade-offs consciously and with the prospect of being held accountable, and (2) to encourage the move toward a more consistent set of standards.

The gains from adopting consistent regulatory standards can be dramatic. If costs and benefits are not balanced in making decisions, it is likely that the returns per dollar in terms of health and safety will be small for some programs and large for others. Such programs present opportunities for saving lives, and cost-benefit analysis will reveal them. Perhaps, as Kelman argues, there is something repugnant about assigning dollar values to lives. But the alternative can be to sacrifice lives needlessly by failing to carry out the calculations that would have revealed the means for saving them. It should be kept in mind that the avoidance of cost-benefit analysis has its own cost, which can be gauged in lives as well as in dollars.

Nonetheless, we do not dispute that cost-benefit analysis is highly imperfect. We would welcome a better guide to public policy, a guide that would be efficient, morally attractive, and certain to ensure that governments follow the dictates of the governed. Kelman's proposal is to adopt an ethical system that balances conflicts between certain unspecified "duties" and "rights" according to "deliberate reflection." But who is to do the reflecting, and on whose behalf? His guide places no clear limits on the actions of regulatory agencies. Rather than enhancing the connections between individual values and state decisions, such a vague guideline threatens to sever them. Is there a common moral standard that every regulator will magically and independently arrive at through "deliberate reflection"? We doubt it. Far more likely is a system in which bureaucratic decisions reflect the preferences, not of the citizens, but of those in a peculiar position to influence decisions. What concessions to special interests cannot be disguised by claiming that it is degrading to make explicit the trade-offs reflected in the decision? What individual crusade cannot be rationalized by an appeal to "public values" that "rise above" values revealed by individual choices?

V

The Means of Environmental Policy: Cost Effectiveness and Market-Based Instruments

16 _Economic Instruments for Environmental Regulation_

Tom H. Tietenberg

Tom H. Tietenberg is Mitchell Family Professor of Economics at Colby College.

I. Introduction

As recently as a decade ago environmental regulators and lobbying groups with a special interest in environmental protection looked upon the market system as a powerful adversary. That the market unleashed powerful forces was widely recognized and that those forces clearly acted to degrade the environment was widely lamented. Conflict and confrontation became the battle cry for those groups seeking to protect the environment as they set out to block market forces whenever possible.

Among the more enlightened participants in the environmental policy process the air of confrontation and conflict has now begun to recede in many parts of the world. Leading environmental groups and regulators have come to realize that the power of the market can be harnessed and channelled toward the achievement of environmental goals, through an economic incentives approach to regulation. Forward-looking business people have come to appreciate the fact that cost-effective regulation can make them more competitive in the global market-place than regulations which impose higher-than-necessary control costs.

The change in attitude has been triggered by a recognition that this former adversary, the market, can be turned into a powerful ally. In contrast to the traditional regulatory approach, which makes mandatory particular forms of behaviour or specific technological choices, the economic incentive approach allows more flexibility in how the environmental goal is reached. By changing the incentives an individual agent faces, the best private choice can be made to coincide with the best social choice. Rather than relying on the regulatory authority to identify the best course of action, the individual agent can use his or her typically superior information to select the best means of meeting an assigned emission reduction responsibility. This flexibility achieves environmental goals at lower cost, which, in turn, makes the goals easier to achieve and easier to establish.

"Economic Instruments for Environmental Regulation," by T. H. Tietenberg, from _Oxford Review of Economic Policy_, 6(1):17–33.

One indicator of the growing support for the use of economic incentive approaches for environmental control in the United States is the favourable treatment it has recently received both in the popular business[1] and environmental[2] press. Some public interest environmental organizations have now even adopted economic incentive approaches as a core part of their strategy for protecting the environment.[3]

In response to this support the emissions trading concept has recently been applied to reducing the lead content in gasoline, to controlling both ozone depletion and non-point sources of water pollution, and was also prominently featured in the Bush administration proposals for reducing acid rain and smog unveiled in June 1989.

Our knowledge about economic incentive approaches has grown rapidly in the two decades in which they have received serious analytical attention. Not only have the theoretical models become more focused and the empirical work more detailed, but we have now had over a decade of experience with emissions trading in the US and emission charges in Europe.

As the world community becomes increasingly conscious of both the need to tighten environmental controls and the local economic perils associated with tighter controls in a highly competitive global market-place, it seems a propitious time to stand back and to organize what we have learned about this practical and promising approach to pollution control that may be especially relevant to current circumstances. In this paper I will draw upon economic theory, empirical studies, and actual experience with implementation to provide a brief overview of some of the major lessons we have learned about two economic incentive approaches— emissions trading and emission charges—as well as their relationships to the more traditional regulatory policy.[4]

II. The Policy Context

(i) Emissions Trading

Stripped to its bare essentials, the US Clean Air Act[5] relies upon a *command-and-control* approach to controlling pollution. Ambient standards es-

---

[1]See, for example, Main (1988).

[2]See, for example, Stavins (1989).

[3]See the various issues in Volume XX of the EDF Letter, a report to members of the Environmental Defense Fund.

[4]In the limited space permitted by this paper only a few highlights can be illustrated. All of the details of the proofs and the empirical work can be found in the references listed at the end of the paper. For a comprehensive summary of this work see Tietenberg (1980), Liroff (1980), Bohm and Russell (1985), Tietenberg (1985), Liroff (1986), Dudek and Palmisano (1988), Hahn (1989), Hahn and Hester (1989a and 1989b), and Tietenberg (1989b).

[5]The US Clean Air Act (42 U.S.C. 7401–642) was first passed in 1955. The central thrust of the approach described in this paragraph was initiated by the Clean Air Act Amendments of 1970 with mid-course corrections provided by the Clean Air Act Amendments of 1977.

tablish the highest allowable concentration of the pollutant in the ambient air for each conventional pollutant. To reach these prescribed ambient standards, emission standards (legal emission ceilings) are imposed on a large number of specific emission points such as stacks, vents, or storage tanks. Following a survey of the technological options of control, the control authority selects a favoured control technology and calculates the amount of emission reduction achievable by that technology as the basis for setting the emission standard. Technologies yielding larger amounts of control (and, hence, supporting more stringent emission standards) are selected for new emitters and for existing emitters in areas where it is very difficult to meet the ambient standard. The responsibility for defining and enforcing these standards is shared in legislatively specified ways between the national government and the various state governments.

The emissions trading programme attempts to inject more flexibility into the manner in which the objectives of the Clean Air Act are met by allowing sources a much wider range of choice in how they satisfy their legal pollution control responsibilities than possible in the command-and-control approach. Any source choosing to reduce emissions at any discharge point more than required by its emission standard can apply to the control authority for certification of the excess control as an "emission reduction credit" (ERC). Defined in terms of a specific amount of a particular pollutant, the certified emissions reduction credit can be used to satisfy emission standards at other (presumably more expensive to control) discharge points controlled by the creating source or it can be sold to other sources. By making these credits transferable, the US Environmental Protection Agency (EPA) has allowed sources to find the cheapest means of satisfying their requirements, even if the cheapest means are under the control of another firm. The ERC is the currency used in emissions trading, while the offset, bubble, emissions banking, and netting policies govern how this currency can be stored and spent.[6]

The *offset policy* requires major new or expanding sources in "non-attainment" areas (those areas with air quality worse than the ambient standards) to secure sufficient offsetting emission reductions (by acquiring ERCs) from existing firms so that the air is cleaner after their entry or expansion than before.[7] Prior to this policy no new firms were allowed to enter non-attainment areas on the grounds they would interfere with attaining the ambient standards. By introducing the offset policy EPA allowed economic growth to continue while assuring progress toward attainment.

The *bubble policy* receives its unusual name from the fact that it treats multiple emission points controlled by existing emitters (as opposed to those expanding or entering an area for the first time) as if they were enclosed in a bubble. Under this policy only the total emissions of each pol-

---

[6]The details of this policy can be found in "Emissions Trading Policy Statements" 51 *Federal Register* 43829 (4 December 1986).

[7]Offsets are also required for major modifications in areas which have attained the standards if the modifications jeopardize attainment.

lutant leaving the bubble are regulated. While the total leaving the bubble must not be larger than the total permitted by adding up all the corresponding emission standards within the bubble (and in some cases the total must be 20 per cent lower), emitters are free to control some discharge points less than dictated by the corresponding emission standard as long as sufficient compensating ERCs are obtained from other discharge points within the bubble. In essence sources are free to choose the mix of control among the discharge points as long as the overall emission reduction requirements are satisfied. Multi-plant bubbles are allowed, opening the possibility for trading ERCs among very different kinds of emitters.

Netting allows modifying or expanding sources (but not new sources) to escape from the need to meet the requirements of the rather stringent new source review process (including the need to acquire offsets) so long as any net increase in emissions (counting any ERCs earned elsewhere in the plant) is below an established threshold. In so far as it allows firms to escape particular regulatory requirements by using ERCs to remain under the threshold which triggers applicability, netting is more properly considered regulatory relief than regulatory reform.

Emissions banking allows firms to store certified ERCs for subsequent use in the offset, bubble, or netting programmes or for sale to others.

Although comprehensive data on the effects of the programme do not exist because substantial proportions of it are administered by local areas and no one collects information in a systematic way, some of the major aspects of the experience are clear.[8]

- The programme has unquestionably and substantially reduced the costs of complying with the requirements of the Clean Air Act. Most estimates place the accumulated capital savings for all components of the programme at over $10 billion. This does not include the recurring savings in operating cost. On the other hand the programme has not produced the magnitude of cost savings that was anticipated by its strongest proponents at its inception.

- The level of compliance with the basic provisions of the Clean Air Act has increased. The emissions trading programme increased the possible means for compliance and sources have responded.

- Somewhere between 7,000 and 12,000 trading transactions have been consummated. Each of these transactions was voluntary and for the participants represented an improvement over the traditional regulatory approach. Several of these transactions involved the introduction of innovative control technologies.

- The vast majority of emissions trading transactions have involved large pollution sources trading emissions reduction credits either created by excess control of uniformly mixed pollutants (those for which the lo-

[8]See, for example, Tietenberg (1985), Hahn and Hester (1989a and 1989b), and Dudek and Palmisano (1988).

cation of emission is not an important policy concern) or involving facilities in close proximity to one another.

- Though air quality has certainly improved for most of the covered pollutants, it is virtually impossible to say how much of the improvement can be attributed to the emissions trading programme. The emissions trading programme complements the traditional regulatory approach, rather than replaces it. Therefore, while it can claim to have hastened compliance with the basic provisions of the act and in some cases to have encouraged improvements beyond the act, improved air quality resulted from the package taken together, rather than from any specific component.

(ii) Emissions Charges

Emission charges are used in both Europe and Japan, though more commonly to control water pollution than air pollution.[9] Currently effluent charges are being used to control water pollution in France, Italy, Germany, and the Netherlands. In both France and the Netherlands the charges are designed to raise revenue for the purpose of funding activities specifically designed to improve water quality.

In Germany discharges are required to meet minimum standards of waste water treatment for a number of defined pollutants. Simultaneously a fee is levied on every unit of discharge depending on the quantity and noxiousness of the effluent. Dischargers meeting or exceeding state-of-the-art effluent standards have to pay only half the normal rate.

The Italian effluent charge system was mainly designed to encourage polluters to achieve provisional effluent standards as soon as possible. The charge is nine times higher for firms that do not meet the prescribed standards than for firms that do meet them. This charge system was designed only to facilitate the transition to the prescribed standards so it is scheduled to expire once full compliance has been achieved.[10]

Air pollution emission charges have been implemented by France and Japan. The French air pollution charge was designed to encourage the early adoption of pollution control equipment with the revenues returned to those paying the charge as a subsidy for installing the equipment. In Japan the emission charge is designed to raise revenue to compensate victims of air pollution. The charge rate is determined primarily by the cost of the compensation programme in the previous year and the amount of remaining emissions over which this cost can be applied *pro rata*.

Charges have also been used in Sweden to increase the rate at which consumers would purchase cars equipped with a catalytic converter. Cars not equipped with a catalytic converter were taxed, while new cars equipped with a catalytic converter were subsidized.

---

[9]See Anderson (1977), Brown and Johnson (1984), Bressers (1988), Vos (1989), Opschoor and Vos (1989), and Sprenger (1989).

[10]The initial deadline for expiration was 1986, but it has since been postponed.

While data are limited a few highlights seem clear.

- Economists typically envisage two types of effluent or emissions charges. The first, an efficiency charge, is designed to produce an efficient outcome by forcing the polluter to compensate completely for all damage caused. The second, a cost-effective charge, is designed to achieve a predefined ambient standard at the lowest possible control cost. In practice, few, if any, implemented programmes fit either of these designs.

- Despite being designed mainly to raise revenue, effluent charges have typically improved water quality. Though the improvements in most cases have been small, apparently due to the low level at which the effluent charge rate is set, the Netherlands, with its higher effective rates, reports rather large improvements. Air pollution charges typically have not had much effect on air quality because the rates are too low and, in the case of France, most of the revenue is returned to the polluting sources.

- The revenue from charges is typically earmarked for specific environmental purposes rather than contributed to the general revenue as a means of reducing the reliance on taxes that produce more distortions in resource allocation.

- The Swedish tax on heavily polluting vehicles and subsidy for new low polluting vehicles was very successful in introducing low polluting vehicles into the automobile population at a much faster than normal rate. The policy was not revenue neutral, however; owing to the success of the programme in altering vehicle choices, the subsidy payments greatly exceeded the tax revenue.

III. First Principles

Theory can help us understand the characteristics of these economic approaches in the most favourable circumstances for their use and assist in the process of designing the instruments for maximum effectiveness. Because of the dualistic nature of emission charges and emission reduction credits,[11] implications about emission charges and emissions trading flow from the same body of theory.

Drawing conclusions about either of these approaches from this type of analysis, however, must be done with care because operational versions typically differ considerably from the idealized versions modelled by the theory. For example, not all trades that would be allowed in an ideal emis-

---

[11]Under fairly general conditions any allocation of control responsibility achieved by an emissions trading programme could also be achieved by a suitably designed system of emission charges and vice versa.

sions trading programme are allowed in the current US emissions trading programme. Similarly the types of emissions charges actually imposed differ considerably from their ideal versions, particularly in the design of the rate structure and the process for adjusting rates over time.

Assuming all participants are cost-minimizers, a "well-defined" emissions trading or emission charge system could cost-effectively allocate the control responsibility for meeting a predefined pollution target among the various pollution sources despite incomplete information on the control possibilities by the regulatory authorities.[12]

The intuition behind this powerful proposition is not difficult to grasp. Cost-minimizing firms seek to minimize the sum of (a) either ERC acquisition costs or payments of emission charges and (b) control costs. Minimization will occur when the marginal cost of control is set equal to the emission reduction credit price or the emission charge. Since all cost-minimizing sources would choose to control until their marginal control costs were equal to the same price or charge, marginal control costs would be equalized across all discharge points, precisely the condition required for cost-effectiveness.[13]

Emission charges could also sustain a cost effective allocation of the control responsibility for meeting a predefined pollution target, but only if the control authority knew the correct level of the charge to impose or was willing to engage in an iterative trial-and-error process over time to find the correct level. Emissions trading does not face this problem because the price level is established by the market, not the control authority.[14]

Though derived in the rarified world of theory, the practical importance of this theorem should not be underestimated. Economic incentive approaches offer a unique opportunity for regulators to solve a fundamental dilemma. The control authorities' desire to allocate the responsibility for control cost-effectively is inevitably frustrated by a lack of information sufficient to achieve this objective. Economic incentive approaches create a system of incentives in which those who have the best knowledge about control opportunities, the environmental managers for the industries, are encouraged to use that knowledge to achieve environmental objectives at minimum cost. Information barriers do not preclude effective regulation.

What constitutes a "well-defined" emissions trading or emission charge system depends crucially on the attributes of the pollutant being controlled.[15]

---

[12]For the formal demonstration of this proposition see Baumol and Oates (1975), Montgomery (1972), and Tietenberg (1985).

[13]It should be noted that while the allocation is cost-effective, it is not necessarily efficient (the amount of pollution indicated by a benefit-cost comparison). It would only be efficient if the predetermined target happened to coincide with the efficient amount of pollution. Nothing guarantees this outcome.

[14]See Tietenberg (1988) for a more detailed explanation of this point.

[15]For the technical details supporting this proposition see Montgomery (1972), and Tietenberg (1985).

To be consistent with a cost-effective allocation of the control responsibility, the policy instruments would have to be defined in different ways
for different types of pollutants. Two differentiating characteristics are of
particular relevance. Approaches designed to control pollutants which are
uniformly mixed in the atmosphere (such as volatile organic compounds,
one type of precursor for ozone formation) can be defined simply in terms
of a rate of emissions flow per unit time. Economic incentive approaches
sharing this design characteristic are called *emission trades* or *emission
charges*.

Instrument design is somewhat more difficult when the pollution target being pursued is defined in terms of concentrations measured at a number of specific receptor locations (such as particulates). In this case the
cost-effective trade or charge design must take into account the *location* of
the emissions (including injection height) as well as the *magnitude* of emissions. As long as the control authorities can define for each emitter a vector of transfer coefficients, which translate the effect of a unit increase of
emissions by that emitter into an increase in concentration at each of the
affected receptors, receptor-specific trades or charges can be defined which
will allocate the responsibility cost-effectively. The design which is consistent with cost-effectiveness in this context is called an *ambient trade* or an
ambient charge.

Unfortunately, while the design of the ambient ERC is not very complicated,[16] implementing the markets within which these ERCs would be
traded is rather complicated. In particular for each unit of planned emissions an emitter would have to acquire separate ERCs for each affected receptor. When the number of receptors is large, the result is a rather complicated set of transactions. Similarly, establishing the correct rate structure
for the charges in this context is particularly difficult because the set of
charges which will satisfy the ambient air quality constraints is not unique;
even a trial-and-error system would not necessarily result in the correct
matrix of ambient charges being put into effect.

As long as markets are competitive and transactions costs are low, the
trading benchmark in an emissions trading approach does not affect the
ultimate cost-effective allocation of control responsibility. When markets
are non-competitive or transactions costs are high, however, the final allocation of control responsibility is affected.[17] Emission charge approaches
do not face this problem.

Once the control authority has decided how much pollution of each
type will be allowed, it must then decide how to allocate the operating permits among the sources. In theory emission reduction credits could either
be auctioned off, with the sources purchasing them from the control authority at the market-clearing price, or (as in the US programme) created

---

[16]Each permit allows the holder to degrade the concentration level at the corresponding receptor by one unit.

[17]See Hahn (1984) for the mathematical treatment of this point. Further discussions can be
found in Tietenberg (1985) and Misiolek and Elder (1989).

by the sources as surplus reductions over and above a predetermined set of emissions standards. (Because this latter approach favours older sources over newer sources, it is known as "grandfathering".) The proposition suggests that either approach will ultimately result in a cost-effective allocation of the control responsibility among the various polluters as long as they are all price-takers, transactions costs are low, and ERCs are fully transferable. Any allocation of emission standards in a grandfathered approach is compatible with cost-effectiveness because the after-market in which firms can buy or sell ERCs corrects any problems with the initial allocation. This is a significant finding because it implies that under the right conditions the control authority can use this initial allocation of emissions standards to pursue distributional goals without interfering with cost-effectiveness.

When firms are price-setters rather than price-takers, however, cost-effectiveness will only be achieved if the control authority initially allocates the emission standards so a cost-effective allocation would be achieved even in the absence of any trading. (Implementing this particular allocation would, of course, require regulators to have complete information on control costs for all sources, an unlikely prospect.) In this special case cost-effectiveness would be achieved even in the presence of one or more price-setting firms because no trading would take place, eliminating the possibility of exploiting any market power.

For all other emission standard assignments an active market would exist, offering the opportunity for price-setting behaviour. The larger is the deviation of the price setting source's emission standard from its cost-effective allocation, the larger is the deviation of ultimate control costs from the least-cost allocation. When the price-setting source is initially allocated an insufficiently stringent emission standard, it can inflict higher control costs on others by withholding some ERCs from the market. When an excessively stringent emission standard is imposed on a price-setting source, however, it necessarily bears a higher control cost as the means of reducing demand (and, hence, prices) for the ERCs.

Similar problems exist when transactions costs are high. High transactions costs preclude or reduce trading activity by diminishing the gains from trade. When the costs of consummating a transaction exceed its potential gains, the incentive to participate in emissions trading is lost.

IV. Lessons from Empirical Research

A vast majority, though not all, of the relevant empirical studies have found the control costs to be substantially higher with the regulatory command-and-control system than the least cost means of allocating the control responsibility.

While theory tells us unambiguously that the command-and-control system will not be cost-effective except by coincidence, it cannot tell us the

magnitude of the excess costs. The empirical work cited in Table 1 adds
the important information that the excess costs are typically very large.[18]
This is an important finding because it provides the motivation for introducing a reform programme; the potential social gains (in terms of reduced
control cost) from breaking away from the status quo are sufficient to justify the trouble. Although the estimates of the excess costs attributable to
a command and control presented in Table 1 overstate the cost savings that
would be achieved by even an ideal economic incentive approach (a point
discussed in more detail below), the general conclusion that the potential
cost savings from adopting economic incentive approaches are large seems
accurate even after correcting for overstatement.

Economic incentive approaches which raise revenue (charges or auction ERC markets) offer an additional benefit—they allow the revenue
raised from these policies to substitute for revenue raised in more traditional ways. Whereas it is well known that traditional revenue-raising approaches distort resource allocation, producing inefficiency, economic incentive approaches enhance efficiency. Some empirical work based on the
US economy suggests that substituting economic incentive means of raising revenue for more traditional means could produce significant efficiency
gains.[19]

When high degrees of control are necessary, ERC prices or charge levels would be correspondingly high. The financial outlays associated with
acquiring ERCs in an auction market or paying charges on uncontrolled
emissions would be sufficiently large that sources would typically have
lower financial burdens with the traditional command-and-control approach than with these particular economic incentive approaches. Only a
"grandfathered" trading system would guarantee that sources would be no
worse off than under the command-and-control system.[20]

Financial burden is a significant concern in a highly competitive global
market-place. Firms bearing large financial burdens would be placed at a
competitive disadvantage when forced to compete with firms not bearing
those burdens. Their costs would be higher.

From the point of view of the source required to control its emissions,
two components of financial burden are significant: (a) control costs and
(b) expenditures on permits or emission charges. While only the former
represent real resource costs to society as a whole (the latter are merely
transferred from one group in society to another), both represent a financial burden to the source. The empirical evidence suggests that when an
auction market is used to distribute ERCs (or, equivalently, when all un-

---

[18]A value of 1.0 in the last column of Table 1 would indicate that the traditional regulatory approach was cost-effective. A value of 4.0 would indicate that the traditional regulatory approach results in an allocation of the control responsibility which is four times as expensive as necessary to
reach the stipulated pollution target.

[19]See Terkla (1984).

[20]See Atkinson and Tietenberg (1982, 1984), Hahn (1984), Harrison (1983), Krupnick (1986),
Lyon (1982), Palmer et al. (1980), Roach et al. (1981), Seskin et al. (1983), and Shapiro and Warhit
(1983) for the individual studies, and Tietenberg (1985) for a summary of the evidence.

Table 1 Empirical Studies of Air Pollution Control

Study	Pollutants Covered	Geographic Area	CAC Benchmark	Ratio of CAC Cost to Least Cost
Atkinson and Lewis	Particulates	St Louis	SIP regulations	6.00[a]
Roach et al.	Sulphur dioxide	Four corners in Utah	SIP regulations Colorado, Arizona, and New Mexico	4.25
Hahn and Noll	Sulphates standards	Los Angeles	California emission	1.07
Krupnick	Nitrogen dioxide regulations	Baltimore	Proposed RACT	5.96[b]
Seskin et al.	Nitrogen dioxide regulations	Chicago	Proposed RACT	14.40[b]
McGartland Spofford	Particulates	Baltimore	SIP regulations	4.18
	Sulphur Dioxide	Lower Delaware Valley	Uniform percentage regulations	1.78
	Particulates	Lower Delaware Valley	Uniform percentage regulations	22.00
Harrison	Airport noise	United States	Mandatory retrofit	1.72[c]
Maloney and Yandle	Hydrocarbons	All domestic DuPont plants	Uniform percentage reduction	4.15[d]
Palmer et al.	CFC emissions from non-aerosol applications	United States	Proposed emission	1.96

CAC = command and control, the traditional regulatory approach.
SIP = state implementation plan.
RACT = reasonably available control technologies, a set of standards imposed on existing sources in non-attainment areas.
[a]Based on a 40 $\mu g/m^3$ at worst receptor.
[b]Based on a short-term, one-hour average of 250 $\mu g/m^3$.
[c]Because it is a benefit-cost study instead of a cost-effectiveness study, the Harrison comparison of the command-and-control approach with the least-cost allocation involves different benefit levels. Specifically, the benefit levels associated with the least-cost allocation are only 82 percent of those associated with the command-control allocation. To produce cost estimates based on more comparable benefits, as a first approximation the least-cost allocation was divided by 0.82 and the resulting number was compared with the command-and-control cost.
[d]Based on 85 per cent reduction of emissions from all sources.

controlled emissions are subject to an emissions charge), the ERC expenditures (charge outlays) would frequently be larger in magnitude than the control costs; the sources would spend more on ERCs (or pay more in charges) than they would on the control equipment. Under the traditional command-and-control system firms make no financial outlays to the government. Although control costs are necessarily higher with the command-and-control system than with an economic incentive approach, they are not so high as to outweigh the additional financial outlays required in an auction market permit system (or an emissions tax system). For this reason existing sources could be expected vehemently to oppose an auction market or emission charges despite their social appeal, unless the revenue derived is used in a manner which is approved by the sources, and the sources with which it competes are required to absorb similar expenses. When environmental policies are not coordinated across national boundaries, this latter condition would be particularly difficult to meet.

In the absence of either a politically popular way to use the revenue or assurances that competitors will face similar financial burdens, this political opposition could be substantially reduced by grandfathering. Under grandfathering, sources have only to purchase any additional ERCs they may need to meet their assigned emission standard (as opposed to purchasing sufficient ERCs or paying charges to cover all uncontrolled emissions in an auction market). Grandfathering is *de facto* the approach taken in the US emissions trading programme.

Grandfathering has its disadvantages. Because ERCs become very valuable, especially in the face of stringent air quality regulations, sources selling emission reduction credits would be able to command very high prices. By placing heavy restrictions on the amount of emissions, the control authority is creating wealth for existing firms *vis-à-vis* new firms.

Although reserving some ERCs for new firms is possible (by assigning more stringent emission standards than needed to reach attainment and using the "surplus" air quality to create government-held ERCs), this option is rarely exercised in practice. In the United States under the offset policy firms typically have to purchase sufficient ERCs to more than cover all uncontrolled emissions, while existing firms only have to purchase enough to comply with their assigned emission standard. Thus grandfathering imposes a bias against new sources in the sense that their financial burden is greater than that of an otherwise identical existing source, even if the two sources install exactly the same emission control devices. This new source bias could retard the introduction of new facilities and new technologies by reducing the cost advantage of building new facilities which embody the latest innovations.

While it is clear from theory that larger trading areas offer the opportunities for larger potential cost savings in an emissions trading programme, some empirical work suggests that substantial savings can be achieved in emissions trading even when the trading areas are rather small.

The point of this finding is *not* that small trading areas are fine; they do retard progress toward the standard. Rather, when political considerations allow only small trading areas or nothing, emissions trading still can play a significant role.

Sometimes political considerations demand a trading area which is smaller than the ideal design. Whether large trading areas are essential for the effective use of this policy is therefore of some relevance. In general, the larger the trading area, the larger would be the potential cost savings due to a wider set of cost reduction opportunities that would become available. The empirical question is how sensitive the cost estimates are to the size of the trading areas.

One study of utilities found that even allowing a plant to trade among discharge points within that plant could save from 30 to 60 per cent of the costs of complying with new sulphur oxide reduction regulations, compared to a situation where no trading whatsoever was permitted.[21] Expanding the trading possibilities to other utilities within the same state permitted a further reduction of 20 per cent, while allowing interstate trading permitted another 15 per cent reduction in costs. If this study is replicated in other circumstances, it would appear that even small trading areas offer the opportunity for significant cost reduction.[22]

Although only a few studies of the empirical impact of market power on emissions trading have been accomplished, their results are consistent with a finding that market power does not seem to have a large effect on regional control costs in most realistic situations.[23]

Even in areas having especially stringent controls, the available evidence suggests that price manipulation is not a serious problem. In an auction market the price-setting source reduces its financial burden by purchasing fewer ERCs in order to drive the price down. To compensate for the smaller number of ERCs purchased, the price-setting source must spend more on controlling its own pollution, limiting the gains from price manipulation. Although these actions could have a rather large impact on *regional financial burden*, they would under normal circumstances have a rather small effect on *regional control costs*. Estimates typically suggest that control costs would rise by less than 1 per cent if market power were exercised by one or more firms.

It should not be surprising that price manipulation could have rather dramatic effects on regional financial burden in an auction market, since the cost of *all* ERCs is affected, not merely those purchased by the price-setting source. The perhaps more surprising result is that control costs are quite insensitive to price-setting behaviour. This is due to the fact that the only control cost change is the net difference between the new larger control burden borne by the price searcher and the correspondingly smaller burden borne by the sources having larger-than-normal allocations of permits. Only the costs of the marginal units are affected.

Within the class of grandfathered distribution rules, some emission standard allocations create a larger potential for strategic price behaviour than others. In general the larger the divergence between the control responsibility assigned to the price-searching source by the emission standards and the cost-effective allocation of control responsibility, the larger the potential for market power. When allocated too little responsibility by the control authority, price-searching firms can exercise power on the selling side of the market, and when allocated too much, they can exercise power on the buying side of the market.

---

[21]ICF, Inc. (1989).

[22]As indicated below, the fact that so many emissions trades have actually taken place within the same plant or among contiguous plants provides some confirmation for this result.

[23]For individual studies see de Lucia (1974), Hahn (1984), Stahl, Bergman and Mäler (1988), and Maloney and Yandle (1984). For a survey of the evidence see Tietenberg (1985).

According to the existing studies it takes a rather considerable divergence from the cost-effective allocation of control responsibility to produce much difference in regional control costs. In practice the deviations from the least cost allocation caused by market power pale in comparison to the much larger potential cost reductions achievable by implementing emissions trading.[24]

V. Lessons from Implementation

Though the number of transactions consummated under the Emissions Trading Program has been large, it has been smaller than expected. Part of this failure to fulfill expectations can be explained as the result of unrealistically inflated expectations. More restrictive regulatory decisions than expected and higher than expected transaction costs also bear some responsibility.

The models used to calculate the potential cost savings were not (and are not) completely adequate guides to reality. The cost functions in these models are invariably *ex ante* cost functions. They implicitly assume that the modelled plant can be built from scratch and can incorporate the best technology. In practice, of course, many existing sources cannot retrofit these technologies and therefore their *ex post* control options are much more limited than implied by the models.

The models also assume all trades are multilateral and are simultaneously consummated, whereas actual trades are usually bilateral and sequential. The distinction is important for non-uniformly mixed pollutants;[25] bilateral trades frequently are constrained by regulatory concerns about decreasing air quality at the site of the acquiring source. Because multilateral trades would typically incorporate compensating reductions coming from other nearby sources, these concerns normally do not arise when trades are multilateral and simultaneous. In essence the models implicitly assume an idealized market process, which is only remotely approximated by actual transactions.

In addition some non-negligible proportion of the expected cost savings recorded by the models for non-uniformly mixed pollutants is attributable to the substantially larger amounts of emissions allowed by the modelled permit equilibrium.[26] For example, the cost estimates imply that the control authority is allowed to arrange the control responsibility in *any* fashion that satisfies the ambient air quality standards. In practice the mod-

---

[24]Strategic price behaviour is not the only potential source of market power problems. Firms could conceivably use permit markets to drive competitors out of business. See Misiolek and Elder (1989). For an analysis which concludes that this problem is relatively rare and can be dealt with on a case-by-case basis should it arise, see Tietenberg (1985).

[25]See Tietenberg and Atkinson (1989) for a demonstration that this is an empirically significant point.

[26]This is demonstrated in Atkinson and Tietenberg (1987).

els allocate more uncontrolled emissions to sources with tall stacks because those emissions can be exported. Exported emissions avoid control costs without affecting the readings at the local monitors. That portion of the cost savings estimated by the models in Table 1 which is due to allowing increased emissions is not acceptable to regulators. Some recent work has suggested that the benefits received from the additional emission control required by the command and control approach may be justified by the net benefits received.[27] The regulatory refusal to allow emission increases was apparently consistent with efficiency,[28] but it was not consistent with the magnitude of cost savings anticipated by the models.

Certain types of trades assumed permissible by the models are prohibited by actual trading rules. New sources, for example, are not allowed to satisfy the New Source Performance Standards (which imply a particular control technology) by choosing some less stringent control option and making up the difference with acquired emission reduction credits; they must install the degree of technological control necessary to meet the standard. Typically this is the same technology used by EPA to define the standard in the first place.

A lost of uncertainty is associated with emission reduction credit transactions since they depend so heavily on administrative action. All trades must be approved by the control authorities. If the authorities are not cooperative or at least consistent, the value of the created emission reduction credits could be diminished or even destroyed.

For non-uniformly mixed pollutants, trades between geographically separated sources will only be approved after dispersion modelling has been accomplished by the applicants. Not only is this modelling expensive, it frequently ends up raising questions which ultimately lead to the transaction being denied. Few trades requiring this modelling have been consummated.

Trading activity has also been inhibited by the paucity of emission banks. The US system allows states to establish emission banks, but does not require them to do so. As of 1986 only seven of the fifty states had established these banks. For sources in the rest of the states the act of creating emission credits is undervalued because the credits cannot be legally held for future use. The supply of emission reduction credits is hence less than would be estimated by the models.

The Emissions Trading Program seems to have worked particularly well for trades involving uniformly mixed pollutants and for trades of nonuniformly mixed pollutants involving contiguous discharge points.

It is not surprising that most consummated trades have been internal (where the buyer and seller share a common corporate parent) rather than

---

[27]See Oates, Portney, and McGartland (1988).

[28]Not all of the cost savings, of course, is due to the capability to increase emissions. The remaining portion of the savings, which is due to taking advantage of opportunities to control a given level of emissions at a lower cost, is still substantial and can be captured by a well-designed permit system which does not allow emissions to increase beyond the command-and-control benchmark. See the calculations in Atkinson and Tietenberg (1987).

external. Not only are the uncertainties associated with interfirm transfers avoided, but most internal trades involve contiguous facilities. Trades between contiguous facilities do not trigger a requirement for dispersion modelling.[29]

It is also not surprising that the plurality of consummated trades involve volatile organic compounds, which are uniformly mixed pollutants. Since dispersion modelling is not required for uniformly mixed pollutants even when the trading sources are somewhat distant from one another, trades involving these pollutants are cheaper to consummate. Additionally emissions trades involving uniformly mixed pollutants do not jeopardize local air quality since the location of the emissions is not a matter of policy consequence.

The establishment of the Emissions Trading Program has encouraged technological progress in pollution control. Although generally the degree of progress has been modest, it has been more dramatic in areas where emission reductions have been sufficiently stringent as to restrict the availability of emission reduction credits created by more traditional means.[30]

Theory would lead us to expect more technological progress with emissions trading than with a command-and-control policy because it changes the incentives so drastically. Under a command-and-control approach technological changes discovered by the control authority typically lead to more stringent standards (and higher costs) for the sources. Sources have little incentive to innovate and a good deal of incentive to hide potential innovations from the control authority. With emissions trading, on the other hand, innovations allowing excess reductions create saleable emission reduction credits.

The evidence suggests that the expectations based on this theory have been borne out to a limited degree in the operating programme. The most prominent example of technological change has been the substitution of water-based solvents for solvents containing volatile organic compounds. Though somewhat more expensive, this substitution made economic sense once the programme was introduced.

It should probably not be surprising that the number of new innovations stimulated by the programme is rather small. As long as cheaper ways of creating credits within existing processes (fuel substitution, for example) are available, it would be unreasonable to expect large investments in new technologies with unproven reliabilities. On the other hand as the degree of control rises and the supply of readily available credits dries up, the demand for new technologies would be expected to rise as well. This expectation seems to have been borne out in those areas where unusually low air quality or stringent regulatory rules have served to limit the available credits.[31]

---

[29]The fact that so many trades have taken place between contiguous discharge points serves as confirmation that substantial savings can be achieved even if the geographic boundaries of the trading area are quite restricted.

[30]For more details see Tietenberg (1985), Maleug (1989), and Dudek and Palmisano (1988).

[31]For the experience in California see Dudek and Palmisano (1988).

This is an important point. Those who fail to consider the dynamic ad
vantages of an economic incentive approach sometimes suggest that if few
credits would be traded, implementing a system of this type has no purpose. In fact it has a substantial purpose—the encouragement of new technologies to meet the increasingly stringent standards.

Introducing the Emissions Trading Program has provided an opportunity to control sources which can reduce emissions relatively cheaply, but
which under the traditional policy were under-regulated due either to their
financially precarious position or the fact that they were not subject to regulation.[32]

Due to the social distress caused by any resulting unemployment, the
control authorities and the courts are understandably reluctant to enforce
stringent emission standards against firms which would not be able to pass
higher costs on to customers without considerable loss of production. Since
many of these sources could control emissions at a lower marginal cost
than other sources, their political immunity from control makes regional
control costs higher than necessary; other sources have to control their own
emissions to a higher degree (at a higher marginal cost) to compensate.

Due to its ability to separate the issue of who pays for the reduction
from the issue of which discharge points are to be controlled, the emissions trading programme provides a way to secure those low cost reductions. The command-and-control policy would assign, as normal, a very
low (perhaps zero) emission reduction to any previously unregulated firm.
Once emissions trading had been established, however, it would be in the
interest of this firm to control emissions further, selling the resulting emission reduction credits. As long as the revenues from the sale at least covered the cost, this transaction could profit, or at least not hurt, the seller.
Because these reductions could be achieved at a lower cost than ratcheting up the degree of control on already heavily controlled sources, non-
immune sources would find purchasing the credits cheaper than controlling their own emissions to a higher degree. Everyone benefits from
controlling these previously under-regulated sources.

Another unique attribute of an emissions trading approach is the capability it offers sources for leasing credits.[33]

Leasing offers an enormously useful degree of flexibility which is not
available with other policy approaches to pollution control. The usefulness
of leasing derives from the fact that some sources, utilities in particular,
have patterns of emission that vary over time while allowable emissions remain constant. In a typical situation, for example, suppose an older utility
would, in the absence of control, be emitting heavily. In the normal course
of a utility expansion cycle the older plant would subsequently experience
substantially reduced emissions when the utility constructed a new plant
and shifted a major part of the load away from the older plant to the new
plant. Ultimately growth in demand on the system would increase the emis-

---

[32]See Tietenberg (1985).
[33]See Feldman and Raufer (1987) and Tietenberg (1989a).

sions again for the older plant as its capacity would once again be needed. The implication of this temporal pattern is that during the middle period, as its own emissions fell well below allowable emissions, this utility could lease excess emission credits to another facility, recalling them as its own need rose with demand growth. Indeed one empirical study of the pattern of the utility demand for and supply of acid rain reduction credits over time suggests that leasing is a critical component of any cost-effective control strategy, a component that neither the traditional approach nor emission charges can offer.[34]

Leasing also provides a way for about-to-be-retired sources to participate in the reduction programme. Under the traditional approach once the deadline for compliance had been reached the utility would either have to retire the unit early or to install expensive control equipment which would be rendered useless once the unit was retired. By leasing credits for the short period to retirement, the unit could remain in compliance without taking either of those drastic steps; it would, however, be sharing in the cost of installing the extra equipment in the leasing utility. Leased credits facilitate an efficient transition into the new regime of more stringent controls.

Unless the process to determine the level of an effluent or emissions charge includes some automatic means of temporal adjustment, the tendency is for the real rate (adjusted for inflation) to decline over time.[35] This problem is particularly serious in areas with economic growth where increasing real rates would be the desired outcome.

In contrast to emissions trading where ERC prices respond automatically to changing market conditions, emission charges have to be determined by an administrative process. When the function of the charge is to raise revenue for a particular purpose, charge rates will be determined by the costs of achieving that purpose; when the costs of achieving the purpose rise, the level of the charge must rise to secure the additional revenue.[36]

Sometimes that process produces an unintended dynamic. In Japan, for example, the charge is calculated on the basis of the amount of compensation paid to victims of air pollution in the previous year. While the amount of compensation has been increasing, the amount of emissions (the base to which the charge is applied) has been decreasing. As a result unexpectedly high charge rates are necessary in order to raise sufficient revenue for the compensation system.

In countries where the tax revenue feeds into the general budget, increases in the level of the charge require a specific administrative act. Evidently it is difficult to raise these rates in practice, since charges have commonly even failed to keep pace with inflation, much less growth in the number of sources. The unintended result is eventual environmental deterioration.

---

[34]Feldman and Raufer (1987).

[35]For further information see Vos (1989) and Sprenger (1989).

[36]While it is theoretically possible (depending on the elasticity of demand for pollution abatement) for a rise in the tax to produce less revenue, this has typically not been the case.

VI. Concluding Comments

Our experience with economic incentive programmes has demonstrated that they have had, and can continue to have, a positive role in environmental policy in the future. I would submit the issue is no longer *whether* they have a role to play, but rather *what kind* of role they should play. The available experience with operating versions of these programmes allows us to draw some specific conclusions which facilitate defining the boundaries for the optimal use of economic incentive approaches in general and for distinguishing the emissions trading and emission charges approaches in particular.

Emissions trading integrates particularly smoothly into any policy structure which is based either directly (through emission standards) or indirectly (through mandated technology or input limitations) on regulating emissions. In this case emission limitations embedded in the operating licenses can serve as the trading benchmark if grandfathering is adopted.

Emissions charges work particularly well when transactions costs associated with bargaining are high. It appears that much of the trading activity in the United States has involved large corporations. Emissions trading is probably not equally applicable to large and small pollution sources. The transaction costs are sufficiently high that only large trades can absorb them without jeopardizing the gains from trade. For this reason charges seem a more appropriate instrument when sources are individually small, but numerous (such as residences or automobiles). Charges also work well as a device for increasing the rate of adoption of new technologies and for raising revenue to subsidize environmentally benign projects.

Emissions trading seems to work especially well for uniformly mixed pollutants. No diffusion modelling is necessary and regulators do not have to worry about trades creating "hot spots" or localized areas of high pollution concentration. Trades can be on a one-to-one basis.

Because emissions trading allows the issue of who will pay for the control to be separated from who will install the control, it introduces an additional degree of flexibility. This flexibility is particularly important in nonattainment areas since marginal control costs are so high. Sources which would not normally be controlled because they could not afford to implement the controls without going out of business, can be controlled with emissions trading. The revenue derived from the sale of emission reduction credits can be used to finance the controls, effectively preventing bankruptcy.

Because it is quantity based, emissions trading also offers a unique possibility for leasing. Leasing is particularly valuable when the temporal pattern of emissions varies across sources. As discussed above this appears generally to be the case with utilities. When a firm plans to shut down one plant in the near future and to build a new one, leasing credits is a vastly superior alternative to the temporary installation of equipment in the old plant which would be useless when the plant was retired. The useful life of this temporary control equipment would be wastefully short.

We have also learned that ERC transactions have higher transactions costs than we previously understood. Regulators must validate every trade. When non-uniformly mixed pollutants are involved, the transactions costs associated with estimating the air quality effects are particularly high. Delegating responsibility for trade approval to lower levels of government may in principle speed up the approval process, but unless the bureaucrats in the lower level of government support the programme the gain may be negligible.

Emissions trading places more importance on the operating permits and emissions inventories than other approaches. To the extent those are deficient the potential for trades that protect air quality may be lost. Firms which have actual levels of emissions substantially below allowable emissions find themselves with a trading opportunity which, if exploited, could degrade air quality. The trading benchmark has to be defined carefully.

There can be little doubt that the emissions trading programme in the US has improved upon the command-and-control programme that preceded it. The documented cost savings are large and the flexibility provided has been important. Similarly emissions charges have achieved their own measure of success in Europe. To be sure the programmes are far from perfect, but the flaws should be kept in perspective. In no way should they overshadow the impressive accomplishments. Although economic incentive approaches lose their Utopian lustre upon closer inspection, they have none the less made a lasting contribution to environmental policy.

The role for economic incentive approaches should grow in the future if for no other reason than the fact that the international pollution problems which are currently commanding centre-stage fall within the domains where economic incentive policies have been most successful. Significantly many of the problems of the future, such as reducing tropospheric ozone, preventing stratospheric ozone depletion, moderating global warming, and increasing acid rain control, involve pollutants that can be treated as uniformly mixed, facilitating the use of economic incentives. In addition larger trading areas facilitate greater cost reductions than smaller trading areas. This also augers well for the use of emissions trading as part of the strategy to control many future pollution problems because the natural trading areas are all very large indeed. Acid rain, stratospheric ozone depletion, and greenhouse gases could (indeed should!) involve trading areas that transcend national boundaries. For greenhouse and ozone depletion gases, the trading areas should be global in scope. Finally, it seems clear that the pivotal role of carbon dioxide in global warming may require some fairly drastic changes in energy use, including changes in personal transportation, and ultimately land use patterns. Some form of charges could play an important role in facilitating this transformation.

We live in an age when the call for tighter environmental controls intensifies with each new discovery of yet another injury modern society is inflicting on the planet. But resistance to additional controls is also growing with the recognition that compliance with each new set of controls is more expensive than the last. While economic incentive approaches to environmental control offer no panacea, they frequently do offer a practical way to achieve environmental goals more flexibly and at lower cost than more traditional regulatory approaches. That is a compelling virtue.

REFERENCES

Anderson, F. R. et al. (1977), *Environmental Improvement Through Economic Incentives*, Baltimore, The Johns Hopkins University Press for Resources for the Future, Inc.

Atkinson, S. E. and Lewis, D. H. (1974). 'A Cost-Effectiveness Analysis of Alternative Air Quality Control Strategies', *Journal of Environmental Economics and Management*, 1, 237–50.

—— and Tietenberg, T. H. (1982), 'The Empirical Properties of Two Classes of Designs for Transferable Discharge Permit Markets', *Journal of Environmental Economics and Management*, 9, 101–21.

—— (1984), 'Approaches for Reaching Ambient Standards in Non-Attainment Areas: Financial Burden and Efficiency Considerations', *Land Economics*, 60, 148–59.

—— (1987), 'Economic Implications of Emission Trading Rules for Local and Regional Pollutants', *Canadian Journal of Economics*, 20, 370–86.

Baumol, W. J., and Oates, W. E. (1975), *The Theory of Environmental Policy*, Englewood Cliffs, N.J., Prentice Hall.

Bohm, P. and Russell, C. (1985), 'Comparative Analysis of Alternative Policy Instruments', in A. V. Kneese and J. L. Sweeney (eds.), *Handbook of Natural Resource and Energy Economics*, Vol. 1, 395–460, Amsterdam, North-Holland.

Bressers, H. T. A. (1988), 'A Comparison of the Effectiveness of Incentives and Directives: The Case of Dutch Water Quality Policy', *Policy Studies Review*, 7, 500–18.

Brown, G. M. Jr. and Johnson, R. W. (1984), 'Pollution control by Effluent Charges: It Works in the Federal Republic of Germany, Why Not in the United States?', *Natural Resources Journal*, 24, 929–66.

de Lucia, R. J. (1974), *An Evaluation of Marketable Effluent Permit Systems*, Report No. EPA-600/5-74-030 to the US Environmental Protection Agency (September).

Dudek, D. J. and Palmisano, J. (1988), 'Emissions Trading: Why is this Throughbred Hobbled?', *Columbia Journal of Environmental Law*, 13, 217–56.

Feldman, S. L. and Raufer, R. K. (1987), *Emissions Trading and Acid Rain Implementing a Market Approach to Pollution Control*, Totowa, N.J., Rowman & Littlefield.

Hahn, R. W. (1984), 'Market Power and Transferable Property Rights', *Quarterly Journal of Economics*, 99, 753–65.

—— (1989), 'Economic Prescriptions for Environmental Problems: How the Patient Followed the Doctor's Orders', *The Journal of Economic Perspectives*, 3, 95–114.

—— and Noll, R. G. (1982), 'Designing a Market for Tradeable Emission Permits', in W. A. Magat (ed.), *Reform of Environmental Regulation*, Cambridge, Mass., Ballinger.

—— and Hester, G. L. (1989a), 'Where Did All the Markets Go? An Analysis of EPA's Emission Trading Program', *Yale Journal of Regulation*, 6, 109–53.

———————(1989b), 'Marketable Permits: Lessons from Theory and Practice', *Ecology Law Quarterly*, 16, 361–406.

Harrison, D., Jr. (1983), 'Case Study 1: The Regulation of Aircraft Noise', in Thomas C. Schelling (ed.), *Incentives for Environmental Protection*, Cambridge, Mass, MIT Press.

ICF Resources, Inc. (1989), 'Economic, Environmental, and Coal Market Impacts of SO2 Emissions Trading Under Alternative Acid Rain Control Proposals', a report prepared for the Regulatory Innovations Staff, USEPA (March).

Krupnick, A. J. (1986), 'Costs of Alternative Policies for the Control of Nitrogen Dioxide in Baltimore', *Journal of Environmental Economics and Management*, 13, 189–97.

Liroff, R. A. (1980), *Air Pollution Offsets: Trading, Selling and Banking*, Washington, D.C., Conservation Foundation.

———————(1986), *Reforming Air Pollution Regulation: The Toil and Trouble of EPA's Bubble*, Washington, D.C., Conservation Foundation.

Lyon, R. M. (1982), 'Auctions and Alternative Procedures for Allocating Pollution Rights', *Land Economics*, 58, 16–32.

McGartland, A. M. (1984), 'Marketable Permit Systems for Air Pollution Control: an Empirical Study', Ph.D. dissertation, University of Maryland.

Main, J. (1988), 'Here Comes the Big Cleanup', *Fortune*, 21 November, 102.

Maleug, David A. (1989), 'Emission Trading and the Incentive to Adopt New Pollution Abatement Technology', *Journal of Environmental Economics and Management*, 16, 52–7.

Maloney, M. T. and Yandle, B. (1984), 'Estimation of the Cost of Air Pollution Control Regulation', *Journal of Environmental Economics and Management*, 11, 244–63.

Misiolek, W. S. and Elder, H. W. (1989), 'Exclusionary Manipulation of Markets for Pollution Rights', *Journal of Environmental Economics and Management*, 16, 156–66.

Montgomery, W. D. (1972), 'Markets in Licenses and Efficient Pollution Control Programs', *Journal of Economic Theory*, 5, 395–418.

Oates, W. E., Portney, P. R., and McGartland, A. M. (1988), 'The Net Benefits of Incentive-Based Regulation: The Case of Environmental Standard Setting in the Real World', Resources for the Future Working Paper December.

Opschoor, J. B. and Vos, H. B. (1989), *The Application of Economic Instruments for Environmental Protection in OECD Countries*, Paris, OECD.

Palmer, A. R., Mooz, W. E., Quinn, T. H., and Wolf, K. A. (1980), *Economic Implications of Regulating Chlorofluorocarbon Emissions from Nonaerosol Applications*, Report No. R–2524–EPA prepared for the US Environmental Protection Agency by the Rand Corporation, June.

Roach, F., Kolstad, C., Kneese, A. V., Tobin, R., and Williams, M. (1981), 'Alternative Air Quality Policy Options in the Four Corners Region', *Southwestern Review*, 1, 29–58.

Seskin, E. P., Anderson, R. J., Jr., and Reid, R. O. (1983), 'An Empirical Analysis of Economic Strategies for Controlling Air Pollution', *Journal of Environmental Economics and Management*, 10, 112–24.

Shapiro, M. and Warhit, E. (1983), 'Marketable Permits: The Case of Chlorofluorocarbons', *Natural Resource Journal*, 23, 577–91.

Spofford, W. O., Jr. (1984), 'Efficiency Properties of Alternative Source Control Policies for Meeting Ambient Air Quality Standards: An Empirical Application to the Lower Delaware Valley', Discussion paper D–118, Washington D.C., Resources for the Future, November.

Sprenger, R. U. (1989), 'Economic Incentives in Environmental Policies: The Case of West Germany', a paper presented at the Symposium on Economic Instruments in Environmental Protection Policies, Stockholm, Sweden (June).

Stahl, L., Bergman, L., and Mailer, K. G. (1988), 'An Experimental Game on Marketable Emission Permits for Hydro-carbons in the Gothenburg Area', Research Paper No. 6359, Stockholm School of Economics (December).

Stavins, R. N. (1989), 'Harnessing Market Forces to Protect the Environment', *Environment*, 31, 4–7, 28–35.

Terkla, D. (1984), 'The Efficiency Value of Effluent Tax Revenues', *Journal of Environmental Economics and Management*, 11, 107–23.

Tietenberg, T. H. (1980), 'Transferable Discharge Permits and the Control of Stationary Source Air Pollution: A Survey and Synthesis', *Land Economics*, 56, 391–416.

——— (1985), *Emissions Trading: An Exercise in Reforming Pollution Policy*, Washington, D.C., Resources for the Future.

——— (1988), *Environmental and Natural Resource Economics*, 2nd edn., Glenview, Illinois, Scott, Foresman and Company.

——— (1989a), 'Acid Rain Reduction Credits', *Challenge*, 32, 25–9.

——— (1989b), 'Marketable Permits in the U.S.: A Decade of Experience', in Karl W. Roskamp (ed.), *Public Finance and the Performance of Enterprises*, Detroit, MI, Wayne State University Press.

——— and Atkinson, S. E. (1989), 'Bilateral, Sequential Trading and the Cost-Effectiveness of the Bubble-Policy', Colby College Working Paper (August).

Vos, H. B. (1989), 'The Application and Efficiency of Economic Instruments: Experiences in OECD Member Countries', a paper presented at the Symposium on Economic Instruments in Environmental Protection Policies, Stockholm, Sweden (June).

17 Environmental Policy Making in a Second-Best Setting

Lawrence H. Goulder

Lawrence H. Goulder is Associate Professor of Economics at Stanford University, University Fellow at Resources for the Future, and Research Associate at the National Bureau of Economic Research.

I. Introduction

Economists have long been interested in ways that taxes and other policy instruments can address environmental problems associated with externalities. This interest dates back at least to Pigou (1938), who showed that taxes could usefully internalize externalities and thereby "get the prices right"—that is, bring prices into alignment with marginal social cost. In the last two decades, there has been increased attention to other, non-tax market instruments—including tradeable emission permits and deposit-refund systems—as tools for dealing with environmental problems in an effective way.

Since the publication of Pigou's classic article, the tradition in environmental economics has been to analyze environmental policies with an almost exclusive attention to the externality of immediate concern and little attention to other distortions or market failures. However, in recent years economists have come to recognize the importance of interactions between environmental policies and other (nonenvironmental) distortions in the economy. In particular, there has been increased attention to the interconnections between environmental taxes and the distortions imposed by preexisting income or commodity taxes.

These interactions were first examined in a seminal contribution by Sandmo (1975), although the insights from this article were largely ignored until recently. Sandmo analyzed the optimal setting of commodity taxes when the production or consumption of one of the commodities generates an externality. He showed that when the government's need for revenue exceeds the level that can be generated by taxes set according to the "Pigov-

"Environmental Policy Making in a Second-Best Setting," by Lawrence H. Goulder was prepared for the University of CEMA Twentieth Anniversary Conference on Applied Economics, Buenos Aires, Argentina, November 12–14, 1998. The original version of this paper appeared in the *Journal of Applied Economics*, 1(2) (November 1998). Section II of the present paper replaces the previous, more technical version of Section II. The author is grateful to Roberton C. Williams III for very helpful comments, and to the National Science Foundation (Grant SBR9613458) and U.S. Environmental Protection Agency (Grant R825313-01) for financial support.

ian principle" (that is, set equal to the marginal environmental damages), then the optimal tax system includes taxes not only on externality-generating goods and services but on other goods and services as well. In Sandmo's analysis, the optimal tax rates on environmentally damaging activities and on ordinary activities are intimately connected.

The interconnections between ordinary and environmental taxes, so central to Sandmo's optimal tax result, also figure importantly in the analysis of the impacts of marginal (that is, less than globally optimizing) environmental reforms. A line of research conducted during this decade shows that one cannot effectively evaluate the impacts of many environmental reforms without paying attention to the magnitudes and types of existing, distortionary taxes such as income, payroll, or sales taxes. There are two important interconnections here. First, as Terkla (1984), Lee and Misiolek (1986), Oates and Schwab (1988), Oates (1993), Repetto et al. (1992), and others have emphasized, the presence of distortionary taxes introduces opportunities to use revenues from new environmental taxes to finance cuts in the marginal rates of the ordinary distortionary taxes. To the extent that revenues from the environmental tax finance marginal rate cuts of this kind, some of the distortions that the ordinary taxes would have generated are avoided. This *revenue-recycling effect* suggests that the overall *gross*[1] costs of environmental taxes will be lower in a second-best world than in a first-best setting.

However, a second interconnection works in the opposite direction. Recent work by Bovenberg and de Mooij (1994a), Bovenberg and van der Ploeg (1994), Bovenberg and Goulder (1996, 1997), Parry (1995, 1997), and others[2] points out that environmental taxes are implicit taxes on factors of production such as labor and capital. By raising the costs of production and the costs of goods in general, environmental taxes (and many other environmental regulations) reduce real after-tax factor returns much like explicit factor taxes do. Thus, environmental taxes function as increments to existing factor taxes, tending to magnify the factor market distortions already generated by preexisting factor taxes. The additional efficiency costs of environmental taxes associated with the reduction in factor returns brought about by higher costs and output prices has been called the *tax-interaction effect*.[3] The larger the rates of preexisting factor taxes, the larger the tax-interaction effect, and thus the higher the gross costs from environmental taxes and other regulations that reduce after-tax returns to factors. The tax-interaction effect implies that, for any given method of recycling the revenues, the gross costs of environmental taxes are higher in a second-best setting with preexisting factor taxes than they would be if there

---

[1]The modifier "gross" indicates that the costs do not net out the policy-generated benefits associated with an improved environment.

[2]For earlier reviews of this recent literature, see Oates (1995) and Goulder (1995a).

[3]Parry (1995) was the first to isolate the tax-interaction and revenue-recycling effects in evaluating the second-best welfare impacts of environmental taxes. He termed these the "interdependency" and "revenue" effects.

were no prior taxes on factors. As will be discussed in more detail later in this paper, the tax-interaction effect tends to be of greater magnitude than the revenue-recycling effect; that is, it is only partly offset by the revenue-recycling effect.

The revenue-recycling and tax-interaction effects are highly relevant to the evaluation of "green tax reforms." A green tax policy of particular interest is a revenue-neutral carbon tax, which would address the prospect of global climate change by discouraging combustion of fossil fuels and the associated emissions of carbon dioxide, a principal contributor to the greenhouse effect. In discussions of carbon taxes, there has been great interest in the possibility that judicious recycling of the revenues from these taxes could cause the overall gross costs of this policy to be become zero or negative. Proponents of carbon taxes certainly would welcome this result, since it implies that policy makers must only establish that there are nonnegative environment-related *benefits* from the carbon tax policy to justify the policy on efficiency grounds. Given the vast uncertainties about the environment-related benefits from carbon abatement, it would significantly reduce the information burden faced by policy makers if they simply needed to determine the sign, rather than magnitude, of the environmental benefits. If one ignores the tax-interaction effect and concentrates only on revenue-recycling (and the revenue-recycling effect), the prospects for a zero-cost carbon tax will seem quite good. But the tax-interaction effect also has a key role here and, as will be discussed below, this latter effect significantly reduces the scope for the zero-cost result.

The absence of a zero-cost result does not imply that carbon taxes are a bad idea; it only means that justifying these taxes requires attention to the magnitudes (not just the sign) of the environmental benefits. Even if revenue-neutral carbon taxes or other green tax reforms do not make environmental improvement a free lunch, they may reduce its cost enough to make it very much worth buying. Indeed, in most analyses (see below) appropriately scaled revenue-neutral green tax reforms yield environmental benefits that exceed their gross costs.

A second area where the revenue-recycling and tax-interaction effects are important is in the choice among alternative policy instruments. Consider, for example, the choice between pollution tax policies (or pollution permits policies involving the auctioning of permits by the government) and freely allocated (or "grandfathered"[4]) emissions permits. The former policies raise revenue and thus are capable of taking advantage of the revenue-recycling effect. The latter policies, in contrast, do not raise revenue and therefore cannot exploit this effect. As discussed below, the tax-

---

[4]In keeping with common practice, we use the terms "grandfathered" and "freely allocated" interchangeably. Strictly speaking, however, grandfathering is not synonymous with free allocation. Grandfathering is a legal provision whereby "old" entities (e.g., firms subject to previous environmental rules) are waived of new regulatory requirements and instead remain bound only to the earlier (and perhaps more lax) regulatory provisions.

interaction effect arises under both policies, but only under the revenue raising policies is the (costly) tax-interaction effect offset by the revenue-recycling effect. Recent work by Parry (1997), Goulder, Parry, and Burtraw (1997), Parry, Williams, and Goulder (1999), Fullerton and Metcalf (1997), and Goulder et al. (1999) reveals that the presence or absence of the revenue-recycling effect can fundamentally affect the overall efficiency impacts of these policies.[5] In fact, when marginal benefits from pollution abatement fail to exceed a certain threshold value, pollution permit policies that fail to enjoy the revenue-recycling effect may be unable to produce any efficiency improvements, no matter what the level of pollution abatement![6] This analysis shows that the decision to give out pollution permits free rather than to auction them (or, equivalent, to employ a pollution tax) comes at a high price in terms of efficiency, and indeed may affect the sign of the overall efficiency impact. Other considerations—such as distributional consequences—may tend to support the use of grandfathered permits rather than auctioned permits or pollution taxes, but this recent literature indicates that the efficiency disadvantage of grandfathered permits is more significant than was previously recognized.

This paper examines the efficiency impacts of pollution taxes and some other pollution-control policies in a second-best setting with prior distortionary taxes in factor markets. It aims to articulate and pull together some key ideas from recent papers on this subject. The next section heuristically describes some of the main results from recent work on the efficiency effects of environmental taxes and quotas (or tradeable permits) in a second-best setting.[7] Section III then elaborates on these results, first by offering additional interpretation related to environmental taxes and the double dividend issue, and then by considering the significance of second-best issues for the choice between taxes and other, non-tax instruments for environmental protection. Section IV briefly depicts some results from investigations that apply this second-best framework to assess the efficiency impacts of environmental taxes and regulations. It first considers the impacts of revenue-neutral environmental taxes; it then examines potential impacts of pollution permits, with a focus on the efficiency implications of the decision whether to auction or freely offer the permits. The final section offers conclusions.

---

[5]Fullerton and Metcalf explain differences in efficiency outcomes in terms of whether policies generate privately-retained scarcity rents, rather than in terms of whether they exploit the revenue-recycling effect. As discussed in Section III, the two issues are intimately connected.

[6]This result, for pollution permits, was foreshadowed by Bovenberg and Goulder's (1996) finding that a carbon tax with lump-sum replacement of the revenues will be efficiency-reducing if marginal environmental benefits from carbon abatement are below a certain threshold (about $50 per ton). Parry (1997) recognized that the same formal analysis applies to the case of pollution quotas and grandfathered pollution permits; thus the same "threshold" issue arises.

[7]This section offers a nontechnical presentation of the results generated in Goulder (1998). Other sections of this paper involve only incidental changes from the corresponding sections in Goulder (1998).

II. Impacts of Environmental Taxes and Quotas in a Second-Best Setting

A. The Conventional, Partial Equilibrium Analysis of Policy Impacts

To understand how environmental policies interact with preexisting factor-market distortions, it helps to consider first the impacts of environmental policies in a setting with no prior distortionary taxes. We can then observe how the situation changes in the presence of distortionary taxes and associated factor-market distortions.

Figure 1 offers the typical partial equilibrium framework for analyzing the welfare effects of an environmental tax or quota.[8] MC denotes the private marginal costs of producing the given commodity, which in this example is coal. MC_{soc} represents the social marginal-cost curve, incorporating the marginal external damage (marginal external cost) MED. MB represents the marginal benefit (demand) curve. If a tax is imposed on coal equal to the marginal external damage, the welfare gain is area B.[9] This is the value of the environmental improvement $(A + B)$ minus the gross costs of the tax (A).[10]

The same figure indicates the impacts of a quota on coal use. Suppose that the government restricts total coal use to the quantity Q_1. The government could do this, for example, by issuing licenses to coal-supplying firms, where the licenses authorize the sale of coal and where the total number of licenses limits aggregate sales to Q_1. (Assume that the licenses are given out free, rather than auctioned, so that the government does not earn revenue in issuing licenses. We will consider shortly the significance of auctioning the licenses.) The diagram indicates that the restriction in coal supply will cause the price of coal to rise by the same amount as in the case of the coal tax. Under this policy, the restriction on coal supply imposes gross costs of A; these gross costs are the lost potential surplus to users of coal such as steel manufacturers or electric utilities. The value of the environmental improvement is again $(A + B)$, and thus the welfare gain is again B.[11]

---

[8]Here the tax is a strict Pigovian tax in that it applies to a commodity with which pollution is associated rather than directly to pollution emissions. Similarly, the quota applies to the commodity (coal) rather than to pollution emissions from coal. The lessons from this section apply equally to taxes and quotas on emissions. For a general examination of issues surrounding the choice between regulating emissions and regulating a commodity closely associated with emissions, see Bovenberg and Goulder (1999).

[9]In the case with nonconstant private marginal costs or nonconstant marginal external costs, the presentation is slightly more complicated but the results are essentially the same.

[10]The environmental economics literature often refers to *abatement costs*. These are usually defined in a way that corresponds, in Figure 1, to the entire area below the MB curve (including the area below the MC curve) over the interval from Q_0 to Q_1.

[11]The efficiency impacts of the tax and quota are the same in this example. However, this example ignores uncertainty by the regulator with regard to firms' costs of coal (or pollution) abatement. In the presence of such uncertainty, taxes and quotas generally have different impacts. See Weitzman (1974) and Stavins (1995).

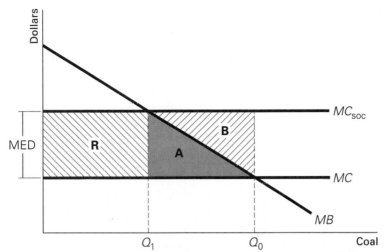

Figure 1 Typical Partial Equilibrium Framework for Analyzing Efficiency Impacts of Environmental Taxes and Quotas

B. Two Complications

Prior distortionary taxes complicate the analysis in two ways. The simple analysis usually assumes that there are no efficiency consequences associated with the transfer of the tax revenue R from those who pay the coal tax to the government and then back to the private sector.[12] However, in an economy with prior taxes, the revenues from an environmental tax can be used to finance reductions in the marginal rates of prior distortionary taxes such as income, payroll, or sales taxes. When revenues are "recycled" in this way, some of the distortions or excess burdens from prior taxes can be avoided. This beneficial efficiency impact is the revenue-recycling effect.

A second complicating effect works in the opposite direction. This second effect, the tax-interaction effect, occurs because the environmental tax or quote tends to reduce the real returns to factors such as labor and capital, discourage the supply of these factors, and thereby exacerbate preexisting distortions in factor markets. The tax-interaction effect is discussed in general terms in a number of recent studies.[13] For concreteness, in the present discussion we will illustrate the tax-interaction effect using our example with coal. In addition, we will describe the tax-interaction effect through its impact on the labor market. A recent paper by Williams (1999) shows that the tax-interaction effect applies to capital in much the same way it applies to labor.

The tax-interaction effect reflects the links from (1) the tax or quota to (2) the cost of living to (3) the real wage and finally to (4) the distortion in

---

[12]In the simplest case, the revenues are returned to the private sector in a lump-sum fashion.
[13]See Parry (1995, 1997), Goulder, Parry, and Burtraw (1997), and Goulder et al. (1999).

the labor market. As suggested by Figure 1, the tax or the quota causes the market price of coal to rise. The higher price of coal raises costs to users of coal, which implies increased prices of goods or services from coal-using industries. One might expect the price-increases to be most pro-nounced in the industries for which coal is a significant, direct input (e.g., electricity and steel). However, higher coal prices affect the costs and out-put prices of other industries too, since other industries use coal indirectly: for example, they use the steel that was made from coal. Through direct and indirect cost-impacts, the higher coal price leads to higher prices in many industries and contributes to a rise in the cost of living. This increase in the cost of living means that a given nominal wage, w, now represents a lower real wage.

By raising the costs of goods and services, environmental policies re-duce the real return to labor. These policies are implicit taxes on labor (and other factors of production). These implicit taxes discourage labor (and other factor) supply, as indicated by Figure 2. In this figure, S_L and D_L rep-resent the supply and demand curves for labor, respectively. Let τ_L denote the prior tax on labor implied by preexisting payroll or income taxes. In this setting, with a prior labor tax, the initial equilibrium labor supply is $L_1 < L_0$. The prior distortion in the labor market is given by the triangular region defined by points a, b, and c. Now consider the labor-market im-pact of the environmental tax or quota. By raising the cost of living and lowering the real wage, the environmental policy induces a shift in the la-

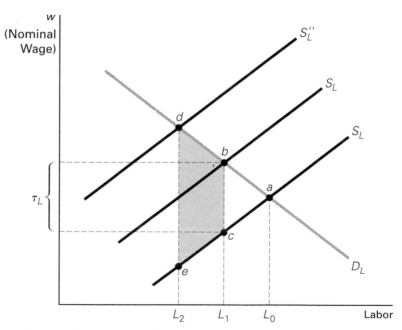

Figure 2   The Tax Interaction Effect

bor supply curve from S_L' to S_L''. This implies a further reduction (to L_2) in the equilibrium labor supply, and a further distortion in the labor market, represented by the trapezoidal area defined by points b, d, e, and c. This area is the tax-interaction effect. As suggested by Figure 2, the tax-interaction effect is an increasing function of the size of the prior tax on labor.[14] In the limiting case where the prior tax τ_L is zero, the tax-interaction effect disappears.

Thus, in a second-best setting, two effects complicate the efficiency analysis of environmental taxes and quotas. The revenue-recycling effect tends to imply lower costs of these policies than in a "first-best" setting with no prior taxes. But the tax-interaction effect tends to imply higher costs. Which effect is stronger? In the simple models developed in recent studies, the tax-interaction effect dominates. If the good to which the environmental tax applies in an average substitute for leisure, the tax-interaction effect is stronger than the revenue-recycling effect.[15] This implies that the costs of environmental taxes and quotas are higher in the presence of prior factor taxes than in their absence—even when the revenues are recycled through cuts in marginal income tax rates.

Why is the tax-interaction effect more powerful? Note that the environmental (coal) tax affects the relative prices of goods and services. It thus "distorts" not only the labor market (by lowering the real wage) but also "distorts" consumers' choices among these goods and services.[16] Recycling the revenues helps return the real wage to its original value and thereby helps reduce the labor-market distortion, but such recycling does not undo the change in relative consumer good prices and the associated "distortion" in consumption choices. For this reason the revenue-recycling effect only partly offsets the tax-interaction effect. The revenue-neutral environmental tax policy effectively substitutes (at the margin) a narrow environmental tax for a broader income tax. This makes the tax system less efficient along the nonenvironmental dimensions captured under the notion of gross cost. (At the same time, the tax system may well be more efficient overall, once one accounts for the environment-related benefits from the tax or quota.)

Figure 3 illustrates these findings. The figure shows the marginal efficiency costs of pollution abatement, at different levels of abatement, where the efficiency costs represented here are gross (that is, exclusive) of the benefits from environmental improvement. The lowermost line depicts the marginal costs of abatement in the "first-best" setting, by which we mean an economy with no distortionary taxes. In a first-best situation, the marginal costs of abatement are the same regardless of whether an environmental tax or quota is imposed.

---

[14]See Parry (1997) for a rigorous demonstration.

[15]We discuss below the significance of the "average substitute" assumption.

[16]The word "distort" is in quotes to acknowledge that we are ignoring environment-related benefits here. While the changes in relative prices of commodities occasioned by the environmental tax may contribute to higher gross costs, these same relative price changes may bring about an overall efficiency improvement, since overall efficiency incorporates the environment-related benefits (reduced pollution) associated with the relative price changes.

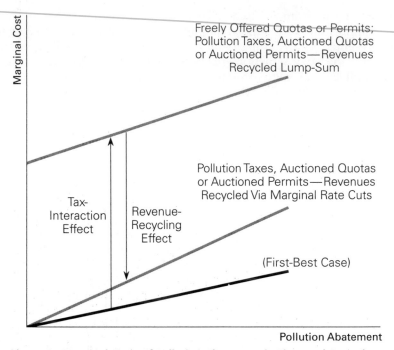

Figure 3　Marginal Costs of Pollution Abatement in First- and Second-Best Settings

The other lines represent the marginal costs in an economy with prior distortionary taxes. The top line depicts the marginal costs of abatement for policies that produce the tax-interaction effect but do not enjoy the revenue-recycling effect. Several policies fall into this category. One is the coal quota just discussed. Another is a system of tradeable coal permits, where the permits are given out free ("grandfathered"). A third is a coal tax policy in which the revenues are returned to the economy lump-sum rather than through cuts in marginal tax rates. In all of these cases, the revenue-recycling effect is absent. For these policies, at all levels of abatement, the marginal costs of abatement are higher than in the first-best case. This is the case even at incremental abatement: the second-best marginal cost curve has a positive intercept, whereas the marginal cost of incremental abatement for these policies is zero (dashed line) in the first-best case.[17] At any level of abatement, the tax-interaction effect is represented by the vertical distance between the top and bottom (dashed) marginal cost curve.

The intercept of the top marginal cost curve represents the critical value for marginal environmental *benefits* from pollution abatement through these policies. If the marginal benefits are (always) below this value, then pollution reductions through one of these policies will always involve costs

---

[17]So long as the prior tax rate on labor is positive, the introduction of these environmental policies augments a preexisting distortion and involves a first-order (i.e., nonincremental) efficiency cost.

that exceed the benefits. Under these circumstances, these policies will be efficiency-reducing regardless of the level of abatement!

The middle line in Figure 3 represents the marginal costs of abatement for policies that exploit the revenue-recycling effect by raising revenues and using these revenues to finance cuts in the marginal rates of prior distortionary taxes. Such policies include environmental taxes, *auctioned* coal quotas or *auctioned* tradeable permits, where revenues are recycled through marginal rate cuts. The revenue-recycling effect is represented by the vertical distance between the top and middle marginal cost curves. Revenue-recycling through marginal rate reductions can significantly reduce the general-equilibrium costs of environmental regulations. At incremental abatement, the revenue-recycling effect fully offsets the tax-interaction effect; hence, the marginal cost of abatement is zero at incremental abatement (as in the first-best case). However, for larger amounts of abatement, the revenue-recycling effect only partly offsets the tax-interaction effect (for the reasons given above), and thus the costs of abatement exceed the costs of comparable abatement in a first-best setting.

Figure 3 illustrates the idea that an environmental policy's potential to yield an overall efficiency gain can depend on whether it exploits the revenue-recycling effect. By definition, a policy yields an efficiency improvement if and only if its (environment-related) benefits exceed its overall gross costs (including the net contribution of the tax-interaction and revenue-recycling effects). The revenue-recycling effect may be necessary to make net benefits positive.

The figure also indicates that second-best considerations tend to imply higher costs from environmental policies. Even so, the news for environmental policy reform is not entirely bad. Note that for policies that exploit the revenue-recycling effect, the general equilibrium marginal costs are initially zero. Note also that, in general, one would expect the (gross) marginal *benefits* from pollution-abatement to be strictly positive at initial amounts of abatement. Together, these ideas imply that these policies generally will be justified on efficiency grounds—so long as the amount of abatement is not too great. In a second-best world, there remains potential for efficiency gains through pollution taxes and other policies that deal with pollution-related externalities.

It should be noted that Figure 3 illustrates the "central case" results from analytical models—that is, the results that stem from the assumption that the good on which the environmental tax is imposed is an average substitute for leisure. Suppose instead, that this good were a weaker than average substitute for leisure, that is, a relative complement to leisure. Analytical studies indicate that in this case, for a sufficiently small environmental tax (or sufficiently small amount of abatement in Figure 3), the revenue-recycling effect will outweigh the tax-interaction effect. Under these circumstances, the costs of abatement are *lower* in a second-best world than in a first-best world—at least up to a certain level of abatement. When a good is a relative complement to leisure, the environmental tax causes a reduction in both the demand for that good and the demand for leisure. The reduced demand for leisure, or increased supply of labor, helps alleviate preexisting labor market distortion. If, on the other hand, the taxed good were a stronger than average substitute for leisure, the tax-interaction effect would overtake the revenue-recycling effect by even more than in the average-substitute case, and the costs of given amounts of abatement would be greater than in the average-substitute case. There is a lack of solid empirical information regarding the extent to which various pollution-related goods are substitutes or complements with leisure. In the absence of such information, the assumption of "average substitutability" seems reasonable. Further empirical work that clarifies these substitutability or complementarity relationships could be of great value to researchers aiming to assess the costs of environmental regulations.

III. Interpretations, Qualifications, and Extensions

A. Can Pollution Taxes Deliver a "Double Dividend"?

In recent years there has been considerable debate about the possibilities for "green tax reform," that is, the substitution of taxes on pollution for ordinary, distortionary taxes. A general argument for such reform is that it makes sense to concentrate taxes on "bads" like pollution rather than "goods" like labor effort or capital formation (saving and investment). To buttress the case for green tax reform, some analysts have argued that the revenue-neutral swap of pollution taxes for ordinary taxes will produce a "double dividend:" not only (1) improve the quality of the environment but also (2) reduce certain costs of the tax system. This argument has occupied a prominent place in the debate about carbon taxes, as mentioned in the introduction. Few analysts deny the first dividend; it is the second dividend that generates controversy.

Can environmental taxes generate the second dividend? Different policy analysts have meant different things by this dividend, and this has led to confusion. Goulder (1995a) distinguishes a "strong" and "weak" version of the double dividend claim, as follows. Let $C(\tau_E \ \Delta\tau_L)$ refer to the gross cost of a revenue-neutral policy involving a new environmental tax τ_E that finances the change (reduction) $\Delta\tau_L$ in preexisting distortionary taxes.[18] Let $C(\tau_E, \Delta T)$ denote the gross cost of a revenue-neutral policy in which a new environmental tax τ_E finances the lump-sum reduction in taxes, ΔT. The weak double dividend claim is:

$$C(\tau_E, \Delta\tau_L) < C(\tau_E, \Delta T)$$

---

[18]In keeping with Section II's focus on labor-market distortions, we use the subscript "L" to refer to the distortionary factor tax. The points raised here apply to economies in which there are several distortionary taxes, including taxes on capital as well as labor.

The above expression asserts that a reform in which the environmental tax's revenues are recycled through cuts in the rates of distortionary tax involves lower gross costs than a policy in which the environmental tax's revenues are returned lump-sum. This weak double-dividend claim is easy to justify: environmental taxes, with revenues devoted to cuts in distortionary taxes, do indeed lower the costs of the tax system *relative to what the costs would be if the revenues were returned lump-sum*. As shown in Goulder (1995a), the weak double-dividend claim is upheld so long as the tax τ_L is appropriately labeled as distortionary. That is, the weak claim is upheld if and only if the tax τ_L has a positive marginal excess burden.

In terms of Figure 3, the weak double-dividend claim is verified by the fact that the marginal cost curve for the environmental tax with lump-sum revenue-replacement lies above the curve for the environmental tax accompanied by cuts in the marginal rates of a distortionary tax. In essence, the weak double-dividend claim amounts to the assertion that, in terms of efficiency, it pays to take advantage of the revenue-recycling effect. Thus it is closely related to the notion that pollution taxes that finance cuts in distortionary taxes are preferable on efficiency grounds to pollution quotas or grandfathered tradeable permits.

The stronger double-dividend claim is

$$C(\tau_E, \Delta\tau_L) \leq 0$$

that is, the revenue-neutral swap of an environmental tax for existing distortionary taxes involves zero or negative gross costs. This is equivalent to asserting that the gross distortionary cost directly attributable to the environmental tax is smaller than the avoided gross distortionary cost stemming from the environmental-tax-financed cut in the distortionary tax. If this strong double-dividend claim held for a carbon tax, then, as noted in the introduction, the tax would be justified on efficiency grounds so long as the environment-related gross *benefits* from the policy were nonnegative.

Is the stronger claim justified? Figure 3 sheds light on the answer. For the strong claim to be valid, the marginal cost curve for the pollution tax accompanied by cuts in distortionary taxes would have to lie on or below the horizontal axis. Clearly the curve does not fulfill this requirement—except at zero abatement. To support the stronger double-dividend claim, the revenue-recycling effect not only would have to fully offset the tax-interaction effect, but also would have to overcome the usual, first-best abatement costs represented by the dashed line. The analytical studies referred to in Section II, which form the basis for the positions of the marginal cost curves in Figure 3, do not support such an outcome. In these studies, for anything but an infinitesimal amount of abatement (infinitesimal environmental tax) the gross costs of a revenue-neutral environmental tax reform are positive.

Some qualifications are in order. As mentioned in the previous section, in most of the aforementioned analytical models the pollution-generating (or "dirty") good is assumed to be an average substitute for leisure. If instead the pollution-generating good were a weaker than average substitute for (stronger than average complement with) leisure, then the double dividend will arise after all—for a sufficiently small environmental tax. Further empirical work to gauge the extent of substitutability or complementarity could shed much light.

Second, more complex theoretical models can provide more scope for the strong double-dividend claim than is offered here.[19] To achieve greater tractability, many of the models examining this issue consider only one factor of production—labor. In models with both capital and labor, an environmental tax reform can produce the second dividend under certain circumstances. Specifically, if the tax system initially is highly inefficient in the sense that one factor is overtaxed relative to the other,[20] and if the environmental tax reform (the combination of the tax itself and the recycling of the revenues) serves to shift the tax burden from the overtaxed to the undertaxed factor, then the reform will produce a *tax-shifting effect* that works toward a more efficient tax system. If this beneficial tax-shifting effect is large enough, it (combined with the revenue-recycling effect) can entirely compensate for usual "first-best" abatement costs and the tax-interaction effect.[21] Thus, under these circumstances, the strong double-dividend materializes after all.

Most empirical studies indicate that in the United States, capital is overtaxed (in efficiency terms) relative to labor.[22] With these initial conditions, an environmental tax reform will produce a favorable tax-shifting effect if it shifts the burden away from capital and toward labor. Bovenberg and Goulder (1997) examine two environmentally motivated, revenue-neutral tax reforms—a Btu tax applied to fossil fuels and an increase in the Federal gasoline tax—and find that the latter policy produces a tax-shifting effect that significantly reduces the gross costs. However, the tax-shifting effect is generally not strong enough to make the gross costs zero or negative, except under extreme values for behavioral parameters. Although the results are somewhat mixed, other simulation studies have tended to support the idea that it is difficult to generate the strong double dividend under plausible parameter values and realistic policy specifications.[23]

The possibility of a (strong) double dividend through a powerful tax-shifting effect is illustrative of a general theme that emerges from recent theoretical work. In virtually all of the theoretical studies, a double

---

[19]Bovenberg (1996), Goulder (1995a), and Bovenberg and Goulder (1999) analyze a range of complicating issues.

[20]In efficiency terms, one factor of production is overtaxed relative to another if the tax on this factor has a larger marginal excess burden per dollar of revenue than the tax on the other factor.

[21]For a theoretical treatment of the tax-shifting issue, see Bovenberg and de Mooij (1994b), and Bovenberg and Goulder (1997).

[22]See, for example, Ballard, Shoven, and Whalley (1985), Fullerton and Mackie (1987), Jorgenson and Yun (1990), Lucas (1990), and Goulder and Thalmann (1993).

[23]Goulder (1995a) surveys these studies.

dividend becomes possible only when two general conditions are met: (1) prior to the introduction of the environmental tax reform, there is a significant inefficiency in the tax system along a nonenvironmental dimension, and (2) the environmental tax reform serves to reduce this "nonenvironmental" inefficiency. If this "non-green" benefit from green tax reform is large enough, it can compensate for the factors that work against the double dividend. The possibility of a double dividend through environmental tax policies that reduce prior inefficiencies in the relative taxation of labor and capital is an illustration of this general theme.[24]

It is important to recognize that the absence of the (strong) double dividend does not vitiate the case for green tax reform. It only means that the positive *sign* of the environmental benefits is not a sufficient condition for justifying such reform. If there is no double dividend, policy makers are obliged to consider the magnitudes of the environmental benefits and compare them with the (positive) gross costs. Also, the absence of a double dividend does not repudiate our intuition that it makes sense to orient the tax system, to a degree, on "bads" (polluting activities) rather than "goods" (labor and capital). *Even if the strong double-dividend claim fails, it is still the case that "Pigovian considerations" should be part of the design of an efficient tax system*: other things equal, the tax on a given good or activity should be higher, the larger the environmental externalities associated with that good or activity. Higher environmental benefits justify higher taxes on polluting activities. It is the larger environmental benefits—not the presumption of zero gross costs—that justify the greening of the tax system.

B. Significance of the Scale of Abatement for the Choice between Taxes and Quotas

The theoretical model indicated that the pollution taxes and auctioned permits have an efficiency advantage over pollution quotas and grandfathered pollution permits to the extent that the former policies exploit the revenue-recycling effect. However, the size of the efficiency advantage generally declines with the amount of abatement. In fact, this advantages approaches zero as the extent of abatement approaches 100 percent. This is illustrated by Figure 4, which is borrowed from Goulder, Parry, and Burtraw (1997), which we will refer to as GPB. Marginal costs rise faster for the pollution tax (or auctioned pollution permit) policy. Eventually—when the extent of abatement is substantial—marginal costs under this policy exceed those for the pollution quota (or grandfathered permit) policy.

---

[24]This theme also is illustrated in the case where the double dividend can arise because the pollution-generating good is a stronger than average complement with leisure. Ignoring environmental considerations, optimal "Ramsey" commodity taxation would tend to justify taxing this relative complement to leisure. In this setting, introducing an environmental tax both serves an environmental purpose and helps eliminate a preexisting inefficiency of the tax system along nonenvironmental dimensions. Thus the situation is conducive to a double dividend.

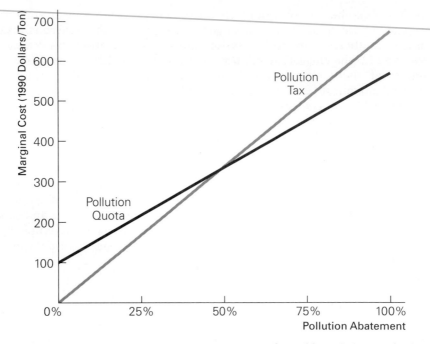

Figure 4   Marginal Costs Over the Entire Range of Possible Emissions Reductions

Why is this so? Consider the pollution tax. Because of this policy's negative impact on labor supply and on emissions, marginal tax revenue declines as the emissions tax rate rises. This means that, with greater abatement, the ability to exploit the revenue-recycling effect diminishes. Eventually, the point is reached where, at the margin, additional abatement (via an incrementally higher pollution tax) raises no more revenue than is raised under the quota policy.[25]

That is the point where the pollution tax and pollution quota marginal cost curves cross. To the right of that point, *at the margin* the tax policy is more costly than the quota policy, because at the margin it has a *negative* revenue-recycling effect (as compared with the negligible revenue-recycling effect of the quota policy). Indeed, if one pursues emissions reductions to the point of 100 percent abatement, the total costs of the two types of policies are identical. This makes sense: at 100 percent abatement neither policy earns any revenue, and thus there is no effective difference between a tax and a quota at that point. Thus the areas under the marginal cost curves from 0 to 100 percent abatement are the same for both policies.

These results demonstrate that the relative superiority (in terms of lower cost) of policies that exploit the revenue-recycling effect diminishes

---

[25]The quota policy does not necessarily raise zero revenue. This policy will tend to raise revenue insofar as quota rents are taxed, and will tend to lose revenue insofar as the policy causes a loss of overall real income and a reduction in the labor tax base.

with the extent of abatement. At low levels of abatement (as would be appropriate if marginal environmental *benefits* are low), these policies have a considerable cost advantage. But at high levels of abatement (as would be justified when marginal environmental benefits are high) the advantage of these policies is much smaller. In the limiting case of 100 percent abatement, these policies have no cost advantage.

C. Impacts of Other Environmental Policies in a Second-Best Setting

Thus far, all of the discussion in this paper has centered on pollution taxes, quotas, and permits. Recent papers by Fullerton and Metcalf (1997) and Goulder, Parry, Williams, and Burtraw (1999) examine the impacts of other policy instruments (in addition to pollution taxes and quotas) in a second-best setting.[26] Among the additional instruments considered in these recent papers are some "command-and-control" policies: namely, mandated technologies and performance standards.

Goulder et al. (1999) show that preexisting taxes also raise the costs of the command-and-control policies relative to their costs in a first-best world. Like emissions taxes and quotas, the command-and-control policies raise production costs and lead to higher output prices. If there are prior distortionary taxes in factor markets, the higher output prices produce the tax-interaction effect, which implies higher costs relative to the costs in a first-best setting.

Although second-best considerations raise the costs of all instruments, they do not increase costs in the same proportion. Indeed, when the amount of pollution-abatement is incremental or "small," preexisting taxes especially raise the costs of non-auctioned quotas or permits, and can put non-auctioned quotas or permits at a cost-disadvantage relative to command-and-control policies. Economists have long favored market-based policies as being more cost-effective than the command-and-control alternatives. Yet in a second-best setting, certain market-based policies can be at a disadvantage. The recent studies by Fullerton and Metcalf and Goulder et al. indicate that the marginal abatement costs of performance standards and technology mandates resemble those of the emissions tax in that marginal costs are zero at the first increment of abatement.[27] This contrasts with the strictly positive costs of initial abatement under a non-auctioned quota. Thus, for "low" amounts of abatement, a command-and-control policy can be less costly than grandfathered permits. However, it should be kept in mind that the command-and-control policies eventually involve higher costs as the amount of abatement becomes very extensive. As discussed in Goul-

---

[26]See also Ng (1980), who analyzed environmental subsidies in the presence of prior tax distortions.

[27]This point was first demonstrated by Fullerton and Metcalf. This was shown for a "technology restriction" policy, which was a constraint on the ratio of labor input to emissions. In their model, this is functionally equivalent to a policy involving a constraint on the ratio of emissions to output.

der et al. (1999), this reflects the inability of these alternative instruments to provide the appropriate prices of inputs and outputs.

It is worth considering further why the marginal cost curves of these alternative instruments emerge from the origin (as in the case of the pollution tax or auctioned quota—with revenues devoted to marginal rate reductions), while the marginal cost curves of grandfathered quotas (or emissions taxes with revenues returned lump sum) do not. Since the mandated technology and performance standard do not raise revenue, it is clear that raising revenue *per se* is not necessary for the zero-marginal-cost-at-initial-abatement property to obtain. One can explain these differences in terms of whether the tax-interaction and revenue-recycling effects cancel at initial abatement. At the first incremental amount of abatement, emissions taxes (with revenues returned through marginal rate cuts) produce a strictly positive tax-interaction effect that is exactly offset by the strictly negative revenue-recycling effect. Hence the marginal abatement costs are zero at initial abatement. The mandated technology and performance standard produce neither a tax-interaction effect nor a revenue-recycling effect. Hence the marginal costs of abatement are again zero at initial abatement.[28] In contrast, under grandfathered quotas there is a strictly positive tax-interaction effect and no offsetting revenue-recycling effect. Hence marginal costs are strictly positive. Thus, the tax-interaction and revenue-recycling effects can explain why marginal costs start out strictly positive under non-auctioned permits or quotas, and start out at zero under the other policies.

These differences at initial abatement can also be linked to the presence or absence of a lump-sum transfer. The government effectuates a lump-sum transfer to individuals when it introduces a pollution tax and returns the revenues lump-sum, when it implements a pollution quota (thus generating quota rents that are not entirely taxed away), or when it introduces a pollution tax and recycles the revenues through cuts in the marginal tax rate on a perfectly inelastically supplied factor of production.[29] In a second-best world, such transfers involve an efficiency cost because they must ultimately be financed through distortionary taxes. In contrast, under the pollution tax or fuels tax (with revenues financing cuts in prior taxes), or under the mandated technology or performance standard, there is no such transfer. Thus the presence or absence of a positive intercept of the marginal cost function corresponds to the presence or absence of this lump-sum transfer.[30]

---

[28]Alternatively, one can view the technology mandate as producing two tax-interaction effects and two revenue-recycling effects. As indicated by Fullerton and Metcalf, the mandated technology is equivalent to the combination of a subsidy to the use of the clean input and a tax on emissions. The subsidy and tax components respectively account for negative (in efficiency terms) and positive revenue-recycling effects, which cancel out, and positive and negative tax-interaction effects, which also cancel out (at the first unit of abatement).

[29]This last case is examined by Bovenberg and de Mooij (1996) and Williams (1998).

[30]Fullerton and Metcalf (1997) point out that pollution regulation through grandfathered permits creates scarcity rents that remain in private (that is, the regulated firm's) hands, and indicate that this accounts for the fact that the marginal costs of incremental abatement are strictly positive. The creation of scarcity rents is an example of the government's bringing about a lump-sum transfer to the private sector.

IV. Some Numerical Results

Thus far we have only considered results from analytical models. Analytical tractability comes at a price in that it necessitates the use of fairly simple models. In this section we briefly display results from some numerical models.[31]

First we present some results that pertain to the double-dividend issue. Here we display and briefly interpret results from the disaggregated computable general equilibrium model employed in Bovenberg and Goulder (1997). We will only sketch the results here; the reader is referred to the Bovenberg-Goulder article for details. In this discussion we also present a sampling of results from other numerical models.

Next we display numerical results indicating how preexisting taxes affect the choice between auctioned and grandfathered emissions permits, in the context of sulfur dioxide (SO_2) and carbon dioxide (CO_2) emissions reductions in the United States.

A. Numerical Explorations of the Double-Dividend Issue

1. Results from Bovenberg-Goulder (1997). Here we examine simulations in which a fossil fuel Btu tax or a consumer gasoline tax increase is implemented in revenue-neutral fashion, with the revenues devoted to reductions in the income tax. An important item to keep in mind when interpreting the results is the relative taxation of capital and labor. In the baseline, or reference equilibrium (and under central values for parameters), the marginal excess burden (MEB) of capital taxes is .43, while the MEB of labor taxes is .31. This means that the tax-shifting effect (see III.A above) works in favor of the second dividend when policies shift the burden of taxation from (overtaxed) capital to (undertaxed) labor. In this regard, note that while the Btu tax tends to fall more or less evenly on capital and labor, the gasoline tax tends to fall mainly on labor (by virtue of its being akin to a consumption tax). Hence the gasoline tax has more potential for tax-shifting that support the second dividend.

Figure 5 shows results when these taxes are introduced with *lump-sum* replacement of the revenues. Figure 5a shows that in the short term, the environmental (Btu and gas) taxes entail a greater GDP sacrifice than the personal income tax. Figure 5b shows that the gasoline tax has a much smaller investment cost than does the Btu tax or income tax. This reflects the fact that the gasoline tax tends to ease the tax burden on capital.

Table 1 shows the effects of these policies on factor prices and quantities. It indicates that the combination of gasoline tax increase and reduction in personal income tax reduces capital's tax burden and raises la-

---

[31]Real-world environmental taxes and other regulations involve "large," as opposed to incremental, changes in the level of pollution. Numerical simulation is usually necessary to evaluate the efficiency implications of these changes.

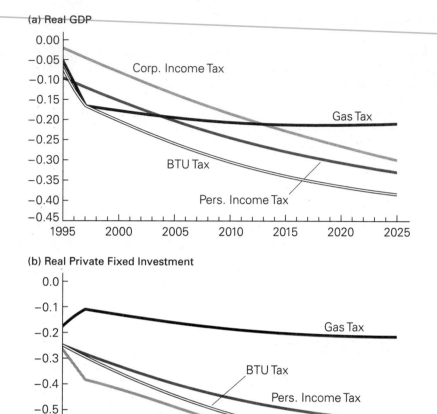

(a) Real GDP

(b) Real Private Fixed Investment

Figure 5 **Aggregate Effects of Energy and Income Tax Policies (percentage changes from reference case)**

bor's. In contrast, the combination of Btu tax and cut in personal income tax does not significantly alter the relative taxation of capital and labor. Thus, the revenue-neutral policy involving the gasoline tax produces a more significant tax-shifting effect.

Table 2 shows welfare effects. These are the monetary equivalent (using the equivalent variation) of the change in utility associated with the policy change. These welfare measures disregard welfare impacts associated with the changes in environmental quality; they refer only to the cost side of the benefit-cost ledger.

Comparing the left and right columns indicates the importance of the revenue-recycling effect; that is, of returning revenues through cuts in marginal tax rates instead of through lump-sum tax cuts. The welfare costs of the revenue-neutral reforms are significantly higher when revenues are returned in lump-sum fashion.

Table 1 Impacts of Taxes on Factor Prices and Supplies
(percentage changes from baseline)

	Years after Policy Introduction			
	1	*2*	*5*	*30*
"Single Tax" Policies:				
Btu Tax, Lump-Sum Repl.				
w	−0.250	−0.390	−0.446	−0.655
r	−0.083	−0.239	−0.179	−0.084
L	−0.124	−0.140	−0.121	−0.049
K	−0.017	−0.035	−0.092	−0.364
Gasoline Tax Increase, Lump-Sum Repl.				
w	−0.722	−1.069	−1.058	−0.983
r	0.095	−0.007	−0.027	−0.005
L	−0.266	−0.335	−0.331	−0.298
K	−0.011	−0.019	−0.031	−0.069
Personal Tax Increase, Lump-Sum Repl.				
w	−0.333	−0.347	−0.404	−0.655
r	−0.104	−0.108	−0.105	−0.053
L	−0.277	−0.274	−0.265	−0.212
K	−0.015	−0.030	−0.072	−0.313
Substitution of Environmental Tax				
For Personal Tax:				
Btu Tax, Personal Tax Repl.				
w	0.083	−0.042	−0.042	0.014
r	0.031	−0.125	−0.074	−0.053
L	0.157	0.139	0.149	0.163
K	−0.001	−0.005	0.019	−0.037
Gasoline Tax Increase, Personal Tax Repl.				
w	−0.375	−0.694	−0.571	−0.307
r	0.216	0.111	0.076	0.057
L	0.013	−0.057	−0.061	−0.084
K	0.004	0.012	0.041	0.252

Note: w, r, L, and K respectively refer to the after-tax real wage, after-tax real rate of return, aggregate real labor supply, and aggregate real capital stock.

Table 2 Welfare Impacts

	Welfare Cost Per Dollar of Revenue	
	Lump-Sum Tax Replacement	Personal Income Tax Replacement
BTU Tax	.656	.318
Consumer-Level Gasoline Tax Increase	.594	.253
Personal Income Tax Increase	.379	—
Corporate Income Tax Increase	.438	.093

Concentrate now on the right column, which displays results from revenue-neutral policies in which the environmental tax revenues finance reductions in the personal tax. There are two main results from this column. First, the second dividend does not arise: the gross welfare costs (i.e., the costs before netting out the environmental benefits) are positive. Second, the welfare cost is lower for the gasoline tax reform, despite the narrower base of the gasoline tax. This reflects the tax-shifting effect: as Table 1 indicated, under the gasoline tax reform the tax burden is shifted from capital to labor, which tends to reduce the gross costs. However, the tax-shifting effect is not strong enough to undo the cost associated with the tax-interaction effect.

Is it possible to make the tax-shifting effect large enough to give the second dividend? Yes. The tax-shifting effect will be stronger to the extent that (1) the initial inefficiencies in the relative taxation of capital and labor are large, and (2) the policy shifts the burden from the overtaxed to the undertaxed factor. To enhance the first condition, we have performed simulations with very elastic capital supply assumptions. Specifically, we assume that the elasticity of substitution in consumption (which affects the household's interest elasticity of saving) is "high" relative to most estimates. To enhance the second condition, we consider a policy in which a gasoline tax is introduced and all the revenues from this tax are recycled through cuts in capital taxes only. This combination produces a large enough tax-shifting effect to yield the second dividend if the intertemporal elasticity of substitution is 1.8 or more. Although this shows that the second dividend can arise, producing this dividend seems to require implausibly high values for the intertemporal elasticity of substitution (most estimates are between 0 and unity[32]).

2. Results from a Sampling of Other Models. Table 3 summarizes results from numerical studies of a revenue-neutral carbon tax policy. The table presents results from seven numerical models. These are the Goulder and Jorgenson-Wilcoxen intertemporal general equilibrium models of the United States, the Proost-Regemorter general equilibrium model of Belgium, the DRI and LINK econometric macroeconomic models of the United States, and the Shah-Larsen partial equilibrium model, which has been applied to five countries, including the United States.[33] The results in Table 3 are for the revenue-neutral combination of an environmental tax (usually a carbon tax) and reduction in the personal income tax, except in cases where this combination was not available.

---

[32]Using time-series data, Hall (1988) estimates that this elasticity is below 0.2. A cross-section analysis by Lawrance (1991) generates a central estimate of 1.1. Estimates from time-series tend to be lower than those from cross-section analyses.

[33]For a more detailed description of these models, see Goulder (1995b), Jorgenson and Wilcoxen (1990, 1996), Shackleton et al. (1996), Proost and Regemorter (1995), and Shah and Larsen (1992). The Shah-Larsen model is the simplest of the models, in part because it takes pretax factor prices as given. Despite its simplicity, the model addresses interactions between commodity and factor markets and thus incorporates some of the major efficiency connections discussed earlier.

Table 3 Numerical Assessments of Welfare Impacts of Revenue-Neutral Environmental Tax Reforms

Model	Reference	Country	Type of Environmental Tax	Method of Revenue Replacement	Welfare Effect
DRI	Shackleton et al. (1996)	U.S.	Phased-in Carbon Tax[a]	Personal Tax Cut	−0.39[b]
Goulder	Goulder (1995b)	U.S.	$25/ton Carbon Tax	Personal Tax Cut	−0.33[c]
"	Goulder (1994)	U.S.	Fossil Fuel Btu Tax	Personal Tax Cut	−0.28[c]
Jorgenson-Wilcoxen	Shackleton et al. (1996)	U.S.	Phased-in Carbon Tax[a]	Capital Tax Cut	0.19[d]
LINK	Shackleton et al. (1996)	U.S.	Phased-in Carbon Tax[a]	Personal Tax Cut	−0.51[b]
Proost-van Regemorter	Proost and van Regemorter (1995)	Belgium	Hybrid of Carbon and Energy Tax	Payroll (Social Security) Tax Cut	−3.45[d]
Shah-Larsen	Shah and Larsen (1992)	U.S.	$10/ton	Personal Tax Cut	−1049.[e]
"	"	India	"	"	−129.
"	"	Indonesia	"	"	−4.
"	"	Japan	"	"	−269.
"	"	Pakistan	"	"	−23.

Notes: [a]Beginning at $15/ton in 1990 (period 1), growing at five percent annually to $39.80 per ton in 2010 (period 21), and remaining at that level thereafter. [b]Percentage change in the present value of consumption; the model does not allow for utility-based welfare measures. [c]Welfare cost per dollar of tax revenue, as measured by the equivalent variation. [d]Equivalent variation as a percentage of benchmark private wealth. [e]Compensating variation in levels (millions of U.S. dollars).

All welfare changes abstract from changes in welfare associated with improvements in environmental quality (reductions in greenhouse gas emissions). Thus they correspond to the gross cost concept discussed above. In the Goulder, Jorgenson-Wilcoxen, and Proost-Regemorter models, welfare changes are reported in terms of the equivalent variation; in the Shah-Larsen model, the changes are based on the compensating variation.[34] In the DRI and LINK macroeconomic models, the percentage change in aggregate real consumption substitutes for a utility-based welfare measure.[35]

---

[34]The equivalent variation is the lump-sum change in wealth which, under the "business-as-usual" or base case, would leave the household as well off as in the policy-change case. Thus a positive equivalent variation indicates that the policy is welfare-improving. The compensating variation is the lump-sum change in wealth that, in the policy-change scenario, would cause the household to be as well off as in the base case. In reporting the Shah-Larsen results we adopt the convention of multiplying the compensating variation by −1, so that a positive number in the table signifies a welfare improvement here as well.

[35]The demand functions in these models are not derived from an explicit utility function. Hence they do not yield utility-based measures.

In most cases, the revenue-neutral green tax swap implies a reduction in welfare, that is, entails positive gross costs. This militates against the double dividend claim. Results from the Jorgenson-Wilcoxen model, however, support the double dividend notion. Relatively high interest elasticities of savings (a high capital supply elasticity) and the assumption of perfect capital mobility across sectors may partially explain this result, at least in the case where revenues from the carbon tax are devoted to cuts in marginal taxes on capital. These assumptions imply large marginal excess burdens from taxes on capital, considerably larger than the MEBs from labor taxes. As indicated above, if the MEB on capital significantly exceeds that on labor, and the environmental reform shifts the tax burden on to labor, the double dividend can arise. Thus, the large MEBs from capital taxes help explain why, in the Jorgenson-Wilcoxen model, a revenue-neutral combination of carbon tax and reduction in capital taxes involves negative gross costs, that is, produces a double dividend. Identifying the sources of differences in results across models is difficult, in large part because of the lack of relevant information on simulation outcomes and parameters. Relatively few studies have performed the type of analysis that exposes the channels underlying the overall impacts. There is a need for more systematic sensitivity analysis, as well as closer investigations of how structural aspects of tax policies (type of tax base, narrowness of tax base, uniformity of tax rates, etc.) influence the outcomes. In addition, key behavioral parameters need to be reported. Serious attention to these issues will help explain differences in results and, one hopes, lead to a greater consensus on likely policy impacts.

B. Preexisting Taxes and the Choice between Auctioned and Non-Auctioned Pollution Permits

Here we display numerical results that bear on the importance of preexisting taxes for the choice between auctioned and non-auctioned (or grandfathered) pollution permits. As the discussion in Section II indicates, these results display the significance of the revenue-recycling effect. Thus the principles here are somewhat broader than the choice between auctioned or grandfathered permits. The results for auctioned permits also would apply to emissions taxes that exploit the revenue-recycling effect by using the revenues to finance cuts in marginal rates of preexisting factor taxes. Likewise, the results for non-auctioned permits apply to emissions taxes that fail to exploit the revenue-recycling effect by returning the revenues in a lump-sum fashion.

1. Sulfur Dioxide Abatement. The GPB study includes an assessment of the costs of reducing emissions of sulfur dioxide (SO_2) from U.S. coal-fired electric power plants. Provisions of the 1990 Clean Air Act Amendments call for such reductions and introduce a system of grandfathered SO_2 emissions permits to achieve them.

Two questions arise. First, how much higher are the costs of reducing SO_2 emissions as a result of preexisting taxes? And how much of the increase in abatement costs could be avoided if the reductions were achieved through a policy that auctioned the permits (or imposed an SO_2 tax) and exploited the revenue-recycling effect, rather than through a policy that grandfathered the permits? Figure 6 gives GPB's best estimates of the answers to these questions. The two solid lines in the figure are the ratios of total costs in a second-best setting (with a positive preexisting tax rate on labor equal to 0.4) to total costs in a first-best setting (with no preexisting tax on labor). In the case of auctioned permits (or pollution taxes), the line is almost perfectly horizontal: this ratio is approximately constant throughout the entire range of possible emissions reductions (0 to 20 million tons). Second-best considerations raise the costs of auctioned permits by about 30 percent, regardless of the extent of emissions abatement. For the actual policy of grandfathered emissions permits, the ratio of total cost is very sensitive to the extent of abatement. Under this policy the ratio begins at infinity, in keeping with the fact that the intercept of the *marginal* cost function is positive for this policy in a second-best world and zero in a first-best world. As the level of abatement approaches 100 percent, the ratio of total costs approaches the ratio for auctioned permits. This is in keeping with the point made in Section III that the efficiency disadvantage of policies that forgo the revenue-recycling effect disappears at 100 percent abatement.

The 1990 Clean Air Act Amendments call for a 10-million-ton (or approximately 50 percent) reduction in SO_2 emissions. There may be significant distributional or political objectives that are served by grandfather-

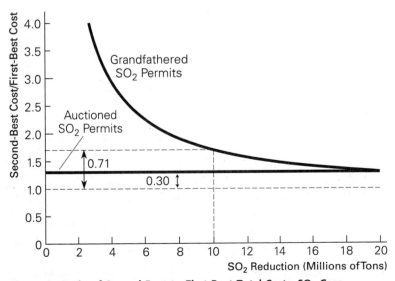

Figure 6   Ratio of Second-Best to First-Best Total Costs, SO_2 Case

ing, but Figure 6's results indicate that they come at a high price in terms of the social cost of abatement. At 10 million tons of abatement, annual total costs under the actual policy are estimated to be 71 percent (or $907 million) higher than they would be in a first-best world. As indicated in this figure, over half of this extra cost could be avoided by auctioning the permits or employing an SO_2 tax. The difference in cost between the two types of policy is $533 million.[36] These results indicate that preexisting taxes and the presence or absence of revenue-recycling have a very substantial impact on the costs of environmental policies.

Figure 7 brings in the benefit side in considering the overall efficiency gains from SO_2 abatement. The overall gains obviously depend on the marginal benefits from SO_2 reductions, and these are highly uncertain. Most estimates are in the range of $100–600 per ton, but some recent estimates are as high as $1000 per ton. The figure displays the net efficiency gains as a function of different values for the marginal benefits, ranging from zero to about $750 per ton.[37] It shows the efficiency gains that result under optimal levels of abatement, that is, abatement levels that equate marginal benefits with marginal costs. For low and intermediate values of the marginal benefits, the efficiency gains are considerably larger when SO_2 permits are auctioned than when they are grandfathered, in keeping with the lower marginal costs of abatement in the former case. Indeed, net gains under grandfathered permits are zero if marginal benefits are below $104 per ton, because in this circumstance the optimal policy is not to regulate SO_2; that is, the optimal reduction in SO_2 is zero. For very high values of the marginal benefits, there is less difference in the net efficiency gains. In fact the net efficiency gains are identical for marginal benefits greater than or equal to about $680 per ton. When marginal benefits go beyond this level, the optimal policy is to eliminate SO_2 emissions entirely. At this point it makes no difference whether permits are grandfathered or auctioned, since no permits are actually provided and thus no revenue can be raised in either case.

2. Carbon Dioxide Abatement. Recent work by Parry, Williams, and Goulder (1999) examines these issues in the context of carbon dioxide (CO_2) emissions abatement in the United States. Figures 8 and 9, based on re-

---

[36]The costs of a 10-million-ton reduction are $2182 and $1649 million under the grandfathering and auctioning of emissions allowances, respectively. Although this paper points out the efficiency drawbacks of the grandfathering element of SO_2 emissions regulation under the 1990 Clean Air Act Amendments, it is not intended to be a wholesale critique of this legislation. We would note that the 1990 legislation achieved major reforms in environmental regulation by introducing a flexible, incentive-based approach to regulation in the form of emissions allowance trading. This approach has a number of theoretical advantages over the traditional, less flexible methods (see, for example, Tietenberg [1985]), and empirical studies already indicate that this approach will yield a dramatic reduction in overall compliance costs, compared to conventional approaches (see, for example, Burtraw [1996], and Ellerman and Montero [1996]).

[37]The marginal benefits are assumed to be constant, that is, independent of the level of abatement.

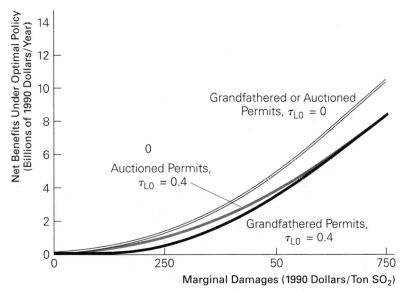

Figure 7   Net Welfare Gain from the Optimal Level of SO_2 Regulation

sults from this study, provide for CO_2 abatement policies the same sort of information as was displayed for SO_2 policies in Figures 6 and 7.

Figure 8 presents the ratio of second-best ($\tau_L = .4$) and first-best ($\tau_L = 0$) total costs, under a carbon (CO_2) tax and a carbon (CO_2) quota.[38] The carbon tax policy exploits the revenue-recycling effect: revenues from the tax are devoted to cuts in the preexisting distortionary (labor) tax. The results are qualitatively similar to the results that were shown in Figure 6. For the carbon tax, the ratio of total costs is virtually unaffected by the extent of carbon emissions abatement. For the carbon quota, in contrast, the ratio of total costs is highly sensitive to the amount of abatement, for the same reasons as were discussed earlier.

Figure 9 shows Parry, Williams, and Goulder's best estimates for net efficiency gains from carbon abatement policies, for a range of values for the marginal benefits from CO_2 abatement. Efficiency gains are considerably larger under the carbon tax than under the carbon quota. In fact, efficiency gains are zero (the optimal amount of abatement is zero) if marginal benefits are below $18 per ton. This reflects the fact that the (gross) marginal costs of CO_2 abatement begin at $18 per ton under the quota policy. Thus, any emissions abatement by way of this type of policy will be ef-

---

[38]The tax and quota policies actually would be oriented toward the use of carbon-based fuels (oil, coal, and natural gas) rather than emissions of CO_2 itself. Emissions from the combustion of these fuels are strictly proportional to carbon content, so that taxing or regulating the use of these fuels is virtually equivalent to taxing or regulating CO_2 emissions. A complication is posed by non-combustion or feedstock uses of these fuels. In the U.S. such uses represent a very small share (less than four percent) of total use.

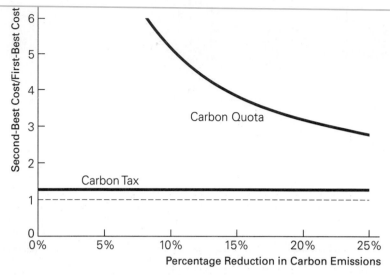

Figure 8   Ratio of Second-Best to First-Best Total Costs, CO_2 Case

ficiency-reducing if the marginal benefits are below this value. Most estimates of the marginal environmental benefits from carbon abatement obtain values below $18 per ton.[39] Thus, these results suggest that any car-

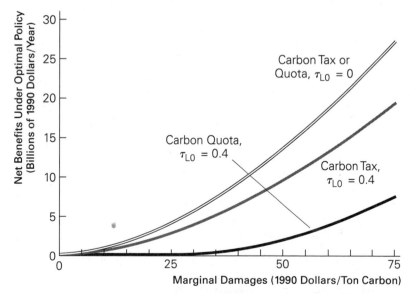

Figure 9   Net Welfare Gain from the Optimal Level of CO_2 Regulation

---

[39]See, for example, Nordhaus (1991), Peck and Teisberg (1993), and Fankhauser (1994).

bon abatement by way of a quota (or freely offered set of carbon permits) will be efficiency reducing![40]

Thus, in the context of regulating SO_2 and CO_2 emissions, second-best interactions have a very substantial effect on the gross costs and net efficiency gains. Preexisting taxes significantly raise the costs of achieving emissions reductions relative to the costs in a first-best setting. And they put policies involving emissions quotas or grandfathered permits policies at a very significant cost disadvantage relative to policies that raise revenue and finance cuts in preexisting taxes. Second-best interactions have first-order consequences.

V. Conclusions

This paper examines the significance of preexisting factor taxes for various environmental policies. It indicates that, under plausible assumptions, prior factor-market distortions raise the costs of revenue-neutral environmental policies, despite the potential to use the revenues from environmental taxes to finance cuts in the marginal rates of preexisting factor taxes. It also shows that prior factor taxes amplify the costs of other environmental policies, including pollution quotas and tradeable pollution permits, relative to what the costs would be in a first-best world.

Two effects underlie these results. The *tax-interaction effect* is the adverse impact in factor markets arising from reductions in after-tax returns to factors (labor) brought about by environmental regulation. In a world with prior taxes on factors, this effect leads to significantly higher costs of regulation relative to what would apply in a first-best world with no preexisting taxes. By generating revenues and using them to reduce preexisting tax rates, pollution taxes and auctioned pollution permits exploit a *revenue-recycling effect* that offsets some of the tax-interaction effect. In contrast, pollution quotas and grandfathered permits enjoy no such offset. Thus the costs of achieving given reductions in pollution are higher under these latter policies.

Even when they take advantage of the revenue-recycling effect, pollution abatement policies through pollution taxes or auctioned permits generally entail positive gross costs. If the good responsible for pollution emissions is an average substitute for leisure, the revenue-recycling effect only partly offsets the gross costs attributable to the tax-interaction effect. This implies that pollution-abatement through these policies is more costly in a second-best setting than it would be in a first-best world, and that the double dividend claim (in its strong form) is not upheld.

---

[40]Several studies suggest that the marginal climate-related damages increase with CO_2 concentrations. If this is the case, and if CO_2 concentrations increase through time, then marginal damages from CO_2 emissions (or marginal benefits from CO_2 emissions abatement) will increase over time. Under such circumstances the prospects for efficiency gains under a quota policy improve with time.

The interactions with factor markets affect the choice among alternative policy instruments. In particular, they put pollution quotas and grandfathered pollution permits at a serious efficiency disadvantage relative to revenue-raising policies whose revenues finance reductions in the marginal rates of existing taxes. Indeed, if the marginal environmental benefits from pollution reductions are below a certain threshold value, then *any* level of pollution abatement through quotas or grandfathered permits is efficiency-reducing. These results emerge from simple analytical models and are confirmed by numerical investigations in specific regulatory contexts.

In recognizing the efficiency advantages of these pollution-tax and auctioned-permit policies over policies involving pollution quotas or grandfathered permits, one should not lose sight of related equity issues. The decision whether to exploit the revenue-recycling effect fundamentally affects the distribution of wealth between taxpayers, on the one hand, and owners and employees of polluting firms, on the other. Clearly, there are important equity issues associated with the differences in distribution. The second-best considerations raised in this paper do not reduce the importance of the equity issues, but at the same time they indicate that the efficiency costs of forgoing the redistribution toward taxpayers are greater than what would be suggested by a first-best analysis.

The tax-interaction effect is relevant to government regulation outside the environmental area. To the extent that government regulations of international trade or agricultural production raise the costs of output and thereby reduce real factor returns, these regulations exacerbate the labor market distortions from preexisting taxes and thus involve higher social costs than would be indicated by partial equilibrium analyses.[41]

REFERENCES

Ballard, Charles, L., John B. Shoven, and John Whalley, 1985. "General Equilibrium Computations of the Marginal Welfare Costs of Taxes in the U.S." *American Economic Review* 75(1):128–38.

Bovenberg, A. Lans, 1996. "Environmental Policy, Distortionary Labor Taxation, and Employment: Pollution Taxes and the Double Dividend." In Carlo Carraro, Yiannis Katsoulacos, and Anastasios Xepapadeas, eds., *Environmental Policy and Market Structure*. Dordrecht: Kluwer Academic Publishers.

Bovenberg, A. Lans, and Ruud A. de Mooij, 1994a. "Environmental Levies and Distortionary Taxation." *American Economic Review* 84(4):1085–9.

Bovenberg, A. Lans, and Ruud A. de Mooij, 1994b. "Environmental Taxation and Labor Market Distortions." *European Journal of Political Economy* 10(4):655–83.

Bovenberg, A. Lans, and Ruud A. de Mooij, 1996. "Environmental Taxation and the Double-Dividend: The Role of Factor Substitution and Capital Mobility." In C.

---

[41]Similarly, Browning (1997) finds that monopoly pricing exacerbates preexisting distortions in factor markets. Hence the efficiency costs of monopoly pricing increase with the magnitude of preexisting factor tax rates. Browning estimates that monopoly pricing in the U.S. is ten times more costly than it would be in the absence of prior factor taxes.

Carraro and D. Siniscalco, eds., *Environmental Fiscal Reform and Unemployment*. Dordrecht: Kluwer.

Bovenberg, A. Lans, and Lawrence H. Goulder, 1996. "Optimal Environmental Taxation in the Presence of Other Taxes: General Equilibrium Analyses." *American Economic Review*, September.

Bovenberg, A. Lans, and Lawrence H. Goulder, 1997. "Costs of Environmentally Motivated Taxes in the Presence of Other Taxes: General Equilibrium Analyses." *National Tax Journal*, forthcoming March 1997.

Bovenberg, A. Lans, and Lawrence H. Goulder, 1999. "Environmental Taxation." In A. Auerbach and M. Feldstein, eds., *Handbook of Public Economics*. New York: North Holland, forthcoming.

Bovenberg, A. Lans, and F. van der Ploeg, 1994. "Environmental Policy, Public Finance, and the Labour Market in a Second-Best World." *Journal of Public Economics* 55:349–70.

Browning, E. K., 1997. "The Welfare Cost of Monopoly and Other Output Distortions." *Journal of Public Economics*, 66:127–44.

Browning, E. K., 1987. "On the Marginal Welfare Cost of Taxation." *American Economic Review* 77:11–23.

Burtraw, Dallas, 1996. "The SO_2 Emissions Trading Program: Cost Savings Without Allowance Trades," *Contemporary Economic Policy*, vol. XIV, no. 2 (April), 79–94.

Ellerman, A. Denny, and Juan Pablo Montero, 1996. "Why Are Allowance Prices So Low? An Analysis of the SO_2 Emissions Trading Program," CEEPR 96-001, Massachusetts Institute of Technology (February).

Fankhauser, Samuel, 1994. "The Social Costs of Greenhouse Gas Emissions: An Expected Value Approach." *The Energy Journal* 15:157–84.

Fullerton, Don, and J. Mackie, 1987. "Investment Allocation and Growth under the Tax Reform Act of 1986." *In Compendium of Tax Research 1987*, Office of Tax Analysis of the U.S. Department of the Treasury, Washington, D.C., pp. 131–171.

Fullerton, Don and Gilbert Metcalf, 1997. "Environmental Controls, Scarcity Rents, and Pre-Existing Distortions." NBER Working paper 6091, July.

Goulder, Lawrence H., 1995a. "Environmental Taxation and the 'Double Dividend': A Reader's Guide." *International Tax and Public Finance* 2(2):157–183.

Goulder, Lawrence H., 1995b. "Effects of Carbon Taxes in an Economy with Prior Tax Distortions: An Intertemporal General Equilibrium Analysis," *Journal of Environmental Economics and Management*, October.

Goulder, Lawrence H., 1998. "Environmental Policy Making in a Second-Best Setting," *Journal of Applied Economics*, 1(2).

Goulder, Lawrence H., Ian W. H. Parry, and Dallas Burtraw, 1997. "Revenue-Raising vs. Other Approaches to Environmental Protection: The Critical Significance of Pre-Existing Tax Distortions." *RAND Journal of Economics*, Winter.

Goulder, Lawrence H., Ian W. H. Parry, Roberton C. Williams III, and Dallas Burtraw, 1999. "The Cost-Effectiveness of Alternative Instruments for Environmental Protection in a Second-best Setting." *Journal of Public Economics* 72(3):329–60.

Goulder, Lawrence H., and Philippe Thalmann, 1993. "Approaches to Efficient Capital Taxation: Leveling the Playing Field vs. Living by the Golden Rule." *Journal of Public Economics* 50:169–96.

Hall, Robert, 1988. "Intertemporal Substitution in Consumption," *Journal of Political Economy* 96(2):339–57.

Jorgenson, Dale W. and Peter J. Wilcoxen, 1990. "Environmental Regulation and U.S. Economic Growth," *RAND Journal of Economics* 21(2), 314–340.

Jorgenson, Dale W. and Peter J. Wilcoxen, 1996. "Reducing U.S. Carbon Emissions: An Econometric General Equilibrium Assessment." In Darius Gaskins and John Weyant, eds., *Reducing Global Carbon Dioxide Emissions: Costs and Policy Options*. Energy Modeling Forum, Stanford University, Stanford, Calif.

Jorgenson, Dale, and Kun-Young Yun, 1990. "Tax Policy and the Cost of Capital." Oxford: Oxford University Press.

Lawrence, Emily, 1991, "Poverty and the Rate of Time Preference: Evidence from Panel Data," *Journal of Political Economy* 99(1):54–77.

Lee, Dwight R., and Walter S. Misiolek, 1986. "Substituting Pollution Taxation for General Taxation: Some Implications for Efficiency in Pollution Taxation." *Journal of Environmental Economics and Management* 13:338–347.

Lucas, Robert E., 1990. "Supply-Side Economics: An Analytical Review." *Oxford Economic Papers* 42:293–316.

Ng, Y. K., 1980. "Optimal Corrective Taxes or Subsidies when Revenue-Raising Imposes an Excess Burden." *American Economic Review* 70:744–51.

Nordhaus, William D., 1991. "To Slow or Not to Slow: The Economics of the Greenhouse Effect." *The Economic Journal* 101:920–37.

Oates, Wallace E., 1993. "Pollution Charges as a Source of Public Revenues." In Herbert Giersch, ed., *Economic Progress and Environmental Concerns*. Berlin: Springer-Verlag, pp. 135–52.

Oates, Wallace E., 1995. "Green Taxes: Can We Protect the Environment and Improve the Tax System at the Same Time?" *Southern Economic Journal* 61(4):914–922.

Oates, Wallace E., and Robert M. Schwab, 1988. "Economic Competition among Jurisdictions: Efficiency Enhancing or Distortion Inducing?" *Journal of Public Economics* 35:333–354, April.

Oates, Wallace E., and Diana L. Strassmann, 1984. "Effluent Fees and Market Structure." *Journal of Public Economics* 24:29–46.

Parry, Ian W. H., 1995. "Pollution Taxes and Revenue Recycling." *Journal of Environmental Economics and Management* 29:S64–S77.

Parry, Ian W. H., 1997. "Environmental Taxes and Quotas in the Presence of Distorting Taxes in Factor Markets." *Resource and Energy Economics* 19:203–220.

Parry, Ian W. H., Roberton Williams, and Lawrence H. Goulder, 1999. "When Can Carbon Abatement Policies Increase Welfare? The Fundamental Role of Distorted Factor Markets." *Journal of Environmental Economics and Management* 37:52–84.

Peck, Stephen C. and Thomas J. Teisberg, 1993. "Global Warming Uncertainties and the Value of Information: An Analysis Using CETA." *Resource and Energy Economics* 15:71–98.

Pigou, A. C., 1938. *The Economics of Welfare* (4th edition). London: Weidenfeld and Nicolson.

Proost, S., and D. van Regemorter, 1995. "The Double Dividend and the Role of Inequality Aversion and Macroeconomic Regimes." *International Tax and Public Finance* 2(2), August.

Repetto, Robert, Roger C. Dower, Robin Jenkins, and Jacqueline Geoghegan, 1992. *Green Fees: How a Tax Shift Can Work for the Environment and the Economy*. World Resources Institute, November.

Sandmo, Agnar, 1975. "Optimal Taxation in the Presence of Externalities." *Swedish Journal of Economics* 77.

Shackleton, Robert, Michael Shelby, Alex Cristofaro, Roger Brinner, Joyce Yanchar, Lawrence Goulder, Dale Jorgenson, Peter Wilcoxen, and Peter Pauly, 1996. "The Efficiency Value of Carbon Tax Revenues." In Darius Gaskins and John Weyant, eds., *Reducing Global Carbon Dioxide Emissions: Costs and Policy Options*. Stanford, Calif.: Energy Modeling Forum.

Shah, Anwar, and Bjorn Larsen, 1992. "Carbon Taxes, the Greenhouse Effect and Developing Countries," World Bank Policy Research Working Paper Series No. 957, The World Bank, Washington, D.C.

Stavins, Robert N., 1995. "Transactions Costs and Tradeable Permits." *Journal of Environmental Economics and Management* 29, 133–147.

Terkla, David, 1984. "The Efficiency Value of Effluent Tax Revenues." *Journal of Environmental Economics and Management* 11:107–23.

Tietenberg, T. H., 1985. *Emissions Trading: An Exercise In Reforming Pollution Policy*. Washington D.C.: Resources for the Future.

Weitzman, Martin L., 1974. "Prices vs. Quantities." *Review of Economic Studies* 41, 477–491.

Williams, Roberton C. III, 1998. "Revisiting the Cost of Protectionism: The Role of Tax Distortions in the Labor Market." *Journal of International Economics*, forthcoming.

Williams, Roberton C. III, 1999. "Tax-Interactions in a Dynamic Model with Capital Accumulation." Working paper, Stanford University.

18 Economic Prescriptions for Environmental Problems: How the Patient Followed the Doctor's Orders*

Robert W. Hahn

Robert W. Hahn is Resident Scholar at the American Enterprise Institute, and Director of the AEI-Brookings Joint Center for Regulatory Studies.

One of the dangers with ivory tower theorizing is that it is easy to lose sight of the actual set of problems which need to be solved, and the range of potential solutions. As one who frequently engages in this exercise, I can attest to this fact. In my view, this loss of sight has become increasingly evident in the theoretical structure underlying environmental economics, which often emphasizes elegance at the expense of realism.

In this paper, I will argue that both normative and positive theorizing could greatly benefit from a careful examination of the results of recent innovative approaches to environmental management. The particular set of policies examined here involves two tools which have received widespread support from the economics community: marketable permits and emission charges (Pigou, 1932; Dales, 1968; Kneese and Schultze, 1975). Both tools represent ways to induce businesses to search for lower cost methods of achieving environmental standards. They stand in stark contrast to the predominant "command-and-control" approach in which a regulator specifies the technology a firm must use to comply with regulations. Under highly restrictive conditions, it can be shown that both of the economic approaches share the desirable feature that any gains in environmental quality will be obtained at the lowest possible cost (Baumol and Oates, 1975).

Until the 1960s, these tools only existed on blackboards and in academic journals, as products of the fertile imaginations of academics. However, some countries have recently begun to explore using these tools as part of a broader strategy for managing environmental problems.

"Economic Prescriptions for Environmental Problems: How the Patient Followed the Doctor's Orders," by Robert W. Hahn, from *Journal of Economic Perspectives*, 3(2):95–114 (Spring 1989).

*This research was funded by the National Science Foundation and the Program for Technology and Society at Carnegie Mellon University. I would like to thank Gordon Hester, Dan Nagin, and the editors for helpful comments. The views expressed herein are those of the author and do not necessarily reflect the views of the Council of Economic Advisers.

This paper chronicles the experience with both marketable permits and emissions charges. It also provides a selective analysis of a variety of applications in Europe and the United States and shows how the actual use of these tools tends to depart from the role which economists have conceived for them.

The Selection of Environmental Instruments

In thinking about the design and implementation of policies, it is generally assumed that policy makers can choose from a variety of "instruments" for achieving specified objectives. The environmental economics literature generally focuses on the selection of instruments that minimize the overall cost of achieving prescribed environmental objectives.

One instrument which has been shown to supply the appropriate incentives, at least in theory, is marketable permits. The implementation of marketable permits involves several steps. First, a target level of environmental quality is established. Next, this level of environmental quality is defined in terms of total allowable emissions. Permits are then allocated to firms, with each permit enabling the owner to emit a specified amount of pollution. Firms are allowed to trade these permits among themselves. Assuming firms minimize their total production costs, and the market for these permits is competitive, it can be shown that the overall cost of achieving the environmental standard will be minimized (Montgomery, 1972).

Marketable permits are generally thought of as a "quantity" instrument because they ration a fixed supply of a commodity, in this case pollution. The polar opposite of a quantity instrument is a "pricing" instrument, such as emissions charges. The idea underlying emissions charges is to charge polluters a fixed price for each unit of pollution. In this way, they are provided with an incentive to economize on the amount of pollution they produce. If all firms are charged the same price for pollution, then marginal costs of abatement are equated across firms, and this result implies that the resulting level of pollution is reached in a cost-minimizing way.

Economists have attempted to estimate the effectiveness of these approaches. Work by Plott (1983) and Hahn (1983) reveals that implementation of these ideas in a laboratory setting leads to marked increases in efficiency levels over traditional forms of regulation, such as setting standards for each individual source of pollution. The work based on simulations using actual costs and environmental data reveals a similar story. For example, in a review of several studies examining the potential for marketable permits, Tietenberg (1985, pp. 43–44) found that potential control costs could be reduced by more than 90 percent in some cases. Naturally, these results are subject to the usual cautions that a competitive market actually must exist for the results to hold true. Perhaps more importantly, the results assume that it is possible to easily monitor and enforce a system of permits or taxes. The subsequent analysis will suggest that the capacity to monitor and enforce can dramatically affect the choice of instruments.

Following the development of a normative theory of instrument choice, a handful of scholars began to explore reasons why environmental regulations are actually selected. This positive environmental literature tends to emphasize the potential winners and losers from environmental policies as a way of explaining the conditions under which we will observe such policies. For example, Buchanan and Tullock (1975) argue that the widespread use of source-specific standards rather than a fee can be explained by looking at the potential profitability of the affected industry under the two regimes. After presenting the various case studies, I will review some of the insights from positive theory and see how they square with the facts.

The formal results in the positive and normative theory of environmental economics are elegant. Unfortunately, they are not immediately applicable, since virtually none of the systems examined below exhibits the purity of the instruments which are the subject of theoretical inquiry. The presentation here highlights those instruments which show a marked resemblance to marketable permits or emission fees. Together, the two approaches to pollution control span a wide array of environmental problems, including toxic substances, air pollution, water pollution and land disposal.

Marketable Permits

In comparison with charges, marketable permits have not received widespread use. Indeed, there appear to be only four existing environmental applications; three of them in the United States. One involves the trading of emissions rights of various pollutants regulated under the Clean Air Act; a second involves trading of lead used in gasoline; a third addresses the control of water pollution on a river; and a fourth involves air pollution trading in Germany and will not be addressed here because of limited information (see Sprenger, 1986). These programs exhibit dramatic differences in performance, which can be traced back to the rules used to implement these approaches.

Wisconsin Fox River Water Permits

In 1981, the state of Wisconsin implemented an innovative program aimed at controlling biological oxygen demand (BOD) on a part of the Fox River (Novotny, 1986, p. 11).[1] The program was designed to allow for the limited trading of marketable discharge permits. The primary objective was to

---

[1]BOD is a measure of the demand for dissolved oxygen imposed on a water body by organic effluents.

allow firms greater flexibility in abatement options while still maintaining environmental quality. The program is administered by the state of Wisconsin in accord with the Federal Water Pollution Control Act. Firms are issued five-year permits which define their wasteload allocation. This allocation defines the initial distribution of permits for each firm.

Early studies estimated that substantial savings, on the order of $7 million per year, could result after implementing this trading system (O'Neil, 1983, p. 225). However, actual cost savings have been minimal. In the six years that the program has been in existence, there has been only one trade. Given the initial fanfare about this system, its performance to date has been disappointing.

A closer look at the nature of the market and the rules for trading reveals that the result should not have been totally unexpected. The regulations are aimed at two types of dischargers: pulp and paper plants and municipal waste treatment plants. David and Joeres (1983) note that the pulp and paper plants have an oligopolistic structure, and thus may not behave as competitive firms in the permit market. Moreover, it is difficult to know how the municipal utilities will perform under this set of rules, since they are subject to public utility regulation (Hahn and Noll, 1983). Trading is also limited by location. There are two points on the river where pollution tends to peak, and firms are divided into "clusters" so that trading will not increase BOD at either of these points. There are only about 6 or 7 firms in each cluster (Patterson, 1987). Consequently, markets for wasteload allocations may be quite thin.

In addition, Novotny (1986) has argued that several restrictions on transfers may have had a negative impact on potential trading. Any transaction between firms requires modifying or reissuing permits. Transfers must be for at least a year; however, the life of the permit is only five years. Moreover, parties must waive any rights to the permit after it expires, and it is unclear how trading will affect the permit renewal process. These conditions create great uncertainty over the future value of the property right. Added to the problems created by these rules are the restrictions on eligibility for trades. Firms are required to justify the "need" for permits. This effectively limits transfers to new dischargers, plants which are expanding, and treatment plants that cannot meet the requirements, despite their best efforts. Trades that only reduce operating costs are not allowed. With all the uncertainty and high transactions costs, it is not surprising that trading has gotten off to a very slow start.

While the marketable permit system for the Fox River was being hailed as a success by economists, the paper mills did not enthusiastically support the idea (Novotny, 1986, p. 15). Nor have the mills chosen to explore this option once it has been implemented. Indeed, by almost any measure, this limited permit trading represents a minor part of the regulatory structure. The mechanism builds on a large regulatory infrastructure where permits specifying treatment and operating rules lie at the center. The new marketable permits approach retains many features of the existing standards-based approach. The initial allocations are based on the status quo, calling for equal percentage reductions from specified limits. This "grand-fathering" approach has a great deal of political appeal for existing firms. New firms must continue to meet more stringent requirements than old firms, and firms must meet specified technological standards before trading is allowed.

Emissions Trading

By far the most significant and far-reaching marketable permit program in the United States is the emissions trading policy. Started over a decade ago, the policy attempts to provide greater flexibility to firms charged with controlling air pollutant emissions.[2] Because the program represents a radical departure in the approach to pollution regulation, it has come under close scrutiny by a variety of interest groups. Environmentalists have been particularly critical. These criticisms notwithstanding, the Environmental Protection Agency Administrator Lee Thomas (1986) characterized the program as "one of EPA's most impressive accomplishments."

Emissions trading has four distinct elements. Netting, the first program element, was introduced in 1974. Netting allows a firm which creates a new source of emissions in a plant to avoid the stringent emission limits which would normally apply by reducing emissions from another source in the plant. Thus, net emissions from the plant do not increase significantly. A firm using netting is only allowed to obtain the necessary emission credits from its own sources. This is called *internal trading* because the transaction involves only one firm. Netting is subject to approval at the state level, not the federal.

Offsets, the second element of emissions trading, are used by new emission sources in "non-attainment areas." (A non-attainment area is a region which has not met a specified ambient standard.) The Clean Air Act specified that no new emission sources would be allowed in non-attainment areas after the original 1975 deadlines for meeting air quality standards passed. Concern that this prohibition would stifle economic growth in these areas prompted EPA to institute the offset rule. This rule specified that new sources would be allowed to locate in non-attainment areas, but only if they "offset" their new emissions by reducing emissions from existing sources by even larger amounts. The offsets could be obtained through internal trading, just as with netting. However, they could also be obtained from other firms directly, which is called *external trading.*

Bubbles, though apparently considered by EPA to be the centerpiece of emissions trading, were not allowed until 1979. The name derives from the placing of an imaginary bubble over a plant, with all emissions exiting at a single point from the bubble. A bubble allows a firm to sum the emission limits from individual sources of a pollutant in a plant, and to adjust

---

[2]Pollutants covered under the policy include volatile organic compounds, carbon monoxide, sulfur dioxide, particulates, and nitrogen oxides (Hahn and Hester, 1986).

the levels of control applied to different sources as long as this aggregate limit is not exceeded. Bubbles apply to existing sources. The policy allows for both internal and external trades. Initially, every bubble had to be approved at the federal level as an amendment to a state's implementation plan. In 1981, EPA approved a "generic rule" for bubbles in New Jersey which allowed the state to give final approval for bubbles. Since then, several other states have followed suit.

Banking, the fourth element of emissions trading, was developed in conjunction with the bubble policy. Banking allows firms to save emission reductions above and beyond permit requirements for future use in emissions trading. While EPA action was initially required to allow banking, the development of banking rules and the administration of banking programs has been left to the states.

The performance of emissions trading can be measured in several ways. A summary evaluation which assesses the impact of the program on abatement costs and environmental quality is provided in Table 1. For each emissions trading activity, an estimate of cost savings, the environmental quality effect, and the number of trades is given. In each case, the estimates are for the entire life of the program. As can be seen from the table, the level of activity under various programs varies dramatically. More netting transactions have taken place than any other type, but all of these have necessarily been internal. The wide range placed on this estimate, 5000 to 12,000, reflects the uncertainty about the precise level of this activity. An estimated 2000 offset transactions have taken place, of which only 10 per-

Table 1 Summary of Emissions Trading Activity

Activity	Estimated Number of Internal Transactions	Estimated Number of External Transactions	Estimated Cost Savings (millions)	Environmental Quality Impact
Netting	5,000 to 12,000	None	$25 to $300 in Permitting costs: $500 to $12,000 in emission control costs	Insignificant in individual cases; Probably insignificant in aggregate
Offsets	1800	200	See text	Probably insignificant
Bubbles:				
Federally approved	40	2	$300	Insignificant
State approved	89	0	$135	Insignificant
Banking	< 100	< 20	Small	Insignificant

Source: Hahn and Hester (1986)

cent have been external. Fewer than 150 bubbles have been approved. Of these, almost twice as many have been approved by states under generic rules than have been approved at the federal level, and only two are known to have involved external trades. For banking, the figures listed are for the number of times firms have withdrawn banked emission credits for sale or use. While no estimates of the exact numbers of such transactions can be made, upper bound estimates of 100 for internal trades and 20 for external trades indicate the fact that there has been relatively little activity in this area.

Cost savings for both netting and bubbles are substantial. Netting is estimated to have resulted in the most cost savings, with a total of between $525 million to over $12 billion from both permitting and emissions control cost savings.[3] By allowing new or modified sources to locate in areas that are highly polluted, offsets confer a major economic benefit on firms which use them. While the size of this economic benefit is not easily estimated, it is probably in the hundreds of millions of dollars. Federally approved bubbles have resulted in savings estimated at $300 million, while state bubbles have resulted in an estimated $135 million in cost savings. Average savings from federal approved bubbles are higher than those for state approved bubbles. Average savings from bubbles are higher than those from netting, which reflects the fact that bubble savings may be derived from several emissions sources in a single transaction, while netting usually involves cost savings at a single source. Finally, the cost savings from the use of banking cannot be estimated, but is necessarily small given the small number of banking transactions which have occurred.

The performance evaluation of emissions trading activities reveals a mixed bag of accomplishments and disappointments. The program has clearly afforded many firms flexibility in meeting emission limits, and this flexibility has resulted in significant aggregate cost savings—in the billions of dollars. However, these cost savings have been realized almost entirely from internal trading. They fall far short of the potential savings which could be realized if there were more external trading. While cost savings have been substantial, the program has led to little or no net change in the level of emissions.

The evolution of the emissions trading can best be understood in terms of a struggle over the nature and distribution of property rights. Emissions trading can be seen as a strategy by regulators to provide industry with increased flexibility while offering environmentalists continuing progress toward environmental quality goals. Meeting these two objectives requires a careful balancing act. To provide industry with greater flexibility, EPA has attempted to define a set of property rights that places for restrictions on their use. However, at the same time, EPA has to be sensitive to the concerns of environmentalists and avoid giving businesses too clear a property right to their existing level of pollution. The conflicting interests of these

---

[3]The wide range of this estimate reflects the uncertainty which results from the fact that little information has been collected on netting.

two groups have led regulators to create a set of policies which are specifically designed to deemphasize the explicit nature of the property right. The high transactions costs associated with external trading have induced firms to eschew this option in favor of internal trading or not trading at all.

Like the preceding example of the Fox River, emissions trading is best viewed as an incremental departure from the existing approach. Property rights were grandfathered. Most trading has been internal, and the structure of the Clean Air Act, including its requirement that new sources be controlled more stringently, was largely left intact.

Lead Trading

Lead trading stands in stark contrast to the preceding two marketable permit approaches. It comes by far the closest to an economist's ideal of a freely functioning market. The purpose of the lead trading program was to allow gasoline refiners greater flexibility during a period when the amount of lead in gasoline was being significantly reduced. (For a more detailed analysis of the performance of the lead trading program, see Hahn and Hester, 1987.)

Unlike many other programs, the lead trading program was scheduled to have a fixed life from the outset. Interrefinery trading of lead credits was permitted in 1982. Banking of lead credits was initiated in 1985. The trading program was terminated at the end of 1987. Initially, the period for trading was defined in terms of quarters. No banking of credits was allowed. Three years after initiating the program limited banking was allowed, which allowed firms to carry over rights to subsequent quarters. Banking has been used extensively by firms since its initiation.

The program is notable for its lack of discrimination among different sources, such as new and old sources. It is also notable for its rules regarding the creation of credits. Lead credits are created on the basis of existing standards. A firm does not gain any extra credits for being a large producer of leaded gasoline in the past. Nor is it penalized for being a small producer. The creation of lead credits is based solely on current production levels and average lead content. For example if the standard were 1.1 grams per gallon, and a firm produces 100 gallons of gasoline, it would receive rights entitling it to produce or sell up to 110 (100×1.1) grams of lead. To the extent that current production levels are correlated with past production levels, the system acknowledges the existing distribution of property rights. However, this linkage is less explicit than those made in other trading programs.[4]

The success of the program is difficult to measure directly. It appears to have had very little impact on environmental quality. This is because the

---

[4]One of the reasons EPA set up the allocation rule in this way was to try to transfer some of the permit rents from producers to consumers. This will not always occur, however, and depends on the structure of the permits market as well as the underlying production functions.

amount of lead in gasoline is routinely reported by refiners and is easily monitored. The effect the program has had on refinery costs is not readily available. In proposing the rule for banking of lead rights, EPA estimated that resulting savings to refiners would be approximately $228 million (U.S. EPA, 1985a). Since banking activity has been somewhat higher than anticipated by EPA, it is likely that actual cost savings will exceed this amount. No specific estimate of the actual cost savings resulting from lead trading have been made by EPA.

The level of trading activity has been high, far surpassing levels observed in other environmental markets. In 1985, over half of the refineries participated in trading. Approximately 15 percent of the total lead rights used were traded. Approximately 35 percent of available lead rights were banked for future use or trading (U.S. EPA, 1985b, 1986). In comparison, volumes of emissions trading have averaged well below 1 percent of the potential emissions that could have been traded.

From the standpoint of creating a workable regulatory mechanism that induces cost savings, the lead market has to be viewed as a success. Refiners, though initially lukewarm about this alternative, have made good use of this program. It stands out amidst a stream of incentive-based programs as the "noble" exception in that it conforms most closely to the economists' notion of a smoothly functioning market.

Given the success of this market in promoting cost savings over a period in which lead was being reduced, it is important to understand why the market was successful. The lead market had two important features which distinguished it from other markets in environmental credits. The first was that the amount of lead in gasoline could be easily monitored with the existing regulatory apparatus. The second was that the program was implemented after agreement had been reached about basic environmental goals. In particular, there was already widespread agreement that lead was to be phased out of gasoline. This suggests that the success in lead trading may not be easily transferred to other applications in which monitoring is a problem, or environmental goals are poorly defined. Nonetheless, the fact that this market worked well provides ammunition for proponents of market-based incentives for environmental regulation.

New Directions for Marketable Permits

An interesting potential application for marketable permits has arisen in the area of nonpoint source pollution.[5] In 1984, Colorado implemented a program which would allow limited trading between point and nonpoint sources for controlling phosphorous loadings in Dillon Reservoir (Elmore et al., 1984). Firms receive an allocation based on their past production and the holding capacity of the lake. At this time, no trading between point and nonpoint sources has occurred.

---

[5]Point sources represent sources which are well-defined, such as a factory smokestack. Nonpoint sources refer to sources whose emission points are not readily identified, such as fertilizer runoff from farms.

As in the case of the Fox river program, point sources are required to make use of the latest technology before they are allowed to trade. The conventional permitting system is used as a basis for trading. Moreover, trades between point and nonpoint sources are required to take place on a 2 for 1 basis. This means for each gram of phosphorous emitted from a point source under a trade, two grams must be reduced from a nonpoint source. Annual cost savings are projected to be about $800,000 (Kashmanian et al., 1986, p. 14); however, projected savings are not always a good indicator of actual savings, as was illustrated in the case of the Fox River.

EPA is also considering using marketable permits as a way of promoting efficiency in the control of chlorofluorocarbons and halons which lead to the depletion of stratospheric ozone.[6] In its notice of proposed rule-making, EPA suggested grandfathering permits to producers based on their 1986 production levels, and allowing them to be freely traded. This approach is similar to earlier approaches which the agency adopted for emissions trading and lead trading.

The applications covered in this section illustrate that there are a rich array of mechanisms that come under the heading of marketable permits. The common element seems to be that the primary motivation behind marketable permits is to provide increased flexibility in meeting prescribed environmental objectives. This flexibility, in turn, allows firms to take advantage of opportunities to reduce their expenditures on pollution control without sacrificing environmental quality. However, the rules of the marketable permits can sometimes be so restrictive that the flexibility they offer is more imaginary than real.

Charges in Practice

Charge systems in four countries are examined. Examples are drawn from France, Germany, the Netherlands, and the United States. Particular systems were selected because they were thought to be significant either in their scope, their effect on revenues, or their impact on the cost effectiveness of environmental regulation. While the focus is on water effluent charges, a variety of systems are briefly mentioned at the end of this section which cover other applications.

Charges in France

The French have had a system of effluent charges on water pollutants in place since 1969 (Bower et al., 1981). The system is primarily designed to raise revenues which are then used to help maintain or improve water qual-

---

[6]EPA's decision to use a market-based approach to limit stratospheric ozone depletion is examined in Hahn and McGartland (1988).

ity. Though the application of charges is widespread, they are generally set at low levels.[7] Moreover, charges are rarely based on actual performance. Rather, they are based on the expected level of discharge by various industries. There is no explicit connection between the charge paid by a given discharger and the subsidy received for reducing discharges (Bower et al., 1981, p. 126). However, charges are generally earmarked for use in promoting environmental quality in areas related to the specific charge. The basic mechanism by which these charges improve environmental quality is through judicious earmarking of the revenues for pollution abatement activities.

In evaluating the charge system, it is important to understand that it is a major, but by no means dominant, part of the French system for managing water quality. Indeed, in terms of total revenues, a sewage tax levied on households and commercial enterprises is larger in magnitude (Bower et al., 1981, p. 142). Moreover, the sewage tax is assessed on the basis of actual volumes of water used. Like most other charge systems, the charge system in France is based on a system of water quality permits, which places constraints on the type and quantity of effluent a firm may discharge. These permits are required for sources discharging more than some specified quantity (Bower et al., 1981, p. 130).

Charges now appear to be accepted as a way of doing business in France. They provide a significant source of revenues for water quality control. One of the keys to their initial success appears to have been the gradual introduction and raising of charges. Charges started at a very low level and were gradually raised to current levels (Bower et al., 1981, p. 22). Moreover, the pollutants on which charges are levied has expanded considerably since the initial inception of the charge program.[8]

Charges in Germany

The German system of effluent charges is very similar to the French system. Effluent charges cover a wide range of pollutants, and the charges are used to cover administrative expenses for water quality management and to subsidize projects which improve water quality (Brown and Johnson, 1984, p. 934, 939, 945). The bills that industry and municipalities pay are generally based on expected volume and concentration (Brown and Johnson, 1984, p. 934). Charges vary by industry type as well as across municipalities. Charges to industries and municipalities depend on several variables, including size of the municipality, desired level of treatment, and age of equipment (Brown and Johnson, 1984, pp. 934, 938).

Charges have existed in selected areas of Germany for decades (Bower et al., 1981, p. 299). Management of water quality is delegated to local

---

[7]Charges cover a wide variety of pollutants, including suspended solids, biological oxygen demand, chemical oxygen demand, and selected toxic chemicals.

[8]For example, Brown (1984, p. 114) notes that charges for nitrogen and phosphorous were added in 1982.

areas. In 1981, a system of nationwide effluent charges was introduced (Bower et al., 1981, p. 226). The federal government provided the basic framework in its 1976 Federal Water Act and Effluent Charge Law (Brown and Johnson, 1984, p. 930). Initially, industry opposed widespread use of charges. But after losing the initial battle, industry focused on how charges would be determined and their effective date of implementation (Brown and Johnson, 1984, p. 932). While hard data are lacking, there is a general perception that the current system is helping to improve water quality.

Charges in the Netherlands

The Netherlands has had a system of effluent charges in place since 1969 (Brown and Bressers, 1986, p. 4). It is one of the oldest and best administered charge systems, and the charges placed on effluent streams are among the highest. In 1983, the effluent charge per person was $17 in the Netherlands, $6 in Germany, and about $2 in France (Brown and Bressers, 1986, p. 5). Because of the comparatively high level of charges found in the Netherlands, this is a logical place to examine whether charges are having a discernible effect on the level of pollution. Bressers (1983), using a multiple regression approach, argues that charges have made a significant difference for several pollutants. This evidence is also buttressed by surveys of industrial polluters and water board officials which indicate that charges had a significant impact on firm behavior (Brown and Bressers, 1986, pp. 12–13). This analysis is one of the few existing empirical investigations of the effect of effluent charges on resulting pollution.

The purpose of the charge system in the Netherlands is to raise revenue that will be used to finance projects that will improve water quality (Brown and Bressers, 1986, p. 4). Like its counterparts in France and Germany, the approach to managing water quality uses both permits and effluent charges for meeting ambient standards (Brown and Bressers, 1986, p. 2).[9] Permits tend to be uniform across similar discharges. The system is designed to ensure that water quality will remain the same or get better (Brown and Bressers, 1986 p. 2). Charges are administered both on volume and concentration. Actual levels of discharge are monitored for larger polluters, while small polluters often pay fixed fees unrelated to actual discharge (Bressers, 1983, p. 10).

Charges have exhibited a slow but steady increase since their inception (Brown and Bressers, 1986, p. 5). This increase in charges has been correlated with declining levels of pollutants. Effluent discharge declined from 40 population equivalents in 1969 to 15.3 population equivalents in 1980, and it was projected to decline to 4.4 population equivalents in 1985 (Brown and Bressers, 1986, p. 10). Thus, over 15 years, this measure of pollution declined on the order of 90 percent.

---

[9]Emission and effluent standards apply to individual sources of pollution while ambient standards apply to regions such as a lake or an air basin.

As in Germany, there was initial opposition from industry to the use of charges. Brown and Bressers (1986, p. 4) also note opposition from environmentalists, who tend to distrust market-like mechanisms. Nonetheless, charges have enjoyed widespread acceptance in a variety of arenas in the Netherlands.

One final interesting feature of the charge system in the Netherlands relates to the differential treatment of new and old plants. In general, newer plants face more stringent regulation than older plants (Brown and Bressers, 1986, p. 10). As we shall see, this is also a dominant theme in American regulation.

Charges in the United States

The United States has a modest system of user charges levied by utilities that process wastewater, encouraged by federal environmental regulations issued by the Environmental Protection Agency. They are based on both volume and strength, and vary across utilities. In some cases, charges are based on actual discharges, and in others, as a rule of thumb, they are related to average behavior. In all cases, charges are added to the existing regulatory system which relies heavily on permits and standards.

Both industry and consumers are required to pay the charges. The primary purpose for the charges is to raise revenues to help meet the revenue requirements of the treatment plants, which are heavily subsidized by the federal government. The direct environmental and economic impact of these charges is apparently small (Boland, 1986, p. 12). They primarily serve as a mechanism to help defray the costs of the treatment plants. Thus, the charges used in the United States are similar in spirit to the German and French systems already described. However, their size appears to be smaller, and the application of the revenues is more limited.

Other Fee-Based Systems and Lessons

There are a variety of other fee-based systems which have not been included in this discussion. Brown (1984) did an analysis of incentive-based systems to control hazardous wastes in Europe and found that a number of countries had adopted systems, some of which had a marked economic effect. The general trend was to use either a tax on waste outputs or tax on feedstocks that are usually correlated with the level of waste produced. Companies and government officials were interviewed to ascertain the effects of these approaches. In line with economic theory, charges were found to induce firms to increase expenditures on achieving waste reduction through a variety of techniques including reprocessing of materials, treatment, and input and output substitution. Firms also devoted greater attention to separating waste streams because prices for disposal often varied by the type of waste stream.

The United States has a diverse range of taxes imposed on hazardous waste streams. Several states have land disposal taxes in place. Charges exhibit a wide degree of variation across states. For example, in 1984, charges were \$14/tonne in Wisconsin and \$70.40/tonne in Minnesota (U.S. CBO, 1985, p. 82). Charges for disposal at landfills also vary widely. The effect of these different charges is very difficult to estimate because of the difficulty in obtaining the necessary data on the quantity and quality of waste streams, as well as the economic variables.

The preceding analysis reveals that there are a wide array of fee-based systems in place designed to promote environmental quality. In a few cases, the fees were shown to have a marked effect on firm behavior; however, in the overwhelming majority of cases studied, the direct economic effect of fees appears to have been small. Several patterns repeat themselves through these examples.

First, the major motivation for implementing emission fees is to raise revenues, which are then usually earmarked for activities which promote environmental quality.[10] Second, most charges are not large enough to have a dramatic impact on the behavior of polluters. In fact, they are not designed to have such an effect. They are relatively low and not directly related to the behavior of individual firms and consumers. Third, there is a tendency for charges to increase faster than inflation over time. Presumably, starting out with a relatively low charge is a way of testing the political waters as well as determining whether the instrument will have the desired effects.

Implementing Market-Based Environmental Programs

An examination of the charge and marketable permits schemes reveals that they are rarely, if ever, introduced in their textbook form. Virtually all environmental regulatory systems using charges and marketable permits rely on the existing permitting system. This result should not be terribly surprising. Most of these approaches were not implemented from scratch; rather, they were grafted onto regulatory systems in which permits and standards play a dominant role.

Perhaps as a result of these hybrid approaches, the level of cost savings resulting from implementing charges and marketable permits is generally far below their theoretical potential. Cost savings can be defined in terms of the savings which would result from meeting a prescribed environmental objective in a less costly manner. As noted, most of the charges to date have not had a major incentive effect. We can infer from this that polluters have not been induced to search for a lower cost mix of meeting environmental objectives as a result of the implementation of charge schemes. Thus, it seems unlikely that charges have performed terribly well

---

[10]The actual application of fees is similar in spirit to the more familiar deposit-refund approaches that are used for collecting bottles and cans.

on narrow efficiency grounds. The experience on marketable permits is similar. Hahn and Hester (1986) argue that cost savings for emissions trading fall far short of their theoretical potential. The only apparent exception to this observation is the lead trading program, which has enjoyed very high levels of trading activity.

The example of lead trading leads to another important observation; in general, different charge and marketable permit systems exhibit wide variation in their effect on economic efficiency. On the whole, there is more evidence for cost savings with marketable permits than with charges.

While the charge systems and marketable permit systems rarely perform well in terms of efficiency, it is important to recognize that their performance is broadly consistent with economic theory. This observation may appear to contradict what was said earlier about the departure of these systems from the economic ideal. However, it is really an altogether different observation. It suggests that the performance of the markets and charge systems can be understood in terms of basic economic theory. For example, where barriers to trading are low, more trading is likely to occur. Where charges are high and more directly related to individual actions, they are more likely to affect the behavior of firms or consumers.

If these instruments are to be measured by their effect on environmental quality, the results are not very impressive. In general, the direct effect of both charges and marketable permits on environmental quality appears to be neutral or slightly positive. The effect of lead trading has been neutral in the aggregate. The effect of emissions trading on environmental quality has probably been neutral or slightly positive. The direct effect of charges on polluter incentives has been modest, although the indirect environmental effect of spending the revenue raised by charges has been significant.

The evidence on charges and marketable permits points to an intriguing conclusion about the nature of these instruments. Charges and marketable permits have played fundamentally different roles in meeting environmental objectives. Charges are used primarily to improve environmental quality by redistributing revenues. Marketable permits are used primarily to promote cost savings.

The positive theory of instrument choice as it relates to pollution control has been greatly influenced by the work of Buchanan and Tullock (1975). They argue that firms will prefer emission standards to emission taxes because standards result in higher profits. Emission standards serve as a barrier to entry to new firms, thus raising firm profits. Charges, on the other hand, do not preclude entry by new firms, and also represent an additional cost to firms. Their argument is based on the view that industry is able to exert its preference for a particular instrument because it is more likely to be well-organized than consumers.

While this argument is elegant, it misses two important points. The first is that within particular classes of instruments, there is a great deal of variation in the performance of instruments. The second is that most solutions to problems involve the application of multiple instruments. Thus, while the Buchanan and Tullock theory explains why standards are chosen over an idealized form of taxes, it does little to help explain the rich array of instruments that are observed in the real world. In particular, under what situations would we be likely to observe different mixes of instruments? Several authors have explored these different issues for instrument choice within this basic framework (Coelho, 1976; Dewees, 1983; Yohe, 1976). The basic insight of this work is that the argument that standards will be preferred to taxes depends on the precise nature of the instruments being compared.

Another weakness in the existing theory is that the instruments are not generally used in the way that is suggested by the theory. Most emissions charges, for example, are used as a revenue raising device for subsidizing abatement activity, but a few also have pronounced direct effects on polluters. Most marketable permit approaches are not really designed to create markets. Moreover, the different Types of trading schemes perform with widely varying success.

The data from the examples given earlier can be used to begin to piece together some of the elements of a more coherent theory of instrument choice. For example, it is clear that distributional concerns play an important role in the acceptability of user charges. The revenue from such charges is usually earmarked for environmental activities related to those contributions. Thus, charges from a noise surcharge will be used to address noise pollution. Charges for water discharges will be used to construct treatment plants and subsidize industry in building equipment to abate water pollution. This pattern suggests that different industries want to make sure that their contributions are used to address pollution problems for which they are likely to be held accountable. Thus, industry sees it as only fair that, as a whole, they get some benefit from making these contributions.

The "recycling" of revenues from charges points up the importance of the existing distribution of property rights. This is also true in the case of marketable permits. The "grandfathering" of rights to existing firms based on the current distribution of rights is an important focal point in many applications of limited markets in pollution rights (Rolph, 1983; Welch, 1983). All the marketable permit programs in the United States place great importance on the existing distribution of rights.

In short, all of the charge and marketable permit systems described earlier place great importance on the status quo. Charges, when introduced, tend to be phased in. Marketable permits, when introduced, usually are optional in the sense that existing firms can meet standards through trading of permits or by conventional means. In contrast, new or expanding firms are not always afforded the same options. For example, new firms must still purchase emission credits if they choose to locate in a non-attainment area, even if they have purchased state-of-the-art pollution control equipment and will pollute less than existing companies. This is an example of a "bias" against new sources. While not efficient from an economic viewpoint, this pattern is consistent with the political insight that new sources don't "vote" while existing sources do.

Though the status quo is important in all applications studied here, it does not explain by itself the rich variety of instruments that are observed. For example, there has been heated controversy over emissions trading since its inception, but comparatively little controversy over the implementation of lead trading. How can economists begin to understand the difference in attitudes towards these two programs?

There are several important differences between emissions trading and lead trading. In the case of lead standards, there appears to be agreement about the distribution of property rights, and the standard that defined them. Refiners had the right to put lead in gasoline at specified levels during specified time periods. Lead in gasoline was reduced to a very low level at the end of 1987. In contrast to lead, there is great disagreement about the underlying distribution of property rights regarding emissions trading. Environmentalists continue to adhere to the symbolic goal of zero pollution. Industry believes and acts as if its current claims on the environment, without any emission reductions, represent a property right.

In the case of lead trading, output could be relatively easily monitored using the existing regulatory apparatus. This was not the case for emissions trading. A new system was set up for evaluating proposed trades. This was, in part, due to existing weaknesses in the current system of monitoring and enforcements. It was also a result of concerns that environmentalists had expressed about the validity of such trades.

The effect that emissions trading was likely to have on environmental quality was much less certain than that of the lead trading program. Some environmentalists viewed emissions trading as a loophole by which industry could forestall compliance, and Hahn and Hester (1986) found some evidence that bubbles were occasionally used for that purpose. The effects of lead trading were much more predictable. Until 1985, there was no banking, so the overall temporal pattern of lead emissions remained unchanged under the program. With the addition of banking in 1985, this pattern was changed slightly, but within well-defined limits.

To accommodate these differing concerns, different rules were developed for the two cases. In the cases of lead trading, rights are traded on a one-for-one basis. In contrast, under emissions trading, rights are not generally traded on a one-for-one basis. Rather, most trades must show a net improvement in environmental quality. In the case of lead, all firms are treated equally from the standpoint of trading. In the case of emissions trading, new firms must meet stringent standards before being allowed to engage in trading.

This comparison suggests that it is possible to gain important insights into the likely performance and choice of instruments by understanding the forces that led to their creation. Analyzing the underlying beliefs about property rights to pollution may be vital both for the political success of the measure and for how well it works in terms of pure economic efficiency.

This view of efficiency is similar to, but should not be confused with, the notion of efficiency advanced by Becker (1983). Becker argues that government will tend to choose mechanisms which are more efficient over those which are less efficient in redistributing revenues from less powerful to more powerful groups. To the extent that his argument is testable, I believe it is not consistent with the facts. For example, the U.S. currently has a policy that directs toxic waste dumps to be cleaned up in priority order. The policy makes no attempt to examine whether a greater risk reduction could be attained with a different allocation of expenditures. Given a finite budget constraint, this policy does not make sense from a purely economic viewpoint. However, it might make sense if environmentalists hoped that more stringent policies would emerge in the future. Or it might make sense if Congress wants to be perceived as doing the job "right," even if only a small part of the job gets done.

A second example can be drawn from emissions trading. It is possible to design marketable permit systems which are more efficient and ensure better environmental quality over time (Hahn and Noll, 1982; Hahn, 1987), yet these systems have not been implemented. Environmentalists may be reluctant to embrace market alternatives because they fear it may give a certain legitimacy to the act of polluting. Moreover, they may not believe in the expected results. Thus, for Becker's theory to hold in an absolute sense, it would be necessary to construct fairly complicated utility functions. The problem is that the theory does not explicitly address how choices are made by lobbyists, legislators and bureaucrats (Campos, 1987).

These choices may be made in different ways in different countries. How can it be explained, for example, that a large array of countries use fees, while only two countries use marketable permits (and the application of permits in Germany is fairly limited)? Noll (1983) has argued that the political institutions of different countries can provide important clues about regulatory strategy. In addition, the comparison of lead trading and emissions trading revealed that the very nature of the environmental problem can have an important effect on interest group attitudes.

Interest group attitudes can be expected to vary across countries. In the Netherlands, Opschoor (1986, p. 15) notes that environmental groups tend to prefer charges while employer groups prefer regulatory instruments. Barde (1986, pp. 10–11) notes that the political "acceptability" of charges is high in both France and the Netherlands. Nonetheless, some French airlines have refused to pay noise charges because the funds are not being used (Barde, 1986, p. 12). In Italy, there has been widespread opposition from industry and interest groups (Panella, 1986, pp. 6, 22). While Germany industry has accepted the notion of charges, some industries have criticized the differential charge rates across jurisdictions. In the United States, environmentalists have shown a marked preference for regulatory instruments, eschewing both charges and marketable permits. These preferences may help to explain the choice of instruments in various countries as well as the relative utilization of different instruments. In addition, interest groups in different countries will share different clusters of relevant experiences, which will help to determine the feasible space for alternatives.

In short, existing theories could benefit from more careful analysis of
the regulatory status quo, underlying beliefs about property rights, and how
political choices are actually made in different countries.

The review of marketable permits and charge systems has demonstrated that regulatory systems involving multiple instruments are the rule
rather than the exception. The fundamental problem is to determine the
most appropriate mix, with an eye to both economic and political realities.

In addition to selecting an appropriate mix of instruments, attention
needs to be given to the effects of having different levels of government implement selected policies. It might seem, for example, that if the problem
is local, then the logical choice for addressing the problem is the local regulatory body. However, this is not always true. Perhaps the problem may
require a level of technical expertise that does not reside at the local level,
in which case some higher level of government involvement may be required. What is clear from a review of implementing environmental policies is that the level of oversight can affect the implementation of policies.
For example, Hahn and Hester (1986) note that a marked increase in bubble activity is associated with a decrease in federal oversight.

Because marketable permit approaches have been shown to have a
demonstrable effect on cost savings without sacrificing environmental quality, this instrument can be expected to receive more widespread use. One
factor which will stimulate the application of this mechanism is the higher
marginal costs of abatement that will be faced as environmental standards
are tightened. A second factor which will tend to stimulate the use of both
charges and marketable permits is a "demonstration effect." Several countries have already implemented these mechanisms with some encouraging
results. The experience gained in implementing these tools will stimulate
their use in future applications. A third factor which will affect the use of
both of these approaches is the technology of monitoring and enforcement.
As monitoring costs go down, the use of mechanisms such as direct charges
and marketable permits can be expected to increase. The combination of
these factors leads to the prediction that greater use of these market-based
environmental systems will be made in the future.

REFERENCES

Barde, J., "Use of Economic Instruments for Environmental Protection: Discussion
Paper," ENV/ECO/86.16, Organization for Economic Cooperation and Devel-
opment, September 9, 1986.
Baumol, W. and Oates, W. *The Theory of Environmental Policy.* Englewood Cliffs,
NJ: Prentice-Hall, 1985.
Becker, G., "A Theory of Competition Among Pressure Groups for Political Influ-
ence," *Quarterly Journal of Economics*, 1983, XCVII, 371–400.
Boland, J., "Economic Instruments for Environmental Protection in the United
States," ENV/ECO/86.14, Organization for Economic Cooperation and Devel-
opment, September 11, 1986.

Bower, B. et al., *Incentives in Water Quality Management: France and the Ruhr Area*. Washington, D.C.: Resources for the Future, 1981.

Bressers, J., "The Effectiveness of Dutch Water Quality Policy," Twente University of Technology, Netherlands, mimeo, 1983.

Brown, G., Jr., "Economic Instruments: Alternatives or Supplements to Regulations?" *Environment and Economics*, Issue Paper, Environment Directorate OECD, June 1984, 103–120.

Brown, G., Jr. and J. Bresser, "Evidence Supporting Effluent Charges," Twente University of Technology, The Netherlands, mimeo, September 1986.

Brown, G., Jr. and R. Johnson, "Pollution Control by Effluent Charges: It Works in the Federal Republic of Germany, Why Not in the U.S.," *Natural Resources Journal*, 1984, *24*, 929–966.

Buchanan, J. and G. Tullock, "Polluters' Profits and Political Response: Direct Controls Versus Taxes," *American Economic Review*, 1975, *65*, 139–147.

Campos, J., "Toward a Theory of Instrument Choice in the Regulation of Markets," California Institute of Technology, Pasadena, California, mimeo, January 26, 1987.

Coelho, P., "Polluters' and Political Response: Direct Control Versus Taxes: Comment," *American Economic Review*, 1976, *66*, 976–978.

Dales, J., *Pollution, Property and Prices*. Toronto: University Press, 1968.

David, M. and E. Joeres, "Is a Viable Implementation of TDPs Transferable?" In Joeres, E. and M. David, eds., *Buying a Better Environment: Cost-Effective Regulation Through Permit Trading*. Madison: University of Wisconsin Press, 1983, 233–248.

Dewees, D., "Instrument Choice in Environmental Policy," *Economic Inquiry*, 1983, *XXI*, 53–71.

Elmore, T. et al., "Trading Between Point and Nonpoint Sources: A Cost Effective Method for Improving Water Quality," paper presented at the 57th annual Conference/Exposition of the Water Pollution Control Federation, New Orleans, Louisiana, 1984.

Hahn, R., "Designing Markets in Transferable Property Rights: A Practitioner's Guide." In Joeres, E. and M. David, eds., *Buying a Better Environment: Cost Effective Regulation Through Permit Trading*. Madison: University of Wisconsin Press, 1983, 83–97.

Hahn, R., "Rules, Equality and Efficiency: An Evaluation of Two Regulatory Reforms," Working Paper 87-7, School of Urban and Public Affairs, Carnegie Mellon University, Pittsburgh, Pennsylvania, 1987.

Hahn, R. and G. Hester, "Where Did All the Markets Go?: An Analysis of EPA's Emission Trading Program," Working Paper 87-3, School of Urban and Public Affairs, Carnegie Mellon University, Pittsburgh, Pennsylvania, 1986. Forthcoming in the *Yale Journal on Regulation*.

Hahn, R. and G. Hester, "Marketable Permits: Lessons for Theory and Practice," *Ecology Law Quarterly*, forthcoming.

Hahn, R. and A. McGartland, "The Political Economy of Instrument Choice: An Examination of the U.S. Role in Implementing the Montreal Protocol," Working Paper 88-34, School of Urban and Public Affairs, Carnegie Mellon University, Pittsburgh, Pennsylvania, 1988.

Hahn, R. and Noll, R., "Designing a Market for Tradable Emissions Permits." In Magat, W. ed., *Reform of Environmental Regulation*. Cambridge, MA: Ballinger, 1982, 119–146.

Hahn, R. and Noll, R., "Barriers to Implementing Tradable Air Pollution Permits: Problems of Regulatory Interaction," *Yale Journal on Regulation*, 1983, *1*, 63–91.

Kashmanian, R. et al., "Beyond Categorical Limits: The Case for Pollution Reduction Through Trading," paper presented at the 59th Annual Water Pollution Control Federation Conference, Los Angeles, CA, October 6–9, 1986.

Kneese, A. and Schultze, C., *Pollution, Prices, and Public Policy*. Washington, D.C.: The Brookings Institution, 1975.

Montgomery, W. D., "Markets in Licenses and Efficient Pollution Control Programs," *Journal of Economic Theory*, 1972, *5*, 395–418.

Noll, R., "The Political Foundations of Regulatory Policy," *Zeitschrift fur die gesamte Staatswissenschaft*, 1983, *139*, 377–404.

Novotny, G., "Transferable Discharge Permits for Water Pollution Control In Wisconsin," Department of Natural Resources, Madison, Wisconsin, mimeo, December 1, 1986.

O'Neil, W., "The Regulation of Water Pollution Permit Trading under Conditions of Varying Streamflow and Temperature." In Joeres, E. and M. David, eds., *Buying a Better Environment: Cost-Effective Regulation Through Permit Trading*. Madison, Wisconsin: University of Wisconsin Press, 1983, 219–231.

Opschoor, J., "Economic Instruments for Environmental Protection in the Netherlands," ENV/ECO/86.15, Organization for Economic Cooperation and Development, August 1, 1986.

Panella, G., "Economic Instruments for Environmental Protection in Italy," ENV/ECO/86.11, Organization for Economic Cooperation and Development, September 2, 1986.

Patterson, D., Bureau of Water Resources Management, Wisconsin Department of Natural Resources, Madison, Wisconsin, telephone interview, April 2, 1987.

Pigou, A., *The Economics of Welfare*, fourth edition. London: Macmillan and Co., 1932.

Plott, C., "Externalities and Corrective Policies in Experimental Markets," *Economic Journal*, 1983, *93*, 106–127.

Rolph, E., "Government Allocation of Property Rights: Who Gets What?," *Journal of Policy Analysis and Management*, 1983, *3*, 45–61.

Sprenger, R., "Economic Instruments for Environmental Protection in Germany," Organization for Economic Cooperation and Development, October 7, 1986.

Thomas, L., memorandum attached to Draft Emissions Trading Policy Statement, Environmental Protection Agency, Washington, D.C., May 19, 1986.

Tietenberg, T., *Emissions Trading: An Exercise in Reforming Pollution Policy*. Washington, D.C.: Resources for the Future, 1985.

U.S. Congressional Budget Office, *Hazardous Waste Management: Recent Changes and Policy Alternatives*, Washington, D.C.: U.S. G.P.O., May 1985.

U.S. Environmental Protection Agency, "Costs and Benefits of Reducing Lead in Gasoline, Final Regulatory Impact Analysis," Office of Policy Analysis, February 1985a.

U.S. Environmental Protection Agency, "Quarterly Reports on Lead in Gasoline," Field Operations and Support Division, Office of Air and Radiation, July 16, 1985b.

U.S. Environmental Protection Agency, "Quarterly Reports on Lead in Gasoline," Field Operations and Support Division, Office of Air and Radiation, March 21, May 23, July 15, 1986.

Welch, W., "The Political Feasibility of Full Ownership Property Rights: The Cases of Pollution and Fisheries," *Policy Sciences*, 1983, *16*, 165–180.

Yohe, G., "Polluters' Profits and Political Response: Direct Control Versus Taxes: Comment," *American Economic Review*, 1976, *66*, 981–982.

19   *It's Immoral to Buy the Right to Pollute (with replies)**

Michael J. Sandel

Michael J. Sandel is Professor of Government at Harvard University.

At the conference on global warming in Kyoto, Japan, the United States found itself at toggerheads with developing nations on two important issues: The United States wanted those countries to commit themselves to restraints on emissions, and it wanted any agreement to include a trading scheme that would let countries buy and sell the right to pollute.

The Administration was right on the first point, but wrong on the second. Creating an international market in emission credits would make it easier for us to meet our obligations under the treaty but undermine the ethic we should be trying to foster on the environment.

Indeed, China and India threatened to torpedo the talks over the issue. They were afraid that such trading would enable rich countries to buy their way out of commitments to reduce greenhouse gases. In the end, the developing nations agreed to allow some emissions trading among developed countries, with details to be negotiated next year.

The Clinton Administration has made emission trading a centerpiece of its environmental policy. Creating an international market for emissions, it argues, is a more efficient way to reduce pollution than imposing fixed levels for each country.

Trading in greenhouse gases could also make compliance cheaper and less painful for the United States, which could pay to reduce some other country's carbon dioxide emissions rather than reduce its own. For example, the United States might find it cheaper (and more politically palatable) to pay to update an old coal-burning factory in a developing country than to tax gas-guzzling sports utility vehicles at home.

Since the aim is to limit the global level of these gases, one might ask, what difference does it make which places on the planet send less carbon to the sky?

It may make no difference from the standpoint of the heavens, but it does make a political difference. Despite the efficiency of international emissions trading, such a system is objectionable for three reasons.

"It's Immoral to Buy the Right to Pollute," editorial by Michael J. Sandel, from *New York Times*, Dec. 15, 1997, p. A29.

*Including replies printed in *New York Times*, Dec. 17, 1997.

First, it creates loopholes that could enable wealthy countries to evade their obligations. Under the Kyoto formula, for example, the United States could take advantage of the fact that Russia has already reduced its emissions 30 percent since 1990, not through energy efficiencies but through economic decline. The United States could buy excess credits from Russia, and count them toward meeting our obligations under the treaty.

Second, turning pollution into a commodity to be bought and sold removes the moral stigma that is properly associated with it, if a company or a country is fined for spewing excessive pollutants into the air, the community conveys its judgment that the polluter has done something wrong. A fee, on the other hand, makes pollution just another cost of doing business, like wages, benefits and rent.

The distinction between a fine and a fee for despoiling the environment is not one we should give up too easily. Suppose there were a $100 fine for throwing a beer can into the Grand Canyon, and a wealthy hiker decided to pay $100 for the convenience. Would there be nothing wrong in his treating the fine as if it were simply an expensive dumping charge?

Or consider the fine for parking in a place reserved for the disabled. If a busy contractor needs to park near his building site and is willing to pay the fine, is there nothing wrong with his treating that space as an expensive parking lot?

In effacing the distinction between a fine and a fee, emission trading is like a recent proposal to open carpool lanes on Los Angeles freeways to drivers without passengers who are willing to pay a fee. Such drivers are now fined for slipping into carpool lanes; under the market proposal, they would enjoy a quicker commute without opprobrium.

A third objection to emission trading among countries is that it may undermine the sense of shared responsibility that increased global cooperation requires.

Consider an illustration drawn from an autumn ritual: raking fallen leaves into great piles and lighting bonfires. Imagine a neighborhood where each family agrees to have only one small bonfire a year. But they also agree that families can buy and sell their bonfire permits as they choose.

The family in the mansion on the hill buys permits from its neighbors—paying them, in effect, to lug their leaves to the town compost heap. The market works, and pollution is reduced, but without the spirit of shared sacrifice that might have been produced had no market intervened.

Those who have sold their permits and those who have bought them, come to regard the bonfires less as an offense against clean air than as a luxury, a status symbol that can be bought and sold. And the resentment against the family in the mansion makes future, more demanding forms of cooperation more difficult to achieve.

Of course, many countries that attended the Kyoto conference have already made cooperation elusive. They have not yet agreed to restrict their emissions at all. Their refusal undermines the prospect of a global environmental ethic as surely as does our pollution trading scheme.

But the United States would have more suasion if these developing countries could not rightly complain that trading in emissions allows wealthy nations to buy their way out of global obligation.

Replies to Michael J. Sandel

From Steven Shavell, Professor of Law and Economics at Harvard Law School

Michael J. Sandel ("It's Immoral to Buy the Right to Pollute," Op-Ed, Dec. 15) discounts the great benefits of trade in pollution rights and advances flawed arguments against it.

Suppose a rich country like the United States would have to spend $50 billion annually to reduce its carbon dioxide emissions by some amount, whereas China could reduce its emissions by this same amount more cheaply, at a cost of $5 billion (say, by installing simple smoke scrubbers in its coal-burning factories).

If trade in emissions credits were allowed, both China and the United States would be better off.

The United States could pay China $30 billion for the right to emit carbon dioxide. This would make China $25 billion better off: it would receive $30 billion and spend only $5 billion to prevent the emissions. The United States would pay $30 billion rather than spend $50 billion to abate the emissions.

And trade would probably lead ultimately to less pollution. When countries know that they can make profits or that ceilings on pollution are easier to meet, they will be more likely to agree to reduce the total amount of permitted pollution over time.

From Robert N. Stavins, Albert Pratt Professor of Business and Government at the John F. Kennedy School of Government, Harvard University, and University Fellow at Resources for the Future

The ink is barely dry on the Kyoto protocol, but Michael J. Sandel argues that the agreement's emissions trading provisions, supported by the Clinton Administration, will foster "immoral" behavior (Op-Ed, Dec. 15).

Was it immoral when the United States used a tradable permit system among refineries to phase leaded gasoline out of the market in the 1980's more rapidly than anyone had anticipated and at a savings of $250 million a year?

Replies to editorial, by Steven Shavell, Robert N. Stavins, Sanford Gaines, and Eric Maskin, from New York times, Dec. 17, 1997.

Is it now immoral that we are reducing acid rain by half through a tradable permit system among electrical utilities, reducing emissions (sulfur dioxide) faster than anyone had predicted and saving up to $1 billion a year for electricity consumers? Is that why the Environmental Defense Fund and others have worked so tirelessly and effectively to implement these emissions-trading programs?

From Sanford E. Gaines, Professor of Law at the University of Houston

Michael J. Sandel (Op-Ed, Dec. 15) invokes the moral argument against emissions trading in the context of reducing greenhouse gas emissions. Maintaining a moral stigma on pollution makes sense for hazardous substances where polluters have choices, for reducing the pollution. But global warming is not such a situation. Does Mr. Sandel really believe he is behaving immorally when he cooks his dinner, switches on a light or turns on a computer to write an Op-Ed article? These activities result in emissions of carbon dioxide. Or is it his utility that should be stigmatized, perhaps for not using nuclear power?

To reduce greenhouse gas emissions, producers and consumers alike need to adopt new technologies. That's a perfect situation to use the power of the market. Mr. Sandel should reserve his moral outrage for those who don't even want the chance to buy the right to pollute because they refuse to accept that the planet can no longer afford cheap energy.

From Eric S. Maskin, Louis Berkman Professor of Economics at Harvard University

Michael J. Sandel (Op-Ed, Dec. 15) neglects an important distinction in his argument against tradable emissions credits. The examples he gives of immoral acts—throwing beer cans into the Grand Canyon or parking in spots reserved for the disabled—are discrete choices: one can do them or not do them, and society can therefore reasonably ban them outright.

But virtually any manufacturing activity entails the creation of some pollution. So the question is not will we pollute, but rather how much. Further, if there is to be pollution, shouldn't we try to trade it off against its economic consequences? Such a trade-off is facilitated by tradable rights.

VI

---

*Transboundary SO$_2$ and Acid
Rain Control*

20 An Interim Evaluation of Sulfur Dioxide Emissions Trading*

Richard Schmalensee

Paul L. Joskow

A. Denny Ellerman

Juan Pablo Montero

Elizabeth M. Bailey

Richard Schmalensee is Dean, Sloan School of Management at the Massachusetts Institute of Technology, and Research Associate at the National Bureau of Economic Research; Paul L. Joskow is James Killian Professor of Economics and Management at the Massachusetts Institute of Technology, and Research Associate at the National Bureau of Economic Research; A. Denny Ellerman is Senior Lecturer at the Sloan School of Management; Juan Pablo Montero is Professor of Industrial Engineering at Catholic University of Chile; and Elizabeth M. Bailey is Consultant at National Economic Research Associates.

Title IV of the 1990 Clean Air Act Amendments established the first large-scale, long-term environmental program to rely on tradable emissions permits—called "allowances" in this program—to control pollution. This program was designed to cut acid rain by reducing sulfur dioxide (SO_2) emissions from electric generating plants to about half their 1980 level, beginning in 1995. It is of interest both as a response to an important environmental issue and as a landmark experiment in environmental policy. This experiment comes at a particularly important time, since emission trading is under serious consideration, with strong U.S. backing, for use to

"An Interim Evaluation of Sulfur Dioxide Emissions Trading," by Richard Schmalensee, Paul L. Joskow, A. Denny Ellerman, Juan Pablo Montero, and Elizabeth M. Bailey, from *Journal of Economic Perspectives*, 12(3):53–68 (Summer 1998).

*We are indebted to the National Acid Precipitation Assessment Program (NAPAP), the U.S. Environmental Protection Agency (EPA), and the MIT Center for Energy and Environmental Policy Research for research support and to the EPA's Acid Rain Division, the Energy Information Administration of the U.S. Department of Energy, Cantor Fitzgerald Environmental Brokerage Services, and personnel of numerous electric utilities (particularly those who responded to our survey) for invaluable cooperation. Robert Stavins and the editors provided valuable comments on earlier drafts. Also, Richard Schmalensee helped design the sulfur dioxide trading program as a Member of the council of Economic Advisers in the Bush Administration, and Paul L. Joskow was a member of the Environmental Protection Agency's Acid Rain Advisory Committee, which helped design the regulations that implemented that program.

deal with global climate change by curbing emissions of carbon dioxide (CO_2). The economic stakes in climate change surpass those in acid rain by several orders of magnitude (Intergovernmental Panel on Climate Change, 1996).

This article summarizes the results to date of our ongoing empirical analysis of compliance costs and allowance market performance under the U.S. acid rain program.[1] Supporting analysis and additional detail are presented and other issues are explored in Ellerman et al. (1997) and our other papers that are cited in what follows.

What Is the Acid Rain Program?

Acid rain (or, more properly, acid deposition) occurs when SO_2 and nitrogen oxides (NO_x) react in the atmosphere to form sulfuric and nitric acids, respectively. These acids then fall to earth, sometimes hundreds of miles from their source, in either wet or dry form. The dominant precursor of acid rain in the United States is SO_2 from coal-fired power plants in the northeast and midwest.

These emissions are the focus of the acid rain program created by Title IV of the Clean Air Act Amendments of 1990. Title IV created a cap on utility SO_2 emissions from electric generating units, to be implemented in two phases. During Phase I, 1995 through 1999, aggregate annual emissions from the 263 dirtiest large generating units—the so-called "Table A units"—must be below a fixed cap. (In 1990 these units accounted for about 22 percent of heat input at U.S. fossil-fueled generating units and about 17 percent of capacity.) In Phase II, 2000 and beyond, virtually all existing and new fossil-fueled electric generating units in the continental United States become subject to a tighter cap on aggregate annual emissions. As the term is used here, an electric generating *unit* is a combustion device (boiler or turbine) used to power one or more electric generators. A typical generating *plant* houses several generating units, which may be of different vintages, scales, or types.

Two provisions, little noted when Title IV was debated, provide that other utility generating units can be voluntarily brought under Title IV regulation in Phase I, thus becoming, along with the Table A units, "affected units." The "substitution" provision was intended to enable owners of Table A units to substitute less costly emission reductions from other units for reductions from the Table A units. The "compensation" provision was designed to prevent owners of Table A units from meeting their emission reduction obligations simply by reducing generation from those particular

---

[1]For discussions of earlier U.S. experience with emissions trading, see Hahn and Hester (1989a,b) and National Economic Research Associates (1994, ch. 2). There is very little experience with this approach outside the United States.

units and increasing generation from other units. Accordingly, this provision required that if generation at a Table A unit was reduced significantly, one or more non-Table A units had to be brought under Phase I regulation to compensate, and increased generation at the latter units had to offset the reduction at the Table A unit. As it happened, generation at Table A units increased substantially in 1995 and 1996.

In both Phase I and Phase II, owners of existing affected units are given fixed numbers of tradable permits, called "allowances," each year following rules that depend primarily on historic emissions and fuel use. Each allowance entitles its holder to emit one ton of SO_2. A small number of additional allowances are auctioned annually by the Environmental Protection Agency (EPA), with the revenues rebated to utilities roughly in proportion to their allowance allocations. New affected units must buy needed allowances from existing units or at the EPA auctions, discussed below. Each affected generating unit must deliver to EPA valid allowances sufficient to cover each year's emissions within 30 days of year's end or incur serious penalties. (Emissions are continuously monitored from affected units, at an average annual cost of about $124,000 per unit.)

Allowances can be bought or sold without restriction to cover emissions anywhere in the continental United States. Permitting allowances to be traded freely anywhere in the United States would be a first-best policy if and only if emissions everywhere in the United States had the same marginal damages, which they plainly do not. However, unrestricted trading would be a reasonable second-best response to worries that the allowance market would otherwise be too thin if marginal abatement costs are inversely correlated with marginal damages. In this case, emissions reductions will tend to be made in the lower-cost, higher-damage places in equilibrium. Large observed reductions in midwest emissions (discussed below) suggest that this condition might be satisfied in fact, though we have seen no formal analysis of this issue.

An allowance can be used in the year it is issued or "banked" for use in any subsequent year. In the early 1990s, analysts predicted allowance prices of about $250–350 per ton in Phase I and $500–700 in Phase II. (The expected time-path must in fact be continuous, since arbitrage conditions and the ability to hold the allowances over time rule out a predictable upward jump in allowance prices at the start of Phase II.)

The acid rain program represents a conceptually important departure from the "command-and-control" tradition that has dominated environmental policy in the United States and abroad. This traditional approach involved prescription of either particular abatement methods, so-called "engineering standards," or maximum emission rates, so-called "performance standards," for a particular pollutant for classes (commonly, types and vintages) of emissions sources. In 1971, for instance, the EPA announced a maximum SO_2 emission rate (expressed in pounds of sulfur per million Btu of fuel burned) for new coal-fired generating units. Additional emission rate constraints, varying substantially in stringency, were placed on existing units under State Implementation Plans, but no limits were imposed on total emissions. The tradable permit approach, in contrast, focuses on total emissions, which are more directly linked to environmental damages.

Holding power generation constant, there are two basic ways to reduce SO_2 emissions from electric generating units: fuel switching, which means burning fuel with less sulfur; and scrubbing, which means operating desulfurization facilities that reduce the amount of SO_2 exiting the stack. Switching to coal with a lower sulfur content has historically raised fuel cost but involved little or no capital cost, while scrubbing involves capital costs of about $125 million on average for a medium-sized 500 megawatt generating unit. Because of differences in location, design, and utilization rate, existing generating units differ considerably in the ease and cost with which they can switch to lower-sulfur fuel or accommodate scrubbers. Any environmental program that imposed the same standards across this heterogeneous population of pollution sources would inflate total cost and would likely impose very high and politically unacceptable costs on some utilities or regions.

Past regulatory policy typically ducked this problem by subjecting new generating units to stricter environmental controls than old units. As a result, utilities faced strong incentives to extend the lives of their old units. By 1985, 83 percent of power plant SO_2 emissions came from units that did not meet the 1971 SO_2 emission rate standard for new units.[2] Any acid rain program would have had to deal with these old units, but their designs and site characteristics varied enormously, and, as a consequence, so did the costs of reducing their SO_2 emissions. One important reason why Congress adopted the nontraditional approach in Title IV was that because of this heterogeneity, there seemed to be no workable "command-and-control" solution to the acid rain problem.[3]

Allowances were given to utilities rather than sold because there was no way that a sales-based program could have passed Congress. Indeed, the only politically live alternative to a simple grant of allowances was to impose an electricity tax that would have forced the customers of "clean" utilities to help pay the clean-up costs of "dirty" utilities. The complex statutory provisions that allocate allowances to individual generating units show clear evidence of rent-seeking, but do not provide strong support for any simple model of government decision-making (Joskow and Schmalensee, forthcoming). On the whole, the states that mined or burned substantial amounts of high-sulfur coal, which had successfully resisted acid rain legislation during the 1980s, did less well in the allowance allocation process than their earlier success on this issue would have suggested.

---

[2]Calculated by the authors from EPA's National Allowance Data Base. These units were too old to be bound by the 1971 standard.

[3]The origins and political economy of this program are discussed in more detail in Joskow and Schmalensee (forthcoming) and in Stavins's article in this issue.

What Happened to Sulfur Dioxide Emissions?

Most of the analysis that follows is based on data at the generating unit level for 1995 and 1996, the first two years this program constrained emissions, and earlier years, and on allowance market data beginning in 1992. Our estimates rely heavily on the EPA's National Allowance Data Base (NADB), Supplemental Data File (SDF), Allowance Tracking System (ATS), and Emissions Monitoring System (EMS).[4]

Figure 1 shows the basic pattern of aggregate emissions from units that were affected under Phase I in both 1995 and 1996. (There were 413 such units; they accounted for 95 percent of emissions from all affected units in 1995 and 98 percent in 1996.) Aggregate SO_2 emissions, shown by the line with squares, declined substantially from 1990 through 1994. The dashed line shows the level of SO_2 emissions that the EPA had forecast for this period if Title IV had not passed. The solid line shows the emission limits imposed by Title IV. About 80 percent of the pre-Phase I emission decline reflected the expansion of the market area served by low-sulfur coal from the Powder River Basin in northeast Wyoming (Ellerman and Montero, 1996). This expansion mainly reflected declines in delivered prices driven by reductions in rail rates, which reflected in turn the continuing productivity benefits of rail deregulation and the introduction of competition into the haulage of coal from the Powder River Basin.

Figure 1 also shows that emissions dropped sharply in 1995 to about 5.3 million tons, 39 percent below total allowances issued or auctioned for that year. Similarly, 1996 emissions were 33 percent below total vintage 1996 allowances. The 6.2 million vintage 1995 and 1996 allowances not needed to cover emissions in these two years were banked for future use. There are two plausible explanations for the dramatic overcompliance seen in these years.

The first explanation involves intertemporal trading and optimization. Allowances have generally been expected to be more expensive in Phase II than in Phase I, so that even when the Phase I constraint on total emissions is not binding, it may be rational to reduce emissions on the margin and save the allowances thus freed up for use in Phase II. This point was widely discussed in the early 1990s, and many analysts argued that some banking of this sort would be efficient throughout Phase I.

For it to be efficient to carry allowances from any periods t to period $t + 1$ in a riskless world, the allowance price must rise at the rate of interest between those periods. In addition, the allowance price must equal operating units' short-run marginal abatement cost.[5] Thus if marginal costs of abate-

---

[4]In addition, we have relied on the trade press, earlier studies of compliance by the Electric Power Research Institute (EPRI), a mail survey of affected utilities that we conducted in the summer of 1996 seeking information about compliance strategies and associated costs (replies covered 37 percent of affected capacity in Phase I), and many telephone interviews with personnel from government agencies, electric utilities, and participants in allowance markets.

[5]Except, of course, for the obvious inequalities that occur for units reducing emissions by either zero or by the maximum possible in the short run.

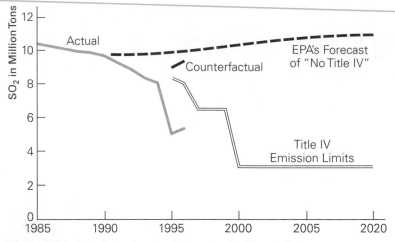

Figure 1 SO$_2$ Emissions, Caps and Forecasts for Phase I Units

Source: Derived from Pechan (1995), EPA's EMS and ATS, and EPA (1996).

ment are non-decreasing, emissions from regulated units must fall along an efficient path with banking from period t to period $t + 1$. At some time T^* in Phase II, the "allowance bank" will be exhausted, and thereafter the allowance price must equal marginal compliance cost. In a riskless world, arbitrage would then ensure that the allowance price at any time t before T^* would equal the marginal cost of compliance at T^*, discounted back to t. In the real world, of course, future abatement costs and market conditions are uncertain, neither T^* nor marginal cost at that time are known for certain, and there is a time-varying "convenience yield" provided by holding allowances, as is the case with other commodities (Williams and Wright, 1991; Bailey, 1998). All else equal, the existence of a positive convenience yield reduces the expected rate of allowance price increases during a period of banking.

The second explanation for substantial overcompliance early in Phase I is that in the aggregate the market underestimated how declines in rail rates would increase the penetration of low-sulfur Powder River Basin coal, and, as a consequence, overinvested in scrubbers and signed long-term contracts for too much low-sulfur coal. This disequilibrium explanation is consistent with the fact that the actual level of banking in 1995 and 1996 far exceeded earlier predictions and with other evidence discussed below.

While only the 263 generating so-called "Table A units" were required to be regulated in Phase I, a much larger than expected number of generating units "volunteered" for such regulation: 182 units in 1995 and 168 in 1996 (with 150 volunteering in both years).[6] As noted above, the provisions

---

[6]In contrast, a much-discussed provision aimed at inducing non-utility sources of SO$_2$ emissions to "opt-in" to the acid rain program had produced only seven industrial opt-in units at two locations by March 1997. See Atkeson (1997) for a discussion.

under which these units opted into Phase I were designed to allow substitution of lower-cost abatement at non-Table A units for higher cost abatement at Table units. However, while some cost-reducing substitution did occur, and we estimate that the volunteers reduced their emissions in aggregate by around 200,000 tons in both 1995 and 1996, our analysis indicates that factors other than abatement cost differences had more impact on the decision to volunteer a unit for Phase I regulation (Montero, 1997a). The process of allocating allowances to volunteers based on past emissions inevitably created adverse selection problems, as units with high past emissions for transitory reasons were given incentives to opt-in to obtain valuable allowances.[7] We estimate that these "substitution and compensation" units received in aggregate 263,000 more allowances in 1995, and 365,000 more in 1996 (20 and 30 percent of their total allocations in these years, respectively), than they would have needed to cover their emissions in the absence of Title IV. In addition, volunteers were exempted from certain NO_x regulations that would have been very costly for some units. Current emissions at these units were reduced somewhat, but the issuance of excess allowances implies a more than compensating increase of emissions elsewhere or in the future. In the end, utilities' substantial use of the "substitution and compensation" provisions did little to reduce compliance costs and caused some increase in total lifetime SO_2 emissions.

How Were Emissions Reduced?

To analyze the extent to which the emissions reduction in 1995 and 1996 was attributable to Title IV, it is necessary to estimate what SO_2 emissions would have been for Phase I units in those years in the absence of Title IV. Our rough estimate of each Phase I unit's 1995 or 1996 counterfactual emissions is the product of its 1993 emissions rate, measured by SO_2 emitted per unit of heat input, times its actual 1995 or 1996 heat input.[8]

Figure 1 shows that total 1995 and 1996 counterfactual emissions for these Phase I units, indicated by the two diamonds, were above actual 1993 emissions by 7.7 and 12.8 percent, respectively. As these differences reflect comparable increases in heat input at affected units, it is clear that compliance with the SO_2 standard was *not* achieved by reducing utilization of units subject to Phase I regulation. Counterfactual emissions were 0.5 and 1.2 million tons above the Phase I cap in 1995 and 1996, respectively,

---

[7]Montero (1997b) discusses the optimal design of voluntary programs of this sort.

[8]The ratio of 1995 and 1996 heat input to 1993 heat input varied relatively little across Phase I units, but did tend to be higher than average for scrubbed units. This pattern casts some doubt on the implicit assumption that heat inputs at affected units were not influenced by Title IV. We considered an alternative counterfactual that avoids this problem (using heat inputs proportional to 1993 inputs and scaled up to match the 1995 and 1996 totals) and obtained results qualitatively similar to those reported in the text.

and roughly four million tons above actual emissions in both years. One-quarter of the total reduction from the counterfactual in these years occurred in Ohio, and 90 percent occurred in the nine high-emissions states extending from Pennsylvania and West Virginia west to Missouri and south to Tennessee and Georgia.

Comparing actual and counterfactual emissions for each unit, we find that the 27 "Table A" units that began operating scrubbers in 1995 or 1996 accounted for about 45 percent of the total reduction in emissions. Almost two-thirds of the reduction due to scrubbing in 1995 and 1996 was contributed by seven units at three large plants. Fuel switching, almost entirely to lower-sulfur coal (rather than, say, to natural gas), accounted for 55 percent of total reductions. While switching to Powder River Basin coal accounted for a large fraction of the reductions in emissions between 1990 and 1993, it only accounted for about 13 percent of the difference between actual and counterfactual 1995 emissions at Phase I units. Switching to low-sulfur (not necessarily low-sulfur) eastern or midwestern coal was much more important. Finally, even though the "substitution and compensation" provisions were much more heavily used than had been anticipated, the Table A units accounted for at least 95 percent of the emission reductions in both 1995 and 1996.

One can learn about the extent to which compliance strategies took advantage of the flexibility allowed by Title IV by comparing units' actual emission rates per unit of heat input with what those rates would plausibly have been in the absence of emissions trading. Figure 2 provides such

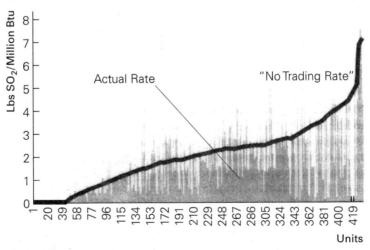

Figure 2 Effect of Trading: 1996

Source: Derived from Pechan (1995), EPA's EMS, and EPA (1996).

a comparison for 1996. (The corresponding graph for 1995 shows a very similar pattern.)

The 431 units covered by Title IV in 1996 are arrayed along the horizontal axis from lowest to highest estimated "no-trading" emission rate. We estimate each unit's no-trading rate as the smaller of its unconstrained emissions rate, which we again take to be its actual 1993 rate, and the maximum legal 1996 emissions rate under a hypothetical no-trading acid rain policy. We assume that this hypothetical policy differs from Title IV only in that allowances cannot be transferred among units, and we take as given each unit's actual allocation of vintage 1996 allowances and its actual fuel use in 1996. Thus each unit's maximum legal emissions rate in this no-trading regime is equal to the ratio of its 1996 allowances (multiplied by 2000 to convert to pounds) to its 1996 fuel use in millions of Btus. The ascending heavy dark line shows the estimated no-trading emissions rates.[9] The grey vertical bars show each unit's actual 1996 emission rate. While there is some tendency for units with higher no-trading emission rates to have higher actual emission rates, the correlation is far from perfect.[10] Figure 2 shows that utilities took advantage of the flexibility provided by Title IV to employ a wide variety of unit-specific compliance strategies, something not possible under traditional command-and-control regimes.

Some units reduced emissions in both 1995 and 1996 to well below their allowance allocations and either transferred allowances to other units or held them for future use, while others reduced emissions relatively little and acquired allowances to be in compliance. About 10 percent of 1995 total emissions (534,000 tons) and 13 percent of 1996 total emissions (689,000 tons) were covered by allowances acquired or transferred from other units, while more than one-third of vintage 1995 and 1996 allowances were banked for future use. Emissions exceeded allowance allocations at 98 generating units in 1995 and 109 generating units in 1996; these were located in 18 of the 24 states with Phase I units. The heterogeneity of unit-specific response strategies depicted in Figure 2 indicates that Title IV was an economically significant departure, as well as a conceptually significant departure, from the traditional "one size fits all" U.S. approach of setting unit-level emission rate standards.

---

[9]The 40-odd units with zero no-trading emissions rates that are shown on the left of the horizontal axis were retired or otherwise off-line in 1996. On the right, high no-trading rates reflect either the receipt of extra allowances (usually as a reward for scrubbing) or a substantially lower heat input in 1996 than in the period used to determine allowance allocations.

[10]Using the 413 generating units affected by Title IV in both 1995 and 1996, let $r(t, t')$ be the correlation between emissions rates in years t and t'. Stable pre-Phase I operating patterns are revealed by values of $r(1988, 1989)$, $r(1989, 1990)$, $r(1990, 1991)$, $r(1991, 1992)$, and $r(1992, 1993)$ that all exceed 0.93. Perhaps because of utilities' preparations for the start of Phase I, $r(1993, 1994)$ falls to 0.89. Reflecting implementation of heterogeneous compliance strategies, $r(1995, 1994)$ falls to 0.72, and $r(1993, 1995)$ is only 0.64. Because compliance strategies are relatively stable, $r(1996, 1995)$ equals 0.91.

What Happened in Allowance Markets?

Figure 3 displays historical information on the pricing of vintage 1995 allowances (in 1995 and earlier) or "current vintage" allowances, where "current vintage" allowances are all those that can be used to offset current emissions. During 1996, vintage 1995 and 1996 allowances are "current vintage" and thus perfect substitutes; vintage 1997 allowances are also "current vintage" during 1997.[11] These data come from five sources: trade press reports; price indices from three private market-making organizations, namely the Emissions Exchange (EX), Fieldston (EATX) and Cantor Fitzgerald (CF); and the EPA's annual March auctions. As directed by the statute, the EPA has implemented a discriminatory auction scheme, in which winning bidders pay what they bid for the small number of allowances EPA auctions each year. The circles in Figure 3 show the clearing prices (lowest winning bids) for vintage 1995 (for 1993–1995) or current vintage (for 1996 and 1997) allowances.

The EPA announced allowance allocations in early 1992 and promulgated associated regulations to permit affected sources to engage in trading and to develop price information before the 1995 compliance deadline. The first allowance transactions were reported in the trade press in mid-1992 at prices of $300 and $265 per allowance—roughly in line with expectations at that time. The March 1993 EPA auction produced a clearing price of $131 for vintage 1995 allowances. This result was dismissed at the

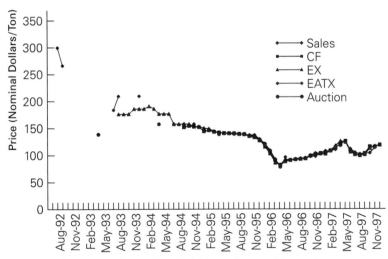

Figure 3 Allowance Prices, 1992–97 (1995 or Current Vintage)

Source: Selected issues of Allowance Price Indications, 1993–97; Cantor Fitzgerald Environmental Brokerage, NY, NY, Compliance Strategy Review, 1992–97; Fieldston, Washington, DC, Exchange Value, 1993–97; Emission Exchange Corp., Escandido, CA.

[11]This section is based on Joskow, Schmalensee, and Bailey (forthcoming).

time as an aberration or a reflection of defects in the auction's design, though, as Figure 3 makes clear, it indicated correctly that earlier projections of Phase I allowance prices were too high. For the remainder of 1993, the few private transactions reported and the Emissions Exchange allowance price index seemed to support the view that the auction results were misleading, though the private transactions pointed to prices in the $150–$200 range rather than the $250–$300 range.

EPA's second auction, in March 1994, cleared at $150 for vintage 1995 allowances, still noticeably below the EX price. Soon thereafter, however, the EX price fell to match the auction price, and the Emissions Exchange (EX) series was validated by price series published by Fieldston (EATX) and Cantor Fitzgerald (CF), two other market-makers. The March auction results in 1995, 1996, and 1997 are virtually identical to the contemporaneous private market prices reflected in these three series.

Figures on trading volume also suggest the emergence of an efficient allowance market, obeying the law of one price, around the middle of 1994. We estimate that 130,000 allowances had been traded on the private market by the end of March 1993, and an additional 226,000 traded in the period from April 1993 to March 1994.[12] Private market volumes for the next three April-March years were sharply higher: 1.6 million, 4.9 million, and 5.1 million allowances, respectively. In contrast, volume in the annual EPA auction has never exceeded 300,000 allowances. There is no obvious standard against which to evaluate these volumes, of course, but the nearly 20-fold increase in the two years after mid-1994 was clearly substantial. It is also worth noting that this increase could not have occurred if the EPA had not implemented Title IV with the intent and effect of keeping transactions costs low—another departure from tradition.

Data from the EPA auctions add a final bit of support to the view that an efficient allowance market emerged as the 1995 Phase I compliance date approached. In the two auctions held in March 1993, average winning bids were 11.5 and 20.6 percent above the lowest winning bids. In the three auctions held in March 1994, the differences between average and lowest winning bids were between 5.7 and 6.4 percent. In the nine subsequent auctions through March 1997, no such difference exceeded 3.4 percent, and all but two were below 2.4 percent. These data are consistent with strong constraints on bidding imposed by a well-developed private market.[13]

---

[12]To obtain the trading volume figures in this paragraph, we excluded intra-utility transfers (including intra-holding-company transfers). Our estimates understate private market activity by excluding unrecorded allowance transfers, unexercised options, and trading in allowance futures, all of which seem to have risen over time, particularly during and after 1995.

[13]Joskow, Schmalensee, and Bailey (forthcoming) discuss the criticisms of the design of the EPA auction that have been advanced by Cason (1993, 1995) and Cason and Plott (1996). Two points are central. First, the critics model the EPA auction as involving purely private values, thus completely ignoring the robust private market that has served since around mid-1994 to provide a common value for allowances. Second, the critics' main theoretical argument is that utilities that voluntarily offer to sell allowances on the EPA auctions have incentives to understate their reservation prices. In fact, most offers to sell have involved reservation prices well above market-clearing levels, and only a trivial number of voluntarily-offered allowances have been sold on the EPA auctions.

When the 1990 Clean Air Act Amendments were under consideration, opponents of the tradable allowance approach argued that the heavily regulated electric power industry would be unlikely to trade in a market for SO_2 emissions. They contended that publicity-shy utilities would be reluctant to buy "licenses to pollute" and that the state public utility commissions would discourage interstate trading.[14] In fact, as of January 1996 only 15 state public utility commissions had explicitly addressed the regulatory treatment of allowance transfers by generic order or informal guideline. Interstate trading does not seem to have been deterred, however. By January 1996, allowances had been transferred across the borders of all 24 states with Phase I affected units and of 10 of the 23 states with only Phase II units. Interviews with staff of all public utility commissions that had not addressed this issue indicated that the main reason guidance had not been issued was that no request for it had been received.

How Much Did It Cost?

We have studied the costs of compliance in detail for 1995; Ellerman et al. (1997) provides details on sources and methods. We find the total (annualized) cost of reducing emissions by 3.9 million tons (relative to the counterfactual) in 1995 to have been about $726 million. (All cost figures include annualized capital costs, along with increases, if any, in operating and fuel costs.) This is an average cost of $187 per ton of emissions reductions, or about $210 per ton on average if emissions reduced at no cost are excluded from the total. (These no-cost reductions all involved switches to low-sulfur Powder River Basin coal that also lowered delivered fuel price.) These per-ton abatement cost figures are at the low end of the range of earlier estimates, which varied from $180 to $307 per ton of emissions reduction for reductions between 3.1 and 4.4 million tons. We estimate emissions reduction through switching to more expensive lower-sulfur coal have cost $153 per ton of emissions reduction on average, while scrubbing costs $265 per ton on average, with considerable variation around both these averages.

There is no shortage of anecdotal evidence that utilities have made good use of the flexibility provided by Title IV, and it is natural to ask how much money this has saved. However, it is unclear what sort of hypothetical command-and-control policy could most instructively be compared with actual performance under Title IV. We have estimated that Title IV saved on the order of 25–34 percent as compared to a regime with the same allocation of allowances to generating units but no ability to transfer allowances from one generating unit to another by trading or intra-company

---

[14]This paragraph is based on Bailey (1996).

reallocation. This is a substantial dollar saving—on the order of $225 million to $375 million per year—but lower in percentage terms than most savings estimates in the literature comparing actual command-and-control policies to ideal tradeable permit regimes (Oates, Portney and McGartland, 1989; Tietenberg, 1985, ch. 3; 1992, p. 403). Perhaps this is because we have chosen a hypothetical alternative that is less inefficient than most actual command-and-control policies or because, as we next discuss, expectation errors prevented cost minimization under Title IV.

Why Have Allowance Prices Been So Low?

Much of the story in the early years of allowances trading was the dawning realization that allowance prices early in Phase I were going to be only around $100, well under half of what had been expected just a few years earlier. Both opponents and supporters of tradeable permits have advanced explanations for this result—but both are probably wrong.

Opponents of the tradeable emissions approach commonly attributed the low allowance prices to some defect in allowance markets, but they have failed to specify what these market defects are or how they have pushed prices down. On the other side, supporters of tradeable permits would be gratified if the difference between actual and expected allowance prices mainly reflected unanticipated innovations that greatly reduced compliance costs. There certainly was some induced innovation. For example, the observed per-ton cost of scrubbing in 1995 was substantially below earlier estimates, and our investigation indicates that this difference reflected unanticipated improvements in instrumentation and controls that reduce personnel requirements, innovative sludge removal techniques, and higher than expected utilization of scrubbed units (which reduces capital cost per ton of sulfur removed). Moreover, new ways were found to adapt midwestern boilers to blends of local and Powder River Basin coals. Although such adaptation was underway prior to 1990, it may well have been accelerated by the passage of Title IV. However, the dramatic gap between actual and expected allowance prices is simply too large to be accounted for by the observed technological improvements.

A more plausible explanation for the very low price of allowances begins by noting that compliance decisions generally had to be made well before the start of 1995. In particular, decisions to build scrubbers required commitments in 1992–93, when information about prices of allowances was highly imperfect. Most of the respondents to our 1996 survey (see note 4, above) who had elected to scrub indicated that expectations of allowance prices in the $300–400 range were "very important" in the choice of scrubbing. Though switching does not require as much advance planning as scrubbing, many utilities signed long-term contracts for low sulfur coal in the 1992–94 period at premium prices reflecting expected coal market conditions in Phase I.

However, it is now clear that market participants considering scrubbing or long-term contracts for lower-sulfur coal underestimated the extent to which declines in rail rates would make it possible to reduce SO_2 emissions reductions at zero or negative cost by switching to Powder River Basin coal and the extent to which falling delivered prices of that coal would drive down the price of lower-sulfur coal from the east and midwest. Thus, until mid-1994 or so, they overestimated allowance prices during at least the early part of Phase I. As a result, there was overinvestiment in scrubbers, and long-term contracts were signed for too much lower-sulfur coal from the east and midwest—some at very high prices. Indeed, a number of respondents to our 1996 survey identified substantial capacity for which they had reversed an initial decision to scrub; a third of these pointed to "low allowance prices" as a reason for reversal, and two-thirds pointed to a fall in low sulfur coal prices relative to scrubber costs.

Once a scrubber is built, however, the decision to run it or not turns on a comparison between the short-run marginal operating cost of using the scrubber to reduce emissions of sulfur by a ton, roughly $65 per ton on average, and the cost of the allowance that would need to be purchased if the scrubber were not run. Because of overinvestment in compliance, the short-run marginal cost of abatement curve was well below the long-run marginal cost curve during 1995 and 1996. A short-run marginal cost of abatement curve that is lower than it would be in long-run equilibrium is consistent with both unexpectedly low allowance prices in the short run and unexpectedly high banking of allowances. This pattern is at least qualitatively consistent with intertemporal equilibrium as well: more banking today postpones the date at which the bank is exhausted (T^* above) and thus reduces the present value of expected marginal abatement cost at that date. It is also consistent with the 6.2 percent increase in emissions from 1995 to 1996 by units that were Phase I affected in both years, a change that can be interpreted as movement toward an efficient equilibrium time-path of emissions but not easily as movement along such a time-path.

What Have We Learned?

Economists have argued for decades that, where the tradable permit approach can be used, it is superior to command-and-control environmental regulation (Tietenberg, 1985). The U.S. acid rain program appears to prove this argument correct in practice. Not only did Title IV more than achieve the SO_2 emissions goal established for Phase I, it did so on time, without extensive litigation, and at costs lower than had been projected. Some of the credit must be attributed to the lower rail rates that widened the area within which low-sulfur Powder River Basin coal could be economically used. Nonetheless, it is important to note that few command-and-control environmental programs, if any, have ever succeeded on all these dimensions.

Viewing the acid rain program as a more general experiment in environmental policy, it is too early to have learned all the lessons it will eventually teach us. Still, we believe several important lessons do follow from our experience to date with Title IV.

First, we have learned that large-scale tradable permit programs can work roughly as the textbooks describe; that is, they can both guarantee emissions reductions and allow profit-seeking emitters to reduce total compliance cost.

Second, one can expect a tradable permit program both to produce surprises and to adapt reasonably efficiently to surprises produced elsewhere in the economy. The big surprise here was the rapid expansion of the market area of Powder River Basin coal, and delayed recognition of this change apparently led to overinvestment and excess emissions abatement. But the market did react to the information contained in allowance prices, and orders for some scrubbers were canceled. The provisions for banking allowances then ensured that emissions reductions that had been reduced in cost by earlier investments were made, even though they were not required by the statute. It is hard to imagine any command-and-control regime adapting as sensibly to such an important exogenous event.

Third, efficient, competitive markets for tradable allowances may take time to develop, and the speed of development may be sensitive to some elements of program design. For example, the allowance auctions that the EPA was required to conduct seem to have facilitated both the price discovery process and the development of the allowance market. While larger auctions with a different design might have done better, only experience with other new programs will help to resolve this point.

Fourth, nothing in the experience with Title IV suggests that tradeable permit programs are a magic tool that can solve any environmental problem at negligible cost. It is clear that one could not use a tradeable permit approach of the sort described here to deal with, for example, an isolated source of toxic emissions with only local effects, since there would not be enough participants to make a market function. Moreover, Title IV rests on accurate emissions monitoring and strict enforcement of the property rights involved. Monitoring and enforcement are likely to pose more serious barriers to the implementation of an international tradeable permit system aimed at emissions of carbon dioxide and other greenhouse gases (Schmalensee, forthcoming).

The Title IV experience to date has demonstrated that the tradable permit approach is a very valuable policy tool that has proven itself superior to traditional methods for dealing with acid rain. However, actual markets do not always perform with frictionless perfection, particularly when they must guide long-lived investments made under conditions of real-world uncertainty.

REFERENCES

Atkeson, Erica, "Joint Implementation: Lessons from Title IV's Voluntary Compliance Programs," Working Paper 97–003, MIT Center for Energy and Environmental Policy Research, May 1997.

Bailey, Elizabeth M., "Allowance Trading Activity and State Regulatory Rulings: Evidence from the US Acid Rain Program," Working Paper 96–002, MIT Center for Energy and Environmental Policy Research, March 1996.

Bailey, Elizabeth M., "Prices and Pricing in the Market for Sulfur Dioxide Emissions," Mimeo, MIT Department of Economics, February 1998.

Cason, T.N., "Seller Incentive Properties of EPA's Emissions Trading Auction," *Journal of Environmental Economics and Management*, September 1993, *25*, 177–95.

Cason, T.N., "An Experimental Investigation of the Seller Incentives in EPA's Emissions Trading Auction, *American Economic Review*, September 1995, *85*, 905–22.

Cason, T.N., and Charles R. Plott, "EPA's New Emissions Trading Mechanism: A Laboratory Evaluation," *Journal of Environmental Economics and Management*, March 1996, *30*, 133–60.

Ellerman, A. Denny, and Juan Pablo Montero, "Why Are Allowance Prices So Low? An Analysis of the SO_2 Emissions Trading Program," Working Paper 96–001, MIT Center for Energy and Environmental Policy Research, February 1996.

Ellerman, A. Denny, Richard Schmalensee, Paul L. Joskow, Juan Pablo Montero, and Elizabeth M. Bailey, *Emissions Trading Under the U.S. Acid Rain Program: Evaluation of Compliance Costs and Allowance Market Performance*, MIT Center for Energy and Environmental Policy Research, October 1997.

Hahn, Robert W., and Gordon L. Hester, "Marketable Permits: Lessons for Theory and Practice," Ecology Law Quarterly, 1989a, *16*, 361–406.

Hahn, Robert W., and Gordon L. Hester, "Where Did All the Markets Go?" *Yale Journal on Regulation*, Winter 1989b, *6*, 109–53.

Intergovernmental Panel on Climate Change (IPCC), *Climate Change 1995. Economic and Social Dimensions of Climate Change: Contribution of Working Group III to the Second Assessment Report of the Intergovernmental Panel on Climate Change.* In J. Bruce, H.P. Lee, and E.F. Haites, eds. Cambridge: Cambridge University Press, 1996.

Joskow, Paul L., and Richard Schmalensee, "The Political Economy of Market-Based Environmental Policy: The U.S. Acid Rain Program," *Journal of Law and Economics*, forthcoming.

Joskow, Paul L., Richard Schmalensee, and Elizabeth M. Bailey. "The Market for Sulfur Dioxide Emissions," *American Economic Review*, forthcoming.

Montero, Juan Pablo, "Volunteering for Market-Based Environmental Regulation: The Substitution Provision of the SO_2 Emissions Trading Program," Working Paper 97–001, MIT Center for Energy and Environmental Policy Research, January 1997a.

Montero, Juan Pablo, "Optimal Design of a Phase-in Emissions Trading Program with Voluntary Compliance Options," Working Paper 97–003, MIT Center for Energy and Environmental Policy Research, July 1997b.

Oates, Wallace E., Paul R. Portney, and Albert M. McGartland, "The *Net* Benefits of Incentive-Based Regulation: A Case Study of Environmental Standard Setting," American Economic Review, December 1989, *79*, 1233–42.

National Economic Research Associates, *Key Issues in the Design of NO_x Emission Trading Programs to Reduce Ground-Level Ozone*, Palo Alto: Electric Power Research Institute, EPRI TR-104245, July 1994.

Pechan, E.H., *The Acid Rain Data Base Version I (ARDBVI)*, E.H. Pechan Associates Inc., Contract no. 68-D3-0005, prepared for the US Environmental Protection Agency's Office of Atmospheric Programs, Acid Rain Division: Washington, DC, 1995.

Schmalensee, Richard, "Greenhouse Policy Architectures and Institutions." In Nordhaus, William, ed. *Economic Issues in Climate Change: Evaluations of the Intergovernmental Panel Report.* Washington: Resources for the Future, forthcoming.

Tietenberg, Thomas H., *Emissions Trading: An Exercise in Reforming Pollution Policy.* Washington: Resources for the Future, 1985.

Tietenberg, Thomas H., *Environmental and Natural Resource Economics*, 3rd Ed. New York: HarperCollins, 1992.

U.S. Environmental Protection Agency (EPA), *1995 Compliance Results: Acid Rain Program*, project # EPA/430-R-96-012, Washington, DC, EPA, July 1996.

Williams, Jeffrey C., and Brian D. Wright, *Storage and Commodity Markets*. Cambridge, UK: Cambridge University Press, 1991.

21 What Can We Learn from the Grand Policy Experiment? Lessons from SO₂ Allowance Trading*

Robert N. Stavins

Robert N. Stavins is Albert Pratt Professor of Business and Government at the John F. Kennedy School of Government, Harvard University, and University Fellow at Resources for the Future.

Economists consistently have urged the use of "market-based" or "economic-incentive" instruments—principally pollution taxes and systems of tradeable permits—to address environmental problems, rather than so-called "command-and-control" instruments, such as design standards, which require the use of particular technologies, or performance standards, which prescribe the maximum amount of pollution that individual sources can emit. At least in theory, a well-designed pollution tax (Pigou, 1920) or tradeable permit system (Crocker, 1966; Dales, 1968; Montgomery, 1972) will minimize the aggregate cost of achieving a given level of environmental protection (Baumol and Oates, 1988), and provide dynamic incentives for the adoption and diffusion of cheaper and better pollution control technologies (Milliman and Prince, 1989).

Despite such advantages, market-based environmental instruments have been used far less frequently than command-and-control standards. In particular, while taxes have been imposed on certain products that are linked to pollution, like gasoline and chemicals, this has typically been done as a way of raising revenue, such as with gas taxes to fund highway construction or chemical taxes to fund cleanup of Superfund toxic waste sites, rather than as incentive devices intended to reduce externalities (Barthold, 1994). But over the past 25 years, the political process has gradually become more receptive to market-oriented environmental tools. Beginning in the 1970s, the Environmental Protection Agency (EPA) offered states the option of employing variants of tradeable permits for the control of local-

"What Can We Learn from the Grand Policy Experiment? Lessons from SO₂ Allowance Trading," by Robert N. Stavins, from *Journal of Economic Perspectives*, 12(3):69–88 (Summer 1998).

*I am indebted to Peter Zapfel for excellent research assistance, and Elizabeth Bailey, Dallas Burtraw, Brad De Long, Denny Ellerman, Lawrence Goulder, Robert Hahn, Paul Joskow, Alan Krueger, Richard Schmalensee, and (especially) Timothy Taylor for valuable comments on a previous version of this article. Any remaining errors are my own.

ized air pollutants. Tradeable-permit systems were used in the 1980s to phase leaded gasoline out of the market and to phase out ozone-depleting chlorofluorocarbons (CFCs). But by far the most ambitious application of these instruments has been for the control of acid rain under Title IV of the Clean Air Act amendments of 1990, which established a sulfur dioxide (SO_2) allowance trading program intended to cut nationwide emissions of SO_2 by 50 percent below 1980 levels by the year 2000.

This essay seeks to identify lessons that can be learned from this grand experiment in economically-oriented environmental policy. Since the SO_2 allowance trading program became binding only in 1995, it might seem premature to search for lessons for future policy. This would be true, were one to consider this policy experiment in isolation. But the SO_2 allowance trading program did not emerge into a policy vacuum; rather, it is but one step in the evolution of market-based environmental policies. Considered in this context, the time is ripe not only for an interim appraisal, but for reflection on what we have learned.

I begin with a brief description of the SO_2 allowance trading system and its performance, relying on the accompanying article by Richard Schmalensee and his colleagues to provide details. I then address questions of positive political economy; for example, given the historical support for command-and-control environmental policy instruments, why was allowance trading adopted for acid-rain control in 1990? Subsequently, I consider normative lessons for the design and implementation of market-oriented environmental policies, and offer some conclusions.

The SO_2 Allowance Trading System and Its Performance

Title IV of the Clean Air Act amendments of 1990 sought to reduce SO_2 emissions by 10 million tons from 1980 levels. The first phase of SO_2 emissions reduction was achieved in 1995, with a second phase of reduction to be accomplished by the year 2000.[1] In Phase I, individual emissions limits were assigned to the 263 most SO_2-emissions intensive generating units at 110 electric utility plants operated by 61 electric utilities, and located largely at coal-fired power plants east of the Mississippi River. EPA allocated each affected unit, on an annual basis, a specified number of allowances related to its share of heat input during the baseline period from 1985–87, plus bonus allowances available under a variety of provisions. After January 1, 1995, these units could emit sulfur dioxide only if they had adequate allowances to cover their emissions. Under Phase II of the program, begin-

---

[1] The law also sought to reduce nitrogen oxide (NO_x) emissions by 2 million tons annually from 1980 levels. A proposal for trading between SO_2 and NO_x was eliminated by Congress.

ning January 1, 2000, almost all fossil-fuel electric power plants will be brought within the system.

Cost-effectiveness is promoted by permitting allowance holders to transfer their permits among one another, so that those who can reduce emissions at the lowest cost have an incentive to do so and sell their allowances to those for whom reducing the cost would be greater. Allowances can also be "banked" for later use. The anticipated result is that marginal abatement costs will be equated across sources, thus achieving aggregate abatement at minimum total cost. In addition to the private market for bilateral trades, an annual auction of allowances withheld from utilities (about 3 percent of total allowances) was established by EPA, with revenues distributed to utilities on the basis of their original allocations. Also, utilities can offer allowances for sale at the annual government-sponsored auction. Finally, compliance is encouraged by a penalty of $2,000 per ton of emissions that exceed any year's allowances, along with a requirement that such excesses be offset the following year.

The SO_2 allowance trading program has performed successfully. Targeted emissions-reductions have been achieved and exceeded; in fact, because of excess reductions in 1995 and 1996 (and because of bonus allowances distributed by the government), utilities have built up an allowance bank of more than six million tons (U.S. Environmental Protection Agency, 1997). Total abatement costs have been significantly less than what they would have been in the absence of the trading provisions. Trading volume has increased over the life of the program, with EPA having recorded more than four million tons of allowance transfers in 1996 among economically unrelated parties (U.S. Environmental Protection Agency, 1997). This robust market has resulted in cost savings of up to $1 billion annually, compared with the cost of command-and-control regulatory alternatives that were considered by Congress in prior years (Kennedy, 1986).

Prospective analysis in 1990 suggested that the program's benefits would approximately equal its costs (Portney, 1990), but recent analysis indicates that benefits will exceed costs by a very significant margin (Burtraw, Krupnick, Mansur, Austin and Farell, 1997). Although the original motivation of the acid-rain control program was to reduce acidification of forest and aquatic ecosystems, the bulk of the benefits result from reduced human risk of premature mortality through reduced exposure to sulfates.

Positive Political Economy Lessons

To understand why the SO_2 allowance trading system was adopted in its particular form in 1990, it is useful to examine first the factors that led to the dominance of command-and-control over market-based instruments in the previous 20 years. To do this, I consider the demand for environmental policy instruments by individuals, firms, and interest groups, and their supply by the legislature and regulatory agencies. This "political market" framework is developed by Keohane, Revesz and Stavins (1997).

Why Have Command-and-Control Instruments Dominated Environmental Regulations?

The short answer is that command-and-control instruments have predominated because all of the main parties involved had reasons to favor them: affected firms, environmental advocacy groups, organized labor, legislators, and bureaucrats.

On the regulatory demand side, affected firms and their trade associations tended to prefer command-and-control instruments because standards can improve a firm's competitive position, while often costing a firm less than pollution taxes or tradeable permits. Command-and-control standards are inevitably set up with extensive input from existing industry and trade associations, which frequently obtain more stringent requirements for new sources and other advantages for existing firms. In contrast, auctioned permits and pollution taxes require firms to pay not only abatement costs to reduce pollution to some level, but also regulatory costs associated with emissions beyond that level, in the form either of permit purchases or tax payments. Because market-based instruments focus on the quantity of pollution, not on who generates it or the methods used to reduce it, these instruments can make the detailed lobbying role of trade associations less important.

For a long time, most environmental advocacy groups were actively hostile towards market-based instruments, for several reasons. A first reason was philosophical: environmentalists frequently portrayed pollution taxes and tradeable permits as "licenses to pollute." Although such ethical objections to the use of market-based environmental strategies have greatly diminished, they have not disappeared completely (Sandel, 1997). A second concern was that damages from pollution—to human health and ecological well-being—were difficult or impossible to quantify and monetize, and thus could not be summed up in a marginal damage function or captured by a Pigovian tax rate (Kelman, 1981). Third, environmental organizations have opposed market-based schemes out of a fear that permit levels and tax rates—once implemented—would be more difficult to tighten over time than command-and-control standards. If permits are given the status of "property rights," then any subsequent attempt by government to reduce pollution levels further could meet with demands for compensation.[2] Similarly, increasing pollution tax rates may be unlikely because raising tax rates is always politically difficult. A related strategic issue is that

---

[2]This concern was alleviated in the SO_2 provisions of the Clean Air Act Amendments of 1990 by an explicit statutory provision that permits do not represent property rights.

moving to tax-based environmental regulation would shift authority from environment committees in the Congress, frequently dominated by pro-environment legislators, to tax-writing committees, which are generally more conservative (Kelman, 1981).[3]

Finally, environmental organizations have objected to decentralized instruments on the grounds that even if emission taxes or tradeable permits reduce overall levels of emissions, they can lead to localized "hot spots" with relatively high levels of ambient pollution. In cases where this is a reasonable concern, it can be addressed in theory, through the use of "ambient permits" or through charge systems that are keyed to changes in ambient conditions at specified locations (Revesz, 1996). Despite the extensive theoretical literature on such ambient systems going back to Montgomery (1972), they have never been implemented, with the partial exception of a two-zone trading system in Los Angeles under the new RECLAIM program.

Organized labor has also been active in some environmental policy debates. In the case of restrictions on clean air, organized labor has taken the side of the United Mine Workers, whose members are heavily concentrated in eastern mines that produce higher-sulfur coal, and have therefore opposed pollution-control measures that would increase incentives for using low-sulfur coal from the largely nonunionized (and less labor-intensive) mines in the Powder River Basin of Wyoming and Montana. In the 1977 debates over amendments to the Clean Air Act, organized labor fought to include a command-and-control standard that effectively required scrubbing, thereby seeking to discourage switching to cleaner western coal (Ackerman and Hassler, 1981). Likewise, the United Mine Workers opposed the SO_2 allowance trading system in 1990 because of a fear that it would encourage a shift to western low-sulfur coal from non-unionized mines.

Turning to the supply side of environmental regulation, legislators have had a number of reasons to find command-and-control standards attractive. First, many legislators and their staffs are trained in law, which predisposes them to favor legalistic regulatory approaches. Second, standards tend to help hide the costs of pollution control (McCubbins and Sullivan, 1984), while market-based instruments generally impose those costs more directly. Compare, for example, the tone of public debates associated with proposed increases in gasoline taxes with those regarding commensurate increases in the stringency of the Corporate Average Fuel Economy standards for new cars.

Third, standards offers greater opportunities for symbolic politics, because strict standards—strong statements of support for environmental protection—can readily be combined with less visible exemptions or with lax enforcement measures. As one recent example of this pattern (albeit from the executive rather than the legislative branch), the Clinton admin-

---

[3]These strategic arguments refer, for the most part, to pollution taxes, not to market-based instruments in general. Indeed, as I discuss later, one reason some environmental groups have come to endorse the tradeable permits approach is that it promises the cost savings of taxes, without the drawbacks that environmentalists associate with tax instruments.

istration announced with much fanfare in June 1997 that it would tighten regulations of particulates and ambient ozone, but the new requirements do not take effect for eight years! Congress has frequently prescribed administrative rules and procedures to protect intended beneficiaries of legislation by constraining the scope of executive intervention (McCubbins, Noll and Weingast, 1987). Such stacking of the deck is more likely to be successful in the context of command-and-control legislation, since market-based instruments leave the allocation of costs and benefits up to the market, treating polluters identically.[4] Of course, the underlying reason why symbolic politics works is that voters have limited information, and so respond to gestures, while remaining relatively unaware of details.

Fourth, if politicians are risk averse, they will prefer instruments that involve more certain effects.[5] The flexibility inherent in market-based instruments creates uncertainty about distributional impacts and local levels of environmental quality. Typically, legislators in a representative democracy are more concerned with the geographic distribution of costs and benefits than with comparisons of total benefits and costs. Hence, aggregate cost-effectiveness—the major advantage of market-based instruments—is likely to play a less significant role in the legislative calculus than whether a politician is getting a good deal for constituents (Shepsle and Weingast, 1984). Politicians are also likely to oppose instruments that can induce firms to close and relocate, leading to localized unemployment. Although there will be winners as well as losers from such relocation, potential losers are likely to be more certain of their status than potential gainers.

Finally, legislators are wary of enacting programs that are likely to be undermined by bureaucrats in their implementation. And bureaucrats are less likely to undermine legislative decisions if their own preferences over policy instruments are accommodated. Bureaucratic preferences—at least in the past—were not supportive of market-based instruments, on several grounds: bureaucrats were familiar with command-and-control approaches; market-based instruments do not require the same kinds of technical expertise that agencies have developed under command-and-control regulation; and market-based instruments can imply a scaled-down role for the agency by shifting decision-making from the bureaucracy to the private sector. In other words, government bureaucrats—like their counterparts in environmental advocacy groups and trade associations—might be expected to oppose market-based instruments to prevent their expertise from becoming obsolete and to preserve their human capital. More recently, however, this same incentive has helped lead EPA staff involved in the SO_2 trading program to become strong proponents of trading for other air pollution problems.

---

[4]But the Congress has nevertheless tried. Joskow and Schmalensee (1998) examine Congressional attempts along these lines in the SO_2 allowance trading program.

[5]Legislators are likely to behave as if they are risk averse, even if they are personally risk neutral, if their constituents punish unpredictable policy choices or their reelection probability is nearly unity" (McCubbins, Noll and Weingast, 1989, p. 22).

Why Has the Chosen Form of Market-Based Approaches Always Been Freely-Allocated Tradeable Permits?

Economic theory suggests that the choice between tradeable permits and pollution taxes should be based upon case-specific factors, but when market-based instruments have been adopted in the United States, they have virtually always taken the form of tradeable permits rather than emission taxes. As already noted, taxes that are related to sources of pollution, like gasoline taxes, serve primarily as revenue-raising instruments, rather than environmental taxes designed to reduce an externality.[6] Moreover, the initial allocation of such permits has always been through free initial distribution, rather than through auctions, despite the apparent economic superiority of the latter mechanism in terms of economic efficiency (Fullerton and Metcalf, 1997; Goulder, Parry, and Burtraw, 1997; Stavins, 1995). The EPA does have an annual auction of SO_2 allowances, but this represents less than 2 percent of the total allocation (Bailey, 1996). While the EPA auctions may have helped in establishing the market for SO_2 allowances, they are a trivial part of the overall program (Joskow, Schmalensee and Bailey, 1996).

Again, many actors in the system have reasons to favor freely allocated tradeable permits over other market-based instruments. On the regulatory demand side, existing firms favor freely allocated tradeable permits because they convey rents to them. Moreover, like stringent command-and-control standards for new sources, but unlike auctioned permits or taxes, freely allocated permits give rise to entry barriers, since new entrants must purchase permits from existing holders. Thus, the rents conveyed to the private sector by freely allocated tradeable permits are, in effect, sustainable.

Environmental advocacy groups have generally supported command-and-control approaches, but given the choice between tradeable permits and emission taxes, these groups strongly prefer the former. Environmental advocates have a strong incentive to avoid policy instruments that make the costs of environmental protection highly visible to consumers and voters; and taxes make those costs more explicit than permits.[7] Also, environmental advocates prefer permit schemes because they specify the quantity of pollution reduction that will be achieved, in contrast with the indirect effect of pollution taxes. Overall, some environmental groups have come to endorse the tradeable permits approach because it promises the cost sav-

---

[6]This pattern holds in Europe, as well. There, environmental taxes have been far more prevalent than tradeable permits, but the taxes employed have typically been two low to induce pollution abatement (Cansier and Krumm, 1997).

[7]For this same reason, private industry may strategically choose to endorse a pollution tax approach, in the hope that consequent public opposition will result in the setting of a less stringent environmental goal. This may seem farfetched, but it appears to be precisely what happened in the closing days of the 1990 Clean Air Act debate in the U.S. Senate. When it had become clear that a 10 million ton SO_2 allowance trading system was about to be passed, electric utilities suddenly proposed an SO_2 emissions tax as an alternative policy instrument.

ings of pollution taxes, without the drawbacks that environmentalists associate with environmental tax instruments.

Freely allocated tradeable permits are easier for legislators to supply than taxes or auctioned permits, again because the costs imposed on industry are less visible and less burdensome, since no money is exchanged at the time of the initial permit allocation. Also, freely allocated permits offer a much greater degree of political control over the distributional effects of regulation, facilitating the formation of majority coalitions. Joskow and Schmalensee (1998) examined the political process of allocating SO_2 allowances in the 1990 amendments, and found that allocating permits on the basis of prior emissions can produce fairly clear winners and losers among firms and states. An auction allows no such political maneuvering.

Why Was a Market-Based Approach Adopted for SO_2 Emissions in 1990?

By the late 1980s, there had already been a significant shift of the political center toward a more favorable view of using markets to solve social problems. The Bush administration, which proposed the SO_2 allowance trading program and then championed it through an initially resistant Democratic Congress, deserves much of the credit here. The ideas of "fiscally responsible environmental protection" and "harnessing market forces to protect the environment" fit well with its quintessentially moderate Republicanism. (The Reagan administration enthusiastically embraced a market-oriented ideology, but demonstrated little interest in employing actual market-based policies in the environmental area.) More broadly, support for market-oriented solutions to various social problems had been increasing across the political spectrum as early as the Carter administration, as evidenced by deliberations and action regarding deregulation of the airline, telecommunications, trucking, railroad, and banking industries. Indeed, by 1990, the phrase "market-based environmental policy" had evolved from being politically problematic to politically attractive. Even leading liberal environmental advocates like Rep. Henry Waxman began to characterize their clean air proposals as using "economic-incentive mechanisms," even if the actual proposals continued to be of the conventional, command-and-control variety.

Given the historical opposition to market-oriented pollution control policies, how can we explain the adoption of the SO_2 allowance trading program in 1990? More broadly, why has there been increased openness to the use of market-based approaches?

For economists, it would be gratifying to believe that increased understanding of market-based instruments had played a large part in fostering their increased political acceptance, but how important has this really been? In 1981, Steven Kelman surveyed Congressional staff members, and found that Republican support and Democratic opposition to market-based environmental policy instruments was based largely on ideological

grounds, with little awareness or understanding of the advantages or disadvantages of the various instruments. What would happen if we were to
replicate Kelman's (1981) survey today? My hypothesis is that we would
find increased support from Republicans, greatly increased support from
Democrats, but insufficient improvements in understanding to explain
these changes.[8] So what else has mattered?

One factor has surely been increased pollution control costs, which
have led to greater demand for cost-effective instruments. By 1990, U.S.
pollution control costs had reached $125 billion annually, nearly a tripling
of real costs from 1972 levels (U.S. Environmental Protection Agency, 1990).
In the case of SO_2 control, it was well known that utilities faced very different marginal abatement costs and would want to use varying abatement
methods, because of differences in the ages of plants and their proximity
to sources of low-sulfur coal. EPA estimates in the late 1980s were that a
well-functioning tradeable-permit program would save 50 percent on costs
that would otherwise exceed $6 billion annually if a dictated technological
solution were implemented (ICF, 1989).

A second factor that was important in the 1990 Clean Air Act debates
was strong and vocal support for the SO_2 allowance trading system from
parts of the environmental community, particularly the Environmental Defense Fund (EDF), which had already become a champion of market-based
approaches to environmental protection in other, less nationally prominent
domains, such as water marketing in California. By supporting allowance
trading, EDF solidified its reputation as a pragmatic environmental organization willing to adopt new strategies involving less confrontation with
private industry, and distinguished itself from other groups (Keohane,
Revesz and Stavins, 1997). When the memberships (and financial resources) of other environmental advocacy groups subsequently declined
with the election of the environment-friendly Clinton-Gore administration,
EDF continued to prosper and grow (Lowry, 1993).

A third key factor in 1990 was the fact that the SO_2 allowance trading
program was designed to reduce emissions, not simply to reallocate them
cost-effectively. In 1990, EDF was able to make powerful arguments for
tradeable permits on the grounds that the use of a cost-effective instrument
would make it politically feasible to achieve greater reductions in SO_2 emissions than would otherwise be possible. Market-based instruments are most
likely to be politically acceptable if they can achieve environmental improvements which otherwise are not politically or economically feasible. It
is not coincidental that the earlier (and successful) lead and chlorofluorocarbon permit trading programs also aimed at reducing emissions, while
EPA's attempts to reform local air quality regulation through its Emissions
Trading Program without incremental improvements in air quality have
been troubled and halting.

---

[8]But there has been some increased understanding of market-based approaches to environmental
protection among policymakers and their staffs, due in part to the economics training that is now
common in law schools, and the proliferation of schools of public policy.

Fourth, many of the economists involved in the deliberations re-garding the SO_2 allowance system took the approach of accepting—implicitly or otherwise—a political goal of reducing SO_2 emissions by 10 million tons. Rather than debating the costs and benefits of that goal, they simply focused on the cost-effective means of achieving it. Separating the benefit-cost calculation about the goals from the instruments used to achieve the goal was important to avoid splintering support for an SO_2 trading program. As evidenced by the failed Republican attempts at "regulatory reform" in 1996, the notion of using explicit benefit-cost calculations as the basis for judging regulations remains highly controversial in political circles. Of course, even if the strategy worked out well in the SO_2 case, there are limitations to the wisdom of separating ends and means: one risks designing a fast train to the wrong station.

Fifth, it is important to note that acid rain was effectively an unregulated problem until the SO_2 allowance trading program of 1990. Hence, there were no existing constituencies for the status quo approach, because there *was* no status quo approach. The demand for a market-based instrument is likely to be greatest and the political opportunity costs of legislators providing support are likely to be least when the status quo instrument is essentially nonexistent. This implies that we should be more optimistic about introducing such market-based instruments for "new" problems, such as global climate change, than for existing, highly regulated problems, such as abandoned hazardous waste sites.

Finally, a caveat is in order. The adoption of the SO_2 allowance trading program for acid rain control—like any major innovation in public policy—can partly be attributed to a healthy dose of chance that placed specific persons in key positions, in this case at the White House, EPA, the Congress, and environmental organizations. Within the White House, among the most active and influential enthusiasts of market-based environmental instruments were Counsel Boyden Gray and his Deputy John Schmitz; Domestic Policy Adviser Roger Porter; Council of Economic Advisers (CEA) Member Richard Schmalensee; CEA Senior Staff Economist Robert Hahn; and Office of Management and Budget Associate Director Robert Grady. At EPA, Administrator William Reilly—a "card-carrying environmentalist"—enjoyed valuable credibility with environmental advocacy groups; Deputy Administrator Henry Habicht was a key supporter of market-based instruments; and Assistant Administrator William Rosenberg was an early convert. In the Congress, Senators Timothy Wirth and John Heinz provided high-profile, bipartisan support for the SO_2 allowance trading system and, more broadly, for a variety of market-based instruments for environmental problems through their "Project 88" (Stavins, 1988). Within the environmental community, EDF Executive Director Fred Krupp, Senior Economist Daniel Dudek, and Staff Attorney Joseph Goffman worked closely with the White House to develop the allowance trading proposal.

Normative Lessons

Within the context of 30 years of federal environmental regulation, characterized by sporadic but increasing reliance on market-based policy instruments, I consider normative lessons from the design and implementation of the SO_2 allowance trading system for design and implementation of tradeable permit systems, analysis of prospective and adopted systems, and identification of new applications.

Lessons for Design and Implementation of Tradeable Permit Systems

The performance of the SO_2 allowance trading system to date provides valuable evidence for environmentalists and others who have been resistant to these innovations that market-based instruments can achieve major cost savings while accomplishing their environmental objectives (Ellerman et al., 1997; U.S. General Accounting Office, 1995). Likewise, we have seen that the system can be implemented without a surge of lawsuits, partly because it was well designed (Burtraw and Swift, 1996) and partly because issues of distributional equity were handled through a congressionally imposed allocation. The system's performance also offers lessons about the importance of flexibility, simplicity, the role of monitoring and enforcement, and the capabilities of the private sector to make markets of this sort work.

In regard to flexibility, tradeable permit systems should be designed to allow for a broad set of compliance alternatives, in terms of both timing and technological options. Allowing flexible timing and intertemporal trading of the allowances—that is, "banking" allowances for future use—has played a very important role in the program's performance (Ellerman et al., 1997), much as it did in the lead rights trading program a decade earlier (Kerr and Maré, 1997). The permit system was based on emissions of SO_2, as opposed to sulfur content of fuels, so that both scrubbing and fuel-switching were feasible options. Moreover, one of the most significant benefits of the trading system was simply that technology standards requiring scrubbing of SO_2 were thereby avoided. This allowed midwestern utilities to take advantage of lower rail rates (brought about by railroad deregulation) to reduce their SO_2 emissions by increasing their use of low-sulfur coal from Wyoming and Montana, an approach that would not have been possible if scrubber requirements had been in place. Also, a less flexible system would not have led to the technological change that may have been induced in scrubber performance and rail transport (Burtraw, 1996; Ellerman and Montero, 1996; Bohi and Burtraw, 1997). Likewise, the economic incentives provided by the trading system have led to induced process innovations in the form of bundling of allowances with coal supplies (Doucet and Strauss, 1994) and the installation of emission reduction technology in exchange for generated allowances (Dudek and Goffman, 1995). The flexibility of the allowance trading system accommodates the dynamic market changes that are occurring because of electric utility deregulation, allowing shifts in industry structure and production methods while assuring that total emissions do not increase.

In regard to simplicity, a unique formula for allocating permits based upon historical data is relatively difficult to contest or manipulate. More generally, trading rules should be clearly defined up front, without ambiguity. For example, there should be no requirements for prior government approval of individual trades. Such requirements hampered EPA's Emissions Trading Program in the 1970s, while the lack of such requirements was an important factor in the success of lead trading (Hahn and Hester, 1989). In the case of SO_2 trading, the absence of requirements for prior approval has reduced uncertainty for utilities and administrative costs for government, and contributed to low transactions costs (Rico, 1995).

Considerations of simplicity and the experience of the SO_2 allowance system also argue for using absolute baselines, not relative ones, as the point of departure for tradeable permit programs. The difference is that with an absolute baseline (so-called "cap-and-trade"), sources are each allocated some number of permits (the total of which is the "cap"); with a relative baseline, reductions are credited from an unspecified baseline. The problem is that without a specified baseline, reductions must be credited relative to an unobservable hypothetical—what the source would have emitted in the absence of the regulation. A hybrid system—where a cap-and-trade program is combined with voluntary "opt-in provisions"—creates the possibility for "paper trades," where a regulated source is credited for an emissions reduction (by an unregulated source) that would have taken place in any event (Montero, 1997). The result is a decrease in aggregate costs among regulated sources, but this is partly due to an unintentional increase in the total emissions cap (Atkeson, 1997). As was experienced with EPA's Emissions Trading Program, relative baselines create significant transaction costs by essentially requiring prior approval of trades as the authority investigates the claimed counterfactual from which reductions are calculated and credits generated (Nichols, Farr and Hester, 1996).

The SO_2 program has also brought home the importance of monitoring and enforcement provisions. In 1990, environmental advocates insisted on continuous emissions monitoring (Burtraw and Swift, 1996), which helps build market confidence (McLean, 1995). The costs of such monitoring, however, are significant. On the enforcement side, the Act's stiff penalties have provided sufficient incentive for the very high degree of compliance that has been achieved.

Another normative lesson is linked with positive issues. Above we emphasized the political advantages of freely allocated permit systems, as employed with SO_2. But the same characteristic that makes such allocation attractive in positive political economy terms—the conveyance of scarcity rents to the private sector—also makes free allocation problematic in normative, efficiency terms (Fullerton and Metcalf, 1997). Goulder, Parry, and Burtraw (1997) estimate that the costs of SO_2 allowance trading would be 25 percent less if permits were auctioned rather than freely allocated, because auctioning yields revenues that can be used to finance reductions in pre-existing distortionary taxes. Furthermore, in the presence of some forms of transaction costs, the post-trading equilibrium—and hence aggregate abatement costs—are sensitive to the initial permit allocation (Stavins, 1995). For both reasons, a successful attempt to establish a politically viable program through a specific initial permit allocation can result in a program that is significantly more costly than anticipated.

Finally, the SO_2 program's performance demonstrates that the private sector can fulfill brokerage needs, providing price information and matching trading partners, despite claims to the contrary when the program was enacted. Entrepreneurs have stepped in to make available a variety of services, including private brokerage, electronic bid/ask bulletin boards, and allowance price forecasts. The annual EPA auctions may have served the purpose of helping to reveal market valuations of allowances, but bilateral trading has also informed the auctions (Joskow, Schmalensee and Bailey, 1996).

Lessons for Analysis of Tradeable Permit Systems

When assessing trading programs, economists have typically employed some measure in which gains from trade are estimated for moving from conventional standards to marketable permits. Aggregate cost savings are the best yardstick for measuring success, not number of trades or total trading volume (Hahn and May, 1994).

The challenge for analysts is to compare realistic versions of both tradeable permit systems and "likely alternatives," not idealized versions of either. It is not enough to analyze static gains from trade (Hahn and Stavins, 1992). For example, the gains from banking allowances should also be modeled (unless this is not permitted in practice). It can also be important to allow for the effects of alternative instruments on technology innovation and diffusion (Milliman and Prince, 1989; Jaffe and Stavins, 1995; Doucet and Strauss, 1994; Dudek and Goffman, 1995), especially when permit trading programs impose significant costs over long time horizons (Newell, Jaffe and Stavins, 1997).

More generally, it is important to consider the effects of the pre-existing regulatory environment. The level of pre-existing factor taxes can affect the total costs of regulation (Goulder, Parry and Burtraw, 1997). Also, because SO_2 is both a transboundary precursor of acid rain and a local air pollutant regulated under a separate part of the Clean Air Act, "local" environmental regulations have sometimes prevented utilities from acquiring allowances rather than carrying out emissions reductions (Conrad and Kohn, 1996). Moreover, because electricity generation and distribution have been regulated by state commissions, a prospective analysis of SO_2 trading should consider the incentives these commissions may have to influence the level of allowance trading.[9]

---

[9]Also, rate-of-return regulation that employs capital investments as a baseline might be expected to lead electric utilities to bias their SO_2 compliance choices toward investments in scrubbers, for example, and away from allowance transactions (Averch and Johnson, 1962).

A set of theoretical arguments suggests that state public utility commissions may have incentives to erect such barriers. Coal interests in some midwestern and eastern states, where high-sulfur coal is mined, were opposed to the concept of allowance trading because it would permit utilities to switch to cleaner western coal. Hence, it is reasonable to suspect that those same interests would pressure state regulatory commissions to erect direct or indirect barriers to trading (Bohi and Burtraw, 1992; Burtraw, 1996). However, the only rigorous analysis that has been carried out of this contention suggests that such pressures have not, if applied, been effective (Bailey, 1996). In any event, it is clear that state regulatory commissions have not encouraged utilities to engage in allowance trading, either (Bohi, 1994). The commissions have been reactive, rather than proactive in terms of accounting and tax treatment of allowance transactions (Rose, 1997), restricting themselves to reviewing and approving plans submitted by utilities. Only the Georgia Public Service Commission has actively ordered utilities in its jurisdiction to monitor the allowance market and purchase allowances when prices are below compliance costs.

It has also been suggested that many electric utilities have been reluctant to consider new options, which is consistent with their reputation as firms that seek to minimize risk, rather than cost (Rose, 1997), but this may change due to the heightened role of competition brought about by electricity deregulation. Also, long-term contractual precommitments have tied many utilities to plans conceived before allowance trading was an option (Coggins and Swinton, 1996). Finally, some utilities may be reluctant to make serious investments in allowances in the face of future regulatory uncertainty (U.S. Energy Information Administration, 1997).

Issues such as these must be taken into account in the analysis of any pollution control program, whether it is market-oriented or command-and-control in nature.

Lessons for Identifying New Applications

Market-based policy instruments are now considered for each and every environmental problem that is raised, ranging from endangered species preservation to what may be the greatest of environmental problems, the greenhouse effect and global climate change. Our experiences with SO_2 trading—and with the earlier programs of lead and chlorofluorocarbon trading—offer some guidance to the conditions under which tradeable permits are likely to work well, and when they may face greater difficulties.

First, SO_2 trading is a case where the cost of abating pollution differs widely among sources, and where a market-based system is therefore likely to have greater gains, relative to conventional, command-and-control regulations (Newell and Stavins, 1997). It was clear early on that SO_2 abatement cost heterogeneity was great, because of differences in ages of plants and their proximity to sources of low-sulfur coal. But where abatement costs are more uniform across sources, the political costs of enacting an allowance trading approach are less likely to be justifiable.

Second, the greater the degree to which pollutants mix in the receiving airshed or watershed, the more attractive a tradeable emission permit (or emission tax) system will be, relative to a conventional uniform standard. This is because taxes or tradeable permits can lead to localized "hot spots" with relatively high levels of ambient pollution. This is a significant distributional issue. Some acid-rain receiving states have attempted to erect barriers to those trades that could increase deposition within their borders.[10] It can also become an efficiency issue, if damages are nonlinearly related to pollutant concentrations.

Third, the efficiency of a tradeable permit system will depend on the pattern of costs and benefits. If uncertainty about marginal abatement costs is significant, and if marginal abatement costs are quite flat and marginal benefits of abatement fall relatively quickly, then a quantity instrument, such as tradeable permits, will be more efficient than a price instrument, such as an emission tax (Weitzman, 1974). Furthermore, when there is also uncertainty about marginal benefits, and marginal benefits are positively correlated with marginal costs (which, it turns out, is a relatively common occurrence for a variety of pollution problems), then there is an additional argument in favor of the relative efficiency of quantity instruments.[11]

Fourth, tradeable permits will work best when transaction costs are low, and the SO_2 experiment shows that if properly designed, private markets will tend to render transaction costs minimal. Finally, considerations of political feasibility point to the wisdom of proposing trading instruments when they can be used to facilitate emissions reductions, as was done with SO_2 allowances and lead rights trading. Policy instruments that appear impeccable from the vantage point of Cambridge, Massachusetts, but consistently prove infeasible in Washington, D.C., can hardly be considered "optimal."

Many of these issues can be illuminated by considering a concrete example: the current interest in applying tradeable permits to the task of cutting carbon dioxide (CO_2) emissions to reduce the risk of global climate change. It is immediately obvious that the number and diversity of sources of CO_2 emissions due to fossil fuel combustion are vastly greater than in the case of SO_2 emissions as a precursor of acid rain, where the focus can be placed on a few hundred electric utility plants (Environmental Law Institute, 1997).

---

[10]For example, as recently as the summer of 1997, legislation emerged in the New York State legislature that would penalize utilities for selling allowances to companies "accused of exacerbating New York's acid rain problem" (*Boston Globe*, June 26, 1997, on-line). Under the legislation, if a trade were found to be "detrimental to environmentally sensitive areas," the Public Service Commission would be directed to impose a fine three times the value of the trade.

[11]One generator of stochastic shocks that frequently affects both marginal benefits and marginal costs—with the same sign—is the weather. For further explanation and specific examples, see Stavins (1996).

Any pollution-control program must face the possibility of "emissions leakage" from regulated to unregulated sources. This could be a problem for meeting domestic targets for CO_2 emissions reduction, but it would be a vastly greater problem for an international program, where emissions would tend to increase in nonparticipant countries. This also raises serious concerns with provisions in the Kyoto Protocol for industrialized countries to participate in a CO_2 cap-and-trade program, while non-participant (developing) nations retain the option of joining the system on a project-by-project basis, an approach commonly known as "joint implementation." As emphasized earlier, provisions in tradeable permit programs that allow for unregulated sources to "opt in" can lower aggregate costs by substituting low-cost for high-cost control, but may also have the unintended effect of increasing aggregate emissions beyond what they would otherwise have been. This is because there is an incentive for adverse selection: sources in developing countries that would reduce their emissions, opt in, and receive "excess allowances" would tend to be those that would have reduced their emissions in any case.

To the limited degree that any previous trading program can serve as a model for the case of global climate change, some attention should be given to the tradeable-permit system that accomplished the U.S. phaseout of leaded gasoline. The currency of that system was not lead oxide emissions from motor vehicles, but the lead content of gasoline. So too, in the case of global climate, great savings in monitoring and enforcement costs could be had by adopting *input* trading linked to the carbon content of fossil fuels. This is reasonable in the climate case, since—unlike in the SO_2 case—CO_2 emissions are roughly proportional to the carbon content of fossil fuels and scrubbing alternatives are largely unavailable, at least at present. On the other hand, natural sequestration of CO_2 from the atmosphere by expanding forested areas is available (even in the United States) at reasonable cost (Stavins, 1997) and is explicitly counted toward compliance with the targets of the Kyoto Protocol. Hence, it will be important to combine any carbon trading (or carbon tax) program with a carbon sequestration program, possibly denominated by forested areas.

In terms of carbon permit allocation mechanisms, auctions would have the advantage that revenues could be used to finance reductions in distortionary taxes. Although free allocation of carbon permits might meet with less political resistance, such free allocation could increase regulatory costs enough that the sign of the efficiency impact would be reversed from positive to negative net benefits (Parry, Williams and Goulder 1997).

Finally, developing a tradeable permit system in the area of global climate change would surely bring forth an entirely new set of economic, political, and institutional challenges, particularly with regard to enforcement problems (Schmalensee, 1996; Stavins, 1998). But it is also true that the diversity of sources of CO_2 emissions and the magnitude of likely abatement costs make it equally clear that only a market-based instrument—some form of carbon rights trading or (probably revenue-neutral) carbon taxes—will be capable of achieving the domestic targets that may eventually be forthcoming from international agreements.

Conclusion

Given that the SO_2 allowance-trading program became fully binding only in 1995, we should be cautious when drawing conclusions about lessons to be learned from the program's development or its performance. A number of important questions remain. For example, little is known empirically about the impact of trading on technological change. Also, much more empirical research is needed on how the pre-existing regulatory environment affects the operation of permit trading programs. Moreover, all the successes with tradeable permits have involved air pollution: acid rain, leaded gasoline, and chlorofluorocarbons. Our experience (and success rate) with water pollution is much more limited (Hahn, 1989), and in other areas, we have no experience at all. Even for air pollution problems, the tremendous differences between SO_2 and acid rain, on the one hand, and the combustion of fossil fuels and global climate change, on the other, indicate that any rush to judgement regarding global climate policy instruments is unwarranted.

Despite these and other uncertainties, market-based instruments for environmental protection—and, in particular, tradeable permit systems—now enjoy proven successes in reducing pollution at low cost. Such cost effectiveness is the primary focus of economists when evaluating public policies, but the political system clearly gives much greater weight to distributional concerns. In the Congressional deliberations that led up to the Clean Air Act amendments of 1990, considerable pressures were brought to bear to allow less switching from high-sulfur to low-sulfur coal to benefit regions dependent on high-sulfur coal mining. Such provisions would have increased compliance costs for midwestern coal-burning utilities (U.S. Congressional Budget Office, 1986), encouraged political pressures for nationwide cost sharing, and greatly reduced the cost-effectiveness of the system. In this way, individual constituencies, each fighting for its own version of distributional equity, negate efficiency and cost effectiveness. In the pursuit of obtaining nicely shaped pieces of the proverbial pie, we all too often end up with a systematically smaller pie. That this did not happen in 1990 was the exception, not the rule.

There are sound reasons why the political world has been slow to embrace the use of market-based instruments for environmental protection, including the ways economists have packaged and promoted their ideas in the past: failing to separate means (cost-effective instruments) from ends (efficiency); and treating environmental problems as little more than "externalities calling for corrective taxes." Much of the resistance has also been due, of course, to the very nature of the political process and the incentives it provides to both politicians and interest groups to favor command-and-control methods instead of market-based approaches.

But despite this history, market-based instruments have moved center stage, and policy debates look very different from the time when these ideas were characterized as "licenses to pollute" or dismissed as completely impractical. Of course, no single policy instrument—whether market-based or conventional—will be appropriate for all environmental problems. Which instrument is best in any given situation depends upon characteristics of the specific environmental problem, and the social, political, and economic context in which the instrument is to be implemented.

REFERENCES

Ackerman, Bruce A., and William T. Hassler, *Clean Coal/Dirty Air*. New Haven: Yale University Press, 1981.

Atkeson, Erica, "Joint Implementation: Lessons from Title IV's Voluntary Compliance Programs," Working Paper 97–003, MIT Center for Energy and Environmental Policy Research, May 1997.

Averch, Harvey, and Leland L. Johnson, "Behavior of the Firm under Regulatory Constraint," *American Economic Review*, 1962, *52*, 1053–69.

Bailey, Elizabeth M., "Allowance Trading Activity and State Regulatory Rulings: Evidence from the US Acid Rain Program," Working Paper 96–002, MIT Center for Energy and Environmental Policy Research, March 1996.

Barthold, Thomas A., "Issues in the Design of Environmental Excise Taxes," *Journal of Economic Perspectives*, Winter 1994, *8*:1, 133–51.

Baumol, William J., and Wallace E. Oates, *The Theory of Environmental Policy*. Second edition. New York: Cambridge University Press, 1988.

Bohi, Douglas R., "Utilities and State Regulators Are Failing to Take Advantage of Emissions Allowance Trading," *The Electricity Journal*, March 1994, 7:2, 20–27.

Bohi, Douglas R., and Dallas Burtraw, "Utility Investment Behavior and the Emission Trading Market," *Resources and Energy*, April 1992, *14*:1/2, 129–53.

Bohi, Douglas R., and Dallas Burtraw, "SO_2 Allowance Trading: How Do Expectations and Experience Measure Up?" *Electricity Journal*, August/September 1997, 67–75.

Burtraw, Dallas, "The SO_2 Emissions Trading Program: Cost Savings Without Allowance Trades," *Contemporary Economic Policy*, April 1996, *14*, 79–94.

Burtraw, Dallas, Alan Krupnick, Erin Mansur, David Austin, and Deidre Farrell, "The Costs and Benefits of Reducing Acid Rain," Discussion Paper 97–31-REV, Resources for the Future, Washington, D.C., September 1997.

Burtraw, Dallas, and Byron Swift, "A New Standard of Performance: An Analysis of the Clean Air Act's Acid Rain Program," *Environmental Law Reporter News & Analysis*, August 1996, *26*:8, 10411–10423.

Cansier, Dieter, and Raimund Krumm, "Air Pollutant Taxation: An Empirical Survey," *Ecological Economics*, 1997, *23*:1, 59–70.

Coggins, Jay S., and John R. Swinton, "The Price of Pollution: A Dual Approach to Valuing SO_2 Allowances," *Journal of Environmental Economics and Management*, January 1996, *30*:1, 58–72.

Conrad, Klaus, and Robert E. Kohn, "The US Market for SO_2 Permits: Policy Implications of the Low Price and Trading Volume," *Energy Policy*, 1996, *24*:12, 1051–59.

Crocker, Thomas D., "The Structuring of Atmospheric Pollution Control Systems." In Harold Wolozin, ed. *The Economics of Air Pollution*. New York: Norton, 1966.

Dales, John H., *Pollution, Property, and Prices*. Toronto: University of Toronto Press, 1968.

Doucet, Joseph A., and Todd Strauss, "On the Bundling of Coal and Sulphur Dioxide Emissions Allowances," *Energy Policy*, September 1994, *22*:9, 764–70.

Dudek, Daniel J., and Joseph Goffman, "The Clean Air Act Acid Rain Program: Lessons for Success in Creating a New Paradigm," 85th Annual Meeting of the Air & Waste Management Association, 95-RA120.06, San Antonio, Texas, 1995.

Ellerman, A. Denny, Richard Schmalensee, Paul J. Joskow, Juan Pablo Montero, and Elizabeth M. Bailey, *Emissions Trading Under the U.S. Acid Rain Program: Evaluation of Compliance Costs and Allowance Market Performance.* Cambridge: MIT Center for Energy and Environmental Policy Research, October 1997.

Ellerman, A. Denny, and Juan Pablo Montero, "Why are Allowance Prices so Low? An Analysis of the SO_2 Emissions Trading Program," Working Paper 96-001, MIT Center for Energy and Environmental Policy Research, February 1996.

Environmental Law Institute, "Implementing an Emissions Cap and Allowance Trading System for Greenhouse Gases: Lessons from the Acid Rain Program," Research Report, Washington, D.C., September 1997.

Fullerton, Don, and Gilbert Metcalf, "Environmental Controls, Scarcity Rents, and Pre-Existing Distortions," NBER Working Paper 6091, July 1997.

Goulder, Lawrence H., Ian W. H. Parry, and Dallas Burtraw, "Revenue-Raising vs. Other Approaches to Environmental Protection: The Critical Significance of Pre-Existing Tax Distortions," *RAND Journal of Economics*, Winter 1997, *28*:4, 708-31.

Hahn, Robert W., "Economic Prescriptions for Environmental Problems: How the patient Followed the Doctor's Orders," *Journal of Economic Perspectives*, Spring 1989, *3*:2, 95-114.

Hahn, Robert W., and Gordon L. Hester, "Marketable Permits: Lessons for Theory and Practice," *Ecology Law Quarterly*, 1989, *16*:2, 361-406.

Hahn, Robert W., and Carol A. May, "The Behavior of the Allowance Market: Theory and Evidence," *The Electricity Journal*, March 1994, *7*:2, 28-37.

Hahn, Robert W., and Robert N. Stavins, "Economic Incentives for Environmental Protection: Integrating Theory and Practice," *American Economic Review*, 1992, *82*, 464-68.

ICF, Inc., "Economic Analysis of Title V (Acid Rain Provisions) of the Administration's Proposed Clean Air Act Amendments (H.R. 3030/S. 1490)." Prepared for the U.S. Environmental Protection Agency, Washington, D.C., 1989.

Jaffe, Adam B., and Robert N. Stavins, "Dynamic Incentives of Environmental Regulations: The Effects of Alternative Policy Instruments on Technological Diffusion." *Journal of Environmental Economics and Management*, November 1995, *29*:3, S43-S63.

Joskow, Paul L., and Richard Schmalensee, "The Political Economy of Market-Based Environmental Policy: The U.S. Acid Rain Program," *Journal of Law and Economics*, April 1998, *41*, 89-135.

Joskow, Paul L., Richard Schmalensee, and Elizabeth M. Bailey, "Auction Design and the Market for Sulfur Dioxide Emissions," National Bureau of Economic Research Working Paper No. 5745, Cambridge, September 1996.

Kelman, Steven P., *What Price Incentives?* Boston: Auburn House, 1981.

Kennedy, David M., *Controlling Acid Rain, 1986.* Case Study C15-86-699.0. Cambridge: John F. Kennedy School of Government. Harvard University, 1986.

Kerr, Suzi, and David Maré, "Efficient Regulation Through Tradeable Permit Markets: The United States Lead Phasedown," Department of Agricultural and Resource Economics, University of Maryland, College Park, Working Paper 96-06, January 1997.

Keohane, Nathaniel O., Richard L. Revesz, and Robert N. Stavins, "The Positive Political Economy of Instrument Choice in Environmental Policy." In Paul Portney and Robert Schwab, eds. *Environmental Economics and Public Policy*. London: Edward Elgar, Ltd., 1997.

Lowry, Robert C., "The Political Economy of Environmental Citizen Groups," unpublished Ph.D. thesis, Harvard University, 1993.

McCubbins, Matthew D., Roger G. Noll, and Barry R. Weingast, "Administrative Procedures as Instruments of Political Control," *Journal of Law, Economics and Organization*, 1987, 3, 243–77.

McCubbins, Matthew D., Roger G. Noll, and Barry R. Weingast, "Structure and Process, Politics and Policy: Administrative Arrangements and the Political Control of Agencies," *Virginia Law Review*, 1989, 75, 431–82.

McCubbins, Matthew and Terry Sullivan, "Constituency Influences on Legislative Policy Choice," *Quality and Quantity*, 1984, 18, 299–319.

McLean, Brian J., "Lessons Learned Implementing Title IV of the Clean Air Act," 85th Annual Meeting of the Air & Waste Management Association, 95-RA120.04, San Antonio, Texas, 1995.

Milliman, Scott R., and Raymond Prince, "Firm Incentives to Promote Technological Changes in Pollution Control," *Journal of Environmental Economics and Management*, 1989, 17, 247–65.

Montgomery, W. David, "Markets in Licenses and Efficient Pollution Control Programs," *Journal of Economic Theory*, 1972, 395–418.

Montero, Juan-Pablo, "Volunteering for Market-Based Environmental Regulation: The Substitution Provision of the SO_2 Emissions Trading Program," Working Paper 97–001, MIT Center for Energy and Environmental Policy Research, January 1997.

Newell Richard G., Adam B. Jaffe, and Robert N. Stavins, "Environmental Policy and Technological Change: The Effects of Economic Incentives and Direct Regulation on Energy-Saving Innovation," paper presented at the 1997 Allied Social Science Association meeting, New Orleans, January 1997.

Newell, Richard G., and Robert N. Stavins, "Abatement Cost Heterogeneity and Potential Gains from Market-Based Instruments." Working paper, John F. Kennedy School of Government, Harvard University, June 1997.

Nichols, Albert L., John G. Farr, and Gordon Hester, "Trading and the Timing of Emissions: Evidence from the Ozone Transport Region," National Economic Research Associates, Cambridge, Massachusetts, Draft of September 9, 1996.

Parry, Ian, Roberton Williams, and Lawrence Goulder, "When Can Carbon Abatement Policies Increase Welfare? The Fundamental Role of Distorted Factor Markets," Working paper, Resources for the Future and Stanford University, September 1997.

Pigou, Arthur Cecil, *The Economics of Welfare*. London: Macmillan and Company, 1920.

Portney, Paul R., "Policy Watch: Economics and the Clean Air Act," *Journal of Economic Perspectives*, Fall 1990, 4:4, 173–81.

Revesz, Richard L., "Federalism and Interstate Environmental Externalities," *University of Pennsylvania Law Review*, 1996, 144, 2341.

Rico, Renee, "The U.S. Allowance Trading System for Sulfur Dioxide: An Update of Market Experience," *Environmental and Resource Economics*, March 1995, 5:2, 115–29.

Rose, Kenneth, "Implementing an Emissions Trading Program in an Economically Regulated Industry: Lessons from the SO_2 Trading Program." In R. Kosobud, and J. Zimmermann, eds. *Market Based Approaches to Environmental Policy: Regulatory Innovations to the Fore*. New York: Van Nostrand Reinhold, 1997.

Sandel, Michael J., "It's Immoral to Buy the Right to Pollute," *New York Times*, December 15, 1997, p. A29.

Schmalensee, Richard, "Greenhouse Policy Architecture and Institutions," MIT Joint Program on the Science and Policy of Global Change, Report 13, November 1996.

Shepsle, Kenneth A., and Barry R. Weingast, "Political Solutions to Market Problems," *American Political Science Review*, 1984, *78*, 417–34.

Stavins, Robert N., "Correlated Uncertainty and Policy Instrument Choice," *Journal of Environmental Economics and Management*, 1996, *30*, 218–32.

Stavins, Robert N., "The Costs of Carbon Sequestration: A Revealed-Preference Approach." Working paper, John F. Kennedy School of Government, Harvard University, November 1997.

Stavins, Robert N., "Policy Instruments for Climate Change: How Can National Governments Address a Global Problem," *The University of Chicago Legal Forum*, forthcoming 1998.

Stavins, Robert N., ed., *Project 88—Harnessing Market Forces to Protect Our Environment: Initiatives for the New President.* A Public Policy Study sponsored by Senator Timothy E. Wirth, Colorado, and Senator John Heinz, Pennsylvania. Washington, D.C.: December 1988.

Stavins, Robert N., "Transaction Costs and Tradable Permits," *Journal of Environmental Economics and Management*, September 1995, *29*, 133–48.

U.S. Congressional Budget Office, *Curbing Acid Rain: Costs, Budget, and Coal-Market Effects.* Washington, D.C., 1986.

U.S. Energy Information Administration, "The Effects of Title IV of the Clean Air Act Amendments of 1990 on Electric Utilities: An Update," DOE/EIA-0582, March 1997, Washington, D.C.

U.S. Environmental Protection Agency, *Environmental Investments: The Cost of a Clean Environment.* Washington, D.C.: U.S. Environmental Protection Agency, 1990.

U.S. Environmental Protection Agency, "1996 Compliance Record: Acid Rain Program," EPA 430-R-97-025, June 1997, Office of Air and Radiation, Washington, D.C.

U.S. General Accounting Office, "Air Pollution: Allowance Trading Offers an Opportunity to Reduce Emissions at Less Cost," GAO/RCED-95-30, Washington, D.C., 1995.

Weitzman, Martin L., "Prices vs. Quantities," *Review of Economic Studies*, 1974, *41*, 477–91.

VII

Global Climate Change

22 Reflections on the Economics of Climate Change

William D. Nordhaus

William D. Nordhaus is A. Whitney Griswold Professor of Economics and on the staff of the Cowles Foundation, Yale University.

Albert Einstein's reaction to quantum mechanics was "God does not play dice with the universe." Yet mankind *is* playing dice with the natural environment through a multitude of interventions—injecting into the atmosphere trace gases like the greenhouse gases or ozone-depleting chemicals, engineering massive land-use changes such as deforestation, depleting multitudes of species in their natural habitats even while creating transgenic ones in the laboratory, and accumulating sufficient nuclear weapons to destroy human civilizations. As natural or social scientists, we need to understand the human sources of these global changes, the potential damage they cause to natural and economic systems, and the most efficient ways of alleviating or removing the dangers. Just as towns in times past decided on the management of their grazing or water resources, so must we today and in the future learn to use wisely and to protect economically our common geophysical and biological resources. This task of understanding and controlling interventions on a global scale can be called managing the global commons.

The issue analyzed in this symposium is the threat of greenhouse warming. Climatologists and other scientists warn that the accumulation of carbon dioxide (CO_2) and other greenhouse gases is likely to lead to global warming and other significant climatic changes over the next century. Many scientific bodies, along with a growing chorus of environmental groups and governments, are calling for severe curbs on the emissions of greenhouse gases. In response, governments have recently approved a framework treaty on climate change to monitor trends and natural efforts, and this treaty formed the centerpiece of the Earth Summit held in Rio in June 1992.[1]

Natural scientists have pondered the question of greenhouse warming for a century. Only recently have economists begun to tackle the issue, studying the impacts of climate change, the costs of slowing climate change,

---

"Reflections on the Economics of Climate Change," by William D. Nordhaus from *Journal of Economic Perspectives*, 7(4):11–25 (Fall 1993).

[1]Formally known a the United Nations Conference on Environment and Development (UNCED), the Earth Summit was the culmination of an effort to reach international agreements on climate, forest, biodiversity and biotechnology, as well as to develop principles for environmentally sound economic development.

and alternative approaches for implementing policies. The intellectual challenge here is daunting for those who take policy analysis seriously, raising formidable issues of data, modeling, uncertainty, international coordination, and institutional design. In addition, the economic stakes are enormous, involving investments on the order of hundreds of billions of dollars a year to slow or prevent climate change.

My purpose here is to provide a non-technical introduction to the economics of climate change. I will sketch the scientific background and uncertainties, survey the results of existing studies of the impacts of climate change, present a summary of a study of efficient policies to slow global warming, and end with the uncertainties that haunt the entire field.

The Scientific Background

What is the greenhouse effect? It is the process by which radiatively active gases like CO_2 selectively absorb radiation at different points of the spectrum and thereby warm the surface of the earth. The greenhouse gases are transparent to incoming solar radiation but absorb significant amounts of outgoing radiation. There is no debate about the importance of the greenhouse effect, without which the Earth's climate would resemble the moon's.[2]

Concern about the greenhouse effect arises because human activities are currently raising atmospheric concentrations of greenhouse gases. The major anthropogenic greenhouse gases are carbon dioxide (emitted primarily from the combustion of fossil fuels), methane, and chlorofluorocarbons (CFCs)—but of these CO_2 is likely to be the most significant over the coming decades. Scientific monitoring has firmly established the buildup of the major greenhouse gases over the last century. Using the standard but problematical metric of the "CO_2 equivalent" of greenhouse gases,[3] atmospheric concentrations of greenhouse gases have risen by over half of the preindustrial level of CO_2.

While the historical record is well established, there is great uncertainty about the potential for future climate change. On the basis of climate models, scientists project that a doubling of the atmospheric concentrations of CO_2 will in equilibrium lead to a warming of the earth's surface of 1 to 5 degree Celsius; other projected and equally uncertain effects include an increase in precipitation and evaporation, a small rise in sea level over the next century, and the potential for hotter and drier weather in midcontinental regions such as the U.S. midwest. Atmospheric scientists have

---

[2]A non-technical description of the science underlying the greenhouse effect is contained in National Academy of Sciences (1992). A thorough survey, full of interesting figures and background, is contained in IPCC (1990).

[3]Because greenhouse gases have differing lifetimes, combining them into a single index of their "CO_2 equivalent" poses complex scientific and economic questions, as Schmalensee (1993) shows.

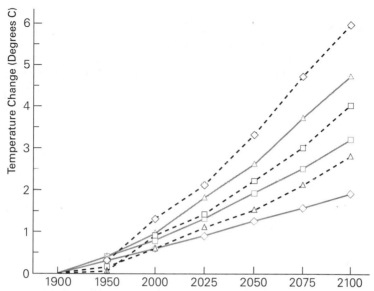

Figure 1 Projections of Global Temperature Increase: IPCC Report and DICE Model

Note: IPCC Report is from Intergovernmental Panel on Climate Change (1990), while DICE model is from Nordhaus (1993). The dashed lines are from IPCC Report and represent, from top to bottom, high estimate, best estimate, and low estimate. The solid lines are from the DICE model and represent, from top to bottom, the 90th, 50th, and 10th percentiles of calculated temperature increases from 500 Monte Carlo runs. In both cases, the changes represent temperature increases from 1900.

engaged in a spirited debate about the climatic impact of increasing greenhouse-gas concentrations, but it is unlikely that the uncertainties will be resolved until this vast geophysical experiment has run its course.

To translate these equilibrium results into a projection of future climate change requires a scenario for emissions and concentrations. Using rudimentary economic modeling, the Intergovernmental Panel on Climate Change (or IPCC), an international panel of distinguished scientists, projected that "business as usual" would produce a 3 to 6 degree C warming in 2100 (relative to 1900) with the best guess being 4 degrees C. The dashed lines in Figure 1 show the high, best, and low estimates from the IPCC.

I have recently used a dynamic optimization model (the DICE model, described more fully later in this paper) to develop a distribution of future temperature increases. Figure 1 shows as solid lines the 10th, 50th, and 90th percentiles of the temperature-increase distribution from the DICE model. In general, economic models project rising relative energy prices and slowing economic growth in the coming decades; as a result, they tend to show lower emissions and temperature trends than the extrapolative approaches often used in the scientific community and exemplified by the IPCC projections. However, virtually all projections are worrisome because climate appears to be heading out of the historical range of temperatures witnessed during the span of human civilizations.

Climate models resemble large macroeconomic models in their ability to answer virtually any question that modelers care to ask. However, the reliability of climate models for global climate changes is unproven, and climate modelers do not expect to be able to forecast regional climates accurately in the foreseeable future. Some believe that there may be "regime changes" in which the climate flips from one locally stable equilibrium to another, say because of changes in ocean circulation. Elaborating bigger and better models will provide fruitful full employment for climatologists well into the next century.

Impacts of Climate Change

What are the likely impacts of projected climate changes over the next century? To begin, we should recognize that in the long march of economic development, technology has increasingly insulated humans and economic activity from the vagaries of climate. Two centuries ago, work and recreation were dictated by the cycles of daylight, the seasons, and the agricultural growing season.

Today, thanks to modern technology, humans live and thrive in virtually every climate on earth. For the bulk of economic activity, variables like wages, unionization, labor-force skills, and political factors swamp climatic considerations. When a manufacturing firm decides between investing in Hong Kong and Moscow, climate will probably not even be on the list of factors considered. Moreover, the process of economic development and technological change tend progressively to reduce climate sensitivity as the share of agriculture in output and employment declines and as capital-intensive space heating and cooling, enclosed shopping malls, artificial snow, and accurate weather or hurricane forecasting reduces the vulnerability of economic activity to weather.

In thinking about the impact of climate change, one must recognize that the variable focussed on in most analyses—globally averaged surface temperature—has little salience for impacts. Rather, variables that accompany or are the result of temperature changes—precipitation, water levels, extremes of droughts or freezes, and thresholds like the freezing point or the level of dikes and levees—will drive the socioeconomic impacts. Mean temperature is chosen because it is a useful *index* of climate change that is highly correlated with or determines the more important variables. Moreover, it must be emphasized that impact studies are in their infancy and that studies of low-income regions are virtually non-existent.

Existing research uses a wide variety of approaches including time-series analysis, engineering studies, and historical analogs. Climate change is likely to have different effects on different sectors and in different coun-

Table 1 Comparison of Estimates of Impact of Global Warming on the United States: Impact on Incomes of CO_2 Doubling
(*in billions of 1988 U.S. dollars per year*)

	Nordhaus	Cline	Fankhauser
Heavily affected sectors			
Agriculture	1	15.2	7.4
Coastal areas	10.7	2.5	2.3
Energy	0.5	9	0
Other sectors	38.1		
Wetland and species loss	b	7.1	14.8
Health and amenity	b	8.4	30.3
Other	b	11.2	12.1
Total: billions of $	50.3	53.4	66.9
(*Percent of output*)	*1.0*	*1.1*	*1.3*

[a]References are Nordhaus (1991), Cline (1992), Fankhauser (1993).
[b]These are included in the total for "other sectors."

tries.[4] In general, those sectors of the economy that depend heavily on unmanaged ecosystems—that is, are heavily dependent upon naturally occurring rainfall, runoff, or temperatures—will be most sensitive to climate change. Agriculture, forestry, outdoor recreation, and coastal activities fall in this category. Countries like Japan or the United States are relatively insulated from climate change while developing countries like India are more vulnerable.

This survey of impacts will concentrate primarily upon the United States, because that is where the evidence is most abundant. In reality, most of the U.S. economy has little direct interaction with climate. For example, cardiovascular surgery and parallel supercomputing are undertaken in carefully controlled environments and are unlikely to be directly affected by climate change. More generally, underground mining, most services, communications, and manufacturing are sectors likely to be largely unaffected by climate change—sectors that comprise around 85 percent of GDP.

A few studies have estimated the impact of an equilibrium CO_2 doubling (2.5 to 3 degrees C) on the United States, and the results of three such surveys are shown in Table 1. The first column of Table 1 shows the results of Nordhaus (1991) updated to 1988 prices. The other two comprehensive studies by Cline (1992) and Fankhauser (1993) use largely the same data base but extend the Nordhaus analysis to other sectors. The convention used in most damage studies is to calculate impacts in terms of today's level and composition of output. Hence, the $53 billion estimate of damage from CO_2 doubling estimated by Cline and shown in Table 1 su-

[4]An early review, emphasizing the potential costs of climate change, is contained in EPA (1989). A more balanced approach, emphasizing the potential for adaptation, is contained in National Academy of Sciences (1992). .

perimposes the estimated impacts that would occur roughly a century from now upon today's economy.

Cline has performed the most detailed economic analysis of the potential impact of climate change on a number of market and non-market sectors, and the overall results are shown in the second column of Table 1. While Cline examined a wide variety of possible impacts, many of the estimates are extremely tenuous and may lean toward overestimating the impacts. For example, Cline's estimates of the impact of losses from storms assume that storms become more severe, whereas both the IPCC and the National Academy studies concluded that the effect of warming on storm intensity is ambiguous. Another example is leisure activities, where he includes only losses to skiing but excludes any gains from the much larger warm-weather industries such as camping, boating, and swimming. In agriculture, Cline relies on estimates that involve little or no adaptation. For health effects, Cline bases his estimates on a study that virtually ignores adaptation. For species loss, Cline takes a very costly decision (that of the Northern spotted owl) and uses that as the basis for valuation. Even with this tendency to see the pessimistic side of global warming, Cline's estimates of impacts are only marginally above those found in other studies (1.1 percent of GNP for a 2.5 degree C warming in Cline, as opposed to 1 percent of GNP for a 3 degree of warming in Nordhaus).

A third approach is a compilation by Fankhauser (1993). This study employs much the same methodology as Nordhaus and Cline but uses additional studies and extends the analysis to the OECD countries and to the world. Fankhauser's results are very close to those in earlier studies, finding a 1.3 percent impact of a 3 degree warming for the United States.

A full assessment of the impact of greenhouse warming must, of course, include regions outside the United States. To date, studies for other countries are fragmentary, and it is not possible to make any general conclusions at this time. A preliminary reading is that other advanced industrial countries will experience modest impacts similar to those of the United States, and some may even have net economic benefits; for example, Fankhauser (1993) extends his analysis and estimates losses from CO_2 doubling of 1.4 percent to OECD countries and 1.5 for the world. Another estimate, more qualitative in nature, is an intensive survey of experts on the economic impacts of climate change (Nordhaus, 1993b). For a 3 degree C warming in 2090, the median response was an economic loss of 1.8 percent of world output. However, there is great uncertainty: the median estimate of the 10th percentile of outcomes is for no impact, while the median estimate of the 90th percentile of outcomes is for a 5.5 percent loss of world output.

All these studies indicate the great uncertainty about the impact of climate change. More recent analysis suggests that the studies reported in Table 1 may well overestimate the impact of climate change because they ignore many ways in which economies can adapt to changing climate. One kind of adaptation ignored in most studies is the buffering of shocks by trade. A study by Reilly and Hohmann (1993) begins with the results of agricultural production-function studies such as those used in Table 1; these studies estimate the impact of climate change on crop yields in individual regions. These yield estimates are then imbedded in a model of international trade. Reilly and Hohmann find that trade tends to reduce the economic impacts by a factor of from five to ten as reactions of supply and demand buffer production shocks. For example, the estimated impact of a substantial (30 percent) yield shock in temperate regions, buffered by the adaptive response in markets, produces a negligible impact on incomes: 0.06 percent of income for the U.S. and 0.08 percent loss for the world over a period of nearly a century. This careful study is a good lesson on how impact estimates often tend to exaggerate losses while ignoring gains and adaptations.[5]

Another approach to measuring impacts is a "Ricardian" analysis that estimates the rents to climate in particular climate zones and then uses these to estimate the impact of climate change on income. The Ricardian approach is useful because it allows all forms of adaptation, whereas the production-function approaches omit all but a few forms of adaptation to changing climate. A study by Mendelsohn, Nordhaus, and Shaw (1993a, b) developed such an approach by examining the impact of climate on U.S. agriculture. This study uses cross-sectional data on climate, farm-land prices, and other economic and geophysical data for almost 3000 counties in the United States.

Applying the model to a global-warming scenario found a range of impacts. The traditional analysis of global warming analyzes the impact upon the grains. Under this approach, the Ricardian model finds annual losses ranging from $6 to $8 billion annually (without CO_2 fertilization in 1988 prices at 1988 levels of farm income). This can be related to gross farm income in 1982 of $175 billion. Strikingly different results emerge if we use a broader approach which includes all agricultural crops. For these, the net impact of warming is slightly positive, ranging from a loss of $0.7 billion to a *gain* of $2 billion per year. The differing results arise because the broader approach weights relatively more heavily the irrigated lands of the American West and South that thrive in a Mediterranean and subtropical climate, a climate that will become relatively more abundant with a warmer climate.

---

[5]One might suspect that there is often an unconscious impulse to find costs and ignore benefits of climate change. A comparison of two sets of studies is instructive in this respect. Almost two decades ago, a series of studies was undertaken to investigate the impact of flights in the stratosphere on global *cooling*. Studies by d'Arge and others (summarized in National Research Council, 1979) found that global cooling of 1° C would impose costs in a number of areas. Of the nine areas of costs identified in the global cooling studies (agriculture, forest products, marine resources, health, locational preferences, fuel demand, housing, public expenditures, and aesthetics), only two were examined in the 1989 EPA study of global warming and *none* were calculated by the EPA to produce benefits. The largest estimated cost in the global cooling studies was the amenity effect of cooling, determined through regional wage differentials. This topic was completely ignored in the EPA studies. One is tempted to say that environmental impact studies can find the cloud behind every silver lining.

The one area where our information is particularly sparse is for developing countries. Small and poor countries, particularly ones with low population mobility in narrowly restricted climatic zone, may be severely affected. Much more work on the potential impact of climate change on developing countries needs to be done.

The Balancing Act in Climate Change Policies

The greenhouse effect is the granddaddy of public goods problems—emissions affect climate globally for centuries to come. Because of the climate externality, individuals will not produce the efficient quantity of greenhouse gases. An important goal of economic research is to examine policies that will find the right balance, on the margin, of costs of action to slow climate change and the benefits of reducing future damages from climate change.

The benefits of emissions reductions come when lower emissions reduce future climate-induced damages. To translate these into a marginal benefit function, it is necessary to follow the emissions through greenhouse-gas concentrations to economic impacts, and then take the present value of the impact of an emission of an additional unit. Graphically, we can depict the marginal damages averted per unit of emissions reduction as the downward-sloping marginal benefit (MB) curve in Figure 2.

The second relationship is the marginal cost of emissions reduction, which portrays the costs that the economy undertakes to reduce a unit of greenhouse-gas emissions (or the equivalent in other policies that would

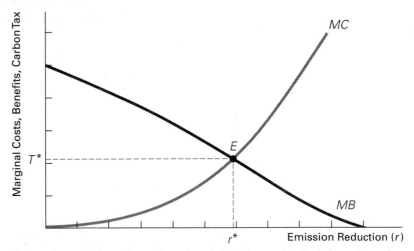

Figure 2 Marginal Costs and Benefits of Greenhouse-Gas Emissions Controls
Note: Efficient policy comes at point E, where marginal cost of further emissions reduction (MC) equals marginal benefit of emissions reductions in slowing climate change (MB). T^* is the efficient carbon tax while r^* is the efficient reduction rate.

slow greenhouse warming). A wide variety of approaches are available to slow climate change. Most policy discussion has focussed on reducing CO_2 emissions by reducing the consumption of fossil fuels through energy conservation, alternative energy sources (some would even contemplate nuclear power), and other measures. Such policies could be implemented through carbon taxes of the kind James Poterba analyzes in this symposium, while some prefer regulations such as tradable emissions permits. Other approaches include reforestation to remove CO_2 from the atmosphere and putting even more stringent controls on CFCs.

Another option, definitely not in the environmentally correct package, would be to offset greenhouse warming through climatic engineering, primarily through measures to change the albedo (reflectivity) of the earth. Such options include injection particles that would increase the backscattering or reflecting of incoming sunlight or stimulate absorption of carbon. Two particularly interesting proposals include shooting smart mirrors into space with 16-inch naval rifles or seeding the oceans with iron to accelerate carbon sequestration.[6] Whatever the approach, economists emphasize the importance of cost-effectiveness—structuring policies to get the maximal reduction in harmful climatic change for a given level of expenditure. Figure 2 shows schematically the marginal cost of cost-effective emissions reductions as MC.

The shape of the cost function for reducing CO_2 emissions has been thoroughly studied, and the effort discussed by John Weyant in this symposium represents the most careful comparative examination of the results of different models. In addition, policies should include other cost-effective measures, and a recent National Academy of Sciences Panel (1992) has compared the costs of a wide variety of measures, including rough estimates of the costs of climate engineering.

From an economic point of view, efficient policies are ones in which the marginal costs are balanced with the marginal benefits of emissions reductions. Figure 2 shows schematically how the efficient rate of emissions reduction and the optimal carbon tax are determined. The pure market solution comes with emissions reductions at 0, where MB is far above the zero MC. Point E represents the efficient point at which marginal abatement costs equal marginal benefits from slowing climate change. The policy can be represented by the efficient fractional reduction in emissions, r^* on the horizontal axis, or by the optimal carbon tax, T^* on the vertical axis.

Empirical Modeling of Optimal Policies

Sketching the optimal policy in Figure 2 demands little more than pencil, paper, and a rudimentary understanding of economics. To move from theory to useful empirical models requires understanding a wide variety of

---

[6]The issues of geoengineering are discussed in National Academy of Sciences (1992, Chapter 28).

empirical economic and geophysical relationships. Work has progressed to the point where the economics and natural science can be integrated to estimate optimal control strategies. In one study, I developed a simple cost-benefit analysis for determining the optimal steady-state control of CO_2 and other greenhouse gases based on the comparative statics framework shown in Figure 2 (Nordhaus, 1991). This earlier study came to a middle-of-the-road conclusion that the threat of greenhouse warming was sufficient to justify low-cost steps to slow the pace of climate change.

A more complete elaboration has been made using an approach I call the "DICE model," shorthand for a Dynamic Integrated Model of Climate and the Economy.[7] The DICE model is a global dynamic optimization model for estimating the optimal path of reductions of greenhouse-gas emissions. The basic approach is to calculate the optimal path for both capital accumulation and reductions of greenhouse-gas emissions in the framework of the Ramsey (1928) model of intertemporal choice. The resulting trajectory can be interpreted as the most efficient path for slowing climate change given inputs and technologies; an alternative interpretation is as a competitive market equilibrium in which externalities or spillover effects are corrected using the appropriate social prices for greenhouse-gas emissions.

The DICE model asks whether to consume goods and services, invest in productive capital, or slow climate change via reducing greenhouse-gas emissions. The optimal path chosen is one that maximizes an objective function that is the discounted sum of the utilities of per capita consumption. Consumption and investment are constrained by a conventional set of economic relationships (Cobb-Douglas production function, capital-balance equation, and so forth) and by a newly developed set of aggregate geophysical constraints (interrelating economic activity, greenhouse gas emissions and concentrations, climate change, costs of abatement, and impacts from climate change).

To give the flavor of the results from the DICE model, consider the economic optimum and compare it to two alternative policies that have been proposed by governments or by the environmental community. The three options are (1) economic optimization as described in the previous paragraph; (2) stabilizing greenhouse-gas emissions at 1990 levels, a target that was endorsed at the Rio Earth Summit by the United States and other governments; and (3) stabilizing climate so that the change in global average temperature is limited to no more than 0.2 degrees C per decade with an ultimate limitation of 1.5 degrees C (compare this with the projections in Figure 1).

Solving the DICE model for the three policies just described produces a time sequence of consumption, investment, greenhouse-gas emissions, and carbon taxes. The carbon taxes can be interpreted as the taxes on green-

---

[7]The basic model and results are presented in Nordhaus (1992a, b), while complete documentation and analysis are forthcoming in Nordhaus (1993a).

house-gas emissions (or the regulatory equivalent, say in auctionable emissions rights) that would lead to the emissions that would attain the policy objectives just described.

Figure 3 shows the resulting carbon taxes. For calibration purposes, in the United States, a carbon tax of $100 per ton would raise coal prices by about $70 per ton, or 300 percent; would increase oil prices by about $8 per barrel; and would raise around $200 billion of revenues (before taking account of emissions reductions). The economic optimum produces relatively modest carbon taxes, rising from around $5 per ton carbon to around $20 per ton by the end of the next century. The stabilization scenarios require must more stringent restraints. For emissions stabilization, the carbon tax would rise from around $40 per ton of carbon currently to around $500 per ton late in the next century; climate stabilization involves current carbon taxes over $100 per ton carbon today rising to nearly $1000 per ton by the end of the next century.

The DICE model can also be used to inquire into the estimated net economic impact of alternative policies. For the global economy, the economic optimum has a net benefit over no controls for the global economy (in terms of the discounted present value measured in 1990 consumption units) of $270 billion. On the other hand, stabilizing emissions or climate imposes major net economic costs. Stabilizing emissions leads to a net present-value loss of around $7 trillion relative to the optimum, while attempting to stabilize climate would have a net present-value cost of around $41 trillion. If these present value figures are converted into consumption annuities using an annuity rate of 4 percent per annum, these strategies represent, respectively, a gain of 0.05 percent and losses of 1.4 and 8.2 per-

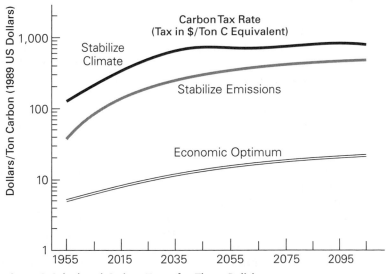

Figure 3 Calculated Carbon Taxes for Three Policies

cent of today's annual gross world output. It would take a major misestimate of either the costs of emissions reductions or of climate-change damages to make the stabilization options economically advantageous.

Several other economic studies have also calculated efficient approaches to slowing global warming. The studies of Manne and Richels (1990, 1992), Peck and Teisberg (1992), and Kolstad (1993) find conclusions roughly similar to those reported here. Other studies—those of Kolstad (1993) as well as earlier studies by the present author (1979, 1991)—also determine the optimal emissions control rates and carbon taxes and show optimal policies in the general range of those determined here.

Two studies derive quite different results, one more optimistic, one more pessimistic. The studies by Jorgenson and Wilcoxen (1991, most strikingly shows a lower set of carbon taxes needed to stabilize greenhouse-gas emissions than those shown here; the reason for the lower carbon taxes seems to reside largely in the slow projected economic growth. By contrast, the study by Cline (1992) proposes much higher control rates. The more stringent controls in the Cline study are due to a number of features—primarily because the Cline result is not grounded in explicit intertemporal optimization and assumes a rate of time preference that is lower than would be consistent with observed real interest rates. Clearly, if we arbitrarily assume a near-zero discount rate (as Cline does), society will undertake massive investments in tangible, human, and environmental capital; who will do all this saving is an unanswered question.

Uncertainties and Anxieties

Most economic studies of the impacts and policies concerning climate change are based on scenarios like the smooth and gradual warming depicted in Figure 1. And, as indicated in the last section, the conclusion that emerges from most economic studies is to impose modest restraints, pack up our tools, and concentrate on more pressing problems. Given the high costs of controls and the modest projected impacts of a 1 to 3 degree C warming over the next half century, how high should global warming be on an international agenda that includes exploding population in the South, nuclear proliferation in the Middle East, collapsing economies in eastern Europe, increasing cycles of poverty and drug use along with stagnating incomes in the West, and sporadic outbreaks of violence and civil war just about everywhere? Given the modest estimated impact of climate change along with these other urgent concerns, we might conclude that global warming should be demoted to a second-tier issue.

Yet, even for those who downplay the urgency of the most likely scenarios for climate change, a deeper anxiety remains about future uncertainties and surprises. Scientists raise the specter of shifting currents turning Europe into Alaska, of mid-continental drying transforming grain belts into deserts, of great rivers drying up as snow packs disappear, of severe storms wiping out whole populations of low-lying regions, of surging ice sheets raising ocean levels by 20 to 50 feet, of northward migration of old or new tropical pests and diseases decimating the temperature regions, of environmentally induced migration overrunning borders in search of livable land. Given the potential for catastrophic surprises, perhaps we should conclude that the major concern lies in the uncertainties and imponderable impacts of climate change rather than in the smooth changes foreseen by the global models.

At present, we do not have the scientific basis for making a firm judgment of the likelihood of one of these catastrophic outcomes. In the survey discussed above (Nordhaus, 1993b), experts were asked about the probability of a 25 percent sustained loss in global income from a 3-degree C warming in 2090 (scenario A) and a 6-degree warming in 2175 (scenario B). The median estimated probability of this catastrophic outcome was 0.5 percent for scenario A and 3 percent for scenario B. On the other hand, the assessment of the catastrophic scenarios varied greatly across respondents and particularly across disciplines. For scenario B, according to the most pessimistic quartile of respondents, the mean probability of this catastrophic outcome was 40 percent. The more pessimistic assessments generally came from natural scientists while the more sanguine views were held by mainstream economists.

Once the door is open to consider catastrophic changes, a whole new debate is engaged. If we do not know how human activities will affect the thin layer of life-supporting activities that gave birth to and nurture human civilization, and if we cannot reliably judge how potential geophysical changes will affect civilization or the world around us, can we use the plain vanilla cost-benefit analysis (or even the Häagen-Dazs variety in dynamic optimization models)? Should we be ultraconservative and tilt toward preserving the natural world at the expense of economic growth and development? Do we dare put human betterment before the preservation of natural systems and trust that human ingenuity will bail us out should Nature deal us a nasty hand?

Faced with this dilemma, we might be tempted to say that such questions are beyond the capability of rational analysis and turn the decisions over to philosophers and politicians. Rather, I believe that natural and social sciences have a central role to play in analyzing potential future outcomes and delineating potential responses. Society often requires that decisions be made in the absence of complete information, whether the decisions be military strategy, oil drilling, or research and development. In each case, a reasoned decision process involves listing the events that may occur, estimating the consequences of the events, judging the probabilities that each of the events will occur, weighing the expected value of the consequences against the expected costs under different courses of action, and choosing the action that maximizes the expected value or utility of the outcome.

Reasoned decision-making under uncertainty is no different for climate-change policy than for other areas, although it may be more complex and require crossing traditional disciplinary boundaries more often.

In thinking through the appropriate treatment of future surprises, to the natural scientists falls the crucial task of sorting through the apocalyptic scenarios and obtaining rough judgments as to the likelihood of different geophysical outcomes so as to distinguish between the likely, plausible, possible, and virtually impossible. To the social scientists falls the issue of assessing the probabilities, determining the values of different outcomes, and devising sensible strategies in the face of such massive uncertainties. To our leaders falls the burden of ultimately deciding how to balance future perils against present costs. For all, this is a fruitful use of our collective talents, full of intellectual challenges and practical payoffs.

REFERENCES

Cline, William, *The Economics of Global Warming.* Washington D.C.: Institute of International Economics, 1992.

EPA, "U.S. Environmental Protection Agency," *The Potential Effects of Global Climate Change on the United States: Report to Congress.* EPA-230-05-89-050, December 1989.

Fankhauser, Samuel, "The Economic Costs of Global Warming: Some Monetary Estimates." In Kaya, Y., N. Nakicenovic, W. D. Nordhaus, and F. L. Toth, eds., *Costs, Impacts, and Benefits of CO$_2$ Mitigation*, Laxenburg, Austria: International Institute for Applied Systems Analysis, CP-93-2, 1993, 85–105.

Gaskins, Darius W., and John P. Weyant, "Model Comparisons of the Costs of Reducing CO$_2$ Emissions," *American Economic Review Papers and Proceedings*, May 1993, *83*:2, 318–30.

IPCC, Intergovernmental Panel on Climate Change. *Climate Change: The IPCC Scientific Assessment.* J. T. Houghton, G. J. Jenkins, and J. J. Ephraums, eds., New York: Cambridge University Press, 1990.

Jorgenson, Dale W., and Peter J. Wilcoxen, "Reducing U.S. Carbon Dioxide Emissions: The Cost of Different Goals." In Moronery, John R., ed., *Energy, Growth, and the Environment.* Greenwich: JAI Press, 1991, 125–28.

Kolstad, Charles D., "Looking vs. Leaping: The Timing of CO$_2$ Control in the Face of Uncertainty and Learning." In Kaya Y., N. Nakicenovic, W. D. Nordhaus, and F. L. Toth, eds., *Costs, Impacts, and Benefits of CO$_2$ Mitigation.* Laxenburg, Austria: International Institute for Applied Systems Analysis, CP-93-2, 1993, 63–82.

Manne, Alan S., and Richard G. Richels, "CO$_2$ Emission Limits: An Economic Cost Analysis for the USA," *The Energy Journal*, April 1990, *11*:2, 51–74.

Manne, Alan S., and Richard G. Richels, *Buying Greenhouse Insurance: The Economic Costs of CO$_2$ Emission Limits.* Cambridge: MIT Press, 1992.

Mendelsohn, Robert, William Nordhaus, and Dai Gee Shaw, "The Impact of Climate on Agriculture: A Ricardian Approach." In Kaya, Y., N. Nakicenovic, W. D. Nordhaus, and F. L. Toth, eds., *Costs, Impacts, and Benefits of CO$_2$ Mitigation.* Laxenburg, Austria: International Institute for Applied Systems Analysis, CP-93-2, 1993a, 173–207.

Mendelsohn, Robert, William D. Nordhaus, and Dai Gee Shaw, "The Impact of Global Warming on Agriculture: A Ricardian Approach," *American Economic Review*, forthcoming 1993b.

National Academy of Sciences (NAS), Committee on Science, Engineering, and Public Policy, *Policy Implications of Greenhouse Warming: Mitigation, Adaptation, and the Science Base*. Washington, D.C.: National Academy Press, 1992.

National Research Council, *Carbon Dioxide and Climate: A Scientific Assessment*. Washington, D.C.: National Academy Press, 1979.

Nordhaus, William D., *The Efficient Use of Energy Resources*. New Haven: Yale University Press, 1979.

Nordhaus, William D., "To Slow or Not to Slow: The Economics of the Greenhouse Effect," *The Economic Journal*, July 1991, *101*, 920–37.

Nordhaus, William D., "How Much Should We Invest in Preserving Our Current Climate?" In Giersch, Herbert, ed., *Economic Progress and Environmental Concerns*. Berlin: Verlag-Springer, 1992a, 255–99.

Nordhaus, William D., "An Optimal Transition Path for Slowing Climate Change," *Science*, November 1992b, *258*, 1315–19.

Nordhaus, William D., *Managing the Global Commons: The Economics of Climate Change*. Cambridge: MIT Press, forthcoming 1993a.

Nordhaus, William D., "Survey on Uncertainties Associated With Future Climate Change," Yale University, processed mimeo, April 1993b.

Peck, Stephen C., and Thomas J. Teisberg, "CETA: A Model for Carbon Emissions Trajectory Assessment," *The Energy Journal*, 1992, *13*:1, 55–77.

Ramsey, Frank P., "A Mathematical Theory of Saving," *The Economic Journal*, December 1928, *38*, 543–59.

Reilly, John, and Neil Hohmann, "Climate Change and Agriculture: The Role of International Trade," *American Economic Review Papers and Proceedings*, May 1993, *83*:2, 306–23.

Schmalensee, Richard, "Comparing Greenhouse Gases for Policy Purposes," *The Energy Journal*, 1993, *14*:1, 245–55.

23   *The Cost of Combating Global Warming: Facing the Tradeoffs*

Thomas C. Schelling

Thomas C. Schelling is Distinguished University Professor of Economics and Public Affairs at the University of Maryland.

At international conferences, people speaking for the developing world insist that it is the developed nations that feel endangered by carbon emissions and want to retard elsewhere the kind of development that has been enjoyed by Western Europe, North America, and Japan. A reduction in carbon emissions in the developing world, they assert, will have to be at the expense of the rich nations. Their diagnosis is wrong, but their conclusion is right. Any costs of mitigating climate change during the coming decades will surely be borne by the high-income countries. But the benefits, despite what spokespeople for the developing world say, will overwhelmingly accrue to future generations in the developing world. Any action combating global warming will be, intended or not, a foreign aid program.

The Chinese, Indonesians, or Bangladeshis are not going to divert resources from their own development to reduce the greenhouse effect, which is caused by the presence of carbon-based gases in the earth's atmosphere. This is a prediction, but it is also sound advice. Their best defense against climate change and vulnerability to weather in general is their own development, reducing their reliance on agriculture and other such outdoor livelihoods. Furthermore, they have immediate environmental problems—air and water pollution, poor sanitation, disease—that demand earlier attention.

There are three reasons the beneficiaries will be in the developing countries, which will be much more developed when the impact of climate change is felt. The first is simple: that is where most people live—four-fifths now, nine-tenths in 75 years.

Second, these economies may still be vulnerable, in a way the developed economies are not, by the time climate change occurs. In the developed world hardly any component of the national income is affected by climate. Agriculture is practically the only sector of the economy affected by climate, and it contributes only a small percentage—three percent in the

"The Costs of Combatting Global Warming: Facing the "Tradeoffs," by Thomas C. Schelling from *Foreign Affairs*, 76(6):8–14 (Nov./Dec. 1997).

United States—of national income. If agricultural productivity were drastically reduced by climate change, the cost of living would rise by one or two percent, and at a time when per capita income will likely have doubled. In developing countries, in contrast, as much as a third of GNP and half the population currently depends on agriculture. They may still be vulnerable to climate change for many years to come.

Third, although most of these populations should be immensely better off in 50 years, many will still be poorer than the rich countries are now. The contribution to their welfare by reduced climate change will therefore be greater than any costs the developing world bears in reducing emissions.

I say all this with apparent confidence, so let me rehearse the uncertainties, which have remained essentially the same for a decade and a half. Arbitrarily adopting a doubling of greenhouse gases as a benchmark, a committee of the U.S. National Academy of Sciences estimated in 1979 that the change in average global surface atmospheric temperature could be anywhere from 1.5 to 4.5 degrees Celsius. (Note that the upper estimate is three times the lower.) This range of uncertainty has still not officially been reduced.

More important than the average warming is the effect it may have on climates. Things will not just get warmer, climatologists predict; some places will, but others will get cooler, wetter, drier, or cloudier. The average warming is merely the engine that will drive the changes. The term "global warming" is mischievous in suggesting that hot summers are what it is all about.

The temperature gradient from equator to pole is a main driving force in the circulation of the atmosphere and oceans, and a change in that gradient will be as important as the change in average temperature. Climatologists have to translate changes in temperature at various latitudes, altitudes, and seasons into changes in weather and climate in different localities. That is another source of uncertainty. Mountains, for example, are hard to work into climate models. Not many people live high in the mountains, so why worry? But India, Pakistan, Bangladesh, and Burma depend on snowfall in the Himalayas for their irrigation.

A further question gets little attention: what will the world be like 75 years from now, when changes in climate may have become serious? If we look back to 1920 and conjecture about what environmental problems then might be affected by climate changes over the coming 75 years, one problem high on the list would be mud. This was the era of muddy roads and narrow tires. Cars had to be pulled out by horses. People could not ride bicycles, and walking in the stuff was arduous. One might think, "If things get wetter or drier the mud problem will get worse or better." It might not occur to anyone that by the 1990s most of the country would be paved.

If the climate changes expected 75 years from now were to happen immediately, the most dramatic consequences would be in the incidence of parasitic and other tropical diseases. Temperature and moisture affect malaria, river blindness, schistosomiasis, dengue fever, and infantile diarrhea, all vastly more dangerous than the radioactive and chemical hazards that worry people in the developed countries.

Alarmists have weighed in with dire predictions of how a warming of tropical and subtropical regions will aggravate the scourge of tropical diseases. But any changes in temperature and moisture need to be superimposed on those areas as they are likely to be 50 or 75 years from now, with better sanitation, nutrition and medical and environmental technology, cleaner water, and the potential eradication of vector-borne diseases.

Malaysia and Singapore have identical climates. There is malaria in Malaysia, but hardly any in Singapore, and any malaria in Singapore gets sophisticated treatment. By the time Malaysia catches up to where Singapore is now, many tropical diseases may have been tamed. One invasive tropical creature, the guinea worm, is already expected to follow smallpox into extinction.

The Marshall Model

The modern era of greenhouse concern dates from the 1992 Rio Conference, attended by President Bush, which produced a "framework convention" for the pursuit of reduced carbon emissions. A sequel is set for Kyoto in December. Countries from the Organization for Economic Cooperation and Development (OECD) are groping for criteria and procedures to determine "targets and timetables." There are proposals for the formal allocation of enforceable quotas, possibly with trading of emission rights. There is disappointment with the lack of convincing progress in the five years since Rio. Many people wonder whether Kyoto will settle anything.

It will not. But five years is to soon to be disappointed. Nothing like a carbon emissions regime has ever been attempted, and it is no country's individual interest to do much about emissions: the atmosphere is a global common where everybody's emissions mingle with everybody else's. The burden to be shared is large, there are no accepted standards of fairness, nations differ greatly in their dependence on fossil fuels, and any regime to be taken seriously has to promise to survive a long time.

There are few precedents. The U.N. budget required a negotiated formula, but adherence is conspicuously imperfect, and the current budget, even including peacekeeping, is two orders of magnitude smaller than what a serious carbon regime would require. The costs in reduced productivity are estimated at two percent of GNP—forever. Two percent of GNP seems politically unmanageable in many countries.

Still, if one plots the curve of U.S. per capita GNP over the coming century with and without the two percent permanent loss, the difference is about the thickness of a line drawn with a number two pencil, and the doubled per capita income that might have been achieved by 2060 is reached in 2062. If someone could wave a wand and phase in, over a few years, a climate-mitigation program that depressed our GNP by two percent in perpetuity, no one would notice the difference.

The only experience commensurate with carbon reduction was division of aid in the Marshall Plan. In 1949–50 there was $4 billion to share. The percentage of European GNP that this amounted to depends on hypothetical exchange rates appropriate to the period, but it was well over two percent, although differing drastically among the countries. The United States insisted that the Europeans divide the aid themselves, and gave them most of a year to prepare.

The procedure was what I call "multilateral reciprocal scrutiny." Each country prepared detailed national accounts showing consumption, investment, dollar earnings and imports, intra-European trade, specifics like per capita fuel and meat consumption, taxes, and government expenditures—anything that might justify a share of U.S. aid. There was never a formula. There were not even criteria; there were "considerations." There was no notion that aid should be allocated to maximize recovery, equalize standards of living, balance improvements in consumption levels, or meet any other objective. Each country made its claim for aid on whatever grounds it chose. Each was queried and cross-examined about dollar-export potential, domestic substitutes for dollar imports, dietary standards, rate of livestock recovery, severity of gasoline rationing, and anything pertinent to dollar requirements. The objective was consensus on how to divide the precious $4 billion.

Although they did not succeed, they were close enough for arbitration by a committee of two people to produce an acceptable division. After the Korean War, when NATO replaced recovery as the objective, the same procedure was used. Again consensus was not reached, but again there was enough agreement for arbitration by a committee of three to decide not only the division of aid but military burdens to be assumed. Multilateral reciprocal scrutiny proved effective, no doubt because an unprecedented camaraderie had been cultivated during the Marshall Plan. And remember, consensus had to be reached by countries as different in their development, war damage, politics, and cultures as Turkey, Norway, Italy, and France. A similar procedure recently led to the European Union's schedule of carbon reductions for its member countries. A difference is that in the Marshall Plan it was for keeps!

Did the Marshall Plan succeed despite, or because of, its lack of formal quantitative criteria and its reliance on looser, more open-ended, pragmatic modes of discourse and argument? In the time available, plan participants could not have agreed on formal criteria. In the end they had to be satisfied with a division. Any argument over variables and parameters would have been self-serving arguments once removed; arguing explicitly over shares was more direct and candid. Had the process gone on several years, more formal criteria might have been forged. The same may occur eventually with carbon emissions.

Setting the Ceiling

Two thousand American economists recently recommended that national emission quotas promptly be negotiated, with purchase and sale of emission rights allowed to assure a fair geographic distribution of reductions. This appears to be the U.S. position for the meeting in Kyoto. It is an elegant idea. But its feasibility is suspect, at least for the present.

One cannot envision national representatives calmly sitting down to divide up rights in perpetuity worth more than a trillion dollars. It is also hard to imagine an enforcement mechanism acceptable to the U.S. Senate. I do not even foresee agreement on what concentration of greenhouse gases will ultimately be tolerable. Without that, any trajectory of global emissions had to be transitory, in which case renegotiation is bound to be anticipated, and no prudent nation is likely to sell its surplus emissions when doing so is clear evidence that it was originally allowed more than it needed.

The current focus of international negotiation is extremely short-term. That is probably appropriate, but the long term needs to be acknowledge and kept in mind. If carbon-induced climate change proves serious, it will be the ultimate concentration of greenhouse gases in the atmosphere that matters. The objective should be to stabilize that final concentration at a level compatible with tolerable climate change. Emissions of the carbon-based gases are the current focus of attention, but the question of concentration is what needs to be settled.

If scientists knew the upper limit to what the earth's climate system could tolerate, that limit could serve as the concentration target. It would probably not matter much climatically how that limit was approached. The optimal trajectory would probably include a continuing rise in annual emissions for a few decades, followed by a significant decline as the world approached a sustainable low level compatible with the ceiling on concentration. That is no argument for present inaction: future technologies that people will rely on to save energy or make energy less carbon-intensive 10, 20, or 30 years from now will depend on much more vigorous research and development, much of it at public expense, than governments and private institutions are doing or even contemplating now.

The ceiling is variously proposed as 450, 550, 650, or 750 parts per million, compared with about 360 parts per million today. The Intergovernmental Panel on Climate Change, the scientific advisory body associated with these conferences, has rendered no opinion on what level of concentration might ultimately become intolerable. Without that decision, there can be no long-range plan.

In the short run, there will almost certainly be innumerable modest but worthwhile opportunities for reducing carbon emissions. National representatives from the developed countries are counting on it. They are proposing reductions of 10 or 15 percent in annual emissions for most developed countries during the coming decade or so. If such reductions are seriously pursued—an open question—a rising trend in emissions would be superimposed on a short-term effort to limit actual emissions.

A program of short-term reductions would help governments learn more about emissions and how much they can be reduced by different measures. But the prevailing sentiment seems to be that emissions can be brought down and kept down in the OECD countries. It is not yet politically correct to acknowledge that global emissions are bound to increase for many decades, especially as nations like China experience economic growth and greater energy use.

When the OECD countries do get serious about combating climate change, they should focus on actions—policies, programs, taxes, subsidies, regulations, investments, energy technology research and development— that governments can actually take or bring about that will affect emissions. Commitments to targets and timetables are inherently flawed. They are pegged some years into the future, generally the further the better. Moreover, most governments cannot predict their policies' impact on emissions.

To pick an unrealistic example, if the United States committed itself to raising the tax on gasoline by ten cents per gallon per year for the next 15 years, any agency could discern whether the tax actually went up a dime per year, and the U.S. government would know exactly what it was committed to doing. But nobody can predict what that tax would do to emissions by the end of 15 years.

Greenhouse Politics

Slowing global warming is a political problem. The cost will be relatively low: a few trillion dollars over the next 30 or 40 years, out of an OECD gross product rising from $15 trillion to $30 trillion or $40 trillion annually. But any greenhouse program that is not outrageously inefficient will have to address carbon emissions in China, whose current emissions are half the United States' but will be several times the U.S. level in 2050 if left unchecked. The OECD countries can curtail their own emissions through regulation, which, although inefficient, is politically more acceptable than taxes because the costs remain invisible. The developed-country expense of curtailing Chinese emissions will require visible transfers of budgeted resources. it will look like the foreign aid it actually is, although it will benefit China no more than India or Nigeria. Building non-carbon or carbon-efficient electric power in China will look like aid to China, not climate relief for the world.

There remains a nagging issue that is never addressed at meetings on global warming policy. The future beneficiaries of these policies in developing countries will almost certainly be better off than their grandparents, today's residents of those countries. Alternative uses of resources devoted to ameliorating climate change should be considered. Namely, does it make more sense to invest directly in the development of these countries?

There are two issues here. One is whether, in benefits three or four generations hence, the return for investing directly in public health, education, water resources, infrastructure, industry, agricultural productivity, and family planning is as great as that for investing in reduced climate change. The second is whether the benefits accrue earlier, to people who more desperately need the help. Is there something escapist about discussing two percent of GNP to be invested in the welfare of future generations when nothing is done for their contemporary ancestors, a third of whom are so undernourished that a case of measles can kill?

If there were aid to divide between Bangladesh and Singapore, would anybody propose giving any of it to Singapore? In 50 or 75 years, when climate change may be a significant reality, Bangladesh probably will have progressed to the level of Singapore today. Should anyone propose investing heavily in the welfare of those future Bangladeshis when the alternative is to help Bangladesh today? People worry that the sea level may rise half a meter in the next century from global warming and that large populated areas of Bangladesh may flood. But Bangladesh already suffers terrible floods.

The need for greenhouse gas abatement cannot logically be separated from the developing world's need for immediate economic improvement. The trade-off should be faced. It probably won't be.

24 Kyoto's Unfinished Business

Henry D. Jacoby

Ronald G. Prinn

Richard Schmalensee

Henry D. Jacoby is the William E. Pounds Professor of Management and Codirector of the Joint Program on the Science and Policy of Global Change at the Massachusetts Institute of Technology; Ronald G. Prinn is the TEPCO Professor of Atmospheric Chemistry, Codirector of the Joint Program on the Science and Policy of Global Change, and Director of the Center for Global Change Science at MIT; Richard Schmalensee is Dean of the Sloan School of Management at the Massachusetts Institute of Technology.

Taking the Long View on Global Warming

Even well-informed observers disagree about what the Kyoto Protocol on Climate Change will accomplish. Some gaze at its text and see a battle won. They cheer the fact that the generally richer nations participating in the protocol agreed to cut their collective emissions of the greenhouse gases that cause global warming to about five percent less than 1990 levels by early in the next century. These optimists also applaud features of the Kyoto accord designed to hold down the costs of achieving these reductions. In computing their emissions, nations can include changes in the six major greenhouse gases emitted because of human activity, not just carbon dioxide, the most important of the six. In addition, countries can factor in reduced carbon dioxide levels from changes in land use and new forestry techniques that take the gas out of the atmosphere. Groups of participating nations may comply jointly and reallocate commitments among themselves, as the European Union (EU) plans to do within a European "bubble," and there is agreement in principle to some form of emissions trading. Joint implementation, under which agents in one country can get credit for reductions they achieve in another, is to be permitted between participating nations, and a new Clean Development Mechanism will provide access to these opportunities in nonparticipating countries, mainly in the developing world. Finally, emissions targets are not rigidly tied to a single year, but to averages over a five-year "commitment period" from 2008 to 2012.

Pessimists, on the other hand, see Kyoto as a costly defeat. They note that there is no solid proof that human-induced climate change will occur or

"Kyoto's Unfinished Business," by Henry D. Jacoby, Ronald G. Prinn, and Richard Schmalensee from *Foreign Affairs*, 77(4):54–66.

that its adverse effects would be serious were it to happen. At the same time, the expense of reducing greenhouse gas emissions to meet the Kyoto targets will be substantial, and pessimists believe that the effort will make participating countries less competitive. In the darkest interpretation, the Kyoto agreement is a pact among rich nations that will cripple their economies for decades to come, made simply because today's political leaders needed to burnish their environmental credentials.

Neither of these schools of thought is correct. Still a third group, whose views are much closer to the mark, believes that Kyoto mainly postpones much-needed work on what may prove a very serious long-term challenge. To them, Kyoto is a quick political fix for a problem created at the First Conference of Parties to the Climate Convention held in Berlin in 1995. The so-called Berlin mandate instructed negotiators to seek short-term, legally binding targets and timetables for emission control for participating countries only. In the run-up to Kyoto, many leaders publicly committed themselves to this idea. Not surprisingly, avoiding embarrassment on this score became the dominant focus of the negotiations. As a result, this group argues, the Kyoto agreement allows political leaders to declare success, but it does not address the larger climate issues at stake.

Even worse, these skeptics fear that by following the Berlin mandate, negotiators at Kyoto may have made it harder, not easier, to meet the long-term challenge. Now the next decade may be spent haggling over these short-term commitments, thereby diverting attention from more important century-scale issues and postponing the involvement of the developing world. The Kyoto agreement might fail to meet even its immediate goals if the lack of domestic support in the United States prevents ratification, which in turn would rationalize inaction by other participating nations. The entire international response to climate change could be discredited, thus increasing the difficulty of collective action in the future, no matter how serious the problem turns out to be.

To some degree, these widely divergent analyses of the Kyoto achievement reflect differing interpretations of its text, key parts of which are still the subject of strong and sometimes bitter international disagreement. Some of these points will be taken up again at the Fourth Conference of the Parties in November, but others may take years to resolve. What is in dispute is not merely the Kyoto text, of course, but the underlying science and economics of global warming. Above all, for the journey from Kyoto to succeed, policymakers will need to spend more time thinking of the long term.

A Global Warming Primer

To start with the basics, climate change can be driven by an imbalance between the energy the earth receives from the sun, largely as visible light, and the energy it radiates back to space as invisible infrared light. The "greenhouse effect" is caused by the presence in the air of gases and clouds that absorb some of the infrared light flowing upward and radiate it back downward. The warming influence of this re-radiated energy is opposed by substances at the surface and in the atmosphere that reflect sunlight directly back into space. These include snow and desert sand, as well as clouds and aerosols. (Aerosols are tiny, submicroscopic solid or liquid particles suspended in the air, such as smoke and fog.)

Water vapor and clouds, which typically remain in the atmosphere for a week or so, are responsible for most of the re-radiated infrared light. Central to the climate change debate, however, are less important but much longer-lasting greenhouse gases, most notably carbon dioxide. Atmospheric concentrations of carbon dioxide and other long-lived greenhouse gases have increased substantially over the past century. As this has happened, the flow of infrared energy to space has been reduced, so that, all else being equal, the earth receives slightly more energy than it radiates to space. This imbalance tends to raise temperatures at the earth's surface. These aspects of the greenhouse effect are not controversial. It is also generally accepted that emissions of carbon dioxide from the combustion of fossil fuels (primarily coal, oil, and natural gas) are the most significant way humans can increase the greenhouse effect, and that this emitted carbon dioxide remains in the atmosphere for a long time, on the order of a century or so.

What is much more uncertain, and the cause of serious scientific debate, is the response of the complex system that determines our climate to changes in the concentrations of greenhouse gases in the atmosphere. Some poorly understood processes in the climate system tend to amplify the warming effect of greenhouse gases, while others, equally poorly understood, tend to counteract or dampen it. Any global warming will likely be delayed because it takes a lot of heat to warm the oceans, but it is not known just how rapidly heat is carried into the ocean depths.

To predict climate, scientists must use mathematical models whose complexity taxes the capabilities of even the world's largest computers. These models are based on incomplete knowledge about the key factors that influence climate, including clouds, ocean circulation, the natural cycles of greenhouse gases, natural aerosols like those produced by volcanic gases, and man-made aerosols like smog. Today's climate models cannot reproduce the succession of ice ages and warm periods over the last 250,000 years, let alone the smaller climatic fluctuations observed over the last century. In addition, climate models are driven by forecasts of greenhouse gas emissions, which in turn rest on highly uncertain long-term predictions of population trends, economic growth, and technological advances.

Burning Down the House?

To help quantify the uncertainty in climate prediction, we and our MIT colleagues have developed a model of global economic development, climate processes, and ecosystems. We have produced seven forecasts of climate change over the next century, each of which assumes no action to restrict future greenhouse gas emissions and can be defended as possible given current knowledge. These forecasts involve changes in global average surface temperature between 1990 and 2100 as small as two degrees Fahrenheit or as large as nine degrees Fahrenheit (roughly one to five degrees centigrade). We cannot sort out which of these paths (or other possible ones) we are heading along, although we are less likely to be on one of the extreme ones. There may be other paths involving rapid climate changes driven by purely natural processes that are not well handled by any current climate models.

Unfortunately, we know even less about the likely impact of climate change. Warming may increase storm damage, for instance, but it may also decrease it. Very little is known about the likely impact on human health or the ability of unmanaged ecosystems to adapt to shifting conditions. Civilization and natural systems have coped with climate change in the past and can, to at least some degree, adapt. What we do know suggests that the changes summarized by the lowest of the seven forecasts would do little harm and might even benefit some countries. Most analysts would agree, however, that the highest of our seven forecasts implies significant risks to a variety of important natural processes including ocean circulation, polar glaciers, and unmanaged ecosystems, as well as agriculture and other human activities. Indeed, for policymakers, the most important finding of climate research to date may be that the range of possible outcomes is so wide. Sound policy decisions must take account of this profound uncertainty, and it is plainly vital to accelerate research aimed at reducing it.

An important complement to the work on forecasts is the search for what has been called a fingerprint—evidence that would clearly reveal human influence on climate. In its 1995 report, the Intergovernmental Panel on Climate Change (IPCC) declared in its *Summary for Policymakers* that "the balance of evidence suggests a discernible human influence on climate." Several scientists, however, subsequently questioned the scientific basis of this summary and the certainty it conveyed. Hence the hunt for definitive evidence of human-induced climate change remains an important research area—mainly because the stronger the human influence on climate, the earlier it will be possible to detect its "signal" despite the "noise" of natural variability in climate over time. The larger the proven human influence on climate, the stronger will be the case for substantial reductions in greenhouse gas emissions.

The current debate about detection does not justify inaction. As our range of forecasts indicates, we know enough to conclude that human activity may produce significant global warming, with substantial adverse impacts. It would be irresponsible to ignore such a risk, just as it would be irresponsible to do nothing when you smell smoke at home until and unless you see flames. It would also be irresponsible, of course, to call the fire department and hose down all your belongings at the slightest whiff of what might be smoke.

What It Takes

The ultimate goal of the climate treaty to which the Kyoto protocol is attached is stabilizing atmospheric concentrations of greenhouse gases at levels that will avoid "danger" to economies and ecosystems. No one knows what the appropriate levels might be, or even if the implicit notion of a sharp line between danger and safety makes sense. The nature of the potential task can be explored, however, by studying an EU recommendation that countries stabilize the amount of carbon dioxide in the atmosphere at roughly twice preindustrial levels, in the long run. Doing this would slow climate change but, according to most climate models, not stop it. For the middle range of MIT model forecasts, following the IPCC path to stabilization at the EU target would lower projected warming between now and 2100 by only about 30 percent, although it would produce a larger percentage reduction in the following century.

Following this EU recommendation would require very sharp cuts in global carbon dioxide emissions, however, and the current signatories to the Kyoto protocol could not do the job by themselves. If the nonparticipating nations were to accept no restrictions, net emissions by participating nations would somehow have to become negative by around the middle of the next century. Even a total ban on use of fossil fuels by all industrialized countries would not reach the target.

Of course, if the nations currently participating in Kyoto reduce their emissions, other nations might also eventually agree to lower theirs. Unfortunately, income growth in the most populous nonparticipating countries—including China, India, Indonesia, and Brazil—seems unlikely to encourage voluntary efforts until the latter part of the next century. Until then, these nations will naturally be more concerned with feeding their children than with protecting their grandchildren from potential global warming. Thus, if the relatively rich participating countries want to stabilize atmospheric concentrations of greenhouse gases, they will have to pay at least some poor countries to reduce their emissions. Achievement of substantial reduction in this way implies international transfers of wealth on a scale well beyond anything in recorded history.

There is no effective political support for such a herculean effort, particularly in the United States. Given the uncertainties discussed above, such an effort would make little economic sense in any event. The groundwork, however, must be laid now to preserve any hope of someday mounting such a response. Future generations will find three legacies especially valuable: participation of all countries in climate-related actions, development of new technologies to lower the cost of emissions control, and the creation of institutions for cost-effective multinational action.

First, a substantial reduction in global emissions will require something close to worldwide participation, so it is essential to build a climate agreement that can encompass countries not currently participating in Kyoto—including most of the developing world. Such an accord must include a way for these countries to gradually accept the burdens of emissions control. Equally important, it must also anticipate a regime to govern climate-related transfers of resources to countries that cannot bear the cost of emissions reduction.

An exclusive emphasis on the relatively wealthy nations participating in Kyoto is a double-edged sword. If rich nations do not control their emissions, poorer ones are unlikely even to consider slowing theirs. But carbon dioxide emission controls will raise the cost in participating countries of manufacturing those goods whose production requires substantial energy. For these products, industries in developing countries will gain an advantage over industries in countries that abide by Kyoto. Once they have invested in production facilities, nonparticipating nations will be more reluctant to take emission-control measures that threaten these activities.

Second, it will be nearly impossible to slow warming appreciably without condemning much of the world to poverty unless energy sources that emit little or no carbon dioxide become competitive with conventional fossil fuels. Only a large R&D effort can have any hope of bringing this about, although it would be cheap relative to the cost of dramatic reductions in carbon dioxide emissions using current technologies. The range of technological options is wide—from using solar power to produce electricity to converting fossil fuels to hydrogen fuel and storing (underground or deep in the ocean) the carbon dioxide produced as a byproduct. Few of the alternatives currently under discussion, however, can be widely used at reasonable costs without fundamental improvements.

Finally, since climate change will be a high-stakes global issue for many decades, the world must begin to develop international institutions that will facilitate policies that minimize the cost of reducing greenhouse gas emissions. For starters, this requires solving the monitoring and enforcement problems necessary to implement efficient international trading of rights to emit greenhouse gases (or to implement internationally harmonized taxes on greenhouse gas emissions). It also requires an institutional structure that can exploit the cheapest abatement opportunities, wherever they may be found, and a decision-making process that can adjust policies to reflect changes in scientific knowledge and economic development.

This is a tall order. The international trade regime developed under the General Agreement on Tariffs and Trade, now the World Trade Organization, hints at the difficulties involved. This regime grew and evolved over time, adding countries and goods along the way, peacefully resolving conflicts between national economic interests, and contributing importantly to global economic growth. By the standards of international affairs, the WTO has been a stunning success, but it took 50 years of hard work—even given an intelligent, forward-looking design at the outset.

A Kyoto Report Card

Kyoto's results are mixed. The agreement failed miserably at including poorer countries. Until the last minute, the negotiating text at Kyoto contained a provision allowing a nonparticipating nation to choose, at any time and on a voluntary basis, a level of emissions control it felt was appropriate to its circumstances. This "opt-in" provision made sense as an opening to wider participation, particularly since some nonparticipating nations, like Singapore, are wealthier than some participants, like Romania. Several nonparticipating countries supported the idea, but the provision was struck from the protocol because key developing countries—especially China and India—strongly opposed adding any avenues that could lead to emissions limits for them. For their part, the developed countries were unwilling to risk deadlock on this issue and let Beijing and New Delhi have their way.

Investment in research and development on new long-term technical options was not even discussed. One phrase calling for parties to "cooperate in scientific and technical research" was tucked away in the text, but that was all; no nation was obliged to devote any resources to R&D. Politicians love to call for more research instead of more regulation, but there is little commitment to the long-term development of greenhouse-friendly technology by those countries most capable of producing it.

The news from Kyoto is more encouraging regarding provisions to facilitate flexible, cost-efficient policies for controlling emissions. Including multiple gases was a step in the right direction. In principle, schemes like the Clean Development Mechanism may encourage making emissions reductions wherever they are least expensive. But these systems give credit for specific emissions reductions, and U.S. experience with similar policies indicates that the administrative and transaction costs of the required project-by-project approval process are likely to limit their benefits substantially. Most important, the Kyoto provision that in principle allows the trading of rights to emit greenhouse gases, if implemented effectively, would yield major reductions in cost.

Other features built into Kyoto to create more flexibility give less cause for celebration. The provision for multicountry "bubbles," within which national emissions limits can be adjusted as long as the total is kept constant, is an artifact of short-term political convenience. The creation of such a bubble for the EU is entirely consistent with other EU institutions. It provides a mechanism for differentiation within the EU while its leaders seek uniform commitments from non-Europeans. The application of the idea to other groups of nations emerged as Washington's defensive response to widespread and continuing opposition to emissions trading. If full-fledged trading were ultimately lost, at least some flexibility might be gained in the short term through government-to-government shifting of quotas. While such arrangements may reduce costs over the next few years, they will not provide flexibility in the long run, and they might make it harder to realize the benefits of full global trading by balkanizing the market.

The inclusion in the Kyoto protocol of credits for "carbon sinks"—increases in the removal of carbon dioxide from the atmosphere because of post-1990 changes in land use and forestry practices—is another double-edged sword. In principle, measures to encourage the use of these sinks should be covered by Kyoto because they may be cost-effective for some countries. Land vegetation is already removing carbon from the atmosphere, on balance, probably spurred by increased plant growth caused by rising atmospheric carbon dioxide. The uncertainties are great, but central estimates in the IPCC report indicate that for the world as a whole, the net removal of carbon dioxide from the atmosphere in this way amounts to about 30 percent of current emissions from the burning of fossil fuels. For countries with large forests, such as the United States, Canada, and Russia, biological sinks may play an important role in their emissions accounting. With stakes this large, and with ambiguity inherent in the protocol's definitions of the 1990 baseline and of increases in removal by sinks, fierce debates about measurement and accounting are already under way. The sinks issue could easily become a troubling diversion.

Finally, it is important to be clear-eyed about the risks involved in the core agreement of the Kyoto protocol: national targets and the 2008–12 timetable. On the positive side, the Kyoto targets are a start toward a long-term solution. If participating countries meet the 5 percent reduction goal and stabilize their emissions at that level for the rest of the century, then—with no restrictions on nonparticipating nations—warming by 2100 will be reduced by about 16 percent. Also, these initial cuts could have important symbolic value, providing incentives for R&D and laying the groundwork for broader national participation. The risk is that these advantages will be lost, and worse, if the emissions reductions agreed to in Kyoto are not met—as they probably will not be. The longer any nation delays adopting serious controls on greenhouse gas emissions, the higher the cost of meeting its Kyoto obligations and the more difficult it will be to generate the requisite domestic political support. The current U.S. policy involves a long delay, which is likely to discourage earlier action by other participating nations fearing a loss of international competitiveness.

The current U.S. climate plan has two main provisions. First, the Clinton administration has asked Congress for $6.3 billion over five years for a technology initiative offering tax incentives and R&D expenditures "to encourage energy efficiency and the use of cleaner energy sources." Second, after a "decade of experience, a decade of data, a decade of technological innovation," the plan holds that whatever administration is in office in 2007 will cap U.S. greenhouse gas emissions and institute a domestic system of tradable rights to emit. Unfortunately, under current policy, the end of the "decade of opportunity" is likely to find U.S. emissions 20 to 25 percent above the 1990 level. The International Energy Agency estimates that by 2000 the United States' emissions will be 16 percent higher than they were in 1990, and climbing. It is simply laughable to forecast that

Washington would then impose a cap on emissions stringent enough to turn the energy economy around in three to five years. Moreover, the administration has promised not to send the Kyoto protocol to the Senate for ratification until developing nations commit to "substantial participation." It is not easy to see when such a condition might be met, particularly if vigorous U.S. action is in any way needed to involve the developing world.

Thus, Kyoto is likely to yield far less than the targeted emissions reduction. That failure will most likely be papered over with creative accounting, shifting definitions of carbon sinks, and so on. If this happens, the credibility of the international process for addressing climate change will be at risk. Other outcomes are possible, of course. Other nations may decide to move forward with emissions control despite U.S. inaction. Changes in U.S. public opinion may accelerate domestic action. Small investments in research may yield unexpectedly large near-term payoffs. Slow economic growth may hold emissions down. Still, even meeting the aggregate Kyoto target will be a hollow victory if it requires spending economic resources and political capital that would be better used to prepare for the vastly greater reductions in global emissions that may be required in the future.

Now, the Hard Part

Even though the dust has not settled from the struggle in Kyoto, preparations have begun for the Fourth Conference of the Parties (COP-4) in November. Its focus should be on the longer term.

It is most important to try again to develop a system that can include developing countries and, if necessary, transfer substantial resources to help them participate in a global effort to control emissions. Two opportunities are apparent, one recently rejected at Kyoto and the other only recently advanced there. First is an amendment to Kyoto that restores the provision that would allow nonparticipating countries to volunteer to control their emissions under flexible terms. For any nation seriously concerned with climate change, this should be a necessary condition for ratification of the Kyoto protocol. If the developing countries' opposition to even voluntary action cannot be overcome, it is probably better to scrap Kyoto and start negotiations again when opinions have changed.

Given success on this point, there may then be room for progress on negotiating the details of the Clean Development Mechanism. The protocol suggests that the "operating entities" that will decide how much credit will be given for specific emission reduction projects under the CDM might serve as intermediaries, helping to reduce transaction costs. If so, the CDM might help bring developing countries into the fold. Most studies find that emissions can be least expensively reduced in those countries, so that nonparticipating nations could, in principle, make a great deal of money selling emissions reductions to participating nations. On the other hand, the

U.S. regulatory experience suggests that because it is hard to estimate precisely what emissions would have been in the absence of particular investments, the CDM could also produce red tape and plenty of administrative jobs but have scant impact on emissions. Much depends on the details to be worked out in COP-4. If those negotiations produce a heavily bureaucratic structure, perhaps burdened with taxes on trades in emissions reduction credits, it may be better to reject this proposal and begin anew.

Dealing seriously with climate change requires a substantial R&D program to produce new technologies that could bring about deep global emissions reductions and still allow robust economic growth. Such an effort should involve several wealthy participating nations. Candidate technologies include nuclear, solar, hydroelectric, geothermal, and hydrogen from fossil fuel. Methods for safe and economical long-term storage of carbon in subterranean reservoirs, the deep ocean, and forests are also important research areas, as are technologies that enhance energy efficiency. In contrast, the U.S. "technology initiative" concentrates on subsidizing the adoption of existing technologies but would spend little in the search for long-term breakthroughs. Efforts elsewhere are similarly dwarfed by the challenge.

Finally, a well-designed, durable institutional structure can significantly reduce the cost of limits on global emissions. Here, the key piece of unfinished business from Kyoto is implementing a system for trading the rights to emit greenhouse gases among participating nations. In negotiating the details of this system, now scheduled for COP-4, a focus on clear definitions, vigilant monitoring, and strict enforcement is essential. Otherwise, the market should be left unfettered. Many nations oppose trading in any form; others want to restrict its use in meeting emissions commitments. If they make it impossible to implement a plausible framework for international trading of emission rights, the Kyoto protocol is headed for a dead end, obviating the point of ratifying it.

The challenge will be developing a framework for international decision-making that can work for several decades. Building these three legacies—inclusion of the developing world, R&D, and flexible provisions for emissions reductions—will be a huge undertaking. But since no serious response to climate change is possible without them, the task merits the same sense of urgency that motivated Kyoto. When it comes to climate change, the world's work has just begun.

VIII

Ecological Values

25 Economic Analysis and Ecosystems: Some Concepts and Issues

R. David Simpson*

R. David Simpson is a Fellow at Resources for the Future.

Introduction

The terms "economics" and "ecology" both come from the same Greek root: "*oikos*," for "house," or "household." Literally, economics means the management of the household, and ecology means the study of its function. Of course, both terms are now used metaphorically. Ecologists study nature's "household," a set of relationships between and among organisms, and between organisms and their abiotic environment. The "household" economists study is society as a whole as it determines how to produce, preserve, and allocate material goods.

If this tracing of origins proves anything, it may only be that etymology can be deceptive. For while there is a laudable trend for economists and ecologists to work together on questions of mutual interest, and there are a number of similarities in analytical and statistical approaches between the disciplines, there are still a great many issues on which economists and ecologists do not necessarily see eye-to-eye. This, at least, has been my experience. Now this may not be surprising. There are many issues on which economists *and economists* do not see eye-to-eye. I can only presume that similar disputes also exist among ecologists.

Moreover, part of the friction between economists and ecologists may stem from what seems a very basic difference in perspectives. At the risk of caricaturizing my discipline, we economists tend to structure our thinking around models of hyper-rational agents making decisions so as to optimize with respect to certain well-defined individual objectives. To an outsider such as me, at least, the life sciences are characterized by a very different paradigm, one in which those agents that replicate themselves are those whose attributes or behaviors are more conducive to survival than are those of the other organisms with which they compete. (This is not to

"Economic Analysis and Ecosystems: Some Concepts and Issues," by R. David Simpson from *Ecological Applications*, (2):342–349 (1998). © 1998 by the Ecological Society of America.

*I thank Paul Ringold, Richard Haeuber, and four anonymous referees for helpful suggestions. All opinions and errors are, however, my own.

say that evolutionary models have not had some impact in economics [see, e.g., Nelson and Winter 1982], nor, I presume, that optimizing models would not be developed by ecologists.)

Despite the facts that there may be differences of opinion within as well as between the disciplines, and that there may be some very fundamental differences in perspective. I feel that at least some arguments between economists and ecologists arise from simple misunderstandings. Economists often base their analyses on a number of restrictive assumptions, and we are often remiss in not advising non-economist readers and listeners of this fact. So, I try in this paper both to describe some basic principles of economic analysis and to clarify the assumptions that underlie them.

I think that much of what I say below represents, if not consensus, at least majority opinion among economists who have thought about ecological issues. You should be aware, though, that the "economic approach" to thinking about ecological and environmental issues for the most part transcends ideological classification. The study of economics should not be confused with advocacy of any particular political platform. As I said above, there are differences of opinion among economists. We are not (necessarily) advocates of *laissez faire*, free market, to-hell-with-the-environment economics any more than are ecologists (necessarily) advocates of the universal restoration of precolumbian ecosystems. Economic tools provide a useful framework that can be used to think about environmental decisions. Different assumptions and interpretations of the data can be used to generate very different conclusions, however.

At the risk of stating the obvious, let me also point out that what I have to say here is necessarily abbreviated and incomplete. I cannot begin to do justice to the breadth and sophistication of work done by economists, or even the work being done by economists working on environmental and ecological issues. When I note below that certain areas are problematic, or that further research is needed, you should recognize that at least some economists—and often more than I can compactly cite—are at work on these unresolved issues.

In what follows I first go through some important concepts in economic analysis, and also highly some important assumptions. Then I discuss some shortcomings in the economic analysis of ecological resources, and I conclude with some observations on what economics tell us about appropriate conservation and preservation policies.

Choices and Values

Economic Decisions as Choices

Economics is sometimes described as the study of which among our unlimited wants we choose to satisfy given our limited resources. These choices involve weighing the satisfaction achieved or the needs met by one alternative against those from another. In practice, this balancing often involves a comparison of what we are willing to pay for one thing as opposed to what we are willing to pay for another. This reduction of the relative value of goods to a comparison of expenditures often has led to a confusion concerning the importance of money in economic analysis. It is ironic that many people believe that economic choices are based (only) on the amount of money involved. It is standard in introductory economics textbooks and courses to note that money is simply a unit of account, of no value except as a means to purchase the things we really do care about.

What is important is not that we make decisions on the basis of dollars. It is, rather, that we make decisions in relative terms. Given a choice between A and B, I must either prefer A to B, prefer B to A, or find A and B equally attractive. Inasmuch as these possibilities are exhaustive, this may not seem controversial. The implication, however, is that absolute values can only be assigned to the achievement of objectives that do not conflict. One cannot, for example, claim to be willing to make any sacrifice both to maintain biodiversity and to improve the lot of the world's poor people, if the only way for the latter to increase their well-being is at the expense of the former. Of course, we sometimes hear arguments to the effect that both objectives could be achieved if only some among us would forego frivolous purchases. I do not intend to debate this proposition here, only to point out that the achievement of what some regard to be the noblest of objectives may require sacrifices that others are unwilling to make.

The Determination of Value

To say that one thing has greater economic value than another is another way of saying that, *under the circumstances*, it would be chose in preference to the other. I have emphasized "under the circumstances" for two reasons. The first is to reiterate what I said above: economic choices are made on the basis of relative comparisons. Not only do we compare one thing to another, but the choice we make may change depending on time, place, and other factors. My second reason for emphasizing that circumstances matter is that groups of people sometimes make the "wrong" choice, because individuals may not consider the effects of their actions on others. I shall say more about this a little later. First, however, let us think about how economic choices are made, and how economic values are determined.

The question of how value is determined dominated economic thought from before the time of Aristotle to the 18th century. Philosophers, when they deigned to consider matters so mundane as economics, were confounded by the "paradox of value." The paradox of value is that things that command great prices are often things that we think of as being of little "intrinsic value." On the other hand, absolutely essential goods are often available at negligible prices. The best example is that of diamonds and water. Life could not exist without water, but most of us go through our whole lives without ever really needing a diamond. Isn't the fact that water is so much less expensive than diamonds evidence that economic value can be completely unrelated to anything socially meaningful?

In fact, there is nothing inconsistent about things that are, in total, immeasurably useful being "worth" less than inessential items. In economics, values are determined "on the margin." By this I mean that the value of something—or, equivalently, how much of it you would trade for something else—is determined by how much *a little bit more* of it is worth in terms of *a little bit more* of something else. Water is so much less valuable than diamonds because it is so much more plentiful. A little more water is, to use a particular appropriate phrase, a drop in the bucket. A few more diamonds may be a few more than most of us will ever have.

It is worth pointing out again, though, that economic values are very much dependent on circumstances. The "marginal" gallon of water might trade for many carats of diamonds in the middle of a desert.

An Important Assumption

The notion of "marginal analysis" that I introduced above is often expressed as the idea that "marginal benefits" should be equal to "marginal costs." Put another way, when one is making optimal decisions between the things that promote one's well-being, one is often supposed to be "indifferent on the margin" between one's options. Another way to think of this is as an analogy to climbing a hill. You want to take that combination of steps that gets you to the highest point on the hill. How do you know when you are at the top of a hill? Well, one condition is that you cannot take a step in any direction and get any higher. This condition—or its mathematical equivalent—is what underlies much of formal economic analysis. If you think about it, though, the strategy of groping around until you cannot get any higher by stepping in any direction can be a dangerous way of scaling a mountain. It may work all right for gently sloping hills with broad, flat summits, but it is not something you would want to try if a misstep could send you plummeting a thousand meters.

Let us relate this analogy to a biological issue. What is the value of biodiversity? That is, at what point is one better off saving the "marginal species" by foregoing development opportunities on the "marginal hectare" of imperiled habitat that supports it? (I have actually performed some such marginal-cost calculations recently [Simpson et al. 1996], but hasten to point out that that work was limited to only one source of value, the use of biodiversity in the development of new pharmaceutical products, and is liberally sprinkled with caveats.) An economic prescription for the optimal preservation of biodiversity might be to convert habitat from its natural condition to use in agriculture until the loss of the marginal species just balances the gain from the marginal hectare of new farmland. It may be unreasonable to suppose, however, that one can simply exterminate X of Y endemic species—or bulldoze X of Y hectares of forest—without affecting those that remain. Experimenting with a little more habitat destruction could prove to be analogous to taking one more step in the search for the summit and falling over a cliff. There appears, at least to a layperson such as me, to be some legitimate concern that no one really knows where the margins of the natural world are. The loss of 1 ha of habitat might lead to the loss of a species, which might lead to the loss of another species, and so forth, until the ecosystem as a whole is greatly degraded.

Even the smoothest of surfaces can appear a ragged jumble of cliffs and crevices when highly magnified, however. While economists often assume that both social and natural systems respond smoothly and continuously to perturbations, this is, at the most literal level, very rarely true. For example, there are a lot of things that people either do or do not buy (new cars, for example). Yet if one looks at aggregate data, the sum of all these individual yes-or-no decisions often appears to be a smooth function of things like changes in prices and incomes. One has to, then, consider what the relevant scale of analysis is. How devastating, for example, are the consequences of *local* environmental degradation? This will depend on the extent of such degradation, as well as on the degree to which goods and services provided by one area can be substituted for another.

The Importance of Substitutes

Substitutability is another important concept in economics. The notion of substitutability links the issues I have just been discussing. Another way of saying what I said about marginal analysis and economic value is that things with lots of close substitutes are not very valuable. On the other hand, things with few substitutes are very valuable. As I also said above, analysis of changes "on the margin" may not be very useful if small changes in some underlying conditions can lead to large, discontinuous changes in the state of the system we are considering. A biological example of this might be the extinction of a keystone species, one for which there is no substitute in performing key ecosystem-stabilizing functions.

Notions of substitutability may seem at first to be rather limited. Some things have close substitutes, but what about unique things? How can we assign a value to a unique asset? I hesitate to make any statement of the form "economists believe that . . . "; as the old joke has it, you could lay every economist in the world end to end and never reach a conclusion. I will say, though, that many people who study economics for an extended period come away convinced that the general public often underestimates possibilities for substitution. While I admit that things are rarely truly redundant, I would also say that there are very few things that are truly unique, in the sense that they have no substitutes.

Having said this, however, it is important to emphasize that the degree to which things are substitutable depends on a number of factors. One is the scale and level of aggregation we are discussing. Baked potatoes and french fries may be pretty good substitutes for each other, but there is no substitute for food in general. This scale-of-analysis issue may explain some disagreements between economists and ecologists. One species may be a substitute for another as a source of food, or one (relatively small) ecosystem may be a substitute for another as a place to live or recreate. Sometimes when economists say something like this, however, ecologists think that the economists are saying that biodiversity or natural ecosystems *as a whole* are not important and valuable.

One would be hard-pressed to find an economist who would take such an extreme position. There is, however, some considerable disagreement within the profession as to exactly what the limits to substitution are. Robert Solow, an economist who won the Nobel Prize for his work on economic growth, wrote a paper in 1974 on economic growth with exhaustible resources. By exhaustible resources, Solow had in mind things like minerals and fossil fuels (whose exhaustion was a great concern during the "energy crisis" years of the 1970s). Renewable resources are also "exhaustible," however, if they can be harvested more rapidly than they renew themselves, and then the same analysis applies. If our continuing well-being depends on our use of exhaustible resources, are we not, sooner or later, doomed? The answer Solow derived is "it all depends." Even if certain resources are essential, we might be able to grow indefinitely, using ever-smaller amounts of the essential resources. The key is to invest enough in other assets (particularly technological know-how) so as to make up for the declining natural-resource base. Of course, this will only work if the other assets in which we can invest are, in fact, substitutes for exhaustible natural resources.

So far as I know, Solow never advocated his theoretical result as a statement of his beliefs; he merely pointed out a mathematical possibility. Nonetheless, some people consider Solow and Herman Daly (see Daly and Cobb 1989) to be the champions in a debate on the relative importance of man-made capital and natural resources. Daly is a proponent of the view that we cannot continue to exploit our natural resources indefinitely. They will eventually reach a point of no return and, when they are gone, we will be stuck with a permanently lower quality of life.

Now it should be clear that neither of the real extremes in such a debate is tenable. Obviously, we cannot destroy *all* (or, to accommodate Solow's result, arbitrarily close to all) of our natural resources and survive. Almost as obviously, if our ancestors had not destroyed *any* of our natural resources, we would have a much lower standard of living. The issue is, at current levels, should we be exploiting our environment more or less intensively? This is really the question of value again. Do we feel that we have reached the point where our natural resources are relatively scarce and hence relatively valuable, or do current human needs justify further depletion? Put in another way, if we destroy some of our remaining natural resources, will those we have left be enough to substitute for them?

Substitutability also depends on the time scale involved. To give a concrete example, consider a recent economic study of the effects of global warming on North American agriculture (Mendelsohn et al. 1994). The authors of that study concluded that such effects would be negligible, and possibly even positive, since, in the fullness of time, farmers could move themselves and their equipment from one region to another. In essence, areas rendered more agriculturally productive could be "substituted" for those regions rendered less productive by changes in climate. Such substitution is easier the more time is available to accomplish it. If climate change happens over several generations, the physical movement of people and equipment from one area to another would be minimized. Rather than current workers driving their tractors from, say, Kansas to Saskatchewan, old farmers and tractors in Kansas would retire, to be replaced by new farmers and tractors in Saskatchewan. A faster pace of climate change would necessitate more rapid, and consequently more costly, changes.

It is also worth nothing that substitution possibilities depend crucially on circumstances. To you and me, a climate-change-induced drought may have little effect. If the wheat harvest in Kansas is low this year, we are often able simply to substitute purchases from the Indiana corn crop. Such options are not available to subsistence farmers in much of the world. For them, there are no substitutes for a failed crop.

Values and Prices

I have had to be careful in what I have written above to avoid using the word "price" instead of "value." Economists often employ the terms interchangeably, but I should not do so without explaining a few things first. One of the biggest sources of confusion—and conflict—between economists and non-economists arises over this matter of "prices" and "values." I noted above that non-economists often think that money is more important in economic analysis than do economists. This misperception may be understandable, however, when so many economists spend a great deal of time talking about "using the market" to effect desirable changes. How can we effect desirable changes when the prices at which things sell are so often distorted? It is not surprising that many people agree with the characterization of economists as scholars who have learned "the price of everything, but the value of nothing."

It is important to understand that economists are not necessarily supporters of the status quo. It is true that many economists believe that a free market, with prices determined by supply and demand, is the best way of allocating *most* goods and services. Arguably, for most of the things about which we care, the free market would do a pretty good job of determining how much is to be produced and consumed. The analysis can get very technical, but the basic principle is that all mutually beneficial transactions take place in a free, competitive market. A competitive market is one in which no individual buyer or seller is large enough so that his/her actions determine the prices at which goods sell. If I am willing to give you at least as much for something as it costs you to provide it, we trade, and we are both better off.

I could go on to describe the circumstances under which the relative prices of things in such a free, competitive market would be a perfect guide to the relative values society ought to place on them. It will probably be obvious, however, that our economic system does not consist entirely of free, competitive markets. One can think of several sources of what are known in the economics profession as "market failures." There are monopolies and what is known as "imperfect competition" when single firms, or groups of firms, control markets. Governments are sometimes blamed for some of these problems, as legislation and regulation can restrict competition or impose unjustified prices. Ironically, though, some important market failures arise because governments do *not* interfere with the price system.

Externalities and Property Rights

Governments must act to correct "externalities." An externality is a consequence of one person's production or consumption that affects others who do not pay for the good produced or consumed. Externalities come in both "positive" and "negative" forms. Pollution is the classical example of the latter. The preservation of biodiversity might be a good example of the former. The environmental amenities that ecosystems produce are examples of externalities. While there are benefits of ecosystem conservation arising from the production and consumption of well-defined goods such as trees and fish, there are other, generally more diffuse, and therefore "external," benefits generated. These may include flood protection, water and nutrient cycling, climate moderation, and natural beauty. Many people, often spread over a wide area, benefit from the provision of these goods and services. The maintenance of pristine ecosystems in a world with competing wants can be an expensive proposition, however. Moreover, when benefits are diffuse but costs are concentrated, there is a misalignment of incentives. Suppose, for example, that I could make $1000 from chopping down and selling the trees on my property. It may well be that each of 10 000 people would be willing to pay a dollar to keep me from doing so, but who is going to organize my neighbors and collect the money to pay me not to cut my trees? Suppose you were one of my neighbors. If you knew that your other neighbors were willing to pay me enough not to chop down my trees, you would have little incentive to pay your share. Everyone would like to "ride for free" on the money someone else pays.

These "free-rider problems" can be overcome by collective action. If externalities are to be corrected, some social consensus must be reached as to how the cost of doing so is to be financed. One way of doing so would be to tax everyone enough to generate enough money to persuade those who are depriving the rest of us of ecosystem services to desist. Another, and effectively equivalent, method is to charge the person depriving the rest of us the amount by which his actions impoverish us. (The equivalence between paying someone to provide a "good" and charging someone for producing a "bad" is the essence of a celebrated result due to Ronald Coase

[1960].) When economists talk about the desirable properties of the price system in allocating goods such as ecosystems and their services, they are generally talking about a price system in which prices reflect the social consequences of an action. A commonly voiced desire among economists is that we "get the prices right." This means that governments should tax actions that are harmful to the environment or subsidize actions that are beneficial (or, in some cases, cut subsidies to harmful actions and cut taxes on beneficial ones).

Before going on, I want to make one important observation. The fact that externalities exist does not obviate the determinants of economic value I discussed above. The value of a good that generates externalities is determined by the same principle as that for any other: how much of the other goods that we (collectively, now) values are we willing to give up to obtain a little more of the good generating externalities? The point I want to make here is that we need to think about the value of ecosystems and environmental amenities in order to make reasonable social decisions concerning their conservation. The fact that many of the things we care about are not traded in the existing economic system makes it more, rather than less, important that we think carefully about what their values really are.

The jokes told about economists can be revealing. Three people—one, of course, an economist—are out on a camping trip, and find that they have brought along a can of beans, but nothing with which to open it. After the economist has ridiculed the suggestions made by her two colleagues for opening the can, they turn to her and say, "Okay, if you're so smart, how do you suggest we solve our problem?" "*Assume* a can opener," she replies smugly.

To many people, the economist's prescription that we "get the prices right" is "assuming a can opener." *How* do we get the prices right? To do so would require that we learn how much each affected person would be willing to pay in order to avoid the externalities others impose on him. Identifying all affected individuals might be a daunting problem even if we could elicit accurate responses from them. In fact, though, it can also be very difficult determining what damages are.

One reason for this difficulty is that economists cannot, in general, do controlled experiments on the problems we really care about. Our options are usually either to interpret real-world data or attempt to conduct experiments in laboratory or survey settings. Inferences derived from the former are often confounded by the innumerable things we can neither control nor measure. Laboratory experiments and surveys may not be reliable because it is so difficult to get subjects to behave the same way in a controlled or hypothetical situation as they would in the "real world."

There is a controversy in economics about whether we should be asking how much a person would be willing to pay to avoid, as opposed to how much he would be willing to accept to endure, environmental externalities; the answers need not always be the same. A discussion of this would be a diversion from the main thrust of this paper; interested readers are referred to Hanneman (1991). Note also that willingness to pay vs.

willingness to accept boils down to questions of the assignation of property rights and the distribution of wealth, which I discuss below.

Existing empirical work on the valuation of environmental amenities
generally falls into one of three categories. One is called "hedonic pricing."
In hedonic pricing, we impute some of the components of the value of one
good to the presence of other goods. The amount one pays for a house, for
example, is related not only to the number of bedrooms and the water-
rightness of the roof, but also to the quality of the air one would be obliged
to breathe while living on the property and the natural beauty one could
enjoy from the front porch.

Closely related is the "travel cost method." The value you place on natural beauty, for example, ought to be reflected in the amount of time and
money you would forfeit to appreciate that beauty. By measuring peoples'
expenditures of time and money in visiting natural ecosystems, we can arrive at some estimate of how they value them. Good reviews of travel cost
and hedonic pricing methods can be found in Freeman (1993).

The third empirical technique often used in the economic valuation
of ecological attributes is direct surveys, or the contingent valuation
method (CVM; a good self-contained introduction is Mitchell and Carson
([1991]). While this method could be employed for valuing any good or
service—we can always simply ask what one would be willing to pay for
something—it is unnecessary for those goods for which we see what people *do* pay.

CVM is the only approach, however, with which we can estimate "existence values"—the moral satisfaction we obtain simply from knowing that
something exists, completely independently of whether we might ever use
or even see it (see Freeman 1993:154). CVM is highly controversial (see,
e.g., Portney 1994, Hanemann 1994, and Diamond and Hausman 1994).

Perhaps the only general conclusions one can draw about the state of
empirical economics is that, first, economists *are* able to explain some very
broad-brush phenomena (e.g., when prices go up, people buy less), but that
we are much less capable of making fine distinctions. The second conclusion is simply that a great deal more work must be done to improve data
and empirical techniques.

There is, at least in theory, a way of obviating the whole issue of empirically valuing externalities, however. Externalities exist because there is
someone to whom the effects of actions are "external." That is, someone is
receiving benefits for which he does not pay, or bearing costs for which he
is not compensated. In economic theory, a "property right" is defined as a
right to negotiate compensation for any cost one suffers or benefit one provides. One way to "get the prices right" would be to assign property rights
to every conceivable asset. For example, if you owned the right to a beautiful view, you could set a price for anyone who wanted to diminish that
view by cutting trees or putting smoke in the air.

Some such de facto property rights now exist. You can, for example,
sue someone whose pollution diminishes your property values; her actions
have compromised your right to enjoy your property. Some organizations

are establishing property rights related to wild species. The CAMPFIRE program in Zimbabwe, for example, grants local communities rights to exploitation of wildlife (Lindberg and Enriquez 1994): the Defenders of Wildlife's "Wolf Reward Program" in the United States pays a landowner who can show that wolves have reproduced on her land (Defenders of Wildlife 1995).

In theory, complete assignation of property rights would solve all the problems arising from externalities. It can be difficult to assign all property rights, however. One problem is that more than one property right may reside in the same physical asset. For example, one person may have the right to use a particular piece of land for residence or recreation, but someone else may wish to purchase an easement to prevent the land from being converted to agricultural or industrial use. In such a case the owner of the easement may need to monitor the landowner to be sure he doesn't use the land for an unauthorized purpose. Another problem is that there are costs, as well as benefits, to the establishment of property rights. While property rights may relieve government of the responsibility of "getting the prices right" (individuals or businesses would set prices and make deals, just as with any other type of private transaction), government would still be required to provide security and adjudicate disputes. The economic theory of property rights (Demsetz 1967, Barzel 1989) holds that property rights come to be established when the benefits of their definition exceed the costs of their enforcement. If this view is correct, some valuation exercise may still be required to determine how much we as a society ought to spend to establish and enforce property rights.

Returning to the opening paragraph of this section, you may still be left with the impression that economists can tell you how to "get the prices right" in theory, but have little notion of how to accomplish this in practice. I must admit that we are not as far along on this as we would like to be. This is an area in which continuing cooperation between economists and ecologists may prove very fruitful.

Conclusions

I have described above how economists argue that society should make decisions concerning the allocation and preservation of resources. It will probably not surprise you—it may well relieve you—that these prescriptions are often not implemented. I must confess that, since my expertise is in economics, I cannot provide a very sophisticated analysis of the political, sociological, and psychological factors that determine how government decisions are made. Let me suggest two factors implicit in what I have said above, however, that may help explain why economists sometimes do not have much influence over the economy (by which I mean to include also the economic factors influencing the biological world).

The first I have hinted at in the preceding section. Especially with respect to ecological issues, we economists are not yet in a position to offer very precise policy advice. We simply cannot measure many things. So, while we can provide a framework for analyzing difficult public choices, to wait for definitive pronouncements from us might result only in "paralysis by analysis." Many economists, recognizing these difficulties, advocate simpler decision rules. Rather than conducting benefit–cost analyses that would likely be deeply flawed anyway, they suggest that we adopt "safe minimum standards" for ecosystem health and integrity (see, e.g., Toman 1996). These standards would be treated as constraints on economic activity, rather than as simply another benefit to be weighed off against others.

The second reason for which economic prescriptions are not always heeded in making decisions concerning how much of the natural world to preserve is that, as I said above, ecological and environmental amenities give rise to a number of "market failures." The costs of preserving these resources are frequently not borne by the same people who receive the benefit. Legal or political action is generally required in order to compel one group to respect another's interests. The assembly of interest groups to achieve these goals can be very difficult. While economists have studied these matters, there is much less consensus in the analysis of complex strategic interactions than there is concerning the analysis of more basic economic models.

I have tried to be fairly neutral in giving this very, very brief overview of how economists go about valuing ecological goods and services. Let me, in concluding, venture some admittedly personal opinions. To reiterate what I said above: economists cannot make any very precise statements about the values of most ecological goods and services. We will get better as we learn more from ecologists; some very good economists are doing such learning now. It will be a long time, however, before we can make as strong statements about the value of ecological goods and services as we can about, say, the value of a potato or a haircut. Things are a lot easier when prices can be observed.

Having said that, though, I'd have to classify myself as an environmental optimist. To repeat something else I said above, the study of economics leads many people—myself included—to believe that substitution possibilities are broader than they may first appear. This has two implications. The first is that the consequences of continued environmental degradation may not be as drastic as some predict. Admittedly, these consequences are at present poorly understood, and we may be taking a huge risk in allowing environmental degradation to continue. Happily, the second implication of broad substitution possibilities is that the costs of preventing degradation are also often much lower than some who have borne them initially predicted. Just as there are often substitutes for goods or services produced by particular ecosystems, there are also often substitutes for the industrial processes, chemical pollutants, agricultural practices, etc., that lead to their degradation.

I fear that economists are too often seen by others as defenders of the status quo and supporters of industrial interests. Because we talk about comparing costs and benefits, and because only some subset of costs and benefits can be easily quantified, it is too often assumed that we simply ignore other considerations. I hope I have made the case that this is not true. In particular, economists generally believe that what is sauce for the goose is sauce for the gander: the same principles by which realistic values of environmental protection are estimated ought also serve to generate realistic estimates of the costs of environmental production.

REFERENCES

Barzel, Y. 1989. The economic analysis of property rights. Cambridge University Press, Cambridge, UK.

Coase, R. 1960. The problem of social cost. Journal of Law and Economics 3(October):1–44.

Daly, H. E., and J. B. Cobb, Jr. 1989. For the common good: redirecting the economy toward community, the environment, and a sustainable future. Beacon, Boston, Massachusetts, USA.

Defenders of Wildlife, 1995. Defenders of Wildlife's wolf reward program: using economic incentives to encourage recovery Defenders of Wildlife, Washington, D.C., USA.

Demsetz, H. 1967. Toward a Theory of Property Rights. American Economic Review Papers and Proceedings. 57(2):347–373.

Diamond, P. A., and J. A. Hausman 1994. Contingent valuation: Is some number better than no number. Journal of Economic Perspectives 8:45–64.

Freeman, A. M., III. 1993. The measurement of environmental and resource values: theory and methods. Resources for the Future, Washington, D.C., USA.

Hanemann, W. M. 1991. Willingness to pay and willingness to accept: How much can they differ?" American Economic Review 81(3):635–647.

———. 1994. Valuing the environment through contingent valuation. Journal of Economic Perspectives 8:19–43.

Lindberg, K., and J. Enriquez. 1994. An analysis of ecotourism's economic contribution to conservation and development in Belize. Volume 1. Summary Report. World Wildlife Fund, Washington, D.C., USA.

Mendelsohn, R., W. D. Nordhaus, and D. Shaw. 1994. The impact of global warming on agriculture: a Ricardian analysis. American Economic Review 84:753–771.

Mitchell, R. C., and R. T. Carson. 1991. Using surveys to value public goods: the contingent valuation method. Resources for the Future, Washington, D.C., USA.

Nelson, R., and S. Winter. 1982. An evolutionary theory of economic change. Belknap, Cambridge, Massachusetts, USA.

Portney, P. R. 1994. The contingent valuation debate: why economists should care. Journal of Economic Perspectives 8:3–17.

Simpson, R. D., R. A. Sedjo, and J. W. Reid, 1996. Valuing biodiversity for use in pharmaceutical research. Journal of Political Economy 104:163–185.

Solow, R. M. 1974. Intergenerational equity and exhaustible resources. Review of Economic Studies, Symposium 1974: 29–46.

Toman, M. A. 1996. Ecosystem valuation: an overview of issues and uncertainties. Pages 25–44 in R. David Simpson and Norman L. Christensen, Jr., editors. Ecosystem function and human activities: reconciling economics and ecology. Chapman & Hall, New York, New York, USA.

26 _Conflicts and Choices in Biodiversity Preservation*_

Andrew Metrick

Martin L. Weitzman

Andrew Metrick is Associate Professor of Economics at Harvard University; and Martin L. Weitzman is Ernest E. Monrad Professor of Economics at Harvard University.

Decisions about endangered species reflect the values, perceptions, uncertainties, and contradictions of the society that makes them. The defining limitation of the economics of biodiversity preservation is the lack of a common denominator or natural anchor. As a society, we have not even come close to defining what is the objective. What _is_ biodiversity? In what units is it to be measured? By contrast, even such a morally loaded field as health economics has at least adopted, in practice, a common denominator of human lives saved as a natural anchor. Until we as a society—in the United States narrowly, and more broadly on the planet Earth—decide what is our objective, all the scientific data imaginable will not help economists to guide policy. At the end of the day, all the brave talk about "win-win" situations, which simultaneously produce sustainable development and conserve biodiversity, will not help us to sort out how many children's hospitals should be sacrificed in the name of preserving natural habitats. The core of the problem is conceptual. We have to make up our minds here what it is we are optimizing. This is the essential problem confounding the preservation of biodiversity today.

We start the paper by showing, in a simple constrained optimization problem, exactly where biodiversity appears in a plausible objective function. Then we indicate for this version the basic properties of a solution. The relevant solution concept is cast in the form of a cost-benefit ranking criterion. We then use this ranking criterion, and this theory, as a vehicle for introducing a normative discussion about the economics of biodiversity preservation. Next, we turn to a positive "revealed preference" analysis of the economics of biodiversity preservation, as acted out in U.S. fed-

---

"Conflicts and Choices in Biodiversity Preservation," by Andrew Metrick and Martin L. Weitzman from _Journal of Economic Perspectives_, 12(3):21–34 (Summer 1998).

*We thank Judson Jaffe for research assistance, and Brad De Long, J.R. DeShazo, Alan Krueger, Rob Stavins, and seminar participants at Stanford for helpful comments. We are especially grateful to Timothy Taylor, whose help in rewriting this final version went far beyond the usual editorial obligations. We also acknowledge support under National Science Foundation grant SBR-9422772.

eral and state government decisions about the preservation of species under the Endangered Species Act. We conclude with a discussion of how economic analysis can help to uncover difficulties in the objectives and in the decision-making process about biodiversity.

The Economics of Diversity Preservation

The analytics of the preservation of biodiversity is plagued by the absence of a workable cost-effectiveness framework, within which, at least in principle, basic questions can be posed and answered. Current approaches to endangered species protection seem almost completely lacking in theoretical underpinnings that might reasonably guide policy. This section introduces a simple analytical framework that we believe represents a useful way of thinking about the economics of diversity. Rather than presenting a broad survey of the literature, we here attempt to home in on what we consider to be the characteristic features of the underlying problem—in the form of a specific model which will lead us to what we call the Noah's Ark Problem.[1] The main underlying issue is how to determine basic priorities for maintaining or increasing diversity. Seen this way, the central task is to develop a cost-effectiveness formula or criterion that can be used to rank priorities among biodiversity-preserving projects under a limited budget constraint.

In talking about biodiversity preservation, there is always a question about what is the appropriate level of discourse. In principle, the basic unit could be at the level of the molecule, cell, organ, individual, species, habitat, ecosystem, or other levels as well. For the purposes of this paper, we take the underlying unit of analysis to be the species, although we believe that the same basic issues and themes of the paper will arise at any level.

Our key point of departure involves conceptualizing the underlying conservation unit—the species—as if it were a library. A library, of course, is full of books, and the books can be thought of as roughly analogous to the genes (or other key characteristics) of the species itself. Naturally, the book collections in various libraries may overlap to some degree. In turn, a book/gene can be thought of as a container of information. To continue the metaphor, a library is at some risk of burning down, with possible loss of the building and the book collection that it houses. Various preventive measures can be undertaken that lower the probability of a fire, such as investing in fire extinguishers—at a cost. Concentrating on the question of how best to allocate scarce fire prevention resources among the various species/libraries allows for a crisp formulation of the generic problem of optimally conserving diversity under a budget constraint.

---

[1]This approach is developed rigorously in Weitzman (1998). There are other approaches in the literature. Solow, Polasky, and Broadus (1993) were the first to present the problem of what to protect as an economic issue. See also Weitzman (1992,1993), Polasky and Solow (1993), and Crozier (1992).

The critical part of the preservation problem is specifying the exact form of the objective function. Recognizing that no single form will satisfy everybody, there are, nevertheless, two broad classes of benefits that belong in the objective function: direct utility from each library, and indirect utility coming from the overall "diversity" of library books. We can define the diversity more explicitly to be the number of different books, or the set consisting of the union of all books, in all the existing libraries. These two categories of benefits are sufficiently universal that virtually all justifications for preservation can be fit within them. Thus, in our setup, the value of a library consists of two components: the building itself and the collection of books that it houses. Each library is housed in a building that has some inherent value as a structure; in the species interpretation, this represents the direct utility of how much we like or value the existence of that species per se. Such valuations can come from many different sources, including commercial values, aesthetic values, and even moral or religious values.

Turning now to the book collections within each library, we would like to express their value in comparable units. But why do we care about the diversity of libraries or books in the first place? Two basic answers are possible. We might like many different books per se, just as we might like many different colors simply because of the more colorful world their sheer variety creates. This would be a kind of aesthetic value of diversity. Or we might want to have different books for the utilitarian reason that they are a potential source of future ideas about new medicines, foods, or whatever. This might be called the information content of a book collection. However, at a sufficiently high level of abstraction, these two answers blur into each other, and become essentially the same. In both cases, the reduced form is that we care about having a large number of different books, or separate prices of information.

The Noah's Ark Problem is intended to be an allegory or parable that renders a vivid image of the core problem of preserving the maximum degree of diversity (plus direct utility) under a budget constraint. The parable goes as follows. Noah knows that a flood is coming. An Ark is available to help save some species/libraries. In a world of unlimited resources, the entire set of species might be saved. Unfortunately, Noah's Ark has a limited capacity; in the Bible, the capacity is given as $300 \times 50 \times 30 = 450,000$ cubed-cubits. Noah must choose which species/libraries are to be afforded more protection—and which less—when there are not enough resources around to protect everything fully. Boarding the Ark is a metaphor for investing in a conservation project, like habitat protection, that improves the survivability of a particular species/library. One especially grim version of the Noah's Ark Problem would make the choice a matter of life or death, meaning that all species/libraries that Noah does not take abroad are doomed. We might call this the Old Testament specification. But it is also possible to conceive of a gentler scenario, in which Noah's decision to take a species/library on board raises somewhat its probability of survival—but the species/library has some lesser (but still positive) chance of surviving the flood regardless.

Let us suppose further that although Noah wishes to solve this problem, he does not want to mess around with an overly elaborate and complicated algorithm. Noah is a practical outdoors man. He needs robustness and rugged performance in the field. As he stands at the door of the ark, Noah wants to use a simple priority ranking list from which he can check off one species at a time for boarding. Noah wishes to have a robust rule in the form of a basic ordinal ranking system so that he can board first species #1, then species #2, then species #3, and so forth, until he runs out of space on the ark, whereupon he battens down the hatches and casts off.

Can we help Noah? Is the concept of such a ranking system sensible? Can there exist such a simple boarding rule, which correctly prioritizes each species? If so, what sort of formula should determine Noah's ranking list for achieving an optimal ark-full of species/libraries? The answer to these questions is essentially positive. Our approach here generates a methodology that has the feel of traditional cost-effectiveness approach and can deal with the conservation of diversity. Here, we will focus on a more intuitive form of the criteria, which is at least useful in suggesting the four fundamental ingredients on which Noah should focus when determining conservation priorities.

Noah will begin with the two broad classes of benefits already defined: direct utility from each species/library, and indirect utility coming from the overall diversity of genes/books. The utility of each species/library will be measured as a combination of commercial, recreational and, yes, emotional reactions to a given species. This will pose difficulties in practice, of course, but conceptually it is reasonably straightforward.

However, thinking about the concept of diversity and how to measure it is much less conceptually straightforward. This component of the objective function represents the non-standard part of the optimization problem. (Otherwise, the Noah's Ark Problem is just a straightforward capital-budgeting problem—just rank and board each species by its expected increase in direct utility per unit of space on the Ark.) In fact, the reader might be forgiven for thinking that the notion of the diversity contributed by a species is sufficiently unorthodox that it is difficult to say anything both general and interesting about the solution to the problem. Fortunately, it turns out that by imposing some further structure on the problem, a quite striking characterization is possible.

We now suppose that the book collections are as if they were acquired by an evolutionary branching process with a corresponding evolutionary tree structure. This critical assumption permits a crisp solution—and besides, it seems warranted in the present context. The particular branching process described here is called the *evolutionary library model*, and it is patterned on the classic paradigm of descent with modification that underlies biological species evolution. The evolutionary library model explains the existence of the current library assemblage as a result of three types of evolutionary-historical events.

1. Each existing library acquires new books at any time by independent sampling, at its own rate, out of an infinitely large pool of different books. The independent acquisition of different new books by each library corresponds to the evolution of genetic traits when species are reproductively isolated, with no gene pool mixing by lateral transfer.

2. New libraries can be created by a speciation event. A new branch library can be founded by adopting a complete copy of the current collection of an existing library, as if all of the existing library's books were cloned or photocopied. Henceforth, however, this new library will become reproductively isolated and acquire its new books independently, as described a moment ago.

3. Libraries can go extinct. When a library is extinguished, its entire collection of books is lost. thus, libraries that have already gone extinct in the past do not show up in the set of currently existing libraries.

The evolutionary library model naturally generates a corresponding evolutionary tree. When a tree structure is present, it seems to induce a way of visualizing and comprehending intuitively relationships among objects that are quite subtle or complicated to describe without the tree. "Tree thinking" represents a prime example of how one picture may be worth a thousand words.

Now let us return to the question of how much a given species/library contributes to distinctiveness or diversity. It is natural to identify the distinctiveness of a library/species with its distance from its nearest neighbor or closest relative—which here means the number of books independently acquired since being split off from its most recent common-ancestor library. In the tree corresponding to an evolutionary branching model, the distinctiveness of a library is represented geometrically by its branch length off the rest of the evolutionary tree. When a species/library goes extinct, the loss of diversity is the length of its branch, which is being snapped off from the rest of the tree. Although this image obviously does not resolve all questions about how to measure diversity in practice, it does open up a way of considering how to do so.

Noah will thus begin by viewing the overall value of a species/library as a sum of two components: 1) the direct utility of the species/library; and 2) the diversity added by the genes/books of this particular species/library. However, there are yet two more considerations that must enter the picture. Any reasonable benefit calculation must weigh the enhanced survivability of the species from being boarded. This gain will be measured by estimating the difference in probability of survival if taken aboard the Ark minus probability of survival if *not* taken aboard. Noah should then calculate the expected gain of taking the species/library aboard the Ark by multiplying the change in survival probability times the sum of direct utility plus diversity value. Finally, Noah must weigh the expected gains against the costs. For the biblical Ark, costs are measured in units of cubed-cubits. In the world today, the relevant concept is the opportunity cost of the project extending an enhanced measure of protection to a particular species/library. If the expected gains are divided by the costs, then Noah will have expected gains per dollar expended.

Now we have at hand the outline of an answer to the Noah's Ark Problem.[2] Noah should take species/libraries on board the Ark in the order of their gains in utility plus diversity, weighted by the increase in their probability of survival, per dollar of cost.[3] A small amount of notation can help make this point concisely. Let the index i stand for a species/library. Consider the following four concepts:

D_i = *distinctiveness* of i = how unique or different is i

U_i = direct *utility* of i = how much we like or value i *per se*

ΔP_i = by how much can the *survivability* of i actually be improved

C_i = how much does it *cost* to improve the survivability of i by ΔP_i

Then we have the following mathematical result. Provided ΔP_i is "relatively small" (for all i) in the usual sense of the prototypical small project justifying cost-benefit investment methodology locally, then a priority ranking based on the criterion:

$$R_i = [D_i + U_i]\left(\frac{\Delta P_i}{C_i}\right)$$

is justified in the sense of giving an arbitrarily close first-order approximation to an optimal policy.[4]

Of course, it will not be easy in practice to quantify the four variables: utility of a species, distinctiveness of a species from other species, increased probability of survival, and cost of increasing the survivability of the species. Nor will it be easy to combine these variables routinely into a simple ranking formula. The real world is more than a match for any model. Instead, the worth of this kind of result is to suggest a framework and to organize a way of conceptualizing biodiversity preservation—a way which begins with this special, but not unreasonable, case, and leads to intuitively plausible results. Perhaps one could come away with a sense that when mak-

---

[2]For an explicit and rigorous derivation of the main result within the optimization framework presented here, along with a detailed discussion of related issues, see Weitzman (1998).

[3]The argument here does assume that the cost of saving a species is "relatively small," so that many species can be saved. As a result, when one gets down to the choice of the last species to board the Ark, it may be that there isn't enough room (or money left) for the next species in line according to its ranking, and so one has to skip down the line a little to find a species where there is enough room (or money left) to accommodate it. However, if the costs of saving a species are "relatively small," then a priority ranking based on the criterion here will be justified in the sense of giving an arbitrarily close first-order approximation to an optimal policy.

[4]We again refer the reader to Weitzman (1998) for a formal derivation of the result.

ing conservation decisions in the name of preserving diversity, it might
seem like a good idea at least to consider these four factors—especially in
a policy world so otherwise lacking clear guidelines for endangered species
protection.

The Endangered Species Act: What Are We Preserving?

We have argued in the previous section that four factors—*utility* of a species;
distinctiveness of a species from other species; increase in *survivability* of
a species following a conservation plan; *cost* of enhancing survivability—
should all play a role in biodiversity preservation. Together, these four factors are used to compute Noah's ranking. But which of the factors actually
matter in practice? On what species do we in the United States actually
spend our scarce time, energy and money? In this section, we attempt to
address such questions by looking at quantifiable actions taken in association with the Endangered Species Act.

Our strategy here will be to look at a number of actual empirical bureaucratic variables that have been gathered and catalogued as a result of
the Endangered Species Act and its amendments. These variables can be
used as proxies for the four theoretical variables that should be important
in the analysis. In the discussion to follow, we explore some of the key
places where the process of the Endangered Species Act gives rise to data
that can help to answer the questions posed above. With these data in hand,
we will then use several proxies for Noah's ranking as the dependent variable regressed on proxy variables for utility of a species, diversity of a
species, increased probability of survival, and cost of this increased survival probability as our explanatory variables.[5] This regression framework
will allow us to identify what factors really seem to matter for the decisions made about preservation of endangered species.[6]

The journey of a species towards protected status begins when some
individual or organization, public or private, suggests formally to the Fish
and Wildlife Service, a division of the Department of Interior, that a species
should be listed under the Endangered Species Act. To be more specific,
several different taxonomic units are eligible for protection under the act,
including species, subspecies, and (for vertebrates) "populations." For the
sake of simplicity, however, we will typically refer to all of the above as
"species," except in the discussion of proxy variables for diversity, when
the distinction between species and subspecies will make a conceptual dif-

---

[5]All of the variables used in this paper can be found in the DEMES database, which is described
and documented in Cash et al. (1997). Readers desiring further information on the variables used in
these analyses should contact the authors to obtain the reference.

[6]Similar empirical studies of the Endangered Species Act can be found in Mann and Plummer
(1993), Tear et al. (1993), Metrick and Weitzman (1996) and Cash (1997).

ference. Once a species has been nominated, the Fish and Wildlife Service then calls on scientific sources, both internal and external to the organization, to determine whether the species is a viable candidate for protection. If the scientific data support listing, then the species may be officially proposed to be listed.

After a species is proposed, there is a 60-day period for public comments, during which any interested parties can go on the record with their opinions about the proposed listing. Virtually all species that reach this stage are eventually listed. Listed species enjoy special protections from harm, and must have official recovery plans created by the Fish and Wildlife Service. Listed species are also eligible for public spending on their recovery. In a 1989 amendment to the Endangered Species Act, Congress required the Fish and Wildlife Service to collect annual spending information from all federal and state authorities and to impute such spending as if on a species-by-species basis. Several steps in this process offer the opportunity to obtain quantitative proxies for Noah's ranking.

A first proxy variable for Noah's rankings is the log of the number of favorable public comments made during the proposal stage. These comments are collected by the Fish and Wildlife Service. Afterwards, summary statistics—that is, number favorable, number unfavorable, number neutral, and total number—are published in the Federal Register. The list of taxa that have received the highest number of favorable public comments reads like a *Who's Who* of the political-environmental landscape, with the northern spotted owl handily topping the list. Naturally, such controversial projects achieve a large number of favorable and unfavorable comments, so focusing only on the favorable side may miss part of the story. However, in a spirit of simplicity, we take these favorable comments as a ranking proxy and do not attempt to explain the complex relationship between the different types of comments.

A second proxy variable for Noah's ranking is the listing decision itself. In our regressions, this will be a dummy variable, taking a value of 1 if a species is listed, and 0 otherwise. Although this variable is not a continuous one, in the way we would expect Noah's rankings to be, it does make sense as an on/off variable for whether a species has been boarded onto the Ark. Since the Ark-boarding policy does use a simple cutoff in which species are either on or off the boat according to Noah's ranking, the use of the on/off decision is a natural proxy. (It also fits in well with similar studies looking for latent rankings, like the decision to buy a car or enter the work force.)

Finally, as a third proxy for Noah's ranking, we use the amount of public money spent from 1989 to 1993 on the recovery of the species. The total amount spent each year has been steadily increasing, and the five-year overall total is $914 million. Four species have each had over $50 million spent on them over this period—chinook salmon, red-cockaded woodpecker, northern spotted owl, and bald eagle—and these four together make up about one-third of the total spending. Most species have had at least some funds spent on them; of the 229 vertebrate species listed as of 1989, all but five have at least $100 of reported spending.[7] Only the costs that can be attributed to individual species are included in our totals.

We use these three different proxies for Noah's ranking because, while each seems reasonable, none seems perfect. If forced to choose a single proxy, we believe that spending is the most appropriate measure of the three because it strikes us as the most direct and least noisy measure of preservation attention.

We next try to identify proxies for our four key decision variables. We first look for proxies for the utility term. It is obviously not possible to quantify every way that humans derive utility from other species. In seeking proxy variables for utility, we choose to focus on the elements that are associated with the class of "charismatic megafauna," a term applied to describe large, popular animals. To get at this effect, we include dummy variables for each taxonomic class within the vertebrates: MAMMAL, BIRD, REPTILE, AMPHIBIAN, and FISH. For the "megafauna" portion, we use the log of the length of a representative individual of the species.

Our next right-hand-side variable is diversity. The contribution of a species to diversity can be quantified, as in the tree diagram of the evolutionary library model, by its genetic distance from other species. This measure can be roughly approximated by its taxonomic uniqueness. We use two dummy variables to capture this idea of distinctiveness. One variable, labeled UNIQUE, takes on a value of 1 if the species is the sole representative of its genus, where a genus is the taxonomic unit immediately above species, and 0 otherwise. A second dummy variable, labeled SUBSPECIES, takes on a value of 1 if a "species" is in fact from the lower taxonomic classification of subspecies or population, and 0 otherwise.

Next, as a proxy measure of a species' survivability or marginal recoverability, we use absolute endangerment. The variable we use comes from the Nature Conservancy, which ranks a comprehensive list of all U.S. vertebrate species (but not subspecies or populations) into a scale from 1 to 5, with 1 being the most endangered and 5 being the least endangered.[8] As long as the most endangered species are also those that would benefit most from small recovery projects—which is all that marginal endangerment means—then this will be a reasonable proxy. One could argue that early intervention is more cost effective, but that is not really the issue here. It is certainly true that there are several examples of species near extinction being saved. These are the cases where, by definition, the gain in survivability has been the highest. These may have been costly projects, but cost is a separate element of the decision.

---

[7]We add $100 to each species reported spending so that we can take the log of the total; this $100 can be thought of as each species' share of a small portion of the program's overhead.

[8]We again refer the reader to Cash et al. (1997) for a complete description of these variables and their sources. The ENDANGERMENT variable used in this paper is of a 1993 vintage, which is slightly different than the most recent measures. We use the 1993 variable because we want to come as close as possible to capturing the endangerment level at the time that the relevant cost decisions were made.

The Fish and Wildlife Service has itself recognized the importance of several of these factors, and they have established a formal priority system to rank species for recovery projects. Their priority system takes into account four factors; in decreasing order of importance they are: "degree of threat," "recovery potential," "taxonomy," and "conflict with development." The first three factors are combined by the Fish and Wildlife Service to form a ranking from 1 to 18 (lower numbers imply higher priority). The fourth factor, which indicates whether or not the recovery of a species conflicts with other public or private development plans, is meant to serve as a tiebreaker among species having the same priority ranking—with those species in conflict with development receiving the advantage. This "conflict" variable can be thought of as a proxy for cost—in this case, an opportunity cost. This proxy gives us at least one representative for each of the four variables in the conceptual solution to the Noah's Ark Problem. In our final test, we include both the priority ranking and the conflict tiebreaker as additional explanatory variables. The formal Fish and Wildlife Service priority system implies that conflict should have a positive effect on spending—a cost-benefit calculation would suggest otherwise.

The results of several regressions using these variables are summarized in Table 1. In all cases, comprehensive data collection is made possible only by restricting the sample to vertebrates; plants and non-vertebrate animals are excluded because of data limitations. We acknowledge that there are many econometric difficulties here: variables are measured at different times, many important considerations are omitted due to data constraints, our proxies are imperfect. For these reasons, we adopt a reduced-form approach and do not claim any structural interpretations. Rather, we hope that readers agree with us that the patterns of behavior are striking enough to yield insights despite the obvious difficulties.

In the regression in the first column, the dependent variable LNCOMMENTS is the log of the number of positive comments received after the species has been proposed. The sample includes all 142 vertebrate full species, subspecies, and populations that have been listed since 1975, when the data first become available. Using the taxonomic class dummies (MAMMAL, BIRD, REPTILE, and AMPHIBIAN—all interpreted relative to FISH, the left-out variable), along with SIZE, ENDANGERMENT, and UNIQUE as explanatory variables, we find only ENDANGERMENT to be significant at the 5 percent level. Note, however, that the coefficient on ENDANGERMENT would appear to be of the wrong sign; the more highly endangered a species is, the fewer favorable comments that it receives. (Recall that the most endangered species receive ENDANGERMENT ratings of 1, and the least endangered species receive ratings of 5.) One interpretation of this coefficient is that species which are not truly endangered must be very "charismatic" to have survived so far in the process, and this same charisma is driving the number of favorable comments. This explanation—that certain key variables proxying for charisma are likely to have been omitted—is a common theme in interpreting the results of these regressions.

Table 1 Regression Results

Regression # Dependent Variable	1 LNCOMMENTS	2 LISTED	3 LNSPEND	4 LNSPEND
MAMMAL	−0.11	0.87*	0.73	0.42
BIRD	0.63	1.21**	0.39	0.59
REPTILE	−0.55	0.82	−1.79**	−1.71**
AMPHIBIAN	0.48	−1.51**	−0.71	−0.78
ENDANGERMENT	0.31*	−1.43**	0.62**	0.85**
SIZE	0.03	0.29*	0.86**	0.66**
UNIQUE	0.33	0.85**	0.06	—
SUBSPECIES	—	—	−0.52	—
PRIORITY	—	—	—	−0.10*
CONFLICT	—	—	—	1.19**
CONSTANT	1.24**	0.97*	9.17**	9.39**
Method of Estimation	OLS	Logit	OLS	OLS
Number of Obs.	142	509	229	229
R^2	.07	.25	.31	.41

Notes: Dependent variables and samples for each regression are (1) LNCOMMENTS: the log of total favorable comments received during the public comments period, as published in the Federal register, the sample includes the 142 vertebrate species listed after 1975; (2) LISTED: 1 if a species is listed (as of 1997) under the ESA and 0 otherwise; the sample includes all vertebrate full species that were ranked G1, G2 or G3 by the Nature Conservancy as of 1993; (3) and (4) LNSPEND: the log of total government spending from 1989 to 1993. The sample includes all taxonomic units (species, subspecies, and populations) that were listed as of 1989. Independent variables: MAMMAL, BIRD, REPTILE, and AMPHIBIAN are dummy variables which equal 1 when the species is a member of that taxonomic class and 0 otherwise. (Coefficients can be interpreted relative to FISH, the excluded dummy variable.) ENDANGERMENT is the Nature Conservancy's Global Endangerment Rank as of 1993. SIZE is the log of the physical length for a typical individual of the species. UNIQUE is a dummy variable equal to 1 if the species is the only species in its genus. SUBSPECIES is a dummy variable equal to 1 if the taxonomic unit is below the level of full species. PRIORITY is the FWS 1-18 priority ranking for the species. CONFLICT is the FWS priority tiebreaker indicating whether or not a species is in conflict with development. (*) and (**) indicate that the relevant coefficient is significant at the five percent and one percent levels, respectively. Please see Cash et al. (1997) for a detailed description of the variables used in these estimations.

In the regression of the second column, the dependent variable is LISTED: a dummy equal to 1 if a species has been listed, and 0 otherwise. The sample includes all vertebrate full species with ENDANGERMENT rankings of 1, 2 or 3. We restrict the sample in this way so that it includes virtually all species that may reasonably be considered candidates for listing; rankings of 4 or 5 are essentially never considered in the first place. Subspecies or populations are not included in the sample because there is no comprehensive database of unlisted units below the level of full species. Several of the factors discussed above appear to play some role in the listing decision. Some dummies for taxonomic class are significant (relative to the excluded dummy for FISH): positive for MAMMAL and BIRD, and negative for AMPHIBIAN. Taxonomic uniqueness appears to play a positive role in the likelihood of listing, as does SIZE and ENDANGERMENT. All in all, the decision of what to place on the official endangerment list seems consistent with our conceptual framework.

The regression in the third column uses the log of the sum of public spending from 1989 to 1993, LNSPEND, as the dependent variable. Here, we use the same regressors as before, with the addition of SUBSPECIES, the dummy variable indicating that the taxnomic unit is below the level of a full species. The sample includes all protected taxonomic units (species, subspecies, and populations) that were listed as of the end of 1989, when the spending data was first collected. There are two important results from this regression. First, the coefficient on SIZE is large and significant. Since the SIZE variable is the log of physical length, its coefficient may be interpreted as an elasticity; it implies an 8.6 percent increase in spending for a 10 percent increase in length. Even more striking, however, is the positive and significant coefficient on ENDANGERMENT. As with the counterintuitive results for the regression in the first column, this sign implies that the more highly endangered a species is, the *less* attention it receives. (Again recall that the most endangered species receive ENDANGERMENT ratings of 1, and the least endangered species receive ratings of 5.) We have argued elsewhere that this result suggests either terribly perverse priority setting, or, more likely, an overpowering role for omitted unobservable charisma-like factors negatively correlated with ENDANGERMENT (Metrick and Weitzman, 1996). In either case, it is difficult to reconcile the sign of the ENDANGERMENT coefficient with the belief that more spending should go to the more highly endangered species, other things being equal. Owing to our belief that spending is the best proxy we have for Noah's ranking, we believe that this regression provides the most striking empirical results in the paper.

The regression in the fourth column is similar to the one in the third column, but adds the regressors PRIORITY (the Fish and Wildlife Service priority ranking from 1 to 18) and CONFLICT (a dummy equal to 1 if the species is in conflict with development according to the Fish and Wildlife Service), while dropping UNIQUE and SUBSPECIES since they are part of the PRIORITY calculation. The results show that while the Fish and Wildlife Service is following their system to some degree, the role played by CONFLICT is far larger than might be anticipated. In fact, this ostensibly least important criterion in the system, supposedly just a tiebreaker, dominates the other three. Although the sign of the CONFLICT coefficient is consistent with the intention of the Fish and Wildlife priority system, its magnitude is out of proportion. Furthermore, the sign on this coefficient is not consistent with the cost-benefit formula laid out earlier; apparently, the Fish and Wildlife Service gives priority to species with high opportunity costs. We believe that the setting of CONFLICT may be endogenous, and that the results of this regression suggest a commingling of supposed objective evaluation of endangerment levels with the preference-based spending decision. In turn, this suggests that the country might better be served by separating the intelligence-gathering and policy-making arms of the Fish and Wildlife Service.

What have we learned from these empirical exercises? First, charismatic megafauna effects do seem to matter a lot; in fact, there is strong evidence that people weigh utility the heaviest of the four criteria. Second, survivability, diversity, and costs do not seem to play their "expected" role in spending decisions. Third, the (ostensibly) scientific part of the priority system seems to be influenced by the same subjective factors that influence spending.

Conclusion

The core of the problem of biodiversity preservation today lies in specifying the objective that we are trying to preserve. We cannot evaluate the overall performance of conservation agencies, like the U.S. Fish and Wildlife Service, without specifying much more clearly what is the "output" on which they are to be graded.

At the end of the day, we must make up our minds about what is the objective function before we can properly use scientific information or formulate rational policies for good stewardship. This means confronting honestly the core problem of economic tradeoffs—because good stewardship of natural habitats, like almost everything else we want in this world, is subject to budget constraints. The evidence suggests that our actual behavior may not reflect a reasoned cost-benefit calculation. If this is true, then we should fix it. If it is not, then we should be honest about our desire to have "charismatic megafauna" effects dominate our decisions.

REFERENCES

Cash, David, "Science, Politics, and Environmental Risk: Regulatory Decision-making in the U.S. Endangered Species Act," Manuscript, J.F.K. School of Government, Harvard University, 1997.

Cash, David, J.R. DeShazo, Andrew Metrick, Todd Schatzki, Stuart Shapiro, and Martin Weitzman, "Database on the Economics and Management of Endangered Species (DEMES)," Manuscript, Department of Economics, Harvard University, 1997.

Crozier, Ross H., "Genetic Diversity and the Agony of Choice," *Biological Conservation*, 1992, *61*, 11–15.

Mann, Charles J., and Mark L. Plummer, "Federal Expenditures on Endangered Species Recovery," Unpublished Manuscript, 1993.

Metrick, Andrew, and Martin L. Weitzman, "Patterns of Behavior in Endangered Species Preservation," *Land Economics*, 1996, *72*:1, 1–16.

Polasky, Stephan, and Andrew Solow, "On the Value of a Collection of Species," *Journal of Environmental Economics and Management*, 1995, *29*, 298–303.

Schatzki, Todd, and Stuart Shapiro, "Ruled or Ruling? Agency Discretion in the Endangered Species Act," Manuscript, J.F.K. School of Government, Harvard University, 1997.

Simpson, R. David, Roger Sedjo, and J. Reid, "Valuing Biodiversity for Use in Pharmaceutical Research," *Journal of Political Economy*, 1996, *104*:1, 163–85.

Solow, Andrew, Stephan Polasky, and James Broadus, "Searching for Uncertain Benefits and the Conservation of Biological Diversity," *Environmental and Resource Economics*, April 1993, *3*:2, 171–81.

Tear, Timothy H., J. Michael Scott, Patricia H. Hayward, and Brad Griffith, "Status and Prospects for Success of the Endangered Species Act: A Look at Recovery Plans," *Science*, 1993, 976–77.

Weitzman, Martin L., "On Diversity," *Quarterly Journal of Economics*, May 1992, *107*:2, 363–405.

Weitzman, Martin L., "What to Preserve? An Application of Diversity Theory to Crane Conservation," *Quarterly Journal of Economics*, February 1993, *108*:1, 157–83.

Weitzman, Martin L., "The Noah's Ark Problem," forthcoming in *Econometrica*, 1998.

IX

Political Economy

27 The Choice of Regulatory Instruments in Environmental Policy*

Nathaniel O. Keohane

Richard L. Revesz

Robert N. Stavins

Nathaniel O. Keohane is a Ph.D. student in Political Economy and Government, Harvard University; Richard L. Revesz is Professor of Law, New York University School of Law; Robert N. Stavins is Albert Pratt Professor of Business and Government at John F. Kennedy School of Government, Harvard University, and University Fellow, Resources for the Future.

I. Introduction

The design of environmental policy requires answers to two central questions: (1) what is the desired level of environmental protection?; and (2) what policy instruments should be used to achieve this level of protection? With respect to the second question, thirty years of positive political reality in the United States has diverged strikingly from the recommendations of normative economic theory. The purpose of this Article is to explain why.

Four gaps between normative theory and positive reality merit particular attention. First, so-called "command-and-control" instruments (such as design standards requiring a particular technology's usage, or performance standards prescribing the maximum amount of pollution that a source can emit)[1] are used to a significantly greater degree than "market-based" or "economic-incentive" instruments (principally pollution taxes or

"The Choice of Regulatory Instruments in Environmental Policy," by Nathaniel O. Keohane, Richard L. Revesz, and Robert N. Stevens from *Harvard Environmental Law Review*, 22:313–367 (1998).

*Helpful comments on a previous version of the Article were provided by: David Charny, Cary Coglianese, John Ferejohn, Don Fullerton, Robert Hahn, James Hamilton, Robert Keohane, David King, Lewis Kornhauser, Robert Lowry, Roger Noll, Kenneth Shepsle, and Richard Stewart. Financial support was provided by the Dean's Research Fund, John F. Kennedy School of Government, and the Filomen D'Agostino and Max E. Greenberg Research Fund at the New York University School of Law. The authors alone are responsible for any errors.

[1]Performance standards could specify an absolute quantity of permissible emissions (that is, a given quantity of emissions per unit of time), but more typically these standards establish allowable emissions in proportional terms (that is, quantity of emissions per unit of product output or per unit of a particular input). This Article uses the term "standard" to refer somewhat generically to command-and-control approaches. Except where stated otherwise, the Article refers to proportional performance standards.

charges[2] and systems of tradeable permits[3]), despite economists' consistent
endorsement of the latter.

At least in theory, market-based instruments minimize the aggregate
cost of achieving a given level of environmental protection,[4] and provide
dynamic incentives for the adoption and diffusion of cheaper and better
control technologies.[5] Despite these advantages, market-based instruments
have been used far less frequently than command-and-control standards.[6]
For example, the cores of the Clean Air Act ("CAA")[7] and Clean Water Act
("CWA")[8] consist of federally prescribed emission and effluent standards,
set by reference to the levels that can be achieved through the use of the
"best available technology."[9]

Second, when command-and-control standards have been used, the required level of pollution abatement has generally been far more stringent
for new pollution sources than for existing ones, possibly worsening pollution by encouraging firms to keep older, dirtier plants in operation.[10]

---

[2]The development of the notion of a corrective tax on pollution is generally credited to Pigou.
See generally Arthur Cecil Pigou, *The Economics of Welfare* (1920).

[3]John Dales initially proposed a system of tradeable permits to control pollution. See generally
John H. Dales, *Pollution, Property, & Prices* (1968). David Montgomery then formalized this system.
See generally W. David Montgomery, "Markets in Licenses and Efficient Pollution Control Programs,"
5 *J. Econ. Theory* 395 (1972). However, much of the literature can be traced back to Ronald Coase.
See Ronald H. Coase, "The Problem of Social Cost," 3 *J.L. & Econ.* 1, 39–44 (1960).

[4]As is well known, a necessary condition for the achievement of such cost-minimization is that
the marginal costs of abatement be equal for all sources. See William J. Baumol & Wallace E. Oates,
The Theory of Environmental Policy 177 (1988). In theory, pollution taxes and systems of marketable
permits induce this effect, at least under specified conditions.

[5]Market-based systems can provide continuous dynamic incentives for adoption of superior technologies, since under such systems it is always in the interest of firms to clean up more if sufficiently inexpensive cleanup technologies can be identified. See Scott R. Milliman & Raymond Prince, "Firm Incentives to Promote Technological Change in Pollution Control," 17 *J. Envtl. Econ. & Mgmt.* 247, 257–61 (1989);
Adam B. Jaffe & Robert N. Stavins, "Dynamic Incentives of Environmental Regulation: The Effects of Alternative Policy Instruments and Technology Diffusion," 29 *J. Envtl. Econ. & Mgmt.* S43, S43–S46 (1995).

[6]Office of Tech. Assessment, Tech. Assessment Board of the 103d Congress, *Environmental Policy Tools: A User's Guide* 27–28 (1995).

[7]See 42 U.S.C. § 7411(a),(b) (1994).

[8]See 33 U.S.C. §§ 1311(b), 1316 (1994).

[9]We use this label as a generic one. The various statutory schemes employ somewhat different
formulations. See, e.g., 33 U.S.C. § 1311(b)(1)(A) (1994) ("best practicable control technology"); id. §
1311(b)(2)(A) ("best available technology"); id. § 1316(a)(1) ("best available demonstrated control technology"); 42 U.S.C. § 7411(a)(1) (1994) ("best system of emission reduction"); id. § 7479(3) ("best available control technology").

[10]New plants ought to have somewhat more stringent standards because their abatement costs are
lower, although such standards should be linked with actual abatement costs, not with the proxy of plant
vintage. When new source standards are sufficiently more stringent, however, they can give rise to an
"old-plant" effect, precluding plant replacements that would otherwise take place. See Matthew D. Mc-
Cubbins et al., "Structure and Process, Politics, and Policy: Administrative Arrangements and the Political Control of Agencies," 75 *Va. L. Rev.* 431, 467 (1989); Richard B. Stewart, "Regulation, Innovation,
and Administrative Law: A Conceptual Framework," 69 *Cal. L. Rev.* 1259, 1270–71 (1981). Empirical evidence shows that differential environmental regulations lengthen the time before plants are retired. See
Michael T. Maloney & Gordon L. Brady, "Capital Turnover and Marketable Pollution Rights," 31 *J.L. &
Econ.* 203, 206 (1988); Randy Nelson et al., "Differential Environmental Regulation: Effects on Electric
Utility Capital Turnover and Emissions," 75 *Rev. Econ. & Stat.* 368, 373 (1993).

The federal environmental statutes further these disparities by bifurcating the regulatory requirements that apply to new and existing sources. For example, under the Clean Air Act, emission standards for new sources are set federally, whereas the corresponding standards for existing sources are set by the states.[11] Similarly, the CAA's Prevention of Significant Deterioration ("PSD") program,[12] which applies to areas with air that is cleaner than the National Ambient Air Quality Standards ("NAAQS),[13] imposes additional emission standards only on new sources.[14] The Clean Water Act sets effluent limitations for both new and existing sources, but these limitations are governed by different statutory provisions.[15]

Third, in the relatively rare instances in which they have been adopted, market-based instruments have nearly always taken the form of tradeable permits rather than emission taxes,[16] although economic theory suggests that the optimal choice between tradeable permits and emission taxes is dependent upon case-specific factors.[17] Moreover, the initial allocation of such permits has been through "grandfathering," or free initial distribution based on existing levels of pollution,[18] rather than through auctions, de-

---

[11]Compare 42 U.S.C. § 7411(a), (b) (1994) (defining federal standards for new sources) with id. § 7410(a) (requiring state plans for existing sources).

[12]See 42 U.S.C. §§ 7470–7479 (1994).

[13]See id. § 7471.

[14]See id. § 7475(a).

[15]Compare 33 U.S.C. § 1316 (1994) (prescribing standards for new sources) with id. § 1311(b) (setting standards for existing sources).

[16]Taxes (so-called unit charges) have been used in some communities for municipal solid waste collection. See Office of Tech. Assessment, supra note 6, at 119–21. Gasoline taxes serve primarily as revenue-raising instruments, rather than environmental (Pigouvian) taxes per se. Interestingly, the European experience is the reverse: environmental taxes are far more prevalent than tradeable permits, although the taxes employed have typically been too low to induce much pollution abatement. See Richard B. Stewart, "Economic Incentives for Environmental Protection: Opportunities and Obstacles" 42 (1996) (unpublished manuscript, on file with New York University). A more comprehensive positive analysis of instrument choice than we provide here would seek to explain this difference between the European and U.S. experiences.

[17]With perfect information, tradeable permits sold at auction have the same effect as a tax. Under conditions of uncertainty, the relative efficiency of tradeable permits and fixed tax rates depends upon the relative slopes of the relevant marginal benefit and marginal cost functions. See Martin L. Weitzman, "Prices v. Quantities," 41 *Rev. Econ. Stud.* 477, 485–90 (1974); Gary W. Yohe, "Towards a General Comparison of Price Controls and Quantity Controls Under Uncertainty," 45 *Rev. Econ. Stud.* 229, 238 (1978); Robert N. Stavins, "Correlated Uncertainty and Policy Instrument Choice," 30 *J. Envtl. Econ. & Mgmt.* 218, 219–25 (1996).

In theory, a hybrid system that incorporates aspects and attributes of both a simple linear tax or a simple tradeable permit system will be preferable, under conditions of uncertainty, to either alone. See Marc J. Roberts & Michael Spence, "Effluent Charges and Licenses Under Uncertain," 5 *J. Pub. Econ.* 193, 196–97 (1976); Louis Kaplow & Steven Shavell, "On the Superiority of Corrective Taxes to Quantity Regulation" 12–14 (National Bureau of Econ. Research Working Paper No. 6251, 1997).

[18]Mandated by the Clean Air Act amendments of 1990, the sulfur dioxide ("SO₂") allowance program (a tradeable permit program to reduce acid rain) provides for annual auctions in addition to grandfathering. However, such auctions involve less than three percent of the total allocation. See Elizabeth M. Bailey, "Allowance Trading Activity and State Regulatory Rulings: Evidence from the U.S. Acid Rain Program" 4 (Mass. Inst. of Tech. Working Paper No. MIT-CEEPR 96-002, 1996). These auctions have proven to be a trivial part of the overall program. See Paul L. Joskow et al., "Auction Design and the Market for Sulfur Dioxide Emissions" 27–28 (National Bureau of Econ. Research Working Paper No. 5745, 1996).

spite the apparently superior ~~mechanism of auctions.~~[19] Despite diversity of available market-based instruments (taxes, revenue-neutral taxes, auctioned permits, and grandfathered permits)[20] and the numerous tradeoffs that exist in normative economic terms, the U.S. experience has been dominated by one choice: grandfathered permits.

Notably, the acid rain provision of the Clean Air Act allocates, without charge, marketable permits for sulfur dioxide emissions to current emitters.[21] Similarly, grandfathered marketable permits are created by the offset mechanism of the nonattainment provision of the CAA.[22] This mechanism permits existing sources to reduce their emissions and sell the resulting reduction to new sources attempting to locate in the area.[23]

---

[19]With perfect information and no transactions costs, trading will result in the economically efficient outcome independently of the initial distribution of permits. See W. David Montgomery, "Markets in Licenses and Efficient Pollution Control Programs" 5 *J. Econ. Theory* 395, 409 (1972); Coase, supra note 3, at 15; Robert W. Hahn & Roger G. Noll, "Designing a Market for Tradeable Emission Permits." in *Reform of Environmental Regulation* 120–21 (Wesley Magat ed., 1982). Under more realistic scenarios, however, there are compelling arguments for the superiority of auctioned permits. First, auctions are more cost-effective in the presence of certain kinds of transactions costs. See Robert N. Stavins, "Transaction Costs and Tradeable Permits," 29 *J. Envtl. Econ. & Mgmt.* 133, 146 (1995). Second, the revenue raised by an auction mechanism can be used to finance a reduction in some distortionary tax. See Lawrence H. Goulder et al., "Revenue-Raising vs. Other Approaches to Environmental Protection: The Critical Significance of Pre-Existing Tax Distortions" 1 (National Bureau of Econ. Research Working Paper No. 5641, 1996). Instruments that restrict pollution production (such as tradeable permits) can create entry barriers that raise product prices, reduce the real wage, and exacerbate preexisting labor supply distortions. However, this effect can be offset if the government auctions the permits, retains the scarcity rents, and recycles the revenue by reducing distortionary labor taxes. See Don Fullerton & Gilbert Metcalf, "Environmental Regulation in a Second-Best World" 6, 25 (1996) (unpublished manuscript, on file with authors). Third, auctions provide greater incentives for firms to develop substitutes for regulated products, by requiring firms to pay for permits rather than giving them rents. See Robert W. Hahn & Albert M. McGartland, "The Political Economy of Instrument Choice: An Examination of the U.S. Role in Implementing the Montreal Protocol, " 83 *Nw. U. L. Rev.* 592, 604 (1989). Fourth, the revenue raised by auctions may provide administrative agencies with an incentive to monitor compliance. See Bruce A. Ackerman & Richard B. Stewart, "Reforming Environmental Law," 37 *Stan. L. Rev.* 1333, 1344–46 (1985). Fifth, grandfathering, if accepted as general practice, could lead unregulated firms to increase their emissions in order to maximize the pollution rights that they obtain if there is a transition to a market-based system. See Donald N. Dewees, "Instrument Choice in Environmental Policy," 21 *Econ. Inquiry* 53, 62–63 (1983).

[20]In a straightforward scheme of effluent taxes, a constant tax is levied on each unit of pollution. In a revenue-neutral framework, the tax revenues are then rebated to the payors, by some method other than the amount of their pollution. In marketable permit schemes, the initial allocation can be performed through an auction, or through grandfathering. In a deterministic setting and abstracting from a set of other issues, a revenue-neutral emission tax can be designed which is equivalent to a grandfathered tradeable permit system. Likewise, under such conditions, a simple emission tax will be roughly equivalent to an auctioned permit system.

[21]See 42 U.S.C. § 7651(b) (1994). The amount of the allocation is capped in Phase I, which is currently in effect, at 2.5 pounds of sulfur dioxide per million BTUs of fuel input consumed. In Phase II, which goes into effect in the year 2000, the cap will be 1.2 pounds of sulfur dioxide per million BTUs of fuel input consumed. See Paul L. Joskow & Richard Schmalensee, "The Political Economy of Market-based Environmental Policy: The 1990 U.S. Acid Rain Program," 41 *J.L. & Econ.* (forthcoming April 1998) (manuscript at 94–95, on file with authors).

[22]See 42 U.S.C. § 7503(a)(1)(A) (1994).

[23]See id. at § 7503(c)(1).

Fourth and finally, there has been a conceptual gap between prior and current political practice. In recent years, the political process has been more receptive to market-based instruments,[24] even though they continue to be a small part of the overall portfolio of existing environmental laws and regulations. After being largely ignored for so long, why have incentive-based instruments begun to gain acceptance in recent years?

Commentators have advanced various explanations for the existence of these four gaps between normative theory and positive reality. While some explanations emerge from formal theories, others take the form of informal hypotheses, purporting to explain certain aspects of environmental policy, but not as a part of a formal theory of political behavior. This Article reviews, evaluates, and extends these explanations. Moreover, this Article places these disparate explanations within the framework of an equilibrium model of instrument choice in environmental policy, based upon the metaphor of a political market.

Informed by intellectual traditions within economics, political science, and law, this framework organizes and synthesizes existing theories and empirical evidence about observed departures of normative prescription from political reality. The scope of the Article, however, is limited in a number of respects. The emphasis is on the control of pollution rather than the management of natural resources. The Article treats Congress, rather than administrative agencies, as the locus of instrument choice decisions; it views legislators (rather than regulators) as the "suppliers" of regulation.[25] Moreover, the Article focuses exclusively on the choice among the policy instruments used to achieve a given level of environmental protection, ranging from tradeable permits to taxes to standards. It does not explore the related issues of how the level of protection is chosen or enforced. Nor does it address why Congress chooses to delegate authority to administrative agencies in the first place.[26] Finally, the Article's outlook is positive, not normative: it seeks to understand why the current set of tools exists, rather than which tools are desirable.

---

[24]Beginning in the 1970s, the U.S. Environmental Protection Agency ("EPA") allowed states to implement trading schemes, as alternatives to command-and-control regulation, in their State Implementation Plans under the Clean Air Act. See Robert W. Hahn, "Economic Prescriptions for Environmental Problems: How the Patient Followed the Doctor's Orders," *J. Econ. Persp.*, Spring 1989, at 95, 101. More significantly, tradeable permit systems were used in the 1980s to accomplish the phasedown of lead in gasoline. See Suzi Kerr & David Maré, "Efficient Regulation Through Tradeable Permit Markets: The United States Lead Phasedown" 3–6 (U. Md. C. Park Working Paper No. 96-06, 1997). Moreover, such systems facilitated the phasedown of ozone-depleting chlorofluorocarbons ("CFCs") and are projected to cut nationwide SO_2 emissions by 50% by the year 2005, see Office of Air Radiation, U.S. Environmental Protection Agency, *1995 Compliance Results: Acid Rain Program* 10–11 (1996), as well as achieving ambient ozone reductions in the northeast and implementing stricter local air pollution controls in the Los Angeles metropolitan region.

[25]We do not intend, however, to deny the importance of executive branch departments and administrative agencies, such as the EPA. For example, the intra-firm emission trading programs of the 1970s were largely the direct creation of EPA.

[26]See generally Morris P. Fiorina, "Legislative Choice of Regulatory Forms: Legal Process or Administrative Process?," 39 *Pub. Choice* 33 (1982).

Part II of the Article reviews the relevant intellectual traditions in economics, political science, and law. Part III presents the key features of our equilibrium framework. Part IV considers the demand for environmental policy instruments, while Part V examines the supply side. Finally, Part VI presents some conclusions.

II. Intellectual Traditions

Positive theories of policy instrument choice find their roots in the broader study of government regulation, a vast literature which has been reviewed elsewhere.[27] For the purposes of this Article, the literature can be divided into three approaches for explaining government regulation: demand-driven explanations, supply-driven explanations, and explanations incorporating the interaction between demand and supply.

A. Demand-Side Analyses

Explanations that focus heavily on the demand for regulation are grounded largely in economics. Not surprisingly, economists have generally concentrated on the demand for economic (rather than social) regulation, devoting most attention to the interests of affected firms. The "economic theory of regulation," initiated by George Stigler[28] and developed further by Richard Posner,[29] Sam Peltzman,[30] and Gary Becker,[31] suggests that much regulation is not imposed on firms but rather demanded by them, as a means of harnessing the coercive power of the state to restrict entry, support prices, or provide direct cash subsidies.[32] A related strand of literature has likewise emphasized rent-seeking behavior.[33]

---

[27]See generally Thomas Romer & Howard Rosenthal, "Modern Political Economy and the Study of Regulation," in *Public Regulation: New Perspectives on Institutions and Policies* 73 (Elizabeth E. Bailey ed., 1987).

[28]See generally George J. Stigler, "The Theory of Economic Regulation," 2 *Bell J. Econ.* 3 (1971).

[29]See generally Richard A. Posner, "Theories of Economic Regulation," 5 *Bell J. Econ.* 335 (1974).

[30]See generally Sam Peltzman, "Toward a More General Theory of Regulation," 19 *J.L. & Econ.* 211 (1976).

[31]See generally Gary S. Becker, "A Theory of Competition Among Pressure Groups for Political Influence," 98 *Q.J. Econ.* 371 (1983).

[32]Stigler's influential paper has been characterized as breaking with a previously dominant view (among economists) that regulation is initiated to correct market imperfections. See Stigler, supra note 28, at 3; see also Posner, supra note 29, at 343. It is worth nothing that as far back as E.E. Schattschneider, political scientists recognized the importance of economic interests among groups pressuring Congress. See E.E. Schattschneider, *Politics, Pressures, and the Tariff* 4 (1935). The "capture theory of regulation" in political science was already well developed by the time of Stigler's work. Stigler's main contribution was less his recognition that economic interests will seek favorable regulation than his introduction of that insight into the economics literature and his application of economic models of behavior (i.e., treating political parties as resource maximizers) to explain policy formulation.

[33]See generally James M. Buchanan & Gordon Tullock, *The Calculus of Consent* (1962); Gordon Tullock, "The Welfare Cost of Tariffs, Monopolies, and Theft," 5 *W. Econ. J.* 224 (1967).

In a number of these economic analyses, the supply side (i.e., the political process itself) is virtually ignored.[34] One paper typifying this demand-driven approach has examined private industry's preferences for regulation and has simply assumed that those policy preferences will prevail.[35] Similarly, another model of the resource allocation decisions of competing interest groups has assumed that the policy outcome depends solely on the relative pressures exerted by interest groups.[36]

Even when they model political processes, economic explanations of regulation have often remained driven by the demand of firms. In Stigler's analysis[37] and Peltzman's elaboration,[38] the state enacts the program of the industry (or, more generally, of the interest group) offering the most resources to the governing party; in other words, regulation goes to the "highest bidder."[39] Thus, private industry will tend to be regulated where and when the benefits to firms from government regulation are highly concentrated, but the costs are widely dispersed.[40] The "government" simply acts to maximize an exogenous "political support function" and thus caters to the more powerful group. Following a conceptually similar tack, another model pictures a single policymaker's decision as responding to a weighted sum of industry interests and environmental interests.[41]

Political actors are included in these analyses, but they are treated as economic agents reacting somewhat mechanically to the resources or the demands of interest groups. In many cases, as in the Stigler-Peltzman model, they have no interest other than collecting political contributions. Moreover, government is treated as a monolith, controlled by a single political party, with regulatory agencies and legislatures combined into a single unit. These accounts leave no room for constituency pressures, variation among legislators, slack between legislative direction and the actions of administrative agencies, or other supply-side phenomena.

---

[34]See generally Jean-Jacque Laffont & Jean Tirole, *A Theory of Incentives in Procurement and Regulation* (1993); Romer & Rosenthal, supra note 27.

[35]See James M. Buchanan & Gordon Tullock, "Polluters' Profits and Political Response: Direct Controls Versus Taxes," 65 *Am. Econ. Rev.* 139, 142 (1975).

[36]See Becker, supra note 31, at 392.

[37]See Stigler, supra note 28, at 12.

[38]See Peltzman, supra note 30, at 214.

[39]The Stigler-Peltzman model is essentially a policy auction. See Stigler, supra note 28, at 12–13; Peltzman, supra note 30, at 212.

[40]Peanut regulation provides an excellent example of the effect of concentrated benefits and diffuse costs. Quotas, import restrictions, and price supports combined in 1982–1987 to transfer an average of $255 million a year from consumers to producers, with a deadweight loss of $34 million. The annual cost to each consumer was only $1.23; each peanut farmer, on the other hand, gained $11,100. Peanut farmers clearly had an incentive to preserve the program, while any individual consumer had little to gain from dismantling it. See W. Kip Viscusi et al., *Economics of Regulation and Antitrust* 331 (1995).

[41]See generally Robert W. Hahn, "The Political Economy of Environmental Regulation: Towards a Unifying Framework," 65 *Pub. Choice* 21 (1990).

B. Supply-Side Analyses

By contrast, political scientists and economists studying the supply side of regulation (and of legislation more generally) have focused on the voting behavior of legislators and the institutional structure of the legislature. The approach typically used by political scientists to explain voting behavior is based upon interview and survey data. On the basis of these sources, Congressmen are seen to be most influenced by colleagues and constituents in deciding how to vote.[42] An alternative approach analyzes roll-call data to estimate the relative importance of ideology, constituent interests, and interest groups in legislative voting.[43] One study found that legislators base their votes not only on the economic interests of their constituents (as the economic theory of regulation assumes), but also on their ideologies.[44] Some scholars, notably Michael Munger and his colleagues, have sought to explain voting behavior by explicitly linking it to campaign contributions.[45] However, just as the Stigler-Peltzman model incorporates politicians but remains fundamentally demand-driven, their approach acknowledges the role of interest groups but is driven by supply-side factors. Some mention is made of the costs to legislators of supplying legislation to interest groups, but the models focus on estimating a "supply price" determined solely by the characteristics of legislators.[46]

A second line of inquiry on the supply side has investigated the role of institutional structure in the legislature. The policy outcome in Congress depends not only on the voting preferences of individual legislators, but also on features such as decision rules, the order of voting, and especially the powers of committees (and their chairmen) to control the agenda of the legislature.[47] Further, expectations of subsequent problems of oversee-

---

[42]See John W. Kingdon, *Congressmen's Voting Decisions* 17 (1989).

[43]See generally Joseph P. Kalt & Mark A. Zupan, "Capture and Ideology in the Economic Theory of Politics," 74 *Am. Econ. Rev.* 279 (1984); James B. Kau & Paul H. Rubin, "Self-Interest, Ideology, and Logrolling in Congressional Voting," 22 *J.L. & Econ.* 365 (1979); Sam Peltzman, "Constituent Interest and Congressional Voting," 27 *J.L. & Econ.* 181 (1984).

[44]See Kalt & Zupan, supra note 43, at 298. Their econometric analysis has been criticized by John Jackson and John Kingdon. See John E. Jackson & John W. Kingdon, "Ideology, Interest Group Scores, and Legislative Votes," 36 *Am. J. Pol. Sci.* 805, 806 (1992).

[45]See generally Arthur T. Denzau & Michael C. Munger, "Legislators and Interest Groups: How Unorganized Interests Get Represented," 80 *Am. Pol. Sci. Rev.* 89 (1986); see also Kevin B. Grier & Michael C. Munger, "Comparing Interest Group PAC Contributions to House and Senate Incumbents, 1980–1986," 55 *J. Pol.* 615, 625–40 (1993).

[46]In empirical studies of interest group contributions, a number of researchers seem to have in mind a "market model" of interest group contributions to legislators where interest groups offer campaign contributions and votes in return for political support. See Jonathan I. Silberman & Garey C. Durden, "Determining Legislative Preferences on the Minimum Wage: An Economic Approach," 84 *J. Pol. Econ.* 317, 328 (1976); Garey C. Durden et al., "The Effects of Interest Group Pressure on Coal Strip-Mining Legislation," 72 *Soc. Sci. Q.* 239, 249 (1991).

[47]See generally Kenneth A. Shepsle & Barry R. Weingast, "Positive Theories of Congressional Institutions," 19 *Legis. Stud. Q.* 149 (1994) (reviewing recent literature on congressional institutions).

ing implementation of regulatory policy by administrative agencies may influence legislators in their choice of regulatory procedures and instruments.[48]

C. Equilibrium Analyses

Compared to the above, relatively few works have taken an equilibrium approach by considering the interaction of the supply and demand for regulation. Those considering such linkages have typically focused on the role of campaign contributions. Several researchers have modeled campaign contributions from profit-maximizing firms to vote-maximizing politicians,[49] where candidates choose optimal policy positions that balance the need to get votes (by moving towards the policy preferences of voters) and the need to secure campaign funds (by moving towards the preferences of contributors).[50] In a similar vein, some analysts have employed game-theoretic models to link campaign contributions by interest groups and policy positions adopted by legislators.[51]

One group considered legislative outcomes directly, modeling the determination of campaign contributions, legislators' floor votes, and constituents' votes, but without advancing a theoretical model of legislative behavior.[52] Another research has explicitly considered the interaction of interest group demand and the legislative supply of policy instruments.[53] In his model, the choice of regulatory instrument is the equilibrium of a game between interest groups (who choose how much to allocate to lobbying in support of their preferred instrument) and legislators (who vote for the instrument that maximizes their support, taking into account the contributions from the interest groups).

Despite the relative scarcity of equilibrium models of positive political economy, the metaphor of a "political market" has frequently been employed in the public choice literature. The works using the market metaphor seem to have had three distinct markets in mind. One market is the market for votes *within* a legislature: legislators are at once demanders and suppliers of votes as they engage in vote trading and

---

[48]See Matthew D. McCubbins et al., "Administrative Procedures as Instruments of Political Control," 3 *J.L. Econ. & Org.* 243, 252–53 (1987); McCubbins et al., supra note 10, at 481.

[49]See generally Uri Ben-Zion & Zeev Eytan, "On Money, Votes, and Policy in a Democratic Society," 17 *Pub. Choice* 1 (1974).

[50]Bental and Ben-Zion extend the model to consider the case where politicians derive utility from adopting a platform close to their personal policy preferences. See Benjamin Bental & Uri Ben-zion, "Political Contribution and Policy—Some Extensions," 24 *Pub. Choice* 1, 1–4 (1975).

[51]See David Austen-Smith, "Interest Groups, Campaign Contributions, and Probabilistic Voting," 54 *Pub. Choice* 123, 128–34 (1987).

[52]See James B. Kau et al., "A General Equilibrium Model of Congressional Voting," 97 *Q.J. Econ.* 271, 288–89 (1982).

[53]See Jose Edgardo L. Campos, "Legislative Institutions, Lobbying, and the Endogenous Choice of Regulatory Instruments: A Political Economy Approach to Instrument Choice," 5 *J.L. Econ. & Org.* 333, 348–49 (1989).

logrolling.[54] Other market models focus on the distribution of wealth resulting *from* legislation: the demanders are the beneficiaries of legislation and the suppliers are the losers, with politicians serving as brokers between the two groups.[55] This Article employs what is perhaps the most prevalent conception of the "political market," one which focuses on the exchange between legislators and constituents or interest groups.[56]

The remainder of this Article develops a new model of a political market involving legislators, constituents, and interest groups in the context of instrument choice in environmental policy. This market framework supplements existing work by simultaneously considering the demand for regulation, the supply of regulatory options, and the equilibrium outcome, that is, the choice of policy instrument in the legislature. In this way, the Article strives to synthesize prior research from the demand side and supply side, using it as a foundation for our own equilibrium framework. This Article also seeks to suggest a richer sense of the supply side than is found in existing equilibrium models,[57] incorporating legislator ideology as well as a fuller description of the opportunity costs of supplying legislation.[58]

III. A Market Framework for Examining Instrument Choice

To develop a framework within which various existing positive political economy theories can be synthesized, consider a "political market" embodied in a legislature and focused on a single "commodity," namely leg-

---

[54]In a "logroll," or vote trade, several legislators might arrange to vote for each others' bills, so that each legislator secures her most preferred outcome in return for supporting other legislators' bills (which she may oppose only slightly if at all). For example, a series of public works projects might prompt a logroll, since each in the series matters a great deal to the representative whose district receives the funds, but is insignificant to other legislators.

[55]See *Public Choice Theory* at xviii (Charles K. Rowley ed., 1993).

[56]In previous work, the identity of demanders and suppliers has varied; the market has been in electoral votes (with legislators "paying" for votes with legislation) and in legislation (with voters paying for the policies with their votes). Peltzman, for one, was clear that the demanders were constituents and the suppliers legislators: "[t]he essential commodity being transacted in the political market is a transfer of wealth, with constituents on the demand side and their political representatives on the supply side." See Peltzman, supra note 30, at 212. In this Article's framework, the market is in units of effective political support (for particular public policies).

[57]See, e.g., Campos, supra note 53, at 338–48.

[58]As noted above, Congress is seen as the locus of policy instrument choice. Extending the framework to cover regulatory agencies and the courts would introduce several interesting but complex issues. For regulatory agencies, for example, it is important to deal with issues such as the principal-agent relationship between the agency and Congress; the degree and nature of congressional oversight; the possibly conflicting goals of the agency head and career bureaucrats; the objective function of the bureaucrats (for example, job security, power, protection of expertise); and the way in which policy demands provide payoffs to the agency.

islators' support for a given instrument in a specific policy context.[59] A schematic view of this political market is provided in Figure 1. Demand for various degrees of support comes from diverse interest groups, including environmental advocacy organizations, private firms, and trade associations. The currency in this market takes the form of resources (monetary and other contributions, and/or endorsements or other forms of support) that can facilitate legislators' reelections. The aggregation of these individual demands is not a simple sum, because the public good nature of regulation means that interest groups can free-ride on the demands of others.

Next, it is assumed that each individual legislator seeks to maximize her expected utility, which involves the satisfaction that comes from being

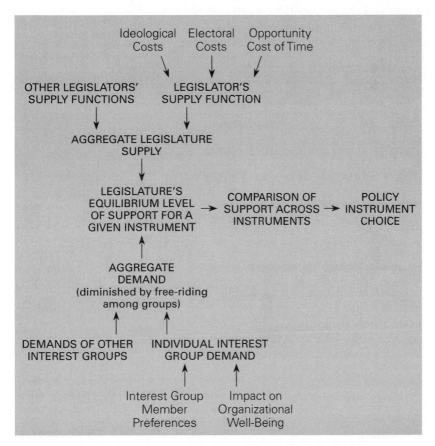

Figure 1 An Equilibrium Framework for Examining the Political Market

---

[59]"Specific policy context" simply refers to the fact that the demand for instruments and the supply of instrument options are both linked to the specific environmental problems for which the instruments are being considered. Also, as discussed below, the legislature in this framework selects a policy instrument from among a range of options, including alternative policy instruments plus the status quo.

a member of the legislature, now and in the future. The result is the legislator's political-support supply function, the shape of which is determined by her ideological predisposition, her perception of her constituents' preferences, and the increasing opportunity cost of providing additional support for the policy instrument (in terms of expended effort, foregone future electoral votes in her home district, and discomfort associated with departures from her ideology). Since each legislator supplies units of a homogeneous product called "effective support" (at differing costs), the individual legislators' supply functions combine to yield an aggregate supply function at the level of the legislature.

Thus, for each instrument, a competitive equilibrium in the legislature is given by the intersection between the aggregate political-support supply function and the aggregation of relevant demands.[60] Levels of effective support provided by individual members of the legislature are hence equivalent to the amounts they are willing to provide at the competitive equilibrium "price," the points of intersection of their supply functions with the infinitely elastic demand they face. The aggregate support is simply the sum over legislators of their individual levels of effective support. The legislative outcome, i.e., the choice of a policy instrument, then depends upon the relative degrees of support generated for alternative policy instruments.

The following sections describe the political market's commodity and currency, and then turn to more detailed expositions of the origins of regulatory demand and supply, respectively. Finally, the Article discusses the nature of political market equilibria and the legislative outcomes that result.

A. The Political Market's Commodity and Currency

Each legislator supplies some degree of support for a given regulatory instrument. Interest groups seek to secure support from legislators in the political market. The commodity of support is seen to be *homogeneous* among legislators. That is, the support produced by one legislator is equivalent to (a perfect substitute for) support produced by any other legislator. This commodity may be characterized as "effective support."[61] It is a measure of impact (output), not of effort (input).

---

[60]It is implicitly assumed that the effective support provided by individual legislators can be observed. This is a reasonable assumption in many but not all situations. Future work should explicitly incorporate this uncertainty.

[61]It might be argued that interest groups ultimately care about votes, which at the level of an individual legislator reduces to a binary variable. But there are several reasons to focus on support, rather than on votes alone. First, this approach facilitates comparisons among several instruments, since the outcome of the legislative process is the instrument that garners the most effective support. Second, empirical analysis has largely failed to link campaign contribution with legislators' votes, see Richard L. Hall & Frank W. Wayman, "Buying Time: Moneyed Interests and the Mobilization of Bias in Congressional Committees," 84 *Am. Pol. Sci. Rev.* 797, 813 (1990), while campaign contributions have been found to be highly correlated with legislators' participation in committees, itself closely linked with the notion of "effective support[.]" See Grier & Munger, supra

To be sure, different legislators require different amounts of effort to produce a unit of effective support. These variations in productivity are due to such factors as the size and effectiveness of members' staffs, their seniority, their committee assignments, and their leadership positions, including committee chairs. Moreover, a legislator's effort may encompass a much larger range of activities than simply voting for a given instrument: among other things, a legislator might hold hearings, attend committee markup meetings, draft or sponsor legislation, insert statements into committee reports, propose amendments, seek to influence colleagues, or make behind-the-scenes deals.[62]

The political currency in this market is seen as the resources necessary for the legislator's reelection: not only votes, but also monetary and other contributions.[63] An environmental interest group, for example, may publicly endorse a candidate for office, or may volunteer time and effort to mobilize votes in a legislator's district. Other forms of "payment" to legislators (such as time spent drafting legislation or policy information for the legislator) are also valued by a legislator seeking reelection, since association with the interest group may increase the legislator's support, and the time saved by the legislator may be spent on activities that generate home district votes. Incorporating home district votes, financial contributions,

---

note 45, at 641; Jonathan I. Silberman & Garey C. Durden, "Determining Legislative Preferences on the Minimum Wage: An Economic Approach," 84 *J. Pol. Econ.* 317, 326–27 (1976). Third, the fate of most prospective legislation is determined before it reaches the floor for a vote. The agenda-setting powers of committees make them virtual arbiters of whether or not bills reach the floor for voting. See Kenneth A. Shepsle & Barry R. Weingast, "The Institutional Foundations of Committee Power," 81 *Am. Pol. Sci. Rev.* 85, 87 (1987). Once a bill reaches the floor, norms of deference may lead many members of Congress to follow committee recommendations, either because of implicit logrolls among committees, see Barry R. Weingast & William J. Marshall, "The Industrial Organization of Congress, or, Why Legislatures, like Firms, Are Not Organized as Markets," 96 *J. Pol. Econ.* 132, 157–58 (1988), or because of recognition of committees' greater expertise. See Kingdon, supra note 42, at 133.

Votes of committee members are usually less critical than the intensity of members' support. See Richard L. Hall, "Participation and Purpose in Committee Decision Making," 81 *Am. Pol. Sci. Rev.* 105, 105–06 (1987); David R. Mayhew, *Congress: The Electoral Connection* 92 (1974). Hence, securing the support of a relatively small number of legislators (each of whom is a highly efficient producer of effective support) may be the primary goal of interest groups, even though the groups ultimately care about the outcome of floor votes. This reality is captured by the above framework, with its focus on levels of "effective support."

[62]One set of researchers describes the range of services legislators can offer interest groups. See Denzau & Munger, supra note 45, at 91. Another group analyzes a similar measure of legislator participation, which they call "political support effort." See Silberman & Durden, supra note 61, at 318. Notably, these models generally treat as an output what in this framework is an input: namely, the effort exerted by the legislator to produce effective support. The above framework incorporates differences among legislators in effectiveness and productivity into the supply side (production of effective support) rather than the demand side (demand of interest groups for support from different legislators). For further discussion of the ways in which members of Congress participate in policy making, especially in committee, see Hall, supra note 61, at 106–08; Richard L. Hall, *Participation in Congress* 40–48 (1996); Hall & Wayman, supra note 61, at 804–15.

[63]Monetary contributions can be used to finance advertising campaigns, literature production and distribution, and other activities that increase the probability of a legislator being reelected.

and nonmonetary contributions in the currency of "resources," the model adopts a monetary numeraire for convenience.

B. Origins of Demand for Environmental Policy Instruments

The Article now explores the nature of demand by firms and individuals, dividing the latter category into three overlapping groups (consumers, workers, and environmentalists), and then considers the role of interest groups in the political market.[64]

1. Firms and Individuals. Firms are affected by environmental regulation through the costs they incur to produce goods and services. Consider a price-taking firm[65] that wishes to maximize its profit from producing a single product and that employs a set of factors in its production, each of which has some cost associated with it. One of these input factors is the set of relevant features of the regulatory environment. In seeking to maximize profits, the firm chooses levels of all its inputs, including the efforts it puts into securing its desired regulatory environment. By solving this maximization problem, the firm derives its demand functions for all its inputs, including its demand for the environmental policy instrument. In this simple model, individual firms have a decreasing marginal willingness to pay to secure particular policy instruments.[66] At a minimum, a firm's demand for a policy instrument is a function of output and input prices, including the "price of legislators' support."[67]

The choice of environmental policy instruments can also have an effect on individuals. For example, individuals can be affected by the level of environmental quality that results from the use of a particular instrument,[68]

---

[64]Of course, individuals and interest groups also play a role on the "supply side" of the political market by affecting legislators' electoral prospects. Individuals vote, while interest groups may spend resources to influence that vote directly (for example, by disseminating information about a legislator's voting record on an issue). Stated in terms of our framework, individuals and interest groups not only exhibit a demand function, but also may also shift legislators' supply functions. See infra Part III.C. This Article attempts to draw a conceptual distinction between these two facets of individual and interest group involvement.

[65]In a competitive market economy, individual firms cannot independently set the price that they will charge (only monopolists can do this); rather, they must accept or "take" the price given by the competitively determined supply-demand equilibrium, and then decide how much to supply at that price.

[66]The maximized objective function is the firm's profit function. Hotelling's Lemma (a basic microeconomic theorem) establishes that the factor demand functions are downward sloping as long as the profit function is convex.

[67]This stylized framework implicitly assumes that firms are profit-maximizing (or cost-minimizing) atomistic units, and thus that there is no significant principal-agent slack between managers and shareholders. There is little doubt that this assumption departs from reality in many cases, but we leave its investigation to future research.

[68]Although attention has been restricted at the outset to the policy instruments used to achieve a given level of protection, the choice of cost-effective instruments can lead to the adoption of more stringent environmental standards, as noted below.

or by the costs of environmental protection as reflected in the prices of the goods and services they buy. Individuals might even derive some direct utility from knowing that a particular type of policy instrument was employed. These effects can be reflected in a utility function, which the consumer maximizes subject to a budgetary constraint. The result is a set of demand functions for all private and public goods, including demand functions for any environmental policy instruments that affect the individual's utility either directly or indirectly. Thus, like firms, individuals can have a decreasing marginal willingness to pay to secure particular policy instruments.[69] Their demand for a policy instrument is a function of their income and of the relative prices of relevant goods, including the price of securing support for their preferred instrument.

Moreover, individuals can be categorized as "consumers," "environmentalists," and "workers"; these three categories are neither mutually exclusive nor exhaustive. Individuals are "consumers" to the degree that the choice of environmental policy instrument affects them through its impact on the prices of goods and services, "environmentalists" to the degree that they are affected by the impact of instrument choice on the level of environmental quality, and "workers" to the degree that they are affected by environmental policy through its impact on the demand for labor, and hence their wages.

2. Interest Groups. Because there are significant costs of lobbying and because the target of demand (i.e., the public policy) is a public good,[70] an individual and even a firm will receive relatively small rewards for any direct lobbying efforts. For individuals, the marginal costs of lobbying are likely to outweigh the perceived marginal benefits over much of the relevant range of lobbying activity, such that individuals will undersupply lobbying, hoping instead to free ride on the efforts of others. Although some large firms maintain offices in Washington, D.C., to facilitate direct lobbying of Congress, most of the demand for public policies from both firms and individuals is transmitted through organized interest groups.

---

[69]The maximized utility function is the individual's indirect utility function. By Roy's Identity (a basic microeconomic truism), the demand functions are derived as downward sloping, as long as the utility functions has the usual properties. It is possible that over a certain region the demand function will be increasing. For example, a unit of support for an instrument will be virtually worthless at very low levels of support, since adoption of that instrument will be extremely unlikely. Assume, however, that the demand function is decreasing over the politically relevant range, in which adoption of the instrument is a realistic possibility. It might be argued that if a legislature were composed of a single legislator and there was perfect information, demand functions for political support would (in the case of support relevant for voting) be a step function with a single step: interest groups would have no willingness-to-pay below some level of (adequate) support, and no willingness-to-pay above a sufficient level of support. But in a multi-member body, more support from individual legislators can always be worth something, and if there is uncertainty about how much support is sufficient, the demand function is likely to be downward sloping over at least some range.

[70]Regulation may not always be nonexclusive. Loopholes, narrowly applying clauses in statutes, and bureaucratic exemptions can all afford special treatment for some firms or narrowly defined categories of consumers. This possibility may provide enough incentive for some individual firms to lobby.

The free-riding problem standing in the way of individual lobbying efforts can also be a significant obstacle to the formation of interest groups.[71] For an interest group to organize, it must overcome the free-riding problem by offering its members enough benefits to make the costs of membership worthwhile. For a citizen group, such as an environmental advocacy organization, these benefits are likely to include: "material incentives," such as newsletters, workshops, or gifts, "solidary incentives," namely the benefits derived from social interaction; and "purposive incentives," such as the personal satisfaction derived from membership in an organization whose activities one supports.[72]

Among citizen groups, taxpayer and consumer organizations may face greater free-riding problems than environmental groups:[73] their lobbying actions are likely to have an even wider range of potential beneficiaries; they may be able to offer fewer material incentives; and they lack the compelling moral mission that may drive the purposive incentives motivating members of environmental groups.

To overcome their own set of free-rider problems, trade associations can offer a range of benefits to member firms that nonmembers do not enjoy, including: influence over policy goals; information on policy developments; reports on economic trends; and participation in an annual convention.[74] Compared with citizen groups, trade associations may have significant advantages in overcoming free-riding: they are usually smaller, making the contributions of each member more significant; and even substantial annual dues may be negligible costs for member firms.[75] Hence, private industry interests may be over-represented in the political process relative to citizen groups.

Importantly, interest groups do not simply aggregate the political demands of their members. Indeed, an interest group's utility maximization function may diverge significantly from those of its members as a result of a principal-agent problem: the members (and donors) are principals who contract with their agent—the interest group (or, more precisely, its professional staff)—to represent their views to the legislature.[76] As in many

---

[71]See Mancur Olson, *The Logic of Collective Action: Public Goods and the Theory of Groups* 43–44 (1965).

[72]See Lawrence S. Rothenberg, *Linking Citizens to Government: Interest Group Politics at Common Cause* 66 (1992); James Q. Wilson, *Political Organizations* 33–35 (1995).

[73]Notably, labor unions are able to overcome free-riding problems through mandatory dues payments. See Olson, supra note 71, at 76; Wilson, supra note 72, at 119. To the extent that these funds are used for lobbying efforts, unions might be expected to be especially well-represented in the political arena. Yet, since unions dedicate most of their campaign contributions to securing favorable labor policy, unions as a group have only rarely been influential (or even active) in environmental policy debates.

[74]See Olson, supra note 71, at 139–41.

[75]See Wilson, supra note 72, at 144.

[76]In the typical principal-agent relationship, the principals (in this case, the firms) know their own interests and wish to ensure that the agent (here the trade association) acts in accordance with those interests. It is conceivable, however, that interest group staff may be leading the charge for policy changes that will benefit member firms, while those firms remain largely ignorant about the policy issues at stake. See Raymond A. Bauer et al., *American Business and Public Policy* 331 (1963).

such contractual relationships, the output exerted by the agents may not be directly observable or controllable by the principal. This principal-agent problem is probably far more serious for environmental advocacy groups than for private industry trade associations.[77]

Principal-agent slack between what the members want and what the interest group actually does arises because the organization's staff has its own self interests. A trade association, for example, may not only want to maximize the profits of its member firms; it may also seek to expand its membership or to increase revenue from member dues. Similarly, the objective function of an environmental group may include not only the level of environmental quality, but also factors such as membership size, budget, and reputation among various constituencies that affect the organization's health and viability.[78]

With these competing interests and constraints in mind, an interest group must decide how to allocate its scarce resources as it lobbies the legislature for its preferred outcome. The total benefits to an interest group of the legislature's support for an instrument rise with the degree of support offered, but there are increasing marginal returns. As in the case of individuals and firms, a unit increased in support when the legislature is already very favorably disposed to one's position is worth less than a unit increase in support by a lukewarm or previously unsupportive legislature. This characteristic produces a downward-sloping demand function: an interest group's marginal willingness-to-pay for support decreases as the legislature's total support increases.

C. Origins of Supply of Environmental Policy Instruments

The Article now considers a legislator who derives utility from a number of relevant interests: making public policy, doing good things for the country or for her district, satisfying ideological beliefs, having prestige and the perquisites of office, and so on. To continue getting utility from these fac-

---

[77]An environmental organization may have a hundred thousand members or more scattered across the country, paying scant attention to the operational proprieties of the organization (let alone the details of its day-to-day activities). Trade associations, on the other hand, may be dominated by a large producer, with an incentive to monitor the association's activities, and their boards of directors may be made up of executives from member firms. Moreover, trade associations have many fewer members, and therefore the stake of each in the organization is greater, and monitoring is more likely to be worthwhile. On the other hand, trade associations have their own set of problems. Among these are the possible necessity of obtaining an expression of consensus from member firms prior to undertaking specific lobbying efforts.

[78]One researcher treats the agency problem in environmental groups extensively, arguing that, because members and patrons cannot observe the outputs or effort of their agents directly, they must instead make funding and membership decisions based on a group's inputs: its expenditures on lobbying, member materials, advertising, and fund raising. See Robert C. Lowry, "The Political Economy of Environmental Citizen Groups" 94–96 (1993) (unpublished Ph.D. dissertation, Harvard University) (on file with the Harvard University Library).

tors, the legislator must be reelected. Assuming that legislators seek to maximize their expected utility, a legislator will choose her level of support for
a proposed policy instrument based on the effort required to provide that
support, the inherent satisfaction she derives from providing that level of
support, and the effects her position will likely have on her chances of reelection.[79]

Accordingly, the legislator's supply function consists of three components: (1) the opportunity cost of efforts required to provide a given degree
of support for a policy instrument; (2) the psychological cost of supporting an instrument despite one's ideological beliefs;[80] and (3) the opportunity cost (in terms of reduced probability of reelection) of supporting an
instrument not favored by one's electoral constituency in terms of reduced
probability of reelection.[81]

The first component emerges from the individual legislator's productivity in providing support. As indicated in Figure 2, the legislator's input is
"effort"[82] and the relevant output is "effective support." Some legislators
may produce "effective support" more efficiently with a given amount of effort thanks to the size and effectiveness of their staffs, their seniority in the
legislature, and their membership and leadership on relevant committees.
By placing a value on the opportunity cost of time and effort, an opportunity cost function can be derived (Figure 3), and from that, the related marginal opportunity cost of effort, represented by the upward-sloping line em-
anating from the origin in Figure 4.[83]

Next, assuming that a legislator derives disutility from acting incon-
sistently with her ideology, the psychological cost of supporting a policy
inconsistent with one's ideological beliefs can be introduced into the framework. As suggested above, this cost would be negative (a benefit) if one
were ideologically predisposed to favor the particular policy. In either case,
it is conceivable that these marginal psychological costs might be increas-

---

[79]This notion of legislators' goals is consistent with other descriptions of Representatives as having three basic objectives: reelection, influence within the House, and good public policy. See Richard
F. Fenno, Jr., *Home Style: House Members in Their Districts* 137 (1978). In our framework, "influence
within the House" and "good public policy" are combined in "being a legislator." If the legislator
wishes to continue to be a legislator in the future, she will also value reelection.

[80]If supporting the instrument is consistent with one's ideological beliefs, then this is a "negative cost," i.e., a benefit.

[81]This is also a "negative cost" (benefit) if supporting the instrument is consistent with one's
constituents' positions.

[82]This includes the use of other resources, but may be thought of as being denominated in units
of time.

[83]In the face of the overwhelming claims on her time and resources—both in Washington and
in her home districts—a member's time and effort carries a significant opportunity cost. See Bauer,
supra note 76, at 412–13; Kingdon, supra note 42, at 216; Fenno, supra note 79, at 141. Effort invested in providing support for one bill could have been spent working on other legislation that would
satisfy ideological goals, reflect voters' objectives, and/or attract votes, dollars, and other resources;
or visiting the home district and supplying constituency services such as help in dealing with the bureaucracy. See Denzau & Munger, supra note 45, at 92–96; Grier & Munger, supra note 45, at 618.
Note that the marginal cost function is assumed in the figure to be linear, simply to keep the explication simple.

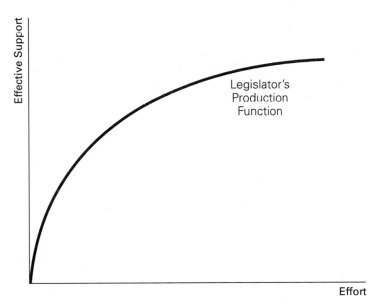

Figure 2 Political-Support Production Function

ing or decreasing (in absolute value) with the degree of support, but for ease of presentation we portray this marginal cost as constant in Figure 4. In this case, the legislator's ideology has no effect on the slope of the combined marginal cost function; rather, ideology shifts the function upwards (for inconsistency with ideology) or downwards (for consistency with ideology).

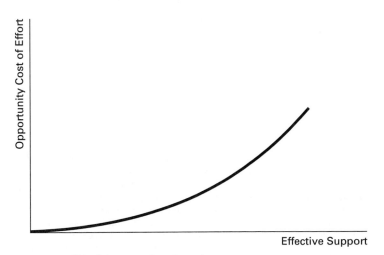

Figure 3 Political-Support Cost Function

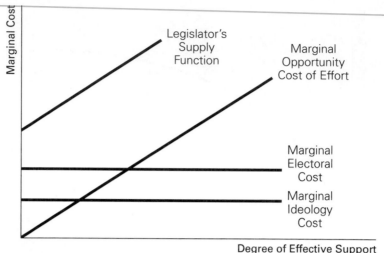

Figure 4 Opportunity Costs and the Supply of Political Support by an Individual Legislator

Finally, the framework incorporates the third component of the legislator's supply function: the opportunity cost corresponding to the reduced probability of reelection given the support of an instrument not favored by one's electoral constituency. Lost votes from constituents unhappy with the legislator's position would directly affect the legislator's chances of reelection, whereas protest and grassroots efforts by interest groups unhappy with the legislator's position could indirectly affect constituents' assessment of the legislator.[84] Again, this is a "negative cost" if supporting the instrument is consistent with one's constituents' positions.[85] As with ideological costs, although these marginal electoral opportunity costs could be increasing or decreasing with the level of the legislator's support, they are drawn as constant (and positive) in Figure 4, to keep things simple.[86]

---

[84]Members of Congress tend to take into account the preferences of the people who voted for them, i.e., their "supporting coalition," see Kingdon, supra note 42, at 60, or their "reelection constituency," see Fenno, supra note 79, at 8. A conservative legislator whose reelection constituency is anti-regulatory, for example, will not be affected by a minority group of environmentalists calling for command-and-control regulation.

[85]Departing from the preferences of constituents reduces the probability of the legislator's reelection. This reduced probability can be evaluated in terms of the resources required to maintain a constant probability of reelection.

[86]Figure 4 represents both ideological costs and electoral costs as being positive; support for the policy is essentially inconsistent both with the legislator's own ideology and her constituents' preferences. It is not inconceivable that these could be of opposite sign, but in a representative democracy, that would be the exception, not the rule. As stated by one author, "If your conscience and your district disagree too often,' members like to say, 'you're in the wrong business.'" Fenno, supra note 79, at 142.

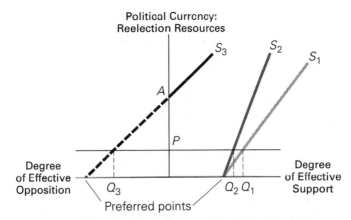

Figure 5 Supplies of Political Support by Individual Legislators

Accordingly, the overall (individual) marginal cost function, or the legislator's supply-of-support function, is simply the vertical summation of these three components: opportunity costs of effort, ideological costs, and constituency costs (Figure 4). The amount of support for a policy instrument that a legislator would supply in the absence of any contributions helpful to advancing the member's goals (including her reelection) is represented in Figure 5 as the "preferred point," the intersection of the supply function with the horizontal axis. In this framework, the legislator can be induced to offer progressively greater degrees of support from this preferred point through offers of "political compensation" that offset the legislator's respective opportunity costs.

Thus, the legislator has an upward-sloping marginal opportunity-cost or supply function, beginning at her preferred degree of support along the horizontal axis. The intersection of the supply function with the horizontal axis can take place at either a positive or a negative degree of support (see S_1 and S_3, respectively, in Figure 5). A politician who is strongly opposed to a given instrument will have a supply function with a negative intercept on the horizontal axis (and a positive intercept on the vertical axis). For such a legislator, a positive, non-marginal shadow price[87] of political compensation is required for any positive degree of support to be forthcoming (see point A in Figure 5).

The legislator's supply function is affected by several exogenous factors. First, an exogenous increase in the negative impact of a given instrument on a legislator's constituents (for example, the construction in the legislator's district of a new factory that would have to pay pollution taxes)

---

[87]the shadow price refers to the implicit price or the marginal valuation of the good or service in question.

may increase the legislator's opportunity costs of supporting that instrument. Conversely, an exogenous increase in the benefits of an instrument to the legislator's constituents (for example, the expansion of a firm in the district that produced a mandated abatement technology) would decrease the legislator's opportunity costs.

Second, the position of the legislator's political party is also relevant. Parties supply funds and organizational support in reelection campaigns. Moreover, leadership posts in the party offer opportunities for increased effectiveness in the legislature. Obviously, parties are likely to be more generous with legislators who are loyal.[88]

Third, the actions of other legislators will have a bearing on the costs of supplying support thanks to the possibilities for vote trading. For example, one legislator may care a great deal about the chosen level of environmental protection, while having only a slight preference for standards over taxes; another legislator may care less about the exact level but have a strong preference for taxes over standards, given her own market-oriented ideology. In a logroll, both legislators could gain from vote trading, with such a logroll affecting both legislators' costs of supplying support for a given instrument.

Fourth and finally, it is both the intent and the consequence of some lobbying activities to shift legislators' supply functions. In other words, in addition to being the primary demanders for alternative forms of regulation, organized interest groups can also play a role in determining the position and shape of legislators' supply functions. Lobbyists might attempt to: affect a legislator's ideologically based perception of the merits of a proposed policy instrument;[89] affect a legislator's perceptions of her constituents' policy preferences;[90] and/or affect a legislator's effort-support production function through provision of information or technical support.[91]

D. Formation of Equilibria and Legislative Outcomes

Up to this point, this Article has focused on the origins of supply and demand for a single policy instrument. However, in many contexts, there will be a *set* of possible instruments considered for achieving a given policy goal: for example, a standard, a tax, and a system of tradeable permits. In addition, there will exist the possibility of doing nothing, i.e., maintaining the status quo. Hence if N alternative instruments are under consideration,

---

[88]Party leaders may conceivably also become effective demanders for policy instrument support by offering various resources to legislators in exchange for support, in which case the parties are essentially functioning as interest groups.

[89]See Kingdon, supra note 42, at 141–42.

[90]See David Austen-Smith & John R. Wright, "Counteractive Lobbying," 38 *Am. J. Pol. Sci.* 25, 29–30 (1994).

[91]See Bauer, supra note 76, at 354–57.

then there will be N + 1 possible choices of action.[92] Each option can define a "political market" for effective support.[93] On the demand side, each policy instrument may have an associated set of interest groups seeking to secure support for it. Moreover, on the supply side, each policy instrument gives rise to its own set of legislator supply functions.[94]

The legislative outcome is the choice of one of the N + 1 alternatives arising from the interactions of interest groups' demands for and legislators' supplies of support for alternative instruments. The degree of aggregate support for each instrument results from an equilibrium established in the legislature, and the outcome in the legislature favors the policy instrument with the greatest degree of total support.

The following sections examine the component parts of this process. First, the nature of the aggregation of demand for a policy instrument across interested individuals and groups, and the aggregation of supplies of support for a policy instrument across members of the legislature, is considered. Then, the formation of equilibria in the legislature for alternative policy instruments and the consequent choice of political outcome is examined. Finally, alternative approaches to modeling this political market are discussed.

1. Aggregation of Demand for Policy Instrument Support. Typically, more than one interest group will be pressing for support from the legislature. How is such interest group demand to be aggregated? In the classic model associated with Stigler[95] and Peltzman,[96] the "winner takes all": the highest bidder wins and gains control over regulation. In another model, competing interest groups participate in a zero-sum game along a single dimension: one group is taxed, the other subsidized, and each tries to improve its lot at the expense of the other.[97] In an actual legislature, interest groups may be opposed to one another or aligned in support of the same instrument.

The most obvious approach for aggregating the demand functions of interest groups might be simply to sum, at each level of willingness-to-pay, the degrees of support that each group demands at that price. Such demand aggregation makes sense for private goods, but the support the legislature provides is essentially a public good. Hence, an efficient approach might involve taking a given level of support and vertically summing what

---

[92] The choice set of instruments is simply taken as given. Important questions remain regarding how it is determined, but these are beyond the scope of this Article.

[93] An interest group can demand and a legislator can supply support for more than one instrument. Although this may at first seem counterintuitive, recall that each legislator's supply function for a given instrument may include the possibility of opposition.

[94] A single legislator may be more efficient at producing support for one instrument than for another and may even have different ideological attitudes towards different instruments. Moreover, the preferences of her reelection constituency may vary across instruments.

[95] See Stigler, supra note 28, at 12–13.

[96] See Peltzman, supra note 30, at 212.

[97] See Becker, supra note 31, at 373–76.

each interest group is (marginally) willing to pay for that degree of support. But such an efficient approach is unlikely to reflect positive reality, as long as free-rider problems among interest groups exist. Therefore, the aggregate demand thus calculated represents the upper bound of actual aggregate demand, that is, the demand experienced in the absence of free-riding.

2. Aggregation of Supply of Policy Instrument Options. In this framework, the degree of support by individual legislators is denominated in terms of homogenous units of "effective support," with differences among legislators already incorporated into the underlying production functions with respect to individual marginal opportunity costs of effort (as well as individual marginal ideological and electoral costs). Therefore, the legislature's supply function can be derived by horizontally summing the supply functions of individual legislators. As noted above, some legislators' supply functions may extend to the left of the vertical axis (for example, S_3 in Figure 5), corresponding to opposition to the instrument in question. Therefore, when the individual legislator supply functions are horizontally added, the aggregate supply function for the legislature represents the relevant net supply of support. Like the supply function for an individual legislator, the aggregate supply function for some instruments may intersect the vertical axis at a positive price.

3. Equilibrium Support in the Legislature for a Policy Instrument. The model treats the legislature as a competitive market for the support of policy instruments. Given the homogeneity of the commodity demanded and supplied, the number of members in the two houses of Congress, and the number of active interest groups, perfect competition is a reasonable first approximation. Under that assumption, the equilibrium, aggregate level of "effective support" provided for the policy instrument is the level for which aggregate supply equals aggregate demand (Q^* in Figure 6). This level is associated with a shadow price (P in Figure 6) representing the aggregate marginal willingness to pay for support in the legislature's equilibrium.

There are two cases of interest in which the aggregate supply and demand functions do not intersect in the politically relevant positive orthant, the northeast part of the graph where both price and quantity are positive. In one case, the demand function intersects the horizontal axis to the left of the legislature's "aggregate preferred point" (see the gap between points B and E_A in Figure 7). In that instance, the maximum support demanded in aggregate by interest groups (at zero price) is lower than the amount that the legislature would provide on its own. In this case of "excess supply," it is reasonable to assume that the legislature would provide support at its preferred point (E_A). With the likelihood of free-riding among interest groups, it would not be surprising if the aggregate demand by interest groups often fell short of the support a strongly committed legislature would provide absent any lobbying. In the above case, the competitive equilibrium price is zero, with each legislator providing support at her own preferred point.

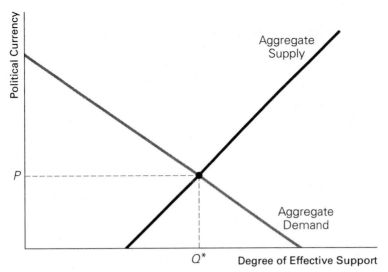

Figure 6 Aggregate Demand and Aggregate Supply of Political Support and the Formation of a Legislative Equilibrium

A second special case arises when a legislature so strongly opposes a policy that its upward-sloping aggregate supply function intersects the vertical axis at a positive price (point C in Figure 7). In this case, the supply function could conceivably lie entirely above the interest groups' aggregate demand function. The political price that such a legislature would require

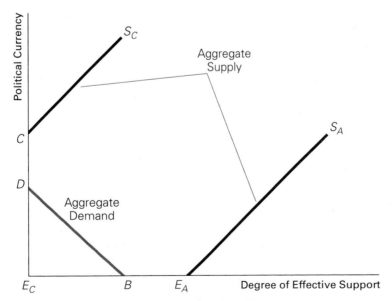

Figure 7 Degenerate Cases in the Political Market

for a positive degree of support is simply greater than the interest groups' overall reservation price for obtaining such support (point D in Figure 7).

In this competitive political market framework, an individual legislator will tend to supply support for a particular policy instrument up to the point where her marginal opportunity costs of doing so are equivalent to the infinitely elastic demand for support she faces from interest groups, represented by the horizontal line through the point P in Figure 5 (derived with the equilibrium in Figure 6). Thus, a set of legislators with supply functions represented by S_1, S_2, and S_3 (Figure 5), would provide effective support of Q_1, Q_2, and Q_3, respectively.

The legislator with supply function S_3 provides a negative level of support, i.e., opposition. An interest group might benefit from contributing to this legislator in the hope of reducing her degree of active opposition,[98] just as it can benefit by increasing the support of a "friendly" legislator. It would take a level of demand (and political compensation) equivalent to point A in Figure 5 to move this same legislator to a position of inaction or indifference. On the other hand, legislators such as those represented by S_1 and S_2 in Figure 5 derive benefits (negative costs) from supporting an instrument, no matter what the position of relevant interest groups. Not surprisingly, such friendly legislators supply even greater levels of support in response to interest group demand.

4. Legislative Outcomes. The previous section discussed the equilibrium level of support for a policy instrument by a single legislator. The next step, then, is to ask how these individual levels of support translate into policy outcomes. One could imagine summing the individual levels of support across legislators to find the aggregate support for an instrument. Such an approach is insufficient, however, because it ignores institutional processes (for example, various kinds of voting rules) that influence collective decisions. In moving from individual support to policy outcomes, therefore, the analysis must take institutional features of the legislature into account.

First, the committee structure of Congress (especially in the House of Representatives) gives different legislators widely different levels of influence over policy.[99] Thus, legislators vary greatly in the effectiveness of the

---

[98]Hall and Wayman examine legislator participation in committees, and argue that interest groups give contributions to "hostile" legislators in order to reduce their participation, i.e., their opposition. See Hall & Wayman, supra note 61, at 803.

[99]Norms of deference, backed up by repeated interactions and the threat of retaliation, give members of committees and subcommittees significant influence over policies under their jurisdiction. See Shepsle & Weingast, supra note 61, at 88–89; Weingast & Marshall, supra note 61, at 158. Agenda-setting or "gate keeping" powers give committees the right to send bills to the floor or table them in committee. Standing committees are also heavily represented on the conference committees that are established to reconcile differences between the chambers before final passage. Power is particularly concentrated in the hands of committee chairs, who hold sway over the committees' agendas and the bills reported to the floor. Given the importance of committee composition, policy outcomes may differ markedly from the preferences of the legislature as a whole; given low committee turnover and the importance of seniority, the status quo may persist long after support in the full legislature has ebbed. See Kenneth A. Shepsle & Barry R. Weingast, "Political Solutions to Market Problems," 78 *Am. Pol. Sci. Rev.* 417, 429 (1984).

support they can supply for a given instrument. However, with the framework's focus on degrees of *effective* support, this reality is already incorporated (through the political support production functions) and has no effect on the appropriate aggregation; it remains one of simple summation of individual equilibria.

Second, legislative outcomes are affected by voting rules. The number of votes necessary for passage (taking into account the veto power of the executive) determines the level and distribution of support needed to pass a bill.[100] Furthermore, the order of voting on amendments and the nature of the final vote also affect the outcome.[101] The question is then how support translates into votes. Whereas the model's "degree of support" is a continuous variable, it produces a binary variable: a vote. Any empirical implementation of this framework would need to address this linkage.[102] For the purposes of this Article, focus can be confined to the reality that, in general, the policy instrument chosen will be the alternative garnering the greatest aggregate support.

5. Alternative Equilibrium Frameworks. Alternative conceptual frameworks of the political market are possible. One potential approach would give greater emphasis to the differences existing among individual legislators in terms of the nature of support they can provide. Thus, instead of quantifying support in terms of perfectly homogenous units of "effective support," the "uniqueness" of support from any single legislator (particularly from powerful members of the legislature) would be interpreted as leading to a set of monopoly political markets, rather than to a single competitive political market.

At one extreme, each member of the legislature is assumed to be a monopoly supplier of her unique type of support and is thus facing a downward-sloping demand for her support. As such, there would exist a set of monopoly equilibria, one for each member of the legislature. In their respective equilibria, each member equates her marginal cost (individual supply function) with the "marginal revenue" function associated with the policy demands she faces, and determines her equilibrium (and utility-maximizing) level of support.

The extreme case of multiple monopoly suppliers appears less reasonable than the perfectly competitive case as an approximation of political reality. However, it does illustrate the potential for alternative models of imperfect competition that may be superior for capturing important characteristics of political markets. Various models of cooperative and noncooperative oligopoly might capture significant elements of legislative rela-

---

[100]In the U.S. Congress, a bill needs a bare majority in the House of Representatives, but may have to clear a higher hurdle in the Senate to bring closure to debate. If the President vetoes the bill, of course, two-thirds majorities in both houses are required to enact legislation.

[101]If modified by successful amendments, a bill will be considered in opposition to the status quo in the final vote. This arrangement favors the status quo and requires that each bill be compared ultimately with the status quo rather than with other alternatives.

[102]Discrete-choice econometric models theoretically based on the existence of an unobserved latent variable are obvious candidates.

tionships.[103] Such explorations will not be dealt with here. Instead, in order to develop a conceptual framework within which existing political economy theories can be organized and synthesized, the basic competitive framework is examined further.

IV. Demand for Environmental Policy Instruments

Demand-side explanations for the choice among environmental policy instruments can be separated into four sectors of regulatory demand: firms, environmentalists, labor, and consumers.

A. Firms

Firms tend to demand the policy instruments promising the highest profits (or the lowest losses) from regulation. While all environmental regulation imposes costs of compliance on firms, not all instruments impose the same costs to achieve a given regulatory goal. Positive political economy explanations of firm demand for environmental regulation can be divided into three principal categories: firm preferences for particular instruments given lower aggregate costs of compliance compared to the industry as a whole; the presence of rents and entry barriers; and differential costs of compliance across firms in a given industry.[104]

1. Lower Aggregate Costs to an Industry as a Whole. All else being equal, firms will tend to prefer regulatory instruments with lower aggregate costs for the industry as a whole. As market-based approaches are likely more cost-effective than command-and-control instruments, the above would suggest that private industry as a whole would generally prefer market-based approaches. However, a crucial distinction exists between the aggregate cost for society and the aggregate cost for private industry. By de-

---

[103]For example, the respective roles played by committee chairs and members may be modeled as a monopolist operating in the context of a competitive fringe.

[104]There are other plausible explanations for firms' preferences. Firms may simply support the continuation of the status quo, which is generally the command-and-control approach, because replacing familiar policies with new instruments can mean that existing expertise within firms becomes less valued. See Steven P. Kelman, *What Price Incentives?* 118–22 (1981); Stewart, supra note 16, at 40. For example, lobbyists—the agents in a principal-agent relationship—may be rationally expected to resist the dissipation of their human capital. See Robert W. Hahn & Robert N. Stavins, "Incentive-based Environmental Regulation: A New Era from an Old Idea," 18 *Ecology L.Q.* 1, 24 (1991). It has also been suggested that market-based instruments may be opposed simply because they are not well understood, and there is at least anecdotal evidence that this has been the case. See Kelman at 96, above; W.P. Welch, "The Political Feasibility of Full Ownership Property Rights: The Case of Pollution and Fisheries," 16 *Pol'y Sci.* 165, 175 (1983). Such lack of understanding can also affect the supply side, and we discuss this later.

THE CHOICE OF REGULATORY INSTRUMENTS IN ENVIRONMENTAL POLICY ~ 587

finition, cost-effective instruments minimize costs to society; they may however vary in proportion of costs imposed on polluters. Accordingly, the use of market-based instruments does not guarantee that firms' compliance costs will be less than the compliance costs of command-and-control regulation.

It would then follow that firms would oppose regulatory instruments that shift a greater cost burden onto industry. For instance, the virtually unanimous opposition by private industry to pollution taxes results from the fact that, under such schemes, firms pay not only their private costs of compliance, but also the costs of tax payments to the government for any residual emissions.[105] Similarly, under tradeable permit schemes, firms bear equivalent costs if the initial distribution of the permits is through an auction. In contrast, under a tradeable permit scheme with grandfathered permits, existing firms do not bear any cost for their residual emissions.[106]

The above suggests that private industry as a whole would prefer grandfathered permits *and* standards to other instruments, since grandfathered permits are cost-effective and the burden placed on industry (at least on existing firms) is minimized. Emissions standards are usually worse for industry in terms of the total-cost criterion, but are likely to be preferred by firms to auctioned permits or taxes.

2. Generation of Rents and Erection of Entry Barriers. Certain types of regulation can actually augment firms' profits through the generation of rents and the erection of entry barriers. In general, firms earn rents if a regulatory instrument drives price above average cost. Assume the case of a command-and-control standard that sets an allowable level of aggregate pollution for each firm, where firms can meet the standard only by reducing output.[107] Assume further that the industry is initially made up of many identical firms, each facing an identical demand, with classical average and marginal cost functions. In the absence of regulation, each firm would produce at the intersection of its marginal and average cost curves, making zero profits. The environmental standard reduces total production and therefore raises price along the aggregate demand curve. If the environmental restriction is not exceptionally severe, the new price will be above average cost for all firms. Firms, therefore, earn rent: the difference between the price they receive for their product and their cost of production.

---

[105]On this point, see Kelman, supra note 104, at 120; see also Frank S. Arnold, *Economic Analysis of Environmental Policy and Regulation* 227 (1995); Robert W. Crandall, *Controlling Industrial Pollution* 70 (1983); Robert W. Hahn & Roger G. Noll, "Environmental Markets in the Year 2000," 3 *J. Risk Uncertainty* 351, 359 (1990). Actually, firms pay less than the full amount of the tax, since a share is passed on to consumers.

[106]Grandfathering distributes the rents from permits to firms that participate in the initial allocation, in contrast with an auction. See Donald N. Dewees, "Instrument Choice in Environmental Policy," 21 *Econ. Inquiry* 53, 59 (1983); Gary W. Yohe, "Polluters' Profits and Political Response: Direct Control Versus Taxes: Comment," 66 *Am. Econ. Rev.* 981, 981 (1976).

[107]See James M. Buchanan & Gordon Tullock, "Polluters' Profits and Political Response: Direct Control Versus Taxes," 65 *Am. Econ. Rev.* 139, 140 (1975).

If entry is prohibited, existing firms will continue earning rents into the future; even if not, rents will last until enough new firms enter to reestablish competitive equilibrium at the new price. Hence, in the above model, firms may prefer standards to no regulation at all, and firms will prefer standards to taxes, since a tax charges for a resource that otherwise would be free.[108]

Firms, however, are not limited to the single response of cutting output. They can also reduce emissions by adopting new technologies or by changing their input mix. In this more general and realistic scenario, depending on the stringency of the standards and other factors, command-and-control standards can still have the effect of providing rents to regulated firms.[109] Here, too, under certain conditions, firms may prefer command-and-control standards to no regulation at all.[110]

It is important to note that the enhanced industry profitability resulting from rents will be sustainable over the long term *only* in the presence of entry restrictions. Thus, firms regulated by a rent-generating instrument, such as command-and-control standards, will benefit if that instrument is linked to a mechanism that imposes barriers to entry. In theory, such a mechanism might prohibit new entry outright; a more politically feasible approach would impose higher costs on new entrants.[111]

The above body of theory explains why private firms (and their trade associations) may have a strong preference for command-and-control standards, which may create rents, and especially for considerably more stringent command-and-control standards for new pollution sources, which create barriers to entry.[112] The indication that firms would support this form of regulation

---

[108]Even if the restriction is severe enough to impose losses on firms, they will prefer standards to taxes, which impose new costs. In the long run, under a tax scheme, firms will exit the industry until a new zero-profit equilibrium is reached; in the short term, firms will lose money. The tax reduces each firm's present value of income, whether it remains in the industry or exits. Firms will therefore oppose the introduction of pollution taxes.

[109]See Michael T. Maloney & Robert E. McCormick, "A Positive Theory of Environmental Quality Regulation," 25 *J.L. & Econ.* 99, 105 (1982).

[110]Pollution restrictions raise both the average and marginal cost curves. Each firm will produce at the level where restricted marginal cost intersects the per-firm demand curve. If the minimum average cost under regulation is to the left of this point, the price (marginal cost) will exceed average cost, and firms will earn rents. Maloney and McCormick identified three conditions that are sufficient for regulation to enhance producer profits: (1) output under regulation corresponds to some cost-minimizing level of output in the absence of regulation; (2) pollution increases with output; and (3) average costs increase more at higher levels of output under regulation. See id. at 104. The necessary and sufficient condition for higher profits is that the intersection of average and marginal cost under regulation lie to the left of the firm's demand curve.

[111]See Stigler, supra note 28, at 3, 5; Eric Rasmusen & Mark Zupan, "Extending the Economic Theory of Regulation to the Form of Policy," 72 *Pub. Choic* 167, 187–89 (1991).

[112]Other barriers to entry result, for example, from the permitting requirements for new sources under the PSD and non-attainment programs under the Clean Air Act, as well as by non-attainment programs' offset requirements for new sources. The positive significance of scarcity rents as a major explanation for the prevalence of particular forms of environmental regulation has important normative implications as well. This is because, in the presence of pre-existing tax distortions, the distribution of these rents can have efficiency implications. See Fullerton & Metcalf, supra note 19, at 44–45. It is ironic that the mechanism that facilitates political acceptance of some environmental policies (transmission of scarcity rents to the regulated sector) may also undo some or all of the welfare gains that would have been forthcoming.

begins to explain the prevalence of such instruments in U.S. environmental law. Furthermore, the theory indicates that, under certain conditions, the regulated industry would be better off than without regulation.

Although the theoretical arguments are strong, there are no conclusive empirical validations of these demand-side propositions. Direct empirical tests of firm demand for regulatory instruments (such as analyses of resources devoted to lobbying for such instruments as a function of firms' stakes in an issue) are virtually nonexistent. Instead, most empirical work in this area simply seeks to measure the benefits an industry receives under regulation. Thus, the work examines not instrument demand itself, but rather the presumed product of such demand.[113]

The above discussion also provides a positive political economy explanation for why market-based instruments have virtually always taken the form of grandfathered tradeable permits, or at least why private firms should be expected to have strong demands for this means of permit allocation. In tradeable permit schemes, grandfathering not only conveys scarcity rents to firms, since existing polluters are granted valuable economic resources for free, but also provides entry barriers, in that new entrants must purchase permits from existing holders.[114]

The preceding discussion does not provide a compelling explanation for the prevalence of command-and-control standards over grandfathered tradeable permits. In principle, either instrument could provide sustainable rents to existing firms. The theory needs to be extended to explain this phenomenon.

3. Differential Costs across Firms in an Industry. An alternative explanation for the landscape of environmental policy instruments arises from the existence of differential costs of environmental compliance across firms. Due to this heterogeneity, a firm may support policy instruments that impose costs on it, as long as those costs affect it less than the industry average, giving it a competitive advantage.[115] For example, firms which could

---

[113]Several researchers employed financial market event analysis in two regulatory cases to test whether the value of regulated firms (measured by stock market prices) was positively affected by the announcement of regulation, as the economic theory of regulation would suggest. They found that cotton dust standards promulgated by the U.S. Occupational, Safety, and Health Administration ("OSHA") raised the asset value of cotton producers, which is consistent with the notion that regulation increased firms' profits by creating rents. See Maloney & McCormick, supra note 109, at 122. However, a more comprehensive study reached the opposite conclusion. See John S. Hughes et al., "The Economic Consequences of the OSHA Cotton Dust Standards: An Analysis of Stock Market Price Behavior," 29 *J.L. Econ.* 29, 58–59 (1986).

[114]One research group provided anecdotal evidence for rent-seeking in the decision making process over EPA's implementation of the Montreal Protocol restricting the use and production of CFCs. See Hahn & McGartland, supra note 19, at 601–10. They argue that a rent-seeking model explains the positions of large producers supporting grandfathered tradeable permits and opposing other implementation schemes, including an auction proposal. See id.

[115]See Robert A. Leone & John E. Jackson, *Studies in Public Regulation* 231, 247 (Gary Fromm ed. 1981); Sharon Oster, "The Strategic Use of Regulatory Investment by Industry Sub-groups," 20 *Econ. Inquiry* 604, 606 (1982).

reduce lead content at relatively low costs (thanks to large refineries) tended to support the gradeable permit system by which the leaded content of gasoline was reduced in the 1980s,[116] while firms with less efficient, smaller refineries were vehemently opposed.[117] Other empirical work, however, has cast doubt on the proposition that firms advocate instruments based on inter-industry or intra-industry transfers.[118]

Another form of cost differential arises as a result of barriers to entry. It is important to maintain the distinction between the entry of new firms and the expansion of existing firms. Entry barriers from environmental regulation generally apply to both situations. Within an industry, firms with no plans to expand would derive greater benefit from entry barriers, potentially discouraging further growth by their competitors.

Conversely, firms with ambitious expansion plans relative to their existing operations would benefit from weaker barriers. Such firms would also try to structure barriers in a manner giving them an advantage relative to newcomers. For example, the "bubble" program of the Clean Air Act creates barriers that are less onerous for existing firms because firms are allowed to engage in intra-firm emissions trading.[119] Under this program, a firm can reduce the emissions of an existing source by an amount at least equal to the emissions of the new source, instead of having to take the more costly step of meeting the command-and-control standard otherwise applicable to new sources.[120] The CAA's banking policies, which allow intra-firm trading across time periods, also make expansion by an incumbent easier than entry by a new firm.

The mechanism for allocating tradeable permits might also produce different winners and losers within an industry. Under a grandfathering

---

[116]See Kerr & Maré, supra note 24, at 31.

[117]See Small Refiner Lead Phasedown Task Force v. EPA, 705 F.2d 506, 514 (D.C. Cir. 1983) (discussing small refineries' opposition). Another example of such intra-industry differentials, and the resulting splintering of lobbying strategy, occurred when the National Coal Association ("NCA") divided over the question of scrubber requirements in clean air legislation. A universal scrubber requirement would have preserved demand for eastern coal, which had higher sulfur content than its cleaner western competition. The NCA split between eastern and western coal producers and stayed out of the debates leading up to the 1977 Clean Air Act Amendments. See Bruce A. Ackerman & William T. Hassler, *Clean Coal/Dirty Air* 31 (1981). Similarly, the largest producers of CFCs (DuPont and Imperial Chemical Industries) supported a ban on CFCs mainly because they were the firms best able to develop substitutes. See Kenneth A. Oye & James H. Maxwell, "Self-Interest and Environmental Management," in *Local Commons and Global Interdependence: Heterogeneity and Cooperation in Two Domains* 191, 198 (Robert O. Keohane & Elinor Ostrom eds., 1995).

[118]Several researchers found that legislators with a paper producer in their districts voted against water pollution control legislation, regardless of whether the producer stood to gain or lose relative to its competitors. See Leone & Jackson, supra note 115, at 247. These authors note that firms may oppose regulation out of uncertainty concerning how the legislation will be implemented, since cost predictions depend on subsequent rulemaking decisions by administrative agencies. Id. at 248.

[119]See 51 Fed. Reg. 43,814, 43,830 (1986). The bubble program typically permits only geographically contiguous trades. Thus, even among existing firms with expansion plans, the benefits of the program depend on where the expansion is contemplated.

[120]Inter-firm trading (as opposed to only intra-firm trading) would eliminate this advantage. See 51 Fed. Reg. 43,814, 43,847–48 (1986).

scheme that allocates permits on the basis of emissions at the time of the scheme's establishment, firms investing in pollution abatement prior to regulation stand to lose relative to their more heavily pollution competitors.[121] Although such investing and expanding firms might conceivably prefer the allocation of permits by means of an initial auction,[122] smaller firms often prefer grandfathering out of concern that auctions will be dominated by larger players.[123]

B. Environmental Organizations

As noted above, the utility of an environmental advocacy group will probably be affected by both the organization's well-being and the level of environmental quality. First, organizational well-being may be measured partly by budgetary resources, which are a function of donor contributions. This financial concern can affect an organization's demand for specific policy instruments if such support attracts members, persuades donors to make contributions, or, more broadly, increases the visibility and prestige of the organization. Hence, an organization's demand for a given policy instrument is likely to be affected by several factors, all else being equal: the likelihood that the instrument will be chosen by policymakers;[124] the degree to which the organization is clearly identified with supporting the instrument; the magnitude of potential funding gains from distinguishing the organization from other environmental groups; and the ability to offer

---

[121]See Hahn & Noll, supra note 105, at 359.

[122]Some supporting evidence is provided by the establishment of a market in takeoff and landing slots at the nation's busiest airports. Since 1968, peak-hour takeoffs and landings have been restricted at LaGuardia, John F. Kennedy, O'Hare, and Washington National Airports. Until 1986, these slots were allocated by a scheduling committee composed of the airlines using a given airport. In that year, the Federal Aviation Administration ("FAA") replaced the committee allocation system with a system of grandfathered tradeable permits. See "Government Policies on the Transfer of Operating Rights Granted by the Federal Government: Hearings before the Subcomm. on Aviation of the House Comm. on Pub. Works and Transp." 99th Cong. 2–4 (1985) (statement of Rep. Norman Y. Mineta). In the months before the proposal was to go into effect, Congress held hearings and considered whether to overrule the FAA. At the hearings, large airlines, which already held most of the slots, supported grandfathering. See, e.g., id. at 55–56 (statement of Robert L. Crandall, CEO, American Airlines); id. at 96 (statement of Steven G. Rothmeier, CEO, Northwest Airlines). In contrast, upstart airlines looking to expand but having few slots, such as People Express, Republic, and Western, vigorously opposed grandfathering, calling for a large percentage of existing slots to be auctioned or distributed by lottery. See, e.g., id. at 71 (statement of Robert E. Cohn, CEO, People Express); id. at 372 (statement of A.B. Magary, Marketing VP, Republic Airlines).

[123]See Hahn & McGartland, supra note 19, at 606. Similarly, since the transition to a grandfathered-permits system is likely to involve less uncertainty than an auction, it might receive disproportionate support from risk-averse firms. Id. at 605.

[124]There is an important distinction between advocacy groups' strategic and tactical decisions. An environmental organization's strategic decision to express demand for a policy instrument and get it on the agenda for consideration tends to be positively related to perceived probability of success, whereas the tactical decision to express demand for an instrument already on the agenda may well be negatively related to probability of success.

donors and members a compelling environmental quality argument in support of the instrument.

A prominent example is provided by the Environmental Defense Fund's
("EDF") enthusiastic and effective support of the SO_2 allowance trading
system adopted as part of the Clean Air Act Amendments of 1990. With the
Bush Administration eager to back up the President's claim of being "the
environmental President," and with key senior staff in the Administration
having strong predispositions to the use of market-based approaches, the
proposal had a strong chance of success. EDF had already become a champion of market-based approaches to environmental protection in other, less
nationally prominent, domains. Now it faced an opportunity to strengthen
that position and solidify its reputation as a pragmatic environmental organization willing to adopt new strategies involving less confrontation with
private industry. By supporting tradeable permits, EDF could seize a market niche in the environmental movement, distinguishing itself further from
other groups. Importantly, EDF was able to make a powerful argument for
tradeable permits on environmental, as opposed to economic, grounds: the
use of a cost-effective instrument would make it politically possible to
achieve greater reductions in sulfur dioxide emissions than would otherwise be the case.[125]

EDF is an outlier in this realm. Most environmental advocacy groups
have been relatively hostile towards market-based instruments. This should
not be terribly surprising. Because of their interest in strengthening environmental protection, environmental organizations might be expected to
prefer command-and-control approaches to market-based schemes for
philosophical, strategic, and technical reasons. On philosophical grounds,
environmentalists have portrayed pollution taxes and tradeable permits as
"license[s] to pollute."[126] Moreover, they have voiced concerns that damages from pollution—to human health and to ecological well-being—are so
difficult or impossible to quantify and monetize that the harm cannot be
calculated through a marginal damage function or captured by a Pigouvian tax rate.[127]

Second, environmental organizations may oppose market-based
schemes on strategic grounds. Once implemented, permit levels and tax
rates may be more difficult to alter than command-and-control standards.
If permits are given the status of "property rights," an attempt to reduce
pollution levels in the future may meet with "takings" claims and demands
for government compensation.[128] This concern, however, can be alleviated
by an explicit statutory provision (like that contained in the acid rain provisions of the Clean Air Act Amendments of 1990) stating that permits do

---

[125]See Hahn & Stavins, supra note 104, at 33 n.180.

[126]See Kelman, supra note 104, at 44. This criticism overlooks the fact that under conventional
command-and-control regulations, firms receive these same licenses to pollute for free. See Hahn &
Stavins, supra note 104, at 37.

[127]See Kelman, supra note 104, at 54–55.

[128]See Hahn & Noll, supra note 105, at 359.

not represent property rights,[129] or by "sunset" provisions that specify a particular period of time during which a permit is valid.

Likewise, in the case of pollution taxes, if increased tax rates become desirable in response to new information about a pollutant or about the response of firms to the existing taxes, adjustment may be unlikely because raising tax rates is politically difficult. Furthermore, taxes have long been treated as "political footballs" in the United States (or as in the recent case of efforts to reduce gasoline taxes). Hence, environmental organizations might oppose pollution taxes out of fear that they would be reduced or eliminated over time. A related strategic reason for environmentalists' opposition of tax instruments is that a shift from command-and-control to tax-based environmental regulation would shift authority from environment committees in the Congress, frequently dominated by pro-environment legislators, to tax-writing committees, which are generally more conservative.[130]

Third, environmental organizations may object to decentralized instruments on technical grounds. Although market-based instruments are theoretically superior in terms of cost-effectiveness, problems may arise in translating theory into practice.[131] For example, an emission tax or tradeable permit scheme can lead to localized "hot spots" with relatively high levels of ambient pollution.[132] While this problem can be addressed in theory through the use of permits or charge systems that are denominated in units of environmental degradation, the design of such systems might be perceived as excessively cumbersome.[133]

C. Labor

Since unions generally seek to protect jobs, they might be expected to oppose instruments likely to lead to plant closings or other large industrial dislocations. Under a tradeable permit scheme, for example, firms might close their factories in heavily polluted areas, sell permits, and relocate to less polluted areas, where permits are less expensive.[134] In contrast, command-and-control standards have generally been tailored to protect aging plants. The threat of factory dislocation is a likely explanation of support from northern, urban members of Congress for the PSD policy in clean

---

[129]See 42 U.S.C. § 765b(f) (1994).

[130]See Kelman, supra note 104, at 139–42. Note that these strategic arguments refer, for the most part, to pollution taxes, not to market-based instruments in general. Indeed, one reason environmental groups such as EDF have endorsed the tradeable permits approach is that it promises the cost savings of taxes without the drawbacks that environmentalists associate with tax instruments.

[131]See Robert W. Hahn & Robert L. Axtell, "Reevaluating the Relationship Between Transferable Property Rights and Command-and-Control Regulation," 8 *J. Reg. Econ.* 125, 126–27 (1995).

[132]See Richard L. Revesz, "Federalism and Interstate Environmental Externalities," 144 *U. Pa. L. Rev.* 2341, 2412 (1996).

[133]See id. at 2412–14.

[134]See Hahn & Noll, supra note 105, at 358.

air regulation, which has discouraged movement of industry out of urban areas in the northeast into high-quality air sheds in the South and West.[135] Depending on the tradeoffs between job creation and preservation effects, labor might support stricter command-and-control standards for new sources.[136]

D. Consumers

To the extent that consumer groups have preferences among environmental policy instruments, one might expect them to favor those instruments that minimize any increases in the prices of consumer goods and services; this would seem to suggest cost-effective (hence, market-based) instruments over command-and-control.[137] In practice, however, these groups typically have not expressed strong demand for environmental policies. As mentioned above, free-riding and limited information are likely to present greater obstacles for consumer organizations than for environmental groups, especially on environmental issues. Thus demand from consumer groups for environmental policy instruments is likely to be muted. Moreover, environmental policy may lie outside the core concerns of consumer groups' constituents. Indeed, when consumer groups do get involved, it may be on "consumer health and safety" issues, where their interests are aligned with those of environmentalists. Calls for cost-effective policies might also be voiced by taxpayer organizations, but again, the minutiae of instrument choice lie outside the scope of these groups' primary concerns. Hence, environmental groups are unlikely to face significant opposition from other public interest organizations.

V. Supply of Environmental Policy Instruments

There are several plausible positive political economy explanations for the nature of the supply of environmental policy instruments. First, legislators and their staffs are thought to be predisposed by their predominantly le-

---

[135]See, e.g., Crandall, supra note 105, at 127–29 (1983); B. Peter Pashigan, "Environmental Regulation: Whose Self-Interests Are Being Protected?," 23 *Econ. Inquiry* 551, 552–53 (1985).

[136]There are other examples of labor concern over the choice of environmental policy instruments. In the 1977 debates over amendments to the Clean Air Act, eastern coal miners' unions fought to include a command-and-control standard that effectively required scrubbing, thereby seeking to ensure continued reliance on cheap, high-sulfur coal from the east, over cleaner western coal. See Ackerman & Hassler, supra note 117, at 31. Likewise, in the debates over the SO_2 allowance trading system in the 1990 amendments to the CAA, the United Mine Workers opposed the system because it would create incentives for the use of low-sulfur coal from largely non-unionized mines in Wyoming's Powder River Basin over high-sulfur coal from eastern, unionized mines. See "Clean Air Reauthorization: Hearing Before the Subcomm. on Energy and Power of the House Comm. on Energy and Commerce," 101st Cong. 455–56 (1989) (statement of Richard L. Trumka, President, United Mine Workers).

[137]It is also possible to distinguish among types of market-based instruments and types of command-and-control instruments, given that any environmental policy instrument that generates privately retained scarcity rents (such as new source performance standards, grandfathered tradeable permits, and others) also raises consumer prices, relative to a policy that does not generate such rents. See Fullerton & Metcalf, supra note 19, at 44.

gal training to favor command-and-control approaches to regulation.[138] Similarly, legislators may need to spend time learning about unfamiliar policy instruments before they can provide substantial support, thereby giving rise to a status quo bias in favor of the current regime of command-and-control regulation.[139] Both these effects may become weaker in the coming years, as a result of the increasing understanding of economics among lawyers as well as among legislators and their staffs.[140]

Second, ideology plays a significant role in instrument choice. A conservative lawmaker who generally supports the free market might be predisposed to support market-based instruments; a legislator with more faith in government and less faith in the private sector might, all else being equal, prefer a command-and-control approach. A 1981 survey of congressional staff members found that support and opposition to effluent charges was based largely on ideological grounds.[141] For example, Republicans who supported the concept of pollution charges offered assertions such as "I trust the marketplace more" or "less bureaucracy" is desirable, without any real awareness or understanding of the economic arguments for market-based programs.[142] Likewise, Democratic opposition was largely based upon analogously ideological factors, with little or no apparent understanding of the real advantages or disadvantages of the various instruments.[143]

Third, constituents react to their perceptions of the costs and benefits to themselves and others of a particular policy, regardless of the real costs

---

[138]See Allen V. Kneese & Charles L. Schulze, *Pollution, Prices, and Public Policy* 116–17 (1975).

[139]See id. at 114–15. This argument assumes that a legislator (or at least her staff) needs to understand an instrument in order to support it. Although such understanding might not be a precondition for voting in favor of the instrument, it is more important for other forms of support, such as insertion of a statement into the legislative history, efforts to get a bill through committee, or attempts to persuade other legislators. Moreover, a lack of understanding may hurt the legislator in her re-election campaign if the press or an opponent seeks to make it an issue. Thus, the greater the prominence of an issue, the more important it will be for a legislator to have a compelling rationale for her position. Responding to this need, interest groups may supply legislators with justifications for supporting given policies. See, e.g., Fenno, supra note 79, at 141–43; Kingdon, supra note 42, at 46–48.

[140]See Hahn & Stavins, supra note 104, at 31, 36. Thus, outreach efforts by economists and others may be thought to have both demand-side and supply-side effects. On the demand side, increased understanding of market-based instruments may have increased the demand for these instruments by various interest groups. On the supply side, increased understanding reduces learning costs for legislators. Since both effects translate into rightward shifts of the respective functions, the outcome is unambiguous in terms of increased degrees of support.

Economists have also played a sometimes significant role as advocates of market-based instruments on efficiency grounds, not only in aspects of environmental policy (such as the U.S. acid rain program) but also in other policy areas, such as the allocation of airport landing spots and the broadcast spectrum. Economists therefore might be seen as acting as "policy entrepreneurs" outside of the interest group-politician nexus (i.e., outside of the strict supply-and-demand framework posited here). See id. at 41.

[141]See Kelman, supra note 104, at 100.

[142]See id. at 100, 104.

[143]See id. at 100–01.

and benefits.[144] The more visible the benefits, the greater the demand for an instrument; the more visible the costs, the greater the opposition and thus the political costs to the legislator. The importance of perceived costs and benefits is a consequence of the limited information most voters have about the details of public policy.[145] Hence, politicians are likely to prefer command-and-control instruments because they tend to hide the cost of regulation in the price increases passed on to consumers.[146] In contrast, though they impose lower total costs, market-based instruments generally impose those costs directly, in the form of effluent or permit charges.[147] Grandfathered permits fare better on the visibility criterion than auctioned permits or taxes, because no money is exchanged at the time of the initial allocation.[148]

Fourth, voters' limited information may also lead politicians to engage in symbolic politics: the use of superficial slogans and symbols to attract constituent support, even when the policies actually implemented are either ineffectual or inconsistent with the symbols employed. Such symbolism offers the legislator political benefits at little opportunity cost. Command-and-control instruments are likely to be well suited to symbolic politics, because strict standards, as strong statements of support for environmental protection, can be readily combined with less visible exemptions.[149] Congress has on several occasions passed environmental laws with strict compliance standards, while simultaneously including lax or insufficient enforcement measures.[150] Tradeable permits and taxes do not offer

---

[144]See, e.g., Matthew D. McCubbins & Terry Sullivan, "Constituency Influences on Legislative Policy Choice," 18 *Quantity & Quality* 299, 301–02 (1984); Robert W. Hahn, "Jobs and Environmental Quality: Some Implications for Instrument Choice," 20 *Pol'y Sci.* 289, 299 (1987).

[145]A rational voter will choose to remain ignorant on most issues, because the costs of gathering information are likely to outweigh the nearly insignificant benefits from voting knowledgeably. See Anthony Downs, *An Economic Theory of Democracy* 212–13 (1957). In contrast, organized interest groups with large stakes in an issue are likely to be well-informed and thus overrepresented in the political process. These issues raised by asymmetric information are particularly relevant to instrument choice, because votes on instrument choice are often much more technical than votes on policy goals, and therefore attract even less attention from average voters. See generally James T. Hamilton, "Taxes, Torts, and the Toxics Release Inventory: Congressional Voting on Instruments to Control Pollution," 35 *Econ. Inquiry* 745 (1997).

[146]See McCubbins & Sullivan, supra note 144, at 306. The point that politicians prefer, all else being equal, regulatory instruments with "invisible" associated costs is related to the more general notion that legislators may seek to disguise transfers to special interests. See Stephen Coate & Stephen Morris, "On the Form of Transfers to Special Interests," 103 *J. Pol. Econ.* 1210, 1212 (1995).

[147]The potential government revenue offered by auctions and taxes is likely to be politically attractive. See Hahn & McGartland, supra note 19, at 608–09.

[148]One commentator emphasized the importance of observable costs and benefits in explaining why Wisconsin chose a largely state-funded pollution-credit program over an effluent charge. See Hahn, supra note 144, at 299. The instrument offered visible job creation, by favoring the construction of new facilities, at the expense of diffuse, less visible costs to widely distributed third parties. In contrast, the market-based alternative would have appeared to sacrifice jobs while its cost-saving benefits would have been less evident. See id. at 299–300.

[149]See Hahn & Noll, supra note 105, at 361. Of course, the reliance on voter ignorance may be countered by better informed interest groups.

[150]See id.

the powerful symbolic benefits of declaring strict standards. Moreover, it may be difficult to have market-based instruments which simultaneously "exempt" certain parties or which are "loosely" enforced.[151]

Fifth, if politicians are risk averse, they will prefer instruments involving more certain effects.[152] With respect to environmental policy instruments, uncertainty is likely to arise with respect to the distribution of costs and benefits among the affected actors and to the implementation of the legislative decision by the bureaucracy. The flexibility inherent in permits and taxes creates uncertainty about distributional effects and local levels of environmental quality.[153] Typically, legislators are more concerned with the distribution of costs and benefits than with a comparison of total benefits and costs.[154] For this reason, aggregate cost-effectiveness, perhaps the major advantage of market-based instruments, is likely to play a less significant role in the legislative calculus than whether a politician is getting the best deal possible for her constituents.[155] Moreover, politicians are likely to oppose instruments (such as tradeable permit schemes) that may induce firms to close business and relocate elsewhere, leading to localized unemployment.[156] Although there will be winners as well as losers from such relocation, potential losers are likely to be more certain of their status than potential gainers. This asymmetry creates a bias in favor of the status quo.[157]

---

[151]But see Joskow & Schmalensee, supra note 21 (examining Congressional attempts to confer benefits on particular firms within the context of the SO_2 allowance trading program).

[152]See Matthew D. McCubbins et al., "Structure and Process, Politics and Policy: Administrative Arrangements and the Political Control of Agencies," 75 *Va. L. Rev.* 431, 437 n.22 (1989) ("Legislators are likely to behave as if they are risk averse, even if they are personally risk neutral, if their constituents punish unpredictable policy choices or their reelection probability is nearly unity.")

[153]See Matthew D. McCubbins & Talbot Page, "The Congressional Foundations of Agency Performance," 51 *Pub. Choice* 173, 178 (1986).

[154]See Hahn & Stavins, supra note 104, at 38–41.

[155]See Kenneth A. Shepsle & Barry Weingast, "Political Solutions to Market Problems," 78 *Am. Pol. Sci. Rev.* 417, 418–20 (1984).

[156]See Hahn & Noll, supra note 105, at 358. Tradeable permits are more likely to be adopted in cases where the industry to be regulated is relatively dispersed and has relatively homogeneous abatement costs. See id. at 363–64. But such homogeneity also means that the gains from a market-based approach are more limited.

[157]The Clean Air Act Amendments of 1977 provide an example of legislation built upon such compromises. See id. at 361–62. Stringent standards for urban non-attainment areas were offset by industry-specific exemptions and by measures preventing relocation of urban factories to less polluted areas, the so-called PSD policy described above. See id. at 361. The winning coalition would likely not have held up under a tradeable permit scheme, which would have allowed rust belt firms to purchase pollution permits from firms in cleaner areas and thus to relocate. See id. On the other hand, a tradeable permit scheme that prevented interregional trading could presumably have protected northern factory jobs just as well.

For the same reason, grandfathering of tradeable permits is more widely to attract a winning coalition than auctions, since grandfathering allows leeway in rewarding firms and distributing the costs and benefits of regulation among jurisdictions. Several prominent researchers have examined the political process of allocating SO_2 emissions permits in the 1990 amendments to the Clean Air Act. See Joskow & Schmalensee, supra note 21. Their focus was on empirically measuring the role of interest group politics and rent-seeking in how those permits were allocated, but another point is made clear by their work: allocating permits by grandfathering can produce fairly clear "winners: and "losers" among firms and states. See id. An auction, on the other hand, would allow no such political maneuvering.

Sixth, command-and-control instruments offer Congress greater control with respect to the implementation of legislative outcomes by administrative agencies. To ensure that the interests of the winning coalition are protected in implementation, Congress may effectively prescribe administrative rules and procedures that favor one group over another.[158] In theory, such a practice protects intended beneficiaries of legislation by constraining the scope of subsequent executive intervention in implementation.[159] If stacking the deck is an important aspect of policymaking, it is more likely to be successful in the context of command-and-control legislation. Market-based instruments leave the allocation of costs and benefits up to the market, treating polluters identically.[160] Standards, on the other hand, open up possibilities for stacking the deck, by building protections in favor of particular constituencies.[161] For example, Congress might favor industry by placing the burden of proof in standard-setting on the administrative agencies, or alternatively help out environmental groups by including citizen-suit provisions allowing legal action to impel standards enforcement.

Seventh, bureaucrats are less likely to undermine the legislative decision if their preferences over policy instruments are accommodated. Administrative decisionmakers are likely to oppose decentralized instruments on several grounds: they are familiar with command-and-control approaches; market-based instruments may not require the same kinds of technical expertise that agencies have developed under command-and-control regulation; and market-based instruments imply a scaled-down role for the agency by shifting decisionmaking from the bureaucracy to private firms, undermining the agency's prestige and its staff's job security.[162]

VI. Conclusions

This Article has attempted to synthesize the seemingly diverse trends of the positive political economy literature by viewing them as relating to component parts of a political market framework. In this framework, interest groups have demands for particular instruments. Legislators, in turn, provide political support for such instruments. The demands of the various interest groups are aggregated, as are the supplies of support from individual legislators. The interaction of such aggregate demand and supply produce a legislature's equilibrium level of aggregate support, with each member simultaneously determining her effective support level. The effective support levels of the various legislators are combined, in an institutional context, to produce the legislature's choice of policy instrument.

---

[158]See McCubbins et al., supra note 152, at 244.
[159]See id. at 261–62.
[160]See Hahn & Noll, supra note 105, at 362.
[161]See id.
[162]See Hahn & Stavins, supra note 104, at 14, 21.

This framework is far from complete, since it focuses on the decisions of individual legislators, while leaving unanswered those questions of how individual (and continuous) legislator support translates into binary votes and how such support or votes are aggregated to the level of the legislature. For example, the model does not deal with the nature of competition among legislators, only briefly considers the role that congressional committees and other institutions play in structuring and influencing instrument choice, and does not explain how instrument choices are framed. Likewise, this is only a competitive legislative model as a first approximation; alternative approaches were discussed briefly. These issues represent promising avenues for extending this framework and building a workable model of instrument choice.

This Article takes a modest step toward a unified framework for positive analysis of policy instrument choice. This framework may permit greater understanding than approaches that focus almost exclusively on one component of the problem at a time. Thus, for example, if one considers only the benefits that a particular industry derives from a proposed regulatory program, one might conclude that a program will be forthcoming if the benefits are sufficiently high. Attention to questions of supply shows why this might not be the case. If the legislature prefers the status quo to the instrument demanded by the interest group, and if the legislature's aggregate supply function is sufficiently inelastic, there may be no equilibrium under which the legislature provides positive support for the demanded instrument. Indeed, the supply function of such a legislature might be above the industry demand function everywhere in the politically relevant domain. Similarly, whether a large shift in the demand for a particular instrument resulting from exogenous factors causes a comparable shift in the actual support provided by the legislature depends on the elasticity of supply. There will be relatively little change in equilibrium support if supply is inelastic, but a far larger change if supply is elastic.

This framework helps us to organize and synthesize available explorations of the four gaps which introduced the Article: three gaps between economic prescription and political reality and one gap between past and current political practices. With respect to the first—the predominance of command-and-control over market-based instruments despite the economic superiority of the latter—firms are likely to prefer command-and-control standards to auctioned permits and taxes. Standards produce rents, which can be sustainable if coupled with sufficiently more stringent requirements for new sources. In contrast, auctioned permits and taxes require firms to pay not only abatement costs to reduce pollution to a specified level, but also costs of polluting up to that level. Environmental interest groups are also likely to prefer command-and-control instruments, for philosophical, strategic, and technical reasons.

On the supply side, command-and-control standards are likely to be supplied more cheaply by legislators for several reasons: the training and experience of legislators may make them more comfortable with a direct standards approach than with market-based approaches; the time needed to learn about market-based instruments may represent significant opportunity costs; standards tend to hide the costs of pollution control while emphasizing the benefits; and standards may offer greater opportunities for symbolic politics. Finally, at the level of the legislature, command-and-control standards offer legislators a greater degree of control over the distributional effects of environmental regulation. This feature is likely to make majority coalitions easier to assemble, because legislative compromise is easier in the face of less uncertainty, and because the winning coalition can better guarantee that its interests will be served in the implementation of policy.

The second gap—that when command-and-control standards have been used, the standards for new sources have been far more stringent than those for existing sources, despite the potentially perverse incentives of this approach—can also be understood in the context of this market framework. Demand for new source standards comes from existing firms, which seek to erect entry barriers to restrict competition and protect the rents created by command-and-control standards. In turn, environmentalists often support strict standards for new sources because they represent environmental progress, at least symbolically. On the supply side, more stringent standards for new sources allow legislators to protect existing constituents and interests by placing the bulk of the pollution control burden on unbuilt factories.

Many of these same arguments can also be used to explain the third gap—the use of grandfathered tradeable permits as the exclusive market-based mechanism in the United States, despite the disadvantages of this allocation scheme. Like command-and-control standards, tradeable permits create rents; grandfathering distributes those rents to firms, while auctioning transfers the rents to government. Moreover, like stringent command-and-control standards for new sources, but unlike auctioned permits or taxes, grandfathered permits give rise to entry barriers. Thus, the rents conveyed to the private sector by grandfathered tradeable permits are, in effect, sustainable.

Moreover, grandfathered tradeable permits are likely to be less costly for legislators to supply. The costs imposed on industry are less visible and less burdensome for grandfathered permits than for auctioned permits or taxes. Also, grandfathered permits offer a greater degree of political control over the distributional effects of regulation, facilitating the formation of majority coalitions. In both these respects, grandfathered permits are somewhat analogous to command-and-control standards.

The fourth and final gap—between the recent rise of the use of market-based instruments and the lack of receptiveness such schemes had encountered in the past—can be credited to several factors. These include: the increased understanding of and familiarity with market-based instruments; niche-seeking by environmental groups interested in both environmental quality and organizational visibility; increased pollution control costs, which create greater demand for cost-effective instruments; attention to new, unregulated environmental problems without constituencies for a status quo approach; and a general shift of the political center toward a more favorable view of using the market to solve social problems. Overall, the image is one of both demand and supply functions for market-based instruments shifting rightward, leading to greater degrees of political support for these market-based instruments over time.[163]

Although some of the current preferences for command-and-control standards simply reflects a desire to maintain the regulatory status quo, the aggregate demand for a market-based instrument is likely to be greatest (and the opportunity costs of legislator support is likely to be least) when the environmental problem has not previously been regulated.[164] Hence, the prospects may be promising with respect to the introduction of such market-based instruments for new problems, such as global climate change, rather than for existing, regulated problems, such as abandoned hazardous waste sites.

Such a market framework can generate empirical work on the positive political economy of instrument choice for environmental regulation. So far, most of the academic work in this area has been theoretical; very few arguments have been subjected to empirical validation. Several of the existing empirical studies have addressed the question of why firms might support particular instruments, rather than whether firms actually provide such support. No empirical studies have constructed demand functions by determining how much firms actually are willing to pay (in the form of lobbying expenses and campaign contributions, for example) to secure particular outcomes. Similarly, no work has sought to determine the nature of demand by interest groups other than industry. In particular, the motives of environmental organizations merit more consideration. This Article discussed the possible self-interested motives of such organizations, and how their demands for particular policy instruments may be motivated by niche-seeking. Whether their expenditures in the political process comport with this theory remains essentially untested.

On the supply side, substantial impediments to empirical work remain. Existing studies have primarily attempted to determine the factors that affect legislative votes on particular programs.[165] In recent years, however, Congress has enacted a greater proportion of legislation by voice vote, rather than recorded vote. There has also been a shift from votes on comparatively narrow bills to votes on omnibus bills, which make it virtually impossible to determine a legislator's actual position with respect to specific components. Thus, the relative dearth of new data makes it difficult to perform studies of legislative voting behavior.

Legislative voting studies also share a substantial problem: distinguishing votes that reflect a legislator's true views about a bill from votes

---

[163]It is also possible that changes in some of the institutional features identified above have affected individual legislators' degrees of support. For example, changes may have occurred that led to particular legislators taking on important committee positions, thus changing their production functions, and hence their opportunity costs.

[164]See Hahn & Stavins, supra note 104, at 42.

[165]See generally Hamilton, supra note 145; see also Pashigan, supra note 135, at 551–54.

cast as part of an implicit or explicit logrolling trade, in which a legislator
votes in favor of a program that she otherwise opposes in order to obtain
a more valuable quid pro quo.[166] Moreover, as argued above, a vote constitutes only one component of the support that a legislator can extend to
a bill. But the other components of support are less well suited to quantitative analysis.[167] Thus, in some cases, the best way to explore empirically
the supply side of the equilibrium framework may be through detailed case
studies of the legislative decisionmaking process.[168]

The market model will, in the end, be an imperfect and incomplete description of political behavior. But there are real advantages to considering instrument choice within this framework, and from developing more
fully the details of the market model and its implications. The ultimate test
of the usefulness of such a framework will be the extent to which it enables reliable predictions of the choices legislatures make, and the extent
to which it facilitates the design of policy instruments that are both economically rational and politically successful.

---

[166]Compare Kau & Rubin, supra note 43, at 380–81 (attempting to measure the importance of
logrolling with a conditional probability model that examined votes as a function of one another)
with Jackson & Kingdon, supra note 44, at 807 (criticizing aspects of Kau and Rubin study).

[167]A pattern of votes on a series of amendments may be used as a proxy for a continuous underlying support variable, overcoming this problem. See Silberman & Durden, supra note 61, at
322–27. Such series of closely related votes, however, are rarely available, particularly in the case of
instrument choice. A different approach has examined the relationship between campaign contributions and degrees of participation in committee activities. See Hall & Wayman, supra note 61, at
805–09.

[168]See generally Ackerman & Hassler, supra note 117.

28 The Political Economy of Market-Based Environmental Policy: The U.S. Acid Rain Program*

Paul L. Joskow

Richard Schmalensee

Paul L. Joskow is James Killian Professor of Economics and Management at the Massachusetts Institute of Technology, and Research Associate at the National Bureau of Economic Research; and Richard Schmalensee is Dean of the Sloan School of Management, Massachusetts Institute of Technology, and Research Associate at the National Bureau of Economic Research.

I. Introduction and Summary

Despite the attractive efficiency properties of "market-based" approaches to internalizing environmental externalities, such as emissions taxes or tradable emissions permit systems, these approaches have rarely been used.[1] United States environmental policy has relied instead on a variety of source-specific "command and control" regulations that specify limits on emis-

"The Political Economy of Market-Based Environmental Policy: The U.S. Acid Rain Program," by Paul S. Joskow and Richard Schmalensee from *Journal of Law and Economics*, 41:37–83 (April 1988). © 1988 by The University of Chicago. All rights reserved.

*The authors are indebted to Amy Ando, Paul Ellickson, and, especially, Elizabeth Bailey for excellent research assistance and to the MIT Center for Energy and Environmental Policy Research for support. They are grateful for aid and guidance to Bruce Braine, Rob Brenner, Denny Ellerman, Dennis Epple, Robert Hahn, Karl Hausker, Brian McLean, Larry Montgomery, Richard Newell, Robert Stavins, Max Stinchcombe, and participants in seminars at Harvard University, Yale University, and the University of Texas, Austin. Despite all this help, only the authors are responsible for the views expressed in this article and any errors it may contain. Richard Schmalensee participated in the preparation of the Bush administration's acid rain proposals and in negotiations between the administration and the Senate in early 1990 on what became the Clean Air Act Amendments of 1990. Paul Joskow was a member of the EPA Acid Rain Advisory Committee, which worked with the Environmental Protection Agency to produce the regulations that implemented the acid rain program called for by that legislation.

[1] For discussions of other environmental programs employing economic instruments, see Thomas H. Tietenberg, *Emissions Trading: An Exercise in Reforming Pollution Policy* (1985); Robert W. Hahn & Gordon L. Hester, "Marketable Permits: Lessons for Theory and Practice," 16 *Ecology L. Rev.* 361 (1989); and National Economic Research Associates, Inc., *Key Issues in the Design of NO_x Emission Trading Programs to Reduce Ground-Level Ozone*, ch. 2 (1994). Roger G. Noll, "Economic Perspectives on the Politics of Regulation," in 2 *Handbook of Industrial Organization* 1254 (R. Schmalensee & R. D. Willig eds. 1989), at 1275, discusses some of the political reasons such programs are rare.

sions rates or mandate particular control technologies. Title IV of the 1990 Clean Air Act Amendments (1990 CAAA, Public Law 101–549) established the first large-scale, long-term U.S. environmental program to rely on tradable emissions permits (called "allowances" in the 1990 legislation) to control emissions. Its target was electric utility emissions of sulfur dioxide (SO_2), the major precursor of acid rain.

Any tradable permit scheme for controlling emissions must specify a quantity cap or emissions ceiling for each of the geographic emissions markets within which emissions permits can be traded. This emissions cap, in turn, defines the total endowment of emissions permits that will be in circulation in each emissions market. Any tradable permit scheme must also adopt a method for distributing those permits—by giving them away, by selling them at auction, or by some other means. The choice necessarily has distributional implications, and, in the presence of transactions costs or other barriers to trading, it has efficiency implications as well.[2] Because emissions permits are valuable and decisions about their distribution are made by political institutions, these decisions are likely to be highly politicized, reflecting rent-seeking behavior and interest group politics. In the U.S. acid rain program, the expectation was that allowances would be worth about $5 billion per year once the program was fully operational.

In this article, we examine how Congress, influenced by the executive branch and various special interests, distributed what was essentially (as we discuss below) a fixed endowment of SO_2 allowances among electric utilities in the process of crafting acid rain legislation. The literature contains essentially no empirical work on the distributional implications of alternative market-based control mechanisms, largely because there have been few applications of such mechanisms.[3] In particular, little attention has been devoted to how interest group politics and associated rent-seeking behavior affect the allocation of permits in a tradable permit system. This is a serious gap in the literature. The political acceptability of market-based mechanisms for internalizing environmental externalities will depend heavily on their distributional implications. Whenever valuable property rights are created by legislation,[4] the associated allocation decisions are

---

[2] On efficiency implications in this context, see Robert N. Stavins, "Transactions Costs and Tradeable Permits," 29 *J. Envtl. Econ. & Mgmt.* 133 (1995).

[3] For related work, see Noll, supra note 1; Bruce A. Ackerman & William T. Hassler, *Clean Coal and Dirty Air* (1981); Robert W. Crandall, "An Acid Test for Congress?" 8 *Regulation* 21 (1984); Robert W. Hahn & Roger G. Noll, "Barriers to Implementing Tradeable Air Pollution Permits: Problems and Regulatory Interactions," 1 *Yale J. Reg.* 63 (1983); and B. Peter Pashigian, "The Effects of Environmental Regulation on Optimal Plant Size and Factor Shares," 27 *J. Law & Econ.* 1 (1984), and "Environmental Regulation: Whose Self-Interests Are Being Protected?" 23 *Econ. Inquiry* 551 (1985).

[4] Technically, the SO_2 allowances created by the 1990 CAAA are not property rights, since Congress can change the number of allowances issued or do away with them altogether without raising a constitutional claim for compensation (see Section 403(f) of the 1990 CAAA). In all other respects, however, allowances are treated as property rights. They are freely tradeable, a variety of market mechanisms are mediating transactions, and the EPA consciously allocated allowances to eligible parties for years beyond 2010 to provide confidence that they would be treated as durable property rights. All this would clearly make it politically difficult to alter allowance allocations in the future in response to new information about costs or benefits of reducing SO_2 emissions.

likely to be highly politicized in much the same way as tax legislation or appropriations bills.[5] Understanding better how the political process deals with such allocational issues can help us to design environmental programs that are both economically efficient and politically acceptable.

It is difficult to apply some of the tools of modern political economic analysis to complex legislation of this sort, particularly when there are no meaningful votes.[6] However, since allowances are homogeneous and can be traded and banked, the distributive implications are easy to quantify. In this case, the allocation of allowances is similar to the allocation of government funds through the legislative appropriations process.[7] The availability of detailed data on the initial allocation of allowances permits analysis of the incidence of individual legislative provisions, as well as analysis of winners and losers under alternative allowance allocation schemes.[8]

The next section provides a brief overview of the tradable SO_2 allowance program created by the 1990 CAAA. Section III reviews important aspects of earlier debates on legislation affecting SO_2 emissions. Section IV discusses the political development of the 1990 acid rain program. Section V examines the comparatively simple allocation of allowances in Phase I of that program, covering calendar years 1995 through 1999. Section VI discusses in more detail the provisions for allocating allowances in the first 10 years of Phase II, 2000–2009. Section VII compares distributional aspects and other features of the resulting allocation and of benchmark alternative allocation schemes. Section VIII presents the results of hypothetical votes by both Houses of Congress between actual and benchmark Phase II allocation patterns. Section IX employs regression analysis to relate differences between actual and benchmark patterns to a variety of variables designed to capture the influence of important interest groups, congressional leadership and committee influence, and state and national electoral politics. Section X presents a few concluding comments.

---

[5]Related research on congressional spending decisions has been performed by Lisa J. Kiel & Richard B. McKenzie, "The Impact of Tenure on the Flow of Federal Benefits to SMSAs," 41 *Pub. Choice* 285 (1983); David P. Baron, "Distributive Politics and the Persistence of Amtrak," 52 *J. Pol.* 883 (1989); and Steven D. Levitt & James M. Poterba, "Congressional Distributive Politics and State Economic Performance," *Pub. Choice* (in press).

[6]See Noll, supra note 1, at 1270–72, for a general discussion of the use of empirical voting models to test interest group theories of legislative politics; see also Joseph P. Kalt & Mark Zupan, "Capture and Ideology in the Economic Theory of Politics," 74 *Am. Econ. Rev.* 243 (1984); Pashigian, "Environmental Regulation," supra note 3; and Sam Peltzman, "How Efficient Is the Voting Market?" 33 *J. Law & Econ.* 27 (1990).

[7]See, for example, Levitt & Poterba, supra note 5, and the literature they discuss.

[8]We have data on the allocation of allowances to individual combustion units, each of which consists of a combustion device (boiler or turbine) used to power one or more generating units, each of which consists of a single electric generator. Most combustion units power a single generating unit, so our use of the term unit for the sake of brevity in what follows should cause no confusion. A generating plant often houses several generating units, which may be of different scales, vintages, or types.

II. The 1990 Acid Rain Program in Brief

Acid rain (or, more properly, acid deposition) occurs when sulfur dioxide (SO_2) and nitrogen oxides (NO_x) react in the atmosphere to form sulfuric and nitric acids, respectively.[9] These acids then fall to earth, sometimes hundreds of miles downwind from their source, in either wet or dry form. In North America, acid rain is a concern mainly in the northeast United States, particularly in the Adirondacks and New England, and in southeast Canada. It has been argued that in those areas acid rain damages aquatic life and harms trees in sensitive forest areas. The dominant precursor of acid rain in the United States is SO_2 from coal-fired and, to a much smaller extent, oil-fired power plants. These emissions are the focus of the tradable allowance program adopted in 1990.[10]

Title IV of the 1990 CAAA represents a fundamental change in the regulatory framework governing air pollution in the United States. Previous air pollution regulations focused on individual *sources*, their emission *rates*, and the application of specific *control technologies* to individual sources with certain attributes. The 1990 acid rain law, on the other hand, focuses on *aggregate* emission levels rather than individual sources, deals with the *emissions* of SO_2 rather than emissions rates, places an aggregate cap on SO_2 emissions, and gives polluters extensive flexibility in choosing whether and how to reduce emissions at specific sources. The importance of this change of approach goes well beyond the introduction of interutility trading. In particular, the 1990 law gave utilities with multiple fossil-fired generating units enormous and unprecedented flexibility in complying with emissions limits even if they traded no allowances at all with other utilities.

Title IV of the 1990 CAAA was advertised as requiring a 10 million ton per year reduction in SO_2 emissions from 1980 levels by the year 2000. To achieve this goal, the law created a cap on SO_2 emissions from electric generating plants of roughly 9 million tons per year, effective in the year 2000 and beyond. This emissions cap was to be achieved in two phases. During Phase I (1995 through 1999), the 261 dirtiest generating units (in 110 gen-

---

[9]U.S. General Accounting Office (GAO), *Allowance Trading Offers an Opportunity to Reduce Emissions at Less Cost*, at 13 (Report GAO/RCED-95-30, December 1994).

[10]Electric utilities accounted for about 70 percent of 1985 U.S. SO_2 emissions: coal-fired units accounted for 96 percent of this total, and oil-fired units accounted for the remainder; U.S. Environmental Protection Agency (EPA), *National Air Pollutant Emission Trends, 1900–1993* (Report EPA-454/R-94-027, October 1994). The other 30 percent of emissions is accounted for by a wide variety of industrial, commercial, and residential boilers and process sources (including smelters and paper facilities), as well as by the use of diesel fuel for transportation. Aside from certain voluntary opt-in provisions contained in the 1990 CAAA, including these other sources in the allowance program was not given serious consideration. These sources are generally individually much smaller than utility sources and are much more diverse. Moreover, there were no systematic "baseline" emissions data available for these sources to provide a basis for allocating allowances to incumbents. On this issue, see Nancy Kete, *The Politics of Markets: The Acid Rain Control Policy in the 1990 Clean Air Act Amendments*, 217–21 (unpublished Ph.D. dissertation, Johns Hopkins Univ., 1992).

erating plants) were required to reduce their emissions by roughly 3.5 million tons per year beginning in 1995.[11] In Phase II (2000 and beyond), virtually all fossil-fueled electric generating plants become subject to the national cap on aggregate annual SO_2 emissions. (All states had Phase II units except Idaho, which had no fossil-fueled generating units, Alaska, and Hawaii.)

The Phase I reductions and the Phase II cap were enforced through the annual issuance of tradable emissions allowances, each of which permits its holder to emit 1 ton of SO_2 in a particular year or any subsequent year.[12] Each unit has 30 days after the end of each year to deliver to EPA valid allowances sufficient to cover its emissions during the year. At that time the EPA cancels the allowances needed to cover emissions. Failure to produce the necessary allowances subjects the utility to substantial financial penalties and the need to make additional future emissions reductions. Allowances good in any particular year but not needed to cover SO_2 emissions in that year may be "banked" for future use. Owners of individual units are free to decide what mix of emissions reductions and allowance transactions they will employ to meet each year's allowance constraint, and essentially no restrictions are placed on emissions reduction techniques. There is also no restriction on who may buy or sell allowances. Brokers have acquired some in hopes of future price increases, for instance, and environmentalists have acquired some in order to reduce emissions more than the law requires.

The units subject to Phase I reductions were issued a total of roughly 5.7 million allowances for each of the 5 years included in Phase I. The basic allocation formula for each unit in Phase I involved multiplying an emissions rate (ER) of 2.5 pounds of SO_2 per million Btus of heat input times baseline heat input (generally the unit's 1985–87 average). As we discuss in Section V, however, there were significant departures from this formula in the final bill, the most important of which was designed to favor the use of eastern high-sulfur coal. Phase I obligations cannot be met by shifting electricity production from a Phase I unit to units not affected by Phase I.

During Phase II, each utility generating unit is allocated a specific number of SO_2 allowances per year out of the roughly 9 million per year made available for the entire country. (When various bonuses are taken into account, about 9.4 million allowances are available annually from 2000 until 2009, and 8.95 million tons are available annually thereafter.) The allocation rules for the years 2000–2009, which we analyze in detail below, are specified in about 30 statutory provisions. The provisions for 2010 and sub-

---

[11]These units are simply listed in table A of the 1990 law; they correspond to 263 combustion units. These units were selected because they had an emissions rate (ER) greater than 2.5 pounds of SO_2 per million. Btus of heat input and a nameplate capacity of at least 100 megawatts.

[12]In fact, these allowances are like checking account deposits; they exist only as records in the EPA's computer-based allowance tracking system. This system contains accounts for all affected generating units and for any other parties that want to hold allowances. It can be used to transfer allowances from one account to another.

sequent years are only slightly less complex. During Phase II, utilities can cover their emissions with the allowances they were allocated, can buy allowances, sell allowances, or bank allowances for future use. Any individual or firm is free to buy and sell allowances as well.

In addition to giving allowances to each generating unit, the EPA has conducted small annual revenue-neutral allowance auctions since 1993. The auctioned allowances are acquired by the EPA by holding back 2.8 percent of the allowances issued to each unit, and each unit in turn receives a pro rata share of the proceeds of the auction. The auction provision was a response to concerns by independent power producers and rapidly growing utilities that an active market for allowances would not emerge, concerns strengthened by assertions during debates on the 1990 CAAA that utilities would hoard their initial allocations and refuse to sell at any price.[13]

This type of flexible compliance mechanism requires an accurate method for measuring emissions and tracking allowances. Title IV requires utilities to install continuous emissions monitoring equipment, and the EPA's regulations contain powerful financial incentives to ensure that these monitors are operating accurately.

After the 1990 legislation was passed, EPA set up an Acid Rain Advisory Committee to assist it in developing the regulations required to implement Title IV and to provide advice on interpreting the statutory language. The EPA also created three internal teams to come to a consensus interpretation of the complex and interrelated allowance allocation provisions contained in Title IV. In order to record and defend its decisions, EPA documented the Phase II allocation methods in detail and produced the National Allowance Data Base (NADB) and Supplemental Data File (SDF).[14] The NADB and SDF are essentially large spreadsheets that display the calculations used to allocate allowances to each of 3,842 existing and planned electric units and, in order to do this, provide a good deal of unit-specific information from which allocations under alternative rules can be computed. These spreadsheets are the main source of data for the analysis that follows.

III. Historical Background on Federal Control of SO_2 Emissions

The structure of the 1990 acid rain program cannot be understood apart from the history of federal efforts to limit electric utility emissions of SO_2. The 1970 Clean Air Act Amendments, the first significant federal air pol-

---

[13]Until recently, some allowances were also held back for sale at a fixed price (which turned out to be well above market prices); any excess supply was later auctioned. Karl Hausker, "The Politics and Economics of Auction Design in the Market for Sulfur Dioxide Pollution," 11 *J. Pol'y Anal. & Mgmt.* 553 (1992), discusses the political economy of these institutions; Paul J. Joskow, Richard Schmalensee, & Elizabeth M. Bailey, "The Market for Sulfur Dioxide Emissions," *Am. Econ. Rev.* (in press).

[14]U.S. Environmental Protection Agency (EPA), Acid Rain Division, *Technical Documentation for Phase II Allowance Allocations* (March 1993).

lution legislation, led to the establishment of national maximum standards for ambient concentrations of SO_2. States were largely responsible for meeting these standards in each local area. The 1970 Amendments also imposed a new source performance standard (NSPS) applicable only to emissions from *new* power plants, which took effect in 1971. According to the NSPS, the emissions rate (ER) for new coal plants could not exceed 1.2 pounds of sulfur dioxide per million Btus of fuel burned (0.8 pounds/mmBtu for oil). These regulations created a significant gap between the emissions rates of many existing plants and the rates permitted for new plants, thus providing a strong incentive to extend the lives of old, dirty plants.[15] Furthermore, in order to help meet the local ambient SO_2 standards, the states required some existing and new power plants to have high smokestacks to disperse emissions over a wider area. By keeping SO_2 in the atmosphere longer, however, tall stacks may increase ambient concentrations at other locations. They also generally encourage the formation of sulfates and sulfuric acid and thus increase the total amount of acid deposition, which may affect geographic areas hundreds of miles away.

Congress next amended the Clean Air Act in 1977. Ambient concentrations of SO_2 were again the focus of attention; acid rain was still not an issue. The political solution that emerged from the 1977 legislation and subsequent EPA rule making satisfied environmentalists, high-sulfur coal interests, and Midwestern utilities.[16] It required coal-fired plants built after 1978 both to meet the ER ≤ 1.2 constraint *and* either (a) to remove 90 percent of potential SO_2 emissions (as determined by the sulfur content of the fuel burned) or (b) to remove 70 percent of potential SO_2 emissions and to operate with ER < 0.6. This "percent reduction" standard required all new coal plants to operate with flue gas desulfurization facilities—generally referred to as "scrubbers"—even if they burned low-sulfur coal.[17] This provision significantly reduced the advantage of low-sulfur coal as a means of compliance and effectively imposed a lower emissions rate on new sources in the West than in the East. As Ackerman and Hassler have stressed, this provision gave environmentalists the tighter NSPS they sought, but it raised the costs of SO_2 control and may well have dirtied the

---

[15]Pre-1970 plants were still subject to controls under State Implementation Plans (SIPs) required by the Clean Air Act to ensure that each state came into compliance with national ambient air quality standards. There was wide variation among the states in the aggressiveness of their SIPs and how they affected existing plants.

[16]For more on this episode, see Ackerman & Hassler, supra note 3, Kete, supra note 10, at 158–59; Richard E. Cohen, *Washington at Work: Back Rooms and Clean Air* (1992), ch. 2; and Paul L. Joskow & Richard Schmalensee, "The Political Economy of Market-Based Environmental Policy: The U.S. Acid Rain Program" (MIT Ctr. for Energy & Environmental Policy Res., Working Paper 96-003, March 1996), Section 3.

[17]Oil-fired units built after 1978 also had to meet the 1971 ER constraint (ER ≤ 0.8) and to remove 90 percent of potential emissions; they faced no percent reduction requirement if ER < 0.2, however. To avoid simply sending SO_2 emissions long distances downwind, the 1977 legislation sharply limited the use of tall smokestacks as a compliance strategy.

air on balance by encouraging utilities to burn high-sulfur coal and by strengthening incentives to extend the lives of old, dirty plants.[18] It is also generally viewed as a victory for high-sulfur coal producers and miners, since the scrubbing provisions reduced what would otherwise have been a very significant economic disadvantage for high-sulfur coal. Conversely, of course, Appalachian and, to a lesser extent, Western producers of low-sulfur coal lost. This legislation was viewed as a victory for most Midwestern and Northeastern coal-burning utilities and their customers, since old plants generally remained relatively lightly controlled,[19] and slow economic growth meant there was little need to build new plants meeting the NSPS.[20] The big losers were those states, mainly in the West, that were using nearby low-sulfur coal and growing rapidly. Scrubbing effectively required these states to engage in costly cleanup of what was already clean coal and to bear a disproportionate share of cleanup costs because they were building a disproportionate share of new fossil-fueled capacity.

Total U.S. emissions of SO_2 peaked in the early 1970s and declined steadily during the 1980s. The focus of Clean Air Act regulation on new generating units, however, served to extend the economic lives of old, dirty plants that were not burdened with significant control costs. As a consequence of this "new-source bias," by 1985 83 percent of power plant SO_2 emissions came from generating units not meeting the 1971 NSPS, and 63 percent were from units with ER $\geq$ 2.5.[21] By 1990, over two-thirds of acid rain precursors emitted by power plants were emitted by plants constructed before 1970s.[22]

Table 1 shows that there were huge interstate differences in aggregate and per capita emissions in the mid-1980s. Differences in per capita emissions reflected differences in the amount of electricity generation per capita (largely reflecting differences in economic and industrial structures), in the use of coal of various types (reflecting accidents of geography and history), and in the vintages of generating plants in use. Per capita emissions tended to be highest in Midwestern states that had grown relatively little since 1970 and that are located near high-sulfur coal deposits. Emissions tended to be lowest in states that had new power plants and had made relatively little use of coal.

---

[18]Ackerman & Hassler, supra note 3.

[19]Controls had been imposed on some old plants by state environmental agencies in order to meet ambient SO_2 standards. The stringency of these controls varied greatly, however, and they were rarely if ever as strict as the NSPS standard. Nonetheless, in part because of these controls, utility SO_2 emissions declined steadily after the mid-1970s, despite increased coal consumption.

[20]In the late 1970s, the technology of choice for meeting incremental generating capacity needs in the East, the South, and portions of the Midwest was nuclear power.

[21]These statistics were calculated using the National Allowance Data Base, described above. As noted above, Phase I covered only large units with ER $\geq$ 2.5.

[22]Kete, supra note 10, at 118.

Table 1 Highest and Lowest Baseline SO$_2$ Emissions per Capita

Pounds/ Capita	Thousands of Tons	State	Pounds/ Capita	Thousands of Tons	State
1,029.5	962.5	West Virginia	53.6	42.7	Utah*
550.9	1,519.7	Indiana	53.5	82.7	Colorado*
548.4	126.7	Wyoming*	52.6	151.3	Virginia
439.3	806.6	Kentucky	44.6	396.8	New York
427.8	138.2	North Dakota	41.8	16.6	Montana*
425.6	2,303.1	Ohio	38.1	60.9	Connecticut
381.7	957.4	Missouri	32.5	68.5	Louisiana*
347.4	1,037.1	Georgia	27.9	62.8	Washington
341.0	807.2	Tennessee	25.9	97.8	New Jersey
281.0	557.5	Alabama	20.7	12.2	Maine
221.8	69.9	Delaware	6.8	3.3	Rhode Island*
197.9	1,174.7	Pennsylvania	4.3	1.3	District of Columbia
177.3	1,013.2	Illinois	.7	.9	Oregon
155.5	373.1	Wisconsin	.6	.2	Vermont*
143.0	72.6	New Hampshire	.5	6.8	California*

Note: Emissions per capita are baseline sulfur dioxide emissions in pounds (from the National Allowance Data Base) divided by the average of 1980 and 1990 population. Baseline emissions for generating units operating in 1985 are generally the product of each unit's 1985 emission rate and its average 1985–87 fuel consumption. Emissions in thousands of tons are baseline generating unit sulfur dioxide emissions in thousands of tons (from the National Allowance Data Base). All states with emissions of 500,000 tons or more are shown except for Florida (635.2) and Texas (641.5). The only state with emissions of 50,000 tons or less not shown is South Dakota (25.8).
*Designated as a "Clean State" under sec. 406 of the 1990 CAAA because baseline average emissions rate (ER) from fossil fuel-fired steam generating units did not exceed 0.8 pounds per million Btu. "Clean States" not shown, with per capital emissions in parentheses, are the following: Arizona (70.50), Arkansas (63.55), Nevada (112.92), New Mexico (101.99), Oklahoma (60.66), and Texas (82.81).

IV. Federal Acid Rain Legislation[23]

Acid rain gradually emerged as a serious environmental and political issue only after 1977 because of pressures from environmental groups, Northeastern states, and, especially, Canadian objections to transborder pollution flows, arising from concerns about the effects of acidic deposition on property, trees, and aquatic life.[24] Many acid rain bills were proposed by

---

[23]Joskow & Schmalensee, supra note 16, treat this history in more depth.

[24]On the early history of this issue, see Ackerman 7 Hassler, supra note 3, at 66; U.S. General Accounting Office (GAO), *An Analysis of Issues Concerning "Acid Rain"* (Report GAO/RCED-85-13, December 1984); and Joseph A. Davis, "Acid Rain to Get Attention as Reagen Changes Course," *Cong. Q.*, March 22, 1986, at 675. To help resolve scientific disputes about the damages caused by acid rain, Congress created the National Acid Precipitation Assessment Program (NAPAP), which spent about $600 million through the end of 1990 (NAPAP, 1989 Annual Report to the President and Congress 7 (June 1990). Its work had no visible effect on the 1990 legislative debates, however; see Leslie Roberts, "Learning from an Acid Rain Program," 251 *Science* 1392 (1991), and "Acid Rain Program: Mixed Review," 252 *Science* 1302 (1991). Among the reasons offered for NAPAP's lack of impact are its focus on "good science" instead of policy-relevant analysis and its lack of political support from the environmental community.

Western and Northeastern senators and representatives during the 1980s.[25] This legislation generally called for reductions of from 6 to 12 million tons of SO_2 emissions per year from 1980 levels, targeted the dirtiest generating units for cleanup, and often involved some variant of the ER ≤ 1.2 constraint that had been applied to new units since 1971. In part because costs of cleanup varied considerably among existing units, these proposals often provided for more flexibility than traditional command and control regulation by, for instance, applying emissions limits at the state level rather than unit by unit.[26] Because the costs of these control strategies would have been heavily concentrated in a few Midwestern states, and projections suggested that electric rates there would have to rise significantly to cover those costs, some of the proposals included a national electricity tax to help to pay for cleanup costs and to "share the pain." Some proposals included mandatory scrubbing, while others did not.

During the 1980s, Midwestern and Appalachian high-sulfur coal-producing states generally opposed *any* new acid rain controls, while Western and Northeastern states opposed both a national electricity tax and any additional scrubbing requirements. Acid rain legislation was effectively blocked in the House by John Dingell (D-Mich.), who became chairman of the powerful House Energy and Commerce Committee in 1981. His main concern was that any legislation amending the Clean Air Act would likely tighten auto emission standards significantly, and he accordingly blocked all such legislation.[27] In the Senate, acid rain legislation was effectively blocked by the majority leader, Robert Byrd (D-W.Va.). West Virginia, with high per capita emissions of SO_2 and high production of high-sulfur coal burned in other states, was potentially a big loser from acid rain legislation. Completing the constellation of major "Just Say No!" forces on acid rain was President Ronald Reagan, who opposed environmental regulation generally.[28]

The political strength of the environmental movement grew dramatically as the decade of the 1980s proceeded, fueled in part by the Reagan administration's apparent intransigence.[29] Population continued to shift to

---

[25]See Cohen, supra note 15, at 36–44; Robert Hanley, "Turning Off Acid Rain at the Source," *N.Y. Times*, December 11, 1983, at A12; Robert W. Crandall, "Air Pollution, Environmentalists, and the Coal Lobby," in *The Political Economy of Deregulation: Interest Groups in the Regulatory Process* (Roger G. Noll & Bruce M. Owen eds. 1983); and the following pages in the indicated annual numbers of the *Congressional Quarterly Almanac*: 1982, at 425–34; 1983, at 340–41; 1984, at 340–42; 1986, at 137; 1987, at 299–301; 1988, at 142–48.

[26]E. H. Pechan & Associates, *Comparison of Acid Rain Control Bills* (EPA Contract No. 68-WA-0038, Work Assignments 94 and 116, OTA Contract Ls-5480.0, November 1989), compare six contemporary acid rain proposals.

[27]See, for instance, Cohen, supra note 16, at 29–32.

[28]Crandall, supra note 3, discusses other obstacles to assembling a winning pro-control coalition during the 1980s.

[29]The Sierra Club's membership increased more than sixfold between 1980 and 1990 (personal communication with Club officials), and the share of respondents agreeing with the following statement increased from 45 percent to 80 percent between 1981 and 1989 (Roberto Suro, "Concern for the Environment," *N.Y. Times*, July 2, 1989, at A1): "Protecting the environment is so important that requirements and standards cannot be too high, and continuing environmental improvements must be made regardless of cost."

the West and South, and the number of high-sulfur coal miners dwindled as high-sulfur coal production fell and productivity improved dramatically.[30] The 1988 presidential election was won by George Bush, who had promised to be "the Environmental President" and had advocated looking "to the marketplace for innovative solutions" to environmental problems. George Mitchell (D-Maine), an ardent proponent of acid rain controls, succeeded Robert Byrd as Senate majority leader. Even before Bush's inauguration, staff at EPA, in the vice president's office, and elsewhere in the executive branch began work on a set of proposed amendments to the Clean Air Act that would deal with acid rain, as well as toxic air pollutants, urban smog, and other air quality issues.[31] Work on acid rain was heavily influenced by an emissions-trading proposal that had been circulated during 1988 by the Environmental Defense Fund (EDF). Though there were concerns about both the workability of the EDF proposal and the size of the emissions reductions it required (12 million tons from 1980 levels), relying on tradable permits to control acid rain would respond to Bush's call to look "to the marketplace" and could reduce control costs. Moreover, it was hoped that EDF's support would provide protection against knee-jerk antimarket attacks from other environmental groups. While some EPA staff clearly preferred traditional command and control methods, strong support developed within the agency, and the basic idea of using tradable permits to control acid rain was adopted by the Bush administration without much internal warfare.

The administration's Clean Air proposal was announced in general terms in June 1989, and draft legislation was released the following month. In the House, the administration's bill went to the Committee on Energy and Commerce, still chaired by John Dingell (D-Mich.). The acid rain Title was sent to the Subcommittee on Energy and Power, chaired by Philip Sharp (D-Ind.). Indiana had large emissions from old dirty plants, and while Sharp had earlier joined in supporting some modest acid rain control proposals, he opposed stringent controls targeted at existing plants without significant cost sharing with other regions. He had advocated paying for acid rain abatement through a national electricity tax.

On the Senate side, the administration's bill went to the Subcommittee on Environmental Protection, chaired by Max Baucus (D-Mont.), of the Committee on Environment and Public Works, chaired by Quentin Burdick (D-N.Dak.). Fifteen of the 16 members of the full committee were also members of the Environmental Protection Subcommittee, and Burdick was not much interested in environmental policy, so all the action was in the Baucus subcommittee. Montana, a state that both produces and uses low-sulfur coal, was one of the losers in the 1977 amendments.

---

[30]Between 1980 and 1990, the average daily employment of miners in Eastern mines (both high-sulfur and low-sulfur) fell from 202,039 to 115,216 (Coal Data (National Coal Association, various years)).

[31]For a contemporary view of this process, see Margaret E. Kriz, "Politics in the Air" Nat'l J., May 6, 1989, at 1098.

The Senate and House committees differed substantially in regional composition and support for environmental legislation.[32] Five of 16 senators on Environment and Public Works were from New England, where concerns about acid rain were high. On the House side, however, New Englanders were outnumbered 41 to 2 on Energy and Commerce. While the Senate committee had representation from neither the states with the highest SO_2 emissions nor the largest Eastern coal-producing states, these states were well represented on Energy and Commerce. Only 31 percent of the senators on Environment and Public Works were from states with (old, dirty) Phase I plants, as compared to 56 percent of representatives on Energy and Commerce. As one might expect, the Senate committee had members who were substantially more inclined to support environmental legislation than their counterparts in the House.

In mid-November, after four days of debate and one day of markup, the Senate Committee on Environment and Public Works approved Clean Air legislation written by its staff by a 15–1 vote.[33] The president threatened to veto the committee's bill unless its costs were reduced substantially, and the bill was poorly received on the Senate floor. In an attempt to produce acceptable legislation, the majority leader, Senator Mitchell, convened a set of closed door sessions involving senators and administration officials beginning in early February. These meetings were open to all senators and their staffs, and states with large stakes in the acid rain Title were well represented when it was discussed.

The Senate negotiators modified the administration's relatively simple rules for determining Phase II allowance endowments. They also brought forward the starting dates of both phases by a year, thus producing greater emissions reductions in 1995 and 2000 than the administration's proposal.[34] In response to efforts by Robert Byrd (D-W.Va.) and other senators from states producing high-sulfur coal, the incremental 1995 reductions were given back as "bonus" allowances for utilities that installed scrubbers rather than switching to low-sulfur coal in Phase I. The incremental reductions in 2000 were given back over the 2000–2009 period through a number of provisions.

---

[32]Joskow & Schmalensee, supra note 16, provide more on the points in this paragraph.

[33]At the insistence of Alan Simpson (R-Wyo.), representing a state that both produced and burned large quantities of low-sulfur coal, the committee bill contained a provision purporting to repeal the "percent reduction" provision of the 1977 amendments. This provision was retained in the final legislation, and the EPA was given 3 years to produce a new NSPS. As of January 1998, however, it had not yet done so. The repeal provision requires that any new NSPS allow no unit to emit more than it would have been allowed to emit under the 1978 NSPS. But this requirement is a "Catch-22," since the 1978 NSPS always requires that emissions be less than the sulfur content of the coal burned (the essence of "percent removal"). Thus the only way to ensure that a unit emits no more than it would have been allowed to emit under the 1978 NSPS is to install a scrubber! In addition, we are told that state regulations effectively require scrubbing in areas where new coal-fired plants have been built, so that there has not been strong industry pressure to revise the 1978 NSPS.

[34]See Kete, supra note 10, at 210.

A major issue in these negotiations and, after an agreement between the administration and the Senate leadership was unveiled in early March 1990, on the Senate floor was the so-called Byrd Amendment. This provision would have provided generous financial aid to high-sulfur coal miners whose jobs were eliminated by Clean Air legislation. The administration and the Senate leadership opposed this amendment and prevailed by a single vote.[35]

The bill subsequently developed in the House also modified the administration's simple allocation rules, but it retained the original administration start dates and ceilings for Phase I and Phase II.[36] Like the Senate bill, it provided incentives for scrubbing. A provision authorizing unemployment and job-training benefits for displaced workers was added on the House floor; it was not restricted to miners and had a much smaller price tag than the Byrd Amendment.

The acid rain Title produced by the conference committee was based mainly on the Senate bill, while the House prevailed on most of the rest of the legislation.[37] A relatively small provision for aiding displaced workers (Title XI) based on the House bill was added,[38] and the Senate's provisions for allocating allowances were modified.

The provisions of the law allocating allowances in Phase I remained fairly simply, but 8 dense pages of about 30 complex and convoluted provisions were developed to govern Phase II allocations. In order to ensure that the intended constraints on *total* Phase II emissions were satisfied in the face of a rising tide of proposed special interest provisions, work on

[35]For discussions of this episode, see Richard E. Cohen, "When Titans Clash on Clean Air," *Nat'l J.*, April 7, 1990, at 849; and Phil Kuntz & George Hager, "Showdown on Clean-Air Bill: Senate Says "No" to Byrd," *Cong. Q.*, March 31, 1990, at 983. Senator Byrd called on longstanding relationships with his Democratic colleagues and on his power as chairman of the Appropriations Committee, and Democrats voted with him (and against the Senate leadership) 38 to 16. In addition, all Republicans from Midwestern and Appalachian coal-producing states voted for the Byrd Amendment, except for Senator Warner (R-Va.), despite strong administration and Republican leadership opposition. Finally, Senators Cochrane (R-Miss.) and McClure (R-Idaho) voted for the Byrd Amendment, and thus against both the White House and the Republican Senate leadership, even though they represented no high-sulfur coal miners. Senator Symms (R-Idaho) was talked out of doing likewise only in the last minute of voting. Given that these three senators were in the bottom 20 in terms of the AFL-CIO's evaluations of lifetime voting records, it seems unlikely that they were casting prolabor votes for ideological reasons. Strategic motives are suggested by the facts that these three senators were in the bottom 10 in terms of the League of Conservation Voters' ratings of 1989–90 voting records and that the president had threatened to veto any legislation containing the Byrd Amendment. It is most plausible that these senators hoped that passage of the Byrd Amendment would force the president to carry out his veto threat and thus likely kill new clean air legislation.

[36]For a detailed comparison of the acid rain provisions of the House and Senate bills, see ICF Resources, Inc. (ICF), *Comparison of the Economic Impacts of the Acid Rain Provisions of the Senate Bill (S. 1630) and the House Bill (S. 1630)* (draft report prepared for the U.S. Environmental Protection Agency, July 1990).

[37]See Cohen, supra note 15, ch. 10; and Alyson Pytte, "A Decade's Acrimony Lifted in the Glow of Clean Air," *Cong. Q.*, October 27, 1990, at 3587.

[38]Of the total authorization of $250 million, less than $29 million had been spent for all displaced workers as of May 1995 (telephone interview, Employment and Training Administration, U.S. Department of Labor).

the Senate/administration bill had quickly incorporated an overarching "ratchet" provision. This provision, which was not controversial and was retained in the final legislation, in effect said that at the end of the day total allocations under (almost) all other provisions would be scaled down to a specified total.[39] This provision had the effect of making negotiations about allowance allocations into a zero-sum game. It also implied that, all else equal, benefits from rules changes that would *decrease* somebody else's allowances would be widely shared. Thus, at least in the negotiations that led up to the passage of the Senate bill, debates about allowance allocations were conducted primarily in terms of proposed rules for *increasing* particular allocations, which were typically supported by arguments about fairness under autarchy.

V. Phase I Allowance Allocations

Table A of the 1990 CAAA lists the Phase I units and specifies allowances to be allocated to each. Eight of these units were added to table A before the Senate bill was passed in April. Though these additions were justified by technical corrections to earlier work, it is interesting that five of the eight units, accounting for 84 percent of the allowances allocated to these units, were located in Minnesota, New York, and Wisconsin. The two Wisconsin units had been retired in 1988, so that adding them to Phase I clearly made their owners better off by the value of the allowances they were given. Since all three of these states had significant acid rain legislation on the books by 1990, adding the Minnesota and New York units to Phase I *and* using their 1985 emissions rates to determine their allowance allocations probably made the owners of these units better off as well.

Most commentators describe the annual table A allowance allocations as equal to emissions (in tons) from baseline fuel use and an ER of 2.5 pounds per million Btus.[40] The EPA's NADB reveals that this formula is only approximately correct. Moreover, table A does not fully describe the Phase I allocations. The table A allocations differ by more than 1 percent from those produced by applying this formula to the NADB data, which we will call the *Basic Rule*, in 44 cases. The absolute value of the differ-

---

[39]When the EPA figured out the allocations required by the statute in 1992, the ratchet's operation reduced Phase II allowances by about 9.6 percent from the total implied by strict application of the other allocation provisions in the bill. The "ratchet" had the effect of reducing annual Phase II "basic" allowances from 9.876 to 8.90 million tons and thus, if "bonus" allowances are taken as fixed, of reducing total annual allowances allocated in the first 10 years of Phase II from 10.115 to 9.139 million tons (EPA, supra note 14, at 5). The large size of the "ratchet" announced in early 1992 was a great surprise to those involved in the process, most of whom had expected a ratchet of less than 5 percent.

[40]See, for instance, Reinier Lock & Dennis P. Harkawik, eds., *The New Clean Air Act: Compliance and Opportunity*, at 24 (1991).

ence exceeded 1,000 allowances per year for 17 units.[41] Most, but not all, of these differences reflect departures from the administration's original table A proposal. In large part, at least, these differences reflect the fact that the NADB contains more recent data than those employed in computations underlying table A.

Table 2 shows that at the state level, the table A allocations of Wisconsin, Indiana, and Missouri are well above those implied by the 2.5 ton/mmBtu Basic Rule, while Pennsylvania's is noticeably lower. The third

Table 2 Phase I Allowance Allocations by State

State	Basic Rule	Table A Difference	Bonuses	Final Allocation	Absolute/% Difference from Rescaled Basic Rule	Extension Allowances
Alabama	230,947	−7	0	230,940	−10,381/−4.30	3,428
Florida	129,792	3,338	0	133,130	−2,492/−1.84	33,248
Georgia	581,599	1	0	581,600	−26,123/−4.30	0
Illinois	353,191	4,709	36,356	394,256	25,201/6.83	0
Indiana	640,855	9,485	66,724	717,064	47,424/7.08	104,323
Iowa	37,555	2,735	1,350	41,640	2,398/6.11	0
Kansas	4,226	−6	0	4,220	−196/−4.44	0
Kentucky	278,637	−387	0	278,250	−12,903/−4.43	82,857
Maryland	140,066	−526	0	139,540	−6,818/−4.66	7,110
Michigan	42,334	6	0	42,340	−1,896/−4.29	0
Minnesota	4,409	−139	0	4,270	−337/−7.32	0
Mississippi	54,609	1	0	54,610	−2,452/−4.30	0
Missouri	345,101	7,889	0	352,990	−7,612/−2.11	0
New Hampshire	32,207	−17	0	32,190	−1,463/−4.35	0
New Jersey	20,811	−31	0	20,780	−966/−4.44	6,242
New York	147,393	3,587	0	150,980	−3,034/−1.97	11,673
Ohio	863,191	89	96,920	960,200	58,237/6.46	167,442
Pennsylvania	536,121	−1,981	0	534,140	−26,063/−4.65	76,441
Tennessee	386,183	247	0	386,430	−17,100/−4.24	111,374
West Virginia	496,528	1,342	0	497,870	−20,961/−4.04	96,131
Wisconsin	130,004	13,376	0	143,380	7,356/5.55	0
Total	5,455,761	43,709	201,350	5,700,820	0/.0	700,000

Note: Basic Rule allocations are computed by multiplying an emission rate of 2.5 times baseline fuel consumption, in tons. The Table A Difference is the difference between the table A and Basic Rule allocations. Bonuses are from sec. 404(h) for the George Neal North unit 1 in Iowa and from sec. 404(a)(3) for units in Illinois, Indiana, and Ohio. The second to last column is the final allocation minus (Basic Rule rescaled to same total)/that difference expressed as a percentage of rescaled Basic Rule. The final column gives annual average Phase 1 extension allowances received, from sec. 404(d), after reallocations among utilities.

---

[41]This does not count large, almost exactly offsetting differences for units 1 and 2 of Georgia Power's Bowen plant. These differences seem almost certain to reflect some sort of error or the correction of another sort of error.

column of Table 2 also shows the effects of two "bonus" provisions: Section 404(h), which affected one unit in Iowa, and Section 404(a)(3), which affected all units in Illinois, Indiana, and Ohio except for three plants that sell mainly to Department of Energy uranium-processing plants.[42] This latter provision was added in response to Midwestern pressures for some form of cost sharing—with care taken not to allocate valuable allowances to plants that sold electricity under cost plus arrangements back to federal facilities. It is worth noting as well that representatives from Indiana and Illinois were chairman and ranking member, respectively, of key House subcommittees. Ohio had the highest total emissions of any state in the country, and two representatives on the House Energy and Power Subcommittee, one of whom (Thomas Luken, D) had been heavily involved in debates over acid rain legislation proposed earlier in the 1980s.

The second to last column in Table 2 shows a comparison of the Final Allocation in the 1990 law with the Basic Rule allocation scaled up to a total of 5,700,820 tons. None of the differences exceed 10 percent of the Basic Rule benchmark, but at an expected price of $200/ton, a thousand-ton annual difference corresponds to a million dollars a year. The positive differences (gains) are much more concentrated than the negative differences (losses); the top three gainers (Ohio, Indiana, and Illinois) accounted for 93 percent of total gains, while the top three losers (Georgia, Pennsylvania, and West Virginia) accounted for 52 percent of the losses. Only four states have positive differences in excess of 5,000 tons per year, while eight states have negative differences of that magnitude.

One hypothesis that explains some of these differences is that the states that burned more coal than they produced, including Indiana and Ohio, focused their attention on acquiring additional allowances, while the states that produced more than they burned, including Pennsylvania and West Virginia, focused their attention on providing incentives for scrubbing and direct financial benefits for displaced coal miners. However, Georgia, which produced no coal, and Illinois, which produced about twice as much as it burned in 1990, conspicuously fail to fit this pattern.[43]

---

[42]Hausker, supra note 13, at 567, notes that the Midwest bonus provision, added late in conference, was the single breach in the zero-sum barrier imposed by the ratchet provision. A third bonus provision, Section 404(e), would provide Phase I allowances to Union Electric in Missouri and Phase II allowances to both Union Electric and Duke Power. Because of pending litigation, however, no allowances had been issued under this provision by late 1995. Only about 4,000 allowances had been allocated under a final bonus provision, Section 404(f), which rewards using conservation or renewable energy to reduce emissions.

[43]Both states had high total emissions and high emissions rates. Georgia had no representation on the Senate Committee on Environment and Public Works or the Senate leadership. On the House side it had nobody on the House Energy and Power Subcommittee and only one junior member (J. Roy Rowland, D) on the full Energy and Commerce Committee. It was represented on the House leadership by the Minority Whip (Newt Gingrich, R). Illinois also had no well-placed representation on the Senate side, but it had the ranking member of the Health and Environment Subcommittee (Edward Madigan, R), a member of both involved subcommittees (Terry Bruce, D), and a third member of the full committee (Cardiss Collins, D). As we discuss below, Georgia fared poorly in both Phase I and Phase II, while Illinois fared well in both phases. Illinois would have appeared to have done even better in Phase I if Illinois Power had applied for scrubber extension allowances, as had been expected when Title IV was being debated.

The last column in Table 2 shows the effects of a final important Phase I provision. In response to pressure from high-sulfur coal states, 3.5 million allowances (the "gain" from moving the start of Phase I from 1996 to 1995) were set aside to encourage the use of "technology" (that is, scrubbers) as an emissions reduction technique in preference to fuel switching. The main beneficiaries of this provision were utilities in Ohio, Tennessee, Indiana, and West Virginia and the high-sulfur coal interests in these and nearby states.[44]

Even though the Phase I allowance allocations have generally been described as following a simple rule, it is clear that the actual allocations were significantly influenced by special interest rent seeking. In addition to the differences between the table A allocations and those implied by the Basic Rule, large special allocations of allowances were given to three of the five states with the highest SO_2 emissions (see Table 1): Ohio, Indiana, and Illinois. All three also had substantial high-sulfur coal mining interests. Pennsylvania, West Virginia, and Kentucky, which had both relatively high aggregate emissions and more important high-sulfur mining interests, were not covered by this special provision. However, these six states plus Tennessee (with emissions just above Kentucky's but few high-sulfur miners) acquired almost all the bonus allowances made available to Phase I units that chose to reduce emissions by scrubbing. Georgia, number 4 in emissions, benefited from neither the special allocation nor the scrubber bonus.

This pattern suggests that Phase I allowances were used partially to compensate three of the high emissions states that were well represented on the key committees. Phase I allowances were also used to subsidize scrubbers in response to high-sulfur coal-mining interests. There is some evidence that the states with important coal-mining interests focused more on increasing scrubber allowances than on securing earmarked allowances. Georgia, which was not represented on the relevant committees, did particularly badly overall in the Phase I allowance allocation process.

VI. Statutory Provisions for Phase II Allocations

Calculations of a generating unit's Phase II allowance allocations generally begin with "baseline" emissions, determined by the recorded emissions rate for 1985 and average heat input from fuel burned during 1985–87.[45] The

---

[44]Again, Georgia got nothing out of the scrubber bonus allowances, but it also had no high-sulfur coal miners to protect. Illinois miners benefited from the scrubbing incentives, and it was generally expected in 1990 that Illinois utilities would apply for a large number of extension allowances. Illinois Power eventually decided not to install scrubbers because its regulators refused to preapprove such investments for rate-making purposes. Illinois Power then became an important early purchaser of allowances.

[45]Special provisions were included for units that were not in operation in 1985 or were still under construction in 1990 when the Act was passed. Emissions rates for 1985 were used in all other cases because NAPAP (see note 24 supra) had constructed particularly good emissions data for that year.

simple rule at the core of Phase II allocates allowances equal to each unit's baseline fuel use times the lesser of its actual 1985 emissions rate and 1.2 pounds of SO_2 per million Btu, expressed in tons. The statute contains over 30 individual provisions that specify exactly how Phase II allowances are to be allocated. These rules fall into three general categories.

The first category contains provisions that specify variations from the simple rule above based on fuel type, unit age, unit capacity, and capacity utilization during the base period. These allocation rules were generally advertised as dealing with various "technical issues" associated with the fuel and operating attributes of units in these categories during the base period. These rules include special provisions for units that operated at low capacity factors during the baseline period due to mechanical problems or unusually low demand along with special allocations for small coal plants for which control options were particularly limited and costly. Other "technical arguments" supporting, for example, a special allocation for units that happened to burn lots of gas during the baseline period because gas prices were unusually low during that time, are more difficult to accept as being "non-political." As we show below, the allocation rules in this first category generally shift allowances from relatively dirty states to relatively clean states, especially those with oil/gas generating units.

The second category of allocation rules consists of those rules that are narrowly focused on special interests—either individual states or individual utilities. Table 3 provides the clearest examples. This table was developed by categorizing all Phase II units by applicable allocation rules and then searching for rules that appeared to be narrowly focused on a single state or a small number of generating units. Table 3 should remove any doubt that interest group politics was at work in the development of the U.S. acid rain program. Some of these provisions are clearly the work of influential legislators. Senator Burdick used his chairmanship of the Committee on Environment and Public Works to ensure that his constituents in North Dakota got special allocations for the lignite-fired units that generate electricity there by inserting Section 405(b)(3). In addition, Congressman Dingell seems to have provided regulatory relief for Detroit Edison through Section 405(I)(2).

It is more difficult to relate some of the other provisions in Table 3 directly to well-positioned congressmen from the states that benefited from them. Florida was not represented in the leadership of either House or Senate, and Senator Bob Graham (D-Fla.) and Congressman Michael Bilirakis (R-Fla.) were the only Floridians on the relevant committees. Nonetheless, Senator Graham managed to secure thousands of incremental allowances for Florida through Section 405(I)(1).[46] Section 405(c)(3) originated in the

---

[46]See Kete, supra note 10, at 207–10. The impact of this provision is capped in the statute at 40,000 allowances annually. Florida may have been treated well in part because it was a large state with competitive races for both senator and governor in prospect for the fall of 1990. (See Table 8 below for the definition of "competitive" used here.) At least one of the other Florida-specific provisions in Table 3 was added to the Senate bill at the insistence of the Republican leadership to give Florida's other senator, Connie Mack (R), something for which he could also claim credit.

Table 3 Incidence of Selected Special Phase II (2000–2009) Provisions

Section	Coverage	No. of Units, States (Systems) Affected	
404(h)	Phase I units 1990 ER < 1.0, ≥60% ER drop since 1980; system ER < 1.0	1	Iowa (Iowa Public Service)
405(b)(3)	Large lignite units with ER ≥ 1.2 in a state with no nonattainment areas	5	North Dakota
405(b)(4)	State has >30 million KW capacity; unit barred from oil use, switched to coal between 1/1/80 and 12/31/85	4	Florida (Tampa Electric)
405(c)(3)	Small unit, ER ≥ 1.2, on line before 12/31/65; system fossil steam capacity >250 MW and <450 MW, fewer than 78,000 customers	2	Missouri (City of Springfield)
405(c)(5)	Small units with ER ≥ 1.2; systems >20% scrubbed, rely on small units, have large units expensive to scrub	23	Ohio (Ohio Edison), Pennsylvania (Pennsylvania Power)
405(d)(5)	Oil/gas units awarded a clean coal technology grant as of 1/1/91	1	Florida (City of Tallahassee)
405(f)(2)	Operated by a utility providing electricity, steam, and natural gas to a city and one contiguous county; or state authority serving same area	48	New York (Consolidated Edison, Power Authority of the State of New York)
405(g)(5)	Units converted from gas to coal between 1/1/85 and 12/31/87 with proposed or final prohibition order	3	Arizona (Tucson Electric), New York (Orange & Rockland Utilities)
405(I)(1)	States with >25% population growth 1980–88 and 1988 electric generating capacity >30 million KW	134	Florida
405(I)(2)	Large units with reduced actual or allowable emissions meeting five conditions on emissions and growth	6	Florida (Florida Power Company), Michigan (Detroit Edison)

House, even though Springfield, Missouri, was represented by a first-term Republican not on Energy and Commerce. Section 405(g)(5) was broadened in conference to include Tucson Electric, even though Arizona was not represented on the conference committee.[47] Finally, Section 404(h) originated in the House, even though the only Iowan on Energy and Commerce, Tom Tauke (R), was not on Energy and Power and was campaigning vigorously (though ultimately unsuccessfully) against an incumbent Democratic senator.

---

[47]Morris Udall (D) of Arizona was appointed to the conference, but specifically to deal with issues other than acid rain; *Cong. Record*, June 6, 1990, at S-7541.

These examples make it clear that the ability of a utility to obtain favorable Phase II allocation provisions in the statute did not necessarily depend on having one or more of the members of its state's congressional delegation on a key committee or in the leadership. States like Florida were of "partisan" political importance because of the presence of close races for the Senate or governor or their expected importance in the next presidential election. Utilities could also gain influence with influential members of Congress representing other areas through their trade associations, PACs, and political contributions. The existence of these alternative pathways through which legislators can be influenced is consistent with the difficulty scholars have had in finding strong empirical linkages between congressional appropriations and the concentration of interest groups in particular states and the seniority and committee assignments of their representatives in Congress.[48] We encounter similar difficulty in the regression analysis discussed below.

As compared with legislation in other areas, we do not believe that there is anything unusual about the provisions in Table 3. The EPA data simply make it easier to identify beneficiaries of these rules than of, say, functionally equivalent provisions in the tax code. Nor do we believe these are the only "special interest" allocation rules included in Title IV—just the most obvious. For example, Section 405(f)(1) provides special bonuses for oil/gas units with very low emissions rates during the baseline period. Units in over 30 states get some benefit from this provision, but the bulk of the benefits are concentrated in California, Florida, and New York.

The third category of Phase II allocation rules provides for general allocations of bonus allowances to units located in groups of states that fall neatly into the "clean" and "dirty" camps. As we discussed above, Section 405(a)(3) allocates 50,000 additional allowances each year to Phase I units located in 10 "dirty" Midwestern states. Section 406 made 125,000 allowances per year available to units in "clean states," which the governor of any of these states could access at his option in lieu of accepting other bonus allowances to which the units were entitled. (See Table 1 for the definition and list of "clean states.") These allocations clearly reflect efforts to "buy off" two sell-organized groups of states with utilities at opposite ends of the dirty/clean spectrum.

VII. Alternative Allocation Rules and the Distribution of Phase II Allowances

Given the number and complexity of Phase II allocation rules, interactions between them, and the global ratchet, it does not appear either practical or interesting to use the EPA data to try to sort out the effects of each in-

---

[48]See Levitt & Poterba, supra note 5, and the references they cite.

dividual provision as we did for Phase I in Table 2. Nor is there any simple, systematic way to tie these provisions to specific interest groups or legislators, since there are no votes to observe either on individual provisions or on the acid rain Title itself in isolation from the rest of the 1990 Amendments. Instead, we have elected to structure our analysis around the allocation patterns produced by the statute and by the four benchmark alternative allocation rules (PR, SR, BC, and CM) defined in Table 4 and discussed in more detail in the next several paragraphs. We perform a variety of direct

Table 4 Initial Phase II Allowance Allocations Considered

Allocation	Code	Correlated with States' Final Allocations		Description
		Total	*Per Capita*	
Proportional Reduction	PR	.882	.811	Baseline emissions ratcheted down by 42.3% to equal total Phase II allowances (i.e., the total in the Final Allocation)
Simple Rule	SR	.989	.985	(1) Units on line before 1986 receive (1985 heat input) × Max (1985 ER, 1.2), expressed in tons; (2) units on line in 1986 or later receive unratcheted basic allowances per Section 405(g); (3) allocations are ratcheted up by 8.5% to equal total Phase II allowances
Base Case	BC	.996	.991	(1) Allowances are allocated using basic provisions in the law that distinguish units by baseline emissions rate, fuel type, and vintage (for units on line in 1986 or later) as described in note 51; (2) allocations are ratch eted down by 1.4% to equal total Phase II allowances.
Final Allocation	FA	. . .	. . .	Actual allocation of Phase II allowances, as provided for in the law
Cost Minimization	CM	.956	.887	Allocation of allowances that minimizes estimated total compliance cost in 2005 on the assumption that transaction costs rule out interstate trading; linear state-level marginal cost curves estimated from table A-16 in ICF, supra note 36, assuming intercepts are $115, as described in note 52 infra

comparisons in this section and then use hypothetical voting and regression techniques for further analysis in Sections VIII and IX, respectively.

A. Alternative Allocations

The *Proportional Reduction* (PR) allocation is a natural starting point for most academic discussions, though it has been found to lack attractive distributional properties in several contexts.[49] The PR allocation implies that in the absence of interstate trading, all states would reduce their emissions by the same proportion to achieve the Phase II emissions cap. This rule implicitly ignores the fact that some states were already clean, and these states generally faced relatively high abatement costs.[50]

The *Simple Rule* (SR) resembles the core rule of the initial administration bill as well as some earlier proposals. Like those bills, it reflects the maximum emissions rate for new coal sources (ignoring the "percent reduction" requirement) in effect since the 1970 Clean Air Act Amendments. Each unit operating in 1985 is initially allocated allowances equal to its baseline fuel use times the lesser of its actual emissions rate and 1.2, expressed in tons. This allocation rule leads to significantly *lower* aggregate allowances than is provided for by Title IV. Thus, these initial allocations are then ratcheted *up* by 8.5 percent so that total allowances under SR equal the actual Phase II cap. The basic idea is to bring old generating units, which account for the bulk of SO_2 emissions, into conformity with the 1971 NSPS in aggregate. Because the ratchet up from this basic principle to the actual Phase II allocations is so large, following this rule makes it possible to meet the statutory emissions limit by allowing all existing coal units to operate with emissions rates substantially above 1.2 pounds per million Btu on average and to provide all other units with allowances well in excess of their baseline emissions.

The *Base Case* (BC) was produced by using the six basic provisions in the final law that distinguish units by baseline emissions rate, fuel type, and age—what we referred to in Section VI as the first category of allocation rules.[51] Our original idea was that differences between the SR and BC

---

[49]See Tietenberg, supra note 1, ch. 5.

[50]See, for instance, Crandall, supra note 3, at 27.

[51]Base Case allowances were allocated as follows before ratcheting down, dividing the results of these formulas by 2,000 to convert to tons. (1) All units that began operation in 1985 or earlier and had ER ≥ 1.2 received baseline fuel use (in Btus) × 1.2, following Section 405(b)(1). (2) All units that began operation in 1985 or earlier and had 0.6 ≤ ER < 1.2 received baseline fuel use × min [actual 1985 ER, maximum allowable 1985 ER] × 1.2, following Section 405(d)(2). (3) All other units (with ER < 0.6) that began operation in 1985 or earlier, except units that derived more than 90 percent of their total fuel consumption (on a Btu basis) from gas during 1980–89 (the ">90 percent gas" units), received baseline fuel use × min [0.6, maximum allowable 1985 ER] × 1.2, following Section 405(d)(1). (4) All >90 percent gas units received baseline fuel use × 1985 ER, following Section 405(h)(1). (5) Units that began operation between 1986 and 1990 received estimated fuel consumption at a 65 percent operating factor × the unit's maximum allowable 1985 ER, following Section 405(g)(1). Finally, (6) all covered units under construction and expected to begin operation after 1990 received estimated fuel consumption at a 65 percent operating factor × min [0.3, the unit's maximum allowable ER], following Sections 405(g)(3) and 405(g)(4).

allocations would have primarily technical rationales, with political influences affecting primarily the difference between BC and the *Final Allocation* (FA) actually employed. As we noted above and will demonstrate below, reality was not so tidy. The high pairwise correlations between FA and each of PR, SR, and BC shown in Table 4 reflect the huge interstate differences in emissions levels.

Finally, we used preenactment, state-level compliance cost estimates from a widely circulated report prepared to inform the legislative process to produce an estimate of the allowance allocation that would have minimized total compliance costs in the absence of interstate trading.[52] Other cost analyses were also developed for and considered in the legislative process and would, of course, imply different cost-minimizing allocations, so the *Cost Minimization* (CM) allocation considered here is more illustrative than definitive. This allocation is of interest both because of actual and perceived market imperfections,[53] and because autarchy was implicitly assumed in much of the actual debate about "fair" allowance allocations. Table 4 shows that the CM allocation is also highly correlated with the FA allocation, again reflecting the importance of baseline interstate differences.

Many in Congress seemed to believe that there would be significant obstacles to interstate allowance trading. It is thus of some interest to use our estimated marginal cost functions, along with consistent estimates of uncontrolled emissions,[54] to estimate the total expected allocation-specific compliance costs in 2005 in the absence of interstate trading. These calculations imply that PR would impose costs about 30 percent above their minimum value, while SR, BC, and FA are estimated to involve total cost between 5 and 10 percent above the minimum. These latter differences seem unlikely to be much above the noise in this exercise. These results suggest that in the presence of transactions costs there was at least a plau-

---

[52]Table A-16 in ICF, supra note 36, contains state-by-state estimates of emissions in 2005 (a) with no controls and (b) with a common marginal cost of control ($572/ton) that was projected to reduce total emissions to near the actual Phase II cap. These data imply a point on each state's estimated marginal cost of abatement schedule for 2005. To determine those schedules fully, we assume linearity and a common intercept. Table A-16 in ICF, supra note 36, gives the total cost of control for the case analyzed, including the cost of reducing utility NO_x emissions by 10.556 million tons. Comparing the total cost of SO_2 control implied by an assumed intercept value with the ICF total cost gives an implied cost per ton of NO_x reductions. An intercept value of $115 gives a cost per ton in the center of the range discussed by ICF, supra note 36, at C-12. (Intercept values of $80 and $150 yielded very similar results; see Joskow & Schmalensee, supra note 16, table 5.) The CM allocation was then computed by equating estimated marginal costs across states and setting total emissions equal to the Phase II cap. ICF, supra note 36, table A-16, projected California and Vermont to have zero SO_2 emissions in 2005 even with no controls; they received zero allowances under CM. At the other extreme, Oregon and the District of Columbia were projected to find it uneconomic to reduce emissions at all, even at an allowance price of $572/ton; their CM allocations equal baseline 2005 emissions.

[53]Stavins, supra note 2.

[54] From ICF, supra note 36, table A-16.

sible *efficiency* case for rejecting PR in favor of any of the other alloca-tions.[55]

B. Gainers and Losers by Type of Generating Unit

Since utility service areas do not map easily into House districts, and since the Senate had somewhat more influence on the final allowance allocations than the House, states are the natural units of political economic analysis. However, most of the Phase II allocation provisions do not relate directly to states but, rather, to generating units with different attributes. The distribution of different types of generating units among the states is thus the main determinant, as a matter of arithmetic rather than of causality, of the effects of different allocation rules on individual states. To understand the latter effects, we begin with an analysis of how those rules treat generating units with different characteristics.

Table 5 summarizes baselines emissions by and allowances allocated to generating units of various types in Phase II under SR, BC, and FA.[56]

Table 5 Emissions and Phase II Allowance Allocations by Unit Type

Unit Type	Baseline Emissions	Implied Initial Allowance Allocations		
		Simple Rule (SR)	Base Case (BC)	Final Allocation (FA)
Dirty: 1.2 ≤ ER:	13,004	5,375	4,887	4,745
ER ≥ 2.5. ≥ 75 MW	9,451	2,901	2,645	2,412
Other dirty	3,553	2,465	2,242	2,333
Moderate: .6 ≤ ER < 1.2	2,793	2,881	3,107	3,186
Clean: ER < .6:	363	394	772	864
Coal	298	323	475	510
Oil/gas	61	67	292	303
Gas (>90%)	4	5	4	50
New: Came on line 1986–90	230	250	238	209
Other: Planned, exempt, etc.	305	239	134	135
Total	16,695	9,139	9,139	9,139

Note: Emissions and allowances are expressed in thousands of tons of SO_2. ER is the baseline emissions rate in pounds of SO_2 emitted per million Btu of fuel burned. Baseline emissions generally equal (1985 emissions rate × 1985–87 average fuel use) for all units on line in 1985.

---

[55]One often-invoked principle of equity is equality of sacrifice. Using the coefficient of variation of states' estimated per capita compliance costs as a measure of inequality of sacrifice, PR is estimated to involve substantially less inequality than the other four allocations (Joskow & Schmalensee, supra note 16, table 5). Using this measure, CM and SR have the least inequality of sacrifice and FA the most. While these estimates must clearly be treated with considerable caution, the outcome of the political process suggests that the equity considerations that drove it are not well summarized by equality of sacrifice.

[56]Since the calculations leading to the CM allocation could only be done at the state level, a breakdown of this allocation by unit type is not possible. PR allocations are directly proportional to baseline emissions.

Under SR, "dirty" units are allocated allowances equal to only about 40 percent of baseline emissions, while both "moderate" and "clean" units receive allocations above their baselines. If the Phase II allowance allocation process had been used partially to "buy off" the states with many dirty generating units, which were the main targets of the whole acid rain program, we would have expected to see allowances allocated to dirty units to be *increased* as we move from SR to BC and from BC to FA. Table 5 shows exactly the opposite: both moves *decrease* the aggregate allowances of dirty units, particularly large, very dirty units. (Table A units fall in this category.) Moreover, all other unit types on line by 1985 receive allowances under FA that in aggregate exceed their baseline emissions. This pattern is consistent with "We're already clean, don't pick on us!" having been a more effective equity argument than any notion of equal sacrifice. It is also consistent with a desire of senators from the "clean" Western states to pay back the Midwestern and Appalachian states for the mandatory scrubbing provision in the 1977 law.[57] Finally, along with the results of Section V, it is also broadly consistent with high-emissions states being willing to accept fewer Phase II allowances in return for more Phase I allowances.

Clean units do much better under BC than under SR.[58] The higher allocation to clean units mainly represents a gain by clean oil/gas units. The formula involved was nominally a response to an argument that these units had burned an "unusual" amount of gas in the base period, so that their baseline emissions were "abnormally"—and thus "unfairly"—low. In connection with both this provision and the "clean states" provision discussed below, it is instructive to consider the possible role of Senator Bennett Johnston (D-La.) in promoting provisions favorable to gas-burning units. Senator Johnston represented a major gas-producing and gas-consuming state and chaired the Energy and Natural Resources Committee. Though this committee had broad oversight authority for federal economic regulation of electric utilities and could have plausibly asserted jurisdiction over aspects of the 1990 legislation, it did not do so. Moreover, it would have been natural for gas-burning electric utilities without more direct influence on the relevant committees to turn to Senator Johnston for assistance.

Differences between BC and FA reflect more than a score of other provisions, some of which appear in Table 3. Their most striking implication in Table 5 is the huge increase in allowances for units burning more than 90 percent gas. This results mainly from the "clean states" provision, Section 406, discussed above. This provision allocated a pool of bonus allowances to units in "clean" states in proportion to generation, not baseline emissions.

Table 5 shows that only the dirtiest large units did less well under FA than under BC, even though their FA endowments were increased by explicit bonuses for Phase I units. Small dirty units (<75 megawatts) receive

[57]See Margaret E. Kriz, "Dunning the Midwest," *Nat'l J.*, April 14, 1990, at 893, on this point.

[58]The lower allocation to "Other" under BC than under SR is an artifact; it primarily reflects a legislative decision to exempt some cogenerators and other units from the program altogether.

more allowances under FA than BC because they are explicitly favored in the final legislation. In fact, because of bonuses for low capacity utilization (rationalized, of course, by arguments that the base period was unusual) and the special provisions affecting Florida and North Dakota listed in Table 3, allowances were also higher for large units with baseline emissions rates between 1.2 and 2.5.

C. Gainers and Losers by State

To examine the state-level implications of alternative allocation rules, we compute the differences between the corresponding implied allocations. The computation reveals that a shift from PR to SR would impose costs mainly on a few Midwestern states and provide benefits to most others. In addition, there is a good deal of similarity in the differences between the three most plausible alternative benchmark allocations (SR, BC, and CM) and the actual allocation (FA).[59] Accordingly, Table 6 displays the states with the largest (in absolute value) differences between FA and the average of the SR, BC, and CM allocations.

Table 6 reveals that Pennsylvania, West Virginia, and Kentucky, which all burn dirty coal and are large net producers of dirty coal, did particularly poorly in Phase II.[60] One hypothesis that explains this is that these states' congressional delegations focused on obtaining benefits for miners, consistent with what we observe for Phase I allocations, both as direct financial assistance and in the form of incentives to scrub, rather than on obtaining additional Phase II allowances. On the other hand, Illinois, which produced more than twice as much high-sulfur coal as it burned, did well in obtaining allowances in both Phases,[61] while Georgia, which produced no coal, did poorly in both Phases. Ohio and Indiana did much better in Phase I than in Phase II; this may reflect an atypically high valuation of near-term benefits.

Many of the clean states did rather well in Phase II, especially California and Louisiana. These states could focus on Phase II allocations since they had no Phase I units. Similarly, less than 40 percent of utility SO_2 emissions in New York and Florida, which also did well in Phase II, were from Phase I units—as compared to over 70 percent in Ohio, Indiana, Illinois, West Virginia, and Georgia. Examination of the Senate and House committee and leadership structures, however, would not suggest that

---

[59]The major exception is Ohio, which receives many fewer allowances under CM than under SR or BC because ICF, supra note 36, estimates it to have the lowest abatement costs in the nation.

[60]Recall that they also did poorly in Phase I; see Table 2. In Phase I, however, they did benefit significantly from the bonus allowances for scrubbing.

[61]Illinois' senators occupied no relevant leadership positions; in the House it was represented by the Minority Leader, Robert Michel (R), and by the Ranking Member of the Subcommittee on Health and the Environment, Edward Madigan (R).

Table 6 States with Largest Phase II Gains and Losses versus Average Benchmark Allowance Allocation

Average Gain			Average Loss		
Absolute	*Percent*	*State*	*Absolute*	*Percent*	*State*
61,727	202.03	California*†	93,666	18.17	West Virginia
58,992	27.58	New York†	88,052	13.95	Pennsylvania*
57,126	15.39	Illinois*†	50,057	15.93	Tennessee
29,839	33.87	Louisiana	31,359	7.65	Kentucky
27,460	5.64	Florida	25,759	16.56	Virginia
27,168	20.65	North Dakota†	20,215	34.04	Washington*
19,311	16.33	Wyoming*	19,943	5.89	Alabama
18,590	35.00	Utah	15,687	4.06	Michigan†
18,190	17.26	Minnesota	14,945	2.82	Indiana†
15,515	30.75	Connecticut	13,984	17.18	New Jersey
13,383	11.12	Iowa	12,889	8.09	Maryland
12,678	11.07	Oklahoma	11,351	2.68	Georgia*
11,880	4.30	Missouri*	9,597	5.30	Wisconsin
11,513	18.21	Nebraska	6,194	4.77	Kansas*

Note: Absolute gains and losses are differences between the state's actual (FA) allowance allocation and the average of its allocations under the SR, BC, and CM benchmarks. Percent gains and losses are absolute gains and losses as percentages of the average of the three benchmark allocations.

*States represented in Senate or House leadership. (The other state represented was Maine, which had an average gain of 2,597 (28.22%).)

†States represented in Senate or House committee leadership. (The other states represented were Montana, which had an average loss of 1,621 (5.24%), and Rhode Island, which had an average gain of 1,117 (47.28%).)

Louisiana or Florida would be winners in this game.[62] Indeed, the two best-positioned congressmen, Chairmen Dingell and Sharp, represented states that wound up doing particularly poorly in Phase II—though Sharp's state, Indiana, did well in Phase I.

Overall, the passage of acid rain legislation aimed at existing dirty units was a loss for the Appalachian and Midwestern coalition that had prevailed in the 1977 debate on SO_2 control. One might have thought that these states,

---

[62]New York and California do not seem likely winners either. New York was represented in the relevant leadership only by the ranking member on Energy and Commerce, Congressman Norman Lent (R). Lent was not generally thought to be nearly as powerful as Chairman Dingell, and Lent's district was not served by Consolidated Edison. California was represented here by Henry Waxman (D), Chairman of Energy and Commerce's Subcommittee on Health and the Environment. Chairman Waxman was primarily concerned with (and only had jurisdiction over) other parts of the 1990 legislation. The Senate majority whip, Alan Cranston (D-CA) took no visible part in the administration-Senate negotiations. California's other senator, Pete Wilson (R), was active in those negotiations, but his focus was on autorelated provisions. As we noted above, some of Louisiana's success in the Phase II "game" may reflect the efforts of Senator Bennett Johnston (D), who had some power in this setting because he chaired the Energy and Natural Resources Committee. California's significant gain on clean oil/gas units would then have been in part a byproduct of Senator Johnston's efforts on behalf of similar units in Louisiana.

which had the most to lose from this legislation, would have been able to
mobilize their well-organized opposition to SO_2 controls and their representation in key leadership positions to obtain a disproportionate share of
the allowances, to help to compensate for their high cleanup costs. However, Table 6 reveals that, with a few exceptions, including Illinois and Ohio,
the opposite generally occurred. Not only did the states that produced and
burned dirty coal lose in the large when they failed to block the passage of
an acid rain law, they also generally lost in the small in the contest over
the allocation of Phase II allowances. West Virginia and Pennsylvania, historically among the most aggressive opponents of acid rain legislation, were
the biggest losers. On the other hand, a broadly distributed set of states
that relied primarily on clean coal and gas-fired generation to produce electricity did well relative to these benchmarks. This result is consistent with
the Phase II allowance allocation game being one of what Wilson has called
"majoritarian politics,"[63] once the 1977 coalition lost its effort to keep the
game from being played at all.

VIII. Hypothetical Votes on Phase II Allocations

As is often the case with complex legislation, the details of Title IV were
largely worked out behind closed doors. There was never a recorded vote
on any aspect of allowance allocations. Since it is very difficult to deny a
determined minority, let alone a majority, the right to offer an amendment
on the Senate floor, the lack of *any* votes suggests, at least, that FA was
some sort of majority rule equilibrium.[64]
    One can explore quantitatively the plausibility of this notion by mak-
ing some assumptions about voting behavior and seeing how obvious alternatives would have fared in hypothetical votes.[65] Because it is impossi-

---

[63]James Q. Wilson, "The Politics of Regulation," in *The Politics of Regulation* (J. Q. Wilson ed.
1980).

[64]To be clear, since there is an alternative allocation with the same total number of allowances
that can defeat any proposed allocation, there is no majority rule equilibrium in a game in which vectors of unit-specific allocations compete for votes. (Proof: Let X be a proposed equilibrium vector of
unit-specific allocations, and let $W(X)$ be the set of elements of X that correspond to units represented
(in whatever sense is relevant) by any arbitrary majority of legislators. Let X' be a vector formed from
X by increasing all elements in $W(X)$ by ϵ and decreasing all other elements by the common amount
necessary to equate the sum of the elements of X' to the sum of the elements of X. Then X' defeats X
under majority rule, so X is not an equilibrium.) However, any votes would not have been on allowance vectors but, rather, on a limited set of alternative allocation rules. (Similarly, tax legislation
is about the rules in the tax code, not the vector of real after-tax household incomes.) As our discussion should have made clear, significant analytical effort would have been required to determine the
incidence of alternative systems of rules, putting proposed amendments to a bill on the floor at a significant disadvantage.

[65]We are unaware of any previous applications of this technique, though we would not be sur-
prised to learn that some exist.

Table 7 Results of Simulated Votes on Phase II Allowance Allocation Changes

Change and Voting Test	States Dropped	Senate			House			Electoral Votes		
		Yea	Nay	Margin	Yea	Nay	Margin	Yea	Nay	Margin
PR → SR:										
None	0	70	24	46	303	126	177	379.5	147	232.5
$\|\Delta\| \geq 5\%$	3	68	20	48	302	102	200	376.5	120	256.5
$\|\Delta\| \geq 10\%$	7	62	18	44	257	99	158	327.5	115	212.5
PR → CM:										
None	0	62	32	30	235	194	41	300.5	226	74.5
$\|\Delta\| \geq 5\%$	1	60	32	28	228	194	34	292	226	66
$\|\Delta\| \geq 10\%$	6	54	28	26	199	184	15	258	212	46
SR → BC:										
None	0	48	46	2	220	209	11	274.5	252	22.5
$\|\Delta\| \geq 5\%$	15	40	24	16	178	91	87	223.5	115.5	108
$\|\Delta\| \geq 10\%$	31	28	6	22	147	3	144	178.5	9	169.5
SR → FA:										
None	0	50	44	6	209	220	−11	261	265.5	−4.5
$\|\Delta\| \geq 5\%$	15	40	24	16	170	113	57	212.5	139	73.5
$\|\Delta\| \geq 10\%$	22	34	18	16	158	75	83	194	92.5	101.5
BC → FA:										
None	0	42	52	−10	207	222	−15	251	275.5	−24.5
$\|\Delta\| \geq 5\%$	19	28	28	0	138	106	32	170	136.5	33.5
$\|\Delta\| \geq 10\%$	34	18	8	10	39	24	15	56	35.5	20.5
CM → FA:										
None	0	48	46	2	242	187	55	290.5	236	54.5
$\|\Delta\| \geq 5\%$	7	40	40	0	197	168	29	236.5	210.5	26
$\|\Delta\| \geq 10\%$	13	38	30	8	193	111	82	230.5	142.5	88

Note: For each change, congressional delegations or electors of states that gain enough to pass the voting test indicated are assumed to vote yea; delegations/electors of states that lose enough are assumed to vote nay. The average of 1988 and 1992 electoral votes was used to tabulate the final three columns.

ble to define the relevant set of alternatives rigorously or to defend ignoring linkages between allowance allocations and other issues in this and other legislation, this approach cannot provide a rigorous test of any hypothesis.[66] Nonetheless, it is interesting to see what can be learned by a simple analysis of hypothetical votes among the alternative Phase II allocations defined in Table 4.

The results of a number of simulated votes are contained in Table 7. It is assumed here that senators and representatives vote for the alternative giving their state more allowances—but only if the difference is noticeable. Given the complexity of the Phase II allocation process, states in

---

[66]On its face, for instance, dropping the special treatment of North Dakota lignite plants (Section 405(b)(3)) would seem to be a clear winner: one small state loses and all others win. But the others do not win much, and Senator Burdick, the powerful chairman of the Environment and Public Works Committee, would have been furious at the amendment's sponsors and supporters.

which actual differences are relatively small could easily have gotten the sign wrong in the heat of debate. Moreover, as others have observed, if constituents are not much affected,[67] legislators may be free to indulge their own preferences—which may depend on ideology, logrolling, PAC contributions, or a host of other factors. We have assumed three different thresholds of concern: any change at all, any change above 5 percent in absolute value, and any change above 10 percent in absolute value. Those legislators whose states' allowance changes do not pass the relevant threshold are assumed to divide their votes evenly; for the sake of clarity they are simply omitted from the vote counts in Table 7. For the sake of completeness we have applied the same calculations to electoral votes (including those of the District of Columbia).

Table 7 makes clear that PR is a political nonstarter as well as potentially expensive (Section VIIA above): a change from PR to SR or to CM passes overwhelmingly in both Houses under any of our thresholds of concern. There are just too many relatively clean states that would suffer under PR for it to gather a majority against any alternative that concentrates the pain in a smaller number of dirty states. This is consistent with SR being at the core of most proposals made during the 1980s and with those proposals having been blocked from passage by powerful legislators from states that this change makes worse off, as discussed above. Once these legislators could no longer simply block acid rain legislation, majoritarian politics increased their pain by reducing the allowances below those they would have received under proportional reduction. This is also broadly consistent with the ultimate rejection of efforts to fashion a cost-sharing program built around a national tax on electricity, a possibility that was seriously discussed during the 1980s. Such a tax would, of course, have benefited precisely those states that lose from a shift from PR to SR, BC, or CM.

A change from SR to BC also passes both Houses, as well as the electoral college. Note that its margin increases uniformly as we impose a stricter voting test. The actual allocation of allowances (FA) defeats CM in the House and electoral college and generally wins in the Senate as well. On the other hand, if we assume that every loss of allowances, no matter how relatively or absolutely small, leads to a "Nay" vote, FA fails in the Senate against BC and in the House against both BC and SR. When even a 5 percent threshold of significance is imposed, however, FA beats both alternatives easily in the House, easily beats SR in the Senate, and needs only a nudge to beat BC in the Senate.

On the whole, Table 7 supports the notion that the Phase II allowance allocation provisions were crafted with sufficient (implicit or explicit) concern for their viability on the floors of both chambers to make them no less attractive than at least some obvious alternatives. If this had not been

---

[67]See, for instance, Kalt & Zupan, supra note 6.

the case, one would expect to have seen votes involving alternative allocation provisions.

IX. Estimating Political Determinants of Allowance Allocations

Our analysis thus far does not suggest that the Phase II allowance allocations can be easily explained by a small number of "standard" political
economy variables. We appear to be dealing with a process of majoritarian politics (once the dam holding back acid rain legislation was broken)
combined with a number of special interest provisions to satisfy narrow
constituencies. Committees of jurisdiction were not unimportant in the legislative process, but, particularly in the Senate and in conference, issue-
specific groups of legislators played critical roles.[68]

Because an abundance of quantitative information is available here,
we can use regression analysis to examine whether and how variables measuring the importance of various interest groups, the presence of senators
and congressmen in leadership positions, and competitive races for Senate, governor, and/or president in particular states help explain the observed
allowance allocation in ways consistent with various theories of distributive politics. This analysis is similar in spirit (and results) to the extensive
literature that relates congressional appropriations to various political variables (and that fails to find strong support for any simple theories of distributive politics).[69]

As above, our analysis concentrates on the Phase II allocation for years
2000–2009, both because it is more complex and important (in expected
dollar terms) than the Phase I allocation and because it involves a larger
sample size. Because of the importance of complex interstate differences
in initial conditions, we focus on explaining *differences* between the states'
actual allocations (FA) and the average of the allocations implied by our
three benchmarks: SR, BC, and CM. (See Table 6 above.) This variable is
defined as ΔPHASEII in Table 8.[70]

We focus on differences in numbers of allowances because allowances
are homogeneous property rights that should have the same market value
no matter to whom they are given. Therefore, the political cost of getting
an incremental allowance for one's own constituents should not depend
heavily on the state in which they happen to reside. Nonetheless, we per-

---

[68]Cohen, supra note 16, stresses that this bill was not atypical of recent experience in this last
regard.

[69]See, for instance, the references cited in note 5, supra.

[70]Joskow & Schmalensee, supra note 16, describe the generally minor differences between the
results for this average variable and those obtained for each of the three differences involving individual benchmark allocations.

Table 8 Variables Employed in Phase II Regression Analysis

Variable	Mean	Max	Min	SD	Description
ΔPHASEII	.00	61.7	−93.7	28.4	Difference between actual (FA) Phase II allowances and the average of allocation under SR, BC, and CM, thousands of tons per year from 2000 to 2009
HSMINERS	1.18	21.6	0	3.64	Estimated number of miners of high-sulfur coal, thousands: product of (fraction of 1992 demonstrated reserves with >1.68 lbs. sulfur per million Btu [from U.S. Energy Information Admin., U.S. Coal Reserves: An Update by Heat and Sulfur Content (DOE/EIA-0529, 1992), table C-1]) and (average daily employment of coal miners in 1990 [from National Coal Assn., Coal Data 1994, at 11–20])
EMISSIONS	348	2,303	.16	473	Baseline SO_2 emissions, thousands of tons
EMRATE	1.49	4.20	.01	1.03	State average SO_2 emission rate from fossil-fueled electric generating units, pounds per million Btu of fuel burned
PHIEXT	16.6	190	0	42.1	Phase I extension allowances requested for generating units in the state, average per year from 1995 to 1999, thousands of tons
SEN	.27	1	0	.45	Competitive Senate election dummy variable: equals one if state has a competitive Senate race in 1990 (races labeled "Best Bets" or noncompetitive in Nat'l J., March 17, 1990, were excluded), zero otherwise
GOVEV	6.14	50.5	0	9.95	Competitive and important governor's election: product of (a dummy variable for competitive governors race, constructed like SEN) and (the average of the state's 1988 and 1992 electoral votes)
SWINGEV	10.0	48.2	.65	8.85	Important swing state: product of ([1 − |RPCT − 53.4|/50], where RPCT is the percentage of the state's popular vote case for Bush in the 1988 Presidential election, and 53.4 is the sample

Table 8 (*continued*)

Variable	Mean	Max	Min	SD	Description
					mean of **RPCT**) and (the average of the state's 1988 and 1992 electoral votes)
HLEAD	.10	1	0	.31	Number of House leadership slots (5 total) filled by the state's delegation
HCR	.12	2	0	.39	Number of House committee (Energy and Commerce) and subcommittee (Energy and Power, Health and Environment) chairmanships and ranking member slots (6) filled by the state's delegation
HCOMM	1.35	8	0	1.84	Number of House committee (Energy and Commerce) slots (43) plus number of subcommittee (Energy and Power) slots (22) filled by the state's delegation
SLEAD	.08	1	0	.28	Number of Senate leadership slots (4) filled by the state's delegation
SCR	.06	1	0	.24	Number of Senate committee (Environment and Public Works) and subcommittee (Environmental Protection) chairmanships and ranking member slots (4) filled by the state's delegation
SSUB	.29	1	0	.46	Number of Senate subcommittee (Environmental Protection) slots (14) filled by the state's delegation
ΔPHASEI	.00	58.2	−26.1	13.7	Actual Phase I allowances minus allocation under rescaled Basic Rule (from Table 2), thousands of tons per year

Note: Except as noted, data are from EPA (principally the NADB) and standard references on U.S. politics. Sample size = 48: Alaska, Hawaii, and Idaho are excluded from the sample, as from the acid rain program, and the District of Columbia is included.

formed a number of experiments involving percentage and per capita differences, without obtaining results qualitatively different from those reported below.

As Table 8 describes, we employed several exogenous variables intended to capture interstate variations in the importance of interest groups involved in debates about acid rain legislation. These include a variable that measures projected job loss in the coal-mining industry as a result of the

legislation (HSMINERS),[71] variables that distinguish between clean and
dirty states with different levels of SO_2 emissions (EMISSIONS) and different emissions rates (EMRATE),[72] and a variable designed to measure interest in relying on scrubbers by applications for Phase I extension allowances to support scrubber investments (PH1EXT).

One might expect that states for which HSMINERS is large would be
very interested in obtaining allowances as compensation for losses of mining jobs. On the other hand, allowances are given to electric utilities, not
miners. It is thus at least equally plausible, particularly in light of some of
the results of Section VII, that representatives of these states would have
neglected the pursuit of allowances in favor of seeking aid for displaced
miners and/or attempting to strengthen incentives to scrub. Thus while
states with high values of HSMINERS cared more than others about the
acid rain program, it is unclear whether that concern should be expected
to produce more or fewer Phase II allowances.

We would expect EMISSIONS and/or EMRATE to have positive coefficients if the "dirty" states were able to use the Phase II allocation process
to make up for some of what they lost through passage of acid rain legislation aimed at existing dirty plants. Negative coefficients, on the other
hand, would be consistent with clean states having been able to use the allocation process to their advantage—the pattern suggested by Section VII.
Finally, we would expect PH1EXT to be negative if the states interested in
scrubbing (either because it was the least-cost control option or because of
pressures to save high-sulfur coal miners' jobs) gave up Phase II allowances
in exchange for greater scrubber incentives during Phase I.

We also computed two sets of more narrowly defined "political" variables. In the spirit of models of partisan distributive politics, variables in
the first set are designed to measure states' electoral importance when the
1990 legislation was being considered. These variables include a dummy
variable indicating whether there was a competitive election for the Senate expected in 1990 (SEN), the national importance of an upcoming competitive governor's race (GOVEV), and a variable that measures the importance of a state as a "swing state" in the 1988 presidential election
(SWINGEV). Since 1990 was an election year, it seems plausible that states
would have had more clout in the zero-sum allowance allocation game if

---

[71]Two other conceptually weaker mining-related variables were computed. (1) Except for Kentucky and West Virginia, which are divided into two regions each, ICF, supra note 36, projections of
mining job losses are based on state-level net employment changes, rather than gross flows out of
high-sulfur mining. (2) Aid actually received by May 1995 under the displaced worker provision (Title XI) that was pushed hard by mining-state representatives (see Section 4, above) amounted to less
than $29 million and could not have been well anticipated in 1990. Both these variables were highly
correlated with HSMINERS, and neither outperformed it significantly in regressions.

[72]We also considered using emissions from or allowances given to Phase I units as independent
variables, but both were almost perfectly correlated with EMISSIONS ($\rho = 0.96$). The share of state
emissions accounted for by Phase I plants did not suffer from this infirmity, but its coefficient never
approached statistical significance in any experiment.

they had a competitive senatorial race (SEN) or if they were an importance state with a competitive gubernatorial race (GOVEV). It also seems plausible that important states that were swing states in the 1988 presidential race (SWINGEV) would have extra bargaining strength.[73] If these electoral importance variables influenced allocations, they should have positive signs. Since the issues in the acid rain program, and in the allowance allocation process in particular, did not reflect a clear split between Democrats and Republicans, we have not included variables measuring party affiliations or ideological ratings of each state's legislators.

The second set of political variables reflects the nonpartisan distributive politics literature, which implies that the ability of an individual legislator or a group of legislators with similar interests to affect acid rain legislation depends, in part, on whether they occupy positions on key committees or subcommittees or hold leadership positions that provide special influence over the provisions of the bill reported to the Senate or the House floor.[74] The variables in this second set include the number of House and Senate leadership posts (HLEAD and SLEAD), the number of House and Senate committee and subcommittee chairmanships and ranking member slots filled by a state's representatives (HCR and SCR), and the number of committee and/or subcommittee slots filled by a state's representatives in the House and Senate (HCOM and SSUB). The leadership in the House (HLEAD) and Senate (SLEAD) generally has seats at any negotiating table about which they care. Committee membership and, especially, chairmanship or service as the ranking minority member can convey issue-specific influence via agenda control.

As we discussed in Section IV, on the House side both the Energy and Commerce Committee (chaired by Congressman Dingell) and two of its subcommittees played important roles in the Clean Air process, though only one of the subcommittees (chaired by Congressman Sharp) dealt with the acid rain program explicitly. Thus HCR counts all chairmen and ranking members involved in Clean Air, while HCOMM gives extra credit for membership on the subcommittee that dealt with the acid rain program. On the Senate side the process was very different. The Senate bill was essentially written in negotiations with the administration in early 1990. While Senator Baucus generally chaired the negotiation sessions, Senator Mitchell assumed the chair at key moments and was heavily involved throughout the process. Similarly, while most senators in the room at any one time were likely to be members of Senator Baucus's Subcommittee on Environmental Protection, the sessions were open to all senators, and many nonmem-

[73]One might also suspect that rich states would have more clout, all else being equal (perhaps because of the presence of campaign contributors), but income per capita had essentially no explanatory power in any equation.
[74]See Barry Weingast & M. Moran, "Bureaucratic Discretion or Congressional Control," 91 *J. Pol. Econ.* 765 (1983); Barry Weingast & W. J. Marshall, "The Industrial Organization of Congress; Or, Why Legislatures, Like Firms, Are Not Organized as Markets," 96 *J. Pol. Econ.* 132 (1988); Kenneth A. Shepsle & Barry R. Weingast, "When Do Rules of Procedure Matter?" 46 *J. Pol.* 206 (1984), and "The Institutional Foundations of Committee Power," 81 *Am. Pol. Sci. Rev.* 85 (1987).

bers participated personally on issues with which they were particularly concerned and had staff in regular attendance. The variables SCR and SSUB attempt to reflect the essential elements of this process.[75] We would expect all the congressional control variables in this second set to have positive coefficients.

Some of our regressions also included ΔPHASEI, a variable, taken from Table 2, that measures how well or poorly a state did in the Phase I allocation process relative to the ER = 2.5 benchmark.[76] Our idea here is that states that did relatively well in Phase I for reasons not reflected in our Phase II independent variables might also have done well in Phase II, reflecting the same unobserved political forces. This variable is clearly endogenous, and its coefficient cannot be given an unambiguous structural interpretation.[77]

Table 9 presents illustrative estimation results for a series of equations in which ΔPHASEII is the dependent variable and alternative combinations of the three sets of variables discussed above are the independent variables. In the equation described in the first column of Table 9, as in all other equations estimated with a large number of plausible independent variables, most coefficients are not significantly different from zero.

Several "political" variables in that equation never had significant coefficients in any specification, and we drop them from further consideration. One of these was SEN, even though all of SEN's correlations with the other independent variables were less than 0.25. In addition, neither HCOMM nor SSUB ever had significant coefficients, perhaps reflecting the general decline in the importance of committees and the concomitant rise in the importance of other issue-specific groups stressed by Cohen.[78] The coefficient of SCR was never significant, even though that of HCR was positive and significant in all specifications.

---

[75]Idaho, with one subcommittee member, Steve Symms (R), was excluded from our sample because it had no fossil-fueled generating units and was thus not included in the allowance allocation process.

[76]This variable does not reflect actual or anticipated extension (scrubber bonus) allowances; it is from the second-last column in Table 2.

[77]Several additional variables were employed in a variety of unsuccessful experiments. One might expect that representatives of states with high electricity rates or expecting to need large numbers of allowances to accommodate growth would both be particularly interested in obtaining incremental allowances and particularly able to argue effectively for them, especially in light of Florida's ability to obtain Section 405(I)(1), but a range of experiments failed to support either hypothesis. (We used the product of the 1980–90 population growth rates and baseline emissions as a measure of growth-related allowance "needs.") Optimistic economists might expect that states with high baseline average or marginal costs would be both eager and able to obtain incremental allowances, all else being equal, but coefficients of such variables (based on ICF, supra note 36, as above) never approached statistical significance. Finally, we attempted to measure the importance of two other Clean Air issues, ozone nonattainment and alternative fuels, that might have been involved in cross-Title deals. Specifically, variables measuring the percentage of each state's population in severe or extreme ozone nonattainment areas and each state's production of corn and natural gas (inputs into alternative fuels) never had significant and sensible coefficients in any specification.

[78]Note 16 supra.

Table 9 Phase II Regression Results

Independent Variable	Dependent Variable = ΔPHASEII					
Constant	−4.032	5.142	1.746	4.094	−2.646	−5.412
	(10.55)	(8.770)	(3.618)	(7.810)	(3.983)	(5.386)
HSMINERS	−.043	−.814	...	...	...	−2.660*
	(1.194)	(1.088)				(.976)
EMISSIONS	−.0311	.023	...	...	...	...
	(.0220)	(.020)				
EMRATE	1.400	−4.642	...	−9.054*	...	...
	(6.534)	(5.849)		(3.708)		
PHIEXT	−.604*	−.421*	−.334*	...	−.466*	...
	(.198)	(.158)	(.078)		(.065)	
SEN	−4.594	...	...	...	...	...
	(9.026)					
GOVEV	.393	.555	...	...	...	...
	(.593)	(.530)				
SWINGEV	−1.012	−.522	...	.942*	1.039*	.854*
	(1.030)	(.731)		(.433)	(.299)	(.404)
HLEAD	−22.79	...	...	...	...	...
	(15.02)					
HCR	30.67*	27.82*	30.47*	...	...	...
	(14.24)	(12.68)	(8.328)			
HCOMM	3.923	...	...	...	...	...
	(3.894)					
SLEAD	.788	...	...	...	...	...
	(13.84)					
SCR	9.549	...	...	...	...	...
	(13.85)					
SSUB	9.481	...	...	...	...	...
	(8.183)					
ΔPHASEI	...	...	...	...	1.140*	.745*
					(.200)	(.260)
R^2	.538	.461	.403	.184	.630	.379
SE	22.67	22.58	22.40	26.20	17.83	23.11

Note: Standard errors are in parentheses. Sample size = 48.
*Significant at 5%.

Finally, the coefficient of HLEAD was generally negative and some-times significant. Four of the five House leadership slots were filled by representatives from Georgia, Illinois, Missouri, and Pennsylvania—all high-emissions states. (The correlation of HLEAD with EMRATE is 0.44.) It seems most likely that there is no real "leadership effect," since a negative effect is implausible and SLEAD never had a positive and significant coefficient. The negative HLEAD coefficient simply tells us that "dirty" states did poorly in Phase II allocations despite being well represented in the House leadership. Accordingly, we drop both HLEAD and SLEAD from further consideration.

Dropping the variables just discussed leads us to the second equation in Table 9. That equation has two groups of independent variables, with high intragroup correlations and low intergroup correlations. The first group consists of four variables that we think of as measuring "dirtiness": HSMINERS, EMISSIONS, EMRATE, and PHIEXT. The lowest of the six pairwise correlations among these variables is 0.38, and the second-lowest is 0.49. The second group consists of three variables that we think of as measuring political/electoral "clout": GOVEV, SWINGEV, and HCR. The lowest of the three pairwise correlations among these variables is 0.58. Within each of these groups, the different variables are conceptually quite distinct. If their performance in regression experiments could also be clearly distinguished, it might be possible to base a structural story on the results. These data, however, are not so kind.

Note first that in the second equation in Table 9, only one variable from each of these two groups has a coefficient that is significant at the 5 percent level. Similarly, in the 18 equations (not shown) with two variables from each group, at most one from each group is significant. In the 12 regressions with only one variable from each of these groups, however, all "dirtiness" coefficients are negative, all "clout" coefficients are positive, all 24 slope coefficients are significant at 5 percent, and 16 are significant at 1 percent. The third and fourth columns in Table 9 show the specifications within this set with the highest and lowest values of R^2, respectively.

These results provide strong evidence that "dirty" states tended to do poorly relative to our benchmarks in Phase II, while states with "clout" tended to do well. Unfortunately, high correlations within our two groups of independent variables make it impossible to use these data to determine with any confidence what elements or aspects of "dirtiness" and "clout" were most important. We are thus unable to discriminate among a large number of plausible structural hypotheses.

We ran the same set of 12 regressions just discussed using ΔPHASEI as the dependent variable and restricting the sample to the 21 Phase I states. All coefficients of both "dirtiness" and "clout" variables were *positive*, though only one of each was significant at 5 percent. These results at least suggest that the dirtiest states concentrated on Phase I, where they did relatively well on average, at the expense of Phase II, where they fared less well. These results also suggest that the "clout" variables are at least correlated with the ability to affect the legislative process positively—at least in the context of acid rain in 1990.

Finally, we re-ran the 12 regressions with one "dirtiness" variable and one "clout" variable on the right, adding ΔPHASEI as a third independent variable. All coefficients of "dirtiness" variables were negative and significant at 5 percent; all coefficients of "clout" variables were positive and significant; and all coefficients of ΔPHASEI were positive and significant. The last two columns of Table 9 show the specifications among these 12 with the highest and lowest R^2 values, respectively. These results suggest that states that managed to do well in Phase I for reasons not correlated with our "dirtiness" and "clout" variables also did well in Phase II. Unfortunately, there seems to be no way to use these data to tell what sorts of forces this effect might reflect, and the complex legislative history summarized above provides no obvious candidates.

This analysis suggests four tentative conclusions. First, and perhaps most important, there does not appear to be any simple, structural theory of distributive politics that is well supported by the data. In particular, the failure of most congressional leadership and committee membership variables seems inconsistent with theories in which power over most legislation is concentrated in the hands of a few people who happen to occupy key positions. This result does not in any sense refute the literature that emphasizes the role of committees, subcommittees, and leadership positions in congressional behavior, however. After all, Congressman Dingell and Senator Byrd managed to block Clean Air legislation for a decade, with the help of a Republican president opposed to new environmental legislation. But, once acid rain legislation got through the gate, the distribution of influential committee assignment and leadership positions did not help much in predicting allowance allocations. As our discussion of Table 3 indicates, some legislators with key committee posts clearly used them to benefit their constituents through the allocation process, but others did not, and several states without obvious influence on the relevant committees or in the leadership did quite well.

Second, there is good evidence that "dirty" states—those on average with many high-sulfur coal miners, high total emissions and emissions rates, and much interest in using scrubbing to comply with Phase I emissions limits—did relatively poorly in the Phase II allowance allocation game, all else equal. There is weak evidence suggesting that the very dirtiest states did relatively well in Phase I, suggesting in turn a willingness to give up Phase II allowances to obtain Phase I allowances from states less concerned with Phase I compliance. Third, there is strong evidence that states with political "clout"—because they were large states that were swing states in the 1988 presidential election, or because they were large states that happened to have competitive gubernatorial campaigns in 1990, or because they had representatives in the House Energy and Commerce leadership—tended to do well in Phase II, and weak evidence that they also did well in Phase I, all else equal.[79]

---

[79]At the suggestion of an editor, we ran a number of regressions using as dependent variables SUM = D(ΔPHASEII) + ΔPHASEI and DIF = D(ΔPHASEII) − ΔPHASEI, where D = $(1.05)^{-5}$ is a discount factor reflecting the 5 years between the starts of Phases I and II. As before, at most one "dirtiness" and one "clout" variable was significant at the 5 percent level in any one regression. In both SUM and DIF regressions involving one variable from each group (12 regressions each), all "dirtiness" coefficients were negative and all "clout" coefficients were positive. In the SUM regressions, none of the "dirtiness" coefficients and eight of the "clout" coefficients were significant. In the DIF regressions, all of the "dirtiness" coefficients were significant, along with six of the "clout" coefficients. These results are consistent, at least, with the notions that the "dirtiest" states gave up Phase II allowances in exchange for Phase I allowances and that "clout" was valuable. Mechanically, however, these results reflect the high correlations between ΔPHASEII and both SUM ($\rho = 0.91$) and DIF ($\rho = 0.80$).

Finally, there is strong evidence that states that did well relative to our Phase I benchmark, holding "dirtiness" and "clout" constant, also did well in Phase II. In a way, this just reaffirms our first tentative conclusion: something not captured by any of our "dirtiness" and "clout" variables produced positive results in both phases. We do not know whether this factor primarily reflects differences in legislators' effectiveness, logrolling on issues outside the acid rain Title (or even completely outside the Clean Air bill), or other effects. Whatever this factor reflects, it appears likely from our earlier work that Illinois had it and Georgia did not.

We do not believe that these regression results should be interpreted as implying that interest group politics, congressional influence, or considerations of state and federal electoral politics did not play an important role in the allocation of SO_2 allowances. Our earlier discussion shows that there is clearly evidence of rent-seeking behavior and congressional influence at work. However, these effects are apparently too subtle and too complex to be captured in any but the crudest way in this kind of summary regression analysis. This is consistent with the results of related work analyzing congressional appropriations.

X. Conclusions

Environmental regulation is an excellent example of interest group politics mediated through legislative and regulatory processes. The history of federal regulations governing power plant emissions of SO_2 represents, in many ways, a classic case. Concentrated and well-organized interests in a few states that produced and burned high-sulfur coal were able to shape the Clean Air Act Amendments of 1970 and, particularly, 1977 to protect high-sulfur coal and impose unnecessary costs on large portions of the rest of the country. During most of the 1980s, the Midwestern and Appalachian utility and mining elements of this coalition managed to use their control over key congressional leadership positions, combined with presidential opposition to new environmental legislation, to block new acid rain legislation. However, once it became clear that acid rain legislation was likely to be enacted as part of a larger reform of the Clean Air Act, our analysis indicates that this coalition was unable to avoid appreciable control costs by obtaining a disproportionate share of emissions allowances.

With regard to Phase I allowances (apart from scrubber bonuses), three of the states with the greatest emissions and cleanup requirements (Ohio, Indiana, and Illinois) did relatively well compared to other states, while four others (Pennsylvania, West Virginia, Kentucky, and Georgia) did relatively poorly. Aside from Illinois, the utilities and, indirectly, high-sulfur coal miners in these states benefited from bonus allowances allocated to Phase I units that scrubbed. However, aside from Illinois, the traditional coalition of high-sulfur coal producers and high-sulfur coal users were not able to claw back a disproportionate share of Phase II allowances. Indeed, they lost even more during the legislative allocation process than they would have if several simple alternative allocation rules had been utilized. Specifically, the relatively larger number of clean states with little to gain per capita were more successful in Phase II than the relatively small number of "dirty" states with much to lose per capita.

If anything, the resulting allocation of Phase II allowances appears more to be a majoritarian equilibrium than one heavily weighted toward a narrowly defined set of economic or geographical interests. It is not strongly consistent with the predictions of standard models of interest group politics or of congressional control. In some cases, influential senators and congressmen managed to capture special benefits for their constituents. In other cases, particular states did much better (or much worse) in the allocation process than might have been predicted by simple theories of distributive politics. On average relatively "dirty" states did poorly in Phase II (perhaps because they were more concerned with Phase I and benefits for miners), while states with political "clout" did relatively well in both Phases. These results do not have great explanatory power, however, and we can only conclude that the fight to grab allowances, within a range of allocations that could not be easily defeated in the Senate or House, reflects both a more complex and a more idiosyncratic pattern of political forces than one might expect from previous work on the political economy of clean air.

Of course, none of this takes away from the fact that Title IV of the 1990 Clean Air Act Amendments put in place a major long-term program to reduce pollution using an innovative tradable emissions permit system. At least in theory, the allowance system gives utilities enormous flexibility in meeting aggregate emissions reductions goals and may thus allow them to meet those goals at much lower cost than under traditional command and control approaches. Demonstrating this theory in the large-scale acid rain program may lead to fundamental changes in environmental policies and significant reductions in their costs.

BIBLIOGRAPHY

Ackerman, Bruce A., and Hassler, William T. *Clean Coal and Dirty Air*. New Haven, Conn.: Yale University Press, 1981.
Baron, David P. "Distributive Politics and the Persistence of Amtrak." *Journal of Politics* 52 (1989): 883–913.
Cohen, Richard E. "When Titans Clash on Clean Air." *National Journal* (April 7, 1990): 849–50.
Cohen, Richard E. *Washington at Work: Back Rooms and Clean Air*. New York: Macmillan, 1992.
Crandall, Robert W. "Air Pollution, Environmentalists, and the Coal Lobby." In *The Political Economy of Deregulation: Interest Groups in the Regulatory Process*, edited by Roger G. Noll and Bruce M. Owen. Washington, D.C.: American Enterprise Institute, 1983.

Crandall, Robert W. "An Acid Test for Congress?" *Regulation* 8 (September/December 1984): 21–28.

Davis, Joseph A. "Acid Rain to Get Attention as Reagan Changes Course." *Congressional Quarterly* (March 22, 1986): 675–76.

Hahn, Robert W., and Hester, Gordon L. "Marketable Permits: Lessons for Theory and Practice." *Ecology Law Review* 16 (1989): 361–406.

Hahn, Robert W., and Noll, Roger G. "Barriers to Implementing Tradeable Air Pollution Permits: Problems and Regulatory Interactions." *Yale Journal on Regulation* 1 (1983): 63–91.

Hanley, Robert. "Turning Off Acid Rain at the Source." *New York Times* (December 11, 1983): A12.

Hausker, Karl. "The Politics and Economics of Auction Design in the Market for Sulfur Dioxide Pollution." *Journal of Policy Analysis and Management* 11 (1992): 553–72.

ICF Resources Incorporated (ICF). "Comparison of the Economic Impacts of the Acid Rain Provisions of the Senate Bill (S. 1630) and the House Bill (S. 1630)." Draft Report Prepared for the U.S. Environmental Protection Agency. Washington, D.C., July 1990.

Joskow, Paul L., and Schmalensee, Richard. "The Political Economy of Market-Based Environmental Policy: The U.S. Acid Rain Program." MIT Center for Energy and Environmental Policy Research Working Paper 96-003. Cambridge, Mass.: MIT, March 1996.

Joskow, Paul L.; Schmalensee, Richard; and Bailey, Elizabeth M. "The Market for Sulfur Dioxide Emissions." *American Economic Review*, forthcoming.

Kalt, Joseph P., and Zupan, Mark. "Capture and Ideology in the Economic Theory of Politics." *American Economic Review* 74 (1984): 243–77.

Kete, Nancy. *The Politics of Markets: The Acid Rain Control Policy in the 1990 Clean Air Act Amendments*. Unpublished dissertation, Johns Hopkins University, 1992.

Kiel, Lisa J., and McKenzie, Richard B. "The Impact of Tenure on the Flow of Federal Benefits to SMSAs." *Public Choice* 41 (1983): 285–93.

Kriz, Margaret E. "Politics in the Air." *National Journal* (May 6, 1989): 1098–1102.

Kriz, Margaret E. "Dunning the Midwest." *National Journal* (April 14, 1990): 893–97.

Kuntz, Phil, and Hager, George Hager. "Showdown on Clean-Air Bill: Senate Says 'No' to Byrd." *Congressional Quarterly* (March 31, 1990): 983–87.

Levitt, Steven D., and Poterba, James M. "Congressional Distributive Politics and State Economic Performance." *Public Choice*, forthcoming.

Lock, Reinier, and Harkawik, Dennis P., eds. *The New Clean Air Act: Compliance and Opportunity*. Arlington, Va.: Public Utilities Reports, 1991.

National Acid Precipitation Assessment Program. *1989 Annual Report to the President and Congress*. Washington, D.C.: U.S. Government Printing Office, June 1990.

National Economic Research Associates, Inc. *Key Issues in the Design of NO_x Emission Trading Programs to Reduce Ground-Level Ozone*. EPRI TR-104245. Palo Alto, Cal.: Electric Power Research Institute, July 1994.

Noll, Roger G. "Economic Perspectives on the Politics of Regulation." In *Handbook of Industrial Organization*, vol. 2, edited by R. Schmalensee and R. D. Willig. Amsterdam: Elsevier, 1989.

Pashigian, B. Peter. "The Effects of Environmental Regulation on Optimal Plant Size and Factor Shares." *Journal of Law and Economics* 27 (1984): 1–28.

Pashigian, B. Peter. "Environmental Regulation: Whose Self-Interests Are Being Protected?" *Economic Inquiry* 23 (1985): 551–84.

Pechan, E. H., & Associates, *Comparison of Acid Rain Control Bills*. EPA Contract No. 68-WA-0038, Work Assignments 94 and 116, OTA Contract L3-5480.0. Washington, D.C.: E. H. Pechan & Associates, November 1989.

Peltzman, Sam. "How Efficient Is the Voting Market?" *Journal of Law and Economics* 33 (1990): 27–63.

Pytte, Alyson. "A Decade's Acrimony Lifted in the Glow of Clean Air." *Congressional Quarterly* (October 27, 1990): 3587–92.

Roberts, Leslie. "Learning from an Acid Rain Program." *Science* 251 (March 15, 1991): 1302–5.

Roberts, Leslie. "Acid Rain Program: Mixed Review." *Science* 252 (April 19, 1991): 371.

Shepsle, Kenneth A., and Weingast, Barry R. "When Do Rules of Procedure Matter?" *Journal of Politics* 46 (1984): 206–21.

Shepsle, Kenneth A., and Weingast, Barry R. "The Institutional Foundations of Committee Power." *American Political Science Review* 81 (1987): 85–104.

Stavins, Robert N. "Transaction Costs and Tradeable Permits." *Journal of Environmental Economics and Management* 29 (1995): 133–48.

Suro, Roberto. "Concern for the Environment." *New York Times* (July 2, 1989): A1.

Tietenberg, Thomas H. *Emissions Trading: An Exercise in Reforming Pollution Policy*. Washington, D.C.: Resources for the Future, 1985.

U.S. Environmental Protection Agency (EPA), Acid Rain Division. *Technical Documentation for Phase II Allowance Allocations*. Washington, D.C.: U.S. Government Printing Office, March 1993.

U.S. Environmental Protection Agency (EPA). *National Air Pollutant Emission Trends, 1900–1993*. EPA-454/R-94-027. Washington, D.C.: U.S. Government Printing Office, October 1994.

U.S. General Accounting Office (GAO). *An Analysis of Issues concerning "Acid Rain."* GAO/RCED-85-13. Washington, D.C.: U.S. Government Printing Office, December 1984.

U.S. General Accounting Office (GAO). *Allowance Trading Offers an Opportunity to Reduce Emissions at Less Cost*. GAO/RCED-95-30. Washington, D.C.: U.S. Government Printing Office, December 1994.

Weingast, Barry, and Marshall, W. J. "The Industrial Organization of Congress; Or, Why Legislatures, Like Firms, Are Not Organized as Markets." *Journal of Political Economy* 96 (1988): 132–63.

Weingast, Barry, and Moran, M. "Bureaucratic Discretion or Congressional Control? Regulatory Policymaking by the Federal Trade Commission." *Journal of Political Economy* 91 (1983): 765–800.

Wilson, James Q. "The Politics of Regulation." In *The Politics of Regulation*, edited by J. Q. Wilson. Cambridge, Mass.: Harvard University Press, 1980.

29   *A Political Economy in an Ecological Web**

Jason F. Shogren

Jason F. Shogren is Stroock Distinguished Professor of Natural Resource
Conservation and Management at the University of Wyoming.

1. Introduction

> And don't let them fob you off with a royal commission or a task force on the
> grounds that economists (or any other experts) will be able to tell them exactly
> the right amount to spend on pollution prevention. No one knows the answer to
> that question. The politicians must decide what the public wants and stake their
> political lives on their decision; they are in a much better position to assess the
> benefits and costs of their action (or inaction) than any body of experts.

> —J. Dales, *Pollution, Property, and Prices*, 1968

If you could tell the President of the United States anything you wanted to
about the interaction of the economy and environment, what would you tell
him? At first, one might be tempted to echo the economist's lament that the
misunderstanding or strategic misdirection of fundamental economic concepts remains a serious obstacle to rational environmental policy.[1] Such frustration, of course, cuts broader than the environment, the US, or the present.
Adam Smith and David Ricardo vilified "oppressive", "miserable", and "mis-

---

"A Political Economy in an Ecological Web," by Jason F. Shogren from *Environmental and Resource Economics* 11(3–4):557–570 (1998). © 1998 Kluwer Academic Publishers.

*Thanks to Joe Aldy, Tom Crocker, David Francis, Sally Kane, Stephan Kroll, Alan Krupnick, Andy Miller, Ray Prince, Sarah Reber, Ray Squitieri, Chad Stone, Mike Toman, and Bob Tuccillo for their insight. Two reviewers provided invaluable comments.

[1]Also see Portney (1990).

[2]Smith (1994, book 4, chapter 9): "Though, by this oppressive policy, a landed nation should be able to raise up artificers, manufacturers, and merchants of its own somewhat sooner than it could do by the freedom of trade a matter, however, which is not a little doubtful—yet it would raise them up, if one may say so, prematurely, and before it was perfectly ripe for them." Smith (1994, book 5, chapter 2): "Such is his distrust in the justice of his assessors that he counterfeits poverty, and wishes to appear scarce able to pay anything for fear of being obliged to pay too much. By this miserable policy he does not, perhaps, always consult his own interest in the most effectual manner, and he probably loses more by the diminution of his produce than he saves by that of his tax." Ricardo (1963): "A country whose financial situation has become extremely artificial by the mischievous policy of accumulating a large national debt, and a conse-quently enormous taxation, is particularly exposed to the inconvenience attendant on this mode of raising taxes. After visiting with a tax the whole round of luxuries; after laying horses, carriages, wine, servants, and all the other enjoyments of the rich, under contribution; a minister is induced to have recourse to more di-rect taxes, such as income and property taxes, neglecting the golden maxim of M[althus]. 'Say, that the very best of all plans of finance is to spend little, and the best of all taxes is that which is the least in amount.'"

chievous" policies that ignored basic human behavior.[2] Charles Schultze declared that "[f]orty years of observing policy debates, including 15 years of participating in them, have not dulled my amazement at how few participants have a grasp of fundamental economic principles and how differently from economist they analyze issues."[3] And the observation that good economics is often bad politics inspired Blinder's corollary to Murphy's Law: "economists have the least influence on policy where they know the most and are most agreed; they have the most influence on policy where they know the least and disagree the most."[4] Their message is clear: good economics does not always win the day when politics drives policy.

In that light, I would sharpen my message—behavior matters more to environmental policy than most people think. The argument that "science defines environmental policy" is correct if the behavioral sciences are integrated into the calculus of ecological equilibrium. Choices can shape nature just as nature can shape our choices. Those policies that artificially separate natural from behavioral phenomena will generate biased predictions, and are ultimately self-defeating. To illustrate, this paper considers omitted economic considerations in four ongoing policy debates, and investigates where additional empirical trade-off analysis could buttress and sharpen the economic viewpoint. This empiricism has a purpose—to increase the costs to policymakers who neglect or downplay the importance of behavior in environmental policy. They can benefit from clear evidence showing that environmental progress could be less expensive by including relevant economic behavior.

Underlying many debates is the polemic notion that somehow economists adhere to unfeeling principles and do not care about the environment or kids or endangered species. Of course, nothing could be further from the truth—economists always have been environmentalists as witnessed by our century-long cry to get prices to reflect true social costs. We are more aware of supply and demand and are therefore more willing to stand up and say that wealth spent here is not spent somewhere else. And that with more rational policy, it is possible to provide more human and environmental health with less wealth. But politicians cannot be expected to act on principle just because the economic data and theory are convincing if the general perception of a principle might not be digestible to the voting public. Appearing to help the environment or kids even at the price of taking aid away in reality will be more appealing to policymakers, no matter how abhorrent to economists. While we cannot out-lawyer or out-engineer advocates in policy debates, politics does understand real and transparent economic costs. Adding more lucid empirical darts to our quiver can only serve to improve our standing in environmental policy debates.

---

[3]See Schultze (1996, p. 27). Schultze was the Chairman of the Council of Economic Advisers during the Carter administration, 1976–80.

[4]See Blinder (1987, p. 1).

2. Risks to Children's Health

Healthy kids—everyone supports that end. Evidence continues to accumulate that suggests children face disproportionate health risks from environmental hazards.[5] These unbalanced risks stem from several fundamental differences in the physiologies and activities of children and adults. As kids develop, their digestive, nerve, and immune systems are more susceptible to toxic pollutants and other environmental hazards. Children eat, drink, and breathe more for their weight, and spend more time outside in exposure to greater amounts of contamination and pollution for their weight than adults. Kids also face potential exposures over their entire lifetime. They are also less able to recognize and to protect themselves. All this suggests children require special attention when designing environmental policy.

Based this argument, in April 1997 President Clinton unveiled a new executive order: EO 13045 "Protection of Children from Environmental Health Risks and Safety Risks" (Federal Register 1997). The EO directs the federal government to safeguard kids from environmental threats through three areas: policy, research coordination, and federal regulatory analysis. First, although many agencies thought this was already part of their mission (e.g., Federal Drug Administration, Health and Human Services), Section 1 requires all agencies to make the protection of children a high priority in implementing their statutory responsibilities and fulfilling their overall missions. Second, Section 3 creates an interagency task force to define a coordinated research agenda to identify research and other initiatives the Administration could take to protect children, and to enlist public input for these efforts. Third, Section 5 requires, for the first time, that agencies examine and explain the effects of their rules on children. Agencies promulgating major regulations that may have a disproportionate impact on children now must (a) evaluate the environmental health or safety effects of the planned regulation on children, and (b) explain why the planned regulation is preferable to other potentially effective and reasonably feasible alternatives considered by the agency. The idea is to link policy decisions to the health science on children, to ensure accountability to the public, and to force agencies to refocus their research agendas. Section 5 is the key to the order and, potentially, the most controversial—it has been called the "kick me" provision and requires an explanation when actions beneficial to kids are passed over. Supporters argue that without Section 5 the order will be merely hortatory and symbolic.

The kids EO raises several issues deserving more empirical attention. First, by maintaining that environmental risk is exogenous, and beyond the control of kids or adults, the EO maintains the false separation of the mechanistic risk assessment and behavioral choice. But risks to kids are not derived from autonomous sources, they are functions of both natural science parameters and their parent's self-protection decisions (Crocker and

---

[5]See, for example, Wargo's (1996) inquiry into pesticide exposure of children.

Shogren 1998). Given the relative marginal effectiveness of different self-protection actions, how people confront risk differs across individuals and situations, even though the natural phenomena that trigger these actions apply equally to everyone. Thus the EO does not address the evidence that suggests the most significant threats to children's health are the behavioral choices frequently associated with poverty, e.g., high discount rates (see, for example, Duncan et al. 1997). Researchers need more information to determine the bias in assessing risks to kids solely in terms of natural science information given that the sources of systematic variation are relative prices, incomes, and other economic and social parameters. Omitting private behavioral responses to risk will result in overestimating the risk to kids, and underestimating the value of reduced risk.

Second, the kids EO was designed purposefully for a few federal agencies who wanted a potential counterweight to the cost-benefit EO 12866—the regulatory review order that already requires similar analysis on costs, small business impact, and other issues, and future regulatory reform aimed at a broader accounting of risk-benefit trade-offs in federal regulations. This issue is tricky, deserving of a fuller account at a later date. For now, a quick point must suffice. While EO 12866 provides significant latitude to agencies and has not served as a strict constraint on behavior, that could change with a new administration. The kids EO provides a potential wedge to divide-and-conquer regulatory decisions if children's health is played as the trump card in the regulatory debate. Suppose a cost-benefit analysis reveals a new regulation is a net loser overall but a net gain to kids, the decision not to implement is no longer clear. The research need is to reduce the knowledge gap on how society evaluates risks to children, and how explicit distributional weights for kids in cost-benefit analysis complicates welfare measurement (see, for example, Harberger 1978).

Finally, the kids EO will pressure agencies to ratchet up their regulatory standards, with a corresponding and potentially unjustified increase in the costs and burdens of regulation. Industry has and will continue to criticize this pressure to raise standards across the board. The additional burden of Section 5 may further delay the regulatory process, and add resource demands to agencies already confronted with budgetary constraints. If agencies do not strengthen the relevant regulatory standards, the EO provides a ready basis to mount judicial challenges to decisions. Every supplement to a rule or regulation provides a new avenue to attack and compromise the core focus of the rule. Whether disclosure produces net economic benefits remains an empirical question.

3. Health Thresholds and the Lost Triangle

Clean air—everyone's for this too. But the U.S. Environmental Protection Agency's (EPA) recent rules to tighten the ozone and particulate matter (PM) ambient air quality standards (NAAQS) triggered an intense debate

in and outside the Administration about the quality of the research used
to support these decisions. The debate ranged from the actual health effects to be ameliorated by these standards and the scientific support underlying these standards to the real economic costs of implementing and
complying with these standards. In the end, President Clinton supported
the tighter federal air pollution standards stating that " . . . I think kids
ought to be healthy." The new standards for PM of 2.5 microns (PM$_{2.5}$) in
diameter call for daily means not to exceed 65 micrograms per cubic meter of air, and for annual means not to exceed 15 micrograms per cubic
meter. The new ozone standards call for concentrations in the air not to
exceed 80 parts per billion over an eight-hour period, and areas that exceed the new standard more than four times per year averaged over a three-
year period would have to take corrective action.

Among the many contentious issues raised in this debate, consider two
points in more detail. First, under the Clean Air Act, the EPA Administrator
sets air quality standards to protect public health with an "inadequate margin of safety." These are *health-based* standards—in principle, the Administrator can and should ignore all economic considerations in setting the degree of stringency. As such, the standards are to be decided based on the
current science that considers whether a statistically significant cause-and-
effect relationship exists between the feared pollutant and health. But in this
debate the underlying science is not at all clear. Even the EPA's science advisory board determined that no "bright line" existed to separate one proposed standard from another as being more protective of public health, including the current standard. And therefore the choice of a standard is a
policy judgment, not a scientific decision (see, for example, Wolff 1997).

Health effects associated with ozone are transitory, and a strong link
between ozone exposure and long-term human health effects or mortality
has not been confirmed by the scientific community. For example, based
on the EPA's own risk analysis, the expected reduction in excess hospital
admissions of asthmatics in the New York City area is about 30 per ozone
season when moving to the proposed standard from the current standard,
compared to total hospital admissions of asthmatics of about 15,000 per
ozone season. The number of children playing outdoors in the nine urban
areas that EPA studied who would experience an ozone-related cough
would be reduced by about 5,000—about 0.2% of outdoor children, and
30–40% of children are outdoor children. The changes in health risk are so
small, uncertain, and overlap from moving to the proposed standard from
the current standard that no clear distinction emerges. The weakness in
the scientific evidence with PM$_{2.5}$ is even more evident given the lack of a
plausible biological mechanism, the limited number of studies considering
PM$_{2.5}$ directly, and the feeble correlation in the studies. Even Dr. Jack Gib-
bons, the President's chief science advisor, recommended delaying the rules
so additional analysis could be performed. Ultimately, the administration
did delay actual implementation until 2002 to allow the EPA to collect additional data; data that should have been on the table before proposing a
change in the current standard.

Economists who scrutinize the econometrics of epidemiology will be more effective in debates over setting health-based standards. The current state of epidemiology is such that econometricians could make significant contributions to estimation procedures. Biases associated with measurement and specification errors are prevalent, especially when self-protection behaviors are left unaccounted for (e.g., Lave and Seskin 1977); ambient concentrations are usually taken to be synonymous with exposure, which is not the case when people change behavior to reduce risk.

For example, consider the case of the Six Cities study, the most important data in the EPA's case for their $PM_{2.5}$ standard (Dockery et al. 1993). The study examined the relationship between air pollution and premature deaths in six American cities, finding that mortality was 26 percent higher in Steubenville, Ohio than Protage, Wisconsin, the two cities with the most and least air pollution of the six considered. But the Six Cities findings are subject to criticism that the study did not correct for differences across cities. Key differences left unaccounted for include temperature, humidity, and income—median family income in Steubenville is about $7000 less than Portage. But the missing point is identical to the argument with kids risk: economic variables affect behavior which affect the risks faced by people, and exclusion of these variables from risk assessment bias predictions (see, for example, Atkinson and Crocker 1992; Kremer 1996). Studies have shown that people persistently below the poverty line are far more likely to become sick than wealthy people for a variety of reasons including habits, lifestyle, less medical screening, and the ability to self-protect (Korenman and Miller 1997). Wealth equals health, as the saying goes. Ignoring this causality will bias the estimated objective risk to these children.

The second point is that although economics has thus far been rejected in standard setting, EO 12866 requires the agency to prepare an economic analysis of the implementation of the proposed and final rules. These analyses included modeling inventories of known emissions sources to identify the most efficient set of control measures to meet the standards in various geographic areas, the health benefits that would be achieved based on projected air quality improvements, and the costs of these measures. The EPA did estimate the costs and benefits of implementation with varying degrees of credulity.

Let us consider one of the more unsubtle positions in the debate—the cost of the ozone standard. The proposed standards will be a significant burden to states. Under the proposed standard, nearly two hundred additional counties containing about fifty million people will be out of attainment. The emissions reductions required to meet the standard are substantial for big areas like Los Angeles (90%) and New York (80%), and for smaller areas like Hartford, CT (80%), Portland, OR (25%), and Huntington, WV (50%). The EPA estimated the costs to reach partial attainment of the ozone standard to be about $2.6 billion per year, based on marginal abatement costs between $3,000 to $10,000/ton(t) of ozone (see Fumento 1997).

But the Clean Air Act does not mandate partial compliance, it calls for full compliance, albeit eventually. As such, the appropriate measure is the costs of full attainment, which according to the President's Council of Economic Advisers could be as high as $60 billion per year.[6]

The EPA responded by claiming that the $10,000/t is a cut-off on the marginal cost curve for ozone abatement, even if reduction is mandated. Their explanation is that nobody will pay more than $10,000/t to reduce ozone pollution either due to new innovations, tradable emission systems, or delayed compliance. The argument presses on to say that these cost figures are exaggerated anyway, and that business estimates of compliance costs are always inflated (see the discussion on acid rain abatement costs in Forster 1993). Marginal abatement exceeding $10,000/t must be irrelevant.

Figure 1 illustrates this lost-cost triangle. Costs are on the vertical axis, and reduced ozone tons on the horizontal axis, up to the point of full compliance. The area under the marginal cost represents the costs of full compliance. But the upper triangle, according to the EPA is extraneous because no one would ever adopt these high-cost technologies—the lost triangle. Unfortunately, only one of the EPA's three reasons for holding costs down actually reduces social costs—innovation. Postponement and redistribution do nothing on their own to change the nature of the marginal abatement cost curve.

Yet the belief in a cost cap persisted straight into a Presidential directive, in which he asks the EPA to encourage ideas like a Clean Air Invest-

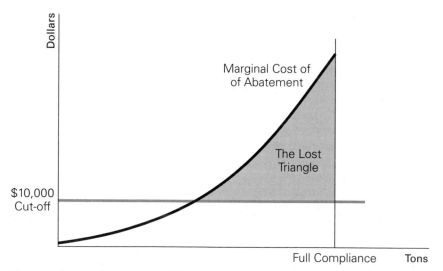

Figure 1. Ozone abatement and the lost triangle.

---

[6]The CEA estimate is based on EPA predictions of emission deficits for non-attainment areas and marginal abatement costs between $30,000 to $80,000 per ton.

ment Fund to cap control costs at $10,000/t. A factory or power plant that faces abatement costs greater than $10,000/t can reach compliance by paying into the fund (tons to complaince@$10,000/t), which will then use the money to buy reductions from other sources. If actual costs exceed $10,000/t, the Fund would be insufficient to cover full compliance, implying that full compliance can only be achieved if costs are lower than the cap. The cap creates an ambiguity about the real costs of this policy since only the degree of compliance that can be afforded will be achieved. Obviously a cap does not remove these costs, and economists must insist that these costs be counted, if for nothing other than keeping the heat on the administration for flexible pollution regulations.

The key empirical question is whether economists are guilty of cost inflation. If we frequently overestimating the costs of environmental compliance, this can be held against us to the point that our future claims can be dismissed as too pessimistic. For example, with the Acid Rain emission trading program, administration and industry economists predicted that abatement costs to achieve targeted emission reductions would range between $170 to $1500 per ton. If these predictions had been realized, high-cost utilities should have demanded more allowances from the low-cost utilities, driving up trading volume and market price. This was not the case. As of the first quarter of 1996, the trading volume between independent parties is estimated at 6.5 million tons, and the going price for an allowance is hovering around $100 per ton. Several reasons exist to explain this gap, such as extra bonus permits, cheap low sulfur coal from Wyoming, and fuel blending.[7] But the fact that realized costs were much lower than predicted provides enough ammunition to tar high-cost estimates for other environmental issues, such as global climate change. A comprehensive survey of *ex ante* cost predictions and *ex post* cost calculations would be a useful addition to our toolbox.

4. Climate Change, Technology, and Behavior

Preventing untold global catastrophe—who could be against that? And central to President Clinton's global climate change policy is technology. The President proposed tax cuts and spending programs up to $5 billion over the next five years in research and development to encourage energy efficiency and the use of less carbon-intensive energy sources. These technologies are presented in a recent Department of Energy report, *Scenarios of U.S. Carbon Reductions*—the five lab study. The report does not, however, present the specific policies or the behavior responses that will trigger the adoption and diffusion of these technologies that supposedly will be used to reduce US carbon emissions by 34 percent in 2010. Rather the

[7]See Burtraw (1996).

report stresses that "a vigorous national commitment" to reduce emissions through energy efficiency alone leaves the impression that these reductions are free.

In times like these, a familiar point like the no-free-lunch cliché is worth making clear with numbers. The free lunch argument comes up again and again in climate change because some policymakers continue to play up the mechanistic while downplaying the behavioral aspects of technology. Engineering studies suggest that from 20 to 25 percent of existing emissions in the greenhouses gases that cause climate change could be eliminated at no additional costs. Climate change policy, so the argument goes, will not really cost the economy anything because low hanging fruit exists in the form of energy-efficient technologies that people do not currently use because they ignore or are ignorant of the benefits. If government could wipe the mud away from the eyes of the nation, we could achieve our policy at no net cost to society.

Economists are typically skeptical of these no-cost, energy-saving arguments heard in climate change policy debates because they do not believe in the free-lunch. The skepticism comes from observing that people do not take advantage of cost-effective, energy-efficient technologies which, in the long run, are good for both the pocketbook and the environment. Economists are not technological pessimists. It is just that we cannot ignore the evidence which suggests people still prefer conventional appliances—at least at current prices. At current prices, many consumers do not experiment with compact fluorescent light bulbs, improved thermal insulation, better heating and cooling systems, and energy-efficient appliances (see Jaffe and Stavins 1994; Nichols 1994). But when prices change so do choices about energy, as our experience with the oil shocks of the 70s shows. Economists see the most effective way to curb excessive energy consumption is to raise its price to reflect the harmful effects on the environment of burning fossil fuels.

Why do people resist new technologies at current prices? People do not see the "no-net costs" as reality when confronted with these technologies. People have or act as if they have a short time horizon, perhaps reflecting their uncertainty about future energy prices and the reliability of the technology. Several studies have estimated that when consumers buy air conditioners, space-heaters, water-heaters, and refrigerators, they implicitly apply a substantial discount to future cost-savings (e.g., Hausman 1979). Due to incomplete markets, their implicit time horizons are shorter than those reflected in market interest rates. People still pay more attention to immediate outlays even when confronted with estimates of future cost savings. And factors other than energy efficiency matter—quality and features, the time and effort to learn about a new technology and how it works. People are also wary about claimed energy savings that might not be realized. Although a technology is cost-effective in its energy use on average, it may not be cost-effective for people who use little energy.

Why does this debate continue? The reason is many policymakers think the market fails when people prefer not to make energy-efficient choices.

Blurring the distinction between a true market failure and preferences frustrates economists who have learned to appreciate the distinction after 200 years of intense debate. A market fails when individual choices diverge from what society wants as a whole; in this case, fewer adoptions than desired.[8] Policy intervention to eliminate a market failure can make society better off, depending on the costs of the intervention.

In contrast, preferences are preferences—individual choices, however fuzzy, do match what society wants. This implies that engineering studies that omit behavioral responses will overestimate the rate of technology adoption. Policies that try to eliminate barriers when people believe these technologies are not cost-effective for them, will usually not pass a benefit-cost test. Intervention to change people's preferences does not necessarily improve social welfare, and can make society worse off. Granted government policies can change how people think, but most economists do not see these campaigns as cost-effective. Changing relative prices is usually seen as a more effective tool to achieve some goal. Adoption rates will increase relative prices change such that the technology now looks profitable. Additional evidence to drive this point home would be most welcome.

5. Endangered Species and Banking on Conservation

Maintaining our ability to function by keeping the web of life intact—what madman would reject that goal? Over the past three centuries, more than 500 of this country's 20,000 know species of plants and animals have become extinct or are missing and possibly extinct. Endangered species protection is a classic example of a public good. The Endangered Species Act (ESA) was passed in 1973 to correct for the market failure associated with the unpriced social benefits of such species—but a new set of problems arose. Although the benefits of protecting endangered species accrue to the

---

[8]Examples of market failure include imperfect capital markets, public information, moral hazards, and externalities. Imperfect capital markets make it difficult for low-income families to get loans to buy goods with longer payback periods. Information has both public and private attributes, and market failure occurs, if once information becomes public, it is too costly to exclude others from using it, and one person's use of information does not preclude another person's use. The public good nature of information results in the under-supply of R&D investment and low adoption rates. Moral hazard exists when a person's actions are hidden from another person. He imposes a cost on the other person, and has insufficient incentive to stop. Consider rental housing—the owner could pay for more energy efficiency, but he has no incentive to invest since it is the renters who benefit because they pay the utility bill. Externalities cause the private marginal cost faced by people to be lower than the social marginal cost, resulting in an oversupply of pollution. For electricity, people to be lower than the social marginal cost, resulting in an oversupply of pollution. For electricity, people do not pay for environmental costs from carbon when they buy coal-based electricity. This makes coal-based electricity more attractive than non-carbon energy sources (e.g., renewable energy).

entire nation, a significant fraction of the costs imposed by the ESA are borne by private landowners. An estimated 75–90 percent of the over 1,000 species of plants and animals that are listed as endangered or threatened under the ESA are found on private land, and many of these landowners complain that the costs of complying are too high. How these landowners choose to protect their investment will affect the success of the ESA.

The pressure to answer the question of whether these costs are too high relative to the social benefits has thrust economists right into the middle of the ESA reauthorization debate. And while a precise cost-benefit analysis of the ESA may be beyond our current reach, thinking about the ESA from this perspective makes sense—if only to force people to realize that trade-offs exist. The main sticking point is a lively and heated debate over how to estimate the economic social value of endangered species protection. The debate spins between two views on how we should value and measure a good that most people will never directly use. Economists have invested significant time and energy assessing the validity of using surveys to measure what a person's hypothetical, non-use value to guarantee the existence of some species that they may or may never see.

At one end, proponents view non-use values as useful indicators of preferences for specific preservation questions that can be reasonably captured in a survey. This side argues that benefits elicited through surveys are valid and usable in policy discussions. Critics dismiss these hypothetical, non-use values as surrogates of general environmental preferences, stating that these beliefs benefits are white noise at best and misleading at worst. The answer most likely lies somewhat in-between: endangered species protection provides valuable services to society that are not fully captured in market prices but probably are not as large as suggested by some survey results. People do place an economic value on species preservation, and it seems worthwhile to try and measure that value to help guide decisions. The problem is that precise estimates are not forthcoming. If, for instance, we crudely summed the benefits estimated by several surveys valuing specific endangered species, the answer suggests an implausible result that people would pay over 1 percent of the U.S. Gross National Product for less than 2 percent of all endangered species (Brown and Shogren 1998). Results such as these reinforce the conclusion that while nonuse values may be a valid concept, the measurement tool is still blunt.

While difficulties still exist in nonmarket valuation, economists can still frame the endangered species debate in benefit-cost terms. Economists seek criteria and conduct analysis to discriminate among species and the resulting extinction of some in recognition of binding budget constraints. Unpleasant choices may have to be made. And while we cannot maximize social value by saving the least costly species, a policy will do poorly that tries to save all and makes no distinctions among species except those governed by "science." Although the idea of extinction unnerves most people, benefit-cost reasoning still has a role because it is questionable whether encyclopedic species protection holds a moral trump card over all other priorities today, such as kids' health. Again the point worth repeating—resources spent on species protection are resources not spent on kids' health.

A second issue is to consider flexible strategies for private landowners. Federal statutes often mandate conservation of natural resources on private land through strict land-use policies, e.g., the Clean Water Act requires minimization of wetlands loss, the ESA requires protection of habitat. Although conflicts between conservation and development are inevitable, a market based approach—conservation banking—offers public officials and landowners a way to work toward a mutually satisfactory resolution of such conflicts.

Conservation banking puts a market value on preservation. A "bank" is established when an investor protects a parcel of land. Public officials then assign credits to the land based on the value of its ecological services and certify the long-term viability of these services. Developers then buy the credits and use them to offset environmental effects on their own land for which they would otherwise be liable. When all credits are purchased the banked land is protected in perpetuity, either by deed restrictions or transfer to a protector, often government.

Unlike traditional land-use policies, which require specific on-site restoration or protection, conservation banking encourages landowners to find the least-cost protection strategy. Landowners with relatively low incremental protection costs conserve land and bank credits, while high-cost developers must buy credits. Both parties gain from the exchange of credits, and so too does society. Banking also increases stakeholder involvement by bringing buyers and sellers together. Regulatory approval and management of a single, large tract of land instead of numerous individual tracts reduces transaction costs and allocates resources on a more regional scale, which minimizes landscape fragmentation. And these benefits are achieved without sacrificing environmental objectives. In practice, the challenge is actually defining "equivalent" ecosystems given so that trades can take place. Different sites offer different ecological services. Measuring and matching the set of services require a fundamental understanding of substitution possibilities.

About 100 wetlands mitigation banks covering well over 20,000 acres are operating nationwide to satisfy the Clean Water Act. In Pembroke Pines, Florida, for example, Wetlandsbank, Inc. has restored 350 acres of wetlands, and they are selling credits for an average of $40,000 each. About 40 habitat banks have emerged in California to ease development pressure on endangered and threatened species. In 1995, for example, Bank of America established the 182-acre Carlsbad Highlands Conservation Bank in Southern California and sold all the credits within a year.

Conservation banking is risky. Banks are created by regulatory agencies with differing missions, which can undermine the security of bank investments. Additionally, banks deal in ecological services that are difficult to match up across regional landscapes. Nevertheless, conservation banks already protect about 32,000 acres and will probably play an increasingly important role in mitigating conservation-development conflicts created by urban expansion that proceeds at a rate of 860,000 acres per year in the United States. Additional research into the nature of flexible regulations such as conservation banking will provide useful insight into how behavior can work for and not against species protection.

6. *Concluding Comments*

Political motives dominate root economic ideas in final decisions—to imagine otherwise would reveal naiveté sufficient to bounce one from Washington, D.C., Paris, Tokyo, or any capital in-between. Scores of economists will testify to this reality in most policy debates (e.g., free trade, deregulation). And while this brief run through the landscape of how the omission of basic economic principles frustrates rational environmental policy may be old news to veterans, hopefully it hints at what to expect for those interested in becoming less apolitical.

Perhaps the small town hick in me shows through, but I must admit to being taken aback by some advocates' unwillingness to accept basic economic principles. And being told that the academic distinctions made by textbook environmental economics add little value to actual public policy debate did make me wonder how exactly we failed in our Econ.101 drills. Neglecting to include positive theories of political behavior in our standard microeconomic models might be one likely culprit (see Hahn 1989). But I also confess that being typecast as a member of the tribe of lemon-sucking economists eventually did turn my disgust into amusement.

What I know now and will not again forget is the power that numbers at your fingertips have in accelerating this change in attitude. Empiricists must continue to generate and push forward an accessible inventory of evidence to withstand the real and artificial fog surrounding environmental policy. Whether good economics ultimately wins out is a long run question—just look at tradable permits. Conceived in 60s, test piloted in the 70s and 80s, implemented at a large scale in the 90s, and now commonplace in discussions of environmental policy for the 21st century, tradable permits have gone native in the political arena. Success stories such as the Acid Rain trading program which reduced emissions by fifty percent at one-half to one-third the cost of a command-and-control approach raise the costs to policy makers who neglect behavioral choices. So, if asked by the President, my response would be: behavior matters—a point worth driving home at every opportunity.

REFERENCES

Atkinson, S. and T. D. Crocker (1992), 'Econometric Health Production Functions: Relative Bias from Omitted Variables and Measurement Error', *Journal of Environmental Economics and Management 22*, 12–24.

Blinder, A. (1987), *Hard Heads, Soft Hearts. Tough-minded Economics for a Just Society*. New York: Addison Wesley.

Brown, G. M., Jr. and J. F. Shogren (1998), 'Economics of the Endangered Species Act', *Journal of Economic Perspectives* (forthcoming).

Burtraw, D. (1996), 'Trading Emissions to Clean the Air: Exchanges Few but Savings Many', *Resources 122*.

Crocker, T. D. and J. F. Shogren (1998), 'Endogenous Risk and Environmental Program Evaluation', in G. Knaap and T. J. Kim, eds., *Environmental Program Evaluation. A Primer*. Urbana, IL: University of Illinois Press, pp. 255–269.

Dockery, D. et al. (1993), 'An Association Between Air Pollution and Mortality in Six U.S. Cities', *New England Journal of Medicine 329*, 1753–1759.

Duncan, G. et al. (1997), 'Does Poverty Affect the Life Chances of Children?' *American Sociological Review* (forthcoming).

Forster, B. (1993), *The Acid Rain Debate. Science and Special Interests in Policy Formation*. Ames, IA: Iowa State University Press.

Federal Register: April 23, 1997 (Volume 62, Number 78, 19883).

Fumento, M. (1997), *Polluted Science. The EPA's Campaign to Expand Clean Air Regulations*. Washington, DC: American Enterprise Institute Press.

Hahn, R. (1989), 'Economic Prescriptions for Environmental Problems: How the Patient Followed the Doctors Orders', *Journal of Economic Perspectives 3*, 94–114.

Harberger, A. (1978), 'On the Use of Distributional Weights in Social Cost-Benefit Analysis', *Journal of Political Economy 86*, S87–S120.

Hausman, J. (1979), 'Individual Discount Rates and the Purchase and utilization of Energy-Using Durables', *Bell Journal of Economics 10*, 33–54.

Jaffe, A. B. and R. N. Stavins (1994), 'The Energy-efficiency Gap: What Does it Mean?' *Energy Policy 22*, 804–810.

Korenman, S. and J. E. Miller (1997), 'Effects of Long-term Poverty on Physical Health of Children in the National Longitudinal Survey of Youth' (Photocopy).

Kremer, M. (1996), 'Integrating Behavioral Choice into Epidemiological Models of AIDS', *Quarterly Journal of Economics 111*, 549–574.

Lave, L. and E. Seskin (1977), *Air Pollution and Human Health*. Baltimore, MD: Johns Hopkins University Press for Resources for the Future.

Nichols, A. L. (1994), 'Demand-Side Management: Overcoming Market Barriers or Obscuring Real Costs?' *Energy Policy 22*, 840–847.

Portney, P. (ed.) (1990), *Public Policies for Environmental Protection*. Washington, DC: Resources for the Future.

Ricardo, D. (1963 (1817), *The Principles of Political Economy and Taxation*. Homewood, IL: Irwin.

Schultze, C. L. (1996), 'The CEA: An Inside Voice for Mainstream Economics', *Journal of Economic Perspectives 10*, 23–39.

Smith, A. 1994 (1776). *An Inquiry into the Nature and Causes of The Wealth of Nations*. New York: The Modern Library.

Wargo, J. (1996), *Our Children's Toxic Legacy. How Science and Law Fail to Protect Us from Pesticides*. New Haven: Yale University Press.

Wolff, G. T. (1996), 'The Scientific Basis For a New Ozone Standard', *Environmental Manager 2*, 27–32.